Lecture Notes in Artificial Intelligence   12799

Subseries of Lecture Notes in Computer Science

More information about this subseries at http://www.springer.com/series/1244

Hamido Fujita · Ali Selamat ·
Jerry Chun-Wei Lin · Moonis Ali (Eds.)

Advances and Trends in Artificial Intelligence

From Theory to Practice

34th International Conference
on Industrial, Engineering and Other Applications
of Applied Intelligent Systems, IEA/AIE 2021
Kuala Lumpur, Malaysia, July 26–29, 2021
Proceedings, Part II

Springer

Editors
Hamido Fujita 🆔
i-SOMET Incorporate Association
Morioka, Japan

Jerry Chun-Wei Lin 🆔
Western Norway University
of Applied Sciences
Bergen, Norway

Ali Selamat 🆔
Universiti Teknologi Malaysia
Kuala Lumpur, Malaysia

Moonis Ali
Texas State University San Marcos
San Marcos, TX, USA

ISSN 0302-9743   ISSN 1611-3349   (electronic)
Lecture Notes in Artificial Intelligence
ISBN 978-3-030-79462-0   ISBN 978-3-030-79463-7   (eBook)
https://doi.org/10.1007/978-3-030-79463-7

LNCS Sublibrary: SL7 – Artificial Intelligence

This Springer imprint is published by the registered company Springer Nature Switzerland AG
The registered company address is: Gewerbestrasse 11, 6330 Cham, Switzerland

Preface

Artificial Intelligence innovations in recent decades have entered a sophisticated stage in providing intelligent interaction between humans and machines, solving problems, and providing advice in many different infrastructures. Machines in different disciplines have become ubiquitous in all aspects of life, including education, governance, science, healthcare, warfare, and industry. Computing machinery has become smaller and faster, and the costs of data storage and communication have greatly decreased. Consequently, big data of vast dimensionality is being intelligently collected and stored in smart databases for use in decision making and prediction for applications such as security and health care, amongst others. Moreover, novel and improved computing architectures have been designed for efficient large-scale data processing, such as big data frameworks, FPGAs and GPUs. Thanks to these advancements and recent breakthroughs in artificial intelligence, researchers and practitioners have developed more complex and effective artificial intelligence-based systems. This has led to a greater interest in artificial intelligence to solve complex real-world problems, and the proposal of many innovative applications.

This volume contains the proceedings of the 34th International Conference on Industrial, Engineering and other Applications of Applied Intelligent Systems (IEA/AIE 2021), which was held online during July 26–29, 2021, in Kuala Lumpur, Malaysia. The IEA/AIE conference is an annual event that emphasizes applications of applied intelligent systems to solve real-life problems in all areas including engineering, science, industry, automation and robotics, business and finance, medicine and biomedicine, bioinformatics, cyberspace, and human-machine interactions. This year, 145 submissions were received. Each paper was evaluated by three to four reviewers from an International Program Committee consisting of 196 members from 37 countries. Based on the evaluation, 87 papers were selected as full papers and 19 as short papers, which are presented in two volumes. We are grateful to all the reviewers for the time spent writing detailed and constructive comments for the authors, and also the authors for the proposal of so many high-quality papers.

The program of IEA/AIE 2021 included eight special sessions:

- Special Session on Data Stream Mining: Algorithms and Applications (DSMAA2021)
- Special Session on Intelligent Knowledge Engineering in Decision Making Systems (IKEDS2021)
- Special Session on Knowledge Graphs in Digitalization Era (KGDE2021)
- Special Session on Spatiotemporal Big Data Analytics (SBDA2021)
- Special Session on Big Data and Intelligence Fusion Analytics (BDIFA2021)
- Special Session on AI in Healthcare (AIH2021)
- Special Session on Intelligent Systems and e-Applications (iSeA2021)
- Special Session on Collective Intelligence in Social Media (CISM2021).

Moreover, two keynote talks were given by Professor Francisco Herrera, from the University of Granada, Spain, and Director of the Andalusian Research Institute "Data Science and Computational Intelligence", and Professor Vincent S. Tseng from the Department of Computer Science, National Yang Ming Chiao Tung University, Taiwan.

We would like to thank everyone who has contributed to the success of this year's edition of IEA/AIE, that is the authors, Program Committee members, reviewers, keynote speakers, organizers and participants.

May 2021

Hamido Fujita
Ali Selamat
Jerry Chun-Wei Lin
Moonis Ali

Organization

General Chairs

Hamido Fujita, Japan
Moonis Ali, USA

Organizing Chairs

Ali Selamat, Malaysia
Jun Sasaki, Japan

Program Chairs

Ali Selamat, Malaysia
Jerry Chun-Wei Lin, Norway

Special Session Chairs

Philippe Fournier-Viger, China
Nor Azura Mohd Ghani, Malaysia

Publicity Chairs

Mohd Hazli Mohamed Zabil, Malaysia
Lim Kok Cheng, Malaysia

Program Committee

Abidalrahman Moh'D, USA
Adel Bouhoula, Tunisia
Adrianna Kozierkiewicz, Poland
Ahmed Tawfik, Egypt
Alban Grastien, Australia
Alexander Ferrein, Germany
Artur Andrzejak, Germany
Ayahiko Niimi, Japan
Barbara Pes, Italy
Bay Vo, Vietnam
Dariusz Krol, Poland
Dinh Tuyen Hoang, Korea
Du Nguyen

Engelbert Mephu Nguifo, France
Eugene Santos Jr., USA
Farid Nouioua, France
Farshad Badie, Denmark
Fevzi Belli, Germany
Flavio Soares Correa da Silva, Brazil
Franz Wotawa, Austria
Giorgos Dounias, Greece
Hadjali Allel, France
Hamido Fujita, Japan
He Jiang, China
Ingo Pill, Austria
Jerry Chun-Wei Lin, Norway
Joao Mendes-Moreira, Portugal
João Paulo Carvalho, Portugal
Jose Maria-Luna, Spain
Krishna Reddy P., India
Ladjel Bellatreche, France
Leszek Borzemski, Poland
Maciej Grzenda, Poland
Mark Levin, USA
Mercedes Merayo, Spain
Nazha Selmaoui-Folcher, Germany
Ngoc-Thanh Nguyen, Poland
Philippe Fournier-Viger, China
Philippe Leray, France
Rui Abreu, Portugal
Sabrina Senatore, Italy
Said Jabbour, France
Shyi-Ming Chen, Taiwan
Sonali Agarwal, India
Takayuki Ito, Japan
Tim Hendtlass, Australia
Trong Hieu Tran, Vietnam
Tzung-Pei Hong, Taiwan
Uday Rage, Japan
Unil Yun, Korea
Van Cuong Tran, Vietnam
Wen-Juan Hou, Taiwan
Wolfgang Mayer, Australia
Xiangdong An, USA
Xinzheng Niu, China
Yun Sing Koh, Australia
Yutaka Watanobe, Japan

Contents – Part II

Data Management, Clustering and Classification

Robotics

Innovative Applications of Intelligent Systems

CPS and Industrial Applications

Defect, Anomaly and Intrusion Detection

Financial and Supply Chain Applications

Bayesian Networks

BigData and Time Series Processing

Information Retrieval and Relation Extraction

Contents – Part I

Artificial Intelligence and Machine Learning

Sematic, Topology, and Ontology Models

Medical and Health-Related Applications

Graphic and Social Network Analysis

Signal and Bioinformatic Processing

Evolutionary Computation

Attack and Security

Natural Language and Text Processing

Fuzzy Inference and Theory

Sensor and Communication Networks

Prediction and Recommendation

F2DeepRS: A Deep Recommendation Framework Applied to ICRC Platforms

Yongquan Xie[1](✉) , Finn Tseng[2], Kristinsson Johannes[2], Shiqi Qiu[2],
and Yi Lu Murphey[1]

[1] University of Michigan-Dearborn, Dearborn, MI 48128, USA
{yongquan,yilu}@umich.edu
[2] Ford Motor Company, Dearborn, MI 48126, USA
{ftseng,jkristin,sqiu2}@ford.com

Abstract. The applications of recommendation system (RS) are ubiquitous in our daily lives. Many RSs have exhibited excellent performances, especially those based on neural networks in recent years. However, many existing methods gained superiority in performance at the expense of hardware or computational costs, which are not applicable to applications that run on information and computation resource constrained (ICRC) platforms. The ICRC applications, such as in-vehicle infotainment system where there is no powerful computer resources, pose new challenges for developing a RS, including uncertainty in the availability of user profile or item content, less powerful computation resources but huge size of user and item pools, etc. With a focus on applications in such context, we developed a Fast and Flexible Deep Recommendation System (F2DeepRS) framework. In this framework, existing user/item knowledge learned by other even non-neural models can be leveraged to make the learning process computationally efficient. And the framework can be flexibly configured to incorporate user/item content information depending on availability. Experiments were conducted using *R2-Yahoo! Music* dataset, which is, to our best knowledge, the largest public dataset publicly accessible to our knowledge. The performance is compared with both traditional and state-of-the-art RS. The results have indicated that the proposed F2DeepRS framework is competitive in preference prediction tasks, and particularly, is very computationally efficient.

Keywords: Recommendation system · Deep learning · Bayesian personalized ranking · Information and computation resource constrained.

1 Introduction

Item recommendation has become an increasingly important component in many information systems in this era where the world has been changed by information

This research is supported by a grant from the Ford Motor Company.

H. Fujita et al. (Eds.): IEA/AIE 2021, LNAI 12799, pp. 3–14, 2021.
https://doi.org/10.1007/978-3-030-79463-7_1

explosion. The applications of item recommendation ubiquitously affect people's daily lives such as product or job advertising and music recommendation. A RS aims to provide the most relevant information to a user by discovering patterns in a dataset the user has interacted with. In this paper, we focus on developing RS on ICRC platforms such as in-vehicle infotainment system and on-board aircraft entertainment system, where computation resources are limited. Although item recommendation have been studied extensively, the problem of making recommendation on an ICRC platform is still complicated by: (1) sheer volume of users and items, i.e., the number of users/items in the pool is huge; (2) uncertainty in the available user or item content data. Unlike the online music or product recommendation website which requires users to create individual profiles, most ICRC systems however, may or may not ask for personal information such as age, gender, occupation, etc. In this situation, the recommendation needs to be flexible with the availability of user/item content information; and (3) limited computing resources. The ICRC platform is not normally equipped with highly powerful computer or server clusters for complex calculation such as those used by Amazon or Google.

Considering the aforementioned challenges, the proposed F2DeepRS framework is designed suitable for the ICRC system in the following aspects: (1) Our method hybridize latent representation and matching function and learns from binarized preference indications, i.e., user's "like" or "dislike" preference, and learns to predict user's such preference to other items. (2) We make the learning and inferencing process of the model light-weighted. The user and item representations are imported from existing prototypes. Representation learning module normally involves large volume of parameters to be learned, which is avoided in our method. (3) The framework can be flexibly reconfigured to include or exclude user or item contents according to specifics of an application, and available contents can be also encoded beforehand for the model to use. The above features distinguish the proposed recommendation method from many existing counterparts. We will review related works in Sect. 2. Some preliminary knowledge is introduced in Sect. 3, followed by the proposed F2DeepRS framework in Sect. 4. The implementation details, experiments and performance evaluation are given in Sect. 5. Finally, Sect. 6 summarizes our work and gives suggestions for the future.

2   Related Works

Current recommendation approaches generally fall into the following categories: collaborative filtering (CF), content-based filtering, latent factor method, matching function learning and hybrid methods. These methods are reviewed in this section to provide an overview.

Collaborative filtering approaches involve collecting a large amount of information on users' behaviors and activities and then predicting what users will like based on their similarity to other users [19]. The fundamental assumption of CF is that if users A and B have similar behaviors or historical item ratings, it is likely they will rate or act on other items similarly. An advantage of CF is that it applies to both explicit data such as users' feedback, and implicit data such as the frequency they click and play a song. A popular series of algorithms belongs to this category is to search similar neighbors. Methods proposed in [3, 12, 20] have made improvements using different strategies. One of the issues with the CF approach is the "cold start problem", in that new users who do not have any historical information for finding similar users and hence difficult to explore interested items.

Content-based filtering approaches analyze item's metadata, or content information for making recommendation. It retrieves items in a user's history record, identifies those have been rated "like", and recommends other items with similar content to the user [14]. A drawback of this approach is that the recommended items are not usually diversified. Conventionally, content features are formatted in manually designed vectors, and similarity between items is measured using distance-based methods like Euclidean distance and cosine similarity. More recently, advanced methods have been developed to extract features using deep neural networks [13]. The deep learning based RS was summarized in [23] and is not reiterated here.

Latent representation learning approaches are mainly based on the theory that a user's rating to an item can be estimated by a matching function that takes the user and item's representations as inputs. Methods such as Bayesian Personalized Ranking (BPR) [17] and Matrix Factorization (MF) [4,11] assume the matching function $h(\cdot)$ to be non-parametric and learn low dimensional user and item latent representations from use-item rating matrix R. The user-item rating matrix R is an extremely sparse matrix because the number of items rated by a user is limited but the total number of items is large. The user/item representations are dense with dimensionality being reduced remarkably. Many variants of this approach have been developed for extending its applications [5, 6, 10]. Neural network is commonly used recently to learn latent representations. These networks generally has a framework as in Fig. 1a. In this approach, two neural network are used to model user and item latent representation mapping functions f_u and f_i, respectively. Users and items are mapped into a common space where their matching score can be obtained by non-parametric functions such as dot product or cosine similarity.

Matching function learning approaches attempt to approximate parametric matching functions $h(\cdot; \theta)$. Neural network is also an excellent and convenient tool to approximate such functions and thus has been widely employed to learn the parameters θ in the matching function. The generic learning framework of this approach is shown in Fig. 1b. Methods of this category include NeuMF[9], NNCF [1], ConvNCF [8], NFM [7], etc. In these methods, the inputs to the matching function approximation module have various forms, such as the sparse rating vectors, user and item representations, or other auxiliary data.

Hybrid methods aim at combining two or more approaches to increase the overall performance. Hybrid CF and content-based methods have been explored extensively [15, 16]. In [6, 18], item content, as well as user content, are integrated

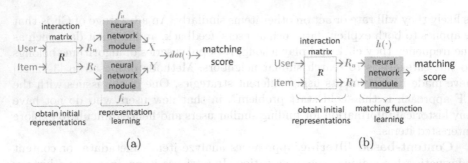

Fig. 1. (a) Neural network-based representation learning framework; (b) Neural network-based matching function learning framework.

into a deep neural architecture in which the user and item latent factor are obtained from the latent factor approach. And authors in [2] combined the latent representation with matching function learning in a DeepCF architecture, which has gained better performance than latent representation and matching function learning alone. From the advanced approaches recently developed, it can be seen that the combination of multiple methods into neural network has become the main stream. The proposed F2DeepRS in this paper is also a hybrid neural network based method of latent representation and matching function learning.

3 Preliminaries

3.1 Problem Description

Suppose the total number of users and items are n_u and n_i respectively, and user-item interaction matrix is $R \in \mathbb{R}^{n_u \times n_i}$, which can be obtained from users' explicit ratings to items or implicit feedback. Throughout this paper, the interaction matrix only refers to user-item like/dislike preference:

$$r_{ui} = \begin{cases} 1, & \text{if } u \text{ likes } i; \\ 0, & \text{if } u \text{ likes } i; \\ \text{N/A}, & \text{no record.} \end{cases} \quad (1)$$

where r_{ui} is an element of R indicating u's preference to i.

The purpose of our task is discriminating a user's "like" preference from "dislike" to an item, which is different from many existing RSs. With this goal, the research does not rank items of "like" preference. The matrix R used in this paper only contains "like" or "dislike" information, which are inferred from explicit or implicit data, e.g., ratings of scale 1 to 5, scores of 2 and 4 can be interpreted as "dislike" and "like" respectively, or a frequently played song can be interpreted as "like" compared with a song played only a few times.

The recommendation problem with user like/dislike preference record is formulated as a preference r_{ui} prediction problem, i.e., it is to fill the missing values "N/A" in R, assuming the preference r_{ui} obeys a Bernoulli distribution:

$$P(r_{ui} = l | p_{ui}) = \begin{cases} p_{ui}, & l = 1; \\ 1 - p_{ui}, & l = 0. \end{cases} \tag{2}$$

where p_{ui} is the probability output by the system and indicates how likely u would like i.

3.2 Bayesian Personal Ranking

The proposed F2DeepRS framework imports latent user and item representations from existing representation learning methods as aforementioned. We leverage Bayesian Personal Ranking (BPR) algorithm [17] as a prototypes in this paper for exemplification. Other representation learning methods will be considered in our future study.

BPR learns user/item representations from items ranked by users and computes scores of unrated items, which are then used to rank the unrated items. The learning is a collaborative process that requires the ranking information from the entire user and item communities U and V. In iterations, it optimizes the user and item latent representations. A personalized user ranking element is denoted by the triplet $\langle u, i, j \rangle$, which denotes user u prefers item i to j. The BPR algorithm uses dot product as the matching function. Its optimization objective is:

$$minimize : \frac{\lambda}{2}(\| X \|^2 + \| Y \|^2) - \sum_{\langle u,i,j \rangle \in \mathcal{D}^{bpr}} ln\sigma(X_u \cdot Y_i - X_u \cdot Y_j) \tag{3}$$

where X_u and Y_i are the latent representations of user u and item i, corresponding to a row vectors of representation matrices X and Y, respectively, $\mathcal{D}^{bpr}$ the set of all user-specific triplets, λ the regularization parameter, and $\sigma(\cdot)$ the sigmoid function.

4 Proposed F2DeepRS

The proposed F2DeepRS framework is presented in Fig. 2. In both subfigures, two embedding layers are included and the weights are initialized by the imported user and item latent representations (X and Y) respectively from BPR. As aforementioned, the BPR algorithm was originally proposed to rank items through estimated user-item matching scores, which is different from our goal of discriminating user's like/dislike preference to items. Therefore, the dataset $\mathcal{D}^{bpr}$ constructed for BPR should be changed to the set of personal preference tuples $\langle u, i, j \rangle$, which means user u likes item i but does not like item j. After building such triplets for all users, the user and item representations are learned by optimizing the objective function in (3).

The user and item representations can be retrieved by the corresponding user/item identifiers. The retrieved user and item representations are then concatenated and sent to the subsequent multilayer perception (MLP) module to learn the matching function. The output p_{ui} is a probability calculated by the sigmoid activation function. The loss function is defined as:

$$\mathcal{L}oss = \frac{1}{|\mathcal{D}|} \sum_{(u,i)\in\mathcal{D}} \ell_{BCE}(l, p_{ui}) \tag{4}$$

where ℓ_{BCE} is the binary cross entropy, $\mathcal{D}$ is the training dataset that contains the user-item pairs $\langle u, i \rangle$ and the corresponding ground truth l indicating user's "like" ($l = 1$) or "dislike" ($l = 0$) preference.

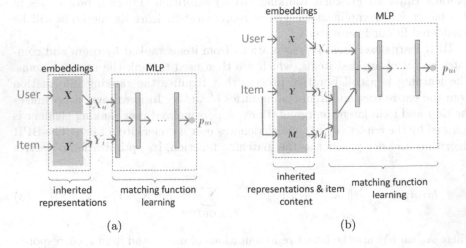

Fig. 2. (a) F2DeepRS without using content; (b) F2DeepRS considering item content.

The second model in Fig. 2b uses the same user and item latent representation initialization and loss function. It additionally includes item content embeddings that are initialized by a pre-trained item content vectors M, which will be introduced later.

It should be mentioned that, the model in Fig. 2b considers the situation where item content is available. However, in a case where the user's content is available, or both are available, a similar embedding layer can be added to the framework. The framework thus can be flexibly extended to different application scenarios. In this paper, more situations are not described and our discussions focus only on whether the model can access to item content as a demonstration.

5   Experiments and Performance Analyses

5.1   Experiments

The dataset of *Yahoo! Music User Ratings of Songs with Artist, Album, and Genre Meta Information, version 1.0* [22] is used for experiments. This dataset represents the Yahoo! Music community's preferences for various songs. This is the largest publicly accessible dataset we can find so far, with split training and testing sets. The dataset contains over 717 million ratings of 136 thousand songs given by 1.8 million users of Yahoo! Music services. In this dataset, it is guaranteed that each user rated at least 20 songs and each item is rated by at least 20 users. The users in the training set and testing set are identical whereas their rated items are non-overlapped. Item genre is hierarchically organized into different "trees". Genre types in the same "tree" are homologous and are thus more similar than genres types in different "trees", which provides useful information that a RS could utilize.

Item genre types are given in categorical values. A commonly method to encode categorical value is the one-hot encoding, which is of low efficiency and cannot reflect between-genre relations. Therefore, we trained dense content vectors for each genre type through discriminating whether two genre types are organized in the same "tree". Specifically, each genre type is initially encoded randomly by a dense vector of a predefined length, and all such vectors compose the content matrix M. A content dataset is constructed to contain the tuples $\langle g_1, g_2 \rangle$ and the ground truth l_g is built, where $l_g = 1$ and $l_g = 0$ indicate genre g_1 and g_2 are from the same and different "tree", respectively. The binary cross-entropy loss is used to update M iteratively. The content matrix M is then transplanted to the model in Fig. 2b.

Both frameworks in Fig. 2 are implemented. The dimension of user/item representations and item genre vectors is empirically set to 64. The number of nodes in MLP is set to 64, 64, 32, 16, 1. Item content vectors M is set to untrainable. The weights of the MLP module are optimized in maximal 80 epochs by the Adam algorithm with learning rate 1e−3. Codes are available at https://github. com/umd-isl-research/F2DeepRS.

For the purpose of comparison, we implemented several different RSs, including the NBCF method proposed in [21] and the BPR algorithm. The BPR algorithm is included to verify the effectiveness of the framework since the proposed F2DeepRS starts from the BPR achievements. Three F2DeepRS models are trained under different configurations: (1) F2DeepRS1: the framework in Fig. 2a, with randomly initialized user and item embedding weights instead of importing from BPR. All weights are updated with the learning rate 1e−3. (2) F2DeepRS2: the framework in Fig. 2a, with imported user and item embedding weights (X and Y) from BPR. Weights of the embedding layers are locked to untrainable. (3) F2DeepRS3: the framework in Fig. 2b, with imported user and item embedding weights (X and Y) from BPR, and imported item content embedding weights M from pre-trained item genre vectors. Weights of the embedding layers are locked to untrainable.

The method DeepCF [2] is also included for performance comparison because it is a model like the proposed framework that hybridizes the modeling of user/item representations and matching function through neural networks. It consists of two neural network modules, both of which can be pre-trained for improved performance (the DeepCF model with pre-trained weights will be referred as "DeepCF+p" in the following texts). Investigations have shown its advantages over many other prestigious methods such as eALS, DMF and NeuMF. However, it cannot inherit weights or knowledge learned by a model working with different mechanisms, e.g., non-neural networks or networks of different architectures, which reduces the flexibility in real applications. Further, it does not have a mechanism to incorporate user/item content information. It would be interesting to see how our proposed models can compete with the state-of-the-art.

The scheme of performance evaluation is as follows. For each user, we sampled a number of items from the entire item pool randomly, then combined them with the items in testing data to be candidates. The size of candidates was made to 100. Let R_u be the recommended items for user u. R_u is obtained by selecting topN=10 items out of the 100 candidates according to the estimation given by different methods, e.g., topN largest matching score output by NBCF, BPR and DeepCF, or topN largest probability above 0.5 output by F2DeepRS. Let T_u be the item list given in testing data with like/dislike preference indicated by u. Then the metrics used to evaluate the recommendation performance include:

$$recall = \frac{|R_u \cap \{T_u | like\}|}{|\{T_u | like\}|} \tag{5}$$

$$negative\ rate = \frac{|R_u \cap \{T_u | dislike\}|}{|\{T_u | dislike\}|} \tag{6}$$

The metric recall (also referred as "hit rate") reflects the ability of a method in recognizing "like" items, while negative rate reflects the ability of avoiding "dislike" items. It should be mentioned that although the Normalized Discounted Cumulative Gain (NDCG) is a metric usually used in some other studies, it is not included in our work because the purpose of our task is not to rank items.

In addition, recommending accuracy is calculated by comparing the predicted preference and the ground truth in testing data. Samples in the two classes (like/dislike) are balanced, so additional metrics are not reported. Recommending accuracy is not applicable to BPR or NBCF because scores calculated by them are used fron item ranking only and does not indicate a user's like/dislike preference.

$$accuracy = \frac{\#\ correct\ predictions}{\#\ items\ in\ testing\ data} \tag{7}$$

5.2   Performance Analyses

The averaged recall and negative rate are plotted in Fig. 3. It is clear that the NBCF algorithm as a conventional collaborative filtering method does not perform as well as the others. Although it generates the best (lowest) negative rate, it is not effective in searching for favoring items for target users. The results demonstrate that NBCF is inefficient in searching similar/neighboring users in a large pool, and can easily miss user interested items.

In contrast, the BPR algorithm improves a lot in finding favoring items. However, when the BPR algorithm generates higher recall, it is also more likely

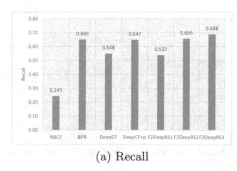 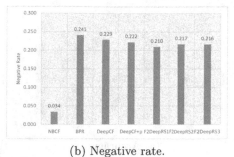

(a) Recall   (b) Negative rate.

Fig. 3. Performance comparison

to include unfavoring items, indicating by the highest negative rate. In terms of the proposed F2DeepRS models in the three configurations, we can see that, even without importing well-learned user/item latent representations, the F2DeepRS1 model yields higher recall compared to NBCF. However, with random initial user/item representations, it does not show advantage over the BPR algorithm, which is a pure user/item latent representation learning method.

In Fig. 3, it is interesting to find that the performance of DeepCF and our proposed models are quite comparable. The models DeepCF and F2DeepRS1 both start from randomized weights. We can see that the DeepCF gains advantage over F2DeepRS1 in recall but lose the advantage in negative rate, and the differences between them are not remarkable. As to DeepCF+p and F2DeepRS2, both of which start from pre-learned knowledge, the advantage of F2DeepRS2 becomes noticeable as it wins in both recall and negative rate. In this experiment, both neural network modules in DeepCF+p are initialized by pre-trained weights, but F2DeepRS2 only imports user and item representations while leaving the weights of matching function learning module still randomly initialized. That demonstrates F2DeepRS2 is more powerful in modeling the like/dislike preference prediction problem.

The model F2DeepRS3, with an extension of item content branch that incorporates item content vectors, wins the highest recall while yielding the lowest negative rate (except for NBCF). As aforementioned, adding a content branch incurs almost none extra computation cost in optimization. The content vectors have been pre-learned to embody content similarities, and therefore assist F2DeepRS3 in identifying more effectively the items a target user would like while filtering out non-preferred ones.

The like/dislike preference prediction accuracy is shown in Fig. 4a. The DeepCF and the proposed F2DeepRS produce almost identical accuracy with random or imported weights correspondingly, with less than 0.4% disparity (DeepCF vs F2DeepRS1, and DeepCF+p vs F2DeepRS2). Generally, importing pre-trained weights or latent representations enhances the accuracy of the two models respectively by about 18%. Additionally, the benefits of considering content information is exhibited again by F2DeepRS3.

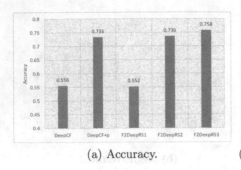
(a) Accuracy.

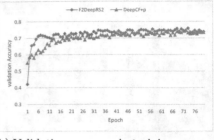
(b) Validation accuracy in training process.

Fig. 4. Comparisons between F2DeepRS and DeepCF.

We particularly analyzed the convergence speed and time cost of DeepCF and F2DeepRS with pre-learned knowledge (DeepCF+p and F2DeepRS2), as they have shown to be very promising recommenders. Under ICRC conditions, a computationally efficient model is more practicable. The validation accuracy is logged during the training process as shown in Fig. 4b. It is noticeable that the DeepCF+p model initially yields better performance than F2DeepRS2. The reason is all the weights of DeepCF+p are pre-trained, but the weights of the matching function learning module in F2DeepRS2 are randomly initialized. Unsurprisingly, randomness makes F2DeepRS2 blindly guess user's preference at the beginning. However, it is encouraging to find the performance of F2DeepRS2 exceeds DeepCF+p in only a couple of epochs and remains relatively stable after 30 epochs, while the accuracy of DeepCF model still creeps upwards slowly until reaching about 50 epochs. The reason might be the concatenation of two neural network modules in DeepCF makes it deeper with more trainable weights than F2DeepRS2 and thus slow the process of weights optimization. As to time cost, on the same implementing platform, the completion of inferencing for every ten thousand users costs DeepCF about 132 s on average. For F2DeepRS2, it is 35 s, saving more than 73% expense in time. F2DeepRS2 demonstrates great efficiency in computation and provides feasible solution for the deployment on ICRC platforms. This may be because the DeepCF needs to pass the initial sparse representations through several layers, while the F2DeepRS2 just needs to index a row of the corresponding user/item embeddings, which reduces the complexity considerably.

6   Conclusion

In this work, we have presented a novel hybrid recommendation framework that integrates the user/item presentations and matching function learning for ICRC platform, which means the system must be computationally friendly, in spite of the huge size of user and item pools. The core ideas are to leverage existing latent user/item representations, and set the goal of predicting barbarized user-item "like" or "dislike" preference instead of item ranking as in many existing methods. We have used of BPR algorithm in our investigation as an example to show the utilization of well-learned representations even if the representations were not derived from non-neural methods. In addition, the proposed framework is flexibly extendable depending on the availability of user or item contents. The effectiveness of incorporating item contents have been shown. The dataset used in this paper has large user and item numbers. In spite of this, the proposed F2DeepRS framework has shown significant efficiency in computation, while keeping performance competitive to both conventional and state-of-the-art methods. The investigation in this paper might be extended in the following aspects. Firstly, strategies to cope with the cold start problem can be combined into our framework, as main focus of the paper is not put on this. In addition, more representation learning methods other than BPR should be tested, and it would be interesting to explore why combining representations learned by a heterogeneous model into our framework is effective.

References

1. Bai, T., Wen, J.R., Zhang, J., Zhao, W.X.: A neural collaborative filtering model with interaction-based neighborhood. In: Proceedings of the 2017 ACM on Conference on Information and Knowledge Management, pp. 1979–1982 (2017)
2. Deng, Z.H., Huang, L., Wang, C.D., Lai, J.H., Philip, S.Y.: DeepCF: a unified framework of representation learning and matching function learning in recommender system. In: Proceedings of the AAAI Conference on Artificial Intelligence, vol. 33, pp. 61–68 (2019)
3. Garg, D., Gupta, P., Malhotra, P., Vig, L., Shroff, G.: Sequence and time aware neighborhood for session-based recommendations: STAN. In: Proceedings of the 42nd International ACM SIGIR Conference on Research and Development in Information Retrieval, pp. 1069–1072 (2019)
4. Hastie, T., Mazumder, R., Lee, J.D., Zadeh, R.: Matrix completion and low-rank SVD via fast alternating least squares. J. Mach. Learn. Res. **16**(1), 3367–3402 (2015)
5. He, J., Li, X., Liao, L.: Category-aware next point-of-interest recommendation via Listwise Bayesian personalized ranking. In: IJCAI, pp. 1837–1843 (2017)
6. He, R., McAuley, J.: VBPR: visual Bayesian personalized ranking from implicit feedback. In: Thirtieth AAAI Conference on Artificial Intelligence (2016)
7. He, X., Chua, T.S.: Neural factorization machines for sparse predictive analytics. In: Proceedings of the 40th International ACM SIGIR Conference on Research and Development in Information Retrieval, pp. 355–364 (2017)
8. He, X., Du, X., Wang, X., Tian, F., Tang, J., Chua, T.S.: Outer product-based neural collaborative filtering. In: Proceedings of the 27th International Joint Conference on Artificial Intelligence, IJCAI 2018, pp. 2227–2233. AAAI Press (2018)
9. He, X., Liao, L., Zhang, H., Nie, L., Hu, X., Chua, T.S.: Neural collaborative filtering. In: Proceedings of the 26th International Conference on World Wide Web, pp. 173–182 (2017)
10. Jiang, Z., Liu, H., Fu, B., Wu, Z., Zhang, T.: Recommendation in heterogeneous information networks based on generalized random walk model and Bayesian personalized ranking. In: Proceedings of the Eleventh ACM International Conference on Web Search and Data Mining, pp. 288–296. ACM (2018)

11. Koren, Y., Bell, R., Volinsky, C.: Matrix factorization techniques for recommender systems. Computer **42**(8), 30–37 (2009)
12. Liu, H., Liu, H., Ji, Q., Zhao, P., Wu, X.: Collaborative deep recommendation with global and local item correlations. Neurocomputing **385**, 278–291 (2020)
13. Liu, Q., Wu, S., Wang, L.: DeepStyle: learning user preferences for visual recommendation. In: Proceedings of the 40th International ACM SIGIR Conference on Research and Development in Information Retrieval, pp. 841–844. ACM (2017)
14. Murthy, Y.S., Koolagudi, S.G.: Content-based music information retrieval (CBMIR) and its applications toward the music industry: a review. ACM Comput. Surv. (CSUR) **51**(3), 1–46 (2018)
15. Park, S., Kim, Y.D., Choi, S.: Hierarchical Bayesian matrix factorization with side information. In: Twenty-Third International Joint Conference on Artificial Intelligence (2013)
16. Porteous, I., Asuncion, A., Welling, M.: Bayesian matrix factorization with side information and Dirichlet process mixtures. In: Twenty-Fourth AAAI Conference on Artificial Intelligence (2010)
17. Rendle, S., Freudenthaler, C., Gantner, Z., Schmidt-Thieme, L.: BPR: Bayesian personalized ranking from implicit feedback. In: Proceedings of the Twenty-Fifth Conference On Uncertainty in Artificial Intelligence, pp. 452–461. AUAI Press (2009)
18. Volkovs, M., Yu, G., Poutanen, T.: DropoutNet: addressing cold start in recommender systems. In: Advances in Neural Information Processing Systems, pp. 4957–4966 (2017)
19. Wang, X., He, X., Wang, M., Feng, F., Chua, T.S.: Neural graph collaborative filtering. In: Proceedings of the 42nd International ACM SIGIR Conference on Research and Development in Information Retrieval, pp. 165–174 (2019)
20. Wang, X., Jin, H., Zhang, A., He, X., Xu, T., Chua, T.S.: Disentangled graph collaborative filtering. In: Proceedings of the 43rd International ACM SIGIR Conference on Research and Development in Information Retrieval, pp. 1001–1010 (2020)
21. Wang, Z., Xie, Y., Murphey, Y.L.: User-specific music recommendation. In: 2019 IEEE Symposium Series on Computational Intelligence (SSCI), pp. 1179–1184. IEEE (2019)
22. Yahoo!: Ratings and classification data (2007). https://webscope.sandbox.yahoo.com
23. Zhang, S., Yao, L., Sun, A., Tay, Y.: Deep learning based recommender system: a survey and new perspectives. ACM Comput. Surv. (CSUR) **52**(1), 5 (2019)

A Novel Rule-Based Online Judge Recommender System to Promote Computer Programming Education

Md. Mostafizer Rahman(✉), Yutaka Watanobe, Uday Kiran Rage, and Keita Nakamura

Graduate Department of Computer Science and Engineering, The University of Aizu, Aizu-Wakamatsu City, Fukushima, Japan
{yutaka,udayrage,keita-n}@u-aizu.ac.jp

Abstract. Reducing students' high dropout rates in the computer programming courses is a challenging problem of great concern in computer science education. Online Judge (OJ) systems were recently being investigated to address this problem and promote computer programming education. Most of the existing OJ systems have been confined only for evaluation purposes, and do not provide any personalized recommendations to enhance the productivity of a student. With this motivation, this paper proposes a novel rule-based OJ recommender system to promote computer programming education. The proposed system involves the following five steps: (i) scoring the programs submitted by a student automatically, (ii) generation of a transactional database, (iii) clustering the database with respect to their scores and other evaluation parameters, (iv) discovering interesting association rules that exist in each of the cluster's data, and (v) providing appropriate recommendations to the users. Experimental results on the data generated by a real-world OJ system demonstrate that the proposed system is efficient.

Keywords: Programming education · Machine learning · Data mining · Clustering · Rule extraction · Online judge

1 Introduction

Computer programming is a fundamental course in computer science education. Many educational organizations (e.g., schools and universities) are redesigning their academic curriculum to effectively meet the basic literacy requirements of programming education. A key obstacle encountered in the traditional class room-based computer programming classes is the students' high failure and dropout rate [1], which can be attributed to several factors such as limited available class time, the limited numbers of classrooms and teachers, and limitations in other forms of logistic support. Online Judge (OJ) systems provide an alternative vital platform for the students to pursue their programming studies over a period of years [3]. In this paper, we focus on improving the services of OJ systems.

© Springer Nature Switzerland AG 2021
H. Fujita et al. (Eds.): IEA/AIE 2021, LNAI 12799, pp. 15–27, 2021.
https://doi.org/10.1007/978-3-030-79463-7_2

Since the introduction of OJ system in International Collegiate Programming Contest [2], many educational institutions have started developing their own OJ systems to accelerate students' learning abilities in programming courses. Few examples include UVa (University of Valladolid) online judge [4], Jutge.org [5], URI (Universidade Regional Integrada) online judge [6], and Aizu Online Judge [7]. To the best of our knowledge, most of the existing OJ systems are only evaluation systems that try to strength the students' programming skills through *"learning-by-doing"* approach. Unfortunately, these systems do not provide any type of personalized recommendation services [8] to the students (or instructors) to improve the computer programming skill set. In this context, there is a need for developing OJ recommender system that can promote computer programming education.

This paper argues that developing an OJ recommender system is a non-trivial and challenging task. The reason is as follows: *"Rule-based recommender systems have been widely studied in eLearning systems (e.g., Moodle) [9]. Since eLearning systems capture only the grades of an exam (or marks attained for each question), they are inadequate to capture the types of bugs that are occurring in a program for each submission. Consequently, these conventional eLearning-based recommender systems cannot be directly extendable to OJ systems, where recommendations have to be provided based on parameters such as number of attempts made by the student to complete a program, type of bugs appeared in the code whenever a student has submitted the program, runtime and memory consumed by an algorithm"*.

In this paper, we propose a novel rule-based OJ recommender system to promote computer programming education. The proposed system initially scores the programs submitted by a student automatically. Next, a transactional database is generated by combining the scores of OJ system with other academic records (e.g., attendance, algorithm assignment, paper exam, and practical exam). Next, clustering is performed on the generated transactional database to group the students into clusters. Next, association rule mining is performed on the sub-database of each students' clusters to discovering interesting association rules. Finally, the generally associated rules are employed to provide personalized recommendation to a student. Please note that the generated information may also help teachers and instructors to take the necessary steps to enhance students' programming and academic performance. Experimental results on the data generated by a real-world OJ system, called Aizu Online Judge (AOJ), demonstrate that the proposed recommender system is efficient.

The remainder of the paper is organized as follows. In Sect. 2, we present a background and related works. Section 3 presents the proposed rule based online judge recommender system. In Sect. 4, we presented the experimental results and discussion. Section 5 draws conclusions with a look at future work.

2   Background and Related Works

2.1   Rule-Based eLearning Recommender Systems

With the rise of online learning it has become a much needed personalized recommender system (RS) for students and instructors. RS provides suggestions to students and instructors for decision making [9]. Most of the recommender systems are built based on the Collaborative Filtering, Content-based Filtering, Knowledge-based Filtering, and Hybrid Systems [10]. When considering automated programming evaluations using eLearning platforms, it fails, instead evaluating programming source codes semi-automatically [11]. In contrast, Online Judge (OJ) systems assess the programming source codes automatically and generate many parameters such as (wrong answer, accepted, cpu time, memory usages, time limit error, etc.). In particular, due to the limitations of automatically evaluating programming source codes, the traditional eLearning recommendation system is not effective for programming education. We solved this problem by using a rule-based eLearning recommendation system for computer programming education. Our rule-based recommendation system provides suggestions using programming assessment parameters and academic scores.

2.2   Online Judge Systems

Online judge or automated programming assessment systems are now widely used as an academic tool in programming classes in many educational institutions, which are playing important roles in improving student programming skills, knowledge, and overall academic performance. The vast amounts of data collected by these systems can help researchers to find students' flaws in programming and thus expands the scope of available improvements. As a result, numerous studies have focused on student programming education via online judge systems and data-driven analyzes have been conducted using the resources of those systems.

In [12], the authors used learning logs of six courses collected from the M2B system. A recurrent neural network (RNN) is used to predict student final grades. This study does not provide any personalized recommendation for students, instead it only predict the grades. Mekterović et al. [13] proposed an automated programming assessment system for conducting programming courses. They created an educational software called Edgar to automatically evaluate programming assignments and other programming-related tasks. In particular, Edgar is not a personalized recommender system or provides suggestions to students, teachers, or instructors.

The proposed rule-based recommendation system can provide recommendations for students, teachers, and instructors using the source code assessment results and academic scores. Our proposed novel rule-based recommendation system is different from other existing studies.

2.3   Clustering Algorithms

Within the context of artificial intelligence (AI) and machine learning (ML), clustering algorithms are frequently used in many real applications. Some prominent clustering algorithms are logistic regression, SVM, decision tree, k-nearest neighbor (KNN), k-means, DBSCAN, CLARA. Among these k-means is widely used clustering algorithm for many real-world applications. This algorithm has two limitations, (i) determining the value of k and (ii) selecting cluster centers randomly. The Elbow method is an effective technique for selecting the ideal number of k value for clustering. We used the modified k-means clustering algorithm [14] for optimal center selection.

2.4   Elbow Method

The elbow method is a proven technique for determining the ideal number of k values for the clustering algorithms. It uses sum square error (SSE) to calculate the optimal number of clusters. Elbow method has reduced unnecessary clustering in datasets. Normally, increasing the value of k then automatically decreases the SSE value. When the SSE value is drastically decreased, the point is caught as the ideal number of clusters. In [15,16], presented the effectiveness of the Elbow method for selecting optimal k value.

2.5   Association Rule Mining

Association rule mining is a kind of unsupervised data mining and knowledge discovery technique. Finding frequent item sets from big data is the key factor of association rules mining [17]. The Apriori and FP-growth algorithms are most effective for association rules mining [18,19]. FP-growth algorithm is much faster than Apriori. In Apriori, to generate candidate itemsets required to scan the database repeatedly. But, FP-growth algorithm is scanned the database only twice to complete the entire process. Let, $I = \{i_1, i_2, i_3, i_4, i_5, \ldots\ldots\ldots, i_d\}$ is a set of all the items in the database. The databases are formed based on a set of transactions $T = \{t_1, t_2, t_3, t_4, \ldots\ldots\ldots, t_N\}$ where every single transaction t_i is a subset of $I(t_i \subseteq I)$. An association rule can be expressed as $R = A \longrightarrow B$, where A, B is a subset of I ($A \subseteq I, B \subseteq I$) and $A \cap B = \phi$. The set of items in A is called antecedent (if), on the other hand, B is called the consequent (then). Confidence (C) and support (S) for a rule R can be expressed as follows:

$$Support, S(R) = \frac{\sigma(A \cup B)}{N} \tag{1}$$

$$Confidence, C(R) = \frac{\sigma(A \cup B)}{\sigma(A)} \tag{2}$$

FP-growth algorithm has two [20] main steps as follows: (i) FP-tree construction, (ii) mining all frequent patterns using FP-tree. Overall, the proposed rule-based OJ recommender system to promote computer programming education is novel and distinct from others.

3   Proposed Rule-Based OJ Recommender System

Our proposed rule-based online judge recommender system has two steps, (i) creation of online judge transactional database (OJ-TDB) and (ii) knowledge discovery from OJ-TDB. Now we describe each step as below.

3.1   Creation of OJ Transactional Database (OJ-TDB)

3.1.1   Partial Transactional Database from OJ System

The Online Judge (OJ) system is a web service for automatically evaluating programs. Users submit program(p) to OJ. The OJ compiles those submitted programs and returns judgments with parameters. The judgements include judge identifier, programming language, verdict of the judge (say, success or type of error), runtime, memory, code size, submission date and judgement date. We now describe the mathematical model to represent the judgements in a transactional database format.

Let $U = \{u_1, u_2, \cdots, u_m\}, m \geq 1$, be the set of users (or students) of an OJ system. Let $P = \{p_1, p_2, \cdots, p_n\}, n \geq 1$, be the set of distinct problems. Let $SID = \{sid_1, sid_2, \cdots, sid_p\}, p \geq 1$, be the set of submission identifiers. Once the user submits a program in any language to an OJ system, a judge in OJ analyzes the program and provides a verdict. Let $V = \{AC, RTE, LTE, WA, CE, PrE, MLE, OLE\}$ be the set of verdicts, where AC = Accepted, WA = Wrong Answer, TLE = Time Limit Error, RTE = Run Time Error, CE = Compile Error, MLE = Memory Limit Error, OLE = Output Limit Error, PrE = Presentation Error.

When users submit the solutions to the AOJ system and the AOJ system responds with this verdict which is either accepted or erroneous (WA, CE, TLE, MLE, RTE, etc.).

Definition 1. *The number of solutions accepted by the AOJ system from the total submissions of a student is called solution accuracy.*

$$Accuracy(Acu) = \frac{Total\ number\ of\ accepted\ solutions}{Total\ number\ of\ submissions} \tag{3}$$

Example 1. If an user (u_1) submits a total of 14 solutions to the AOJ system, only 8 out of 14 solutions have been accepted by the AOJ. Then, according to Eq. (3), the solution accuracy of user (u_1) is about 57 %.

The output of the OJ system, denoted as $OP_{oj} = \{s_r, u_s, p_t, v_u, acu_v\}$, where $s_r \in SID$, $u_s \in U$, $p_t \in P$, $v_u \in V$, $acu_v \in Acu$. The sample output of the OJ system is shown in Table 1.

3.1.2   Partial Transactional Database from Learning Management System

Learning Content Management System (LCMS) has a huge impact on education. Thousands of courses are administered by LCMS on a daily basis around

Table 1. Sample submission logs of an OJ system

SID	U	P	V	Acu
917006	u_1	p_1	AC	57
917007	u_2	p_2	WA	64
917008	u_3	p_7	RTE	89

the world. Online exams, quiz, grading are all smoothly conducted by LCMS. LCMS has limitations in automatically evaluating the submitted programs but it is evaluated semi-automatically [11]. The output generated by LCMS for a problem, denoted as $OP_{lcms} = \{u_r, p_t, grade\}$, where $grade = \{A^+, A, B, C, D, F\}$. The sample grading data generated by a LCMS is shown in Table 2.

Table 2. Sample scores produced by the LCMS

U	Programming assig. (PA)	Coding exam (CoE)	Paper exam (PE)
u_1	110	90	101
u_2	100	79	97
u_3	94	80	104

3.1.3 Joining the LCMS and OJ Transactional Databases

The tables OJ and LCMS are joined with one another to produce a joined transactional database (J-TDB). That is, J-$TDB = OP_{oj} \bowtie OP_{lmcs} = \{SID, U, P, V, Acu, PA, CoE, PE\}$. This J-TDB will be mined to discover knowledge, which will be used to improve the programming skills of the users. A sample of J-TDB by using the Tables 1 and 2 is shown in Table 3.

Table 3. Sample J-TDB by using the Tables 1 and 2

SID	U	P	V	Acu	PA	CoE	PE
917006	u_1	p_1	AC	57	110	90	101
917007	u_2	p_2	WA	64	100	79	97
917008	u_3	p_7	RTE	89	94	80	104
917009	u_1	p_2	TLE	57	110	90	101
917010	u_3	p_1	AC	89	94	80	104

3.1.4 Creation of OJ Transactional Database (OJ-TDB)

Once we have converted the attributes' value of Table 3 into IDs for experimental uses, we called it online judge-transactional database (OJ-TDB). The values of attributes are converted into IDs according to Table 4.

Table 4. Conversion of values of the attributes into IDs

ID (x)	Value	Attributes	ID (x)	Value	Attributes
1	P_1		80	$\geq 80\%$	
2	P_2	Problems (P)	81	$65\% - 79\%$	Programming Assign. (PA)
.	.		82	$45\% - 64\%$	
57	P_{57}		83	$< 45\%$	
60	$\geq 75\%$		90	$\geq 80\%$	
61	$60\% - 74\%$	Accuracy (Acu)	91	$65\% - 79\%$	Coding Examination (CoE)
62	$45\% - 59\%$		92	$45\% - 64\%$	
63	$< 54\%$		93	$< 45\%$	
70	AC		100	$\geq 80\%$	
71	CE		101	$65\% - 79\%$	Paper Examination (PE)
72	MLE		102	$45\% - 64\%$	
73	OLE	Verdicts (V)	103	$< 45\%$	
74	PrE				
75	RTE				
76	TLE				
77	WA				

Let, define the IDs of attributes A = {{P}, {Acu}, {V}, {PA}, {CoE}, {PE}} where problems (P) = $\{x|x \in \mathbb{N}, 1 \leq x \leq 57\}$, accuracy (Acu) = $\{x|x \in \mathbb{N}, 60 < x \leq 63\}$, verdict (V) = $\{x|x \in \mathbb{N}, 70 \leq x \leq 77\}$, PA = $\{x|x \in \mathbb{N}, 80 \leq x \leq 83\}$, CoE = $\{x|x \in \mathbb{N}, 90 \leq x \leq 93\}$, PE = $\{x|x \in \mathbb{N}, 100 \leq x \leq 103\}$. So, all the sets P, Acu, V, PA, CoE, and PE are the subset of A ($P \subseteq A, Acu \subseteq A, V \subseteq A, PA \subseteq A, CoE \subseteq A, PE \subseteq A$).

After converting the value of the attributes to IDs, a sample online judge transactional database (OJ-TDB) is shown in Table 5. Later OJ-TDB has been used for all the experimental purposes.

Table 5. A sample OJ transactional database (OJ-TDB)

U	P	Acu	V	PA	CoE	PE
u_1	29	57	70	81	90	100
u_9	17	61	72	80	92	102
u_{21}	6	63	77	81	93	103
u_{11}	39	62	73	82	91	102

3.2 Framework of Rule-Based OJ Recommender System

The framework of online judge recommender system is shown in Fig. 1. We now explain this framework. The entire process of knowledge discovery and rule mining have been divided into two phases. First, we clustered the OJ transactional database (OJ-TDB) using k-means clustering algorithm. Based on the numerical analysis of each cluster, we extracted useful hidden features that are not plainly visible in the data.

In second phase, we applied the FP-growth pattern mining and association rule mining algorithm to each cluster. Diversifying various parameters such as minimum support and confidence of the FP-growth algorithm, we obtained several interesting patterns and association rules from each cluster. The framework of our proposed rule-based OJ recommender system is shown in Fig. 1

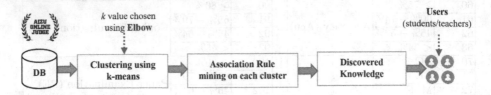

Fig. 1. The framework of the proposed rule-based OJ recommender system

4   Experimental Results and Discussion

The AOJ system [7] has more than 5 million source code archives, 80,000 users, and 2,500 different interesting problems. The experimental OJ transactional database was generated by combining the data produced by the AOJ and the conventional learning management system. The generated database contained 81 items and 57,822 transactions. Similar data generated by the AOJ system was also employed for other research purposes [21,22].

Figure 2 shows the frequency distribution of items in transactional database. The X-axis represents the ranking of items in descending order of their *frequency* values. The Y-axis represents the *frequency* of an item. The following two observations can be drawn from this figure: (i) The distribution of items' frequencies follow long-tail (or exponential) distribution, and (ii) Few items (especially, top-20) items have high frequencies, while remaining items have relatively low frequencies in the data. This long-tail distribution of items posses challenges in developing an efficient recommender system. We employ clustering technique to address the long-tail distribution problem.

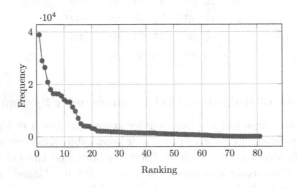

Fig. 2. Ranking of the attributes based on frequencies

4.1   Identifying Optimal k Value Using Elbow and Clustering

Clustering using k-means algorithm is an important step in our system. It influences the overall performance of our recommender system. Identifying the appropriate k value is a key task in our clustering step. We employed elbow method to identify the right k value. Figure 3 shows the SSE values generated by the Elbow method for various k values. It can be observed that their is not much variation in the SSE values when k is increased from 4 to 8. Henceforth, k-means clustering was performed on the database by setting $k = 4$.

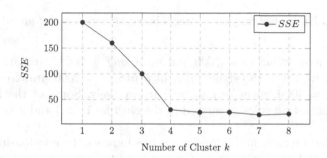

Fig. 3. Elbow method for selecting optimal number of clusters

Now our data resources are grouped into four (4) clusters. The similarity characteristics of the students in each cluster are very identical. Then, we analyzed the clustering data using a data analytical tool and presented the results in the following sections.

4.2   Extracting Association Rules

For each cluster, we applied frequent pattern mining and association rule mining algorithm to extract patterns and association rules. Several data pre-processing steps have been performed to extract the hidden association rules from each cluster. The association rules determined the actual relationship between submission logs and class performance scores. We used Python library [23] function to implement this experiment.

Figure 4 describes the number of frequent patterns getting generated in various clusters at different minimum support ($minSup$) values. The following two observations can be drawn from this figure (i) increase in $minSup$ value has decreased the number of patterns being generated at different $minSup$ values for various clusters. It is because many patterns have failed to satisfy the increased $minSup$ value (ii) Clusters 2 and 3 have generated large number of patterns at any given number of $minSup$ value. Cluster 4 has generated lowest number of patterns at any given $minSup$.

Finally, we have extracted association rules from each cluster by setting optimal $minConf$ and $minSup$ threshold values. For clusters 1 and 4, we set a

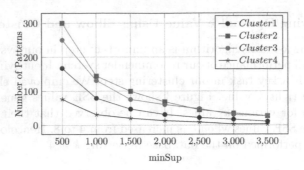

Fig. 4. Number of frequent patterns based on various *minSup* values

threshold value of $minSup = 1500$ and $minConf = 90\%$. Similarly, for clusters 2 and 3, we set a threshold value of $minSup = 2000$, $minConf = 90\%$ and $minSup = 3000$, $minConf = 90\%$ respectively. Some of the interesting and useful association rules generated in the clusters 1, 2, 3 and 4 are shown in Table 6.

The association rules in Table 6 for clusters indicate the relationship between programming and academic scores. Cluster 1 students are involved with (*i*) the higher scores on academic exams, (*ii*) the higher solution accuracy, and (*iii*) the highest number of accepted verdicts. Cluster 2 students are connected with (*i*) the higher PE and PA scores, (*ii*) the lower CoE scores, (*iii*) the higher value of solution accuracy, and (*iv*) the higher number of accepted verdicts.

So far, the activities of the students of cluster 1 and cluster 2 are enthusiastic and their level of knowledge and skills in programming and theories are satisfactory. Moreover, we have some recommendations based on the extracted features and rules of these two clusters (1 and 2) as follows:

– Take special treatment for extraordinary students.
– General assignment problems are too easy for them, so more difficult problems can uplift their programming skills and knowledge.
– Encourage students to participate in programming competitions, lectures, workshops, as well as read other codes.
– Get involved in creating project development experience.

In Table 6, the extracted association rules for cluster 3 students are related to (*i*) the lower CoE scores, (*ii*) the lower solution accuracy, (*iii*) maximum number of error verdicts, and (*iv*) the moderate number of PE and PA scores. Similarly, cluster 4 students are involved with (*i*) the very lower PE, CoE, and PA scores, (*ii*) the lower value of solution accuracy, (*iii*) a large number of error verdicts, and (*iv*) a few accepted verdicts.

After analyzing the hidden features and association rules from different perspectives, we have identified some flaws in the programming and academic performance of cluster 3 and cluster 4 students. A set of supportive measures can be helpful for those students to improve programming skills as well as academic performance. The recommendations are as follows:

Table 6. Extracted association rules for the students of clusters 1, 2, 3 and 4

Cluster	Rules
	R1: $PE \geq 80\%$ && V_AC && $PA \geq 80\% \longrightarrow Acu(\geq 75\%)$
	R2: $PE(65\% - 79\%)$ && $V\_AC \longrightarrow Acu(\geq 75\%)$
Cluster 1	**R3:** $PE \geq 80\%$ && $V\_AC \longrightarrow Acu(\geq 75\%)$
	R4: V_AC && $PA \geq 80\% \longrightarrow Acu(\geq 75\%)$
	R5: V_AC && $CoE(45\% - 64\%) \longrightarrow Acu(\geq 75\%)$
	R1: $PE(45\% - 79\%)$ && $V\_AC \longrightarrow Acu(\geq 75\%)$
	R2: V_AC && $PA(65\% - 79\%)$ && $CoE < 45\% \longrightarrow Acu(\geq 75\%)$
Cluster 2	**R3:** $PE(65\% - 79\%)$ && V_AC && $CoE < 45\% \longrightarrow Acu(\geq 75\%)$
	R4: V_AC && $CoE(45\% - 64\%) \longrightarrow Acu(\geq 75\%)$
	R5: V_AC && $PA(45\% - 79\%) \longrightarrow Acu(\geq 75\%)$
	R6: $V\_CE \longrightarrow Acu(< 45\%)$
	R1: $PE(45\% - 64\%)$ && $Acu < 45\% \longrightarrow CoE < 45\%$
	R2: $PE(65\% - 79\%) \longrightarrow CoE < 45\%$
	R3: $V\_AC \longrightarrow Acu \geq 75\%$ && $CoE < 45\%$
Cluster 3	**R4:** $Acu < 45\% \longrightarrow CoE < 45\%$
	R5: $PE(45\% - 64\%)$ && $Acu \geq 75\% \longrightarrow CoE < 45\%$
	R6: $Acu \geq 75\%$ && $V\_AC \longrightarrow CoE < 45\%$
	R7: $Acu < 45\%$ && $PA(45\% - 64\%) \longrightarrow CoE < 45\%$
	R1: $Acu >= 75\% \longrightarrow CoE < 45\%$
	R2: $V\_AC \longrightarrow CoE < 45\%$
	R3: $PE < 45\%$ && $Acu < 45\%$ && $PA < 45\% \longrightarrow CoE < 45\%$
Cluster 4	**R4:** $PE < 45\%$ && $Acu < 45\% \longrightarrow CoE < 45\%$
	R5: $PE < 45\%$ && $PA < 45\% \longrightarrow CoE < 45\%$
	R6: $Acu \geq 75\%$ && $V\_AC \longrightarrow CoE < 45\%$
	R7: $PA < 45\%$ && $CoE < 45\% \longrightarrow PE < 45\%$

- According to extracted features and rules, special assistance can be provided to students to improve programming and academic performance.
- Ensure understanding of programming and algorithms in lectures and observe students' responses.
- Encourage students to solve exercise problems through self-knowledge and understanding.
- Monitor the submission activities in the AOJ system.

5   Conclusion

In this research, we have proposed a novel rule-based recommender system for online Judge systems. The proposed system clusters students based on source code submission logs with class performance scores, then applied a pattern mining algorithm to extract association rules. Important features and rules are identified in each cluster. These features and rules can be used as supportive materials for programming and academic activities. Also, the interaction and interdependence between programming and academic performance have been focused in this research. Recommendations have been provided for the promotion of programming education on the basis of extracted features and rules. In such cases, the online judge system provides practical help to students desiring to extend their programming education capabilities.

Acknowledgement. This research was funded by the Japan Society for the Promotion of Science (JSPS) KAKENHI (Grant Number 19K12252).

Conflict of Interest. The authors declare that they have no conflict of interests.

Ethics Approval. This research was approved by the Research Ethics Examination Boards, The University of Aizu, Japan.

References

1. Margulieux, L.E., Morrison, B.B., Decker, A.: Reducing withdrawal and failure rates in introductory programming with subgoal labeled worked examples. Int. J. STEM Educ. **7**(1), 1–16 (2020). https://doi.org/10.1186/s40594-020-00222-7
2. ICPC. https://icpc.global/icpc/
3. Wasik, S., Antczak, M., Badura, J., Laskowski, A., Sternal, T.: A survey on online judge systems and their applications. ACM Comput. Surv. (CSUR) **51**(1), 1–34 (2018)
4. Revilla, M.A., Manzoor, S., Liu, R.: Competitive learning in informatics: the UVa online judge experience. Olympiads Inf. **2**, 131–148 (2008)
5. Petit, J., et al.: Jutge.org: characteristics and experiences. IEEE Trans. Learn. Technol. **11**(3), 321–333 (2018)
6. Bez, J.L., Tonin, N.A., Rodegheri, P.R.: URI online judge academic: a tool for algorithms and programming classes. In: Proceedings of the 2014 9th International Conference on Computer Science Education, Vancouver, BC, Canada, pp. 149–152 (2014)
7. Watanobe, Y.: Aizu online judge (2018). https://onlinejudge.u-aizu.ac.jp
8. Saito, T., Watanobe, Y.: Learning path recommendation system for programming education based on neural networks. Int. J. Distance Educ. Technol. (IJDET) **18**(1), 36–64 (2020)
9. Klašnja-Milićević, A., Ivanović, M., Nanopoulos, A.: Recommender systems in e-learning environments: a survey of the state-of-the-art and possible extensions. Artif. Intell. Rev. **44**, 571–604 (2015)
10. Khanal, S.S., Prasad, P.W.C., Alsadoon, A., Maag, A.: A systematic review: machine learning based recommendation systems for e-learning. Educ. Inf. Technol. **25**(4), 2635–2664 (2019). https://doi.org/10.1007/s10639-019-10063-9
11. Yusof, N., Zin, N.A.M., Adnan, N.S.: Java programming assessment tool for assignment module in moodle e-learning system. In: Proceedings of the International Conference on Teaching and Learning in Higher Education in conjunction with Regional Conference on Engineering Education and Research in Higher Education, Malaysia, pp. 767–773 (2012)
12. Okubo, F., Yamashita, T., Shimada, A., Konomi, S.: Students' performance prediction using data of multiple courses by recurrent neural network. In: Proceedings of the 25th International Conference on Computers in Education (ICCE), Christchurch, New Zealand, pp. 439–444 (2017)

13. Mekterović, I., Brkić, L., Milašinović, B., Baranović, M.: Building a comprehensive automated programming assessment system. IEEE Access **8**, 81154–81172 (2020)
14. Rahman, M.M., Watanobe, Y.: An efficient approach for selecting initial centroid and outlier detection of data clustering. In: Proceedings of the 18th International Conference on Intelligent Software Methodologies, Tools and Techniques (SoMeT19), Kuching, Malaysia, pp. 616–628 (2019)
15. Marutho, D., Hanadaka, S.H., Wijaya, E., Muljono: The determination of cluster number at k-mean using elbow method and purity evaluation on headline news. In: Proceedings of the 2018 International Seminar on Application for Technology of Information and Communication, Semarang, Indonesia, pp. 533–538 (2018)
16. Yuan, C., Yang, H.: Research on k-value selection method of k-means clustering algorithm. J-Multidiscip. Sci. J. **2**(2), 226–235 (2019)
17. Kamsu-Foguem, B., Rigal, F., Mauget, F.: Mining association rules for the quality improvement of the production process. Expert Syst. Appl. **40**(4), 1034–1045 (2013)
18. Yuan, J., Ding, S.: Research and improvement on association rule algorithm based on FP-growth. In: Proceedings of the International Conference on Web Information Systems and Mining, China, pp. 306–313 (2012)
19. Wang, P., An, C., Wang, L.: An improved algorithm for mining association rule in relational database. In: Proceedings of the International Conference on Machine Learning and Cybernetics, Lanzhou, China, pp. 247–252 (2014)
20. Han, J., Pei, J., Yin, Y.: Mining frequent patterns without candidate generation. In: Proceedings of the 2000 ACM SIGMOD International Conference on Management of Data, New York, USA, pp. 1–12 (2000)
21. Rahman, M.M., Watanobe, Y., Nakamura, K.: Source code assessment and classification based on estimated error probability using attentive LSTM language model and its application in programming education. Appl. Sci. **10**(8), 2973 (2020)
22. Rahman, M.M., Watanobe, Y., Nakamura, K.: A neural network based intelligent support model for program code completion. Sci. Program. **2020**, 1–18 (2020)
23. Kiran, R.U.: FP-growth library (2020). https://github.com/udayRage/pami_pykit/tree/master/traditional/fpgrowth

Using Machine Learning to Predict Salaries
of Major League Baseball Players

Cheng-Yu Lee[1], Ping-Yu Hsu[1], Ming-Shien Cheng[2]([✉]), Jun-Der Leu[1], Ni Xu[1],
and Bo-Lun Kan[1]

[1] Department of Business Administration, National Central University, No. 300, Jhongda Road,
Jhongli City 32001, Taoyuan County, Taiwan (R.O.C.)
984401019@cc.ncu.edu.tw

[2] Department of Industrial Engineering and Management, Ming Chi University of Technology,
No. 84, Gongzhuan Road, Taishan District, New Taipei City 24301, Taiwan (R.O.C.)
mscheng@mail.mcut.edu.tw

Abstract. Major League Baseball is one of the most watched sports in the world. In recent years, in addition to focusing on the performance of a player and his team, a player's salary has also been a focus of fan discussion, always generating discussion and beginning to examine whether a player's performance really matches his worth. Therefore, how to evaluate the salary of players has always been a hot topic. The most direct basis is the performance of players in the game. In addition to the statistical performance of players on the field, many scholars have also proposed some new variables that may affect the salary of players. At present, there have been many studies on the salary of major league baseball, and there are many reasons for the influence of salary. Some scholars even divide the players into pitcher and hitter for analysis. Therefore, this study focused on the players into the compensation to the annual salary increase do interval, using machine learning methods, such as limit gradient (XGBoost) to do a classification prediction model, From the research results, it can be concluded that the new variables are helpful for the increase of accuracy.

Keywords: MLB · XGBoost · Predicting salaries · Classification

1 Introduction

Major League Baseball (MLB) is one of the top professional baseball leagues and one of the events attracting huge attention in the world. In addition to the players and the team's performance, players' salaries are also the focus of discussion among fans. Every time a team spends a lot of money to sign a star player, there is a discussion and fans start examining whether the player's performance matches his worth.

The basis for evaluating a player's salary has attracted much research attention. The most direct basis is the performance of the player in the game. In addition to the performance of players on the field, many scholars have proposed some variables that may affect players' salary, such as all-star selections, golden glove awards, health status,

H. Fujita et al. (Eds.): IEA/AIE 2021, LNAI 12799, pp. 28–33, 2021.
https://doi.org/10.1007/978-3-030-79463-7_3

age, and fielding position (Meltzer 2005). Golden glove awards, race (Palmer and King 2006), MVP awards, all-star selections and market demographics, age (Hakes and Turner Hakes and Turner 2011), are all off-court variables that influence the player's salary. There are many other factors that may influence players' salaries off the field. Therefore, this study aims to explore more external factors that influence players' salaries. In this study, in addition to the variables mentioned in previous literature that influence players' salaries, external factors that may influence players' salaries are also included in the model, such as players' team, team winning percentage, team ranking and other advanced baseball data. According to the research literature, there is no research on the prediction of the salary increase of players by using the classification method.

Based on the above background and problems, this study uses the classification method in machine learning to construct the model and predict the range of players' salary increase, and sets up two types of model: pitcher model and hitter model. We used the classification method–XGBoost which was a popular tool used in Kaggle competition in recent years, and was a decision tree algorithm to achieve Gradient Boosting. This method is suitable for regression analysis and classification, with strong explanatory power and fast prediction speed.

This paper organized as follow: (1) Introduction: Research background, motivation and purpose. (2) Related work: Review of scholars researches on the variables affecting salary and classification model–XGBoost. (3) Research methodology: Content of research process in this study. (4) Result analysis: Experimental results and the discussion of the test results. (5) Conclusion and future research: Contribution of the study, and possible future research direction is discussed.

2 Related Work

Magel and Hoffman (2015) adopted all the above mentioned variables—listed in Tables 1 and 2, so the player variables adopted in this study are mainly the player variables mentioned in the study of Magel and Hoffman (2015). With the development of computer technology, there have been more advanced methods of baseball statistics in recent years. The evaluation of players' performance is not only based on basic data, but also on advanced baseball data, such as team ranking, team winning rate, whether the player is in the contract year (listed in Table 3), were also added. These added variables have not been used in previous studies.

3 Research Methodology

The research architecture is shown in Fig. 1. The collected data about the two main players were collated and their performance and salary were combined and classified by year. After the classification is completed, the feature was screened. After the screening, the three machine learning methods mentioned above were used for classification prediction. The methods mentioned in the experiment flow chart are further explained in the following sections.

Table 1. The variables of pitchers

Variable	Scholars
W (Wins)	(Magel and Hoffman 2015)
L (Losses)	(Magel and Hoffman 2015)
ERA (Earned Run Average)	(Magel and Hoffman 2015)
GS (Game Started)	(Magel and Hoffman 2015)
GF (Game Finished)	(Magel and Hoffman 2015)
CG (Complete Games)	(Magel and Hoffman 2015)
SHO (Shutouts)	(Magel and Hoffman 2015)
SV (Saves)	(Magel and Hoffman 2015)
IP (Inning Pitched)	(Magel and Hoffman 2015; Scully 1974)
H (Hits)	(Magel and Hoffman 2015)
R (Run Scored)	(Magel and Hoffman 2015)
ER (Earned Runs)	(Magel and Hoffman 2015)
BB (Based on Ball)	(Magel and Hoffman 2015)
IBB (International Based on Ball)	(Magel and Hoffman 2015)
SO (Stricksout)	(Magel and Hoffman 2015)
HBP (Times Hit by a Pitch)	(Magel and Hoffman 2015)
BK (Balks)	(Magel and Hoffman 2015)
WP (Wild Pitches)	(Magel and Hoffman 2015)
BF (Batters Faced)	(Magel and Hoffman 2015)
AGE (Age)	(Magel and Hoffman 2015; Hochberg 2011; Hakes and Turner 2011; Dinnerstein 2007; Palmer and King 2006; Meltzer 2005)

Table 2. The variables of hitters

Variable	Scholars
PA (Plate Apperances)	(Meltzer 2005)
AB (At-Bats)	(Dinnerstein 2007; Palmer and King 2006; Scully 1974)
R (Runs)	(Magel and Hoffman 2015)
2B (Doubles Hits)	(Magel and Hoffman 2015)
3B (Triples Hits)	(Magel and Hoffman 2015)
HR (Home Runs)	(Dinnerstein 2007)
RBI (Runs Batted In)	(Dinnerstein 2007; Palmer and King 2006)
SB (Stolen Bases)	(Hochberg 2011)
CS (Caught Stealing)	(Magel and Hoffman 2015)
BB (Bases on Ball)	(Magel and Hoffman 2015)
SO (Strikesout)	(Magel and Hoffman 2015)
AVG (Batting Average)	(Magel and Hoffman 2015; Dinnerstein 2007; Scully 1974)
OBP (On-Base-Percentage)	(Magel and Hoffman 2015; Hakes and Turner 2011; Dinnerstein 2007; Palmer and King 2006; Scully 1974)
SLG (Slugging Percentage)	(Magel and Hoffman 2015; Dinnerstein 2007, Palmer and King 2006; Scully 1974)
OPS (On-base Plus Slugging	(Magel and Hoffman 2015; Hochberg 2011; Hakes and Turner 2011)
OPS+	(Magel and Hoffman 2015)
TB (Total Bases)	(Magel and Hoffman 2015)
GDP (Ground-into-Double Play)	(Magel and Hoffman 2015)
HBP (Hit by Pitch)	(Magel and Hoffman 2015)
SH (Sacrifice Hits)	(Magel and Hoffman 2015)
SF (Sacrifice Flies)	(Magel and Hoffman 2015)
IBB (International Based on Balls)	(Magel and Hoffman 2015)
AGE (Age)	(Magel and Hoffman 2015; Hochberg 2011; Hakes and Turner 2011; Dinnerstein 2007; Palmer and King 2006; Meltzer 2005)

The materials used in this study are from Baseball Reference, a well-known baseball data website in the United States, and Cots Contracts, a website that specializes in investigating MLB players' salary. The following is a brief introduction to both sites.

Table 3. Added variables by this study

Variable	Description
Team rank (Total)	The overall ranking of the league's 30 teams (Calandra 2020)
Team rank (Division)	The ranking of the division of the team (Calandra 2020)
Team	Player's team (Calandra Calandra 2020)
Win Rate	The winning percentage of the player's team (Calandra 2020)
Year	Players' qualifications in the major leagues (Brown 2019)
WAR(Win Above Replacement)	Assess the value of winning or losing a player can bring to the team
Free Agent or not (FA/NFA)	Is it a free agent at the end of the year
Next Year C/UC	Is it still in the contract next year

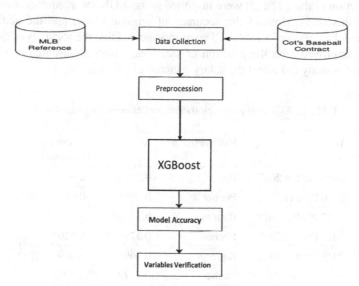

Fig. 1. Research process

Baseball Reference is a website owned by Sports Reference. Founded in 2004, Baseball Reference has primary and advanced data from several professional baseball leagues around the world and is an essential search tool for many baseball fans and practitioners. Baseball Reference is currently the 3rd largest baseball website in the world with traffic second to MLB.com and MLBTradeRumors.com. Baseball Reference holds data on Major League Baseball (MLB), Minor League Baseball (MiLB), Independent League Baseball, Nippon Professional Baseball, Korea Baseball Organization (KBO) and Mexican League, but it has no data on Chinese Professional Baseball League (CPBL). Sean

Forman, the founder of the site, decided to add CPBL data to Baseball Reference in April 2020, recommended by CPBL STATS, and updated the data daily. Founded in 2005, Cots Contracts provides information on the salaries of all players on the 30 teams of MLB. The data include details of player contracts, such as incentive bonuses, installments of salary, and airfare and lodging allowances for family members, in addition to the basic player salaries. It also records the total income of each player at retirement. The site has salary data for any player who has participated in MLB.

4   Research Results

All the classification models used in this study adopt 80% of the data set as the training set and the remaining 20% as the test set. After the training of the three classification models is completed, the data of the test set were imported into the model, and finally the accuracy was verified with the actual value. The results of each model are described below.

The variables of the pitcher and hitter mentioned in previous literature on player salary prediction (Tables 1, 2, 3) were imported to the XGBoost prediction model constructed by this study. Both of the accuracy of original model and the adding new variables model are shown in Table 4. The results showed that the accuracy of the model was greatly improved after the addition of variables, which represented that the new variables in this study did affect the salary increase of players.

Table 4. XGBoost accuracy (before and after adding variables)

Year	Batter/Pitcher	Accuracy	Accuracy (Adding)
2016 Predict 2017	Batter	0.2656	0.6094
2016 Predict 2017	Pitcher	0.2951	0.623
2017 Predict 2018	Batter	0.35	0.6
2017 Predict 2018	Pitcher	0.3793	0.6207
2018 Predict 2019	Batter	0.2698	0.619
2018 Predict 2019	Pitcher	0.3279	0.5082

From the above results, it can be concluded that the new variables are helpful for the increase of accuracy.

5   Conclusion and Future Research

In this study, we established a salary prediction system for pitchers and hitters, and used the player performance data to model, and verified whether the added variables affect the player salary. The results show that among the variables newly added, Year, WAR and FA/NFA have strong explanatory power for the prediction system constructed in this study. However, this does not mean that other newly added variables cannot affect salary, but that the above three variables are more important in terms of their characteristics compared with other newly added variables.

According to the experimental results of this study, the variables and analysis methods used in this study can be referred to when the team negotiates salary contracts with the players' agent. This not only can reduce the possibility of overestimating the player's salary, accurately grasp the team's salary cap and the player needed, but also help the agent to more accurately judge the player's value.

The limitations of this study can be summarized as follows. First, players are paid on an average annual basis. For example, a player signs a contract with a salary of USD 36 million for three years, but his annual salary is recorded as USD 12 million. Even if the player has good performance, the salary is still USD 12 million in the next year. Therefore, the prediction accuracy of the player's actual salary is greatly affected. Second, although many senior players do not have outstanding performance, they still receive a high salary because of their high reputation and the support of fans. Although their performance on the field has deteriorated, the team has to maintain their salary, so that the accuracy of the model is affected. Third, some players hide their physical health status, because once they are found to suffer poor health by the team, their values are affected. Therefore, their performances decline even if they get paid a high salary, thus affecting the accuracy of the model.

References

Brown, M.: (2019). https://www.forbes.com/sites/maurybrown/2019/02/11/inside-the-numbers-the-player-salary-battle-lines-between-mlb-and-the-mlbpa/#44e659ee5c14

Calandra, W.: The MLB has a competitive balance issue, and it's related to money and pay-roll inequalities (2020). https://georgetownvoice.com/2020/02/18/the-mlb-has-a-competitive-balance-issue-and-its-related-to-money-and-payroll-inequalities/

Dinerstein, M.J.R.M.: Free Agency and Contract Options: How Major League Baseball Teams Value Players. 1 (2007)

Hakes, J.K., Turner, C.: pay, productivity and aging in major league baseball 35(1), 61–74 (2011)

Hochberg, D.: The effect of contract year performance on free agent salary in major league baseball (2011)

Magel, R., Hoffman, M.: Predicting salaries of major league baseball players. Int. J. Sports Sci. 5(2), 51–58 (2015)

Meltzer, J.: Average salary and contract length in major league baseball: when do they diverge? (2005)

Palmer, M., King, R.: Has salary discrimination really disappeared from major league baseball? 32(2), 285–297 (2006)

Scully, G.W.: Pay and performance in major league baseball. 64(6), 915–930 (1974)

Efficient Prediction of Discharge and Water Levels Using Ensemble Learning and Singular-Spectrum Analysis-Based Denoising

Anh Duy Nguyen[1], Viet Hung Vu[1], Minh Hieu Nguyen[1], Duc Viet Hoang[1], Thanh Hung Nguyen[1], Kien Nguyen[2], and Phi Le Nguyen[1(✉)]

[1] Hanoi University of Science and Technology, Hanoi, Vietnam
{duy.na184249,hung.vv162050,hieu.nm151338,
viet.hd183666}@sis.hust.edu.vn, {hungnt,lenp}@soict.hust.edu.vn
[2] Graduate School of Engineering, Chiba University, Chiba, Japan
nguyen@chiba-u.jp

Abstract. This work addresses forecasting two essential factors in river hydrodynamics, which are discharge (Q) and water (H) levels. The accurate forecast of the two has long been a challenge in hydrological researches and flood prediction. While the traditional statistical models fail to capture the peak discharge during flooding seasons (i.e., due to the excessive level values), the simulation's numerical models face the difficulty of precise input parameters (e.g., measured values of surface zones, root zones, etc.). The emerging deep learning shows a lot of potential in solving the challenges of Q and H prediction. However, applying deep learning in such a context is not straightforward due to the following critical issues. First, the amount of training data is insufficient due to the data collection is non-trivial. Second, although lacking, the collected data incurs noises (e.g., measurement errors). We aim to overcome those shortcomings in a newly proposed deep learning model that accurately predicts Q and H. The model is a new ensemble of the one-dimensional convolutional neural network (1D-CNN), long short term memory (LSTM) models, to handle the insufficient data issue. Moreover, we adopt the Singular-Spectrum Analysis technique to eliminate noise from the collected data. The experimental results show that our proposed approach outperforms existing methods.

1   Introduction

Rivers have been playing many vital roles, such as contributing to crop irrigation or even the existence of life. In general, the variations of river flows largely impacts various aspects of the ecosystem (e.g., the climate, environment, human, etc.). Hence, understanding the river's discharge and water levels in the future may help to deal with various problems effectively, including potential disasters (e.g., flood, drought), water resources distribution (e.g., depending on seasons),

© Springer Nature Switzerland AG 2021
H. Fujita et al. (Eds.): IEA/AIE 2021, LNAI 12799, pp. 34–46, 2021.
https://doi.org/10.1007/978-3-030-79463-7_4

or freshwater maintenance, etc. The predicted results potentially help administrators, government, policymakers, and environmentalists to make better decisions [1,2]. Accordingly, many hydrological research efforts aim to analyze and predict the river flow accurately in the literature. The existing approaches can be divided into two main categories: physical-based numerical (e.g., simulation) and data-driven ones.

The methods of the former approach have several limitations. First, they usually require precise input data, which is difficult to measure, for example, the data from atmospheric circulation, the evolution of long-term weather processes, etc. [3]. By conceptualizing the physical strategies and their properties, the methods can extract hydrological variables' inherent behaviors. However, these methods are not generic but usually require special knowledge and techniques in the field (i.e., hydrological researchers). Another limitation of the approach is using complex mathematical models, which have unique dedicated numerical formulas. They cause struggles in the estimation of a considerable number of parameters and high computational cost. Moreover, these models are specialized for the rivers of specific regions, hence do not apply to others.

The latter approach can further be classified into traditional statistical and artificial intelligence, dealing with linear and non-linear data, respectively. The traditional statistical models, also known as Box-Jenkins methodology [4], include the Autoregressive (AR), the Autoregressive Moving Average (ARMA), and the Autoregressive Integrated Moving Average (ARIMA). They are widely and effectively applied to dealing with time-series data in general and predicting river hydrological data in particular [5,6]. However, the models have the disadvantage of applicability to only linear data. Artificial intelligence (deep learning) models have emerged recently following great success in many domains, such as computer vision, speech recognition, and wireless communications, etc. Several works follow this approach to fit the measured hydrology, run-off process to establish the prediction models [7–9]. Y Sudriani et al. proposed a deep learning approach with LSTM recurrent network to forecast five-day-ahead discharge in Cimandiri river [10]. An Adaptive Metropolis-Markov Chain Monte Carlo-Wavelet Regression model to improve the hydrologic time series forecasting accuracy was introduced in [11]. In [12], the authors propose deep models that utilize spatial information and temporal data for flood prediction. Although the deep-learning approach shows extensive ability in providing high predictive accuracy, they require a large amount of data to train the models. Moreover, deep learning models' performance strongly depends on the quality of the data and the setting of hyper-parameters. Especially if the training data is not clean enough, the noise may degrade the prediction accuracy significantly.

There are two challenging issues in dealing with the rivers' discharge (Q) and water (H) levels prediction using deep learning. The first one is the lack of training data for the deep learning model. That is because the data concerning discharge and water level is challenging to collect. The insufficiency will make the model lack generality and lead to inaccurate prediction. Second, data interruptions may occur for the collected data due to the monitoring device's failure or other external causes. Besides, the outliers may appear in hydrological data because of, for example, the sudden weather change. Hence, there is noise and outliers in the training data, which will disturb the model's training process and degrade the model's accuracy.

This work proposed a novel deep learning model of the discharge and water level prediction, which can overcome the issues. On the one hand, to fill in the lack of training data, we leverage ensemble learning that uses multiple base learners trained with different hyper-parameters to learn various knowledge about the dataset. These pre-trained base learners then generate training data for meta-leaner. By doing so, we can extract more information from the dataset and increase the training data's diversity. On the other hand, to deal with noise and outlier in the data, we exploit the Singular-Spectrum Analysis (SSA) technique in the data processing. SSA can split the original data into three components: trends, periodic, and noise. The first two are meaningful information used to train the model, while the last will be eliminated. The main contributions of the paper are as follows.

- We newly introduce ensemble learning and SSA in the Q and H prediction.
- We propose the new deep learning model, an ensemble of several submodels consisting of two main components: the base learners and the meta-learner. Each base learner combines multiple 1D-CNN and LSTM layers responsible for extracting the short-term and long-term temporal correlations of the data. The meta-learner includes two LSTM layers, which aim to extract essential features from the original data and retrieve the learned knowledge from the base learners.
- We propose a pre-processing data method based on the SSA technique, which helps remove the noise and outlier from the original data before feeding it into the models.

2 Preliminaries

2.1 Problem Description

We aim to obtain the information from m previous timesteps and produce the discharge (Q) values and water level (H) of the next n timesteps. To prepare data for training and evaluating phases, we define a so-called sliding window, a grid acting upon the initial series. The sliding window is a frame with a $(m + n)$ size, sliding through all the datasets and making snapshots. When shifting the window by one timestep, we capture a snapshot of $(m + n)$ consecutive steps. That snapshot is then extracted as follows. The first m steps of suitable features are then taken to make up the input set, and for the remaining n ones, Q and H values are extracted to put in the output set. The targeted problem now can be mathematically represented as follows.

Input: $x_i, x_{i+1}, \ldots, x_{i+m-1}$
Output: $\tilde{y}_{i+m}, \tilde{y}_{i+m+1}, \ldots, \tilde{y}_{i+m+n-1}$

$$= \underset{y_{i+m}, y_{i+m+1}, \dots, y_{i+m+n-1}}{\operatorname{argmax}} p(y_{i+m}, y_{i+m+1}, \dots, y_{i+m+n-1} | x_i, x_{i+1}, \dots, x_{i+m-1}),$$

where x_{i+j} $(j = 0, \dots, m-1)$ is the input vector at the j-th timestep; y_{i+m+k} $(k = 0, \dots, n-1)$ is a vector represents Q, H values at the $(i+m+k)$-th timestep.

2.2   One Dimensional Convolutional Neural Network (1-D CNN)

One-Dimensional CNN has been shown experimentally to produce positive results in various challenging sequential tasks with little or no data feature engineering. Let the input time series have the length of m timesteps and the width of k features, the 1-D convolution kernels by default always have the same width k as the time series, while their length can be varied and fine-tuned later on. With this design, the kernels move in only one direction of length m from the beginning of the series toward its end, performing convolution operation. Specifically, while sliding through the length of the time series, the convolution kernels are element-wise multiplied with the corresponding part of the series. The results then are summed and concatenated by $z_i = \sum_{j=0}^{kl} x_{ij} * \mathcal{K}_j$ $(i = 0, \dots, m-l)$, where $\mathcal{K}$ is a kernel of length l, x_i is the i-th block of the input time series, and z_i is the i-th element of the extracted feature map. During the training process, number of convolution kernels are tuned to extract the most useful set of feature maps - the inner relationship of the time series.

2.3   Long Short Term Memory (LSTM)

Recurrent neural network (RNN) is powerful in handling time series data. However, former RNN units struggle with a critical weakness, which is the unstable gradient (i.e., exploding or vanishing gradient). In both cases, the gradient accumulated through each timestep becomes too large or too small to perform further calculation, resulting in a halt in the training process and a failure to capture the long dependency lying in the time series as a consequence. LSTM is then developed to perfectly address the mentioned issue. An LSTM cell introduces three new special units, called *gates*: Input Gate (i), Forget Gate (f), Output Gate (o). By leveraging these gates, the LSTM cell can decide which information is worth keeping and how much that information should be remembered. The outstanding advantage of LSTM compared to other forms of RNN is the ability to learn long-term dependencies. For each timestep t, x_t denotes the input data, c_t is the cell state, c_t is defined as the potential candidate for replacing memory cell, u_t denotes the update gate and f_t, o_t are the outputs of updated forget gate and output gate, respectively. The cell decides whether or not to update c_t using c_t and c_{t-1} base on the values of f_t and u_t.

   The sigmoid function (i.e., σ) is used to compute both forget gate and output gate, with the input is the previous hidden state a_{t-1} and the current input x_t. Therefore, the output range of both gates is $(0, 1)$ - the closer to lower bound is the indication of forgetting and ignoring, and the closer to upper bound represents keeping and storing, inversely. Besides, to aid in regulating the network, a $tanh$ function generates a vector of potential candidate values, c_t, that could be added to the current state. $tanh$ function is used due to the output of $tanh$ can be either positive or negative, allowing for increases and decreases in the state; this can help to overcome the vanishing, exploding gradient problem and make the model converge faster. To get hidden state at timestep t, cell state needs to be calculated first. The previous cell state c_{t-1} do pointwise multiplication with the forget vector f_t, which has the possibility of dropping irrelevant values in the cell state if it gets multiplied by values near 0. Then by adding $u_t * c_t$, the cell state c_t is updated to new values that the network finds relevant. Last we have the output gate that decides what the next hidden state should be. The generated cell state is put through another $tanh$ function and multiply the result by o_t, so that the cell only output the essential parts to hidden state a_t and forward it to the next recurrence. To sum up, the forget gate decides what is relevant to keep from previous steps; the update gate decides what information is relevant to add from the current step; the output gate determines what the next hidden state should be. All three components make up an LSTM with a great ability to memorize relations in the time sequence itself.

2.4　Singular-Spectrum Analysis (SSA)

SSA decomposes a time series into a number of components with simple structures such as a trend, periodic, and noise. By using SSA, we can remove the noise and extract important information from the series. Basically, SSA is performed in two main stages: *Decomposition* and *Reconstruction*. The first stage consists of two steps. The first step (i.e.. *Embedding step*) is to transfer the raw input sequence $\mathbf{x} = (x_1, x_2, \ldots, x_M)$ of length M into a sequence of the so-called *Lagged Vectors* $L_i = (x_i, \ldots x_{i+L-1})^T$, $i = 1, \ldots, K = M - L + 1$, where L is a tunable parameter. These vectors are then iteratively transposed to form the columns of the $(L \times K)$ *Trajectory Matrix*

$$\mathbf{X} = \begin{bmatrix} x_1 & x_2 & \cdots & x_K \\ \vdots & \vdots & \vdots & \vdots \\ x_L & x_{L+1} & \vdots & x_{L+K-1} \end{bmatrix}.$$

$\mathbf{X}$ is a *Hankel* matrix X with equal elements on the skew-diagonals. The trajectory matrix is then decomposed into a sum of bi-orthogonal elementary matrices by the second step named *Singular Value Decomposition (SVD)*, where d is the trajectory matrix's rank. Specifically, Decomposing $\mathbf{X} = \mathbf{U}\mathbf{S}\mathbf{V}^T$, where $\mathbf{U}$, $\mathbf{V}$ are two $L \times L$ and $K \times K$ unitary matrices containing the orthonormal set of the left and right singular vectors of $\mathbf{X}$, respectively; $\mathbf{S}$ is a diagonal matrix whose diagonal elements $\sigma_1, \ldots, \sigma_d$ are the singular values of $\mathbf{X}$ (i.e., σ_i are sorted in the decreasing order). Accordingly, $\mathbf{X}$ can be represented as the sum of elementary matrices $\mathbf{X_i}$ $(i = 1, ..., d)$, $\mathbf{X} = \sum_{i=1}^{d} \sigma_i \mathbf{U}_i \mathbf{V}_i^T = \sum_{i=1}^{d} \mathbf{X}_i$, where $\mathbf{U}_i$ and $\mathbf{V}_i$ are the i-th left and right singular vectors of $\mathbf{X}$, respectively.

The second stage, i.e., *Reconstruction stage*, comprises of two steps: *Grouping* and *Transformation*. In the first step, the elementary matrices are divided into m groups. The summation of the matrices in each group makes a resultant matrix. Let $I_i = \{i_1, ..., i_{k_i}\}$ be the indices of the i-th group, then the i-th resultant matrix is given by $\mathbf{X}^{I_i} = \mathbf{X}_{i_1} + ... + \mathbf{X}_{i_{k_i}}$. Accordingly, the trajectory matrix can be represented as the sum of these m resultant matrices $\mathbf{X} = \mathbf{X}^{I_i} + ... + \mathbf{X}^{I_m}$. The last step in SSA is to transform each resultant matrix into a one dimensional series of length M using the so-called *diagonal averaging* method. Let $\mathbf{Y} = \{y_{ij}\}, i = 1, ..., L; j = 1, ..., K$ be a $L \times K$ matrix, and denote by $L^* = \min(L, K)$, $K^* = \max(L, K)$ and $N = L + K - 1$. Let $y_{ij}^* = y_{ij}$ if $L < K$ and $y_{ij}^* = y_{ji}$, otherwise. The diagonal averaging method transfers matrix $\mathbf{Y}$ into a series $g_0, ..., g_{N-1}$ as follows

$$
g_k = \begin{cases}
\frac{1}{k+1} \sum_{u}^{k+1} y_{u,k-u+2}^* & 0 \le k < L^* - 1 \\
\frac{1}{L^*} \sum_{u=1}^{L^*} y_{u,k-u+2}^* & L^* - 1 \le k < K^* \\
\frac{1}{N-k} \sum_{u=k-K^*+2}^{N-k+1} y_{u,k-u+2}^* & K^* \le k < N.
\end{cases}
$$

The formula corresponds to averaging the elements along the diagonals $i+j = k+2$ of matrix $\mathbf{Y}$. Applying this diagonal averaging method on $\mathbf{X}^{I_i}$ provides a time series of length N. Consequently, the initial input time series $\mathbf{x}$ is represented as the sum of m series: $\mathbf{x} = \mathbf{x}_1 + ... + \mathbf{x}_m$.

3 SSA-Assisted CNN-LSTM Ensemble Prediction Model

3.1 SSA-Based Data Pre-processing

Initially, we leverage Singular-Spectrum Analysis (SSA) for preprocessing data before feeding into the prediction model. The reason for choosing SSA is that it is a model-free technique independent of the model chosen, thus, it can be applied to any data. Recall that in the SSA method, after the embedding step, the input time series is transferred into a trajectory matrix $\mathbf{X}$. The trajectory matrix $\mathbf{X}$ then is decomposed into a sum of elementary matrices $\mathbf{X_i}$ $(i = 1, ..., d)$, i.e., $\mathbf{X} = \sum_{i=1}^{d} \sigma_i \mathbf{U}_i \mathbf{V}_i^T$. Intuitively, singular value σ_i can be interpreted as a scaling factor that determines the relative importance of $\mathbf{X}_i$ to the trajectory matrix $\mathbf{X}$. Therefore, the first few elementary matrices $\mathbf{X}_i$ contribute much greater impact than that of the last few elementary matrices. In other words, it is likely that the last elementary matrices (the ones with small values of the singular value) represent noises in the time series data. Therefore, our idea is that by filtering out these *noises*, we can fully extract the time series's meaningful information such as the trend, the periodic and seasonal information, which can help to improve the prediction model's accuracy.

Let $\mathbf{x}$ be the input time series, then our proposed data pre-process method is as follows. First, We leverage SSA's *Decomposition stage* to transfer $\mathbf{x}$ into the trajectory matrix $\mathbf{X}$, which is decomposed into the sum of elementary matrices, i.e., $\mathbf{X} = \sum_{i=1}^{d} \mathbf{X}_i = \sum_{i=1}^{d} \sigma_i \mathbf{U}_i \mathbf{V}_i^T$, where σ_i are sorted in the decreasing order. Second, following the *Grouping step*, we divide the elementary matrices into three groups. The first contains matrices representing the data trend. The second comprises the ones describing the periodic; and the last group includes all noise-liked matrices. We let the first group contain only the first elementary matrix, whose singular value σ_1 is the greatest. For the remaining matrices, we propose a correlation-based clustering algorithm as follows. We construct a correlation matrix representing the correlation of $d-1$ elementary matrices $\mathbf{X}_2, ..., \mathbf{X}_d$. Based on the correlation matrix, we cluster these $d-1$ elementary matrices into two groups such that the matrices in the same group have a high correlation with each other. Among the two groups, the one containing elementary matrices with small singular values is the noise, and the other represents the periodic. Consequently, we obtain three resultant matrices $\mathbf{X}_1, \mathbf{X}_2, \mathbf{X}_3$ that represent the trend, periodic, and noise, respectively. We eliminate the noise, i.e., $\mathbf{X}_3$, while remaining $\mathbf{X}_1, \mathbf{X}_2$. Finally, we apply the *Diagonal average* to generate two time series $\mathbf{x}_1, \mathbf{x}_2$ from $\mathbf{X}_1$ and $\mathbf{X}_2$. Finally, we obtain the output $\mathbf{y}$ as the sum of these two time series, i.e., $\mathbf{y} = \mathbf{x}_1 + \mathbf{x}_2$, which then is used to train the model.

3.2 Base Learners

A base learner is a combination of multiple 1D CNN layers and LSTM layers. 1D-CNN is used to extract the non-linear relationships between short term temporal data and identify deep, time-independent features. Besides, LSTM is developed to capture and memorize long term relationships. Therefore by combining the two, we aim at extracting the most relational information from the past data. Moreover, with the use of 1-D CNNs, by precalculating the dimensions and tuning the number of kernels, we can utilize the base learners to make predictions for various timesteps in the future. The difference among base learners lies in the fact that they are trained with different epochs, which results in other convergent points. Intuitively, it can be seen that each base learner trained with a particular number of epochs can learn a specific aspect of the input data. The trained base learners are then used to generate data to train the meta-learner. By analyzing the correspondence between the outputs of base learners and the targeted output values, it is possible to assign each output a weight value, which together with the input contributes to the final prediction of the ensemble model.

3.3 Ensemble Methodology

Our proposed meta-learner consists of two LSTM layers. The first LSTM layer receives the same input data as the base learners and is responsible for re-extracting and reprocessing that information to formulate a context information. The information extracted by the first LSTM layer then is used as the initial state for the second LSTM layer. Moreover, the second LSTM layer also makes use of

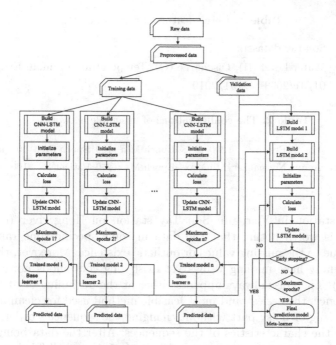

Fig. 1. The training flow of the proposed ensemble model

the knowledge learnt by the base learners to enhance the prediction accuracy. Specifically, the training process is performed as follows (illustrated in Fig. 1).

1. The full data set is divided into three sub-sets: the training data x_{train}, the evaluation data x_{eval}, the testing data x_{test}. The training data and the evaluation data is pre-processed using SSA as described in Sect. 2.4.
2. The first training phase starts with the base learners (i.e., $\mathcal{M}_1, ..., \mathcal{M}_N$, where N is a tunable hyper-parameter). All the base learners are trained with the same x_{train} set, but with different numbers of epochs.
3. After finishing the first training phase, we obtain N trained base learners. x_{eval} is fed into all the trained·base learners to obtain predicted results. Let the results obtained from the base learner $\mathcal{M}_i$ $(i = 1, ..., N)$ be $\tilde{y}_i$, then $\tilde{y}_i$ are concatenated and reshaped to form a new data set $\tilde{y}^*$.
4. $\tilde{y}^*$ and the evaluation data x_{eval} is used to train the meta-learner at the second training stage. First, x_{eval} is fed into the first LSTM layer to extract significant features. Then, the output of the first LSTM layer, denoted as $\tilde{x}_{eval}$ and the predicted results of the base learners, i.e., $\tilde{y}^*$, are used as the input of the second LSTM layer.

4   Performance Evaluation

4.1   Datasets, Hyper-parameter, and Metrics

In this section, we evaluate the performance of our model in comparison to others. We use the real daily data collected from a river basin's hydrological

Table 1. Detail features of the dataset

	Son tay dataset
Metrics	Water Level (H), Discharge (Q), Temperature, Rainfall, Evaporation
Time range	01/01/2008– 12/31/2019

Table 2. The configurations of ensemble network

Batch size	128	Epoch	200	iEpoch Min	100	Epoch Step	50	m	30
Optimizer	Adam	Normalizer	MinMax	iEpoch Max	250	Patient	100	n	1–7

monitoring station in Vietnam: Son Tay station on Hong river (detailed in Table 1). It is worth noting that the data in some specific time range is not consistent due to the missing values or outliers' existence. Moreover, the dataset does not usually have missing values yet exist long continuous noise segments (for months). The noise always appears either at the beginning or at the end of the data. Hence, the easiest and most feasible method used for cleaning is dropping the missing or noisy part without changing the sequence's order, therefore still keeping the characteristics of the sequences. After the data being cleaned, all of the values were normalized to points in $[-1;1]$ and divided in the ratio 0.6 for training dataset, 0.2 and 0.2 for validation and test dataset before going through preprocessing. Figure 2 visualizes Q & H values after cleaning noisy data. Table 2 summarizes the detail hyper-parameters of our Ensemble model. The iEpoch Min and iEpoch Max represent the minimum and maximum the base learner's number of epochs. The iEpoch step indicates the difference in the number of epochs between two consecutive base learners.

The performance metrics used in the evaluation including The Nash–Sutcliffe model efficiency coefficient (NSE) score, Mean Square Error (MSE), Mean Absolute Error (MAE), and Mean Absolute Percentage Error (MAPE). MAE and MSE are two metrics measuring L1 and squared L2 differences that depend on evaluating the dataset's size. Simultaneously, NSE and MAPE are independent of size and measure how well the predictions approximate the observed data, the error rate in percentage, respectively. We conduct two main experiments. In the first experiment, namely, one-step-ahead prediction, we use the data of the

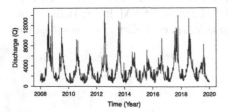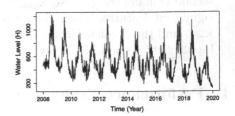

Fig. 2. SonTay dataset

Table 3. One-step-ahead forecasting for Son Tay dataset

Metrics/Models		SSA ensemble	Ensemble	LSTM [10]	ANN [8]	ARIMA [6]
Q	NSE	**0.99**	0.97	0.94	0.71	0.90
	MSE	**14264**	19755	104972	747259	72629
	MAE	**85**	194	220	637	183
	MAPE	**0.0316**	0.0719	0.0919	0.261	0.0736
H	NSE	**0.986**	0.96	0.93	0.76	0.94
	MSE	**288.38**	613.7	1041	5173	645
	MAE	**11.96**	17.31	24.7	55.7	17.5
	MAPE	**0.0366**	0.0545	0.0978	0.2	0.0586

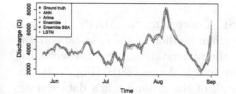 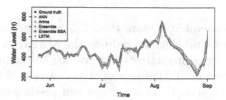

Fig. 3. Performance comparison in predicting Q & H in August 2019

past thirty days to predict the Q value and H value of the next day. The second experiment uses the same input data as the first one, but it tries to predict the Q value and H value multiple days ahead. Specifically, the prediction span in the second experiment ranges from one to seven days. We leverage the iterative prediction method, in which the predicted values of the n-th day are fed into the model to predict the value of the $(n + 1)$-th day. We compare our proposed approach's performance with five benchmarks, namely ARIMA [6], ANN [8], LSTM [10], CNN-LSTM, and ensemble learning model without SSA. To ease the presentation, we name our proposed model *SSA Ensemble.*

4.2   One-Step-Ahead Prediction

The one-step-ahead prediction accuracy of the models are represented in Table 3. It can be seen that the SSA ensemble model achieves the best performance. Compared to the statistic, machine learning-based models, which are proposed in [6,8], the SSA ensemble model improves the NSE by 23% and 4.6% compared to ANN and ARIMA, respectively; the MAPE achieved by SSA ensemble is lower than 16.3% that of ANN and 2.2% that of ARIMA. The use of ensemble architecture also positively affects the prediction accuracy compared to the model using only LSTM. This is reflected by the performance gap of SSA ensemble and ensemble models to the LSTM model. Finally, by leveraging SSA to preprocess data, the SSA ensemble model improves the performance significantly compared to the ensemble model. The performance gap of SSA ensemble to

Table 4. Multi-step-ahead Forecasting for Son Tay Dataset

Metrics/Models		SSA ensemble	Ensemble	LSTM [10]	ANN [8]	ARIMA [6]
Q	NSE	**0.81**	0.78	0.71	0.61	0.36
	MSE	**504201**	564745	573311	1021919	602559
	MAE	**424**	531	543	836	550
	MAPE	**0.137**	0.21	0.247	0.397	0.226
H	NSE	**0.83**	0.80	0.68	0.54	0.72
	MSE	**3696**	4613	5512	10008	4704
	MAE	**37.8**	50.9	59	83.5	56.6
	MAPE	**0.107**	0.179	0.234	0.391	0.190

ensemble is more than 2% in terms of NSE. Concerning the MAPE, the SSA ensemble model reduces the MAPE by 4% when predicting the Q value and 2% when predicting the H value. To facilitate the understanding, we also visualize the prediction results of discharge and water level in August 2019 (Fig. 3). It can be seen that our model can predict the peak of the ground truth data during the raining season, which can bring great benefit to flood prediction.

4.3 Multi-step-ahead Prediction

Table 4 summarizes the average performance evaluation of all the models in terms of NSE, MSE, MAE, and MAPE score. In general, similar to the first experiment, our approach with SSA pre-processed input achieves the best performance in all scenarios. On average, our approach with SSA improves 14% compared to LSTM, and 3% compared to the ensemble model concerning NSE score; the SSA ensemble model reduces the MAPE by 11% and 7% compared to ensemble model and LSTM model, respectively. Figure 4 represents the models' detail accuracy when varying the output timestep from 1 to 7. It can be observed that the accuracy of all models decreases when increasing the output timestep. However, the SSA ensemble model outperforms the others in all scenarios. Moreover, when the output timestep is relatively small, i.e., less than 4, the decreasing slope in our model is also the smallest among all.

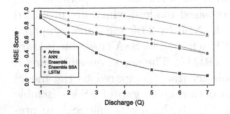 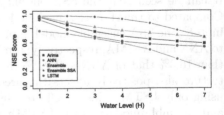

Fig. 4. Multi-step-prediction NSE scores of all approaches

5   Conclusion

This paper studied the discharge and water level prediction problem. We proposed an effective approach that leverages the SSA technique to pre-process the data and the ensemble learning approach to enhance the prediction accuracy. We performed experiments on the dataset collected from Son Tay station in Vietnam. The experimental results showed our proposed model's superiority to the existing approaches. Specifically, concerning one-step-ahead prediction, our model improves the NSE score by at least 2% compared to other models, and up to 23% in the best case. Concerning the multi-step-ahead prediction, the average NSE achieves by our proposed models is higher than at least 3%, and up to 45% compared to the others.

Acknowledgement. Minh Hieu Nguyen was funded by Vingroup Joint Stock Company and supported by the Domestic Master/PhD Scholarship Programme of Vingroup Innovation Foundation (VINIF), Vingroup Big Data Institute (VINBIGDATA), code VINIF.2020.ThS.BK.08.

References

1. Tsakiri, K., Marsellos, A., Kapetanakis, S.: Artificial neural network and multiple linear regression for flood prediction in Mohawk river, New York. Water **10** (2018)
2. Meshram, S.G., Ghorbani, M.A., Shamshirband, S.: River flow prediction using hybrid PSOGSA algorithm based on feed-forward neural network. Soft Comput. **23**, 10429–10438 (2019)
3. Andreolli, I., Collischonn, W., Haas, R., Tucci, C.E.M.: Forecasting river uruguay flow using rainfall forecasts from a regional weather-prediction model. J. Hydrol. **305**, 87–98 (2005)
4. Jenkins, G., Box, G.E.P.: Distribution of residual autocorrelations in autoregressive-integrated moving average time series models. J. Am. Stat. Assoc. **65**, 1509–1526 (1970)
5. Al-Masudi, R.K.: Fitting ARIMA models for forecasting to inflow of Dokan reservoir. J. Babylon Univ. 1675–1685 (2013)
6. Kisi, O., Adnan, R.M., Yuan, X., Curtef, V.: Application of time series models for streamflow forecasting. Civ. Environ. Res. **9**, 56–63 (2017b)
7. Shamshirband, S., Chau, K.-W., Fotovatikhah, F., Herrera, M., Ardabili, S.F., Piran, M.J.: Survey of computational intelligence as basis to big flood management: challenges research directions and future work. Eng. Appl. Comput. Fluid Mech. **12**, 411–437 (2018)
8. Panwar, S., Chakrapani, G.J., Khan, M.Y.A., Hasan, F.: Neural network model for discharge and water-level prediction for Ramganga river catchment of Ganga basin, India. Hydrol. Sci. J. **61**(11), 2084–2095 (2016)
9. Lin, J.Y., Cheng, C.T., Chau, K.W.: Using support vector machines for long-term discharge prediction. Hydrol. Sci. J. **51**, 599–612 (2006)
10. Sudriani, Y., Ridwansyah, I., Rustini, H.A.: Long short term memory (LSTM) recurrent neural network (RNN) for discharge level prediction and forecast in Cimandiri river, Indonesia. In: IOP Conference Series: Earth and Environmental Science, vol. 299, July 2019

11. Wang, Z., Liu, C., Yang, M., Sang, Y., Shang, L.: Bayesian-combined wavelet regressive modeling for hydrologic time series forecasting. Chin. Sci. Bull. **58**, 3796–3805 (2013)

12. Pain, C.C., Hua, R., Fanga, F., Navon, I.M.: Rapid spatio-temporal flood prediction and uncertainty quantification using a deep learning method. J. Hydrol. **575**, 911–920 (2019)

An Efficient Transformer-Based Model for Vietnamese Punctuation Prediction

Hieu Tran[2,3,4], Cuong V. Dinh[1], Quang Pham[5], and Binh T. Nguyen[2,3,4][✉]

[1] Dublin City University, Dublin, Ireland
[2] AISIA Research Lab, Ho Chi Minh City, Vietnam
ngtbinh@hcmus.edu.vn
[3] University of Science, Ho Chi Minh City, Vietnam
[4] Vietnam National University, Ho Chi Minh City, Vietnam
[5] Singapore Management University, Singapore, Singapore

Abstract. In both formal and informal texts, missing punctuation marks make the texts confusing and challenging to read. This paper aims to conduct exhaustive experiments to investigate the benefits of the pre-trained Transformer-based models on two Vietnamese punctuation datasets. The experimental results show our models can achieve encouraging results, and adding Bi-LSTM or/and CRF layers on top of the proposed models can also boost model performance. Finally, our best model can significantly bypass state-of-the-art approaches on both the novel and news datasets for the Vietnamese language. It can gain the corresponding performance up to 21.45% and 18.27% in the overall F1-scores.

Keywords: Transfer learning · Transformer models · Punctuation prediction

1 Introduction

In different languages, punctuation is a collection of symbols designating a sentence structure to slow down, remark, or expose emotion. Using punctuation marks is an essential step in writing to make each sentence or paragraph easy to read and understand. In many formal and informal texts, the misuse of punctuation marks frequently happens due to the lack of knowledge in grammars or human mistakes [1,2]. Along with developing Automatic Speech Recognition (ASR) systems, speech transcripts may not have any punctuation marks. Accordingly, selecting relevant punctuation marks to transcribed text is vital to ensure one can correctly understand the text.

Punctuation prediction is an indispensable problem in multiple languages. Some studies treat this problem as a sequence labeling task and settle it using neural networks in recent years. There have been various approaches to punctuation prediction in different languages (English, Chinese, and Slovenia) in recent years, achieving particular accomplishments. Previous studies utilize both statistic models and traditional deep neural networks to settle the missing punctuation

H. Fujita et al. (Eds.): IEA/AIE 2021, LNAI 12799, pp. 47–58, 2021.
https://doi.org/10.1007/978-3-030-79463-7_5

marks problem [3–6]. One of the earliest works on the English language is in [7], where the authors presented the stacked RNNs model to learn more hierarchical aspects. It can be followed by a layer-wise multi-head attention mechanism to focus on the relevant contexts at each time step and capture the features directly from each hierarchical level. Makhija and colleagues [8] utilized the BERT language model to capture contextualized word embeddings, fed into a hybrid of BiLSTM and CRF layer after that. The authors evaluate the model's effectiveness on the IWSLT2012 English dataset, and these models achieve an overall F1-score of 81.4%, which is higher than the previous models' score. Fang et al. [9] tried using the same architecture for the Chinese punctuation prediction task. The experiment of this model shows the pre-trained language model also accomplish on Chinese characteristics. Furthermore, this work indicates that the CRF layer does not make performance increase clearly, so it has little effect on this problem. Wang and co-workers [10] addresses the punctuation prediction problem like machine translation instead of sequence labeling. The authors use Transformer architecture and two softmax layers: the label softmax and word softmax. The combination of word sequence information and labeling information significantly improves compared to the previous models.

In previous Vietnamese studies, Quang et al. [1] apply the CRF model and a set of appropriate features for solving the punctuation prediction problem. To inspect the model's effectiveness, the authors ask some volunteers to insert punctuation marks into a small dataset and compare them with their model. The model has achieved approximately human performance. Thuy and colleagues [2] investigate the deep neural networks Bi-LSTM model in two novels and news dataset. To enhance the model for capturing more complex data structures, the authors add an attention mechanism on top of the Bi-LSTM model. It makes the model can focus on particular syllables in the past while predicting the current punctuation mark. This study also benchmarks the traditional CRF method by replacing the softmax layer. Cross-Entropy loss is not suitable for the different distribution of punctuation marks. This work proposes to use the focal loss that can give more weights to rare classes in the data. The experiment results show the combination between the Bi-LSTM model and the attention mechanism outperforms the others. Besides that, the CRF method is not very useful in this problem.

More recently, the release of Transformer [11] architecture is the inspiration for some robust models such as BERT [12], ELECTRA [13], and XLM-RoBERTa [14]. They have dramatically improved the state-of-the-art results on various downstream natural language tasks. These pre-trained models learn useful contextual representations from massive unlabeled datasets using self-supervised pre-training objectives, such as masked language modeling. It can predict the original masked word based only on its context from a masked input sentence. These advantages motivated us to apply them for our punctuation prediction task.

This paper contributes to using the pre-trained Transformer models such as BERT, ELECTRA, and XLM-RoBERTA on two large-scale Vietnamese novel and news datasets. We also extend our proposed method by incorporating a BiLSTM layer and a CRF layer compared with the previous work. We consider adding a BiLSTM and/or CRF layer on top of the pre-trained models to captures semantics and long-range dependencies in the input sentence. Results show that the transfer learning method is useful in the punctuation prediction problem.

The rest of this paper can be organized as follows. Section 1 briefly introduces the punctuation prediction problem and discusses all related works of the problem. Section 2 describes the model architecture of punctuation prediction, and Sect. 3 presents experimental results on two Vietnamese datasets. The paper ends with the conclusion and further work.

2 Methodology

2.1 Problem Formulation

Similar to the previous studies [1,2,5], we represent the punctuation prediction task as a sequence labeling problem and find an appropriate model for this task. It is worth noting that we label each word by its immediately following punctuation. In this paper, we consider six standard punctuation marks in the Vietnamese language: the period (.), the comma (,), the colon (:), the semicolon (;), the question mark (?), the exclamation mark (!), and space. We use the label O to indicate that a given the word is not followed by any punctuation.

For instance, let us consider the following sentence in the Vietnamese language.[1]

> Năm ngoái, dù có doanh số bán quảng cáo sụt giảm nghiêm trọng trong khoảng thời gian đầu năm, Facebook đã chứng kiến doanh thu phục hồi vào những tháng sau đó nhờ nhu cầu tiếp cận khách hàng tăng cao của các doanh nghiệp nhỏ.

(Last year, despite a dramatic decline in ad sales in the early part of the year, Facebook saw its revenue rebound in the following months, thanks to rising demand for customer access by small businesses.)

Typically, one can label the above paragraph as follows:

> Năm/O ngoái/Comma dù/O có/O doanh/O số/O bán/O quảng/O cáo/O sụt/O giảm/O nghiêm/O trọng/O trong/O khoảng/O thời/O gian/O đầu/O năm/Comma Facebook/O đã/O chứng/O kiến/O doanh/O thu/O phục/O hồi/O vào/O những/O tháng/O sau/O đó/O nhờ/O nhu/O cầu/O tiếp/O cận/O khách/O hàng/O tăng/O cao/O của/O các/O doanh/O nghiệp/O nhỏ/Period

Remarkably, the word case information is not available for the punctuation prediction problem since all the words are lower case during the data processing step.

---

[1] https://vnexpress.net/facebook-hay-google-manh-hon-4226827.html.

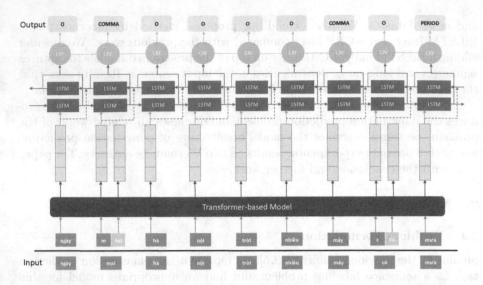

Fig. 1. The first proposed neural network architecture by combining LSTM and CRF. The input sentence means "Hanoi is cloudy and rainy tomorrow".

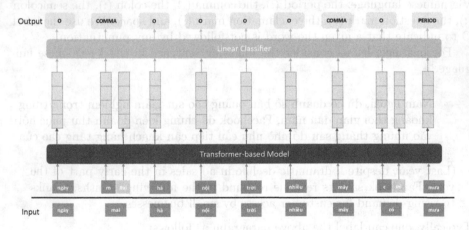

Fig. 2. The second proposed standalone neural network architecture (without using LSTM and CRF). The input sentence means "Hanoi is cloudy and rainy tomorrow".

2.2   Our Proposed Techniques

Data Processing. The dataset described in Sect. 3.1 is not segmented into sentences. Consequently, we split the data into multiple paragraphs with a maximum length of 128 words but still have to ensure that they start after the end punctuation mark. We also replace all numbers in the dataset with <NUM> token, and this helps to reduce the influence of different numbers. It is important to note that all words in this dataset are lowercase, and some special characters are excluded.

To fine-tune the Transformer-based models such as BERT and ELECTRA, one needs to insert two particular tokens, [CLS] and [SEP], into the input. The [CLS] is encoded, including all representative information of the whole input sentence. Meanwhile, the use of [SEP] token is to separate different sentences of an input. We only need to insert the [SEP] to the end of every input data. The advantage of these models is that they can handle words that are not part of the vocabulary. The tokenizer takes the input sentence and relies on the vocabulary to decide whether to keep the whole word or slice it into subwords, containing the first subword and subsequent subwords starting with the # (sharp) symbol. As every word in each sentence has its label, we need to assign the corresponding labels from the first subword to subsequent subwords. Finally, we convert the new input to the sequence of indices with the same length. We also pad the sequences with the [PAD] token if their length is less than a given threshold.

Feature Extraction. In the text classification tasks, one usually trains a model to predict the CLS token encoded, including all representative information of the whole input sentence. Nevertheless, in the sequence labeling tasks, we can feed the last hidden state, which encloses all words of each input sentence's hidden ones into later layers. We also include the subsequent subwords inside the last hidden state to take the hidden state's first subword to represent the whole word and use it for prediction.

Models. More recently, pre-trained language models have shown to be useful in learning common language representations by utilizing a large amount of unlabeled data. These models have achieved great results in many downstream natural language processing tasks. In what follows, we describe our chosen architectures for implementation in this paper:

- BERT stands for Bidirectional Encoder Representations from Transformers. The model contains multiple bidirectional Transformer encoders, and each encoder layer is composed of a multi-head self-attention. However, BERT Encoder slightly differs from the canonical Transformer, which uses a GELU [15] activation rather than the standard RELU. BERT uses Word Piece [16] to tokenize the input sentence into tokens.
  Each token is represented by the sum of the token embedding, segment embedding, and positional embedding. All these things make it possible for BERT to learn contextualized word representations. BERT uses masked language modeling objective and next sentence prediction for pre-training. In the masked language modeling task, some percentage of tokens can be selected at random as the masked tokens and then predicting only these tokens. In the next sentence prediction task, BERT treats this task as a binary classification and indicate whether the second sentence is the following sentence of the first sentence.
- ELECTRA (Efficiently Learning an Encoder that Classifies Token Replacements Accurately) uses a new pre-training approach that is substituted token

detection. Instead of replacing the input tokens with masked tokens, this method corrupts the input by replacing some tokens with incorrect tokens. And then, the model tries to determine which tokens from the original input have been replaced. This setup requires two Transformer models in pre-training: a generator and a discriminator. After pre-training, one can remove the generator and keep the discriminator for fine-tuning in downstream tasks. ELECTRA also uses a Word Piece tokenizer like BERT.

- XLM-RoBERTa is the first multilingual model that can outperform traditional monolingual pre-trained models. This model is the combination of XLM [17] and RoBERTa [18]. Specifically, XLM-RoBERTa relies on masked language modeling objective and cross-lingual language modeling objective without next sentence pre-training objective. Unlike BERT, XLM-RoBERTa uses the Sentence Piece model [19] for tokenizing the input sentence instead of using Word Piece tokenizer. The Sentence Piece implements two segmentation algorithms, including the byte-pair-encoding and unigram language model. It is an effective way to tackle the out-of-vocab problems.

We examine to stack a Bidirectional Long Short-Term Memory network (BiLSTM) and Conditional Random Field (CRF) layer on the top of output representations.

- BiLSTM was proposed to deal with the vanishing gradient problem encountered by traditional RNNs. A typical LSTM layer consists of three gates, input gate, output gate, and forget gate. These gates control how the information in a sequence of input comes into, stores in, and leaves the network. With the bidirectional term, this layer looks at the sequence from left to right in the forward stage and observes from right to left in the backward stage. The advantage of this layer is it can captures long-distance dependencies across the sequences from both past and future contexts.
- CRF tries to learn the conditional probability over label sequences given a particular observation sequence, rather than a joint probability over both label and observation sequences. Instead of directly using cross-entropy loss, we pass the outputs from the previous layer through the CRF layer to compute all possible classes' probability or the negative log-likelihood loss. This layer helps to choose labels based on both past and current dependencies.

The summary of the proposed model can be illustrated in Figs. 1 and 2.

Performance Metrics. We measure the performance of our models on precision, recall, and F1-score. Following the previous work, we only consider six punctuation marks, including comma, period, colon, semicolon, question mark, and exclamation. The best model is the model that dominates in the average micro F1-score.

3   Experiments

In this section, we compare the effectiveness of a multilingual pre-trained model and a monolingual pre-trained model. We make use of multilingual BERT[2] and XLM-RoBERTa,[3] both models trained on large-scale data, in 100 languages. For the monolingual model, we choose the viELECTRA model, which is released by [20], this model trained on 60 GB of Vietnamese texts. All these models contain 12 Encoder layers, 768 hidden units, and we use Adam optimizer with a learning rate of 5e-5 and weight decay of 0.01. In the Bi-LSTM layers, we stack two layers, and the number of unit cells in each of the LSTM layers is half of the pre-trained model hidden size. The results in Table 2 and Table 3 are selected from the highest scores in 15 epochs. We also provide all the source codes[4] for reproducing experiments.

3.1   Datasets

Our models are tested by performing experiments on the two large-scale Vietnamese datasets, as described by Quang et al. [1]. The novel dataset contains 111,601 sentences on the training set and 44,081 sentences on the test set. Meanwhile, the size of the news dataset is over three times the novel dataset. It contains 440,866 sentences on the training set and 145,768 on the test set. Comma and period are punctuation marks with the most percentage of occurrence in both datasets, but the others are significantly different. Specifically, the number of colon and semicolon marks is so small, and they have only a few tens or a few hundred in the novel dataset. In the news dataset, the smallest number of punctuation marks are semicolons and exclamation marks. See Table 1 for more information about punctuation mark distributions.

3.2   Results

We compare our models with the combination of BiLSTM and Attention from previous work [2] that achieves the highest overall f1-score in both Vietnamese datasets.

In the novels dataset, mBERT, XLM-RoBERTa, and viELECTRA improve the overall F1-score by 12.01%, 18.56%, and 21.12%, respectively. Because of the poverty of semicolon marks in both training and test set, our proposed models fail to predict the semicolon, leading to zero correction even when these models are pre-trained on a massive corpus.

---

[2] https://github.com/google-research/bert/blob/master/multilingual.md.
[3] https://github.com/facebookresearch/XLM.
[4] https://github.com/heraclex12/VN-Punc-Pretrained-LMs.

Table 1. The number of punctuation marks on both training and test sets in Vietnamese novels and news datasets.

Punctuation	Novel		News	
	Training	Test	Training	Test
COMMA	50909	21231	482435	160472
PERIOD	66519	29643	419580	138967
COLON	742	1153	32177	10728
QMARK	14899	5271	13902	4468
EXCLAM	30183	9167	7384	2333
SEMICOLON	48	43	5675	2045

There are many grammatical errors in the news dataset, and existing foreign words that lead to the performance improvements are slightly different. The performance of the "mBERT" is improved further by 13.49%. On the other hand, the performance improvement of both XLM-RoBERTa and viELECTRA respectively fall to 16.75% and 18.29%. Compared with the novels dataset, the distribution of punctuation marks is more balanced. Thus, our models can predict all the punctuation marks well, though the performance still needs further improvement.

As shown in Tables 2 and 3, all our models outperform the previous model. Especially, fine-tuning viELECTRA reaches the highest performance compared to other fine-tuning models. However, there are a few observations contrary to our expectations. All our additional layers could not obtain the expected outcomes, with less than 1% improvement in the overall F1-score. It indicates that the influence of dependencies in the BiLSTM layer and CRF layer is not much. Finally, the combination of the "viELECTRA" and CRF layer achieves 71.97% in overall F1-score, which is the best performance in the Vietnamese novels dataset, and 21.45% higher in absolute difference from the previous work. On the other hand, the combination of viELECTRA, BiLSTM, and CRF dominates the Vietnamese news benchmark. It achieves 80.98% in overall F1-score and outperforms the previous model 18.31% in an absolute score.

3.3 Discussion

Experimental results show that the transfer learning method is effective. All fine-tuning models outperform the previous model on both the Vietnamese novels dataset and news dataset. Our models employ robust architecture to learn different aspects of the language in both left and right contexts and allow our models to focus on essential words in the sentence. Another reason is our models benefit from the weights that we have learned on a lot of training data. Both of the above reasons make our models decide the meaning of the words based on the context, instead of getting a particular meaning. We assume that incorporating a Bi-LSTM layer or a CRF layer can boost the performance, but it is not

Table 2. The performance of our proposed models in Vietnamese novel dataset. We consider six punctuation marks in our experiments and compare the proposed models with the state-of-the-art method for the punctuation prediction task in the Vietnamese language [2].

Model	Avg	,	.	:	?	!	;
BiLSTM+Att [2]	56.52	56.10	55.86	21.43	70.34	52.09	0.00
	45.67	38.45	47.33	0.95	65.60	54.30	0.00
	50.52	45.63	51.24	1.81	67.89	53.18	0.00
mBERT	62.26	60.47	63.47	28.57	75.44	55.64	0.00
	62.80	56.13	67.93	3.82	75.77	61.90	0.00
	62.53	58.22	65.63	6.73	75.61	58.60	0.00
+CRF	62.74	59.45	65.28	29.22	75.23	55.81	0.00
	62.51	57.49	66.31	3.90	75.92	61.78	0.00
	62.62	58.45	65.79	6.89	75.57	58.64	0.00
+LSTM	62.92	59.83	64.93	22.86	75.82	56.52	0.00
	62.17	56.87	66.12	0.69	75.26	62.17	0.00
	62.54	58.31	65.52	1.35	75.54	59.21	0.00
+LSTM+CRF	63.31	60.49	64.53	25.00	77.23	58.13	0.00
	62.03	55.98	66.41	1.47	75.47	62.06	0.00
	62.67	58.15	65.46	2.78	76.34	60.03	0.00
XLM-RoBERTa	69.72	67.21	73.12	40.15	80.96	60.01	0.00
	68.44	64.33	72.21	4.6	78.03	68.65	0.00
	69.08	65.74	72.66	8.25	79.47	64.04	0.00
+CRF	69.36	66.53	72.64	40.57	80.55	60.65	0.00
	68.94	65.15	72.40	7.46	79.74	68.35	0.00
	69.15	65.83	72.52	12.6	80.14	64.27	0.00
+LSTM	69.34	66.72	76.62	35.96	81.33	59.90	0.00
	68.67	64.70	72.31	5.55	79.34	68.22	0.00
	69.01	65.70	72.47	9.62	80.32	63.79	0.00
+LSTM+CRF	70.34	66.53	73.83	34.92	80.46	63.01	0.00
	68.15	65.78	71.50	3.82	79.76	64.58	0.00
	69.23	66.15	72.65	6.88	80.11	63.78	0.00
viELECTRA	71.84	69.66	75.79	41.28	81.18	61.15	0.00
	71.44	67.19	75.43	**7.81**	81.01	71.24	0.00
	71.64	68.40	75.61	**13.13**	81.10	65.81	0.00
+CRF	**72.17**	**70.29**	**75.97**	48.41	80.95	61.27	0.00
	71.77	**68.39**	75.32	5.29	**81.45**	**71.26**	0.00
	71.97	**69.32**	75.65	9.54	**81.20**	**65.89**	0.00
+LSTM	71.27	68.53	74.67	32.52	81.75	62.20	0.00
	71.06	67.49	75.70	5.81	79.91	67.79	0.00
	71.17	68.00	75.18	9.86	80.82	64.87	0.00
+LSTM+CRF	71.66	68.02	74.46	34.31	**82.44**	**65.47**	0.00
	71.44	68.31	**77.10**	5.55	79.45	64.40	0.00
	71.55	68.16	**75.76**	9.56	80.92	64.93	0.00

Notes: The 1st line in each row is Precision, the 2nd line is Recall, and the 3rd one is F1-score.

Table 3. The performance of our proposed models in Vietnamese news dataset. We consider six punctuation marks in our experiments and compare the proposed models with the state-of-the-art method for the punctuation prediction task in the Vietnamese language [2].

Model	Avg	,	.	:	?	!	;
BiLSTM+Att [2]	69.63	68.30	72.09	61.54	61.01	35.71	29.25
	56.97	52.42	68.13	29.87	51.30	7.50	4.92
	62.67	59.32	70.06	40.22	55.73	12.40	8.43
mBERT	77.48	73.50	83.06	64.25	68.67	**42.95**	36.09
	74.89	69.01	85.92	49.58	65.35	11.62	13.89
	76.16	71.18	84.46	55.97	66.97	18.29	20.06
+CRF	77.58	73.47	83.32	64.80	68.36	41.96	36.98
	74.61	68.66	85.64	49.00	66.05	12.09	15.55
	76.06	70.98	84.46	55.80	67.18	18.77	21.89
+LSTM	77.79	73.60	83.53	65.12	68.08	42.57	36.97
	74.63	68.91	85.57	48.04	65.44	11.66	10.61
	76.17	71.18	84.54	55.29	66.74	18.30	16.49
+LSTM+CRF	77.78	73.33	83.86	65.19	69.57	40.72	36.49
	74.66	69.18	85.32	48.31	64.28	12.13	11.69
	76.19	71.20	84.59	55.50	66.82	18.69	17.70
XLM-RoBERTa	80.61	76.70	86.22	67.64	74.96	44.97	38.56
	78.27	72.90	88.47	54.19	72.09	14.96	18.63
	79.42	74.75	87.33	60.18	73.50	22.45	25.12
+CRF	80.48	76.54	86.31	66.09	75.96	42.89	36.47
	78.40	73.01	88.48	56.28	72.07	14.62	18.78
	79.42	74.73	87.38	60.79	73.96	21.80	24.79
+LSTM	80.89	76.73	86.72	67.88	75.12	45.49	43.45
	78.29	73.21	88.24	54.73	71.08	13.84	14.77
	79.57	74.93	87.47	60.60	73.05	21.23	22.04
+LSTM+CRF	80.83	76.58	86.72	68.67	75.59	45.45	40.58
	78.28	73.31	88.17	53.68	71.24	14.36	13.69
	79.54	74.91	87.44	60.62	73.35	21.82	20.48
viELECTRA	81.86	77.78	88.06	68.18	**76.94**	41.70	37.53
	80.07	**75.42**	89.16	59.13	**74.40**	18.52	20.24
	80.96	**76.59**	88.60	63.33	**75.65**	25.65	26.30
+CRF	81.82	77.73	88.06	68.46	76.06	42.27	36.40
	80.08	75.37	**89.22**	**59.29**	74.10	**19.46**	20.15
	80.94	76.53	88.64	63.55	75.07	**26.65**	25.94
+LSTM	82.07	78.01	88.23	68.76	76.65	40.69	36.49
	79.85	75.06	89.19	58.28	73.16	17.70	20.54
	80.95	76.51	88.71	63.08	74.87	24.67	26.28
+LSTM+CRF	**82.12**	**78.06**	**88.29**	**69.09**	75.97	40.92	**38.29**
	79.87	74.98	89.19	59.23	73.93	18.17	**22.05**
	80.98	76.49	**88.74**	**63.78**	74.93	25.18	**27.99**

Notes: The 1st line in each row is Precision, the 2nd line is Recall, and the 3rd one is F1-score.

significant. The possible reason is that the pre-trained models already consist of deep networks, making the architecture more complicated is a redundant option.

4   Conclusion

This paper has conducted extensive experiments to investigate the various pre-trained Transformer-based models for the Vietnamese language's punctuation prediction problem and consider two categories of models: monolingual and multilingual. The experimental results show that the monolingual Transformer-based models are better than the multilingual models, and our proposed models outperform the previous works for the Vietnamese language. It can demonstrate that using a transfer-learning method can provide high efficiency in the punctuation prediction task. Besides, we also stack LSTM and/or on top of the pre-trained models and achieve promising results. Our best model dominates other approaches in both datasets. We can conduct an overall F1-score of 21,45% on the novel dataset and 18.27% on the news dataset.

For future work, we plan to expand two Vietnamese datasets to distribute classes more balanced. It can help our model learn better in the minority class. We also aim to analyze our proposed model's robustness on other informal texts that are more challenging in the real world. Instead of treating the missing punctuation mark problem as a sequence labeling task, we can deal with this problem as the punctuation restoration task, using another approach like machine translation. In this approach, the input sentence does not contain any punctuation marks, and then the model generates and outputs that sentence with the correct punctuation marks.

References

1. Pham, Q.H., Nguyen, B.T., Cuong, N.V.: Punctuation prediction for vietnamese texts using conditional random fields. In: Proceedings of the Tenth International Symposium on Information and Communication Technology, SoICT 2019, pp. 322–327 (2019)
2. Pham, T., Nguyen, N., Pham, Q., Cao, H., Nguyen, B.: Vietnamese punctuation prediction using deep neural networks. In: Chatzigeorgiou, A., et al. (eds.) SOF-SEM 2020. LNCS, vol. 12011, pp. 388–400. Springer, Cham (2020). https://doi.org/10.1007/978-3-030-38919-2_32
3. Beeferman, D., Berger, A., Lafferty, J.: Cyberpunc: a lightweight punctuation annotation system for speech. In: Proceedings of the 1998 IEEE International Conference on Acoustics, Speech and Signal Processing, vol. 2, pp. 689–692, May 1998 (1998)
4. Huang, J., Zweig, G.: Maximum entropy model for punctuation annotation from speech (2002)
5. Lu, W., Tou Ng, H.: Better punctuation prediction with dynamic conditional random fields, pp. 177–186 (2010)
6. S. Peitz, M. Freitag, A. Mauser, and H. Ney, "Modeling punctuation prediction as machine translation," in IWSLT, 2011

7. Kim, S.: Deep recurrent neural networks with layer-wise multi-head attentions for punctuation restoration. In: ICASSP 2019–2019 IEEE International Conference on Acoustics, Speech and Signal Processing (ICASSP), pp. 7280–7284 (2019)
8. K. Makhija, T. Ho, and E. Chng, "Transfer learning for punctuation prediction," in 2019 Asia-Pacific Signal and Information Processing Association Annual Summit and Conference (APSIPA ASC), pp. 268–273, 2019
9. Fang, M., Zhao, H., Song, X., Wang, X., Huang, S.: Using bidirectional LSTM with Bert for Chinese punctuation prediction. In: 2019 IEEE International Conference on Signal, Information and Data Processing (ICSIDP), pp. 1–5 (2019)
10. Wang, F., Chen, W., Yang, Z., Xu, B.: Self-attention based network for punctuation restoration. In: 2018 24th International Conference on Pattern Recognition (ICPR), pp. 2803–2808 (2018)
11. Vaswani, A., et al.: Attention is all you need (2017)
12. Devlin, J., Chang, M.-W., Lee, K., Toutanova, K.: Bert: pre-training of deep bidirectional transformers for language understanding (2019)
13. Clark, K., Luong, M.-T., Le, Q.V., Manning, C.D.: Electra: pre-training text encoders as discriminators rather than generators (2020)
14. Conneau, A., et al.: Unsupervised cross-lingual representation learning at scale (2020)
15. Hendrycks, D., Gimpel, K.: Bridging nonlinearities and stochastic regularizers with Gaussian error linear units, ArXiv, vol. abs/1606.08415 (2016)
16. Wu, Y., et al.: Google's neural machine translation system: bridging the gap between human and machine translation (2016)
17. Lample, G., Conneau, A.: Cross-lingual language model pretraining (2019)
18. Liu, Y., et al.: Roberta: a robustly optimized bert pretraining approach (2019)
19. Kudo, T., Richardson, J.: SentencePiece: a simple and language independent subword tokenizer and detokenizer for neural text processing. In: Proceedings of the 2018 Conference on Empirical Methods in Natural Language Processing: System Demonstrations, (Brussels, Belgium), pp. 66–71. Association for Computational Linguistics, November 2018 (2018)
20. The, V.B., Thi, O.T., Le-Hong, P.: Improving sequence tagging for vietnamese text using transformer-based neural models (2020)

Study of Hybridized Support Vector Regression Based Flood Susceptibility Mapping for Bangladesh

Zakaria Shams Siam[1], Rubyat Tasnuva Hasan[1], Soumik Sarker Anik[1], Fahima Noor[1], Mohammed Sarfaraz Gani Adnan[2], and Rashedur M. Rahman[1(✉)]

[1] Department of Electrical and Computer Engineering, North South University, Dhaka 1229, Bangladesh
{zakaria.siam,rubyat.tasnuva,soumik.anik,fahima.noor, rashedur.rahman}@northsouth.edu
[2] Department of Urban and Regional Planning, Chittagong University of Engineering and Technology, Chittagong, Bangladesh
sarfarazadnan@cuet.ac.bd

Abstract. Flooding has become an exceedingly complex problem in many developing countries of the world including Bangladesh. Currently, Bangladesh is using MIKE 11 hydrodynamic model for flood forecasting. Previous studies indicated that hybridized machine learning models, especially support vector regression (SVR) models outperform standalone machine learning and other numerical models in mapping flood susceptibility. However, no study has been conducted on the flood dataset of Bangladesh using hybridized SVR model to predict flood susceptibility. In the present study, we have collected and modeled the recent flood inundation dataset of Bangladesh in terms of nine flood factors and explored their relative importance rank using the random forest (RF) algorithm. Then, we employed a genetic algorithm (GA) optimized SVR with radial basis function (RBF) kernel (hybridized GA-RBF-SVR) model along with the stand-alone RBF-SVR and multilayer perceptron (MLP) models to predict the flood susceptibility map for the whole country. The result of the hybridized SVR model is very promising to be employed in decision making to deal with the flood forecasting problem in Bangladesh.

Keywords: Flood susceptibility mapping · Flood inventory · Machine learning · Random forest · Hybridized support vector regression · Multilayer perceptron

1 Introduction

Bangladesh, located in the South Asian region, is one of the most flood prone countries globally. Due to the deltaic geographical setting, flat topography, shallow riverbed, high monsoon precipitation, high population density, and high discharge of sediments, the country is highly vulnerable to annual flood events of various types [1]. Different types of floods occur in Bangladesh every year including river, pluvial, flash, tidal and

© Springer Nature Switzerland AG 2021
H. Fujita et al. (Eds.): IEA/AIE 2021, LNAI 12799, pp. 59–71, 2021.
https://doi.org/10.1007/978-3-030-79463-7_6

storm surge-induced floods [2]. Since flooding is an outcome of complex interactions among various geomorphological, hydrological and anthropogenic processes, predicting a flood event is challenging. Flood susceptibility mapping (FSM) is a useful way of predicting the flood potentials of an area. From 1995–96, Bangladesh has been using MIKE 11 hydrodynamic model incorporating GIS for flood forecasting [3]. However, these numerical models' prediction accuracy gets affected due to the non-linear and dynamic attributes of floods and the restriction in data availability [4]. Different machine learning (ML) models of FSM have been deployed in previous studies to address low prediction accuracy in numerical flood modeling [5, 6]. Among these ML models, support vector regression (SVR) has been the most popular model to map flood susceptibility [4]. The performance of flood susceptibility modeling can be improved by integrating different metaheuristic optimization algorithms with ML models to build hybridized ML algorithms [4]. Evidence from various studies indicated that the hybridized models perform better in terms of generalization, performance, accuracy and robustness compared to the traditional standalone ML models [4].

Very few studies have been conducted on the FSM of Bangladesh using ML techniques. To the best of our knowledge, no study has been conducted to prepare a flood susceptibility map at the country level in Bangladesh using hybridized SVR model. Rahman et al. [5] presented flood inundation mapping using multiple ML algorithms including multilayer perceptron (MLP), analytical hierarchy process (AHP), logistic regression (LR) and frequency ratio (FR). Talukdar et al. [6] provided flood inundation mapping of the Teesta River basin using different bagging algorithms such as bagging with random forest (RF) and other models. Islam et al. [7] assessed flood susceptibility mapping in the Teesta River basin using random subspace (RS), RF, MLP and support vector machine (SVM). However, recent studies [4] have shown that hybridized SVR model provides better results than other machine learning models in flood susceptibility mapping. Hence, this study seeks to predict flood susceptibility for the whole area of Bangladesh exploiting the hybridized SVR model: Genetic Algorithm-Radial Basis Function-Support Vector Regression (GA-RBF-SVR) model and compare it with the standalone SVR with radial basis function (RBF) kernel (RBF-SVR) model and MLP model. We considered nine flood influencing factors to explore the hybridized SVR model's efficacy to produce more accurate FSM at the country scale in Bangladesh.

The structure of this paper is as follows. Section 2 describes the related works. Section 3 deals with the detailed description of the dataset. Section 4 describes the methodology. Section 5 discusses the results. Finally, Sect. 6 concludes with possible future works.

2 Related Works

In this section, we have discussed some related works exploring hybridized ML models to produce efficient FSM. Rahmati et al. [4] studied different hybridized ML models to create a flood susceptibility map for Iran's Amol city. They integrated the SVR model combining wavelet kernel function and two metaheuristic optimization algorithms: grey wolf optimizer (GWO) and bat optimizer (Bat). The study showed the greater efficacy of Wavelet-SVR-GWO than other models. They also demonstrated that both of the hybridized models performed much better than the standalone SVR model.

Jahangir et al. [8] exploited MLP to develop a spatial flood forecast model in the Kan River basin in Iran. They used seven flood triggering factors in their study. After developing the MLP model, the study compared it with the Soil Conservation Service (SCS) model. The MLP model heavily outperformed the SCS model in their study, where the values of the root-mean-squared error test were 0.16 for MLP and 0.21 for SCS. The study concluded that the hybrid utilization of GIS and MLP could bring excellent efficiency for predicting floods.

Wang et al. [9] provided assessed floods in Shangyou County of China using hybridized convolutional neural network (CNN) and SVM models. A total of 13 flood factors and 108 observed flood locations were taken into consideration. Two CNN algorithms for FSM were presented in their study. They demonstrated that all the proposed CNN models produced better results than SVM and the CNN-SVM hybrid model increased the prediction capability of SVM.

All the studies described above yielded excellent prediction accuracy in FSM using hybridized ML models. However, no study has been conducted in Bangladesh employing hybridized ML models. Hence, our present study aims to develop a hybridized model for FSM in Bangladesh.

3 Data Acquisition

This section describes the dataset collected and used in this study. Bangladesh has been chosen as the case study area. Bangladesh is a small South Asian country and it is partitioned into five main topographic sectors: Chittagong region, North Bengal region, Tippera-Comilla region, northeastern region and southwestern region [10]. The country consists of three main rivers, Padma, Meghna, and Jamuna, with many tributaries. The country's environment is mainly characterized by a tropical climate. The annual mean temperature fluctuates between 25 °C to 35 °C [5]. The annual rainfall ranges between 1200 mm and 6500 mm.

A total of nine flood conditioning factors were used to develop FSM in this study (Table 1). All these variables can either directly or indirectly influence the occurrence of flooding [11]. Heavy rainfall is generally associated with flooding [12]. LULC is an anthropogenic parameter that influences flood susceptibility, as it determines the rate of evapotranspiration and terrain infiltration that indirectly causes flooding [5–11]. Geological characteristics of an area are associated with the drainage pattern, which is related to floodplain formation [13]. Soil heavily influences rainfall-runoff mechanisms and is also responsible for the water infiltration in an area [5–12]. Due to earth's gravity, flood always moves from places of higher altitudes to lower altitudes and hence, the probability of flood increases in low elevated areas [14]. Hence, elevation is much important in determining flood susceptibility. Slope controls the streaming speed of flood waters and if the slope of a location declines, the probability of floods in that area also increases [15]. Both flood depth and flood duration have a direct contribution to the occurrences of floods [5]. Hence, we have selected all these nine factors as the independent variables of our study.

Table 1 shows the independent variables, classification of these variables and their sources.

Table 1. Classification of 9 flood conditioning factors

Factors	Classification	Source
Rainfall	i) 0 to 200 mm; ii) 201 to 400 mm; iii) 401 to 600 mm; iv) Above 600 mm	Bangladesh Agricultural Research Council (BARC)
Elevation	i) 0–3 m; ii) 3–10 m; iii) 10–30 m; iv) 30–75 m; v) 75–300 m; vi) Above 300 m	Bangladesh Agricultural Research Council (BARC)
Slope	i) Less than 10.8°; ii) 10.8 to 28.8°; iii) 28.8 to 57.6°; iv) 57.6 to 108°; v) 108 to 162°; vi) Greater than 162°	Bangladesh Agricultural Research Council (BARC)
Land Use / Land Cover (LULC)	i) Water; ii) Evergreen Needleleaf Forest; iii) Evergreen Broadleaf Forest; iv) Deciduous Needleleaf Forest; v) Deciduous Broadleaf; vi) Closed Shrublands; vii) Open Shrublands; viii) Woody Savannas; ix) Savannas; x) Grasslands; xi) Permanent Wetlands; xii) Cropland; xiii) Urban and Built-up; xiv) Cropland; xv) Natural Vegetation Mosaic; xvi) Snow and Ice; xvii) Barren or Sparsely Vegetation	Earth Explorer
Geology	i) Alluvial Deposit; ii) Alluvial Fan Deposit; iii) Bedrocks; iv) Coastal Deposit; v) Deltaic Deposit; vi) Jaintia Group; vii) Paludal Deposit; viii) Residual Deposit; ix) Suma Group; x) Tipam Group; xi) Lake; xii) Ocean and River	U.S. Geological Survey
Soil Tract	i) Brahmaputra Alluvium; ii) Tista Slit; iii) Madhupur Tract; iv) Gangetic Alluvium; v) Barind Tract; vi) Coastal Saline; vii) Hill Tract; viii) Miscellaneous	Bangladesh Agricultural Research Council (BARC)

(continued)

Table 1. (*continued*)

Factors	Classification	Source
Drainage Area	i) Imperfectly Drained; ii) Very Poorly Drained; iii) Poorly Drained but Surface Drains Late; iv) Poorly Drained but Surface Drains Early; v) Moderately Well Drained; vi) Well Drained	Bangladesh Agricultural Research Council (BARC)
Flood Depth	i) No flooding; ii) Flooding < 0.30 m; iii) Flooding 0.30–0.90 m; iv) Flooding 0.91–1.83 m; v) Flooding 1.84–3.05 m; vi) Flooding > 3.05 m	Bangladesh Agricultural Research Council (BARC)
Flood Duration	i) No Flooding; ii) Short; iii) Medium; iv) Long	Manual extraction from flood inundation dataset

For the flood susceptibility model, we considered flood inundation area as the dependent variable. For mapping flood inundation, this study used National Oceanic and Atmospheric Administration (NOAA) Visible Infrared Imaging Radiometer Suite (VIIRS) data for the food events of July 21, 2020, July 27, 2020 and August 8, 2020 prepared by United Nations Institute for Training and Research (UNITAR) [16]. Further processing was done to identify the Upazilas that the flooding areas belonged to and perform the geoprocessing of the flood inundated shape files in ArcGIS software. We prepared the flood inundated area variable by combining these three shapefiles in ArcGIS. In the combined shape file, the flooding locations were assigned the value of 1 whereas the non-flooding locations were assigned the value of 0. Finally, the flood conditioning factors were added to their corresponding flooding or non-flooding areas to produce the processed dataset. Total 544 locations containing the flooding and non-flooding areas in the designated dates were identified. We used the 10-fold cross-validation technique to divide the dataset containing 544 samples into the train and test data.

4 Methodology

This section describes the methodology of our study. The overall design of the complete methodology of this study is illustrated in Fig. 1.

After preparing the dataset described in Sect. 3, we have first explored the relative importance rank of the collected nine predictors using random forest (RF) algorithm by observing the %IncMSE and IncNodePurity measures of all the predictors. RF is a powerful ML technique to rank the independent variables according to their degree of importance for explaining the dependent variable. The %IncMSE refers to the mean decrease accuracy, and the IncNodePurity refers to the mean decrease gini of the predictors. The higher values of %IncMSE and IncNodePurity measures correspond to being

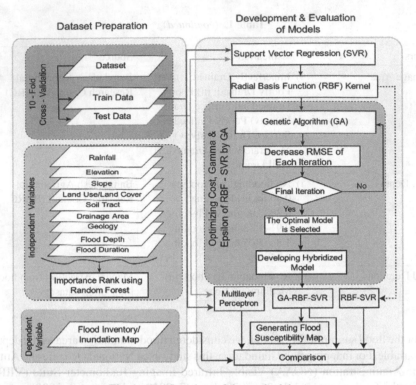

Fig. 1. The flowchart of the methodology

more important predictors. Other studies [17, 18] have also implemented this method to find out the importance of flood susceptibility predictors.

Then, we have exploited three ML methods for modeling flood susceptibility based on the selected independent and dependent variables: radial basis function kernel-support vector regression (RBF-SVR), hybridized genetic algorithm-radial basis function kernel-support vector regression (GA-RBF-SVR) and multilayer perceptron (MLP). SVR is a supervised learning model that can solve regression problems and execute forecasting or prediction in the short run [4]. It is very good at reducing generalization errors. SVR produces the function (1) that can describe the connection between input and output data.

$$f(x) = w^T \psi(x) + b \tag{1}$$

where $x \in R^n$ is the input vector data containing the features, $w \in R^n$ denotes the weight vector, b refers to the bias and $\psi(x)$ is the non-linear mapping function. By solving this mapping function with Lagrangian formulation, we get Lagrangian multipliers and the kernel function. Multiple kinds of kernel functions are used in SVR such as linear, polynomial, exponential RBF, gaussian RBF etc. In general, if the total number of training examples is fairly large compared to the number of features, the RBF kernel should be used [19] which is the most generalized form of kernelization and represented mathematically in (2).

$$K(x_1, x_2) = \exp(-\frac{\|x_1 - x_2\|^2}{2\sigma^2}) \tag{2}$$

where, σ is represented as the variance and the hyperparameter, $\|x_1 - x_2\|$ is the Euclidean interval between two points.

The SVR model learns by finding the optimal w values in (1). However, in RBF-SVR, the model's generalization performance strongly depends on the selected values of its parameters, cost (C), epsilon (ϵ) and gamma. The soft margin cost function parameter, C involves trading the penalty of error for stability. A faulty selection of C makes the empirical risk minimization and the model complexity minimization imbalanced. Also, when the value of the free parameter of RBF, gamma is higher, nearby points carry greater influence. If lower, then farther points are also considered to determine the decision boundary. Moreover, ϵ influences the smoothness of the response of SVR and also the number of support vectors. Hence, its value controls both the generalization capability and the model complexity. To find the optimal values of these three parameters of RBF-SVR in a specific search domain, we have first employed the grid search algorithm with a 10-fold cross-validation technique. We have trained 2000 SVR models in total ranging the values of gamma from 0.1 to 2 with an interval of 0.1 and the values of C from 0.1 to 10 with an interval of 0.1. We have set the value of ϵ to 0.1. We then tested all these trained 2000 RBF-SVR models on the test dataset using 10-fold cross-validation technique and measured their corresponding regression errors. Finally, we came up with the best RBF-SVR model from these 2000 trained models with the least regression error. We have used the root-mean-squared error (RMSE) metric to calculate the regression error for model validation. RMSE computes the difference between the predicted values by the model and the observed values. Equation (3) describes the formula of RMSE.

$$RMSE = \left[\frac{1}{N} \sum_{n=1}^{N} (y_n - y_{p.n})^2 \right]^{\frac{1}{2}} \tag{3}$$

where, y_n are the observed values and $y_{p.n}$ are the predicted values.

However, the grid search algorithm takes much time searching for the optimal values of hyperparameters in the specified range. Hence, searching the optimal values with it is not always feasible. In this regard, we have integrated genetic algorithm (GA), a parallel and heuristic optimization algorithm inspired by the theory of natural selection, with the RBF-SVR model to build the hybridized GA-RBF-SVR model to reduce the RMSE further. In GA, high fitness individuals are survived whereas low fitness individuals are eradicated. After several iterations, high fitness individuals are obtained. To find the optimal values of C, ϵ and gamma in the specified range with the help of GA, we have defined the negative value of the mean RMSE of the hybridized model over the test samples in 10-fold cross-validation as the fitness function for the iteration process of GA. Hence, we have maximized the fitness function values (the negative mean RMSE values) of the individuals to minimize the positive RMSE of the model. Thus, GA assists in finding out the optimal RBF-SVR model parameters in the specified range more efficiently than the grid search algorithm by minimizing RMSE and time complexity.

We have set the population size to 50 and the maximum iteration number to 100. The crossover and mutation probability were set to 0.8 and 0.1 respectively. Using GA, we have searched over the real values of ϵ ranging from 0 to 1, gamma ranging from 0.001 to 2 and C ranging from 0.0001 to 10 to get the least RMSE. This model was also tested and evaluated using the 10-fold cross-validation technique.

Next, we have applied the MLP model to predict flood susceptibility, which minimizes empirical risk. We have set 2 hidden layers with the first hidden layer having ten neurons and the second hidden layer having three neurons. We have used the backpropagation learning algorithm. We have set the learning rate to 0.0001, the threshold value to 0.1 and the maximum iteration number to 10^6. We have tested this model using 10-fold cross-validation as well.

Finally, we have explored the comparison among the three models using the RMSE metric and the 10-fold cross-validation technique to select the best performing model to plot the flood susceptibility map. We have used the R programming language in RStudio to apply all these three ML models and perform model validation and comparison. The final flood susceptibility map was plotted using ArcGIS. For plotting the flood susceptibility map, we determined the flood susceptibility scores using (4).

$$Flood\ Susceptibility\ Score = \sum_{i=1}^{n} w_i x_i \qquad (4)$$

where, n denotes the number of flood predictors which is 9 in our study. x_i denotes the feature and w_i denotes the weight of that feature.

After obtaining the optimal weight values for all the nine features and then calculating each location's corresponding predicted flood susceptibility score using (4), we stored these scores ranging from 0 to 1. Using the equal interval method, we have then divided these scores into 'Very Low' (from 0 to 0.2), 'Low' (from 0.2 to 0.4), 'Medium' (from 0.4 to 0.6), 'High' (from 0.6 to 0.8) and 'Very High' (from 0.8 to 1) susceptibility categories. Then we transferred these values to the district-based Bangladesh map collected from Bangladesh-Subnational Administrative Boundaries [20]. Next, we have colored the map according to the predicted flood susceptibility scores. Finally, we have compared this flood susceptibility map to the observed flood inundation map for assessing the effectiveness of our hybridized model.

5   Results and Discussion

In this section, we have presented and discussed all the results. First, we have delineated the relative importance rank of all the collected features. Then we have employed the hybridized GA-RBF-SVR, RBF-SVR, and MLP models to predict flood susceptibility and explored the comparison among them to ascertain the efficacy of the hybridized SVR model in mapping flood susceptibility.

First, we have determined the %IncMSE and IncNodePurity measures for all the flood conditioning factors in mapping flood susceptibility using RF to observe the relative importance rank of all the predictors illustrated in Fig. 2.

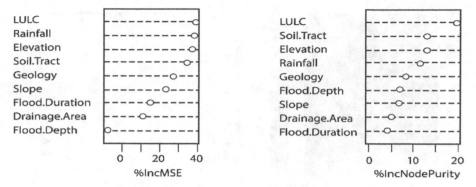

Fig. 2. Relative importance rank of the predictors using RF

From Fig. 2, it is evident that LULC, rainfall, elevation, and soil tract are the most important four factors, while drainage area and flood depth are the least contributing predictors for predicting flood susceptibility according to the %IncMSE measures. Talukder et al. [6] found that LULC and elevation contribute the most to trigger flood compared to the other attributes. Also, Bui et al. [12] showed that soil is highly crucial in triggering flash floods. Our findings are consistent in this regard.

While applying the RBF-SVR model using the grid search technique, the optimal value of C turned out to be 1.2, and the optimal gamma turned out to be 0.4 in the specified range while ϵ was set to 0.1 for minimizing the time complexity. The values of the weight matrix, w for the selected best RBF-SVR model turned out to be -18.30 for rainfall, 47.59 for LULC, -56.78 for elevation, -76.11 for slope, -38.69 for soil tract, -1.83 for flood depth, -18.22 for drainage area, 5.04 for geology and 31.19 for flood duration. The bias value turned out to be 0.39. We have shown the contour plot in Fig. 3(a) illustrating the performance of each of the trained 2000 RBF-SVR models. Here, C and gamma values have been plotted along the X and Y axis, respectively, while along the Z-axis indicated by the color bar delineates the mean squared error (MSE) values that are just the squared values of RMSE. The calculated least RMSE value for the optimal RBF-SVR model turned out to be 0.28 considering all nine predictors. In GA-RBF-SVR, after 100 iterations, the optimal values of C, ϵ and gamma turned out to be 1.62, 0.48, and 0.09, respectively, in the specified search domain, and the corresponding least RMSE was 0.18. Thus, we are observing a great accuracy boost in prediction while exploiting the hybridized model. Figure 3(b) illustrates the fitness values or negative RMSE values in each generation within the 100 iterations of GA.

Finally, the employed MLP model produces an RMSE value of 0.46. We tried different architectures of MLP having a different number of hidden layers and neurons exploiting different learning algorithms. However, in each case, we either got larger RMSE values, or the model did not converge. Fig. 4 illustrates the comparison among the RBF-SVR, GA-RBF-SVR, and MLP models using the RMSE metric and the 10-fold cross-validation technique. Notably, in Fig. 4 the hybridized GA-RBF-SVR model performs much better than the other two models. This performance plot proves the efficacy of the GA-RBF-SVR model in predicting the flood susceptibility map with the least prediction error. Hence, we decided to plot and analyze the flood susceptibility map

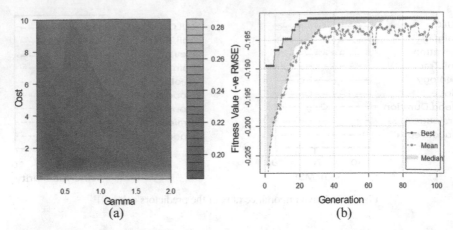

Fig. 3. (a) Performance of RBF-SVR models; (b) Fitness values in each generation in GA

of Bangladesh using the predicted flood susceptibility scores given by the hybridized GA-RBF-SVR model only.

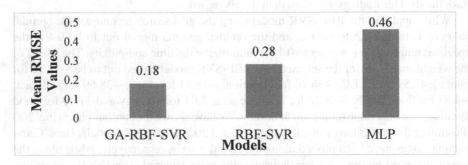

Fig. 4. RMSE-based comparison among the 3 models

Using the prediction results made by the optimal GA-RBF-SVR model, we have generated the flood susceptibility map of Bangladesh in 2020 that shows areas with different degrees of flood susceptibility (Fig. 5 (b)). This map was then compared to the observed flood inundation map of Bangladesh for the same year (Fig. 5 (a)) to verify the flood susceptibility map produced by the hybridized SVR model.

The NAWG Flood Preliminary Impact [21] and the HCTT Response Plan Monsoon Floods 2020 [22] were used to understand the degree of flooding in different regions of Bangladesh. The reports include a detailed flood analysis of the monsoon 2020. The original flood map shows that Rangpur, situated near the northern part of Bangladesh, did not face much flooding. Around 15.30% of the area was inundated in flood. Our model was able to show this region as a very low flood susceptible area. The model also shows Rajbari to have very low flood susceptibility. Around 15.43% area of Rajbari was inundated during the monsoon. Our model determines the south-eastern region like Khagrachari as a low flood susceptible zone. This district experienced flash floods

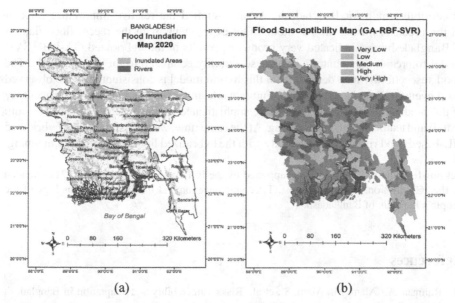

Fig. 5. (a) Flood Inundation Map, 2020 of Bangladesh; (b) Flood Susceptibility Map, 2020 of Bangladesh using the Hybridized GA-RBF-SVR Model.

only once (in 2019) in the past five years [23]. Around 45.52% of the northern district, Netrakona, was inundated with a flood, and our model shows medium level susceptibility for this region. Both flood maps show Tangail, a central district, to be a medium flood susceptible region, where around 50% of the area was inundated. Both Fig. 5(a) and Fig. 5(b) show parts of Jamalpur, a north-central region of Bangladesh, to be highly prone to flooding. Throughout the monsoon of 2020, around 73.49% of the area in this district was inundated. Rajshahi, Dinajpur, Shatkira, and Gaibandha are some of the districts that experienced heavy inundation. Our model marked these districts as high flood susceptible regions. The Eastern part of Sylhet also faced heavy inundation, which is determined to be a very highly flood susceptible region by our model. Districts like Narayanganj, Kishoreganj, Magura and Faridpur were also heavily inundated during the monsoon period, and our model marked those places to be very highly susceptible to flooding. The continuous geographical and environmental changes may cause a slight estimation difference in some regions in our flood susceptibility map. Overall, if we compare both the flood susceptibility map of our model and the original flood map of Bangladesh in 2020, we can see practical and expected outcomes. Thus, this direct comparison proves the efficacy of our chosen optimal GA-RBF-SVR model in generating an effective flood susceptibility map for the whole area of Bangladesh.

6 Conclusion and Future Works

This study collected nine significant flood predictors and flood inundation dataset and then employed RBF-SVR, GA- RBF-SVR, and MLP models to generate the flood susceptibility map for Bangladesh. We also studied the relative importance rank of all the predictors using the RF model. Our experiments with the recent flood dataset of Bangladesh have indicated very promising results of the hybridized GA-RBF-SVR model to predict the country's flood susceptibility compared to the other models. The flood susceptibility map derived from this hybrid model is consistent with the observed flood events of Bangladesh in 2020. Future works may focus on increasing the accuracy of the prediction with the help of more sophisticated hybridized ML models for both spatial and temporal flood forecasting. At the same time, we will integrate the hybridized ML-based flood risk assessment study with the hybridized flood susceptibility mapping.

Acknowledgements. This work is supported by the ICT Innovation Fund (2020-21) provided by the ICT division, Ministry of Post, Telecommunication and Information Technology of the People's Republic of Bangladesh.

References

1. Rahman, A., Alam, M., Alam, S., et al.: Risks vulnerability and adaptation in Bangladesh Human Development Repositor (2007)
2. Rahman,R., Salehin, M.: Flood risks and reduction approaches in Bangladesh. In: Disaster Risk Reduction Approaches in Bangladesh, Tokyo, Springer (2013)
3. Leon, M., Barua, P., Sarker, P., et al.: Annual Flood Report 2019. IOP Publishing FFWC (2020). http://www.ffwc.gov.bd/images/annual19.pdf
4. Rahmati, O., Darabi, H., Panahi, M.: Development of novel hybridized models for urban flood susceptibility mapping. Sci. Rep. **10**(1), 1–19 (2020)
5. Rahman, M., et al.: Flood susceptibility assessment in Bangladesh using machine learning and multi-criteria decision analysis. Earth Syst. Environ. **3**(3), 585–601 (2019). https://doi.org/10.1007/s41748-019-00123-y
6. Talukdar, S., Ghose, B., Pham, Q.: Flood susceptibility modeling in Teesta River basin, Bangladesh using novel ensembles of bagging algorithms. Stoch. Env. Res. Risk Assess. **34**, 2277–2300 (2020)
7. Islam, T., Talukdar, S., Mahato, S.: Flood susceptibility modelling using advanced ensemble machine learning models. Geosci. Front. **12**(3), 101075 (2020)
8. Jahangir, M., Reineh, S., Abolghasemi, M.: Spatial predication of flood zonation mapping in Kan River Basin, Iran, using artificial neural network algorithm. Weather Clim. Extremes **25** (2019)
9. Wang, Y., Fang, Z., Hong, H., Peng, L.: Flood susceptibility mapping using convolutional neural network frameworks. J. Hydrol. **582** (2020)
10. Islam, M., Sado, K.: Development of flood hazard maps of Bangladesh using NOAA- AVHRR images with GIS. Hydrol. Sci. J. **45**, 337–355 (2000)
11. Adnan, MSG., Talchabhadel, R., Nakagawa, H., Hall, W.: The potential of tidal river management for flood alleviation in south western Bangladesh. Sci. Total Environ. **731** (2020)
12. Bui, D., Hoang, N., Costache, R.: A novel deep learning neural network approach for predicting flash flood susceptibility: a case study at a high frequency tropical storm area. Sci. Total Environ. **701**, 134413 (2019)
13. Dt, B., Td, P., Jafaari, A.: A novel hybrid approach based on a swarm intelligence optimized extreme learning machine for flash flood susceptibility mapping. CATENA **179**, 184–196 (2019)

14. Coulthard, T., Frostick, L.: The Hull floods of 2007: implications for the governance and management of urban drainage systems. J. Flood Risk Manag **3**, 223–231 (2010)
15. Kassogué, H., Bernoussi, A., Maâtouk, M.: Two scale cellular automaton for flow dynamics modeling (2CAFDYM). Appl. Math. Model. **43**, 61–77 (2017)
16. Map detail United Nations Institute for Training and Research. https://www.unitar.org/maps/map/3073
17. Vafakhah, M., Pourghasemi, H., Katebikord, A., Loor, S.: Comparing performance of random forest and adaptive neuro-fuzzy inference system data mining models for flood susceptibility mapping. Arabian. J. Geosci **13**, 1–6 (2020)
18. Quang-Thanh, B., Quoc-Huy, N.: Verification of novel integrations of swarm intelligence algorithms into deep learning neural network for flood susceptibility mapping. J. Hydrol. **581**, 124379 (2019)
19. Prajakta, P., Shaw, K., Malathi, P.: Speaker dependent speech emotion recognition using MFCC and Support Vector Machine. In: 2016 International Conference on Automatic Control and Dynamic Optimization Techniques (ICACDOT), Pune (2016)
20. Bangladesh Subnational Administrative Boundaries. https://data.humdata.org/dataset/administrative-boundaries-of-bangladesh-as-of-2015
21. Monsoon flood preliminary impact and KIN assessment. https://reliefweb.int/sites/reliefweb.int/files/resources/nawg_monsoon_flood_preliminary_impact_and_kin_20200725_final_draft.pdf
22. Response Plan Monsoon Floods (2020). https://www.humanitarianresponse.info/en/operations/bangladesh/document/hctt-monsoon-flood-humanitarian-response-plan-monitoring-dashboard-30
23. Dhaka tribune. https://www.dhakatribune.com/bangladesh/nation/2020/09/27/4th-time-flood-thakurgaon-records-worst-rain-in-a-decade

A Fusion Approach for Paper Submission Recommendation System

Son T. Huynh[1,2,3], Nhi Dang[1,2,3], Phong T. Huynh[1,2,3], Dac H. Nguyen[3,4], and Binh T. Nguyen[1,2,3(✉)]

[1] University of Science, Ho Chi Minh City, Vietnam
ngtbinh@hcmus.edu.vn
[2] Vietnam National University, Ho Chi Minh City, Vietnam
[3] AISIA Research Lab, Ho Chi Minh City, Vietnam
[4] John Von Neumann Institute, Ho Chi Minh City, Vietnam

Abstract. Building a recommendation system to support researchers in the conference or journal selection process to submit their work has been one interesting topic during the last few years. The current state-of-the-art approaches usually use the available information of one paper submission: the title, the abstract, and the list of keywords. In this paper, we propose a new approach for the paper submission recommendation problem by constructing a suitable architecture to extract the useful information from the "Aims and Scopes" of journals and combine the textual features computed from the title, the abstract, and the list of keywords of the paper submission. We collect one dataset with 414512 papers related to computer science to measure the performance of our proposed method. The experimental results show that a fusion approach of these features can significantly bypass the state-of-the-art techniques and contribute to the relevant research topic.

Keywords: Paper submission recommendation · Text embedding · Recommendation system · Deep neural networks

1 Introduction

Nowadays, there have been many applications for different aspects of recommendation systems in our daily lives, from big companies to startups. Each company can utilize recommendation algorithms to deep dive into historical user data and give customers better suggestions or insights. Satisfying users and allowing them a better customer experience for each product can boost the related business as efficiently as possible besides optimizing any potential cost. Consequently, many companies like Google, Facebook, Amazon, eBay, Spotify, or Netflix have been investing a lot in improving their recommendation algorithms in different company products. There are various recommendation systems related to academics, including paper submission system [1], collaboration recommendation [2,3], and paper suggestion [4].

© Springer Nature Switzerland AG 2021
H. Fujita et al. (Eds.): IEA/AIE 2021, LNAI 12799, pp. 72–83, 2021.
https://doi.org/10.1007/978-3-030-79463-7_7

Submitting new papers at conferences or scientific journals is always one of the significant milestones for researchers to extend their research and collaborate with others. Besides having good results and better preparation for the submitted papers, both young and experienced researchers have to decide which venues are the best for submission. Sometimes, this decision is quite challenging and time-consuming when the total number of both conferences and journals is quite large [5]. Moreover, each conference or journal has its specific topic, aims and scopes, and quality ranking. As a result, there is a need for a paper recommendation system for supporting researchers in choosing the best revenue for their work, especially for young researchers (postdocs, Ph.D. students, or Master students). There have been several works of building such a recommendation system. Wang et al. [1] extracted useful features (the Chi-square statistics, the term frequency-inverse document frequency (TF-IDF)) from each submission's abstract. They trained a suitable recommendation model using linear logistic regression to achieve an accuracy of 61.37% in one dataset collected from different conferences and journals in computer science. Son and colleagues later [5,6] improved the paper submission recommendation algorithm's performance in the dataset of Wang et al. by combining different types of features (including deep learning features) and using various models. One can find other interesting results at [7–10].

Each conference or scientific journal has clear aims and scopes to help researchers easily submit appropriate submissions to the corresponding conference or journal. There is no paper submission recommendation system using this type of information to enhance such a system's performance to the best of our knowledge. This paper investigates the paper recommendation problem by considering four different available attributes when submitting one scientific work, including the title, the abstract, the list of keywords, and the aims of scopes of each journal considered. We collect one dataset of 414512 papers with 331464 papers in the training dataset and 83048 academic journal articles in the testing dataset. It is worth noting that the paper submission recommendation system's primary purpose is to suggest the list of top K relevant journals for given paper submission of users. We construct the corresponding architecture to combine the information related to each conference or scientific journal's aims and scopes with a feature selection from the submission's available attributes (the title, the abstract, and the keywords). The experimental results show that applying our feature engineering of using additional aims and scopes of each journal or conference can enhance the corresponding paper submission recommendation system's performance. Our approach mostly outperforms other state-of-the-art methods [1,5,6] using the title, the abstract, and the keywords of each submission in terms of Accuracy@K (K = 1, 3, 5, 10).

2 Methodology

In this section, we describe our approach in different steps: data processing, feature selection, and modeling for a paper submission recommendation system.

2.1   Data Processing

Data processing is a crucial step in many natural language processing problems to transform the raw text into a form that computers can understand and efficiently apply different embedding methods or deep learning models to extract useful features. In this work, as we aim to use two different types of data: the available attributes of each paper submission (the title, the abstract, and the list of keywords) and the aims and scopes of each journal or conference, one can employ the following data processing steps:

1. Lowercase text to make all texts have the same format and avoid the first letter of the sentence or nickname.
2. Remove not-be-alphabet text containing insignificant semantic to the problem (for instance, a word "pre-treatment" or an email "author@gmail.com").
3. Remove single letters that likely do not have pretrained weights in well-known pretrained word vectors like FastText Common Crawl[1].
4. Remove words within stopwords downloaded from the *Natural Language Toolkit* (NLTK[2]) and additional stopwords we define.
5. Remove unnecessary space from the beginning to the end of the text after doing four steps above.

Table 1 depicts one example related to the data processing of three available attributes of one paper submission. Table 2 describes the corresponding process for the aims and scopes of each journal or conference.

2.2   Feature Selection

In this study, we consider two groups of features: Feature Group I and Feature Group II.

Feature Group I. For Feature Group I, we use seven different combinations of available attributes of each paper submission: Title(T), Abstract(A), Keywords(K), Title + Abstract (TA), Title + Keywords (TK), Abstract + Keywords (AK), Title + Abstract + Keywords (TAK). For this group, we apply two different state-of-the-art methods to extract features from these three attributes and/or combine the feature extracted from the aims and scopes (S) in our proposed architecture. We employ two different methods [5,6] to compute feature vectors from the title, the abstract, and the keywords in our experiments. It is worth noting that these two methods are the state-of-the-art methods in the dataset of Wang et al.

We modify the recommendation algorithm described in [6] by adjusting the parameters to fit the new dataset better. We increase the number of filters of Convolution 1D to enhance feature extraction from model input, put dropouts to avoid overfitting in Deep Learning Neural Network [11], and increase the number

---

[1] https://fasttext.cc/docs/en/english-vectors.html.
[2] https://gist.github.com/sebleier/554280.

Table 1. The data processing step for three available attributes: Abstract, Title, and Keywords.

	Original data	Processed data
Title	Malnutrition and its effects in severely injured trauma patients	malnutrition effects severely injured trauma patients
	Vitamin D deficiency in adult fracture patients: prevalence and risk factors	vitamin deficiency adult fracture patients prevalence risk factors
Abstract	Background To be a level I trauma center in the Netherlands a computed tomography (CT) scanner...	background level trauma center netherlands computed tomography ct scanner...
	Purpose Although vitamin D levels are not routinely monitored in outpatient fracture patients, identification of fracture...	purpose vitamin levels routinely monitored outpatient fracture patients identification fracture ...
Keywords	Penetrating injury, Diagnostics, Trauma, CT scan	penetrating injury diagnostics trauma ct scan
	Vitamin D, Vitamin D deficiency, Risk factors, Fracture, Fracture healing	vitamin deficiency risk factors fracture healing

of hidden nodes in every fully-connected layer. Finally, we use crawl-300d-2M[3] as the pre-train embedding matrix, which has 600 billion tokens and 2 million word vectors trained on Common Crawl. It can make using crawl-300d-2M more efficiently in vectorization.

As depicted in Fig. 2, the input data can be one of seven different combinations of features: T, A, K, TA, AK, TK, and TAK. We feed the input data through one Convolution 1D layer with 1800 filters and the kernel size as two. This layer is connected with a layer Dropout having the rate of 0.5. This amount of information is then computed by using the layer Global-MaxPooling. We use two fully connected layers where each block consists of a layer fully-connected layer with n_i units and a dropout of 0.3. In experiments, we choose $n_1 = 1000$ and $n_2 = 500$.

Feature Group II. For Feature Group II, using each journal's aim and scope in the dataset, we compute the corresponding paper-journal similarity vector, as illustrated in Fig. 1. Assume that there are N journals or conferences in our dataset. For each journal and given paper submission, we apply one embedding method to embed the processed text concatenating all the title, the abstract, the list of keywords of the submission, and the processed text containing the corresponding aim and scope. Then, we compute the similarity between these

---

[3] https://fasttext.cc/docs/en/english-vectors.html.

embedded vectors to represent the matching value between the paper and the journal. Applying this step, namely "paper-journal similarity extraction", for all N journals or conferences, we can derive a feature vector of N dimensions.

Table 2. The data processing step for aims and scopes of journals or conferences.

Revenue	Aims&Scopes	Processed data
European Journal of Trauma and Emergency Surgery	Trauma causes individual patterns of injury and involves shock, fractures, soft tissue and organ injuries. Treatment therefore requires ...	trauma causes individual patterns injury involves shock fractures soft tissue organ injuries treatment requires
Journal of Cluster Science	The journal publishes the following types of papers: (a) original and important research;(b) authoritative comprehensive reviews or short overviews of topics of current interest; (c) brief	journal publishes following types papers original important research authoritative comprehensive reviews short overviews topics currentinterest brief

Combining these two groups of features, we can obtain seven new features for each paper submission: Title + Aims and Scopes (TS), Abstract + Aims and Scopes (AS), Keyword s+ Aims and Scopes (KS), Title + Abstract + Aims and Scopes (TAS), Title +Keywords + Aims and Scopes (TKS), Abstract + Keywords + Aims and Scopes (AKS), Title + Abstract + Keywords + Aims and Scopes (TAKS).

2.3 Modeling

In this section, we describe three different models using in our experiments.

Models Using Title, Abstract, and Keywords. With a given paper submission, depending on each combination among seven types of input data, we extract the corresponding feature vector via the feature selection process for Feature Group I. For each journal or conference in the dataset, we use the cosine similarity distance to compute the relevant scores between the paper submission and other papers accepted in that journal or conference. The matching score between the paper submission and the journal or conference is the maximum value of all these relevant scores. Finally, we sort these matching scores among N journals and conferences in the dataset from the top to the least to choose the top K relevant ones.

Models Using Aims and Scopes. Given a paper submission, through the step of Paper-Journal Similarity Extraction, we derive the associated feature vector and feed this vector into multiple perceptron layers as described in Fig. 3. In this proposed architecture, the feature vector goes through a layer Batch-Normalization [12] with Keras [13] default implementation. After that, we define a block consisting of one fully connected layer (with n_i units and the activation function RELU) and one Dropout layer with 40% dropout of nodes. In experiments, we use four different blocks with $n_1 = 2000$, $n_2 = 1500$, $n_3 = 1000$, and $n_4 = 500$. Finally, we compute the final matching scores between the paper submission and each journal via the final layer with the Softmax activation function and sort them in an ascending order to return the top list of recommended items.

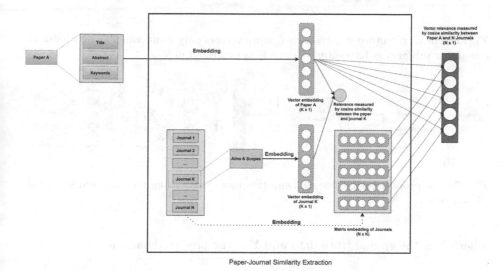

Paper-Journal Similarity Extraction

Fig. 1. Paper-journal similarity extraction.

Our Proposed Fusion Model. Our primary model for the paper submission recommendation system leverages both Feature Group I and Feature Group II. As described in Fig. 4, we combine all two feature vectors computed from these feature groups into one final feature vector and put them into one dense layer of 1000 hidden nodes and one Dropout layer with the rate of 30%. Finally, we feed this computed feature vector into the final layer of 500 hidden nodes using the activation function Softmax to return the recommended results.

2.4 Evaluation Metrics

In this experiment, we use $Accuracy@N$ as a measure to evaluate our proposed methods' performance, where N = 1, 3, 5, 10. The formulation of $Accuracy@N$ can be computed as follows:

$$p_{top_N}(X, Y) = \frac{\sum_{x_i \in N, y_i \in N} P_{top_N}(x_i, y_i)}{|Y|},$$

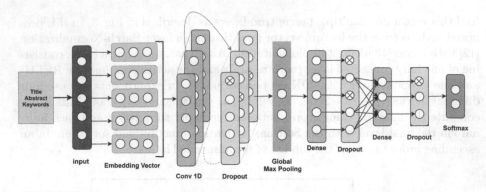

Fig. 2. The architecture of extracting feature vectors only using available attributes of one paper submission for Feature Group I, as described in [6].

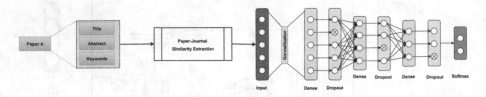

Fig. 3. The proposed paper recommendation model only using the aims and scopes of all journals.

where X is the ground truth data and Y is the predicted one, and

$$P_{top_N}(x_i, y_i) = \begin{cases} 1 & \text{if } y_i \text{ is in the top N list of recommended items by } x_i \\ 0 & \text{otherwise} \end{cases}$$

3 Experiments

In this paper, we run all experiments on a computer with Intel(R) Core(TM) i7 2CPUs running at 2.4GHz with eight GB of RAM and an Nvidia GeForce RTX2080Ti GPU.

During this study, we read data and process data by pandas and NumPy package. In the data processing step, we use different Python packages, including Textblob, NLTK, and Regex package, as tools to clean data. Additionally, due to the size of both training and testing datasets, we have to use a multiprocessing package to run multi-threads, thus making the model significantly faster. For the modeling procedure, we apply the Scikit-learn package to run model Multi-Perceptron and Keras package to run custom Multi-Perceptron and our deep learning models. Finally, we use pickle to store models' weights for predicting purpose in the future without training.

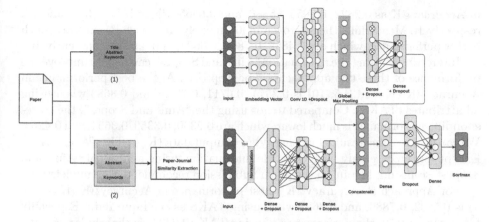

Fig. 4. Our proposed fusion model using four attributes: the title, the abstract, the list of keywords, and the aim and scope of each journal.

3.1 Dataset

This experiment evaluates our problem-solving method and compares the previous results with a completely new dataset. These are papers in the field of computer science from the publisher Springer[4].

Firstly, we searched in the Springer website with a chosen keyword as "computer science" and crawled about 2000 journal names. We retrieve all papers, the aims & scopes for each journal, and the corresponding journal ranking. Specifically, there are more than 6 million available papers in this query. We then cleaned the data by removing the journals with no aims/scopes and ranking. After that, we continued to clean scientific papers by removing all not having any abstract or keywords or belonging to journals previously filtered out. Finally, we only keep journals having over 600 articles, and for other journals, we only got papers during the last five years (2016–2020).

After the data collection process, we obtain one dataset having 414512 papers: 331464 papers for the training dataset and 83048 papers for the testing dataset. We collect the corresponding aims and scopes in the journal website for all journals in this dataset for doing necessary experiments.

3.2 Results

We compare the performance of three different methods: only using the title, the abstract, and the keywords; only using the aims and scopes of journals; and a combination of these features. One can see more details in our experimental results in Figs. 5 and 6.

First, we compare models and techniques without using any "Aims and Scopes" information in our dataset. The experimental results show that using the approach in [5] (namely Approach A), one can obtain the corresponding performance

---

[4] https://www.springer.com/.

in Accuracy@K as 0.2822, 0.5055 0.5886, and 0.6865, where K = 1, 3, 5, and 10, respectively. Meanwhile, the approach in [6] (namely Approach B) can gain much better performance, which are 0.4852, 0.7865, 0.8624, and 0.9333, consecutively.

Interestingly, using the information "Aims and Scopes" can help to improve the performance of these two approaches. For Approach A, the best performance in Accuracy@K (K = 1, 3, 5, 10) is 0.3574, 0.6711, 0.7672, and 0.8683 when using all attributes (TAKS). Compared to not using the "Aims and Scopes", the corresponding performance is much lower, which are 0.2330, 0.3359, 0.3694, and 0.4254. We can get the same results for other types of input data (K, A, TK, TA, and AK). Except for the case only using the title information, using additional "Aims and Scopes" seems not helpful to the paper submission recommendation model.

For Approach B, Accuracy@K's best performance in Accuracy@K (K = 1, 3, 5) is 0.5002, 0.7889, and 0.8627 when using TAKS as the input data. Especially for Accuracy@10, the performance of using TAK (0.9333) is slightly larger than using TAKS (0.9323). The six remaining types of input data, using the "Aims and Scopes", can enhance the paper recommendation model's performance.

It is worth noting that only using the feature vector extracted from the "Aims and Scopes" with the cosine similarity measure can outperform using Approach A for seven types of input data. The corresponding Accuracy@K for this case is 0.4142, 0.7228, 0.8170, and 0.9079. It implies that the similarity between the concatenating text (the title, the abstract, and the keywords) and the aims/scopes of the journal can indicate choosing relevant journals for the paper submission process.

The experimental results show the importance of using the information "Aims and Scopes" with the paper submission recommendation problem (Tables 3, 4 and 5).

Table 3. The performance of Approach A in our dataset.

Feature	Top1	Top3	Top5	Top10
T	**0.0406**	**0.0734**	**0.0918**	**0.1248**
TS	0.0159	0.0384	0.0494	0.0845
K	0.2822	0.5055	0.5886	0.6865
KS	**0.3145**	**0.5662**	**0.6605**	**0.7779**
A	0.0873	0.1320	0.1849	0.2520
AS	**0.2915**	**0.5567**	**0.6614**	**0.7792**
TK	0.1763	0.2595	0.2923	0.3590
TKS	**0.3275**	**0.5937**	**0.6887**	**0.7978**
TA	0.1229	0.1788	0.2020	0.2688
TAS	**0.2839**	**0.5539**	**0.6582**	**0.7763**
AK	0.1984	0.2901	0.3298	0.3970
AKS	**0.3612**	**0.6662**	**0.7611**	**0.8603**
TAK	0.2330	0.3359	0.3694	0.4254
TAKS	**0.3574**	**0.6711**	**0.7672**	**0.8638**

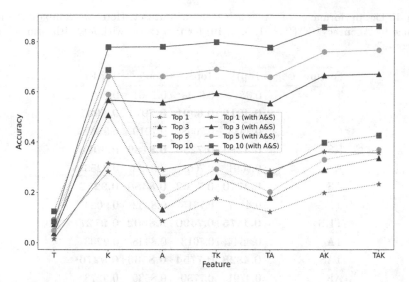

Fig. 5. The performance of different features for Approach A. Here, we compare the performance by Accuracy@K (K = 1, 3, 5, 10) for two cases: without/with using "Aims and Scopes".

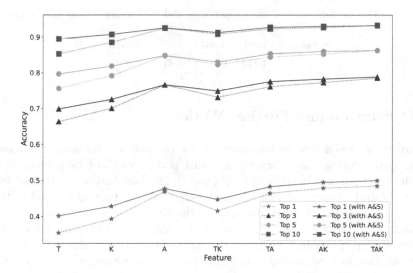

Fig. 6. The performance of different features for Approach B.

Table 4. The performance of Approach B in our dataset. Here, we compare the performance by Accuracy@K (K = 1, 3, 5, 10) for two cases: without/with using "Aims and Scopes".

Feature usage	Top1	Top3	Top5	Top10
T	0.3542	0.6634	0.7561	0.8532
TS	**0.4015**	**0.6991**	**0.7971**	**0.8951**
K	0.3933	0.7008	0.7919	0.8852
KS	**0.4284**	**0.7256**	**0.8189**	**0.9075**
A	0.4691	0.7661	0.8482	0.9253
AS	**0.4770**	**0.7662**	**0.8488**	**0.9258**
TK	0.4157	0.7315	0.8232	0.9084
TKS	**0.4475**	**0.7490**	**0.8302**	**0.9127**
TA	0.4644	0.7613	0.8448	0.9233
TAS	**0.4828**	**0.7754**	**0.8536**	**0.9276**
AK	0.4791	0.7730	0.8530	0.9273
AKS	**0.4951**	**0.7830**	**0.8602**	**0.9304**
TAK	0.4852	0.7856	0.8624	**0.9333**
TAKS	**0.5002**	**0.7889**	**0.8627**	0.9323

Table 5. The performance of our proposed model only using "Aims and Scopes".

Feature	Top1	Top3	Top5	Top10
S	0.4142	0.7228	0.8170	0.9079

4   Conclusion and Further Works

We have proposed a new fusion approach for the paper submission recommendation system using the information "Aims and Scopes" of each journal. We have designed the architecture of combining the textual features extracted from the "Aims and Scopes" of journals with other feature vectors computed from available information of paper submission (the title, the abstract, and the list of keywords). The experimental results show that using the additional information of journals can significantly enhance the state-of-the-art methods related to the paper submission recommendation algorithm. In the future, we aim to extend our results for different datasets and apply new embedding methods to improve the proposed algorithms' performance.

Acknowledgement. This research is funded by Vietnam National University Ho Chi Minh City (VNU-HCM) under grant number C2021-18-03. We want to thank the University of Science, Vietnam National University in Ho Chi Minh City, and AISIA Research Lab in Vietnam for supporting us throughout this paper.

References

1. Wang, D., Liang, Y., Xu, D., Feng, X., Guan, R.: A content-based recommender system for computer science publications. Knowl.-Based Syst. **157**, 1–9 (2018)
2. Chaiwanarom, P., Lursinsap, C.: Collaborator recommendation in interdisciplinary computer science using degrees of collaborative forces, temporal evolution of research interest, and comparative seniority status. Knowl.-Based Syst. **75**, 161–172 (2015)
3. Liu, Z., Xie, X., Chen, L.: Context-aware academic collaborator recommendation, pp. 1870–1879 (2018)
4. Bai, X., Wang, M., Lee, I., Yang, Z., Kong, X., Xia, F.: Scientific paper recommendation: a survey. IEEE Access **7**, 9324–9339 (2019)
5. Son, H., Phong, H., Dac, N., Cuong, D.V., Binh, N.T.: S2RSCS: an efficient scientific submission recommendation system for computer science. In: 33th International Conference on Industrial, Engineering and Other Applications of Applied Intelligent Systems (2020)
6. Son, H.T., Tan Phong, H., Dac, N.H.: An efficient approach for paper submission recommendation. In: IEEE TENCON 2020, pp. 726–731 (2020)
7. Feng, X., et al.: The deep learning-based recommender system "pubmender" for choosing a biomedical publication venue: development and validation study. J Med. Internet Res. **21**, e12957 (2019)
8. Pradhan, T., Pal, S.: A hybrid personalized scholarly venue recommender system integrating social network analysis and contextual similarity. Future Gener. Comput. Syst. **11**, 1139–1166 (2019)
9. Medvet, E., Bartoli, A., Piccinin, G.: Publication venue recommendation based on paper abstract. In: 2014 IEEE 26th International Conference on Tools with Artificial Intelligence, pp. 1004–1010, November 2014
10. Safa, R., Mirroshandel, S., Javadi, S., Azizi, M.: Venue recommendation based on paper's title and co-authors network, vol. 6 (2018)
11. Srivastava, N., Hinton, G., Krizhevsky, A., Sutskever, I., Salakhutdinov, R.: Dropout: a simple way to prevent neural networks from overfitting. J. Mach. Learn. Res. **15**, 1929–1958 (2014)
12. Ioffe, S., Szegedy, C.: Batch normalization: accelerating deep network training by reducing internal covariate shift. In: Proceedings of the 32nd International Conference on International Conference on Machine Learning, ICML 2015, vol. 37, pp. 448–456. JMLR.org (2015)
13. Chollet, F., et al.: Keras (2015)

One-Class Classification Approach Using Feature-Slide Prediction Subtask for Feature Data

Toshitaka Hayashi[1]([✉]) [iD] and Hamido Fujita[2,3] [iD]

[1] Faculty of Software and Information Science, Iwate Prefectural University, Takizawa, Japan

[2] i-SOMET, Inc., Morioka, Japan
HFujita-799@acm.org

[3] Regional Research Center, Iwate Prefectural University, Takizawa, Japan

Abstract. One-class classification is machine learning problem where training data has only one class. Recently, various subtask-based one-class classification methods are proposed for image data. However, these methods are specialized for image. Applying them to feature data is difficult. In this paper, feature-slide prediction subtask is proposed for feature data. These additional feature vectors are annotated as how features are slid. Then, multi-class classifier is trained using self-labeled dataset. Since this classification model is built using data from only one-class, accuracy of feature-slide prediction for seen data is high relative to unseen data. Accordingly, OCC could be made using feature slide prediction subtask. Proposed methods are experimented using imbalanced-learn dataset.

Keywords: Machine learning · One-class classification · Subtask

1 Introduction

In recent years, machine learning is introduced to various fields. Especially, supervised learning is widely applied with annotation by experts [1, 2]. However, such methods require a large volume of data. Moreover, the model can predict only classes in training data. Thus, supervised learning is not applicable where only one class is collectible as training data. This problem is called one-class classification (OCC) [3], which is an important issue in ML and related to anomaly detection [4], novelty detection [5]. Intrusion detection [6], and zero-shot learning [7].

In OCC, two types of classes exist, seen class and unseen class. These classes are either training data, are not. The objective of OCC is to determine if the input data is seen or unseen. Many algorithms are proposed, for example; early studies such as OCSVM [8], Local Outlier Factor [9], and Isolation Forest [10] are popular and effective methods to vector data. However, these methods are not suitable for image data since there is no feature extraction process, such as the convolutional layer [11].

Recently, DL-based OCC methods are proposed for image datasets [11]. These methods are roughly classified into two groups, fake-unseen-samples approach [12] or subtask approach [13, 14]. Especially, the subtask approach shows good accuracy [13, 14]. These

© Springer Nature Switzerland AG 2021
H. Fujita et al. (Eds.): IEA/AIE 2021, LNAI 12799, pp. 84–96, 2021.
https://doi.org/10.1007/978-3-030-79463-7_8

methods train the DL model and use the error for OCC. Such an idea could be extended to other data types, such as vector data. However, these tasks are specialized to image data [13, 14]. Thus, applying the existing subtask approach to vector data is not practical or suitable for such a purpose. Therefore, considering effective subtask for vector data is an important challenge.

In this paper, a novel subtask, namely feature-slide prediction, is proposed for OCC in vector data. This task uses a self-labeled dataset, which includes additional feature vectors created by sliding dimensions of original vectors. These additional vectors are annotated as to how features are slid. Then, a multi-class classifier is trained using a self-labeled dataset. Since this classification model is built using data from only one class, the accuracy of feature-slide prediction for seen data is high relative to unseen data. Accordingly, OCC could be made using feature-slide prediction subtask as shown in the case study provided in this paper.

The proposed framework, namely OCFSP, is experimented with using an imbalanced-learn dataset. Moreover, the result is compared with other OCC algorithms.

The organization of the paper is as follows. Section 2 describes related work. Section 3 presents the proposed OCC framework. Section 4 provides experiment results and discussions. Finally, Sect. 5 gives the conclusion and future work.

2 Related Work

OCC is promising research area because it has ability to detect unseen samples, which is weak point of supervised learning. In this problem, only one class is seen as training data, and other classes are unseen. Since the model is trained from one class, data balance is not a problem. Thus, OCC is possible solution for data imbalance problem [23]. Moreover, ensemble learning [23, 24] is applied to one-class classifiers [17, 19]. These methods train one-class classifiers for each class. Then, the class label is predicted based on all classifiers. This classifier is effective for unseen samples. Thus, a one-class ensemble could replace binary or multi-class classifiers [17].

General OCC framework is as shown in Fig. 1. In training step, the behavior of a seen class is determined based on some algorithms. Then, prediction is made using whether testing data includes seen behavior.

In this framework, training from one class is an important component. In other words, how to determine the behavior of a seen class, and how to detect unseen classes are challenges of OCC.

One-class Support Vector Machine (OCSVM) applies mapping function for seen data into feature vector space. In such vector space, unseen samples are considered origin O. Then, the maximum margin hyper-plane between mapped seen vectors and O is computed [8]. In contrast, Local Outlier Factor (LOF) computes outlier scores of a sample using the neighbor samples [9]. Such kind of scoring becomes large where data is far from the neighbor samples [9]. Additionally, Isolation Forest (IF) is the technique to detect outlier using tree structure with random split. In such tree, outlier is isolated with high probability since it is far from normal samples [10]. Furthermore, recent studies extend these algorithms [15–17]. In addition, cluster-based method generates clusters from seen class. Then, data which is not assigned to cluster are considered as unseen [18].

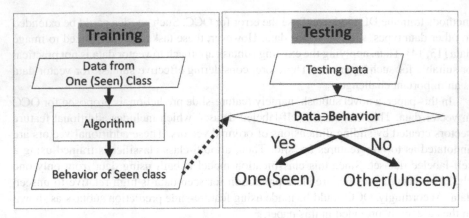

Fig. 1. One-class classification Framework

Apart from these studies, DL-based OCC are developed for image data [11]. These methods are roughly classified into two groups, fake-unseen-sample approach or subtask approach. The first approach generates fake-unseen-samples [12]. However, this method is difficult since there is none information for unseen samples.

In contrast, another approach trains DL models as subtask, and use the model error for OCC [13, 14]. Since unseen class does not exist in training data, the model error of seen class is small relative to unseen class. Second approach shows better results than the first one. Various subtasks are proposed such as classification of geometric transformation [13], perturb classification [22], and image transformation to only one image [14]. However, these subtasks are specialized for image data. Thus, applying to feature data is not suitable. Accordingly, this paper proposes novel subtask for feature data.

3 One-Class Classification using Feature-Slide Prediction

In this section, novel one-class classification algorithm is presented. In particular, feature-slide prediction is proposed as new subtask for feature data.

Figure 2 shows the framework, which consists of two stages, training and testing. In which, only seen data is utilized as training data.

In the training stage, additional data is generated by sliding feature vectors. Then, self-labeled dataset is created by gathering original and additional data. In which, self-label represents how feature vectors are slid. Then after, classification model is trained using self-labeled dataset. Finally, threshold value is computed based on feature-slide prediction accuracy.

In the testing stage, additional data is generated in the same way as training. Then, feature-slide prediction is applied, and the accuracy is computed. If accuracy is higher than a threshold value, data is treated as seen class. Otherwise, data is unseen class.

In the following paragraphs, mathematical descriptions are provided.

Data is defined as d-dimensional feature vector X, as shown in Eq. (1).

$$X = (X_1, X_2, \ldots, X_d) \tag{1}$$

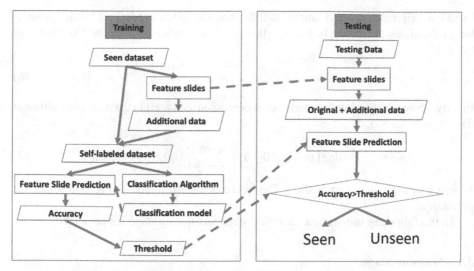

Fig. 2. One-class classification using feature-slide prediction

Where d is number of dimension. The objective in OCC is predicting class label Y that is defined as in Eq. (2).

$$Y = \{S, U\} \tag{2}$$

Where S and U are seen and unseen class, respectively. This study propose feature slide prediction subtask. Such task generates additional data A. In particular, feature slide T is computed to generate additional data A from X as Eq. (3).

$$T(X, z) : X \to A$$
$$A = \{A_1, \dots, A_z\} \tag{3}$$

In which, z is number of applied slides where $0 < z < d$ because d-dimensional data has d-1 possible slides. Moreover, volume of A increases related to z. Additionally, the components of A are defined as Eq. (4).

$$A_1 = (X_2, X_3, \dots, X_d, X_1)$$
$$\vdots$$
$$A_z = (X_{z+1}, \dots, X_d, X_1, \dots, X_z) \tag{4}$$
$$\vdots$$
$$A_{d-1} = (X_d, X_1, \dots, X_{d-1})$$

In which, original feature vector X is slid forward by the number of the slide.

These original and additional data are annotated using self-label L as in Eq. (5).

$$L = \{0, 1, \dots, z\} \tag{5}$$

In which, original data is self-labeled as 0. In contrast, additional data are labeled as number of the slides. Accordingly, feature slide prediction subtask g is defined as following Eq. (6).

$$g : X, A \rightarrow L \tag{6}$$

Finally, score of data related to seen class is computed using original data X and additional data A as in Eq. (7).

$$score(X) = log\Big(g(X) = 0|X\Big) + \sum_{k=1}^{z} log(g(A_k) = k|A_k\Big) \tag{7}$$

Where k is the value of each slide. This score is log-likelihood and related to correct prediction.

In the following sub-sections, training stage and testing stage are presented.

3.1 Training Stage

In the training stage, dataset Dtr is defined as Eq. (8):

$$Dtr = [Xtr_1, Xtr_2, \ldots, Xtr_N] \tag{8}$$

Where N is number of the data.

Besides, additional datasets are created by sliding Dtr as in Eq. (4). These datasets are defined as in Eq. (9):

$$Atr_1 = \Big[Atr_{1,1}, Atr_{1,2}, \ldots, Atr_{1,N}\Big]$$
$$\vdots \tag{9}$$
$$Atr_z = \Big[Atr_{z,1}, Atr_{z,2}, \ldots, Atr_{z,N}\Big]$$

Besides, Self-labeled dataset $Dself$; is created by merging Dtr and Atr as in Eq. (10):

$$Dself = [Dtr, Atrc_1, \ldots, Atr_z] \tag{10}$$

Then, self-label L is assigned to these dataset as shown in Eq. (5). Besides, feature-slide classifier g is trained using Dself and L as shown in Eq. (6). In such process, existing classification algorithms are applied. Since training is done using only seen class, this classifier has high accuracy for seen class relative to unseen class.

3.2 Testing Stage

In the testing stage, input is $Xtest$, and additional data $Atest$ are generated from $Xtest$ as shown in Eq. (4). These data are merged to self-labeled testing set $Dtest$ as shown in Eq. (11):

$$Dtest = [Xtest, Atest_1, \ldots, Atest_z] \tag{11}$$

Then, score of *Xtest* is computed as Eq. (12).

$$\text{score}(Xtest) = log(g(Xtest) = 0|Xtest) + \sum_{k=1}^{z} log(g(Atest_k) = k|Atest_k) \quad (12)$$

Finally, seen-unseen classification f is established using Eq. (13).

$$f(Xtest) = \begin{cases} S(score(Xtest) \geq \lambda) \\ U(score(Xtest) < \lambda) \end{cases} \quad (13)$$

Where λ is a threshold value, which is determined in a heuristic optimal way.

4 Experiment

The proposed method (OCFSP) has been validated using data listed in Sect. 4.1. The measurement of evaluation is shown in Sect. 4.2. The experiment results are shown in Sect. 4.3.

4.1 The Data

In the experiment, an imbalanced-learn dataset [20] is used for evaluation. This dataset consists of 27 sub-datasets for binary classification and is provided by an imbalanced-learn package [20] on Python.

Table 1 shows information of datasets, such as dimension, number of each class, and Imbalance Ratio (IR). All datasets are normalized based on min-max. In the experiment, one class is treated as seen class, and another class is concluded as unseen class.

Table 1. Details of imbalanced datasets in experiment

Data	Dimension	Minority	Majority	IR
ecoli	7	35	301	8.60
optical_digits	64	554	5066	9.14
satimage	36	626	5809	9.28
pen_digits	16	1055	9937	9.42
abalone	10	391	3786	9.68
sick_euthyroid	42	293	2870	9.80
spectrometer	93	45	486	10.80
car_eval_34	21	134	1594	11.90
isolet	617	600	7197	12.00

(continued)

Table 1. (*continued*)

Data	Dimension	Minority	Majority	IR
us_crime	100	150	1844	12.29
yeast_ml8	103	178	2239	12.58
scene	294	177	2230	12.60
libras_move	90	24	336	14.00
thyroid_sick	52	231	3541	15.33
coil_2000	85	586	9236	15.76
arrhythmia	278	25	427	17.08
solar_flare_m0	32	68	1321	19.43
oil	49	41	896	21.85
car_eval_4	21	65	1663	25.58
wine_quality	11	183	4715	25.77
letter_img	16	734	19266	26.25
yeast_me2	8	51	1433	28.10
webpage	300	981	33799	34.45
ozone_level	72	73	2463	33.74
mammography	6	260	10923	42.01
protein_homo	74	1296	144455	111.46
abalone_19	10	32	4145	129.53

4.2 Measurement of the Evaluation

Evaluation is done using the Area under the ROC Curve (AUC). This curve is a graph plotting the performance in all possible thresholds. In which the x-axis and y-axis are FPR and TPR, respectively. These values are computed as given in Eqs. (14), (15) and Table 2. In which, Positive and Negative are corresponding to minority and Majority class, respectively.

$$\text{TPR} = \frac{TP}{TP + FN} \tag{14}$$

$$\text{FPR} = \frac{FP}{FP + TN} \tag{15}$$

4.3 Experiment Result

In the experiment, all datasets are split into training and testing set by 60% and 40% ratios. This split is using five different random seeds, and the average score is reported. Moreover, these experiments are implemented using two libraries, imbalanced-learn [20] and scikit-learn [21].

Table 2. Confusion matrix

		Predicted	
		Positive	Negative
Actual	Positive	TP	FN
	Negative	FP	TN

Then, the training set is split into minority and Majority data, and the one-class classifiers are trained separately. Moreover, an ensemble of both classifiers is computed as Eqs. (16) and (17).

$$Score_{ensemble}(X) = Score_{minority}(X) - Score_{Majority}(X) \qquad (16)$$

$$f(X) = \begin{cases} minority(Score_{ensemble}(X) \geq \lambda) \\ Majority(Score_{ensemble}(X) < \lambda) \end{cases} \qquad (17)$$

In the feature-slide prediction, Decision Tree (DT) and Logistic Regression (LR) are applied as classification algorithm. These algorithms are selected based on processing time.

Table 3 shows average AUC of imbalanced-learn datasets. Z represents number of the slides applied to original data. Thus, $Z + 1$ class classification is executed as feature-slide prediction. The best scores are marked in bold font.

Table 3. AUC for OCFSP using DT and LR classifier

Z	DTminor	DTmajor	DTensemble	LRminor	LRmajor	LRensemble
1	59.21	52.19	60.01	70.47	54.53	74.32
2	61.88	54.36	63.52	73.05	56.45	77.31
3	64.21	57.27	66.79	74.14	**56.60**	78.17
4	65.49	57.75	68.15	74.78	56.08	78.55
5	65.27	58.53	68.49	74.93	55.12	78.64
6	66.31	58.59	69.18	75.03	54.60	78.71
7	66.75	59.01	69.91	75.26	53.97	78.85
8	67.73	59.50	71.09	75.35	53.68	78.98
9	67.67	59.78	71.27	75.37	53.47	79.02
10	68.66	59.48	71.89	**75.38**	53.29	**79.03**
11	68.64	59.84	71.96	75.38	53.07	78.99
12	68.57	59.76	72.09	75.33	52.83	78.93

(*continued*)

Table 3. (*continued*)

Z	DTminor	DTmajor	DTensemble	LRminor	LRmajor	LRensemble
13	68.72	59.58	72.35	75.18	52.64	78.80
14	68.54	59.47	72.22	75.08	52.51	78.69
15	69.04	59.67	72.83	74.93	52.34	78.57
16	69.10	59.93	72.99	74.92	52.17	78.56
17	68.90	59.53	72.67	74.91	52.05	78.55
18	69.15	59.54	73.00	74.90	51.98	78.52
19	69.54	59.56	73.39	74.90	51.94	78.48
20	69.50	59.56	73.41	74.89	51.91	78.48
21	70.38	59.54	74.32	74.89	51.88	78.46
22	70.88	59.66	74.55	74.89	51.87	78.46
23	70.46	59.58	73.93	74.89	51.84	78.44
24	70.53	59.67	74.33	74.91	51.85	78.48
25	70.88	59.76	74.53	74.92	51.82	78.51
26	**70.97**	59.72	74.73	74.93	51.83	78.52
27	70.65	59.63	74.43	74.95	51.86	78.53
28	70.77	59.75	74.67	74.96	51.85	78.54
29	70.75	**59.84**	**74.89**	74.97	51.87	78.56

In Table 3, AUC is small, where the z value is small. The reason is considered as random prediction leads to high accuracy where a number of the class is small. In such a case, feature-slide prediction for unseen class becomes unfairly high accuracy.

On the other hand, the AUC score decreases where the z value is large. This may be due to feature-slide-prediction becomes unpredictable for even seen class, where the number of the class label is large. Moreover, processing speed is affected due to the size of the self-labeled dataset increases with the corresponding number of slides z. Accordingly, an appropriate selection of z value becomes necessary.

Additionally, Table 4 shows the results for each dataset in imbalanced-learn. The reported score is using the best z values for both DT and LR classifiers. In some datasets, z is larger than the dimension of the data. In such a case, the reported result is AUC score where $z = d - 1$.

In Table 4, DT is appropriate for the majority classifiers. In contrast, LR is better for minority classifiers and ensemble classifiers. Moreover, the performance for the minority classifier is better than the majority classifier. The reason is considered as OCC framework aims to determine the behavior of seen class. In general, finding common behavior from small samples is easy relative to doing the same from large samples. Thus, the minority classifier shows a higher AUC score relative to the majority classifier.

Table 4. AUC for each dataset in imbalanced-learn.

Dataset	DTminor	DTmajor	DTensemble	LRminor	LRmajor	LRensemble
ecoli	53.9 ± 4.9	50.2 ± 1.8	52.3 ± 5.1	88.3 ± 5.7	22.7 ± 6.0	**91.2 ± 3.4**
optical_digits	94.2 ± 0.6	74.8 ± 1.1	**98.1 ± 0.1**	87.0 ± 0.6	49.3 ± 0.8	88.1 ± 0.9
satimage	86.6 ± 0.8	65.0 ± 1.1	**88.6 ± 0.5**	74.7 ± 0.7	46.3 ± 1.2	73.4 ± 0.7
pen_digits	**99.3 ± 0.3**	88.6 ± 0.6	99.8 ± 0.0	83.4 ± 0.6	68.0 ± 0.9	89.9 ± 0.6
abalone	62.8 ± 3.5	49.8 ± 0.2	62.7 ± 3.5	66.9 ± 0.9	59.6 ± 0.6	**71.9 ± 1.4**
sick_euthyroid	67.6 ± 3.0	48.9 ± 1.0	68.0 ± 2.9	**76.3 ± 2.4**	43.2 ± 4.1	66.9 ± 2.2
spectrometer	70.1 ± 8.9	66.0 ± 6.1	89.0 ± 4.1	63.6 ± 12	48.8 ± 10	**91.7 ± 3.3**
car_eval_34	94.6 ± 3.0	57.0 ± 2.1	94.8 ± 2.8	**98.6 ± 0.4**	61.7 ± 3.4	98.1 ± 0.5
isolet	73.9 ± 4.9	47.2 ± 0.4	72.3 ± 4.9	79.1 ± 2.1	36.4 ± 2.2	**79.9 ± 2.1**
us_crime	70.8 ± 5.0	69.8 ± 1.0	80.0 ± 4.1	79.8 ± 4.2	77.8 ± 3.5	**86.6 ± 1.4**
yeast_ml8	53.0 ± 3.6	56.2 ± 1.9	**58.4 ± 2.6**	50.5 ± 2.4	52.5 ± 2.2	51.1 ± 2.4
scene	61.8 ± 3.3	50.9 ± 1.3	63.3 ± 3.0	63.8 ± 3.3	43.9 ± 3.5	**65.2 ± 3.2**
libras_move	80.5 ± 5.1	87.4 ± 2.4	94.2 ± 2.3	88.5 ± 7.4	87.4 ± 6.1	**95.8 ± 4.1**
thyroid_sick	63.9 ± 1.2	50.0 ± 0.4	64.7 ± 1.1	80.4 ± 2.0	59.9 ± 1.0	**80.4 ± 1.4**
coil_2000	57.0 ± 1.6	51.1 ± 0.9	58.7 ± 1.6	65.7 ± 1.5	38.4 ± 1.2	**65.9 ± 1.5**
arrhythmia	66.4 ± 4.2	44.0 ± 2.1	63.3 ± 3.9	66.3 ± 3.3	40.6 ± 2.0	**66.8 ± 3.3**
solar_flare_m0	49.8 ± 4.7	66.3 ± 1.3	59.7 ± 5.0	57.6 ± 3.8	66.7 ± 5.5	**68.3 ± 3.5**
oil	55.8 ± 9.8	61.4 ± 3.4	**64.1 ± 9.3**	53.6 ± 7.4	60.1 ± 4.3	55.2 ± 7.3
car_eval_4	**99.2 ± 0.2**	54.8 ± 2.1	97.7 ± 1.3	99.4 ± 0.1	42.2 ± 4.0	97.7 ± 0.9
wine_quality	61.6 ± 5.5	64.2 ± 3.5	**70.1 ± 4.7**	58.9 ± 2.7	59.5 ± 3.4	69.8 ± 3.3
letter_img	97.5 ± 0.5	64.7 ± 2.8	**98.4 ± 0.1**	90.9 ± 1.2	58.7 ± 0.7	90.2 ± 0.4
yeast_me2	53.0 ± 1.1	49.4 ± 0.3	52.4 ± 1.2	83.3 ± 2.7	31.3 ± 3.3	**83.3 ± 2.8**
webpage	69.3 ± 0.6	82.1 ± 0.8	88.9 ± 0.4	70.9 ± 1.7	79.4 ± 0.5	**91.1 ± 0.9**
ozone_level	67.1 ± 3.6	43.2 ± 1.1	65.8 ± 4.3	**81.3 ± 3.3**	34.7 ± 4.7	80.5 ± 3.3
mammography	73.2 ± 2.9	43.0 ± 3.1	66.1 ± 2.1	81.8 ± 2.2	53.4 ± 1.1	**87.6 ± 1.9**
protein_homo	61.1 ± 2.2	79.9 ± 0.7	**84.2 ± 1.0**	78.0 ± 0.8	69.2 ± 0.9	83.7 ± 0.6
abalone_19	66.3 ± 2.6	49.8 ± 0.1	66.2 ± 2.6	**67.0 ± 3.2**	41.2 ± 3.0	62.6 ± 3.1
Avg	70.75	59.84	74.89	75.38	53.29	**79.03**

4.4 Comparison with Other OCC Algorithms

Table 5 shows the comparison with other OCC algorithms. OCSVM, LOF, and IF are well-known algorithms. Moreover, the GMM-based method extends GMM clustering to predict unseen classes [18]. These methods are implemented in the scikit-learn library [21]. In the experiment, default parameters are applied. The reported scores are average AUC for ensemble classifiers.

Table 5. Comparison with other OCC algorithm (ensemble classifier)

Methods	Average AUC(ensemble)
OCSVM [8]	65.4
LOF [9]	80.1
IF [10]	81.2
GMM-based method [18]	**81.4**
OCFSP-DT ($z = 29$)	74.9
OCFSP-LR ($z = 10$)	79.0

OCFSP outperform OCSVM. Moreover, OCFSP-LR shows comparable performance with other OCC methods. Accordingly, this method could be considered as one of the alternative solutions for OCC.

As the discussion, OCFSP performance is related to the applied classification algorithms. Thus, other classification algorithms should be experimented with for finding the best classifier. Moreover, OCFSP has issues with processing time and data volume. These value increases are related to the number of slides z. Furthermore, several slid vectors are similar. In such a case, feature-slide classification is unpredictable for even seen data.

The second and third problems could be solved by reducing the number of feature slides. In particular, eliminating or fusing similar feature slides are considered. Such a solution reduces the number of self-label. In another solution, score computation could be changed as forgiving misprediction into similar self-labels.

5   Conclusion and Future Work

In this paper, feature-slide prediction is proposed as a new subtask for OCC. In particular, the self-labeled dataset is created by sliding feature vectors. Then, this dataset is trained by a supervised classification algorithm. Since the training is computed using seen data, accuracy for seen class is considered high relative to unseen class. Accordingly, OCC is computable based on the accuracy of feature-slide prediction. Proposed OCFSP is experimented with using an imbalanced-learn dataset and shows comparable performance with other OCC methods.

As future work, other classification algorithms should be tried for feature-slide prediction. In which a deep learning classifier would be promising. Moreover, similar feature slides should be eliminated or fused for reducing the number of self-label. Furthermore, score computation should be reconsidered for improving accuracy. Finally, this idea could be extended to other data types such as image or time-series; for example, sliding or shuffling RGB channels are considered.

Acknowledgements. This study is supported by JSPS KAKENHI (Grants-in-Aid for Scientific Research) #JP20K11955.

References

1. Litjens, G., et al.: A survey on deep learning in medical image analysis. Med. Image Anal. **42**, 60–88 (2017)
2. Huang, X., Lei, Q., Xie, T., Zhang, Y., Hu, Z., Zhou, Q.: Deep transfer convolutional neural network and extreme learning machine for lung nodule diagnosis on CT images. Knowl. Based Syst. **204**, 106230 (2020). https://doi.org/10.1016/j.knosys.2020.106230
3. Gautam, C., Tiwari, A., Tanveer, M.: KOC+: Kernel ridge regression based one-class classification using privileged information. Inf. Sci. **504**, 324–333 (2019)
4. Gautam, C., Balaji, R., Sudharsan, K., Tiwari, A., Ahuja, K.: Localized multiple kernel learning for anomaly detection: one-class classification. Knowl. Based Syst. **165**, 241–252 (2019)
5. Sadooghi, M.S., Khadem, S.E.: Improving one class support vector machine novelty detection scheme using nonlinear features. Pattern Recogn. **83**, 14–33 (2018). https://doi.org/10.1016/j.patcog.2018.05.002
6. Mazini, M., Shirazi, B., Mahdavi, I.: Anomaly network-based intrusion detection system using a reliable hybrid artificial bee colony and AdaBoost algorithms. J. King Saud Univ. Comput. Inf. Sci. **31**(4), 541–553 (2019)
7. Socher, R., Ganjoo, M., Manning, C.D., Ng, A.Y.: Zero-shot learning through cross-modal transfer. In: Proceedings of the 26th International Conference on Neural Information Processing Systems (NIPS 2013), vol. 1, pp. 935–943. Curran Associates Inc., Red Hook (2013)
8. Schölkopf, B., Platt, J.C., Shawe-Taylor, J., Smola, A.J., Williamson, R.C.: Estimating the support of a high-dimensional distribution. Neural Comput. **13**(7), 1443–1471 (2001). https://doi.org/10.1162/089976601750264965
9. Breunig, M.M., Kriegel, H.P., Ng, R.T., Sander, J.: LOF: identifying density-based local outliers. In: ACM SIGMOD Record (2000)
10. Liu, F.T., Ting, K.M., Zhou, Z.: Isolation forest. In: 2008 Eighth IEEE International Conference on Data Mining, Pisa, Italy, pp. 413–422 (2008)
11. Ruff, L., et al.: Deep one-class classification. In: Proceedings of the 35th International Conference on Machine Learning (PMLR), vol. 80, pp. 4393–4402 (2018)
12. Yang, Y., Hou, C., Lang, Y., Yue, G., He, Y.: One-class classification using generative adversarial networks. IEEE Access **7**, 37970–37979 (2019). https://doi.org/10.1109/ACCESS.2019.2905933
13. Golan, I., El-Yaniv, R.: Deep anomaly detection using geometric transformations. In: Proceedings of the 32nd International Conference on Neural Information Processing Systems (NIPS 2018), pp. 9781–9791. Curran Associates Inc., Red Hook (2018)
14. Hayashi, T., Fujita, H., Hernandez-Matamoros, A.: Less complexity one-class classification approach using construction error of convolutional image transformation network. Inf. Sci. **560**, 217–234 (2021)
15. Karczmarek, P., Kiersztyn, A., Pedrycz, W., Al, E.: K-means-based isolation forest. Knowl. Based Syst. **195**, 105659 (2020). https://doi.org/10.1016/j.knosys.2020.105659
16. Liu, F., Yu, Y., Song, P., Fan, Y., Tong, X.: Scalable KDE-based top-n local outlier detection over large-scale data streams. Knowl. Based Syst. **204**, 106186 (2020). https://doi.org/10.1016/j.knosys.2020.106186
17. Silva, C., Bouwmans, T., Frélicot, C.: Superpixel-based online wagging one-class ensemble for feature selection in foreground/background separation. Pattern Recogn. Lett. **100**, 144–151 (2017)
18. Hayashi, T., Fujita, H.: Cluster-based zero-shot learning for multivariate data. J. Ambient Intell. Humaniz. Comput. **12**(2), 1897–1911 (2020). https://doi.org/10.1007/s12652-020-02268-5

19. Silva, C., Bouwmans, T., Frélicot, C.: Superpixel-based online wagging one-class ensemble for feature selection in foreground/background separation in foreground/background. Pattern Recogn. Lett. **100**, 144–151 (2017)
20. Krawczyk, B., Galar, M., Woźniak, M., Bustince, H., Herrera, F.: Dynamic ensemble selection for multi-class classification with one-class classifiers. Pattern Recogn. **83**, 34–51 (2018)
21. Lemaitre, G., Nogueira, F., Aridas, C.K.: Imbalanced-learn: a Python toolbox to tackle the curse of imbalanced datasets in machine learning. J. Mach. Learn. Res. **18**, 1–5 (2017)
22. Pedregosa, F., et al.: Scikit-learn: machine learning in Python. J. Mach. Learn. Res. **12**(85), 2825–2830 (2011)
23. Gao, L., Zhang, L., Liu, C., Wu, S.: Handling imbalanced medical image data: a deep-learning-based one-class classification approach. Artif. Intell. Med. **108**, 101935 (2020). https://doi.org/10.1016/j.artmed.2020.101935
24. Sun, J., Li, H., Fujita, H., Binbin, F., Ai, W.: Class-imbalanced dynamic financial distress prediction based on Adaboost-SVM ensemble combined with SMOTE and time weighting. Inf. Fusion **54**, 128–144 (2020). https://doi.org/10.1016/j.inffus.2019.07.006
25. Zhou, L., Fujita, H.: Posterior probability based ensemble strategy using optimizing decision directed acyclic graph for multi-class classification. Inf. Sci. **400**, 142–156 (2017). https://doi.org/10.1016/j.ins.2017.02.059

Data Management, Clustering and Classification

A Novel Approach for Enhancing Vietnamese Sentiment Classification

Cuong V. Nguyen[1,2,3], Khiem H. Le[1,2,3], and Binh T. Nguyen[1,2,3(✉)]

[1] AISIA Research Lab, Ho Chi Minh City, Vietnam
ngtbinh@hcmus.edu.vn
[2] University of Science, Ho Chi Minh City, Vietnam
[3] Vietnam National University, Ho Chi Minh City, Vietnam

Abstract. Sentiment analysis has become an essential and fundamental task in natural language processing that has many useful applications. There exist various methods for solving the sentiment classification problem using traditional machine learning models, deep neural networks, and transfer learning methods. It is still interesting for Vietnamese sentiment classification problems to understand the impact of different ensemble techniques and deep learning approaches for building the most suitable model. This work aims to study the Vietnamese sentiment classification on one public dataset used in the Vietnamese Sentiment Analysis Challenge 2019 and another large-scale dataset, namely "AISIA-Sent-002", which was collected from the Vietnamese e-commerce websites by ourselves. We explore five distinct ensemble schemes, including the classic methods (Uniform Weighting and Linear Ensemble) and the feature importance-based advanced methods (Gating Network, Squeeze-Excitation Network, and Attention Network) for Vietnamese sentiment analysis. We do these ensemble techniques with five individual deep learning models: TextCNN, LSTM, GRU, LSTM + CNN, and GRU + CNN. Extensive experiments on two datasets show that the ensemble methods perform much better than any individual model and significantly outperform the competition's winning solution with a large margin. Finally, we aim to publish our source codes to contribute to the current research community related to natural language processing.

Keywords: Ensemble · Feature importance · Gating Network · SE Network · Attention Network

1 Introduction

Sentiment analysis, one of the fundamental tasks in natural language processing [2,13], has been extensively investigated for many years and had many applications in data mining, information retrieval, social networks, and e-commerce [4,28]. A vast number of companies and corporations have had their customer

---

C. V. Nguyen and K. H. Le—Equal contribution.

H. Fujita et al. (Eds.): IEA/AIE 2021, LNAI 12799, pp. 99–111, 2021.
https://doi.org/10.1007/978-3-030-79463-7_9

support teams that continuously collect users' feedback and suggestions about different products, mobile/web applications, and even websites. They consider this opportunity to extract valuable information from users' comments, detect all sentiments, get all recommendations associated with the current products, such as new features, new designs, potential bugs, security concerns, and service enhancement. Although there may be many negative or subjective reviews from customers, a ratio of these comments can be advantageous to provide the company with another perspective on each product's pros and cons. For instance, one can use sentiment analysis to measure users' satisfaction when releasing new features or a new pricing plan for different users on an e-commerce website. If most of the users give negative feedback, it means there are many inevitable works to improve the new features or change the new pricing plan to keep or increase customers' engagement.

Many studies are related to the sentiment classification problem, especially for English, Arabic, and Chinese. Tang and colleagues proposed an efficient approach using gated recurrent neural networks to employ vector-based document representation and capture semantics of sentences and the associated relations from one document. The proposed method could surpass many state-of-the-art (SOTA) methods on four large-scale review datasets from IMDB and Yelp Dataset Challenge [23]. Xu et al. presented Cached Long Short-Term Memory neural networks to obtain the general semantic information in long texts and give better performance than state-of-the-art models on three publicly available document-level sentiment analyses datasets. Zhang et al. utilized the word embedding method, Word2Vec, to compute semantic features from comment texts in the selected domain and the Chinese language and used the SVMperf [8] to study a sentiment classification model. The experiments on the data set of Chinese comments on clothing products show that their proposed technique can achieve a better performance than other methods in terms of precision, recall, and F1-score. Using GloVe [20] as a critical embedding method to extract semantic features from tweets, Jianqiang et al. trained a suitable sentiment classification model on five different Twitter data sets. They showed promising experimental results in terms of accuracy and F1-score. One could also use a transfer learning method for the sentiment classification problem by applying pre-trained models such as BERT [5] that could surpass other state-of-the-art techniques [22,29], especially for the Arabic language [6].

Related to the Vietnamese sentiment analysis, Hung et al. [27] investigated the topic classification and sentiment analysis for a Vietnamese education survey system using the Bag-of-Structure technique and traditional machine learning methods. Phan and colleagues [21] applied a Skip-gram based model to study the sentiment analysis on unstructured documents using Vietnamese text comments about locations. Phu et al. collected a Vietnamese Students' Feedback Corpus dataset from one university in Vietnam and applied traditional and deep-learning approaches for sentiment classification and topic classification. Other works related to the Vietnamese language's sentiment classification problem can be found at [12,16–18,25]. According to our knowledge, it is still fascinating to understand the impact of different ensemble techniques and deep learning approaches for Vietnamese sentiment classification problems.

In this work, we focus on studying the Vietnamese sentiment classification on two datasets and exploring five deep learning-based baseline models: TextCNN, LSTM, GRU, LSTM + CNN, and GRU + CNN, for the problem. The experimental results show that these five individual models can significantly surpass the competition's winning solution in terms of F1-score. After that, we investigate five distinct ensemble schemes, Gating Network, Squeeze-Excitation (SE) Network, Attention Network, Uniform Weighting, and Linear Ensembling, for these individual models and measure the impact of these ensemble techniques on the performance of the sentiment classification problem. In the experiments, using ensemble techniques can perform much better than any individual model with promising results. On the AIVIVN dataset, Gating Network could obtain the best performance in the metrics of AUC (98.59%) and F1-score (93.82%), and Attention Network could achieve the best result in term of ACC (94.14%). On our large-scale dataset "AISIA-Sent-002", SE Network shows its dominance of performance in all the metrics of ACC (93.63%), F1-score (93.26%), and AUC (98.48%).

2 Methodology

This section presents the Vietnamese sentiment classification problem. It describes different individual models and five ensemble networks that can take advances of feature embeddings from multi models and enhance the problem's performance.

2.1 Sentiment Classification

We now explain the sentiment classification problem studied in this paper. Sentiment analysis is the text classification that identifies the polarities given a text, document, paragraph, or sentence. The polarities can be positive, negative, neutral, or emotions with multiple levels. In this work, we aim at investigating the binary classification problem for Vietnamese sentiment analysis, where our model can predict positive or negative sentiment given a user review. Figure 1a illustrates a fundamental architecture of an individual classifier model.

In recent years, with the rising of deep learning due to its outstanding performance in solving many tasks in NLP, classification models for sentiment classification are usually implemented by a deep neural network. It is powerful in learning useful insights from data and transform them into a good feature representation. A deep learning model of NLP consists of two main components. The first one is word embedding, which can be done by employing a pre-trained embedding model, such as, e.g., Word2vec [14], Glove [20], and Fasttext[1]. The second component is a deep neural network, usually formed by Convolutional Neural Network (CNN) and Recurrent Neural Network (RNN), to learn feature representation and make the inference. In this work, we employ five different

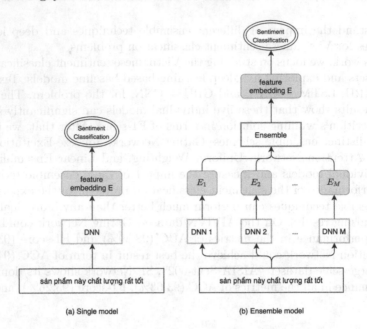

(a) Single model   (b) Ensemble model

Fig. 1. An overall architecture for Vietnamese sentiment classification, where the input review is "'Sản phẩm này có chất lượng rất tốt'" ("This product has a very good quality"). (a) A general individual model using deep neural network. (b) A general ensemble model which combines different feature embeddings from multiple models.

architectures of deep neural networks, including TextCNN [9], LSTM/GRU [24], LSTM + CNN/GRU + CNN [10,15], which are successfully used for sentiment classification problem.

Specifically, let $D = \{x_i, y_i\}_{i=1}^n$ be a training dataset including n pairs of $\{(x_i, y_i)\}_{i=1}^n$, where x_i is a input sentence and y_i is the corresponding label in $\{0, 1\}$. Here, the labels 0 and 1 indicate a positive and negative sentiment, respectively. A deep neural network aims to learn an embedding function f : $X \rightarrow E$, which maps a sample x from the data space X to a K-dimensional feature embedding space $\mathbb{E}$. All parameters of the function f can be optimized end-to-end by minimizing the loss function, which is usually implemented by the cross-entropy loss.

2.2 Our Proposed Architectures

Figure 1b shows a general ensemble architecture that combines multiple feature embeddings learned from individual models. Suppose that $\{E_1, E_2, ..., E_m\}$ is a set of feature embeddings, where m is the number of models. It is a fascinating question that given multiple feature embeddings, how could one combine those features in the right way to boost the performance?

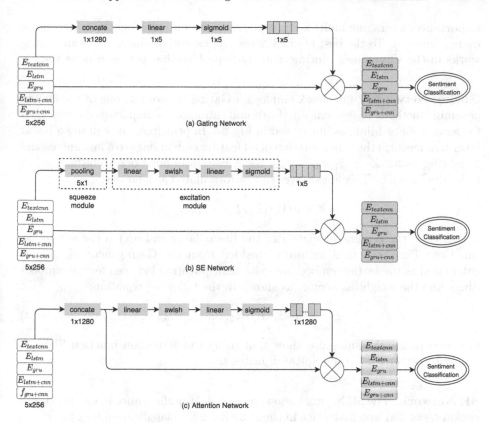

Fig. 2. Our proposed ensemble networks for enhancing Vietnamese sentiment classification, those are (a) Gating Network, (b) SE Network, (c) Attention Network.

Typically, one can choose two popular ensemble methods. The first one is the uniform weighting or the average weighting, as shown below:

$$E = [\frac{\sum_{i=1}^{m} E_i}{m}]. \tag{1}$$

Another one is the concatenation of feature embeddings, namely linear ensemble in our work, as depicted as follows:

$$E = [E_1, E_2, ..., E_m] \tag{2}$$

Remarkably, both methods do not care much about the importance of features despite different features that impact the target output. For this reason, in this work, we are very curious to analyze the effect of different ensemble methods on the sentiment classification problem, especially for the Vietnamese language. Besides using the two techniques above, we consider three other ensemble techniques, including Gating Network, SE Network, and Attention Network. It is worth noting that these approaches emphasize dynamically learning the feature importance, leveraging multi-feature embeddings, and boosting the performance more efficiently. To the best of our knowledge, exploring different ensemble networks in the Vietnamese sentiment analysis problem has not been done yet.

Gating Networks. Our work employs a Gating network as one of the chosen ensemble methods to dynamically learn and estimate the importance coefficients for feature embedding, as illustrated in Fig. 2a. In principal, one can use a linear layer to transform the concatenation of all feature embeddings to a m-dimensional weighting vector $Z = [z_1, z_2, ..., z_m]$. Here, $m = 5$ in our work according to five individual models. This linear layer can be formulated as follows:

$$Z = \sigma(W([E_1, E_2, ..., E_m]), \tag{3}$$

where W is the parameter matrix of the linear layer and $\sigma(.)$ is the activation function. Then, the final feature embedded from the Gating network can be calculated as the feature embedding-wise multiplication between feature embeddings and the weighting vector, as shown in the following equation:

$$E = [E_1 \cdot z_1, E_2 \cdot z_2, ..., E_m \cdot z_m] \tag{4}$$

Our experimental results also show that using the activation function Sigmoid performs better than using SoftMax instead.

SE Network. The SE Network shows an excellent performance in image classification tasks and won first place in the ILSVRC 2017 classification task [7]. It can improve the representational power by explicitly modeling the interdependencies among different channels of convolutional features in various image classification tasks. Inspired by the success of SE Network in the computer vision, we utilize the SE mechanism to gain better the importance of each feature embedding in the sentiment classification problem. As shown in Fig. 2b, the SE Network has three main modules as follows:

Squeeze. This module can be described as accumulating summary statistics of each feature embedding using 1D-pooling techniques, such as Max or Average, to squeeze a K-dimensional feature embedding into a scalar value that represents the global information represented for that feature embedding. Feature embeddings are squeezed into an m-dimensional statistic vector $S = [s_1, s_2, ..., s_m]$, and one can measure each s_i according to the global max 1D pooling:

$$s_i = \frac{\sum_{j=1}^{K} e_{ij}}{K}, \quad i \in \{1, 2, ..., m\} \tag{5}$$

Excitation. This module aims to learn the weight for each feature embedding based on the statistic vector S above. We use two linear layers in our work to dynamically learn the corresponding weights of each embedding feature. The first linear layer transforms the statistic vector into a latent vector with a reduction factor by working as an encoder. The second linear layer, working as a decoder, transforms the latent vector into a weighting vector. One can put an activation function between these two layers. Formally, the m-dimensional weighting vector $Z = [z_1, z_2, ..., z_m]$ can be calculated as:

$$Z = Sigmoid(W_2 SiLU(W_1 S)),$$ (6)

where W_1 and W_2 are two matrices of parameters of two layers, respectively.

Re-scaling. This module aims to re-scale feature embeddings by calculating feature embedding-wise multiplication between feature embeddings and the weighting vector learned above. Thus, the final embedding from the SE Network can be shown as below:

$$E = [E_1 \cdot z_1, E_2 \cdot z_2, ..., E_m \cdot z_m]$$ (7)

Attention Network. In recent years, Attention techniques [11,26] have been proved to be very successful in many natural language processing tasks. We utilize the Attention technique to automatically determine the importance coefficients for each embedding feature, as demonstrated in Fig. 2c. Unlike all methods above, we use two linear layers working as an encoder and a decoder with SiLU activation placed in the middle to transform the concatenation of feature embeddings to the weighting vector with the dimension of $m \times K$. In our experiments, we choose m as 5, the number of individual models and K as 256 is the dimension of the feature embedding. Formally, the $m \times K$-dimensional weighting vector $Z = [z_1, z_2, ..., z_{m \times K}]$ or $Z = [z_{ij}]$, where $i \in 1, 2, ..., m$ and $j \in 1, 2, ..., K$, can be calculated as follows:

$$Z = Sigmoid(W_2 SiLU(W_1 S))$$ (8)

where W_1 and W_2 are two parameter matrices of two linear layers. The final feature embedded from the Attention network can be computed as the feature-wise multiplication between feature embeddings and the weighting vector, by the following equation:

$$E = [e_{ij} \cdot z_{ij}],$$ (9)

where $i \in \{1, 2, ..., m\}$ and $j \in \{1, 2, ..., K\}$.

3   Experiments

We conduct all experiments on a workstation with Intel Core i9-7900X CPU, 128 GB RAM, and two GPUs RTX-2080Ti.

3.1   Datasets

To investigate the effectiveness of the proposed ensemble networks for Vietnamese sentiment analysis, we employ the public data AIVIVN, including user reviews of Vietnamese e-commerce pages used for the Vietnamese Sentiment Analysis Challenge 2019[1]. We also collected another large-scale dataset, which was collected from different Vietnamese e-commerce websites by ourselves. The AIVIVN dataset consists of around 16K training user reviews and 11K testing user reviews, while our dataset "AISIA-Sent-002" collected contains more than 450K user reviews, including 358,743 positive reviews and 100,699 negative reviews [15]. For our experiments, we consider a subset of around 15K training reviews and 170K reviews for evaluation. The statistics of the datasets can be described in Table 1.

Table 1. Two Vietnamese datasets used in our work.

AIVIVN Dataset	Positive	Negative	Total
Train	8690	7383	16073
Test	5767	5214	10981
AISIA-Sent-002	Positive	Negative	Total
Train	11765	3235	15000
Test	137833	30210	168043

3.2 Implementation

Our source codes are all implemented by Pytorch [19]. All the individual model architectures and the proposed ensemble networks for Vietnamese sentiment analysis are designed and implemented from scratch. We use Fasttext embedding of Vietnamese version[2], whose embedding dimension is 300, as word embedding layer. All architectures are trained with a batch size of 256, shuffle for training, sentence padding with a max length of 100, Adam optimizer with a learning rate of 1e−3, and weight decay of 1e−3, maximum epochs of 20, the dimensionality of each feature embedding of 256. We train each model of TextCNN, LSTM, GRU, LSTM + CNN, and GRU + CNN independently and save the best checkpoint, which will be weights-frozen and used as a feature extractor in the proposed ensemble architectures. We measure the performance of all proposed approaches through the metrics of ACC, F1, and AUC.

3.3 Experimental Results

Tables 2 and 3 illustrate the effectiveness of all proposed ensemble methods in enhancing the performance of Vietnamese sentiment analysis.

Overall, one can see that the ensemble methods except Uniform Weighting achieve a better performance than any individual model in all the metrics. They

---

[1] https://www.aivivn.com/contests/1.

[2] https://fasttext.cc.

Table 2. The experimental results of three proposed ensemble networks and other baseline methods along with the winning solution on **AIVIVN dataset**. The metrics of ACC and AUC are not provided by competition organizer.

Methods	ACC	F1	AUC
AIVIVN 2019 Sentiment Champion	–	90.012	–
TextCNN	93.24	92.85	98.17
LSTM	92.21	91.61	97.91
GRU	92.72	92.26	98.09
LSTM + CNN	93.96	93.65	98.46
GRU + CNN	93.75	93.39	98.51
Uniform Weighting	93.91	93.56	98.55
Linear	94.13	93.79	98.56
Gating Network	94.12	**93.82**	**98.59**
SE Network	94.00	93.63	98.57
Attention Network	**94.14**	93.80	98.58

Table 3. The experimental results of three proposed ensemble networks and other baseline methods on **AISIA-Sent-002**.

Methods	ACC	F1	AUC
TextCNN	92.86	92.37	98.07
LSTM	92.50	92.04	97.88
GRU	92.45	91.98	97.97
LSTM + CNN	93.17	92.87	98.28
GRU + CNN	93.14	92.66	98.30
Uniform Weighting	93.53	93.11	98.47
Linear	93.61	93.23	**98.48**
Gating Network	93.56	93.14	98.47
SE Network	**93.63**	**93.26**	**98.48**
Attention Network	**93.63**	93.25	**98.48**

remarkably surpass the winning solution of the competition "AIVIVN 2019 Sentiment Champion", which is the weighted ensemble of TextCNN [9], VDCNN [3], HARNN [30], and Self-Attention RNN [26] and achieves the best F1-score as 90.012%. Furthermore, the classical ensemble method, Uniform Weighting, performs less than the individual model (LSTM + CNN) in the dataset of AIVIVN. It can indicate that we need a better ensemble method to combine and take advantage of different models (Gating Network, SE Network, or Attention Network, as regarded in this paper). Specifically, in **AIVIVN dataset**, Gating Network shows the best performance in the metrics of F1-score (93.82%), AUC

(98.59%), and very competitive result in term of ACC (94.12%) in comparison with Attention Network (94.14% in ACC). While, in **AISIA-Sent-002**, SE Network shows its dominance in all the metrics of ACC (93.63%), F1-score (93.26%), and AUC (98.48%).

3.4 Ablation Study

Impact of the Number of Models on the Ensemble Performance. To investigate the impact of the number of individual models on ensemble performance, we run the proposed ensemble networks of Uniform Weighting, Linear, Gating Network, SE Network, and Attention Network in two settings. The first setting is the ensembling of three models, and the second is an ensemble of five models, as illustrated in Fig. 3. We observe that the combination of more models consistently gains a better performance in all the ACC, F1, and AUC metrics. It demonstrates the importance of the increasing number of individual models on the ensemble's performance.

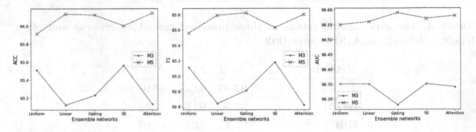

Fig. 3. The effect on the model performance with the number of individual models selected. Here, M3 represents the ensemble of three individual models (which are TextCNN, LSTM, GRU) and M5 denotes the ensemble of all five individual models.

Impact of the Dimension of Feature Embeddings on the Ensemble Performance. To explore the impact of feature embedding dimension on ensemble performance, we set feature embedding dimensions from each model at 128, 256, and 512. We run the proposed ensemble networks of Gating Network, SE Network, and Attention Network on different types of feature embeddings. The results are shown in Fig. 4. We observe that increasing the embedding dimension does not improve the ensemble method's performance during the evaluation. The results present that most of ensemble networks gain the best performance at the embedding dimension of 256.

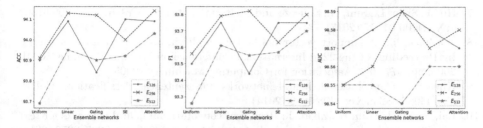

Fig. 4. The impact of feature embedding dimension on ensemble performance. Here, E_{128}, E_{256} and E_{512} represent the corresponding scenarios choosing the embedding dimension of 128, 256, and 512, respectively.

4 Conclusion

This paper has investigated the Vietnamese sentiment classification by exploring the impact of different ensemble methods on the performance with five individual models, TextCNN, LSTM, GRU, LSTM + CNN, and GRU + CNN. We have conducted all experiments on the AIVIVN dataset for a well-known sentiment competition in Vietnam and compare five ensemble schemes (Gating Network, SE Network, Attention Network, Uniform Weighting, and Linear Ensemble) with other methods. We use three standard metrics of ACC, F1, and AUC for measuring the performance of different approaches. The experimental results show the outstanding performance of the proposed ensemble networks compared with other methods. Notably, they can perform much better than the winning solution of the competition by a large margin. Finally, we aim to publish all our source codes and the dataset at https://github.com/lhkhiem28/Enhancing-Vietnamese-Sentiment-Analysis-with-Ensemble-Networks.

References

1. Bojanowski, P., Grave, E., Joulin, A., Mikolov, T.: Enriching word vectors with subword information. CoRR, abs/1607.04606 arXiv:1607.0460 (2016)
2. Chakriswaran, P., Vincent, D.R., Srinivasan, K., Sharma, V., Chang, C.Y., Reina, D.G.: Emotion AI-driven sentiment analysis: a survey, future research directions, and open issues. Appl. Sci. **9**(24), 5462 (2019)
3. Conneau, A., Schwenk, H., Barrault, L., Lecun, Y.: Very deep convolutional networks for text classification (2016)
4. Contratres, F.G., Alves-Souza, S.N., Filgueiras, L.V.L., DeSouza, L.S.: Sentiment analysis of social network data for cold-start relief in recommender systems. In: Rocha, Á., Adeli, H., Reis, L.P., Costanzo, S. (eds.) WorldCIST'18 2018. AISC, vol. 746, pp. 122–132. Springer, Cham (2018). https://doi.org/10.1007/978-3-319-77712-2_12
5. Devlin, J., Chang, M.W., Lee, K., Toutanova, K.: Bert: Pre-training of deep bidirectional transformers for language understanding (2019)
6. ElJundi, O., Antoun, W., El Droubi, N., Hajj, H., El-Hajj, W., Shaban, K.: hulmona: The universal language model in Arabic. In: Proceedings of the Fourth Arabic Natural Language Processing Workshop, pp. 68–77 (2019)

7. Hu, J., Shen, L., Sun, G.: Squeeze-and-excitation networks. CoRR, abs/1709.01507 arXiv:1709.01507 (2017)
8. Joachims, T.: A support vector method for multivariate performance measures. In: Proceedings of the 22nd International Conference on Machine Learning, ICML 2005, pp. 377–384. Association for Computing Machinery (2005)
9. Kim, Y.: Convolutional neural networks for sentence classification. CoRR, abs/1408.5882 arXiv:1408.5882 (2014)
10. Lai, S., Xu, L., Liu, K., Zhao, J.: Recurrent convolutional neural networks for text classification. In: Bonet, B., Koenig, S. (eds.) AAAI, vol. 333, pp. 2267–2273 (2015)
11. Luong, M.T., Pham, H., Manning, C.D.: Effective approaches to attention-based neural machine translation. CoRR, abs/1508.04025 arXiv:1508.04025 (2015)
12. Mai, L., Le, B.: Aspect-based sentiment analysis of vietnamese texts with deep learning. In: Nguyen, N.T., Hoang, D.H., Hong, T.-P., Pham, H., Trawiński, B. (eds.) ACIIDS 2018. LNCS (LNAI), vol. 10751, pp. 149–158. Springer, Cham (2018). https://doi.org/10.1007/978-3-319-75417-8_14
13. Medhat, W., Hassan, A., Korashy, H.: Sentiment analysis algorithms and applications: a survey. Ain Shams Eng. J. 5(4), 1093–1113 (2014)
14. Mikolov, T., Sutskever, I., Chen, K., Corrado, G., Dean, J.: Distributed representations of words and phrases and their compositionality. In: Proceedings of the 26th International Conference on Neural Information Processing Systems, NIPS 2013, vol. 2, pp. 3111–3119. Curran Associates Inc. (2013)
15. Nguyen, C.V., Le, K.H., Tran, A.M., Nguyen, B.T.: An efficient framework for Vietnamese sentiment analysis. In: Proceedings of The 18th International Conference on Intelligent Software Methodologies, Tools, and Techniques (SoMeT) (2020)
16. Nguyen, H.Q., Nguyen, Q.U.: An ensemble of shallow and deep learning algorithms for Vietnamese sentiment analysis, pp. 165–170 (2018)
17. Nguyen-Thanh, T., Tran, G.T.: Vietnamese sentiment analysis for hotel review based on overfitting training and ensemble learning (2019)
18. Nguyen-Thi, B.-T., Duong, H.-T.: A Vietnamese sentiment analysis system based on multiple classifiers with enhancing lexicon features. In: Duong, T.Q., Vo, N.-S., Nguyen, L.K., Vien, Q.-T., Nguyen, V.-D. (eds.) INISCOM 2019. LNICST, vol. 293, pp. 240–249. Springer, Cham (2019). https://doi.org/10.1007/978-3-030-30149-1_20
19. Paszke, A., et al.: Pytorch: an imperative style, high-performance deep learning library. In: Advances in Neural Information Processing Systems, pp. 8024–8035 (2019)
20. Pennington, J., Socher, R., Manning, C.D.: Glove: Global vectors for word representation. In: Empirical Methods in Natural Language Processing (EMNLP), pp. 1532–1543 (2014)
21. Phan, D.H., Cao, T.D.: Applying skip-gram word estimation and SVM-based classification for opinion mining Vietnamese food places text reviews. In: Proceedings of the Fifth Symposium on Information and Communication Technology, SoICT 2014, pp. 232–239. Association for Computing Machinery (2014)
22. Radford, A., Wu, J., Child, R., Luan, D., Amodei, D., Sutskever, I.: Language models are unsupervised multitask learners (2019)
23. Tang, D., Qin, B., Liu, T.: Document modeling with gated recurrent neural network for sentiment classification. In: Proceedings of the 2015 Conference on Empirical Methods in Natural Language Processing, pp. 1422–1432 (2015)

24. Tang, D., Qin, B., Liu, T.: Document modeling with gated recurrent neural network for sentiment classification. In: Proceedings of the 2015 Conference on Empirical Methods in Natural Language Processing, pp. 1422–1432. Association for Computational Linguistics (2015)

25. Trinh, S., Nguyen, L., Vo, M., Do, P.: Lexicon-based sentiment analysis of Facebook comments in Vietnamese language. In: Król, D., Madeyski, L., Nguyen, N.T. (eds.) Recent Developments in Intelligent Information and Database Systems. SCI, vol. 642, pp. 263–276. Springer, Cham (2016). https://doi.org/10.1007/978-3-319-31277-4_23

26. Vaswani, A., et al.: Attention is all you need. CoRR, abs/1706.03762 arXiv:1706.03762 (2017)

27. Vo, H.T., Lam, H.C., Nguyen, D.D., Tuong, N.H.: Topic classification and sentiment analysis for Vietnamese education survey system. Asian J. Comput. Sci. Inf. Technol. **6**, 27–34 (2016)

28. Wang, G., Sun, J., Ma, J., Kaiquan, X., Jibao, G.: Sentiment classification: the contribution of ensemble learning. Decis. Support Syst. **57**, 77–93 (2014)

29. Xie, Q., Dai, Z., Hovy, E., Luong, M.T., Le, Q.V.: Unsupervised data augmentation for consistency training (2019)

30. Yang, Z., Yang, D., Dyer, C., He, X., Smola, A., Hovy, E.: Hierarchical attention networks for document classification. In: Proceedings of the 2016 Conference of the North American Chapter of the Association for Computational Linguistics: Human Language Technologies, pp. 1480–1489 (2016)

Consistency Assessment of Datasets in the Context of a Problem Domain

Bogumila Hnatkowska$^{(\boxtimes)}$ [ID], Zbigniew Huzar [ID], and Lech Tuzinkiewicz [ID]

Department of Applied Informatics, Wroclaw University of Science and Technology,
50-370 Wroclaw, Poland
{bogumila.hnatkowska,zbigniew.huzar,
lech.tuzinkiewicz}@pwr.edu.pl

Abstract. Datasets have many applications, e.g., are used for software testing or serve as training data in artificial intelligence. In any case, they must be of good quality, i.e., be consistent with the domain represented by the dataset. The work aims to propose an approach to checking the consistency between a dataset and its domain. It is assumed that the collected data has a form of uninterpretable records, except for the knowledge of the attributes' names. The domain is represented by an ontology in the form of a UML class diagram. The proposed method consists of two stages: first, a UML class diagram is generated from a dataset, and then it is compared with the diagram representing the domain ontology with the use of defined measures. A case study illustrates the proposed approach. It has been shown that the proposed measures help to find inconsistencies and improve data quality. The proposed method enables the quality assessment of a data sample.

Keywords: Dataset · Domain ontology · UML class diagrams

1 Introduction

Datasets can be used in many different contexts, such as developing new software systems, as a knowledge base for a given field or as training data in learning processes. They usually express knowledge related to some area of application. As datasets may come from various sources, there is no guarantee that they will be of good quality in terms of compliance, completeness, consistency, and accuracy with respect to a given domain [1].

The notion of data quality, its characteristics, and measures are discussed in ISO 25xxx recommendation series. Data quality refers to the degree to which data quality characteristics have to satisfy stated and implied needs when data is used under specified conditions. In particular, it may refer to [1]:

- data domain values and possible restrictions (e.g., business rules governing the quality required for the characteristics in a given application);
- relationships of data values (e.g., consistency);
- metadata.

H. Fujita et al. (Eds.): IEA/AIE 2021, LNAI 12799, pp. 112–125, 2021.
https://doi.org/10.1007/978-3-030-79463-7_10

The paper addresses the problem of data consistency – data in a dataset should be consistent with business rules and be instances of a conceptual data model.

The paper aims to present an approach to assessing a dataset's consistency with a given application domain. The approach is based on the following assumptions.

The dataset is assumed to be given in the form of a data frame $DF = <H, B>$, where header H is a set of attribute names and B is a set of tuples (records). The application domain is represented by an ontology expressed as a UML class diagram.

While the form of the dataset seems to be natural, the form of the class diagram requires some explanation. Domain ontologies can be expressed in many languages. Nowadays, the OWL can be considered as one of the most popular. An ontology that is represented in OWL can also be represented in the form of a UML class diagram [2]. The problem of representing the domain ontology by UML class diagrams is considered in [3].

Generally, the dataset and the domain can cover different ranges. Therefore, it is also assumed that we concentrate only on the concepts found in both the dataset and the class diagram, more strictly on the set of attribute names along with their data types, which have the same semantics and data types on the class diagram. Identification of data types can be automated, but it requires domain expert knowledge to determine whether an attribute with a given name and type represents the same concept in a class diagram.

In our previous works [4, 5], we presented an algorithm that constructs a class diagram for a given data frame. That allows us to translate the problem of checking the consistency between a data set and its application domain into that of checking the consistency between two class diagrams: a class diagram CF representing the data frame and a class diagram CD representing the domain.

To assess the consistency of class diagrams, a number of measures have been introduced. Classes and binary associations are compared using elementary measures. Then, based on these measures, a global measure was proposed to compare class diagrams. Measure values help in finding inconsistencies and improving the dataset.

The structure of the paper is as follows. The next section briefly discusses related works. Subsection 3.1 outlines the algorithm of class diagram generation from datasets. Proposed measures for class diagrams comparison are defined in Subsect. 3.2. To illustrate the application of the proposed measures, a case study is presented in Sect. 4, and the final section concludes the paper.

2 Related Works

The problem posed – checking the consistency of a dataset against the domain ontology – seems new. To the best of the authors' knowledge, no papers are addressing a similar problem. However, the mechanisms used in solving the problem can be compared to a number of works found in the literature.

The first group of mechanisms concerns the extraction of knowledge from a dataset. First of all, extraction requires the identification of dependencies among the data. A short overview of the different types of these dependencies is given in [6]. Our work concentrates solely on functional dependencies. In general, the problem of identification and analysis of functional dependencies is of polynomial computational complexity. To reduce the complexity of the UML class diagram construction algorithm, some heuristics were applied in our previous works [4, 5, 7].

The obtained class diagram – a conceptual model of the dataset – is compared with another UML class diagram that is assumed to be the domain's ontology model. This assumption is justified by the work [2], which presents a practical approach to the construction of a UML class diagram from an OWL ontology. Thus, class diagrams can be proposed as an efficient means of representing a domain ontology. An exhausted analysis of problems in transforming and validating an ontology represented by OWL into a UML class diagram is discussed in detail in [8].

The second group of mechanisms is related to approaches comparing two class diagrams. The problem of comparison is not new but has been considered in different contexts. Below, short comments on selected works are presented.

For example, the identification of similarities and differences between the elements of matched class diagrams was considered in [9]. The aspects taken into consideration are lexical naming and similarities between attributes and behaviors. Basic measures that compare selected aspects are integrated with complex ones that are empirically validated and calibrated.

The aim of [10] is to introduce a framework that can be used to compare class models in model repositories. The relational structures of two class models in the form of graphs are compared. The algorithm for calculating the distance between the compared diagrams is of polynomial complexity.

A more general problem of comparison of two UML specifications taking into account both static and dynamic aspects is presented in [11], while our approach concentrates on the static aspect. The selection of similarities between UML diagrams after their transformation into so-called Structure-mapping Engines within a static approach may be compared to our one.

Another approach is presented in [12], where UML class diagrams are compared in the context of software reuse. The idea is to compare classes based on their semantics and next to compare the structure of the entire class diagrams. A similar idea is applied in our approach.

3   Assessment Method of Dataset Consistency

The idea of the proposed method is to compare two class diagrams. The first is derived from the dataset, the second represents the ontology under consideration. Subsection 3.1, presents the method of class diagram derivation, and Subsect. 3.2, the proposed method of class diagram comparison.

3.1   Derivation of Class Diagram from Dataset

This section shortly describes the algorithm used for the generation of a class diagram from a dataset. The details of the algorithm are given in [4, 5, 7]. Here only a general idea is presented.

The algorithm goes through three main stages: *preprocessing, processing, and postprocessing*. The date frame is read during the *preprocessing* stage. It is assumed that the frame is available in a single file. Functional dependencies between attributes are identified based on the data values. For practical reasons, the algorithm considers the functional dependencies of a set containing 1 to 4 attributes.

Processing is the main stage in the algorithm. It is divided into three steps: *finding partitions*, *processing partition elements*, and *processing reminder*. The first step (*finding partitions*) is the result of a divide-and-conquer strategy in which we try to split the attribute set into disjoint subsets called partitions. Each partition is the source of a single class diagram and contains attributes linked by functional dependencies. Attributes outside any partition are members of so-called reminders. To limit the number of functional dependencies considered by the algorithm, certain heuristics are used. Simpler dependencies take precedence over more complex ones, which can eventually be ignored.

During the *processing partition elements* step, each partition is processed in turn. The activity splits the attributes which belong to the partition into separate containers (classes) by applying a normalization process known from databases, adapted to the object-oriented paradigm. This means that classes can be joined with association classes, self-association, or generalizations. The first generated class for the partition is called a root class. Root classes play an important role later in the generation process.

In the last step (*processing reminder*), the reminder is processed. In general, it is processed in the same way as partitions and may result in a new class diagram (containing only 1 class in specific cases).

The *postprocessing* stage serves two purposes. The first allows refactoring the generated diagrams by introducing new generalization relationships. This step requires the a-domain expert's involvement and answers to questions about the similarity of selected attributes' semantics. According to a domain expert, if two (or more) attributes belonging to different classes have the same semantics, one of them will be replaced with a generalization relationship. The second goal is to join the diagrams generated by partitions/reminder into a consistent graph. The root classes are linked to connect separate diagrams. Two root classes are only linked when there is no path between them. Such simplification serves to limit the number of connections shown in the class diagram.

The algorithm application is demonstrated below. Suppose we have a data set to be processed – see Table 1. It comes from the university's domain and presents data about courses (*Course Id, Course Name*), students' groups (*Group Id*), and students enrolled in groups (*Index, First Name, Surname*). The data set contains additional labels used – if they are present – as (potential) class names. The generation algorithm in the postprocessing stage replaces anonymous class names with labels if possible. The way of solving potential conflicts (e.g., a label boundary does not cover all class attributes) is presented in [7].

As one can observe, a course can have many related groups. A group can have many students enrolled, and one student can be a member of many groups.

The algorithm starts with the identification of functional dependencies: *GroupId* $\rightarrow$ *CourseId*, *CourseId* $\rightarrow$ *CourseName*, *Index* $\rightarrow$ {*FirstName, Surname*}. After that, it tries to split the attributes into manageable groups called partitions. A partition should contain relatively independent columns. There are two partitions in the data set: {*Index, FirstName, Surname*} and {*CourseId, CourseName, GroupId*}. The remainder is empty.

Table 1. Exemplary data set

Course		Group		Student	
CourseId	CourseName	GroupId	Index	FirstName	Surname
INZ01W	Java	GR01	10100	John	Scott
INZ01P	Java	GR02	10100	John	Scott
INZ01W	Java	GR01	10101	John	Novak
INZ01P	Java	GR02	10101	John	Novak
INZ02S	Project Management	GR03	10101	John	Novak
INZ02S	Project Management	GR03	10102	Eva	Novak
INZ02S	Project Management	GR04	10100	John	Scott

Each partition is processed separately, resulting in a class subdiagram. The first partition is a source for one class (*Student*), the second – for two classes: *Group* and *Course* related by one to many associations (see Fig. 1).

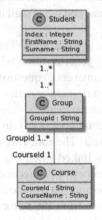

Fig. 1. Class diagram generated for the data set from Table 1

During the refactorization stage, an expert is asked if *CourseId* and *GroupId* columns have the same semantics. If the answer were 'yes', the association between *Group* and *Course* classes would be replaced with generalization.

The root classes from both partitions (*Student* and *Group*) are joined with many to many associations.

3.2 Class Diagram Comparison

It is assumed that there are two class diagrams: *CD* – represents the ontology of a given application domain, and *CF* – derived from the dataset *DF*. Both diagrams are refactored; each association class is replaced by a class with two associations on its ends; each generalization relationship is handled by copying all parents' attributes and associations to each child (the generalization is removed).

In further, the following notation is used:

- c.name — the name of the class c
- attr.name — the name of the attribute $attr$
- attr.type — the type of the attribute $attr$
- c.attr — set of attributes of the class c
- c.attr.name — set of names of the attribute $attr$ in the class c
- ass.end — set of classes at the ends of the association ass
- cd.cl — set of classes of the class diagram cd
- cd.ass — set of associations of the class diagram cd

When comparing the diagrams, we consider in turn: attributes, classes, and associations.

In the preliminary step, we determine the correspondence between the CF diagram attributes and the CD diagram attributes. This can be done in two manners, automatically or manually. In automatic mode, an attribute a_1 from CF is consistent with an attribute a_2 from CD if they have the same name, that is, $a_1.name = a_2.name$, and the data type of a_1 is consistent with the data type of a_2, $a_1.type \subseteq a_2.type$. In real cases, this demand may be too restrictive. It is assumed that attribute names are unique in a data frame (otherwise, they won't be distinguishable). On the other side, different classes can have attributes with the same names. Therefore, in manual mode, an expert can define the mapping between the attributes from CF and CD diagrams. However, the requirement for consistency of types is still valid. In further, for the sake of simplicity, we assume the use of automatic mode.

Class correspondence is determined on the basis of two measures: a measure of consistency and a measure of class similarity. Class comparison is based on a comparison of their attributes.

The measure of the consistency of a class c_1 with respect to a class c_2 is the value determined by the formula (1):

$$con(c_1, c_2) = \frac{|c_1.attr.name \cap c_2.attr.name|}{|c_2.attr.name|} \quad (1)$$

and the measure of the similarity of a class c_1 to a class c_2 is the value determined by the formula (2):

$$sim(c_1, c_2) = \frac{|c_1.attr.name \cap c_2.attr.name|}{|c_1.attr.name \cup c_2.attr.name|} \quad (2)$$

Pay attention that $con(c_1, c_2) \neq con(c_2, c_1)$, but $sim(c_1, c_2) = sim(c_2, c_1)$, and $0 \leq con(c_1, c_2) \leq 1$ and $0 \leq sim(c_1, c_2) \leq 1$.

For each class c on CF diagram, we identify on CD diagram such class c' that is the most consistent with c (the equivalent of c), noted $c' = eq(c)$, which satisfies the condition given below:

$$con\left(c, c'\right) = \max\{con(c, c_1)|c_1 \epsilon CD.cl\} \quad (3)$$

and, if there are two classes c' and c'' such that $con\left(c, c'\right) = con\left(c, c''\right)$ then we select as the equivalent such class c' for which

$$sim\left(c, c'\right) \geq sim\left(c, c''\right)$$

For each class c from the CD diagram, the following set is defined:

$$MC(c, CF) = \left\{ c' \in CF \middle| c' = eq(c) \right\} \tag{4}$$

A measure of the consistency of the set of classes $MC(c, CF)$ from the CF diagram with respect to the class c from the CD diagram is defined by Eq. (5):

$$con(c, CF) = \frac{|c.attr.name \cap \bigcup_{c' \in MC(c,CF)} c'.attr.name|}{|c.attr.name|} \tag{5}$$

If $MC(c, CF) = \varnothing$ or $c.attr.name = \varnothing$ then $con(c, CF) = 0$.

Now the CF diagram is compared to the CD diagram at the class level. The measure of the consistency of the CF diagram with respect to the CD diagram at the class level is defined as:

$$con_{cl}(CF, CD) = |CD.cl|^{-1} \sum_{c \in CD.cl} con(c, FD) \tag{6}$$

To compare the CF and CD diagrams at the association level, we first need to define the necessary conditions for the associations being compared. An association ass_1 from CF can be compared to an association ass_2 from CD if:

(1) $|ass_1.end| = |ass_2.end|$,
(2) each class $c \in ass_1.end$ has its equivalent class $c' \in ass_2$, noted $c' = eq(c)$, and
(3) each multiplicity m defined at the class $c \in ass_1.end$ satisfies $m \subseteq m'$, where m' is the multiplicity at the end of the class $eq(c)$.

Let $con(ass_1, ass_2)$ be the consistency measure of an association ass_1 from CF with respect to an association ass_2 from CD, noted $ass_2 = eq(ass_1)$. The following four cases for association comparison are considered.

(1) If for an association ass_1 from CF, there exists an association ass_2 from CD such that the above given conditions are satisfied, then by definition $con(ass_1, ass_2) = 1$.
(2) If a binary association ass_1 may be compared only to a derived association ass_2 that is a composition of other binary associations, say, $ass_2 = ass'_1 \circ ass'_2 \circ \cdots \circ ass'_k$ then by definition $con(ass_1, ass_2) = 1/k$.
(3) A very specific is the case for a binary association ass_1 such that $eq(c_1) = eq(c_2)$ where $c_1, c_2 \in ass_1.end$. The case is interpreted as a decomposition of the class $eq(c_1)$ into two associated classes c_1', c_1'', and the association ass_1 is compared to an nonexistent association '*' what is expressed as $con(ass_1, *)$. The value of $con(ass_1, *) = 1$ if multiplicities at both ends of ass_1 are 1 or 0..1; $con(ass_1, *) = 0, 5$ if these multiplicities are * or 1..* at one end and 0..1 or 1 for the other end; $con(ass_1, *) = 0$ otherwise.

(4) If for an association ass_1 there does not exist an association for comparison, then by definition $con(ass_1, *) = 0$.

Now, the comparison of the CF diagram with the CD diagram at the level of associations is expressed by the measure:

$$con_{ass}(CF, CD) = |CF.ass|^{-1} \sum_{ass_1 \in CF.ass} con(ass_1, eq(ass_1)) \qquad (7)$$

Finally, the measure of consistency of the CF diagram with the CD diagram may be defined as:

$$CON(CF, CD) = \alpha con_{cl}(CF, CD) + \beta con_{ass}(CF, CD) \qquad (8)$$

where $\alpha, \beta \geq 0$ and $\alpha + \beta = 1$.

4 Case Study

The demonstration of the measured calculations and their use in assessing the consistency of a data frame with respect to a specific domain is based on a case study. The case study refers to an external data source, i.e., https://relational.fit.cvut.cz/dataset/Classi cModels. We have selected the *ClassicModels* database from many available databases as a reference domain because of its understandability. The database keeps data about products, orders, customers, and employees. We have excluded one table from it (Payments), as it seems to be loosely related to order. The database model is given in the form of a class diagram in Fig. 2. The class diagram was prepared by an expert and served as the domain model. The data types were mapped to UML primitive data types: *int* into *Integer*, *double* into *Real*, anything else into *String*. The names of columns in the data frame as well as in the class diagram have a prefix representing the table from which the data come from.

The database contains the data from which we have prepared an initial data frame in the form of a csv file. The file consists of all records kept in the database after joining all its tables (2996 records in total). The data frame is a view of the selected database containing all attributes of the selected tables. The data frame was cleaned. The columns representing foreign keys (in different tables) were removed manually, which reduced the number of columns from 55 to 49. The implementation of the prototype tool based on csv is due its popularity, but the method is not limited to that format.

The initial data frame was input for two groups of test cases:

- Vertical slices of the data frame – 1 test case and its improvement.
- Horizontal slices of the data frame – 2 test cases, one with improvement.

The test cases have been set up to validate the proposed method for a small (the first test case) and a large number of attributes (the second test case).

4.1 Vertical Slices of Data Frame

The test is a projection of the initial data frame limited to the attributes of product and product line tables (*Product*, and *ProductLine* classes in Fig. 2).

A class diagram generated for this test is presented in Fig. 3a. As was expected, the diagram contains two classes linked by one to many association. However, the *ProductLine* class looks not as expected. Firstly, it doesn't contain two fields, *pln_htmlDescription* and *pln_Image*. These columns are empty in the dataset, therefore the generating algorithm could not decide to which class they should belong. Secondly, the *p_productDescription* field is a part of the *ProductLine* class instead of the *Product* class. One can observe these problems when reading metrics values at the class level. Consistency measure for *ProductLine* classes is equal to 0.66, and their similarity – 0.4. Consistency measure for *Product* classes is equal to 1.0, and their similarity – 0.86. Consistency at the class level is equal to 0.83. There is no problem with the association consistency, which is equal to 1.0. Therefore, the generated class diagram is consistent with its domain at 0.92.

The problem with classes was caused by the fact that the *p_productDescription* attribute has to define functionally other fields in *ProductLine* class or be defined by one of them. To fix this problem, it is enough to break the functional dependency.

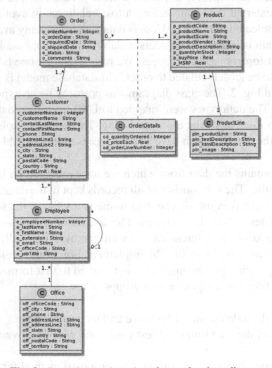

Fig. 2. Domain ontology in a form of a class diagram

We have changed the product description for the product with the code S10_2016 to be the same as for the product with the code S18_1589 from another product line. As a result, we obtain a diagram presented in Fig. 3b, which is entirely consistent with the ontology (consistency equal to 1.0) even if the generated *ProductLine* class does not contain all original class attributes.

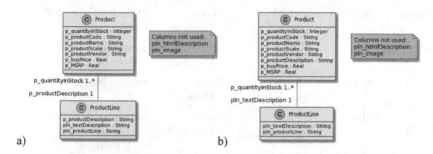

Fig. 3. Class diagram generated for a test case (a – before fix, b – after the fix)

4.2 Horizontal Slices of Data Frame

The quality of a data set strongly depends on the number of records and their diversity. To demonstrate the influence, we prepared two test cases selections of the input data frame with an increasing number of records (all attributes are present). The first sample contains records for a selected product only (code set to S10_1678), 28 records in total. We did not expect the generated diagram to be highly consistent with the ontology because of the limited perspective. The second sample contains records for the first 10 products ordered alphabetically (138 records).

The diagram generated for the first sample is presented in Fig. 4a, and for the second sample in Fig. 4b.

The existing functional dependencies among attributes allowed to extract six classes and six binary associations in the first case. The tool could not infer all class names based on the labels assigned to the columns; therefore, anonymous names (*Dummy4*, *Dummy5*) are used instead.

Detailed measure calculations for the consistency checking between class diagram from Fig. 4a and Fig. 2 are given in Table 2.

Employee and *Office* classes are fully consistent with their equivalent classes, which means that they contain only attributes from the original range. The lowest consistency has the *Dummy4* class because it is a mixture of many other classes. To fix that problem, a higher diversity of its attributes is necessary. The *Dummy5* and its association with the *Order* class are pointed out as probably mistaken (there is no equivalent association in the domain model because of multiplicity constraints).

The considered testing data frame is good enough for the representation of customers and employees. The same can be said about the representation of offices but not their connection to order. The path between their equivalent classes has a length equal to 3, which means that the association is probably accidental.

Table 2. Detailed metrics calculation for class diagrams from Fig. 4a (data frame) and Fig. 2 (ontology).

FD class – c_1	CD class – c_2	Con(c_1,c_2)	FD ass – a_1	CD ass – a_1	con(a_1, a_2)
{Customer, Dummy5}	Customer	0.81	Customer – Employee	Customer – Employee	1.00
Employee	Employee	1.00	Order – Customer	Order – Customer	1.00
Order	Order	0.57	Customer – Dummy4	Customer – Product	0.33
Dummy4	Product	0.44	Order – Dummy4	Order – Product	0.50
Office	Office	1.00	Order – Dummy5	No equivalent because of multiplicity	0.00
			Order – Office	Order – Office	0.33
con_{cl}		0.64	Con_{ass}		0.53
CON(FD, CD) = 0.58					

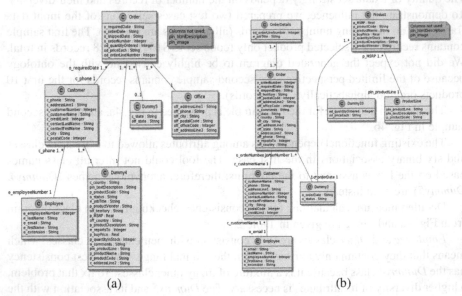

Fig. 4. (a) The class diagram generated for 1 product (on the left), (b) The class diagram generated for 10 products (on the right).

The diagram generated for the second sample (4b) is more consistent with the domain. *OrderDetail* class reflects an accidental functional dependency between *od_orderLineNumber* and *e_jobTitle* columns and can be easily eliminated. The *Order* class attributes are split among two connected classes (*Order* and *Dummy3*) when the anonymous class can be removed if one removes a dependency between *o_OrderDate* and *o_status* fields. Similar to the previous case, we have one class *Order*, which is a mixture of other classes.

Detailed metrics calculations for the consistency checking between the class diagram from Fig. 4b and Fig. 2 are given in Table 3.

The values of consistency metrics are a little better for the extended data sample, both at the class level and association level. After small fixes, i.e., replacing the value of *e_jobTitle* for one person (this field has the same values for all records), and removing the dependency between *o_orderDate* and *o_status* attributes, the consistency at the class level increased to 0.71, at the association level to 0.65, and the assessment of the diagram to 0.68.

Table 3. Detailed metrics calculation for class diagrams from Fig. 4a (data frame) and Fig. 2 (ontology).

FD class – c_1	CD class – c_2	Con(c_1,c_2)	FD ass – a_1	CD ass – a_1	Con(a_1, a_2)
{OrderDetails, Dummy10}	OrderDetails	1.00	Customer – Employee	Customer – Employee	1.00
Dummy3	Order	1.00	Order – Dummy3	No equiv.	0.00
Product	Product	1.00	Order – Customer	No equiv.	0.00
ProductLine	ProductLine	0.66	Product – ProductLine	Product – ProductLine	1.00
Customer	Customer	1.0	OrderDetails – Order	No equiv.	0.00
Order	Office	0.53	Product – Dummy10	Product – OrderDetails	1.00
			Dummy10 – Dummy3	OrderDetails – Order	1.00
con_{cl}		0.69	con_{ass}		0.57
CON(FD, CD) = 0.63					

It should be mentioned that the process of assessing the data set's quality is supported by a working version of the software that allows to compare class diagrams and determine the measures' values. This software parses class diagrams described in plantUML, builds their models based on specifications, and then transforms these diagrams by replacing association classes and generalization relationships with their equivalent constructs. It then counts and prints the values of all metrics. The tool runnable version (jar file) with the test samples and generated diagrams used in the case study can be found in [13].

5 Conclusions

Data can come from different sources, including business, computers, the Internet, and other digital devices producing a large amount of data. Nowadays, there has been a change in the understanding of the meaning and value of data.

The proposed method visualizes the data in the form of a class diagram. Such a diagram can be compared with existing representations of the domain from which the data comes. The solution presented in the article aims to determine the quality of a data sample by assessing the degree of data consistency with the domain ontology. The consistency is assessed by a set of measures.

The presented method can be used for:

- Gain knowledge to interpret data in the context of the problem domain.
- Assess the quality of the sample data.
- Improve the data quality based on the obtained results of consistency measurements.

The method is still under development, including the detailed procedure of dataset quality assessment.

Choosing conceptual modeling and ontologies to support data quality evaluation is a novel approach that can be part of analytics systems. In the future, we intend to prove the usefulness of the proposed measures by experimenting with external experts.

References

1. Fleckenstein, M., Fellows, L.: Modern Data Strategy. Springer, Cham (2018). https://doi.org/10.1007/978-3-319-68993-7
2. Sadowska, M., Huzar, Z.: Representation of UML class diagrams in OWL 2 on the background of domain ontologies. E-Informatica Softw. Eng. J. **13**(1), 63–103 (2019)
3. Robles, K., Fraga, A., Morato, J., Llorens, J.: Towards an ontology-based retrieval of UML class diagrams. Inf. Softw. Technol. **54**, 72–86 (2012)
4. Hnatkowska, B., Huzar, Z., Tuzinkiewicz, L.: A data-driven conceptual modeling. In: Jarzabek, S., Poniszewska-Marańda, A., Madeyski, L. (eds.) Integrating research and practice in software engineering. SCI, vol. 851, pp. 97–109. Springer, Cham (2020). https://doi.org/10.1007/978-3-030-26574-8_8
5. Hnatkowska, B., Huzar, Z., Tuzinkiewicz, L.: Extracting class diagram from hidden dependencies in data sets. Comput. Sci. **21**(2), 197–223 (2020)
6. Liu, J., Li, J., Liu, C., Chen, Y.: Discover dependencies from data – a review. IEEE Trans. Knowl. Data Eng. **24**(2), 251–264 (2012)
7. Hnatkowska, B.: Visualization of structural dependencies hidden in a large data set. In: Hernes, M., Wojtkiewicz, K., Szczerbicki, E. (eds.) ICCCI 2020. CCIS, vol. 1287, pp. 427–439. Springer, Cham (2020). https://doi.org/10.1007/978-3-030-63119-2_35
8. Sadowska, M.: Creating and validating UML class diagrams with the use of domain ontologies expressed in OWL 2. Doctoral Thesis, Faculty of Computer Science and Management, Wroclaw University of Science and Technology (2020)
9. Mojeeb, A.A., Moataz A.: UML class diagrams: similarity aspects and matching, LNCS, vol. 4, no. 1, pp. 41–47 (2016)
10. Cech, P.: Matching UML class models using graph edit distance. Expert Syst. Appl. **130**, 206–224 (2019)

11. Wei-Jin, P., Doo-Hwan, B.: A two-stage framework for UML specification matching. Inf. Softw. Technol. **53**, 230–244 (2011)
12. Zongmin, M., Zhongchen, Y., Li, Y.: Two-level clustering of UML class diagrams based on semantics and structure. Inform. Softw. Technol. (in Print)
13. Hnatkowska, B.: Class diagram comparison tool (2021). github.com/bhnatkowska/ClassDiag ramComparison

Effects of Performance Clustering in User Modelling for Learning Style Knowledge Representation

Chin-Wei Teoh[1], Sin-Ban Ho[1(✉)] (iD), Khairi Shazwan Dollmat[1], Ian Chai[1],
Wan-Noorshahida Mohd-Isa[1], Chuie-Hong Tan[2], Sek-Kit Teh[1],
and Manzoor Shahida Raihan[1]

[1] Faculty of Computing and Informatics, Multimedia University, 63100 Cyberjaya, Malaysia
{sbho,shazwan.dollmat,ianchai,wan.noorshahida.isa}@mmu.edu.my
[2] Faculty of Management, Multimedia University, 63100 Cyberjaya, Malaysia
chtan@mmu.edu.my

Abstract. The transformation of education from the era of face-to-face teaching to the era of e-learning has promoted the rise of technological approaches for educational teaching. This new educational norm is currently confronting challenges especially in terms of analysing student performance in e-learning platforms. Furthermore, differences in how students receive and process learning information has focused attention on analysing student learning style. Therefore, this research has introduced two important investigations, which are analysing the relationship between student learning style behaviours and their learning performance in e-learning platforms, as well as combining the K-means algorithm with the Principal Component Analysis (PCA) feature reduction technique to produce a clustering model. By comparing based on Felder-Silverman (FS) learning style dimensions, students who have similar learning style dimensions would produce similar learning performance in the e-learning platform. The PCA method has successfully increased the silhouette coefficient of the K-means clustering model. The clustering model grouped students into different clusters based on student learning characteristics.

Keywords: K-means clustering · Felder-Silverman learning styles · Principal Component Analysis · Elbow method · Silhouette coefficient · Educational data mining · User modeling · Knowledge representation

1 Introduction

Traditionally, face-to-face learning with the presence of educators has been seen as the primary source of transmitting knowledge to students [1]. However, educational norms have evolved from generation to generation due to the emergence of educational technology [2]. Challenges such as study time constraints, and geographic separation between

© Springer Nature Switzerland AG 2021
H. Fujita et al. (Eds.): IEA/AIE 2021, LNAI 12799, pp. 126–137, 2021.
https://doi.org/10.1007/978-3-030-79463-7_11

students' homes and places of study have motivated the emergence of educational technology as an alternative solution to deliver knowledge to students. Undoubtedly, nowadays students have started to adapt to a new educational norm, accessing e-learning web platforms for learning new knowledge [2].

The rise of e-learning web platforms has created an opportunity for researchers in the education domain to collect relevant data related to student learning style (LS) and learning characteristics. In this case, it is beneficial for educators to analyse student learning trends and collect some insight, which is useful for educators to come out with better decisions when structuring teaching methods [3]. This situation has created a domain called educational data mining.

There are two important techniques to choose for educational data-mining: supervised and unsupervised [4]. Supervised methods are applied for data which contain class labels. Unsupervised techniques, on the other hand, are applied for data without class labels. Clustering has been applied as one of the most significant unsupervised methods to analyse student performance in online learning [5]. Researchers have applied a clustering method to identify hidden patterns or insight in the educational data, which is helpful for educators to understand student learning performance in e-learning [6].

Clustering is the algorithm of grouping objects into classes of similar objects. In this case, partition-based algorithms such as K-means can decompose the set of objects into clusters where the optimal number of clusters can be determined through several methods such as the elbow method, silhouette coefficient, Calinski-Harabasz index, gap statistic, and others [7]. On the other hand, Principal Component Analysis (PCA) has been applied to transform high dimensional data into lower dimensional data and the K-means algorithm is then applied to cluster the data [8].

2 Background Study

The research conducted by Wanli Xing proposes a K-means clustering method to analyse a group of students' performances in various massive open online courses (MOOC) design features [9]. The combination of K-means clustering and the elbow method has produced reasonably accurate results in analysing the progress of the student's performance [10]. Similar studies conducted by Marutho et al. have proven that applying the elbow method to determine the optimal number of clusters can help to improve clustering model performance [11].

Selecting a midpoint position of a bad cluster will cause a K-means clustering model with high errors [12]. Therefore, the elbow method can help in determining the optimal number of clusters easily through observing the curve point of the plot, known as the "bend point of the elbow" [11]. Mathematically, the formula of the elbow method can be described as the following Eq. (1).

$$W = \sum_{r=1}^{k} \frac{1}{n_r} D_r \tag{1}$$

where W is the average internal sum of squares, k denotes the number of clusters, n_r denotes the number of data points in cluster r, and D_r denotes the sum of the average Euclidean distance between all data points against the centroid in a cluster.

Nonetheless, a study has pointed out the disadvantage of the elbow method. The elbow method applies the sum of squared errors (SSE) as a metric and then traverses the number of cluster points to determine the bend point. If the condition of noise within the data increases, the possibility of causing ambiguous results in the plot will increase [13]. Consequently, it is difficult to determine the optimal point of clusters.

Therefore, a similar study has suggested alternative methods to be applied instead of only elbow methods. For instance, the silhouette coefficient and gap statistic methods can be applied as alternative solutions. In this case, the silhouette coefficient can help to determine the optimal number of clusters by calculating the mean of intra-cluster distance and the average nearest-cluster distance to all clusters. The silhouette score range is between −1 and 1, where 1 denotes the ideal condition of all clusters being well apart [14]. Furthermore, the approach of Principal Component Analysis (PCA) on the data pre-processing stage is suggested to be conducted for high dimensional data before building the clustering model. In this case, PCA can transform high dimensional data into lower dimensional data. Consequently, PCA can improve the compression and clustering model for data visualization purposes.

El-Bishouty et al. indicated learning styles have a significant effect on student learning progress. Thus, the Felder-Silverman (FS) learning style model has become an insight benchmark for teachers to design e-learning courses. The study shows that the design of the course has a positive impact on student learning performance [15]. Furthermore, another study has indicated a positive correlation between learning styles and academic

Table 1. Felder-Silverman learner dimension.

Dimension	Learning styles	
Processing (LS1):	Active	Reflective
	Prefers to perceive knowledge through active activities such as experimentation and applying the knowledge into real life	Prefers to think alone and observe rather than perform actions like experimentation
Perception (LS2):	Sensor	Intuitive
	Prefers to solve problems through a standard method, fact, data or experiment	Prefer to solve problem through principles, theory or innovation and dislikes any form of repetition
Input (LS3):	Visual	Verbal
	Prefers to engage with information in the form of images, charts, or diagrams	Prefers to engage with information in the form of words and discussion
Understanding (LS4):	Sequential	Global
	Understands better via a step-by-step approach or structured information	Understands better on seeing the big picture without going through specific details or relationships in the knowledge

performance [16]. Table 1 describes the definition of each dimension in the FS learning style model [17].

3   Methodology

There were 71 undergraduates from different years of a computer science programme who participated in a Python programming course. All participants had to answer a set of Index of Learning Style (ILS) questions before they proceed to the learning phase. The result of the ILS were analysed based on the FS learning style model. Throughout the experiment, all participants went through assigned learning materials. After that, all participants attempted multiple-choice questions, and the total test scores, as well as time taken to complete a test, were recorded. Figure 1 summarizes our research work, which was subsequently analysed with scripts written in Python with the Pandas data analysis library.

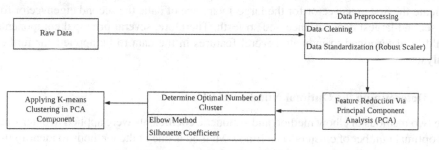

Fig. 1. Research methodology.

3.1   Data Preprocessing

Data Preprocessing is an important phase before cluster modelling. At first, the data cleaning process was conducted on imported datasets as per the attributes in Table 2, where missing values were checked on every attribute located on the datasets. At the same time, exploratory data analysis was conducted to perform an initial investigation on data where the relationship between attributes on the data could be analysed.

Table 2. Raw data attributes descriptions.

Attributes	Description
LS1, LS2, LS3, LS4	Score of learning style dimension 1, 2, 3, 4 (*Range: −11 to 11*)
Total Time (min)	Total Time completion to complete a test in minute
Convert_100%	Total mark for test in percentage

K-means clustering, a distance-based algorithm, was most affected by the range of features due to the similarity of data and was influenced by the distance between data points and an outlier. Therefore, scaling of timely completion and total quiz scores attributes were conducted, and then the effect of scaling was measured through Euclidean distance. In this case, robust scaling as a standardization technique was selected to scale the range of data based on mean and standard deviation.

3.2 Feature Reduction via Principal Component Analysis (PCA)

By considering the advantage of PCA as an unsupervised algorithm that helps to construct a new set of properties with the combination of the old set of properties, PCA has been selected to conduct feature reduction. Initially, the covariance matrix was to be calculated to investigate the variance and covariance of the data. In this case, the eigenvector value denotes the direction of data variance to be calculated whereas the eigenvalue denotes the magnitude of data variance also to be calculated. Next, the eigenvectors were to be sorted in descending order concerning the eigenvalues. In this case, the result would indicate the first eigenvector for the largest variance of data, the second eigenvector for the second-largest data variance and so forth. Therefore, several principal components could be determined to indicate several features in the data to be applied for further analysis.

3.3 Determining the Optimal Number of Cluster

The two methods of elbow method and silhouette coefficients were applied to determine the optimal number of clusters. The Elbow Method is one of the methods to identify the optimal number of clusters through the bend point or curve point of a plot. On the other hand, a higher silhouette score can help to identify the optimal number of clusters.

3.4 Applying K-means Clustering to PCA

After the optimal number of clusters had been selected, we performed K-means clustering through appropriate visualization tools to display the cluster output. In this case, the K-means clustering model would be trained with a maximum number of iterations of 300 of the Elkan algorithm and the initialization method of K-means++.

4 Results and Discussion

4.1 Learning Style and Time Taken for Quiz

In the first part of the research, the objective is to study the relationship between learning style and the time taken to complete a quiz. As mentioned in the proposed method, there were four different dimensions of learning styles. In terms of the first learning style dimension (LS1), Fig. 2 shows that the number of students under active and reflective styles are quite balanced.

However, some active style students took between 100 until 140 min to complete the test, which were longer than reflective style students. In the second learning style dimension (LS2), there were more intuitive style students than sensing style students. The time completion between sensing and intuitive styles are roughly similar. In the third learning style dimension (LS3), there were more verbal style students than visual style students. The majority of verbal and visual styles students took between 40 and 120 min to complete the test, but students with a verbal style took a longer time than the others. In the fourth learning style dimension (LS4), there were more global style students than sequential style students. At the same time, global style students were slower than sequential style students. This means that the sequential style students were faster since they followed the steps without relating the big picture to the specific details in the knowledge.

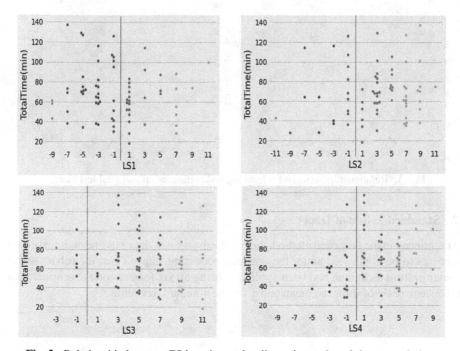

Fig. 2. Relationship between FS learning styles dimension and total time completion.

Next, the learning style dimension against the total test mark would be discussed. Figure 3 indicates that there is no significant relationship between total test mark with first (LS1) and fourth learning style (LS4) dimensions. Nonetheless, statistically significantly more intuitive style students achieved excellent results between 90% and 100% than sensing style students in LS2. Similarly, statistically significantly more verbal style students achieving a score of between 90% and 100% than visual style students in LS3.

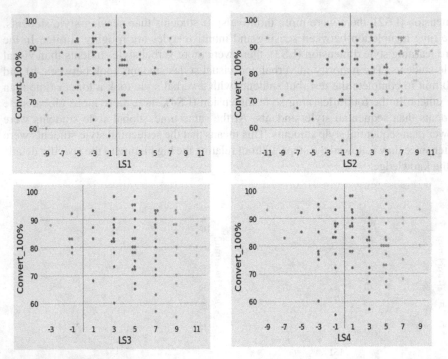

Fig. 3. Relationship between FS learning styles dimension and total test mark.

4.2 Standardization of Data

As mentioned in the proposed method, the standardization of data was one of the essential processes to be conducted under the data preprocessing stage. Thus, the robust scaler standardization technique had been applied to bring all six features on the original data to the same scale of 0 for the mean and 1 for the standard deviation.

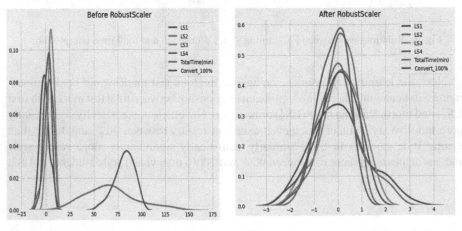

Fig. 4. Data distribution on all six features before and after robust scaler is applied.

Figure 4 shows how all features skew in different directions before the standardization technique was applied. After the standardization technique had been applied, all features had been scaled into the same range of mean and standard deviation. Furthermore, the robust scaler method had helped to minimize the influence of outliers on the data.

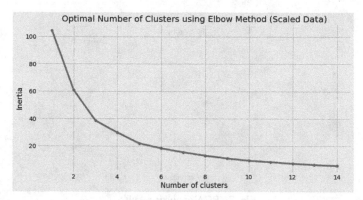

Fig. 5. Elbow method to determine optimal number of clusters of post-scaled data.

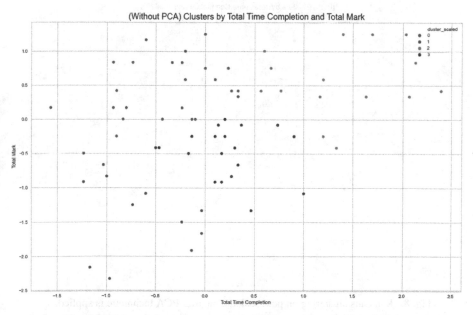

Fig. 6. K-Means clustering on post-scaled data without PCA technique.

Next, an unsupervised machine learning method, clustering had been applied to identify data clusters between total time completion and total mark features. Initially, the elbow method had identified an optimal number of clusters on post-scaled data was either four or five, as illustrated in Fig. 5. For the sake of simplicity, the optimal number of clusters selected were four. By comparing to the silhouette coefficient, a cluster of four achieves a score of 0.34, which is on the low-end point. Figure 6 shows the K-means clustering method applied to all four clusters on post-scaled data without the PCA technique.

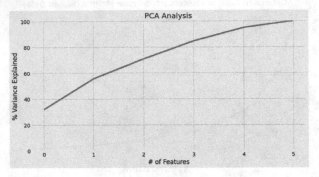

Fig. 7. PCA analysis result.

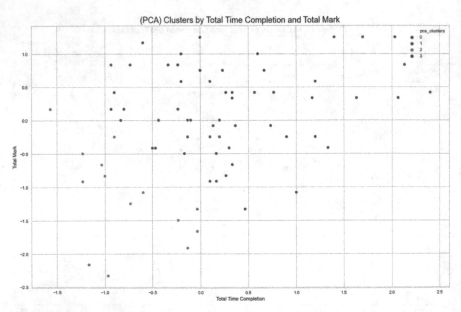

Fig. 8. K-means clustering on post-scaled data after PCA technique is applied.

We subsequently conducted the feature reduction via the PCA method. From Fig. 7, the number of principal components selected was two. The first principal component contains roughly 70% of the variance and the percentage of variance ratio for the first and second PCA components were approximated at 0.32 and 0.24 respectively. Thus, the features were reduced from 6 to 2. Next, we applied the K-means clustering method on the lower-dimensional scaled data. The silhouette score had been increased from 0.34 to 0.59 on the same number clusters of four. There were significant improvements and distinction between all clusters in terms of total time completion and total mark features.

From the K-means clustering output in Fig. 8, there are four significant clusters in the relationship between time completion and total test mark features. The yellow cluster has the characteristic of spending a short time to complete a test but achieves the lowest test mark. Meanwhile, the green cluster has the characteristic of consuming an average amount of time to complete a test and achieve an average mark better than students under the yellow cluster. Although students under the blue cluster had an almost similar average minutes of time to complete a test as the green cluster, students under the blue cluster were more likely to achieve an average excellent mark than students under the green cluster. Lastly, students under the red cluster have the characteristic of taking the longest amount time to complete the test, but achieve the highest test score.

5   Conclusion

The first part of the research study was to identify the relationship between the FS learning style and student time taken to complete a test as well as test marks. In the time completion aspect, active, intuitive, and global styles students were taking a longer time of approximately 40–100 min to complete tests than students with the opposite dimensions. Meanwhile in the test mark aspect, the intuitive and verbal styles students were more likely to achieve a score between 90% and 100% than students with the opposite dimensions. Moreover, students with similar learning style dimensions produce similar learning performance in the e-learning platform.

The second part of the research work was applied to the K-means algorithm to cluster the data. Before that, the standardization method was applied to the original data; then the PCA technique was used to reduce the original six features into two features. As a result, K-means clustering was applied, then four clusters were shown. The silhouette score on the cluster model increased after the PCA was applied. From the clustering result, some students took a shorter time to complete the test but achieved the lowest test mark. On the other hand, some students took a longer time, more than 40 min, but achieved the highest test marks.

By comparing to other research work with a similar method of K-means algorithm in clustering student performance in programming assessment, this research study has applied the PCA technique in the data prepossessing stage to enhance the clustering performance in the student academic performance [18]. However, the drawbacks of K-means clustering are that it cannot produce a good cluster when the data is in a complex geometric shape, and has a high computational time when the number of the data points is large. Therefore, future work may improve on this by using another clustering algorithm, such as Gaussian Mixtures, which is more flexible on elliptical clusters and takes a shorter time to converge on a local minimum of data.

Acknowledgments. The authors appreciate the financial support given by the Fundamental Research Grant Scheme, FRGS/1/2019/SS06/MMU/02/4.

References

1. Castro Hoyos, A.A., Velasquez, J.D.: Teaching analytics: current challenges and future development. IEEE J. Latin-Am. Learn. Technol. IEEE R. Iberoamericana Tecnologias Aprendizaje **15**(1), 1–9 (2020). https://doi.org/10.1109/RITA.2020.2979245
2. Al Kurdi, B., Alshurideh, M., Salloum, S.A.: Investigating a theoretical framework for e-learning technology acceptance. Int. J. Electr. Comput. Eng. **10**(6), 6484–6496 (2020)
3. Romero, C., Ventura, S.: Educational data mining and learning analytics: an updated survey. WIREs: Data Min. Knowl. Discov. **10**(3), e1355 (2020). https://doi.org/10.1002/widm.1355
4. Salal, Y.K., Abdullaev, S.M., Kumar, M.: Educational data mining: student performance prediction in academic. Int. J. Eng. Adv. Technol. **8**(4C), 54–59 (2019)
5. Jasser, J., Ming, H., Zohdy, M.A.: Situation-awareness in action: an intelligent online learning platform (IOLP). In: Kurosu, M. (ed.) HCI 2017. LNCS, vol. 10272, pp. 319–330. Springer, Cham (2017). https://doi.org/10.1007/978-3-319-58077-7_25
6. Nagesh, A.S., Satyamurty, C.V.: Application of clustering algorithm for analysis of student academic performance. Int. J. Comput. Sci. Eng. **6**(1), 381–384 (2018)
7. Hossain, M.Z., Akhtar, M.N., Ahmad, R.B., Rahman, M.: A dynamic K-means clustering for data mining. IJEECS **13**(2), 521–526 (2019). https://doi.org/10.11591/ijeecs.v13.i2.pp5 21-526
8. Fortuna, F., Maturo, F.: K-means clustering of item characteristic curves and item information curves via functional principal component analysis. Qual. Quant. **53**(5), 2291–2304 (2018). https://doi.org/10.1007/s11135-018-0724-7
9. Xing, W.: Exploring the influences of MOOC design features on student performance and persistence. Distance Educ. **40**(1), 98–113 (2019)
10. Omar, T., Alzahrani, A., Zohdy, M.: Clustering approach for analyzing the student's efficiency and performance based on data. J. Data Anal. Inf. Process. **8**(3), 171 (2020). https://doi.org/10.4236/jdaip.2020.83010
11. Marutho, D., Handaka, S.H., Wijaya, E.: The determination of cluster number at k-mean using elbow method and purity evaluation on headline news. In: 2018 International Seminar on Application for Technology of Information and Communication, pp. 533–538. IEEE Press, New York (2018). https://doi.org/10.1109/ISEMANTIC.2018.8549751
12. Syakur, M.A., Khotimah, B.K., Rochman, E.M.S., Satoto, B.D.: Integration k-means clustering method and elbow method for identification of the best customer profile cluster. In IOP Conference Series: Materials Science and Engineering, vol. 336, no. (1), p. 012017. IOP Publishing (2018)
13. Yuan, C., Yang, H.: Research on K-value selection method of K-means clustering algorithm. J-Multi. Sci. J. **2**(2), 226–235 (2019). https://doi.org/10.3390/j2020016
14. Dinh, D.-T., Fujinami, T., Huynh, V.-N.: Estimating the optimal number of clusters in categorical data clustering by Silhouette coefficient. In: Chen, J., Huynh, V.N., Nguyen, G.-N., Tang, X. (eds.) KSS 2019. CCIS, vol. 1103, pp. 1–17. Springer, Singapore (2019). https://doi.org/10.1007/978-981-15-1209-4_1
15. El-Bishouty, M.M., et al.: Use of Felder and Silverman learning style model for online course design. Educ. Tech. Res. Dev. **67**(1), 161–177 (2019). https://doi.org/10.1007/s11423-018-9634-6
16. Nja, C.O., Umali, C.U.B., Asuquo, E.E., Orim, R.E.: The influence of learning styles on academic performance among science education undergraduates at the University of Calabar. Educ. Res. Rev. **14**(17), 618–624 (2019). https://doi.org/10.5897/ERR2019.3806

17. Ho, S.-B., Teh, S.-K., Chan, G.-Y., Chai, I., Tan, C.-H.: Sequential and global learning styles as pathways to improve learning in programming. In: Alfred, R., Iida, H., Ag. Ibrahim, A.A., Lim, Y. (eds.) ICCST 2017. LNEE, vol. 488, pp. 1–10. Springer, Singapore (2018). https://doi.org/10.1007/978-981-10-8276-4_1

18. Qoiriah, A., Harimurti, R., Nurhidayat, A.I.: Application of K-Means algorithm for clustering student's computer programming performance in automatic programming assessment tool. In International Joint Conference on Science and Engineering (IJCSE 2020), pp. 421–425. Atlantis Press (2020). https://doi.org/10.2991/aer.k.201124.075

A Novel Perspective of Text Classification by Prolog-Based Deductive Databases

Kiet Van Nguyen[1,2]([⊠]), Tin Van Huynh[1,2], and Anh Gia-Tuan Nguyen[1,2]

[1] University of Information Technology, Ho Chi Minh City, Vietnam
{kietnv,tinhv,anhngt}@uit.edu.vn
[2] Vietnam National University, Ho Chi Minh City, Vietnam

Abstract. Natural language processing has been studied extensively worldwide and has been implemented into various applications, including text classification. Especially, the significant development of social networking platforms has led to a considerable increase in data. Thus, it becomes the fertile data domain to carry out a series of studies on text classification. Various studies on this task are conducted in many languages but still have many limitations with Vietnamese. This is why we aim to do this study to classify Vietnamese texts from two Vietnamese benchmark datasets. Despite many studies on machine learning models in this study, any research work using facts and rules in a deductive database to classify Vietnamese text classification has not been studied. In particular, we design a system architecture based on facts and rules in a deductive database for text classification in Vietnamese. Our experiments show our results are positive on two Vietnamese datasets. The best performances from the experiments achieve 93.18% of F1-score for the UIT-ViNames dataset, 76.79% and 69.96% for the sentiment detection and the topic classification on the UIT-VSFC dataset, respectively. Although the experimental results are not better than the previous studies, these results are the premise for developing solutions for natural language processing problems on the deductive database, a successful pilot in implementing text classification on the Prolog-based deductive database.

Keywords: Text classification · Sentiment analysis · Deductive database · Prolog

1 Introduction

Text classification is a well-known topic of natural language processing or computational linguistics, which has currently attracted numerous study efforts from the research community. The automated text classification task is categorized as supervised learning task, including sentiment analysis [2,11,30], emotion textual classification [6,13], hate speech detection [14,27]. For sentiment analysis, there are several state-of-the-art approaches such as deep learning and transfer learning-based models. However, there are few researches related to rule-based

© Springer Nature Switzerland AG 2021
H. Fujita et al. (Eds.): IEA/AIE 2021, LNAI 12799, pp. 138–148, 2021.
https://doi.org/10.1007/978-3-030-79463-7_12

approaches, and Prolog-based deductive database [10,32]. Although there are few Vietnamese studies [18] on Prolog, there are no studies for text classification in Vietnamese. In this paper, we aim to conduct experiments based on the rule-based approach using the Prolog-based deductive database. Or otherwise, we aim to answer the question: Does the Prolog-based deductive database approach achieve positive results on the text-classification datasets?

In this paper, we introduce a novel approach based on the Prolog-based deductive database for classifying Vietnamese texts automatically. In our experiments, we implement this approach on two types datasets: UIT-VSFC [29] for classifying students' feedback and UIT-ViNames [25] for detecting name's gender. In particular, we have three main contributions described as follows.

- We propose a new Prolog-based deductive database system to predict the category of Vietnamese texts. In particular, we design the facts and rules that are suitable for the Vietnamese text-classification problems.
- We achieve positive results with F1-score of 76.79% and 69.96% for sentiment and topic on UIT-VSFC, respectively. In addition, we also obtain a better performance of 93.18% in F1-score on the UIT-ViNames dataset.

The content of the paper is structured as follows. Section 2 presents background and related work. Section 3 describes our datasets that we use for conducting experiments. Section 4 presents the text-classification approach based on the deductive database with designing facts and rules. Section 5 describes our experiments on the Vietnamese datasets and the performance comparison. Finally, Sect. 6 draws conclusions and gives future directions.

2 Background and Related Work

2.1 Deductive Databases and Prolog

Deductive Database (DDBs) [3] is a database system with a deductive approach based on facts and rules through a declarative language - an artificial language in which these systems determine what to obtain rather than how to achieve it. The deduction mechanism of this system can deduce new facts from the database by interpreting these rules. The architecture used for deductive databases is closely related to the relational data architecture, particularly to the domain relational calculus formalism. This system is also associated with the logic programming language as Prolog. The deductive database work based on logic has been implemented on the Prolog tool. Datalog is a variant of Prolog to define facts and rules declaratively in conjunction with a set of relations. Although the language structure of Datalog is similar to that of Prolog, its operational semantics executed is still different.

A deductive database program consists of two main components: facts and rules. Facts are described as how relations are specified, except that it is unnecessary to comprise the attribute names. A tuple in a relation presents a real-world fact whose meaning is partly defined by the attribute names. A deductive database determines the meaning of an attribute value in a tuple based on its position within the tuple. Rules that are similar to relational facts present virtual relations that are not stored but can be determined by applying deductive mechanisms based on the rule designations. The primary difference between rules and facts is that rules may involve recursion and hence generate virtual relations that cannot be defined in terms of basic relational facts.

2.2   Text Classification

The strong development of the Internet in the world has generated a vast volume of data. In particular, the growth of social media continuously creates a huge amount of texts which are valuable sources to exploit and analyze in revolution 4.0. With great potential, text classification has attracted much attention from scientists in the natural language processing or computational linguistics. In English, there is a range of text-classification publications in many problems. However, relatively few papers have been conducted on Vietnamese text because Vietnamese is a low-resource language. There are different methods for text classification consisting of rule-based [1,15], traditional machine learning-based [5,9], neural network-based [8,12,20,23,28,31] and transfer learning-based [4,33]. In recent years, neural network-based models have attracted large attention from scientists in the works. However, in this paper, we aim to evaluate the novel perspective of Vietnamese text classification by the Prolog-based deductive database. In particular, we propose a new framework based on Prolog for text classification.

In Vietnam, there have been several studies efforts for text classification tasks [7,19,21,26,29], as well as contributing Vietnamese data for the research community. In particular, there are some contributions to benchmark datasets (UIT-VSFC [29], VLSP-ABSA [19], UIT-VSMEC [6], UIT-ViNames [25]) and methods [7,22,27]. In this paper, we focus on conducting experiments on the two benchmark datasets: UIT-VSFC [29] and UIT-ViNames [25]. On the UIT-VSFC dataset, Nguyen et al. [7] gained the highest result by the BiLSTM model with 92.79% on sentiment and 89.70% on the topic label. With the UIT-ViNames dataset, To et al. [25] gained the highest result by the BiLSTM model with 95.89%. However, so far, there has not been any Prolog-based deductive database evaluation for the two datasets. However, we aim to conduct experiments based on the rule-based approach using the Prolog-based deductive database. Or otherwise, we want to answer the question: Does the Prolog-based deductive database approach achieve positive results on the Vietnamese text-classification datasets?

3   Datasets

In our experiments, we implement deductive database based on facts and rules in deductive database into benchmark text-classification datasets such as UIT-ViNames [25] and UIT-VSFC [29].

3.1   The UIT-ViNames Dataset

The first dataset that we use in our experiments is UIT-ViNames. This dataset was proposed by To et al. [25]. There are 26,852 Vietnamese full names in this dataset, which are annotated with 1 for male and 0 for female. They gathered name information of students from a number of Vietnamese universities. In particular, this dataset has become diverse of name thanks to the students of these universities from many different provinces in Vietnam with a variety of naming cultures for people. Furthermore, To avoid revealing any personal information of students, the data only includes the students' names and genders. UIT-ViNames contains 26,850 samples with a widely even distribution of the two genders. Males account for 57.71% of the dataset, while females occupy 42.29%.

3.2   The UIT-VSFC Dataset

Besides, UIT-VSFC (Vietnamese Students' Feedback Corpus for Sentiment Analysis) [29] is also used in this study. This dataset was constructed from students' feedback from a university for the text classification task. This dataset consists of 16,175 items with two classification parts that are important: sentiments and topics. For the sentiment, each student's feedback is labeled by three emotional labels: Positive, Negative, and Neutral. Meanwhile, with the topic part, the feedback is annotated by four labels: Curriculums, Lecturers, Facilities, and Others. Specifically, while positive and negative labels share a similarly high percentage with over 45%, a neutral label accounts for a small portion in the dataset with only approximately 5%. Moreover, there is an imbalance in the topic part data in the UIT-VSFC dataset. It is statistically shown that student feedback is mostly concerned with two Lecturer and Curriculum aspects. Specifically, more than 90% belong to these two labels, while both Facility and Others only make up nearly 10%.

4   Text Classification Models Based on Deductive Databases

In this section, we introduce a new approach based on the Prolog-based deductive database for text classification in Vietnamese (Fig. 1).

4.1   Overview of Our Proposed Architecture

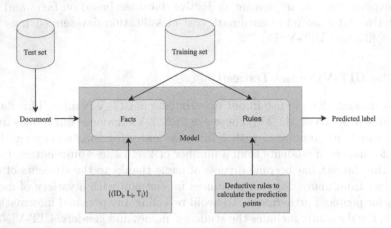

Fig. 1. The overview architecture of text classification based on the deductive database.

4.2   Design of Facts

First of all, we find an approach to represent data as facts. In particular, we represent annotated texts (T) (sentences or comments) that have a unique ID, along with their labels (L) as $\{ID_i, T_i, L_i\}$, for each text (T) there will be a unique ID. Table 1 presents several facts of the two datasets. Besides, we conduct some pre-processing steps on that texts as follows: Each text will be split into single words by spaces, and then these single words will be converted to lists corresponding to each text.

Table 1. Designed facts for the two text-classification tasks in Vietnamese.

Dataset	Text	Label
UIT-VSFC	Giảng viên hướng dẫn tận tình và chu đáo. (The lecturer is enthusiastic and thoughtful.) **Fact: text(1, pos, [giảng, viên, hướng, dẫn, tận, tình, và, chu, đáo]).**	Positive
	Nội dung môn học chưa đúng với đề cương. (Course contents are incompatible with the syllabus.) **Fact: text(2, neg, [nội, dung, môn, học, chưa, đúng, với, đề, cương]).**	Negative
	Em không có bất cứ một lời phê bình nào. (I have no comments.) **Fact: text(3, neu, [em, không, có, bất, cứ, một, lời, phê, bình, nào]).**	Neutral
UIT-ViNames	Võ Minh Đủ (Vo Minh Du) **Fact: text(1, male, [võ, minh, đủ]).**	Male
	Nguyễn Thị Hiền (Nguyen Thi Hien) **Fact: text(2, female, [nguyễn, thị, hiền]).**	Female

4.3   Design of Rules

Our selected algorithm is Naive Bayes to conduct experiments in this paper. Because this algorithm is really suitable for designing deductive rules. This algorithm is very successful in previous works [17,24]. Based on the design of facts, we design rules to calculate the prediction points for text classification. Table 2 shows our designed rules for Vietnamese text classification.

Table 2. Designed rules for text classification in Vietnamese.

No.	Rules	Explanation
1	condition_probability (DataPoint, Label, PL)	This rule generates a list PL of conditional probabilities of each attribute-value pair in DataPoint, given Label
2	class_probability(Label, LP)	This rule calculates the probability of Label which is a percentage of samples in Label in the whole dataset
3	probabilities(DataPoint, LP)	This rule generates likelihoods of DataPoint belonging to each class
4	multiples(LP, P)	This rule multiplies the probabilities in LP
5	maximum(PL, C)	This rule finds the class attached the highest probability from the list of class probabilities
6	predict(Text, Label)	This rule predicts the Label of Text

```
%Prolog-based rules using Naive Bayes for Vietnamese text classification.

%Input: texts, and output: C including a predicted class and its probability.
predict(Text, C) :- probabilities(Text, W), maximum(W, C).

probabilities(X, W) :- setof(Class, N^E^text(N, Class, E), Cs), findall(Class/P, (member(Class, Cs),
    condition_probability(X, Class, PL), class_probability(Class, CP), multiple(PL, PS), P is PS*CP), W).

maximum([E], E) :- !.
maximum([E/M|T], Y/N) :- maximum(T, Z/K), (M>K, Y/N=E/M; Y/N=Z/K), !.

multiple([], 1) :- !.
multiple([_/P|L], Ps) :- multiple(L, Px), Ps is Px*P.

condition_probability([], _, []).
condition_probability([AV|L], Class, [AV/P|PL]) :- findall(ID, text(ID, Class, _), All), length(All, N),
findall(ID, (text(ID, Class, AVL), member(AV, AVL)), W), length(W, M), P is M/N, condition_probability(L, Class, PL).

class_probability(Class, CP) :- findall(ID, text(ID, _, _), All), length(All, N), findall(ID, text(ID , Class, _), W),
    length(W, M), CP is M/N.

%Prolog-based facts represent data

text(1, 1, [võ, minh, dủ]).
text(2, 0, [nguyễn, thị, hiền]).
text(3, 1, [võ, thanh, minh]).
...
```

Fig. 2. An simple program of text classification based on facts and rules of deductive database.

4.4   An Simple Program Example of Text Classification

We design a general Prolog-based deductive database framework for any text-classification dataset. In particular, it is really easy to adapt a new dataset by only re-defining facts. Figure 2 shows the simple text classification program based on facts and rules of the deductive database.

5   Experiments

5.1   Experimental Settings

In our experiments, we set up facts and rules on SWI-Prolog[1]. For UIT-ViNames, the framework consists of only 8 computing rules and 18,795 facts for the training set, 2,686 facts for the development set, and 5,370 facts for the test set. For UIT-VSFC, the framework uses the same number of rules as UIT-ViNames and comprises 11,426 facts for the training set, 1,538 facts for the development set, and 3,166 facts for the test set.

In order to compare previous works, we follow metrics used in previous work [7, 25] to evaluate our proposed system.

5.2   Experimental Results and Discussion

We achieve the positive results on the two datasets. We report the final performances of our proposed system on the two datasets in Table 3 and Table 4. On the development set, our system reaches the F1-score of 78.65% for the sentiment task and 71.76% for the topic task on the UIT-VFSC dataset and the F1-score of 93.28% on UIT-Names. On the test set, our system achieves the F1-score of 76.79% for the sentiment task and 69.96% for the topic task on the UIT-VFSC dataset and the F1-score of 93.18% on UIT-Names.

Table 3. Experimental results on the UIT-VSFC dataset.

	Development set	Test set
Sentiment detection task	78.65	76.79
Topic detection task	71.76	69.96

Table 4. Experimental results on the UIT-ViNames dataset.

Dataset	Development set	Test set
UIT-ViNames	93.28	93.18

---

[1] https://www.swi-prolog.org/.

Table 5. Performance comparison on the test sets of UIT-VSFC and UIT-ViNames with the previous work.

Dataset		Our system	Best performance
UIT-VSFC	Sentiment	76.79	92.79 [7]
	Topic	69.96	89.70 [7]
UIT-ViNames		93.18	95.89 [25]

Comparison with the previous work [7,25], although our results are lower than the best results on these two datasets, we come up with the first design for the text classification in Vietnamese based on the Prolog-based deductive database. Table 5 presents a performance comparison on the two datasets with the previous work. The UIT-ViNames dataset is more simple than the UIT-VFSC dataset. In addition, Huynh et al. [7] and To et al. [25] use powerful and complex methods based on deep learning and ensemble techniques. The performance difference between our system and the previous best-performance method is relatively small on the UIT-ViNames, whereas our experimental results on UIT-VSFC are lower significantly than that of the previous best-performance method. However, the design of our proposed system is more simple than that of the previous systems.

6 Conclusion and Future Work

In this paper, we presented a novel Prolog-based deductive database approach for the text classification task in Vietnamese. Our experiments were conducted on the two Vietnamese benchmark datasets: UIT-VSFC and UIT-ViNames. Before conducting our experiments, we designed facts and rules to be suitable for the Vietnamese text-classification datasets. Although the experimental results were not better than the previous studies, these results are the premise for developing solutions for natural language processing tasks on the Prolog-based deductive database. In addition, we found that our system performed well on shorter texts (on the UIT-ViNames dataset) rather than long and complex texts (on the UIT-VSFC dataset).

In future work, motivated by the previous work [16], we try to improve performances of our proposed system by implementing constraints on facts and rules. Or, complex machine learning methods like deep neural network-based learning or BERT-based transfer learning can be explored on Prolog. With this design of these rules and facts, it is simple but effective to adapt on many textual classification datasets on various languages such as English, Chinese or other low-resource languages.

References

1. Abdallah, S., Shaalan, K., Shoaib, M.: Integrating rule-based system with classification for Arabic named entity recognition. In: Gelbukh, A. (ed.) CICLing 2012. LNCS, vol. 7181, pp. 311–322. Springer, Heidelberg (2012). https://doi.org/10.1007/978-3-642-28604-9_26
2. Agarwal, A., Xie, B., Vovsha, I., Rambow, O., Passonneau, R.J.: Sentiment analysis of Twitter data. In: Proceedings of the Workshop on Language in Social Media (LSM 2011), pp. 30–38 (2011)
3. Gallaire, H., Minker, J., Nicolas, J.M.: Logic and databases: a deductive approach. Read. Artif. Intell. Databases. 231–247 (1989)
4. Garg, S., Ramakrishnan, G.: BAE: BERT-based adversarial examples for text classification. In: Proceedings of the 2020 Conference on Empirical Methods in Natural Language Processing (EMNLP), pp. 6174–6181. Association for Computational Linguistics, November 2020. https://doi.org/10.18653/v1/2020.emnlp-main.498, https://www.aclweb.org/anthology/2020.emnlp-main.498
5. Hartmann, J., Huppertz, J., Schamp, C., Heitmann, M.: Comparing automated text classification methods. Int. J. Res. Market. **36**(1), 20–38 (2019)
6. Ho, V.A., et al.: Emotion recognition for Vietnamese social media text. arXiv preprint arXiv:1911.09339 (2019)
7. Huynh, H.D., Do, H.T.T., Van Nguyen, K., Nguyen, N.L.T.: A simple and efficient ensemble classifier combining multiple neural network models on social media datasets in Vietnamese. arXiv preprint arXiv:2009.13060 (2020)
8. Jacovi, A., Sar Shalom, O., Goldberg, Y.: Understanding convolutional neural networks for text classification. In: Proceedings of the 2018 EMNLP Workshop BlackboxNLP: Analyzing and Interpreting Neural Networks for NLP, pp. 56–65. Association for Computational Linguistics, Brussels, November 2018. https://doi.org/10.18653/v1/W18-5408, https://www.aclweb.org/anthology/W18-5408
9. Joachims, T.: Text categorization with support vector machines: learning with many relevant features. In: Nédellec, C., Rouveirol, C. (eds.) ECML 1998. LNCS, vol. 1398, pp. 137–142. Springer, Heidelberg (1998). https://doi.org/10.1007/BFb0026683
10. Julián-Iranzo, P., Sáenz-Pérez, F.: A fuzzy datalog deductive database system. IEEE Trans. Fuzzy Syst. **26**(5), 2634–2648 (2018)
11. Kenyon-Dean, K., et al.: Sentiment analysis: it's complicated! In: Proceedings of the 2018 Conference of the North American Chapter of the Association for Computational Linguistics: Human Language Technologies, vol. 1 (Long Papers), pp. 1886–1895 (2018)
12. Lai, S., Xu, L., Liu, K., Zhao, J.: Recurrent convolutional neural networks for text classification. In: Proceedings of the AAAI Conference on Artificial Intelligence, vol. 29 (2015)
13. Li, W., Xu, H.: Text-based emotion classification using emotion cause extraction. Expert Syst. Appl. **41**(4), 1742–1749 (2014)
14. MacAvaney, S., Yao, H.R., Yang, E., Russell, K., Goharian, N., Frieder, O.: Hate speech detection: challenges and solutions. PLoS ONE **14**(8), e0221152 (2019)
15. Madabushi, H.T., Lee, M.: High accuracy rule-based question classification using question syntax and semantics. In: Proceedings of COLING 2016, the 26th International Conference on Computational Linguistics: Technical Papers, pp. 1220–1230 (2016)

16. Morawietz, F.: Chart parsing and constraint programming. In: COLING 2000 Volume 1: The 18th International Conference on Computational Linguistics (2000)
17. Narayanan, V., Arora, I., Bhatia, A.: Fast and accurate sentiment classification using an enhanced Naive Bayes model. In: Yin, H., Tang, K., Gao, Y., Klawonn, F., Lee, M., Weise, T., Li, B., Yao, X. (eds.) IDEAL 2013. LNCS, vol. 8206, pp. 194–201. Springer, Heidelberg (2013). https://doi.org/10.1007/978-3-642-41278-3_24
18. Nguyen, D.T., Van Nguyen, K., Pham, T.T.: Implementing a subcategorized probabilistic definite clause grammar for Vietnamese sentence parsing. Int. J. Nat. Lang. Comput. **2**(4), 27 (2013)
19. Nguyen, H.T., et al.: VLSP shared task: sentiment analysis. J. Comput. Sci. Cybern. **34**(4), 295–310 (2018)
20. Nguyen, L.T., Nguyen, K.V., Nguyen, N.L.T.: Constructive and toxic speech detection for open-domain social media comments in Vietnamese. arXiv preprint arXiv:2103.10069 (2021)
21. Nguyen, P.X., Hong, T.T., Van Nguyen, K., Nguyen, N.L.T.: Deep learning versus traditional classifiers on Vietnamese students' feedback corpus. In: 2018 5th NAFOSTED Conference on Information and Computer Science (NICS), pp. 75–80. IEEE (2018)
22. Nguyen, Q.T., Nguyen, T.L., Luong, N.H., Ngo, Q.H.: Fine-tuning BERT for sentiment analysis of Vietnamese reviews (2020)
23. Nguyen, V.D., Van Nguyen, K., Nguyen, N.L.T.: Variants of long short-term memory for sentiment analysis on Vietnamese students' feedback corpus. In: 2018 10th International Conference on Knowledge and Systems Engineering (KSE), pp. 306–311. IEEE (2018)
24. Schneider, K.-M.: Techniques for improving the performance of Naive Bayes for text classification. In: Gelbukh, A. (ed.) CICLing 2005. LNCS, vol. 3406, pp. 682–693. Springer, Heidelberg (2005). https://doi.org/10.1007/978-3-540-30586-6_76
25. To, H.Q., Nguyen, K.V., Nguyen, N.L.T., Nguyen, A.G.T.: Gender prediction based on Vietnamese names with machine learning techniques (2020)
26. Tran, T.K., Phan, T.T.: Capturing contextual factors in sentiment classification: an ensemble approach. IEEE Access **8**, 116856–116865 (2020). https://doi.org/10.1109/ACCESS.2020.3004180
27. Van Huynh, T., Nguyen, V.D., Van Nguyen, K., Nguyen, N.L.T., Nguyen, A.G.T.: Hate speech detection on Vietnamese social media text using the bi-GRU-LSTM-CNN model. arXiv preprint arXiv:1911.03644 (2019)
28. Van Huynh, T., Van Nguyen, K., Nguyen, N.L.T., Nguyen, A.G.T.: Job prediction: from deep neural network models to applications. In: 2020 RIVF International Conference on Computing and Communication Technologies (RIVF), pp. 1–6. IEEE (2020)
29. Van Nguyen, K., Nguyen, V.D., Nguyen, P.X., Truong, T.T., Nguyen, N.L.T.: UIT-VSFC: Vietnamese students' feedback corpus for sentiment analysis. In: 2018 10th International Conference on Knowledge and Systems (KSE), pp. 19–24. IEEE (2018)
30. van Thin, D., Nguyen, V.D., van Nguyen, K., Nguyen, N.L.T.: A transformation method for aspect-based sentiment analysis. J. Comput. Sci. Cybern. **34**(4), 323–333 (2018)
31. Wang, J.H., Liu, T.W., Luo, X., Wang, L.: An LSTM approach to short text sentiment classification with word embeddings. In: Proceedings of the 30th Conference on Computational Linguistics and Speech Processing (ROCLING 2018), pp. 214–223 (2018)

32. Williams, M.H., et al.: Prolog and deductive databases. Knowl.-Based Syst. **1**(3), 188–192 (1988)
33. Yu, S., Su, J., Luo, D.: Improving BERT-based text classification with auxiliary sentence and domain knowledge. IEEE Access **7**, 176600–176612 (2019)

Improving Human Emotion Recognition from Emotive Videos Using Geometric Data Augmentation

Nusrat J. Shoumy[1]([⊠]), Li-Minn Ang[2], D. M. Motiur Rahaman[1], Tanveer Zia[1], Kah Phooi Seng[3], and Sabira Khatun[4]

[1] School of Computing and Mathematics, Charles Sturt University, Wagga, NSW, Australia
nshoumy@csu.edu.au
[2] School of Science and Engineering, University of the Sunshine Coast, Sippy Downs, QLD, Australia
[3] School of Engineering and IT, University of New South Wales, Canberra, Australia
[4] Faculty of Electrical and Electronics Engineering, Universiti Malaysia Pahang, Pekan, Pahang, Malaysia

Abstract. Emotional recognition from videos or images requires large amount of data to obtain high performance and classification accuracy. However, large datasets are not always easily available. A good solution to this problem is to augment the data and extrapolate it to create a bigger dataset for training the classifier. In this paper, we evaluate the impact of different geometric data augmentation (GDA) techniques on emotion recognition accuracy using facial image data. The GDA techniques that were implemented were horizontal reflection, cropping, rotation separately and combined. In addition to this, our system was further evaluated with four different classifiers (Convolutional Neural Network (CNN), Linear Discriminant Analysis (LDA), K-Nearest Neighbor (kNN) and Decision Tree (DT)) to determine which of the four classifiers achieves the best results. In the proposed system, we used augmented data from a dataset (SAVEE) to perform training, and testing was carried out by the original data. A combination of GDA techniques using the CNN classifier was found to give the best performance of approximately 97.8%. Our system with GDA augmentation was shown to outperform previous approaches where only the original dataset was used for classifier training.

Keywords: Multimodal data · Emotion recognition · Data augmentation · Data classification · Neural network

1 Introduction

Affective computing is a field that allows a new form of human computer interaction that enables computers to recognize, feel, understand and interpret human emotions. It is an emerging multidisciplinary research field that is increasingly drawing the attention of researchers and practitioners in various fields [1]. Research in affective computing

© Springer Nature Switzerland AG 2021
H. Fujita et al. (Eds.): IEA/AIE 2021, LNAI 12799, pp. 149–161, 2021.
https://doi.org/10.1007/978-3-030-79463-7_13

covers many fields, where one major area for development is emotion recognition. Emotion recognition is the ability to identify other peoples' feelings continuously for each moment within a time duration and understand the connection between his/her feelings and related expressions. It is a challenging task for experts from various research fields, such as psychology, physiology and computer science [2]. Ekman [3] proposed a model stating that humans have the ability to identify six basic universal emotions which are sadness, happiness, anger, fear, disgust and surprise. Emotions can also be expressed in terms of one or more dimensions by relating them to the intensity levels of emotions [4]. A theory proposed by Mehrabian and Russell [5, 6] stated that all emotions can be represented by three dimensions: pleasure, arousal and dominance. In their proposed work, authors, Mehrabian and Russell, intended to classify the emotions captured through the video data into discrete emotion categories (Ekman model). The emotion recognition researches are mainly divided into two areas: (i) Single modality for emotion classification, such as facial expressions in images or video, or speech or electroencephalogram (EEG) signals; and (ii) multi-modal emotion classification models by combining different emotion modalities. Single modality data (videos) is adopted for the proposed work in this paper, whereas multimodal systems are left for future works.

One of the major limitations faced by any recognition system is the lack of data for training the classifier. When large datasets are used for training, then, during testing, the more likely it is that there will be a closely matched training example. Therefore, the performance accuracy is likely to rise when there are more training data. However, there are insufficient data in many of the currently available datasets. One way to overcome this problem is to augment the data to increase the number of data samples. There are many ways to augment data. One such way is data warping augmentations. Data warping augmentations works in a way such that existing images are transformed but their label is preserved. This includes augmentation techniques like geometric and color transformation, random erasing, adversarial training, etc. Additionally, data augmentation also overcomes the system over-fitting problems [7]. In our proposed emotion recognition system, new data augmentation phases are employed to tackle the problems caused by lack of data for classifier training.

An essential part of the emotion recognition system is the classification of data. State-of-Art classifiers include neural networks (NN), naïve-bayes (NB), LDA, support vector machine (SVM), fuzzy logic, DT and genetic algorithm [8]. In the field of emotion recognition in images, CNN has particularly produced exceptional performance in terms of performance accuracy [9], while classifiers such as NB [10], LDA [11] and DT [12] has also shown great promise. For this experiment, four different classifiers (CNN, LDA, kNN and DT) were used separately for image classification to compare the performance accuracy.

In this paper, we aim to evaluate and compare the effect of different well-established GDA techniques and classifiers on performance accuracy of an emotion recognition model. This was performed in three phases: data augmentation, feature extraction and finally, classification. The experiments were carried out on the publicly available and well-established Surrey Audio-Visual Expressed Emotion (SAVEE) dataset in order to recognize the six basic expressions along with a neutral state.

The rest of this paper is organized as follows. Section 2 presents related literature review and previous related works. The proposed approaches are discussed in Sect. 3. This is followed by results and analysis along with their comparison in Sect. 4, and finally conclusion for the proposed works with future directions in Sect. 5.

2 Related Work

In this section, related works on video/images emotion analysis and augmented emotion data are discussed. Table 1 shows an overview of the researches discussed in this section.

2.1 Emotion Recognition in Video/Images

Different classifiers including CNN, SVM, deep neural network (DNN) and others have been used in recent approaches in the area of emotion recognition. These classifiers can learn multiple levels of representation and abstraction that allow algorithms to discover complex data patterns.

A research work by Wang et al. [13] focused on micro-expression recognition and used the ORL, Yale, YaleB facial databases and Chinese Academy of Sciences Micro-Expression (CASME) databases to detect five types of micro-expressions (attention, disgust, repression, surprise and tense). The extreme learning machine (ELM) and kNN were used as classifiers with maximum accuracy of approximately 45% on the CASME dataset.

Chen et al. [14] proposed audio and video emotion analysis for the Cohn-Kanade (CK+, GEMEP-FERA 2011 dataset and Acted Facial Expression in Wild (AFEW) 4.0 dataset. The SVM was used to classify the emotions into seven basic emotions to obtain an accuracy of 89.6%.

Xu et al. [15] proposed a method for video emotion recognition using the YouTube emotion (YT) dataset, VideoStory-P14 and YF-E6 datasets. The videos were classified into eight emotions (anger, anticipation, disgust, fear, joy, sadness, surprise and trust) using SVM and CNN. The highest achieved performance accuracy was 56.3% with YT dataset.

Recent research work by Zhu et al. [16] proposed a depression diagnosis method using DNN for classification. This paper used the AVEC2013 and AVEC2014 databases in conjunction with deep convolutional neutral networks (DCNN) to classify emotions into different range of depression severity. The achievement of the system was computed through mean absolute error (MAE) and root mean square error (RMSE), where best performance achieved was 7.47 and 9.55 respectively.

A current paper by Kaya et al. [17] proposed a video-based emotion recognition using the Emotion Recognition in the Wild (EmotiW) 2015/2016 datasets with DCNN to obtain seven emotion classes (angry, disgust, fear, happy, neutral, sad and surprise) and achieved an accuracy of 52.11%.

In [18], Raheel et al. created an emotion recognition system to detect facial expression using EEG. The data for this experiment was acquired through participants who were asked to express their facial expressions while watching video clips and simultaneously, EEG data was recorded. Five facial expressions (smile, looking up, looking down, eye wink and eye blink) were classified using k-nearest neighbor (kNN), NB, SVM and multi-layer perceptron (MLP). The highest classification accuracy was achieved by kNN with 81.60%.

Zamil et al. [19], proposed an emotion detection model from speech signals using Berlin Database of Emotional Speech (Emo- DB) dataset and Ryerson Audio-Visual Database of Emotional Speech and Song (RAVDESS). Logistic Model Tree (LMT) classifier was used to categorize seven different emotions. This performance accuracy of this model was a maximum of 70%.

A recently published paper by Lingampeta et al. [20] proposed a system to classify and validate different human emotions from the speech signals. Five datasets (Emo-DB, SES, IEMOCAP, IITKGP-SEHSC, and IITKGP- SESC) were obtained for this experiment and LDA, KNN and SVM classifiers were used to classify the data into four emotion categories (anger, fear, happy and neutral). The SVM gave the best accuracy with 93.5% for the IITKGP-SEHSC dataset.

2.2 Data Augmentation in Emotion Recognition

Data augmentation methods are widely used because of the small size of publicly available datasets. Among the many data augmentation methods, GDA are the most widely used due to being less complex, having faster transformations and label preservation.

In a recent work by Ahmed et al. [21], rotation, shearing, zooming, horizontal flip, rescale was applied to the data collected from various datasets (CK and CK+, FER2013, MUG, KDEF & AKDEF, KinFaceW-I and II). CNN was used to classify the data into seven basic emotions, achieving performance accuracy of up to 96.24%.

Salama et al. [22] proposed multi-modal emotion recognition framework featuring EEG signals and facial videos using DEAP dataset. Here, a combination of data augmentation (noise signal addition, flipping, updating color and adjusting brightness) and ensemble learning techniques are applied together with data and score fusion methods. Then 3D-CNN and SVM classifiers are used to obtain model prediction accuracy. This system attains accuracies of 96.13% and 96.79% for valence and arousal respectively.

In [23], Cho et al. proposed a system to recognize stress level using videos of breathing pattern of the subjects. Thermal videos were captured for this specific experiment and a unidirectional sliding cropper with a square window was used augment the data. Using CNN as classifier performance accuracy reaches 84.59% accuracy in recognizing two levels of stress (no-stress, stress) and 56.52% in recognizing three levels of stress (none, low, high-level stress).

A research by [24] proposed recognition of six basic emotions using CNN. GDA techniques such as face detection, cropping, resize, adding noise and data normalization were applied to JAFFE, CK+ and MUG datasets and feature extraction was carried out. The system achieved up to 97.06% in terms of performance accuracy.

Finally, in a recent paper by Porcu et al. [2], emotion recognition in facial images were carried out on KDEF, CK+ and ExpW datasets. The dataset was augmented with horizontal reflection, translation, random rotation and generative adversarial network (GAN). CNN classifier was used with the highest achieved accuracy being 83.3%.

Table 1. Overview of literature review in emotion recognition and data augmentation.

Author	Dataset	Augmentation	Classifier	Performance accuracy (%)
Wang et al. [13]	ORL, Yale, YaleB, CASME	–	ELM, kNN	45
Chen et al. [14]	CK+, GEMEP-FERA 2011, AFEW 4.0	–	SVM	89.6
Xu et al. [15]	YT, VideoStory-P14, YF-E6	–	CNN, SVM	56.3
Zhu et al. [16]	AVEC2013, AVEC2014	–	DCNN	–
Kaya et al. [17]	EmotiW 2015/2016	–	DCNN	52.11
Raheel et al. [18]	Self-made	–	kNN, NB, SVM, MLP	81.60
Zamil et al. [19]	Emo-DB, RAVDESS	–	LMT	70
Lingampeta et al. [20]	Emo-DB, SES, IEMOCAP, IITKGP-SEHSC, and IITKGP-SESC	–	SVM	93.5
Ahmed et al. [21]	CK and CK+, FER2013, MUG, KDEF & AKDEF, KinFaceW-I and II	Rotation, shearing, zooming, horizontal flip, rescale	CNN	96.24
Salama et al. [22]	DEAP	Noise signal addition, flipping, updating color and adjusting brightness	3D-CNN, SVM	96.13 and 96.79 for valence and arousal respectively
Cho et al. [23]	Self-made	Unidirectional sliding cropper	CNN	84.59
Pitaloka et al. [24]	JAFFE, CK+, MUG	Cropping, resize, adding noise data normalization	CNN	97.06

(*continued*)

Table 1. (*continued*)

Author	Dataset	Augmentation	Classifier	Performance accuracy (%)
Porcu et al. [2]	KDEF, CK+, ExpW	Horizontal reflection, translation, random rotation, GAN	CNN	83.3

3 Proposed System

The main purpose of the proposed work is to investigate the effectiveness of data augmentation techniques in combination with different classifiers for emotion recognition in emotive videos. The overall framework of the proposed emotion recognition system is shown in Fig. 1. The rest of the section gives detailed explanation to each part of the proposed system.

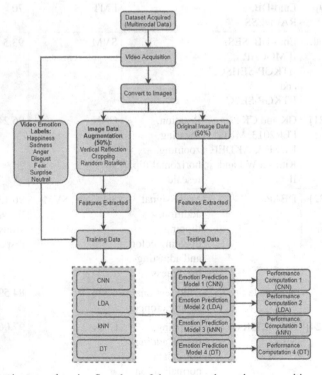

Fig. 1. A comprehensive flowchart of the proposed emotion recognition system.

3.1 Data Preprocessing

Firstly, a suitable dataset was selected, in our case, a multimodal dataset (SAVEE) was acquired. Details of this dataset are discussed in the next Sect. 4.1. The videos which contained human faces showing seven different emotions (happiness, sadness, surprise, fear, anger, disgust and neutral) were extracted from the dataset for further analysis. Since the videos that were obtained only contains human faces (single subject facing the camera), no other face detection operation was carried out separately. The videos were then converted to image frames as losslessly as possible for further processing using a simple video to image tool.

3.2 Geometric Data Augmentation

Next, 50% of the images from each of the seven different emotion categories were separated as training samples. Various augmentation techniques were implemented to increase these training images, which were: horizontal reflection (HR), rotation (R) and cropping (CR). These techniques are described in detail below:

- Horizontal reflection (HR): The HR technique generates a mirrored image from the original one along the vertical direction.
- Rotation (R): The image rotation technique causes the image to rotate between 90° to the left or right or to any specified degree. In this experiment, the image was rotated 14° to the right. The reason for using 14° was that rotating it any further made the important parts of the face go outside of the boundary box.
- Cropping (CR): The CR technique crops a section of the original image and resizes the cropped image to a specific resolution. The size of the cropped image should be large enough to contain a part of the face that is relevant. In this experiment, the cropped image size was 200 by 150 pixels.

Figure 2 shows a few examples of the GDA techniques that were applied in this paper along with their original data sample. These approaches seek to increase the size of the training set by generating new copies of the original images for the emotion model training process.

3.3 Facial Feature Extraction

The next step in the process was to extract the facial features using OpenFace, an open-source face recognition software that uses facial action units (AU) to track facial movements [25]. OpenFace implements state-of-the-art algorithms for facial behavior analysis, including facial landmark detection, head pose tracking, eye gaze and estimate of the facial AU. In this experiment, we focused on the use of facial landmarks to train the emotion recognition system. Sixty-eight facial landmarks which corresponds to the facial features (eyes, eyebrows, nose-tip [32], mouth and facial outline) were detected for each training image sample. An example of the 68 facial landmarks detected is shown in Fig. 3.

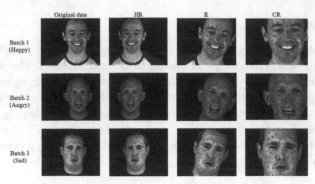

Fig. 2. Examples of GDA implemented images (HR: horizontal reflection, R: rotation, CR: cropped) for a few training samples (happy, angry, sad).

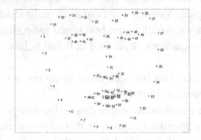

Fig. 3. Example of facial landmark position detected in OpenFace software [26].

In order to train the classifier to predict facial expressions, a function vector is first generated by:

$$\vec{F}_{i,j} = (f_1, f_2, f_3, \ldots, f_n), f = (x, y) \tag{1}$$

where i and j represents the i-th facial landmark set for the j-th training sample, n denotes the number of extracted landmarks (here, $n - 68$), and $= f(x, y)$ is the Cartesian coordinate for the landmark f [27].

3.4 Facial Expression Classification

The emotion labels associated with each video and the augmented images are used to train the different classifiers to create the prediction model for each classifier. Then, the proposed system is evaluated with four classifiers which are CNN, LDA, kNN and DT. Each classifier is briefly described below:

- CNN: Convolutional neural network or CNN is a machine learning algorithm for a system to understand the features of the training data with foresight and remember the features. This algorithm is then able to guess what is the class of the new image fed to the machine based on its training data.

- LDA: Linear Discriminant Analysis or LDA can be as a tool for classification, dimension reduction, and data visualization. For classification, LDA attempts to determine which variables (or their combinations) have the best discriminate boundary between two or more group [28].
- kNN: The k-nearest neighbors (kNN) or kNN is a supervised machine learning algorithm that can be used to solve both classification and regression problems. In classification problems, kNN works by finding the distances between a test sample and the training examples supplied, selecting the specified number examples (k) closest to the test sample, then votes for the most frequent class or label.
- DT: Decision trees or DT are non-parametric supervised learning method used for classification and regression. DT works by learning basic decision rules estimated from the data features of the training samples, then creates a model that predicts the value of a test sample.

The reason for these techniques being chosen was to use well-established, state-of-the-art methods so that we may compare our approaches in terms of the performance when data augmentation is implemented.

The emotion prediction models are then able to process the testing images and predict one of the seven human emotions (anger, sadness, surprise, happiness, disgust, fear or neutral). The aim of this experiment is to evaluate the effect of each GDA technique and classifier on the performance of the emotion prediction model, which is computed using 50% test images from the dataset that do not include any images used to train the model in order to carry out unbiased evaluation.

4 Experimental Results

In the first section, the database used is described. In the following sections, the experimental results for each GDA and classifier are compared.

4.1 Dataset

The experiments were performed using the publicly available dataset: Surrey Audio-Visual Expressed Emotion (SAVEE) dataset. The SAVEE dataset consists of recordings from four English male actors in seven different emotions (anger, sadness, surprise, happiness, disgust fear and neutral). The actors spoke a total of 480 English sentences (120 utterances per actor) with 15 sentences per emotion except for neutral which had 30 sentences. The sampling rate for audio was 44.1 kHz and 60 fps for video [29]. In this work, 1260 images were captured to be used from the SAVEE dataset, 180 images for each facial expression. The selected images were divided into two parts, which was 50% for training and 50% for testing.

4.2 GDA Comparison

The emotion recognition model evaluation process was performed by training the proposed system with augmented SAVEE image data and testing with the original image data from the dataset. The SAVEE dataset augmented images with the considered geometric augmentation techniques were as follows: (1) 180 images created with HR; (2) 180 images created with CR (200 by 150 pixels) of each image; (3) 180 images created with R (14° rotation to the right). The size of the training database was 540 images when using all 3 h, CR, and RR techniques. The GDA techniques were processed with CNN, LDA, kNN and DT classifiers to be categorized into specific emotion labels. The testing data which consisted of 50% of un-augmented, original data from the SAVEE dataset was input into the prediction models of the individual classifiers and the performance accuracy of each classifier was obtained.

Table 2 summarizes the values of the overall emotion recognition accuracy achieved considering different geometric augmentation techniques and classifiers. The best performance accuracy achieved with CNN classifier was a combination of HR, CR and R which was 97.8%, and when no GDA technique was applied an accuracy rate of 85.4% was achieved. HR technique produced little change compared to no GDA with an accuracy of 85.2%, while CR and R had a slightly decreased accuracy of 80.1% and 83.5% respectively. This decrease might have been caused by the reduction of facial data in the images when cropped or rotated. This trend is repeated for each classifier with best accuracy for LDA, kNN and DT being 92.8%, 90.9% and 89.2% respectively when a combination of the GDA techniques are used. In a paper by Nguyen et al. [30], SAVEE dataset was used on a PathNet-based transfer learning method. The best performance achieved by that paper was 93.75%. In another recently published paper, Avots et al. [31], an accuracy of 77.4% was obtained for SAVEE dataset when CNN was used for classification.

It can be seen that the approach combining all the augmented techniques outperforms the rest and CNN classifier achieved the best performance. By incorporating additional images and modalities to the training database, the performance is likely to increase, which would be the target for our future experiments.

Table 2. Emotion recognition accuracy achieved with the SAVEE dataset considering different augmentation techniques and classifiers.

Data augmentations	Performance accuracy			
	CNN (%)	LDA (%)	kNN (%)	DT (%)
No GDA	85.4	78.0	73.2	68.2
HR	85.2	77.8	73.0	68.0
CR	80.1	75.1	70.1	65.9
R	83.5	76.0	71.7	65.6
HR, CR and R	97.8	92.8	90.9	89.2

5 Conclusion

This paper has presented an emotion recognition model using GDA techniques to extrapolate the obtained dataset and evaluated with four well-known classifiers: CNN, LDA, KNN and DT. The results demonstrate that GDA transformations, specifically, combination of HR, CR and R, provide performance improvements up to 30% with respect to the case where DA is not used. It can be seen through this experiment that a large amount of data is required for more accurate emotion recognition in images and that in place of small datasets or small number of images, augmented images provide an alternative to make up for lack of data. However, the downside to data augmentation is that manipulating images causes data loss, and because of computational complexity, large quantities of images need extra processing time. The outcome of this experiment in this paper emphasizes the significance of training data for emotion recognition tasks and the effectiveness of the right GDA technique when large datasets are not available. Future works to be considered are the use of GAN on image datasets to create a synthetic novel dataset for emotion recognition system from facial images with better precision and accuracy. The use of audio and EEG modalities with GDA techniques will also be considered.

References

1. Kleinsmith, A., Bianchi-Berthouze, N.: Affective body expression perception and recognition: a survey. IEEE Trans. Affect. Comput. **4**, 15–33 (2013). https://doi.org/10.1109/T-AFFC.2012.16
2. Porcu, S., Floris, A., Atzori, L.: Evaluation of data augmentation techniques for facial expression recognition systems. Electronics **9**(11), 1892 (2020). https://doi.org/10.3390/electronics9111892
3. Ekman, P., Friesen, W.V.: Constants across cultures in the face and emotion. J. Pers. Soc. Psychol. **17**, 124–129 (1971). https://doi.org/10.1037/h0030377
4. Frijda, N.H., Mesquita, B.: The analysis of emotions. In: Mascolo, M.F., Griffin, S. (eds.) What Develops in Emotional Development?, pp. 273–295. Springer US, Boston (1998). https://doi.org/10.1007/978-1-4899-1939-7_11
5. Mehrabian, A.: Comparison of the PAD and PANAS as models for describing emotions and for differentiating anxiety from depression. J. Psychopathol. Behav. Assess. **19**, 331–357 (1997). https://doi.org/10.1007/BF02229025
6. Mehrabian, A.: Pleasure-arousal-dominance: a general framework for describing and measuring individual differences in temperament. Curr. Psychol. **14**, 261–292 (1996). https://doi.org/10.1007/BF02686918
7. Shorten, C., Khoshgoftaar, T.M.: A survey on image data augmentation for deep learning. J. Big Data **6**(1), 1–48 (2019). https://doi.org/10.1186/s40537-019-0197-0
8. Gavali, P., Banu, J.S.: Deep convolutional neural network for image classification on CUDA platform. In: Deep Learning and Parallel Computing Environment for Bioengineering Systems, pp. 99–122. Elsevier (2019). https://doi.org/10.1016/B978-0-12-816718-2.00013-0
9. Shoumy, N.J., Ang, L.M., Seng, K.P., Rahaman, D.M.M., Zia, T.: Multimodal big data affective analytics: a comprehensive survey using text, audio, visual and physiological signals. J. Netw. Comput. Appl. **149**, 1–24 (2020). https://doi.org/10.1016/j.jnca.2019.102447

10. Setchi, R., Asikhia, O.K.: Exploring user experience with image schemas, sentiments, and semantics. IEEE Trans. Affect. Comput. **10**(2), 182–195 (2019). https://doi.org/10.1109/TAFFC.2017.2705691

11. Bartlett, M.S., Littlewort, G., Frank, M., Lainscsek, C., Fasel, I., Movellan, J.: Recognizing facial expression: machine learning and application to spontaneous behavior. In: Proceedings of IEEE Computer Society Conference on Computer Vision and Pattern Recognition, vol. 2, pp. 568–573 (2005). https://doi.org/10.1109/CVPR.2005.297

12. Dapogny, A., Bailly, K., Dubuisson, S.: Dynamic pose-robust facial expression recognition by multi-view pairwise conditional random forests, vol. 3045, pp. 1–14 (2016). https://doi.org/10.1109/ICCV.2015.431

13. Wang, S.-J., Chen, H.-L., Yan, W.-J., Chen, Y.-H., Fu, X.: Face recognition and micro-expression recognition based on discriminant tensor subspace analysis plus extreme learning machine. Neural Process. Lett. **39**(1), 25–43 (2013). https://doi.org/10.1007/s11063-013-9288-7

14. Chen, J., Chen, Z., Chi, Z., Fu, H.: Facial expression recognition in video with multiple feature fusion. IEEE Trans. Affect. Comput. **3045**, 1 (2016). https://doi.org/10.1109/TAFFC.2016.2593719

15. Xu, B., Fu, Y., Jiang, Y.-G., Li, B., Sigal, L.: Heterogeneous knowledge transfer in video emotion recognition, attribution and summarization. IEEE Trans. Affect. Comput. **3045**, 1–13 (2015). https://doi.org/10.1109/TAFFC.2016.2622690

16. Zhu, Y., Shang, Y., Shao, Z., Guo, G.: Automated depression diagnosis based on deep networks to encode facial appearance and dynamics. IEEE Trans. Affect. Comput. **9**(4), 578–584 (2018). https://doi.org/10.1109/TAFFC.2017.2650899

17. Kaya, H., Gürpınar, F., Salah, A.A.: Video-based emotion recognition in the wild using deep transfer learning and score fusion. Image Vis. Comput. **65**, 66–75 (2017). https://doi.org/10.1016/j.imavis.2017.01.012

18. Raheel, A., Majid, M., Anwar, S.M.: Facial expression recognition based on electroencephalography. In: 2019 Proceedings of the 2nd International Conference on Computing, Mathematics and Engineering Technologies (iCoMET), pp. 1–5. IEEE (2019). https://doi.org/10.1109/ICOMET.2019.8673408

19. Zamil, A.A.A., Hasan, S., Jannatul Baki, S.M., Adam, J.M., Zaman, I.: Emotion detection from speech signals using voting mechanism on classified frames. In: Proceedings of the 1st International Conference on Robotics, Electrical and Signal Processing Techniques, ICREST 2019, pp. 281–285. IEEE (2019). https://doi.org/10.1109/ICREST.2019.8644168

20. Lingampeta, D., Yalamanchili, B.: Human emotion recognition using acoustic features with optimized feature selection and fusion techniques. In: Proceedings of the 5th International Conference on Inventive Computation Technologies, ICICT 2020, pp. 221–225 (2020). https://doi.org/10.1109/ICICT48043.2020.9112452

21. Ahmed, T.U., Hossain, S., Hossain, M.S., ul Islam, R., Andersson, K.: Facial expression recognition using convolutional neural network with data augmentation. In: Proceedings of the Joint 8th International Conference on Informatics, Electronics and Vision (ICIEV 2019) and Proceedings of the 3rd International Conference on Imaging, Vision and Pattern Recognition (icIVPR 2019), pp. 336–341. IEEE (2019). https://doi.org/10.1109/ICIEV.2019.8858529

22. Salama, E.S., El-Khoribi, R.A., Shoman, M.E., Wahby Shalaby, M.A.: A 3D-convolutional neural network framework with ensemble learning techniques for multi-modal emotion recognition. Egypt. Inform. J. (2020). https://doi.org/10.1016/j.eij.2020.07.005.

23. Cho, Y., Bianchi-Berthouze, N., Julier, S.J.: DeepBreath: deep learning of breathing patterns for automatic stress recognition using low-cost thermal imaging in unconstrained settings. In: Proceedings of the 7th International Conference on Affective Computing and Intelligent Interaction, ACII 2017, pp. 456–463 (2018). https://doi.org/10.1109/ACII.2017.8273639

24. Pitaloka, D.A., Wulandari, A., Basaruddin, T., Liliana, D.Y.: Enhancing CNN with prepro-cessing stage in automatic emotion recognition. Procedia Comput. Sci. **116**, 523–529 (2017). https://doi.org/10.1016/j.procs.2017.10.038
25. Baltrusaitis, T., Zadeh, A., Lim, Y.C., Morency, L.P.: OpenFace 2.0: facial behavior analy-sis toolkit. In: Proceedings of the 13th IEEE International Conference on Automation Face Gesture Recognition, FG 2018, pp. 59–66 (2018). https://doi.org/10.1109/FG.2018.00019
26. Pampouchidou, A., et al.: Quantitative comparison of motion history image variants for video-based depression assessment. EURASIP J. Image Video Process. **2017**(1), 1–11 (2017). https://doi.org/10.1186/s13640-017-0212-3
27. Silva, C., Sobral, A., Vieira, R.T.: An automatic facial expression recognition system evaluated by different classifier. In: X Workshop de Visão Computacional (WVC 2014) (2014). https://doi.org/10.13140/2.1.2789.2801
28. Belhumeur, P.N., Hespanha, J.P., Kriegman, D.J.: Eigenfaces vs. Fisherfaces: recognition using class specific linear projection. In: Buxton, B., Cipolla, R. (eds.) Computer Vision— ECCV '96: 4th European Conference on Computer Vision Cambridge, UK, April 15–18, 1996 Proceedings, Volume I, pp. 43–58. Springer Berlin Heidelberg, Berlin, Heidelberg (1996). https://doi.org/10.1007/BFb0015522
29. Haq, S., Jackson, P.J.B.: Speaker-dependent audio-visual emotion recognition. In: Pro-ceedings of the VSP 2009—International Conference of Audio-Visual Speech Processing University of East Anglia, Norwich, UK, 10–13 September 2009, pp. 1–6 (2009)
30. Nguyen, D., Sridharan, S., Nguyen, D.T., Denman, S., Dean, D., Fookes, C.: Meta transfer learning for emotion recognition. arXiv (2020)
31. Avots, E., Sapiński, T., Bachmann, M., Kamińska, D.: Audiovisual emotion recognition in wild. Mach. Vis. Appl. **30**(5), 975–985 (2018). https://doi.org/10.1007/s00138-018-0960-9
32. Chew, W.J., Seng, K.P., Ang, L.M.: Nose tip detection on a three-dimensional face range image invariant to head pose. In: Proceedings of the International Multiconference of Engineers and Computer Scientists, vol. 1, pp. 18–20 (2009)

Applying Method of Automatic Classification Tools to Make Effective Organizing of Photos Taken in Childcare Facilities

Takaaki Yamaga[1], Takayuki Inoue[2], Hiroki Uemura[3], Wakaho Otoyama[4], and Jun Sasaki[1(✉)]

[1] Graduate School of Software and Information Science, Iwate Prefectural University, 152-52 Sugo, Takizawa, Iwate, Japan
g231s034@s.iwate-pu.ac.jp, jsasaki@iwate-pu.ac.jp
[2] Faculty of Social Welfare, Iwate Prefectural University, Takizawa, Japan
[3] Department of Early Child Care, Seiwa Gakuen College, Sendai, Japan
[4] Graduate School of Education, Gunma University, Maebashi, Japan

Abstract. In recent years, there has been a steady increase in the use of photos in Japanese childcare facilities to provide parents with growth records such as newsletters and photo albums. We have been developing a photo sharing system for childcare facilities that is used for the daily training of childcare workers, thereby improving the quality of childcare and childcare education. However, sorting and organizing the photos into newsletters, albums, and other growth records for each child, from among the large number of photos taken in childcare facilities, is an extensively time-consuming task. To address this problem, we have considered applying existing automatic photo classification tools for organizing photos. In this paper, we report the evaluation results of the performance of two major photo classification tools applied to 1,900 photos posted to the photo sharing system. Experimental results indicate that the existing tools had very low classification accuracy for children's photos compared to those of adults and took a long time to classify many photos. Based on these results, we will propose a work procedure to efficiently organize photos.

Keywords: Quality of childcare · Photo classification · Face recognition · Growth record · Photo sharing system

1 Introduction

Recent years have witnessed a steady increase in the use of photos in Japanese childcare facilities to provide parents with newsletters, albums, and other growth records, improving the quality of childcare. For example, personal photos are useful for reviewing the growth of a child. In addition, there are online distribution services that provide newsletters and photo sharing services between childcare facilities and the child's parents. As these services are usually developed by companies, there is an economic problem. If people working in a childcare facility can themselves organize the photos and distribute

© Springer Nature Switzerland AG 2021
H. Fujita et al. (Eds.): IEA/AIE 2021, LNAI 12799, pp. 162–172, 2021.
https://doi.org/10.1007/978-3-030-79463-7_14

or share them easily, the economic problem is resolved and the quality of childcare and other services can be improved. The Japanese Ministry of Economy, Trade and Industry has introduced information and communication technology (ICT) to reduce the workload, improve the quality of childcare, and actively encourage the introduction of ICT in childcare. In fact, the authors have been conducting research on improving the efficiency of childcare operations at childcare facilities using ICT [1]. However, one of the challenges is that sorting and organizing photos for each child from the large number of photos taken in childcare facilities and creating albums and newsletters is time-consuming. In addition, it is difficult for a childcare facility to share photos with other childcare facilities and parents.

Our research aims to improve the quality of childcare and education and reduce the workload in childcare facilities by using ICT. In this paper, we describe the conventional research and issues on improving the quality of childcare and education, and reduction of workload in Sect. 2, related studies on image recognition in Sect. 3, and the development of a new photo sharing system in Sect. 4 We propose a photo classification method in Sect. 5. In Sect. 6, we present the experimental results on the performance of two major automatic photo classification tools. The discussion and conclusion are presented in Sects. 7 and 8, respectively.

2 Improving the Quality of Childcare and Reduction of Workload

There has been substantial research on the quality of childcare in various countries. For example, Akgündüz et al. examined the extent to which disadvantaged children are able to access high-quality early childhood education and care in the Netherlands [2]. Cárcamo et al. suggested several measures to improve childcare quality [3]. Gregoriadisa et al. attempted to initiate a discussion about the need to build a strong and equal partnership between kindergarten and childcare programmers and to move towards a more coherent approach in the Greek early childhood education system [4]. Araujo et al. used a fixed-effects identification strategy to assess how differences in the quality of childcare affect the communication, fine motor, and problem-solving skills of infants and toddlers [5]. Robinson reported the findings of an investigation into the constructs of quality from two stakeholder groups of parents and educators [6]. Bjørnestad et al. explored the quality of toddler childcare in Norway using the Infant Toddler Environment Rating Scale-Revised Edition [7].

Conventional research has shown that information sharing and communication between workers and parents is important for improving the quality of childcare. However, little research has been conducted on applying ICT to improve the quality of childcare. In addition, education and training for workers in childcare facilities is crucial for improving the quality of childcare. Conventionally, gathering training at one place has been the main style, but under the current circumstances in COVID-19, online training and web meetings are safer and more effective. There are also fields of ICT utilization; however, these are beyond our research scope.

In the business world, various systems have been developed to reduce the workload in childcare facilities. The main purpose of these systems is to reduce the workload of the management of toddlers and create communication opportunities between workers and parents through newsletters, albums, and other records. However, few studies have been conducted on the burden of classifying children's photos required to create newsletters, albums, and other records.

3 Related Study on Image Recognition

In recent years, image recognition technology has advanced remarkably. Many researchers have proposed methods using a variety of techniques. For example, Oku-mura et al. proposed an identity-verification system using continuous face recognition improved by managing the check-in behavior of event attendees such as facial directions and eye contact (eyes are open or closed) [8]. Wang et al. proposed a deep ranking model that employs deep learning techniques to learn the image similarity metric directly has a higher learning capability than models based on hand-crafted features. We can find many other papers related to image recognition and face recognition [9–17] in the archive (arXiv) provided by Cornell University. Schroff et al., developed a face recognition and clustering system named "Facenet" [10], which provides high accuracy face recognition system. Cheng et al. improved the person re-identification performance using a new con-volutional neural network algorithm [11]. In addition, several other studies have been conducted on photo classification [18–22]. As a result of these studies, the face recog-nition rate and its performance have improved, and they have been applied to various devices such as smartphones. However, since the face recognition rate of infants has not been clarified, there is still doubt about the adaptability of existing face recognition tools in actual childcare facilities. In this study, we conducted experiments to clarify whether existing image recognition tools can be applied to young children. Specifically, we ana-lyzed the automatic photo classification of preschool children by using the photos taken in an actual kodomo-en (center for early childhood education and care) by the photo sharing systems "OgaPhoto" and "Ogasta" explained in the next section.

4 Development of a New Photo Sharing System

Our project has developed a photo sharing system using "OgaPhoto" and "Ogasta" and applied it to six kodomo-ens.

Figure 1 shows the proposed photo sharing system. OgaPhoto is an application for smartphones. Workers in a kodomo-en can use OgaPhoto to take pictures of children and upload them to the server along with relevant comments. The server provides a web application service named Ogasta that provides photo sharing service among workers. Using this system, the photos are uploaded automatically to the dedicated server and can be shared easily among workers in kodomo-ens. Subsequently, the workers evaluate the photos from the viewpoint of quality of childcare or education and accordingly assign marks. As a result, this operation affords valuable education and training experience to the workers.

Figure 2 shows the expected effects of the developed system. The captured photos can be used to create a portfolio, which is a record and history of growth for each child. Additionally, this system increases business efficiency as well as improves childcare quality, because the workload of creating photo-based newsletters and albums for parents is reduced. However, photo classification requires considerable effort and time and can thus be cumbersome.

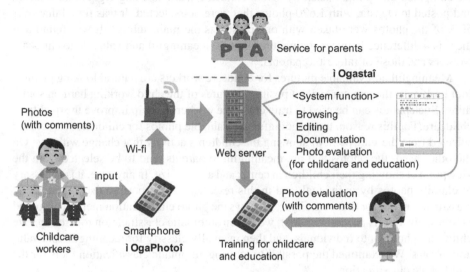

Fig. 1. Configuration of developed photo sharing system (OgaPhoto and Ogasta).

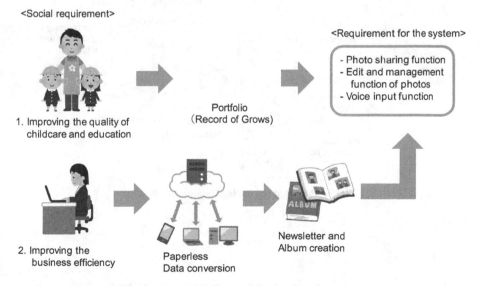

Fig. 2. Expected effects of the developed system.

5 Proposed Photo Classification Method in Childcare Facilities

Typically, many pictures are taken at childcare facilities, some of which are adopted for newsletters and albums, while others are discarded. Photographic classification is needed to select meaningful and valuable data. Therefore, before considering the classification method, we compared the photos that were adopted and those that were not. Concretely, we compared 280 photos taken by actual childcare workers using OgaPhoto, selected and posted to Ogasta, with 1,620 photos that were not selected. It was found that over 50% of the photos were taken with one person as the main subject. It was found that there is a difference between the pictures that are meaningful and valuable to childcare workers and those of interest to parents.

Meaningful and valuable pictures for childcare workers are natural looking pictures (not looking at the camera and not posing), pictures of the child working hard on something. Such photos can be used to train childcare workers to help improve the quality of childcare. For this reason, the meaningful and valuable photos for childcare workers are selected from the viewpoint of showing the children's activity that change with age. On the other hand, the photos that are meaningful to parents tend to be selected from the viewpoint of showing their children in center and a large size. In any case, it is necessary to classify photos by individual, and in this research, we propose to use an automatic classification tool for that part. Figure 3 shows the photo classification method proposed in this study. In this proposal, at first, we use an automatic classification tool to separate children's photos into individuals, and then manually classify for meaningful and valuable photos. We examined the possibility of using automatic classification tools for the child photo classification.

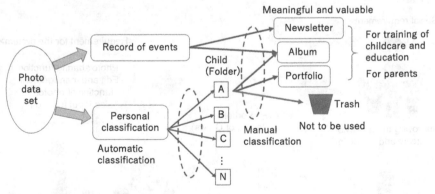

Fig. 3. Proposed photo classification method.

6 Experiments

6.1 Experimental Condition

An automatic photo classification tool was used for personal classification in the proposed photo classification method shown in Fig. 3. In the first step of this research, we used an existing automatic photo classification tool and conducted an experiment to evaluate its applicability. The experimental conditions are listed in Table 1. The automatic photo classification tool targeted two of the most popular application tools (G: "Google Photo" and M: "Microsoft Photo"). We focused on these two tools because they are adaptive to the actual experimental device environment.

Using these two tools, 1,900 photos taken in a class of 3-year-olds at an actual kodomo-en were input into the tools and evaluated from the viewpoint of individual classification accuracy and classification time. Folders were created for each child when the target photos were entered into each tool. Table 2 lists the results of comparing the number of personal folders created one week after entering the photos, the number of photos saved in the folders, and the accuracy (accuracy) of the photos in the folders. As listed in Table 2, Tool G has a smaller number and variance of extracted photos than Tool M, resulting in higher accuracy. The accuracy is defined as follows:

$$a_m = \frac{1}{n} \sum_{i=1}^{n} \frac{C_n}{A_n} \times 100. \tag{1}$$

where a_m is the accuracy in folder "m", n is the number of photos, A_n is the number of extracted photos, and C_n is the number of correct photos.

The total number of extracted photos N_a is calculated by as follows:

$$N_a = \sum_{i=1}^{n} A_i. \tag{2}$$

and the dispersion s^2 of the accuracy can be calculated as

$$s^2 = \frac{1}{n} \sum_{i=1}^{n} (a_i - \overline{a})^2. \tag{3}$$

where, $\overline{a}$ is the average of the accuracy.

It is generally claimed that the accuracy of face recognition of this type of tool ranges from 80% to 99% [9]. For example, the accuracy of face recognition of FaceNet is 99.63% [23] and that of Amazon Web Services (AWS) and Microsoft Azure "Face API" are 99% and 80%–87%, respectively [24]. This performance was obtained for adults facing the front of the camera. In our face recognition experiment on photos of children, we found that the accuracy was approximately 50%, as listed in Table 2, which was extremely low compared to that of adults.

6.2 Accuracy Comparison

The experimental results are presented in Table 2. As a result of performing photo classification for one month on 1,900 input photos, 61 folders were created for tool G

Table 1. Experimental conditions.

Target photos	Photos for the class of 3-year-olds in a kodomo-en in Hachinohe city in Japan
Total number	1,900 photos
Period wherein photos were taken	November, 2019–October, 2020
Automatic classification tools	Application "Google Photo" (tool G)
	Application "Microsoft Photo" (tool M)

Table 2. Accuracy comparison result (extraction time is one month)

	tool G	tool M
Number of created folders	61	44
Number of photos in a folder	5–103 Photos	3–61 Photos
Accuracy in a folder	26.92–100%	2.04–100%
Average accuracy	49.47%	52.23%
Dispersion	347.1	942.4

and 44 folders were created for tool M. As listed in Table 2, we can determine the number of photos in a folder and the fact that the accuracy of the photos varied. To compare the tools under the same conditions, the accuracy of the photos for the same folder (Child A, B, C, …, W) and the number of extracted photos for the same folder (child A, B, C, …, W) are shown in Figs. 4 and 5, respectively. Figure 4 indicates that there is no significant difference between the two tools in terms of photo accuracy, but tool M has a larger variation. Figure 5 shows that the tool M extracts a smaller number of photos in many folders and tool G seemed to be able to extract more stable and relatively more accurate photos. Regarding the total number of recognized photos, there is a difference of nearly three times between G and M; thus, G is a superior tool to obtain a large number of classified photos.

6.3 Comparison of Start Time for the Classification

If a user enters a large number of photos in each tool, it will take a long time to start sorting (start creating folders). Therefore, we conducted an experiment to investigate the relationship between the number of photos input at one time and the duration until the start of the classification. The experimental results are shown in Fig. 6. Tool M did not start sorting after 20 photos were entered. As the number of input sheets increases, the classification start time increases, but when it exceeds 100 sheets, the time decreases to approximately 200 sheets (295 s); subsequently, the classification start time tends to gradually increase. The upper limit of the number of sheets could not be confirmed in the experimental duration of 1 h (3,600 s). With tool G, automatic classification started when only 20 photos were input and the minimum time (752 s) was reached when 100 photos

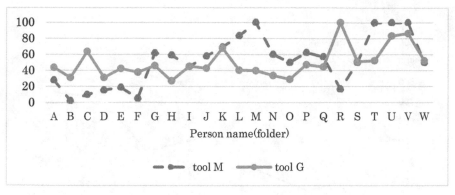

Fig. 4. Comparison of accuracy for the same person (a_m).

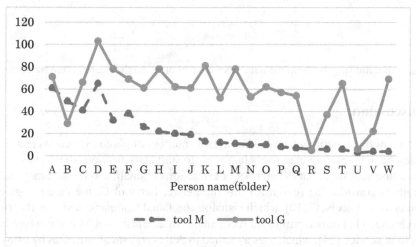

Fig. 5. Comparison of the total number of extracted photos (N_a).

were entered, with the duration increasing thereafter, such that classification did not start in 1 h from 600 sheets. In this case, the upper limit was considered to be approximately 500 photos. Typically, when a childcare worker manually classifies 100 photos, it takes 10 s or more for each photo, taking a total of 1,000 s. If the user adopts tool G in the input units of 100 photos, it is thought that the sorting duration can be shortened compared to manual classification. However, it is also necessary to measure the photo classification completion duration until a satisfactory result is obtained.

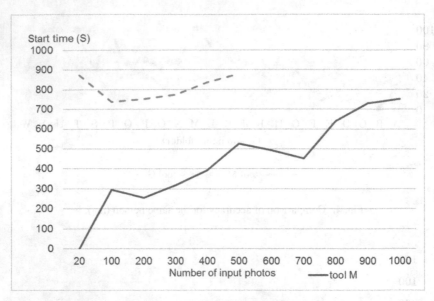

Fig. 6. Relationship between the number of input photos and the classification start time.

7 Discussion

As a result of the experiment, tool G has a stable number of photo extractions and better accuracy, but it takes a comparatively large time to start classification. Tool M has a short classification start time, but the number of extractions is small, and the accuracy varies. The authors consider the reason for this difference. For tool G, the face recognition system used is "FaceNet" [10], which visualizes 68 facial landmarks and uses the triplet loss technique [11] to perform facial recognition. In contrast, tool M is the Azure Face recognition service [24], which uses a method to detect statistical attributes by using 27 face landmarks. Owing to the difference in the number of landmarks and the method, it is thought that the difference in the automatic classification start time and the difference in accuracy will occur.

The issues to be considered in future investigations are as follows:

- Further improve the accuracy of face recognition in early childhood using a combination of artificial intelligence and work procedures,
- Clarify satisfactory classification-end conditions and determine the optimum number of photos to be input to the automatic classification tool,
- Research on the extraction of valuable and meaningful photos for childcare workers and parents using machine learning and deep learning technologies.

8 Conclusion

In this paper, we describe conventional research on improving the quality of childcare and education. Then, a new photo sharing system (with OgaPhoto and Ogasta) was developed for use in training childcare workers. In addition, we proposed a photo classification method for childcare facilities by applying automatic photo classification tools. Next, we conducted an experiment to clarify the applicability of existing automatic classification tools using photos taken at actual childcare facilities and posted them to Ogasta. As a result, it was found that tool G is superior to tool M in terms of accuracy stability and number of extracted photos. However, tool G has the disadvantage that the start time will be longer if the number of input photos is large. In the future, based on these results, we plan to propose a realistic, optimal, overall photo classification workflow and evaluate it at actual childcare facilities.

Finally, we would like to thank Midorinokaze Educale of a childcare and education facility for providing photo data sets, Iwate Information Technology Co., Ltd. for implementing the photo sharing system, and the Telecommunications Advancement Foundation for their funding and cooperation in this research. We would like to thank Editage (www.editage.com) for English language editing.

References

1. Yamaga, T., et al.: Development of efficient childcare recording system for childcare facilities. In: Annual Conference of Japan Processing Society of Japan, no. 1, pp. 51–52 (2020)
2. Akgündüz, Y.E., Plantenga, J.: Equal Access to High Quality Child Care in the Netherlands (2012). https://doi.org/10.1332/policypress/9781447310518.003.0005
3. Cárcamo, R.A., Vermeer, H.J., De la Harpe, C., van der Veer, R., van IJzendoorn, M.H.: The quality of childcare in chile: its stability and international ranking. Child Youth Care Forum 43(6), 747–761 (2014). https://doi.org/10.1007/s10566-014-9264-z
4. Gregoriadis, A., Tsigilis, N., Grammatikopoulos, V., Kouli, O.: Comparing quality of childcare and kindergarten centres: the need for a strong and equal partnership in the greek early childhood education system. Early Child Dev. Care 186, 1142–1151 (2016)
5. Araujo, M.C., Dormal, M., Schady, N.: Child care quality and child development. Int. J. Whole Schooling SPECIAL ISSUE (2017)
6. Robinson, C.: Constructing Quality Childcare: Perspectives of Quality and Their Connection to Belonging, Being and Becoming. IDB Working Paper Series, No. IDB-WP-779 (2017)
7. Bjørnestad, E., Os, E.: Quality in Norwegian childcare for toddlers using ITERS-R. EECERJ 26(1), 111–127 (2018)
8. Okumura, A., Handa, S., Hoshino, T., Tokunaga, N., Kanda, M.: Identity verification using face recognition improved by managing check-in behavior of event attendees. In: Ohsawa, Y., et al. (eds.) JSAI 2019. AISC, vol. 1128, pp. 291–304. Springer, Cham (2020). https://doi.org/10.1007/978-3-030-39878-1_26
9. Wang, J., et al.: Learning fine-grained image similarity with deep ranking. Computer Vision Pattern Recognition (2014)
10. Schroff, F., Kalenichenko, D., Philbin, J.: Facenet: a unified embedding for face recognition and clustering. Computer Vision Pattern Recognition (2015)
11. Cheng, D., Gong, Y., Zhou, S., Wang, J., Zheng, N.: Person re-identification by multi-channel parts-based CNN with improved triplet loss function. Computer Vision Pattern Recognition (2016)

12. Li, Z., Snavely, N.: MegaDepth: learning single-view depth prediction from internet photos. Computer Vision Pattern Recognition (2016)
13. Shi, Y., Jain, A.K.: Docface: matching ID document photos to selfies. Computer Vision Pattern Recognition Michigan State University East Lansing (2018)
14. Wang, M., Deng, W.: Deep face recognition: a survey. Computer Vision Pattern Recognition (2018)
15. Zuo, H., Lang, H., Blasch, E., Ling, H.: Covert photo classification by deep convolutional neural networks. Mach. Vis. Appl. **28**, 623–634 (2017)
16. Deng, J., Guo, J., Xue, N., Zafeiriou, S.: ArcFace: additive angular margin loss for deep face recognition. Computer Vision Pattern Recognition (2018)
17. Wang, H., et al.: CosFace: large margin cosine loss for deep face recognition. Computer Vision Pattern Recognition (2018)
18. Hou, Y.: Photo content classification using convolutional neural network. In: ICAITA (2020)
19. Sarker, M.K., Rashwan, H.A., Talavera, E., Furruka Banu, S., Radeva, P., Puig, D.: MACNet: multi-scale atrous convolution networks for food places classification in egocentric photo-streams. In: ECCV 2018 (2018)
20. Yang, F., et al.: Exploring deep multimodal fusion of text and photo for hate speech classification. In: Proceedings of the Third Workshop on Abusive Language Online, pp. 11–18 (2019)
21. Makienko, D., Seleznev, I., Safonov, I.: The effect of the imbalanced training dataset on the quality of classification of lithotypes via whole core photos. In: Creative Commons License Attribution 4.0 International (2020)
22. Waldrop, L.E., Hart, C.R., Parker, N.E., Pettit, C.L., McIntosh, S.: Utility of machine learning algorithms for natural background photo classification. Cold Regions Research and Engineering Laboratory (2018)
23. A.I. Lionbridge and Japan Ltd, July 2020. https://lionbridge.ai/ja/articles/face-recognition-ai/. (in Japanese)
24. X. Nikkei, August 2019. xtech.nikkei.com/atcl/nxt/cpbook/18/00031/00002/. (in Japanese)

Land Use/Land Cover Change Analysis Due to Tourism in the Chittagong Hill Tracts of Bangladesh

Fayezah Anjum, Hasan Mohiuddin Zilany, Syed Shahir Ahmed Rakin,
Md. Abdul Hoque, Aina-Nin Ania, Md. Asadut Zaman, Jebun Nahar Moni,
and Rashedur M. Rahman(✉)

Department of Electrical and Computer Engineering, North South University,
Dhaka, Bangladesh
{fayezah.anjum,hasan.zilany01,syed.rakin01,abdul.hoque05,
aina.ania,asadut.zaman,nahar.moni,
rashedur.rahman}@northsouth.edu

Abstract. Bangladesh is a country in South Asia with full of natural beauty, from beaches to hilly regions, forests, and waterfalls. The tourism sector of the country has been emerging over the past few years and creating employment, innovation, and new infrastructures. The tourist spots of Bangladesh are scattered all over the country. This paper focuses mainly on the hilly areas of Chittagong Hill Tracts (CHT), namely Bandarban, Rangamati, and Khagrachari. This paper aims to analyze the change in land cover due to the growth in tourism in the Chittagong Hill Tracts using Remote Sensing. The use of remote sensing (RS) together with Google Earth Engine (GEE) has been proved to be effective in monitoring and analyzing land use/land cover changes (LULC). The purpose of this study is to use the application of multi-temporal satellite image data and GEE for monitoring changes in land cover and analyzing the dynamics and change in the built-up area of Chittagong Hill Tracts due to tourism over the past ten years. The performance of the classification of the land cover change is evaluated, and the accuracy assessment is determined from the confusion matrix. The error analysis, limitations, and possible work scope in the future are also discussed in this paper.

Keywords: Land use and land cover change · CART · Remote sensing · GEE · Tourism · CHT

1 Introduction

The Chittagong Hill Tracts (CHT) is in the southeastern part of Bangladesh, and it consists of the three hilly districts of Bandarban, Rangamati, and Khagrachari. CHT covers an area of 13,294 square kilometers, and the estimated population of this region is about 1.6 million. The CHT is ethnically and culturally diverse. Its geographically distinct features make it one of the most popular tourist destinations in Bangladesh. It is

H. Fujita et al. (Eds.): IEA/AIE 2021, LNAI 12799, pp. 173–184, 2021.
https://doi.org/10.1007/978-3-030-79463-7_15

characterized by mountainous, rugged terrain and forests, waterfalls, and lakes, which contributes to the breathtaking beauty of this area.

The tourism sector is one of the fastest-growing industries in the global market. Tourism is often considered as a tool for infrastructural development and economic growth in developing countries like Bangladesh. The tourism sector of Bangladesh has been emerging over the past few years and creating employment, innovation, and new infrastructure. It helped to increase the brand image of the country on an international level. The official phrase of the tourism industry of Bangladesh is "Beautiful Bangladesh." Although the proportion of foreign tourists in the country is not that big in number, it has millions of domestic tourists who go on vacation in the different parts of the country. The tourist spots of Bangladesh are scattered all over the country. A few of the famous tourist destinations are Cox's Bazar, Sylhet, Chittagong Hill Tracts (CHT), Sundarban, and Sajek. This paper focuses mainly on the hilly areas of CHT, namely Bandarban, Rangamati, and Khagrachari. The aim of this paper is to analyze the land use/land cover change (LULC) due to the growth in tourism in the Chittagong Hill Tracts using Remote Sensing.

Land cover is described as the physical and biological cover of the surface of the Earth. It documents how much of a particular region is covered by different areas such as agricultural regions, forests, natural areas, wetlands, and water bodies. It can be determined by analyzing high-resolution satellite images. The use of remote sensing (RS) together with Google Earth Engine (GEE) has been proved to be effective in monitoring and analyzing land use/land cover changes.

Data acquisition is made using two different satellites: Landsat 7 for the year 2010 to 2013 and Landsat 8 for the years 2013 to 2020. Two major land cover classes, non-built up area (non-urban) and built-up area (urban), are used. The map is plotted with the Built-up Index (BU) band to get a clearer difference between urban and non-urban areas. In the GEE, there are several machine learning classifier packages for supervised classification using multi-temporal Landsat images. For example, Random Forests (RF), Classification and Regression Trees (CART), Support Vector Machine (SVM), and many others. These kinds of supervised classifiers are useful in classifying remote sensing images. For this research purpose, supervised classification is applied on desired years on the area of interest, using Classification and Regression Trees (CART) classifier in the GEE. The performance of the classification of the land cover change is evaluated, and the accuracy assessment is determined from the confusion matrix.

In this study, the purpose is to use the application of multi-temporal satellite image data and GEE for monitoring land cover changes and analyzing the dynamics of the Chittagong Hill Tracts' built-up area due to tourism. CHT is one of the most famous tourist regions in Bangladesh. Its unparalleled natural beauty attracts people who want to get away from the hustle and bustle of daily city lives.

The structure of this paper is as follows. Section 2 presents a number of works in this area. Section 3 refers to the methodology where Sect. 4 presents the results and discussion. Section 5 refers to conclusion and possible future works.

2 Related Works

The authors in [1] used remote sensing and geographical information system to analyze and predict the change in land cover in the city of Kathmandu in Nepal. It has been found over the period of 20 years, from 1990 to 2010, the Kathmandu district has lost a significant amount of forests, agricultural land, and water bodies due to the expansion of urban areas in this region. They have used Landsat 5 TM and Landsat 8 TM for 1990 and 2010 data. In the past, the three hill districts have been the subject of study for the land cover changes [2]. One of the instances is where the Halda River, which flows through Khagrachari district in 2 no. Patachora union, from where the river starts the journey, has been a subject to the study of land cover changes over the last 40 years where they have used the data from the ASTER satellite and Landsat Satellite for 3 years. These data were used for measuring possible land use/land cover changes in the Halda River [2]. There was another instance where Cox's Bazar has been the subject of study where the land cover change had to be analyzed due to deforestation and forced migration of the Rohingya refugees. In order to accommodate the refugees, a lot of lands had to be taken in order to set up camps and settlement areas. The people involved with the research had to study the land cover changes from 1988 to 2018, given that these lands were fairly unused for human accommodation purposes in the past. Here, the images from Landsat-8, Landsat-5, and Sentinel-2 were used for the combined 30 years. For classification purposes, CART Classifier, Support Vector Machine, Random Forest, and Max Entropy were used where all of them apart from the Max Entropy were commonly used for the purpose of Land Cover Changes [3]. In the paper [4], the authors generated land cover maps for the study area Bangladesh for 2005 using the GEE platform. It is a part of the 20-year change in land use/land cover analysis in the Ganges Basin. In this study, the authors suggested a method of using the GlobeLand30 (GLC30) product to obtain reference data for the supervised classification in order to address the issue of the lack of ground truth data.

In another study [5], the authors used a supervised classification method to determine the change in land in cover with the shifting of shoreline in Nijhum Dwip of Bangladesh. Landsat images of 1998, 2008, and 2018 were used. Image classification was done using Maximum Likelihood Classification. The well-known technique, normalized difference vegetation index (NDVI), was used in this study to monitor how the greenness of vegetation cover declined over the three years. The NDVI maps demonstrated an apparent decline in the greenness of the mangroves. This study used the confusion matrix method for the accuracy assessment of the classified images. The study's main result proved that during the time period of 1998–2018, 285 hectares of mangrove forest has disappeared, agricultural land was reduced, and there has been a significant increase in the settlement area. This shows that the land cover in Nijhum Dwip has changed due to sea-level rise, increase in population, and human settlement.

3   Methodology

The flowchart shown below in Fig. 1 outlines the conceptual framework used in the study to detect and analyze the land cover change in the desired study area. There are four key steps, which includes: i) acquisition and preparation of data; ii) training and classification; iii) land use/land cover change classification and change detection; iv) accuracy assessment. In this section, we will discuss the methodology of the whole study.

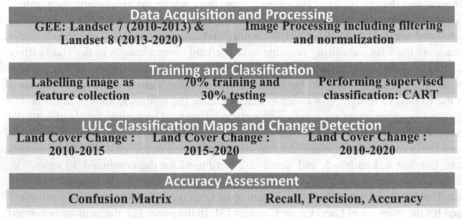

Fig. 1. Flowchart of the methodology

3.1   Data Acquisition and Processing

3.1.1   Data Acquisition

This study has used satellite images of three time periods: 2010, 2015, and 2020. Due to cloud coverage we could not get any clear image set in 2015, so we have used 2016 image set for Bandarban area. Two different satellites were used: Landsat 7 for the year 2010 to 2013 and Landsat 8 for the years 2013 to 2020. All the dataset used and top of atmosphere images (TOA) were obtained from the Google Earth Engine (GEE) repository. The images were preprocessed by filtering (cropping, dates, and cloud cover) and normalization (NDBI, NDVI, BU) to minimize the atmospheric disturbances in the dataset. The images were filtered to have less than 5% cloud cover. For each study area, all the processing and computation were done in one single script of GEE. We have used 3 scripts for Bandarban, Rangamati and Khagrachari respectively.

We have also tried to implement some nontraditional methods to acquire data. Using VIIRS Nighttime Day/Night Band Composites is one of the efficient ways to detect buildings and such. As the region of interest consists mostly of rural and remote areas, implementing nighttime lights as a feature was not possible.

3.1.2 Image Processing

Landsat data are used for classification. A higher degree of accuracy in the data can be obtained during classification if the resolution of satellite data is higher. Landsat data have several bands based on their wavelength. Landsat 7 data have total 8 bands, and Landsat 8 data have 11 bands.

In this study, two major land cover classes, non-built up area (non-urban) and built-up area (urban), are used applying Normalized Difference Vegetation Index (NDVI) and Normalized Difference Build up Index (NDBI), respectively. The indices like NDVI and NDBI were derived from the primary bands of satellite imagery. These bands accurately classify the Landsat imagery and produce land cover maps by eliminating shadows of hills and buildings.

Normalized Difference Vegetation Index (NDVI) is the most frequently used vegetation index to perceive the vegetation or greenery's richness. The internal structure of plant leaves gives it a high reflectance in Near Infrared (NIR). This high NIR and high absorption in Red Spectrum are used to calculate NDVI as given in the following Eq. (1):

$$NDVI = (NIR - Red)/(NIR + Red) \tag{1}$$

For calculating NDVI for Landsat 7 data: NDVI = (Band 4 – Band 3)/(Band 4 + Band 3)
For calculating NDVI for Landsat 8 data: NDVI = (Band 5 – Band 4)/(Band 5 + Band 4)

The Normalized Difference Built-Up Index (NDBI) is used for the analysis of the built-up area. Each index has their own calculation methods. It separates the built-up area from the background, and it is the normalized difference between Short-wave infrared (SWIR) and NIR bands. It is calculated, as shown in Eq. (2):

$$NDBI = (SWIR - NIR)/(SWIR + NIR) \tag{2}$$

For calculating NDBI for Landsat 7 data, NDBI = (Band 5 – Band 4)/(Band 5 + Band 4)
For calculating NDBI for Landsat 8 data, NDBI = (Band 6 – Band 5)/(Band 6 + Band 5)

Built-up Index (BU) was used for better results. BU is an index for analyzing urban patterns using NDBI and NDVI, and it allows BU to map the built-up area automatically. It is calculated, as shown in Eq. (3):

$$BU = NDBI - NDVI \tag{3}$$

All these indexes were calculated and added to the bands in the images, which help in the land cover classification.

NDVI and NDBI were used as they are some of the most well-known techniques. But there are some methods which are arguably better. Enhanced Vegetation Index (EVI) is an alternate version of NDBI. They are quite similar, but EVI responds better with daylight change. NDBI and UI (Urban Index) are not capable of verifying the distribution of built-up areas and bare land areas. Enhanced Built-Up and Bareness Index (EBBI) overcomes this problem. Despite of these facts, NDBI and NDVI are still widely used for their proven effectiveness.

3.2 Training and Classification

Two major land cover classes, non-built up area (non-urban) and built-up area (urban) are used in this study. The map was plotted with the BU band to get a clearer difference between urban and non-urban areas. Then the resulting satellite image of the desired study area is labeled manually. The labeling of images as a feature collection is done to perform supervised classification. The samples obtained through labeling the images on a specific area are divided into 70% training data and 30% testing data.

Image classification can be done in both supervised classification and unsupervised classification techniques. For this research purpose, supervised classification is applied on desired years on the area of interest, using Classification and Regression Trees (CART) classifier in the GEE.

CART was introduced by Leo Breiman, Jerome Friedman, Richard Olshen, and Charles Stone in 1984. It is based on decision tree predictive model which explains how an outcome variable's values can be predicted based on other values. Decision Trees are used to create a model that would predict the value of a target based on the values of the several input variables. In the CART algorithm, the input and output are connected by a series of nodes, where each node is divided into two branches and leading to leaf nodes. In the case of Classification trees, the leaf node represents class labels within which a target variable would likely fall into. In Regression trees, it represents continuous variables, and the tree is used to predict its value. In the remote sensing area of studies, the Tree-based classifier such as CART is widely used, mainly for its robustness and simplicity.

3.3 Land Cover Classification Maps and Change Detection

The supervised classification using CART was applied on the three time periods of 2010, 2015, and 2020 for a specific study area, for instance, the first area of interest, Bandarban. The classified result for the desired area can be displayed.

The various land features available on the earth's surface can be explained by observing the Land use/land cover (LULC) using the GEE. Land use gives an idea of how the land is being utilized for different uses, such as agricultural and residential areas. On the other hand, land cover change refers to the changes in the physical land types over a time period, such as human settlements and built-up areas.

In this research, the main aim is to analyze the land cover change between the time periods 2010–2015, 2015–2020, and 2010–2020 in the specific area of study, i.e., Bandarban, and observe the change in the built-up area which is correlated with the increase in tourism of Bandarban over the past ten years. We had to work with year 2016 for Bandarban instead of 2015, due to some issues mentioned later.

4   Results and Discussion

All the steps mentioned in the methodology were implemented in all the three areas of study: Bandarban, Rangamati, and Khagrachari, in three separate GEE scripts. The objective is to find and analyze the land cover change in these districts of Chittagong Hill Tracts (CHT) between the time periods 2010–2016, 2016–2020, and eventually the land cover change over the last ten years from 2010 to 2020. As it was discussed at the beginning of the paper, over the past few years, there had been an increase in tourism in the CHT of Bangladesh, especially Bandarban. The divine beauty of these places attracts many tourists in those areas. The increase in tourism led to an increase in urbanization due to the building of hotels and resorts in the famous tourist spots. Our primary goal is to illustrate this observation by analyzing the land cover change and to find an increase in the built-up areas using remote sensing data.

After performing the supervised classification using CART on the three years 2010, 2016, and 2020, the classified result for the desired area was obtained. Then the land use/land cover change (LULC) between the three-time periods 2010–2016, 2016–2020 and the overall change in land cover during the past 10 years in the Bandarban district is illustrated by Fig. 2 given below.

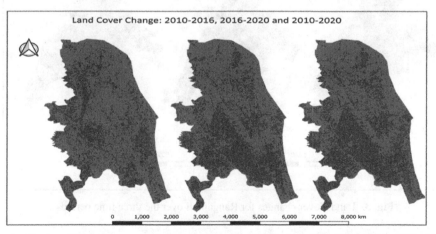

Fig. 2. The Land Cover Change for Bandarban, between the time periods: 2010–2016, 2016–2020 and 2010–2020 respectively.

In this study, the performance of the classification of the land cover change is based on a metric by the use of confusion matrix that is often used to assess the accuracy and performance of a classification model. When the data is imbalanced, Kappa values can give a more realistic view of the model's performance. Equation (4) shows the formula to calculate the Kappa value.

$$\text{Kappa} = (\text{Total Accuracy} - \text{Random Accuracy})/(1 - \text{Random Accuracy}) \quad (4)$$

Where,

$$\text{Total Accuracy} = (TP + TN)/(TP + TN + FP + FN)$$

$$\text{Random Accuracy} = ((TN + FP) * (TN + FN) + (FN + TP) * (FP + TP))/(\text{Total} * \text{Total})$$

The land use/land cover change (LULC) for the second study area, the district of Rangamati, between the three time periods 2010–2015, 2015–2020 and 2010–2020 is illustrated by Fig. 3.

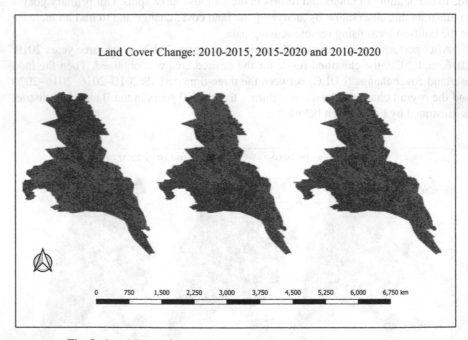

Fig. 3. Land Cover changes for Rangamati over the three time periods.

The land use/land cover change (LULC) for the third study area, the district of Khagrachari, between the three time periods 2010–2015, 2015–2020 and 2010–2020 is illustrated by Fig. 4 as shown below.

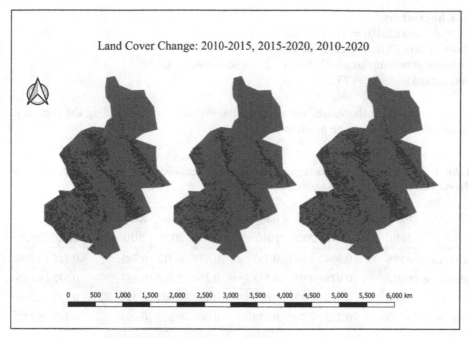

Fig. 4. Land Cover changes for Khagrachari over the three time periods.

One of the objectives was to analyze how its tourism contributed to the increase in built-up area over the past ten years from 2010 to 2020. From the results obtained from the research and the generated map of the change in the land cover map by the classification model, it can be seen that there has been a visible change in the land cover over the years. Figure 2 of the LULC of Bandarban for the time period 2010–2020 shows the increase in built-up areas. The model generates that theBuilt-up area has more than doubled from 2010 to 2020.The increase in built-up area for three regions can be found by the difference between the built-up areas during the years 2010 and 2020 and given below.

A. Bandarban:
Built-up area in 2010 = 515.597 km^2
Built-up area in 2020 = 1233.957 km^2
Increase of built-up area = 718.194 km^2
Built-up area has more than doubled for Bandarban, from 2010 to 2020

B. Rangamati:
Built-up area (2010) = 1850.34 km^2
Built-up area (2020) = 3545.79 km^2
Increase in built-up area = 3545.79 − 1850.34 = 1695.45 km^2
Percentage increase = 91.6%

C. Khagrachari:

Built-up area (2010) = 1358.96 km^2

Built-up area (2020) = 2353.34 km^2

Increase in built-up area = 2353.34 − 1358.96 = 994.38 km^2

Percentage increase = 73.2%

By considering the values for all three, the overall results including the accuracy, precision and recall can be given in Table 1.

Table 1. The accuracy, precision, and recall results obtained over three time periods for Bandandan, Rangamati, and Khagrachari

	Bandarban			Rangamati			Khagrachari		
	2010	2016	2020	2010	2015	2020	2010	2015	2020
Accuracy	0.896	0.904	0.887	0.747	0.633	0.713	0.785	0.752	0.836
Precision	0.972	0.978	0.979	0.553	0.204	0.482	0.657	0.542	0.686
Recall	0.908	0.910	0.892	0.629	0.424	0.594	0.299	0.172	0.506
Random accuracy	0.733	0.735	0.742	0.574	0.606	0.573	0.693	0.705	0.682
Kappa	0.61	0.638	0.562	0.406	0.069	0.328	0.302	0.157	0.483

Table 2. Percentage increase in built-up areas for all three areas.

	Bandarban	Rangamati	Khagrachari
Increase in built-up areas	718.36 km^2	1695.45 km^2	994.38 km^2
Percentage increase in built-up areas	139.3%	91.6%	73.2%

Table 2 depicts the overall built-up index for the three study areas. We can see that the percentage increase in built-up areas is given, all three areas had their increase in built-up areas for the last ten years. Based on the three areas, we can find the average percentage increase in built-up areas for each area.

$$Average \ \% \ Increase \ in \ bulit\text{-}up \ areas = \frac{139.3 + 91.6 + 73.2}{3} = 101.3\% \ per \ area$$

The land cover changes for the years 2010 to 2020 is correctly classified by the model, and the percentage change in the built-up index is also visible. Regarding the accuracy of the result, they have been given in Table 1 where the accuracies for Bandarban for the three periods were 0.896, 0.904, and 0.887 respectively. For the case of Rangamati, the accuracies are 0.747, 0.633, and 0.713 respectively; in the case of Khagrachari, the accuracies are 0.785, 0.752, and 0.836 respectively.

Despite the accuracies, the average percentage increase in built-up areas is calculated to be 101.3% per area, meaning each district had their built-up areas to increase by 101.3% in average considering the three areas. According to the article "Tourism Booming with Economy", about 70% of tourists prefer visiting Cox's Bazar and Chittagong Hill Tracts, followed by Sundarban and Sylhet [6, 8]. As per different tourist operators, the number of domestic tourists from 60 lakh per year to 70 lakh per year from 2016 to 2017. About 778,143 inbound tourists were recorded in the year 2017, and the country made revenue of $97.05 million from foreign tourists, according to the tourism board of Bangladesh. According to another article published in the Financial Express, in 2014, we had about 0.16 million foreign tourists [7, 9]. Though this is slightly reduced to 0.14 million in 2015. We had an increasing amount of foreigners to 0.20 million in 2016, about 0.26 million in 2017, around 0.27 million in 2018, and about 0.20 million up to the mod of the year 2019.

5 Conclusion and Future Work

This paper focuses mainly on the hilly areas of Chittagong Hill Tracts (CHT), namely Bandarban, Rangamati, and Khagrachari. The land use/land cover change (LULC) due to tourism growth in the Chittagong Hill Tracts is analyzed using Remote Sensing data. The GEE was used for tracking the changes in the land cover and analyzing the dynamics and change in the built-up area of Chittagong Hill Tracts (CHT) due to tourism over the past ten years. The performance of the classification of the land cover change is evaluated, and the accuracy assessment is determined from the confusion matrix. The land cover change for the years 2010 to 2020 is correctly classified by the model, and the percentage change in the built-up index is also visible. The limitations of the study, i.e., the lack of statistical data, unavailability of the tourism growth in CHT areas, and the cloud cover problems of the satellite data, indicate the possible future works that can be done based on this current study. Also, further works include predicting the land cover change for the future years based on the past data.

References

1. Wang, S.W., Gebru, B.M., Lamchin, M., Kayastha, R.B., Lee, W.-K.: Land use and land cover change detection and prediction in the Kathmandu district of Nepal using remote sensing and GIS. Sustainability **12**, 3925 (2020). https://doi.org/10.3390/su12093925
2. Chowdhury, M., Hasan, M.E., Abdullah-Al-Mamun, M.M.: Land use/land cover change assessment of Halda watershed using remote sensing and GIS. Egypt. J. Remote Sens. Space Sci. **23**(1), 63–75 (2020)
3. Ahmed, N., Islam, M.N., Hasan, M.F., Motahar, T., Sujauddin, M.: Understanding the political ecology of forced migration and deforestation through a multi-algorithm classification approach: the case of Rohingya displacement in the southeastern border region of Bangladesh. Geol. Ecol. Lands. **3**(4), 282–294 (2018)
4. Yu, Z., et al.: Land use and land cover classification for Bangladesh 2005 on google earth engine. In: Proceedings of the 2018 7th International Conference on Agro-Geoinformatics (Agro-Geoinformatics), Hangzhou, China, 6–9 August 2018

5. Islam, M., Saiful, M., Asraf, U., Mallik, A.H.: Assessing the dynamics of land cover and shoreline changes of Nijhum Dwip (Island) of Bangladesh using remote sensing and GIS techniques. Reg. Stud. Marine Sci. **41**, 101578 (2021) https://doi.org/10.1016/j.rsma.2020.101578

6. Rahman, M.R.: The Socio-economic importance of Tourism and its impact on the Livelihood in South Asia. Theseus, May 2016. https://www.theseus.fi/handle/10024/116404. Accessed 15 Jan 2021

7. Sharif, R., Islam, M.A.: Critical Analysis of Growth Trend & Growth Pattern of Hill Track: A Study on Khagrachari Hill District, Bangladesh, 20 January 2017. http://www.sciencepublishinggroup.com/journal/archive?journalid=241&issueid=2410101. Accessed 15 Jan 2021

8. https://www.thedailystar.net/business/news/tourism-booming-economy-1673479

9. https://thefinancialexpress.com.bd/economy/tourist-arrivals-rise-in-five-years-1569469201

Robotics

Estimation Method for Operational Environment Complexity by a Robotic Team

Denis A. Beloglazov, Maria A. Vasileva$^{(\boxtimes)}$, Victor V. Soloviev,
Vladimir A. Pereverzev, and Viacheslav H. Pshihopov

JSC «SDB of Robotics and Control Systems», Taganrog, Russia
`marv@sfedu.ru`

Abstract. The paper presents the estimation method for operational environment complexity by a robotic team. Its distinguishing feature is the way to organize the intragroup information exchange between the team members, identifying the robots that, due to some restrictions, are not able to adequately estimate the complexity of the surrounding area. Overcoming the restrictions implies assistance from group members, meanwhile, their reasons may be of different origin, for example, faulty individual sensors or sensors' visibility range being overlapped with environmental elements.

Upon the method application, an unambiguous (explicit) idea concerning the information sources and receivers and their necessary list, is formed, which makes the exchange of data more efficient and the estimation process more accurate.

A special function set has been developed for environment complexity estimation; using this function set implies representing the surrounding area as a plane divided into sectors with their dimensions corresponding to the team robot size. The transition from three-dimensional to two-dimensional space is carried out by projecting onto a flat surface the coordinates of the environment elements.

The presented function set is approximated with high precision by an artificial neural network that can be used for further evaluations.

Keywords: Robotic team · Environment complexity estimation · Artificial neural networks · Training · Keras

1 Introduction

Robots are widely used in various fields of human life. Further development of robotics is aimed at creating robots that can autonomously solve tasks and act as part of groups. On the one hand, this eliminates the dependence of robots on the human operator. On the other hand, it allows the production of robots of simple design, operating as part of heterogeneous groups of small and large numbers. For the operation of robots in the environment, it is necessary to improve the methods of planning trajectories of movement, mapping methods, and methods of environmental estimation [1–6].

Most works on robotics [1–6] insufficient attention to the analysis of the properties of the environment, which the robot interacts with while performing the tasks set. This

© Springer Nature Switzerland AG 2021
H. Fujita et al. (Eds.): IEA/AIE 2021, LNAI 12799, pp. 187–198, 2021.
https://doi.org/10.1007/978-3-030-79463-7_16

approach is not correct, as the robot does not function separately from the environment but is involved in it.

This paper presents a method that allows a robotic team to receive the numerical estimations of the complexity of the local areas of the environment basing on their sensor system data. Its peculiarity lies in the ability of group members to determine the need for exchanging data between themselves at any given time, the amount of information transmitted, as well as their sources and receivers. The obtained complexity estimates can be used in various ways, to enhance the efficiency of planning the motion trajectories for both individual robots and the team.

2   Developing the Method of Environment Complexity Estimation

While the robotic team is working to achieve their goals in a certain environment, the task of its estimation arises to determine the possible counteraction or the presence of potentially dangerous obstacles, etc. This estimation can be performed in various ways: by a team leader, by each of the robotic team members separately, by each of the robotic team members considering the data from the nearest neighbors.

The proposed options have their own implementation features, advantages, and disadvantages.

The option of obtaining the complexity estimation of local areas of the environment using the team leader requires the team members to transfer the information about the surrounding area formed by each of the group robots, to the leader, as shown in Fig. 1. This makes the robotic team centralized or dependent on the leader.

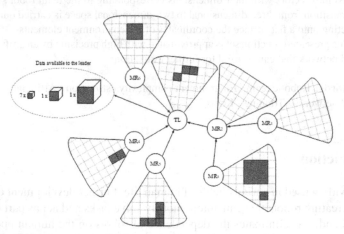

Fig. 1. Data transfer from the mobile robots team members to the leader TL. TL – team leader; MRi – Mobile robot, being part of the team

The algorithm for determining the complexity of the environment for the i-th robot by the group leader includes the following steps (Algorithm 1).

Algorithm 1 Determining the complexity of the environment for the i-th robot by the group leader

---

 1: **Notation**: Environment ε, Mobile robot MR, Team Leader TL, Complexity C, Mobile robot position P

 2: Input: ε, MR

 3: $TL \leftarrow$ FindTeamLeader(MR)

 4: **for** MR_i in MR **do**

 5:     $p \leftarrow$ GetPosition(MR_i)

 6:     $e \leftarrow$ GetEnviroment(MR_i)

 7:     P.push_back(p)

 8:     ε.push_back(e)

 9: **end for**

10: $C \leftarrow$ CostComplexityByTL(P, ε)

11: **for** MR_i in MR **do**

12:     SendComplexityToMR(C_i)

13: **end for**

The availability of data on the external environment allows the leader to calculate the estimates of the complexity of environment local areas for each of the team members. Such systems, even with the frequent change of the leader, have significant drawbacks, which are primarily associated with the need to transfer large amounts of information between group members.

The method of obtaining an estimation of the environment section complexity by each of the group robots separately has obvious drawbacks related to the impossibility of detecting individual objects due to their location or the characteristics of the sensor elements used. This means that there is a high probability that the i-th robot will receive an estimate of the environment that does not correspond to reality. As a result, the probability of the robot getting into undesirable situations increases.

The method of obtaining an estimation of the environment section complexity by each of the group robots taking into consideration the data from the nearest neighbors appears to be the most interesting of all presented above. Its peculiarity lies in the strict limitation and focus of the processes of information interaction between the group members, i.e. have an accurate understanding of the list of transmitted information, their sources, and consumers.

As is seen from Fig. 2, there are various alternatives for locating medium elements in the operating area of the robot sensor system. In each of the cases, we may observe sensor systems blind spots being formed which restrict their abilities to receive information (the form of the shading, which depends on the sensor type being used area and their location, is in this case shown schematically).

Knowing the current position of the i-th robot in space and the characteristics of its sensor system (visibility, viewing angle, beam pitch, orientation, etc.), you can determine the coordinates of the location of the blind area, as shown in Fig. 3. These data are necessary for organizing the exchange of information between groups of robots.

Information concerning the blind spots, formed by adjacent robots of the group, can have a different look:

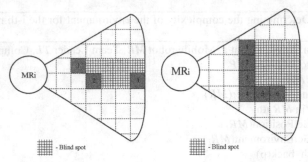

Fig. 2. Schematic visualization of the sensor system blind spots of the i-th robot. a) – obstacle № 3 is in the in the sensor system blind spot; б) – obstacles № 5, 6 are in the in the sensor system blind spot

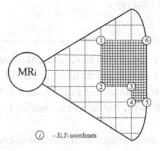

Fig. 3. Parameters characterizing the location of the sensor system blind spots of the i-th robot

– estimation of the complexity of the environment area, restricted by the blind spots
– the coordinates and parameters of the environment area, restricted by the blind spots

The peculiarity of the first case is the occurrence of situations where the i-th robot can have N different estimations of the events happening:

$$E = \{e_{1,2}, \ldots, e_N\}, \tag{1}$$

where E – is a range of possible complexity estimations of the environment area under consideration; e_i – is the estimation area formed by the i-th robot.

The presence of a set of the E environment estimations poses an urgent task of combining or choosing between them. The easiest way to solve this problem is to use max/min operations:

$$e_c = \max(E) = \max\{e_{1,2}, \ldots, e_N\}, \tag{2}$$

$$e_c = \min(E) = \min\{e_{1,2}, \ldots, e_N\}, \tag{3}$$

where e_c – is complexity estimation of the environment area, adopted for the current group robot.

This results in environment estimation being carried out by a single robot at any given time with the views of other robots being neglected. This means that part of the information is lost and is not used.

This problem can be solved by using the following expression to determine the value of e_c:

$$e_c = \sum_{i=1}^{N} e_i w_i, \tag{4}$$

where w_i – weight coefficient.

An obvious disadvantage of using weight coefficients is the need to obtain their numerical values.

An alternative to the formation, exchange, and subsequent merging of N different estimates of the local environment area are to transfer data on the number and coordinates of obstacles in the blind spots of the sensor systems of the group robots. The essential advantage of this approach is its great simplicity.

As an example, let us consider the situation shown in Fig. 4, where two robots see the same piece of the area from different angles. For MR1 robot, the considered area contains only one obstacle with the number 1, since the rest are in the dark zone of the sensor system. The MR2 robot sees all 4 obstacles, and its complexity estimation will differ significantly from that received by the MR1. The choice of which of the estimates to use in the future depends on the specific situation and in most cases is complicated and very ambiguous.

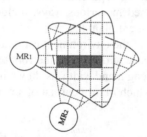

Fig. 4. Differences in estimations of the environment area complexity for MR_1 и MR_2

The process of information exchange between the robots of the group is not constant. It is initialized at strictly specified points in time, the definition whereof requires an analysis of the data obtained by the sensor systems of robots.

In the elementary case, what is covered by the visibility range of the i-th robot sensor system are the objects of the environment. No other robots in the group are visible. This situation does not require the identification of robots that need assistance in estimating the environment sector. As a result, the i-th robot evaluates the environment using only the sensory information available to it. In the case of the dimming zones of the sensor system, data on the obstacles located in them cannot be obtained from other robots of the group.

A more complicated case involves the discovery of one or more members of a group in the vicinity of the i-th robot. Their location and orientation affect whether the information will be exchanged or not. In case one of the following conditions is fulfilled, the i-th robot transfers its information about the local area of the environment:

– the robot is within the visibility area of another robot sensor system
– the principal axes of the robot sensory systems (PAR) intersect at the point belonging to the working area of each of them (Fig. 5).

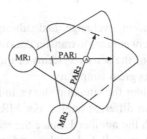

Fig. 5. Intersection of principal axes of the robot sensory systems of robots group

During its movement in the environment, the i-th robot performs an estimate of its complexity, which characterizes its capabilities for its unobstructed overcoming. The information obtained can be used in various ways, including so that to improve the effectiveness of the robot movement planning.

Let us consider the process of the environment estimation by the i-th robot in more detail. We shall imagine the space surrounding the robot in the form of a sector with certain geometric dimensions: length and width, as shown in Fig. 6. The sector is divided into rows Ri and columns Ci, which in turn consist of smaller subdivisions – cells.

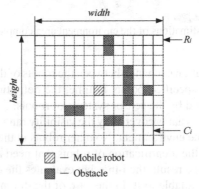

Fig. 6. Sectoral representation of the area surrounding the robot

The sizes of the cells that form the rows and columns correspond to the security zone around the i-th robot, generating the estimation of the complexity of this area.

At each time ti€{T} of estimation the environment complexity, the robot is located at its center. Detected by sensor systems of robots of the group (the current robot and its nearest neighbors) elements of the environment (obstacles, etc.) are distributed over the sector cells. This results in forming opinions concerning certain cells being occupied which are represented in the digital form (1 – if the cell is occupied, 0 – if the cell is free).

Ri rows are considered passable if they do not contain cells occupied by obstacles, as shown in Fig. 7, a. Otherwise, the rows are not passable, as shown in Fig. 7, b. The same is true for columns.

a)   b)

Fig. 7. Row passability R_i a) – unpassable row R_i; b) – passable row R_i

Given the position and the number of obstacles in the sector, it is possible to determine its complexity. To do so, we use the following analytical equation:

$$P = 0,4 \cdot \frac{C_O}{ASec} + 0,3 \cdot \frac{R_I}{R_A} + 0,3 \cdot \frac{I}{A} \tag{5}$$

where P – is the estimation of passability complexity for the i-th robot of the sector; Co – the number of cells in the sector, which are occupied by the obstacles; C_{ASec} – the total number of the cells in the sector; R_I – the number of the unpassable rows; R_A – the total number of the rows; C_I – the number of the unpassable columns; C_A – the total number of the columns.

In the event, if there are rows or columns in the space that are fully occupied by obstacles, it is advisable to take the value of P equal to 1.

The estimation of the maneuvering complexity, which the i-th robot will have to perform when overcoming a sector, can be obtained based on the following expression:

$$M = \frac{\sum_{i=1}^{N} P_i}{N} \tag{6}$$

Where M – is the estimation of the maneuvering complexity for sector overcoming; P_i – the estimation of the passability complexity for the i-th subsector of the area with the dimensions length/N, height/N; N – the number of subsectors.

The use of expression (6) implies a partition of the estimated sector into N adjacent equal size subsectors, as shown in Fig. 6.

The method for determining the environment complexity by the i-th robot, considering the information from its nearest neighbors, includes the following sequence of steps.

At first the parameters of the sensor system blind zones being calculated by the i-th robot. Next, the condition for the initialization of data exchange between neighboring robots of the group is checked. Then information to/from neighboring group members being transmitted/received. A shared overview of the environment being formed, considering information from neighboring members of the group. Finally, performs an estimation of the complexity of the current local area environment.

Table 1. Advantages and drawbacks of the methods for environment complexity estimation

Method name	Advantages	Drawbacks
The estimation by the group leader	The ability to manipulate the information available to each member of the group; the possibility of obtaining an adequate estimation of the environment complexity by each of the robots of the group	The need to select a group leader; the need to transmit large amounts of information between the group leader and its members; the need for calculations for all members of the group by its leader; high probability of duplication of data on the environment from different robots
Separate estimation by each of the group members	The possibility of obtaining an assessment of the environment complexity without waiting for data from the rest of the group; no need to transfer/receive data between group members	High probability of getting inadequate environment complexity assessment
Assessment by each of the group members considering the information provided by other group members	The ability to manipulate the information available to several members of the group; the efficiency of the information exchange between team members being enhanced; the possibility of obtaining an adequate environment complexity assessment for the i-th group robot	The need to solve problems of local positioning and navigation for each of the robots of the group

As mentioned above, each of the methods for forming estimation of environment's areas has certain advantages and disadvantages, which are presented in Table 1. Upon analysis of Table 1, the developed method is more efficient than the considered analogs while reducing the amount of data transferred between members groups (Fig. 8).

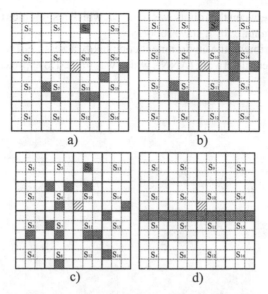

Fig. 8. The division of the sector under estimation into N adjacent S_i sub-sectors with 3x3 size; a) – the presence of 7 obstacles in the environment; b) – the presence of 11 obstacles in the environment; c) – the presence of 14 obstacles in the environment; d) – the presence of 12 obstacles in the environment, which form an impassable row

3   Experimental Trial of the Method of Forming Assessment of the Environment Sections Complexity

The proposed method for assessing the complexity of the environment allows the robots of the group to form a map of its passability. As a result, the robots moving trajectories can be planned more effectively.

A study of the trajectory planning effectiveness regarding the environment sections complexity was carried out basing on the task of a robotic group moving in a column. As shown in Fig. 9a, in front of the lead column there is a lengthy obstacle. The lead robot rebuilds the motion trajectory, assessing this area as impassable. Therefore, the lead robot adjusts the motion trajectory, assessing this area as impassable. The information about the obtained assessment of the complexity of the visible part of the environment is transmitted to the slave robot, which allows it to plan hitherto a new trajectory of movement taking into account the characteristics of the operating environment, as is shown in Fig. 9b.

Then the team motion continues through to the passable section. As soon as the obstacle is bypassed, sections of poor passability are marked in the visibility range of the lead robot. This information is considered by the slave robot when planning the trajectory. It allows passing the complex section with an enhanced safety zone.

The experiment's result shows the environment complexity assessment by a robotic team when moving in a particular system allowed raising safety parameters and shorten the trajectory of the robotic motion. This is conveniently illustrated by Figs. 9a and 9d, where the distance between the robots was reduced, which testimonies to a more efficient motion trajectory planning by a slave robot.

During the experiment, the environment complexity assessment was performed by a direct propagation neural network (ANN), which was trained to approximate expressions (5), (6).

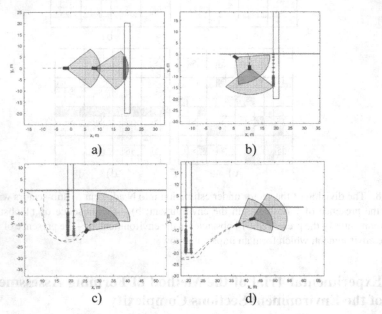

a)

b)

c)

d)

Fig. 9. The simulation results of the motion trajectories planning by a robotic team, considering the method of assessment generation as to the environment sections complexity

The data on sector cells being occupied by obstacles S_i is fed into the net at the input, with values of P and M being fed back at the output. The results of the ANN testing in the Keras environment are displayed in Table 2.

Table 2. Results of ANN testing, performing the assessment of the environment

№	Desired ANN output signal values		The actual ANN output signal values	
	P	M	P	M
1	0.59	0.36	0.59	0.35
2	0.79	0.51	0.72	0.48
3	0.73	0.55	0.76	0.53
4	0.5	0.24	0.5	0.23
5	0.74	0.46	0.70	0.46

The presented method and the algorithms laid down in it, including the ANN, were implemented and tested on a hardware basis, namely wheeled robotic vehicle, whose appearance and technical characteristics are presented in Fig. 10.

The process controller of wheeled robotic vehicle operates based on the Linux operating system and the ROS framework [7, 8]. With the help of ROS, the possibility of information interaction between the operator's control point (laptop) and mobile robots via a Wi-Fi network is implemented. The transition from the three-dimensional space to the two-dimensional space surrounding the robot, which uses the method for the complexity assessment of the environment section, is relatively simple and lies upon projecting the detected obstacle points onto a horizontal surface.

Fig. 10. Appearance of wheeled robotic vehicles

4   Conclusion

The paper presents a method for assessing the environment complexity by a group of mobile autonomous robots. Its peculiarity lies in the possibility of identifying members of a group, which, due to certain limitations, are unable to make a correct assessment of the environment on their own and provide them with support from their closest neighbors. The information about what data is required for each of the robots in the group reduces the amount of information transmitted.

Given the values of numerical complexity estimates of the environment sections, the robots of the group can become more effective at planning the trajectories of their movement, bypassing the areas of the environment which are obviously difficult to overcome.

Analytical equations being applied to assess the environment can be approximated with high accuracy by an artificial neural network. This renders the assessment function set more flexible.

The results of the practical application of the proposed method proved its effectiveness, but also revealed several features that should be considered. First, the proposed method involves the transition from three-dimensional to two-dimensional space to obtain estimates. This is relatively easy to do in the case of ground robots, however, for other types of robots, an adaptation of the method will be required. Secondly, the application of the method is impossible without solving the problem of local positioning and navigation, since the data from the robot sensor systems of the group can be significantly distorted. This problem is currently being solved by using methods such as SLAM [9, 10], which give good results. With the advent of [11, 12], one can say that the complexity of the problem of local positioning and navigation is significantly reduced.

Acknowledgment. The study is supported by the Russian Science Foundation grant No. 18-19-00621 at Joint stock Company «Scientific-Design bureau of Robotics and Control Systems».

References

1. Mohanarajah, G., Usenko, V., Singh, M., D'Andrea, R., Waibel, M.: Cloud-based collaborative 3D mapping in real-time with low-cost robots. IEEE Trans. Autom. Sci. Eng. 423–431 (2015). https://doi.org/10.1109/TASE.2015.2408456. ISSN 1545-5955
2. Peter, F., et al.: Collaborative navigation for flying and walking robots. In: IEEE/RSJ International Conference on Intelligent Robots and Systems (IROS), pp. 2859–2866 (2016). https://doi.org/10.3929/ethz-a-010687710
3. Gadd, M., Newman, P.: Checkout my map: version control for fleetwide visual localisation. In: IEEE/RSJ International Conference on Intelligent Robots and Systems (IROS), pp 5729–5736 (2016). https://doi.org/10.1109/IROS.2016.7759843
4. Contreras, L., Kermorgant, O., Martinet, P.: Efficient decentralized collaborative mapping for outdoor environments. In: International Conference on Robotic Computing, Laguna Hills, United States, January 2018. https://doi.org/10.1109/IRC.2018.00017
5. Jessup, J., Givigi, S.N., Beaulieu, A.: Merging of octree based 3D occupancy grid maps. In: IEEE International Systems Conference Proceedings Ottawa, ON, Canada, April 2014. https://doi.org/10.1109/SysCon.2014.6819283
6. Gulli, A., Pal, S.: Deep learning with Keras. Implement Neural Networks with Keras on Therano and TensorFlow/translated from English by A. A. Slinkin. DMK Press (2018). 294 p. illustated
7. Joseph, L.: Mastering ROS for Robotics Programming. Packt Publishing (2015). ISBN 978-1-78355-179-8
8. Fairchild, C., Harman, T.L.: ROS Robotics by Example. Packt Publishing (2016). ISBN 978-1-78217-519-3
9. Krinkin, K., Filatov, A., Filatov, A.: Modern multi-agent SLAM approaches survey. In: Proceedings of the FRUCT20, 776 p (2017). ISSN 2305-7254, ISBN 978-952-68653-0-0
10. Cadena, C., et al.: Past, present, and future of simultaneous localization and mapping: toward the robust-perception age. IEEE Trans. Robot. **32**(6), 1309–1332 (2016). https://doi.org/10.1109/TRO.2016.2624754
11. Dubé, R., Cramariuc, A., Dugas, D., Nieto, J., Siegwart, R., Cadena, C.: SegMap: 3D Segment Mapping using Data-Driven Descriptors. https://arxiv.org/abs/1804.09557 (2017)
12. Bloesch, M., Omari, S., Hutter, M., Siegwart, R.: ROVIO: robust visual inertial odometry using a direct EKF-based approach. In: Proceedings of the IEEE/RSJ Conference on Intelligent Robots and Systems (IROS) (2015)

A Cloud-Based Robot Framework for Indoor Object Identification Using Unsupervised Segmentation Technique and Convolution Neural Network (CNN)

Raihan Kabir[1]([✉]), Yutaka Watanobe[1], and Md. Rashedul Islam[2]

[1] Department of Computer Science and Engineering, University of Aizu, Fukushima, Japan
yutaka@u-aizu.ac.jp
[2] Department of Computer Science and Engineering, University of Asia Pacific, Dhaka, Bangladesh

Abstract. Nowadays autonomous indoor mobile robot is getting more attention in many application areas. A cloud-based multi-robot framework provides highspeed data processing and inter robot's communication efficiently for the indoor mobile robot system. However, efficient detection and recognition of the environmental objects are vital issues for indoor mobile robots. Thus, this paper proposes a cloud-based multi-robot system, where Indoor objects are detected using a new unsupervised object segmentation model and object identification using cloud-based Convolutional Neural Networks (CNN) model. In the object segmentation model, a segmentation algorithm is developed with the combination of Canny edge detection, Floodfill, and BoundingBox image processing technique for efficiently segmenting the objects of the indoor environment. After detecting objects, a cloud-based CNN model with SoftMax classifier is used for classifying objects. Besides, an iterative learning is introduced in our proposed model for identifying unknown objects. Some indoor images captured by the camera are used to test the proposed system. To validate the proposed model, a benchmarked object image dataset from an open resource repository is used in this paper to train the CNN model. The model shows good object detection and identification result and the cloud-based framework enhance the usability of the proposed system.

Keywords: Cloud robot · Object identification · Unsupervised segmentation · Canny edge detection · Convolutional Neural Networks (CNN) · Indoor mobile robot

1 Introduction

The mobile robot is invented with the ability to move autonomously to perform tasks in the application area. A large scale of business industries has tasks and workload which are overhead for the manpower. There are several tasks, such as sorting for parcel delivery, storing product in the warehouse, provide service in the hospital, mall, and house, assist in the office, and others may be done by the robot with the replacement

© Springer Nature Switzerland AG 2021
H. Fujita et al. (Eds.): IEA/AIE 2021, LNAI 12799, pp. 199–211, 2021.
https://doi.org/10.1007/978-3-030-79463-7_17

of human. Thus, the uses of the indoor robot are getting interest day by day in many indoor seances. A statistic of the International Federation of Robotics (IFR) discloses that the sale of domestic service robots is increased by 42 million during 2016–2019 [1]. To perform the daily task efficiently in an indoor environment, the robot needs an expert system or intelligence for recognizing its environment. Also, communication between robots needs to be automated and efficient for deploying in the environment. When these robots need to move through an environment to perform their actions, it is essential to understanding the environment and different objects in that environment. Thus, indoor object detection is very useful for those robots. If those robots are able to detect all the objects in their view space they can move for performing their work accurately. Also, shared storage and high computation power is needed for processing data and generating the robot action. Thus, the main motivation of this paper is to develop a cloud-based automatic, and reliable multi-robot system that can detect objects efficiently using image processing and machine learning techniques.

Object detection using machine learning techniques is very much popular. Several researchers have investigated image processing-based object detection models, processing the environmental knowledge, and managing cloud-base station for storing and sharing data. However, the performances are suboptimal and there are several scopes to enhance performance and integrate the unsupervised object segmentation technique with the cloud-based mobile robot. Thus, the main purpose of this research is to propose a model to achieve this goal.

F. Al-Hafiz, et al. 2018, proposed an automatic segmentation algorithm for Red blood cells (RBCs) using thresholding and Canny detector [2]. This model uses boundary-based methods to automatically computes the threshold image and then apply canny detector to segment red blood cells in bioimages. The accuracy rate of 87.9% of their proposed segmentation method.

L. Vasil, et al. 2018, proposed an approach that helps a mobile robot to recognize a target and follow that target dynamically [3]. In their proposed approach, the problem to recognize the target is considered an image classification task. This task was attempted by using a deep convolutional neural network (CNN). A sequence of images obtained from the robot uses as input in the CNN and the successive target following problem is implemented using a 2D range data. This proposed method has been implemented on a mobile platform named KUKA youBot omnidirectional using robot operating system middleware and this robot is equipped with a 2D LiDAR and an onboard USB camera.

P. Espinace, 2013, proposed a technique that is indoor scene identification, such as, an Office or a Kitchen, for an indoor mobile robot [4]. The authors use object category classifiers to extract low-level visual features of the indoor objects and a contextual relation of the low-level visual features of the objects. For increasing detection accuracy and efficiency, they used a 3D range sensor that helps to implement an attention mechanism for gathering geometrical and structural information.

Rahman, et al. 2019, proposed an optimal energy-efficient task offloading model for the cloud-based multi-robot system [5]. In the proposed task offloading scheme, the primary robot accumulates and processes data from other local robots to improve the offloading process. The proposed system described a warehouse scenario for parcel sorting and distribution. The proposed model enhanced the performance of bandwidth connectivity, path planning, global and local offloading for energy-efficient offloading, and available resource utilization to the cloud.

L. Bergamini, et al. 2020, presents a framework based on Deep Convolutional Neural Networks (DCNN) for predicting multiple objects using both single and multiple grasps pose all at once with an input single RGB image [6]. They thankful to a novel loss function and their framework is trained with an end-to-end fashion and they match their model accuracy with a state-of-art smaller architecture, that gives the unparalleled real-time performances. During the experimental tests, and to makes their application reliable and work on real robots they implemented the system using the ROS framework and tested it on a Baxter collaborative robot.

R. Wanga, et al. 2019, proposed a method of Object instance detection with pruned Alexnet and extended training data [7]. In their proposed method they used BING-Pruned Alexnet (B-PA). They first utilize BING (Binarized Normed Gradient) for computing bounding boxes and then they utilize a pruned neural network for recognition purposes. They also reduced neurons and cut the fully connected layers on the classic Alexnet architecture for object instance detection.

Badawy et al. 2019, proposed a cloud-based computing model that provides a real-time environment for mobile robots to enhance reliability and usability [8]. The proposed mobile robot architecture provides a data flow mechanism between mobile robots and cloud servers. The image clustering algorithm and the neural gas algorithm are adopted for the mobile robot and the cloud server. The experimental results show 25% to 45% enhancement in the total response time.

In the real indoor environment, there are multiple objects presets in the single image computed by the robot camera. To understanding the environment during robot movement, the object should be separated and recognized separately. However, most of the researches does not consider object separation for processing, or some objection segmentation models are not well worked. Alternatively, high configured RCNN may recognize objects of an image separately. But the RCNN demands high computation power and execution time. Thus, this paper proposes an efficient object segmentation model for separating different objects of an image captured by robots and a cloud-based CNN model for extracting features of object images and classify indoor objects. Besides, the cloud robot system provides a communication framework between robots, a cloud database for data sharing, and shared computational power.

The rest of this paper is as follows. Section 2 presents the details about the proposed model of this paper, Sect. 3 presents the experimental results and discussion part, and Sect. 4 concludes the paper.

2 Proposed Model

A general system model of the cloud-based indoor robot framework is presented in Fig. 1. In this proposed framework, there are two stations, the first one is cloud-base station and the second one is the robot local station. In the cloud-base station, all data are stored (such as Collected images, Training data, Trained model, and other essential Data) and this data is analyzed (such as preprocessed, Segmented, trained, and classified), and robot action is generated and sent to the robot to perform the action.

In the local robot station, indoor images are captured and sent to the cloud database for analysis. The cloud-base station processes the data, makes the decision, and sent to the robot. The next action has been performed by the robots using some motor driver and robot operating system (ROS). The temporary data and performed action data are stored in the cloud database.

Using this proposed model multiple robots can be manipulated. Each robot will communicate with the cloud-base station and their captured data can be analyzed and classified using the trained model and the next action will be generated and sent to the particular robot using their particular robot id.

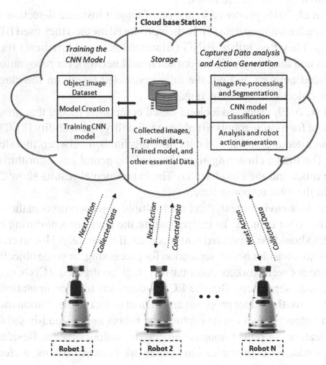

Fig. 1. Block diagram of the proposed model.

2.1 Data Analysis and Action Generation in Cloud-Base Station

Figure 2 presents the block diagram of data analysis and action generation of the proposed cloud-base station. The proposed recognition system is combined with two processes. The first process performs the training process of the CNN model and the second is the testing process. In those processes, a new unsupervised object segmentation technique is applied to separate the objects of the input image and features of those objects are extracted using the CNN model. The extracted features are used for the classification process. In the classification process, the objects are classified using the SoftMax classifier using the trained CNN model. Based on the classification result, the system generates the next robot instruction (avoid the object obstacle or accept as target). Additional new and non-classified objects are trained again with the CNN model incrementally.

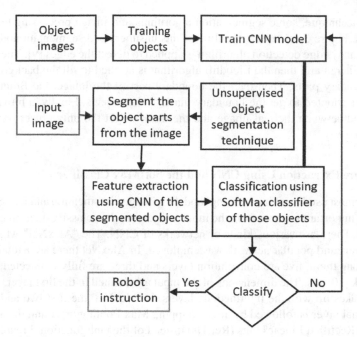

Fig. 2. Block diagram of Data analysis and action generation part in Cloud-base station.

2.2 Segmentation

Generally, object segmentation from an image of a random and dynamic background is the most challenging task. Without an efficient segmentation, the classification performance is suboptimal. In this proposed model, the input image is segmented using a new unsupervised segmentation technique.

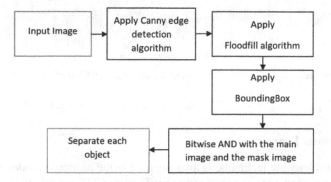

Fig. 3. Flow diagram of segmentation process of captured images.

In this technique, some segmentation algorithms and image processing techniques are applied. Figure 3 represents the flow of this unsupervised segmentation algorithm. First, the Canny edge detection algorithm is applied to detect the edges [9]. The detected edges are filtered and then the Floodfill algorithm is applied to fill the background and get the boundary parts. Then over the boundary part of the image, the BoundingBox algorithm is adopted to get the boundary mask of the objects. Finally, a bitwise AND is calculated between the real image and the mask to get the only object parts of the original image.

2.3 Feature Extraction Using CNN and the SoftMax Classifier

CNN is the most used machine learning model for image classification and recognition. It can extract important features from the input images and then classify their images using a classifier. There are various kinds of networks of CNN. The "AlexNet" which is the most common and popular network was employed. In AlexNet there are a total of eight layers, among them, five are convolution layers and three are fully-connected layers in the network [10, 11]. The dimensions of the input are defined in the first layer. The bulk of CNN makes up with the intermediate layers. In AlexNet, the first two and the fifth convolutional layer is followed by an overlapping Max Pooling layer and the activation function is Rectified Linear Units (ReLUs) instead of the tanh function. Figure 4 shows the architecture of the Convolutional Neural Network that is used in the proposed model. In Fig. 4 the 8th layer (Fc8) is the classification layer. In this layer, a Softmax classifier is used. The output of the last fully-connected layer is the input of the 1000-way softmax which produces a distribution over the 1000 class labels. Softmax is very useful because it converts the scores to a normalized probability distribution.

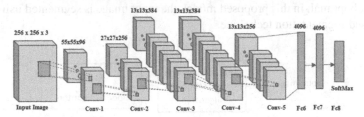

Fig. 4. The architecture of Convolutional Neural Network (CNN) used in the proposed model.

2.4 Incremental Learning

An Incremental learning technique is also engaged in the proposed model. In this technique, the segmented objects are classified using the CNN model. If the objects are classified by the classifier then it gives the next robot instruction else the non-classified objects are trained again with the CNN model incrementally.

2.5 The Cloud-Based Multi-robot Communication Framework

To share the computation power and inter-communication between multi-robots of robot station and cloud-base station, a layered framework is important. The cloud-based system supports a multi-robot system to provide on-demand communication in industrial applications [12] Fig. 5 presents the different layers of cloud robot system communication and task management. This system consists of a supervisory control layer, cloud-base station layer, network layer, and physical layer that contains multi robots.

At the top of the framework, there is a supervisory control layer. In the cloud robot system, the supervisory control layer is used to monitor and guide to robots (if needed) remotely by a human through a cloud-base station. Robot movement can be monitored by this layer through a Cloud-base Station. This layer also can manage the cloud database and adjust the configuration of the whole system accordingly.

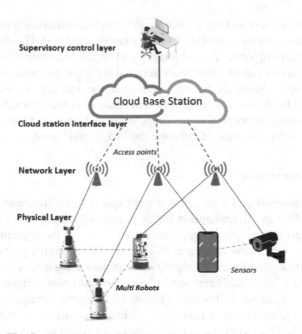

Fig. 5. Cloud-based multi-robot communication framework.

The Cloud-base Station has definite tasks to perform. a) store sensor data from robots of the physical layer, b) analyze the stored data for generating actions for the robots, c) store all the intermediate data and generated action data of this proposed model to perform the next action of the robot. The cloud-base station has a cloud database to store all data of this system. It also maintains the communication between the multiple robots of the physical layer.

The Network layer provides the communication between the robots, sensors, and the cloud-base Station. It consists of several access points (AP) to establish the communication bridge between the physical layer and the Cloud-base Station interface layer. Using the APs, the robots can gain a continuous stream depending on their location using IEEE 802.11 WLANs.

The Physical layer contains multiple robots and some sensors (for monitoring the robot's action). This layer provides the facilities for collecting data of robots and sent them to the cloud-base Station. Also provides communication between Robots and sensors using their local ad-hoc network.

3   Experimental Results and Discussion

3.1   Dataset

To validate the proposed object segmentation and object detection using the cloud-based robot, a benchmarked dataset called the COCO dataset is used [13]. This dataset contains 80 different classes of objects, 123,287 images, and 886,284 instances. However, in this research, 11 classes of indoor objects are selected for the experiment and validation. as the selected object classes are person, chair, tv, laptop, cat, dog, mouse, remote, cell phone, clock, and book. The dimensions of input images of the selected dataset is 256 * 256 * 3. For the testing purpose of the proposed model, some random indoor images from the dataset as well as some of our captured images were used.

3.2   Object Segmentation

This developed unsupervised segmentation technique is formulated using Canny edge detection, floodfilled and BoundingBox image processing algorithm, which is used for segmenting objects of the input image. Figure 6 and 7 present the segmentation process and results. Figure 6 (A) shows the input RGB image, (B) edged image using the Canny algorithm. After that, the Floodfilled algorithm is applied and got the Foreground of the Floodfilled image (C, D) and Foreground part of the real image (E), A BoundingBox algorithm is applied and got the bounding-box of the foreground image. A bitwise AND with the main image and the mask BoundingBox image, segment the Objects of the real input image (G, H). Those segmented objects are used as input to the CNN model in the training and classifying process.

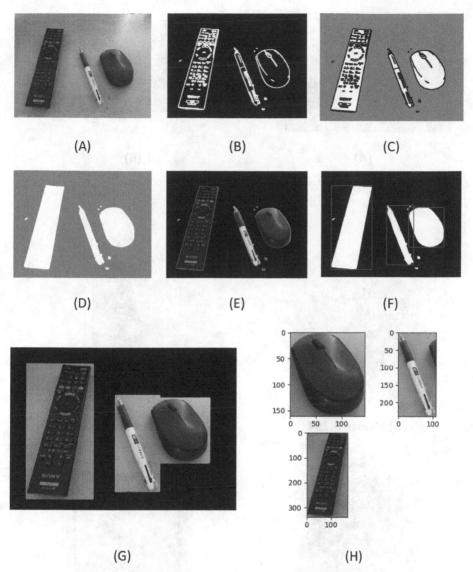

Fig. 6. (A) Input image, (B) Detected edge using Canny algorithm, (C) Inverted Floodfilled image, (D) Foreground of Floodfilled image, (E) Foreground part of the real image, (F) BoundingBox of the foreground, (G) Bitwise and with the main image and the mask boundingbox image, (H) Segmented Objects.

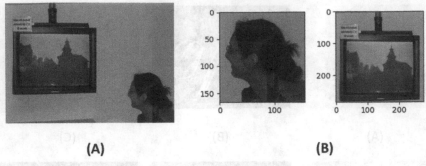

(A)   **(B)**

Fig. 7. (A) Input image, (B) Segmented objects.

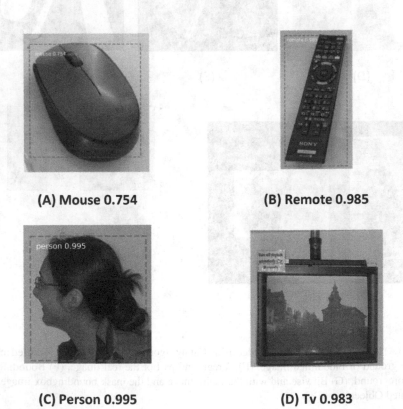

(A) Mouse 0.754   **(B) Remote 0.985**

(C) Person 0.995   **(D) Tv 0.983**

Fig. 8. (A, B, C, D) Classified objects of the segmented images.

3.3 Classification Results

In this section, the segmented objects are used as input in the CNN model to classify the segmented object. Using this process, multiple objects can be classified from one input image. Figure 8 shows the classification output results. The segmentation technique used in the proposed model helps to separate the object's area from the input images effectively. The optimally separated object images help to increase the object recognition accuracy. Moreover, the proposed CNN model extracts efficient features that help to improve the classification accuracy using the SoftMax classifier. According to the experimental results, our proposed methods achieve better object classification accuracy.

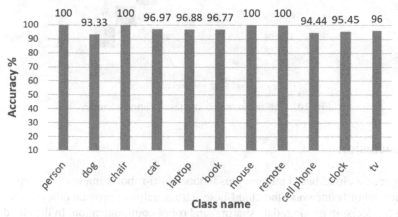

Fig. 9. Individual class classification accuracy.

In the evaluation process of the proposed model, 120 random images from the benchmark dataset and 50 captured images are segmented and 310 segmented objects are extracted. The detected objects are classified using the cloud-based CNN model and we got the average accuracy of indoor object identification is 97.10%. Figure 9 shows the Individual object class classification accuracy.

The proposed model achieves 100% accuracy of "Remote", "mouse", "Person" and "Chair" objects. Figure 10 shows the confusion matrix of identification accuracy.

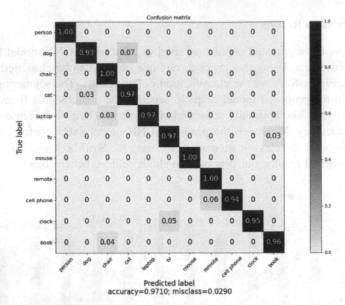

Fig. 10. Confusion matrix of classification accuracy.

4   Conclusion

In this paper, a cloud-based autonomous indoor multi-robot framework is proposed. In this cloud robot framework, the cloud-base station helps to provide efficient data processing for decision making, data sharing, and robot communication. In the cloud-base station, data analysis has different steps such as object segmentation, feature extraction, and classification to recognize the indoor objects and targets. A convolutional neural network (CNN), trained with an object image dataset, is used to identify indoor objects for a mobile multi-robot system. In this framework, the indoor input images captured from the robots are sent to the cloud-base station. The input images are segmented using the proposed segmentation algorithm to detect all objects in an image. A deep learning technique i.e., CNN is used to extract the features from segmented objects and fed to the classifier for classification. As a classifier algorithm SoftMax classifier is used to classify those objects. As a result, the average acceptance of indoor object identification is 97.10% which leads to a better result and helps to improve the environmental knowledge of a cloud-based indoor multi-robot system and it can be useful to make the next robot instruction efficiently.

References

1. Fortunati, L.: Robotization and the domestic sphere. New Media Soc. **20**(8), 2673–2690 (2017). https://doi.org/10.1177/1461444817729366
2. Al-Hafiz, F., Al-Megren, S., Kurdi, H.: Red blood cell segmentation by thresholding and Canny detector. Procedia Comput. Sci. **141**, 327–334 (2018). https://doi.org/10.1016/j.procs.2018.10.193

3. Popov, V.L., Ahmed, S.A., Topalov, A.V., Shakev, N.G.: Development of mobile robot target recognition and following behaviour using deep convolutional neural network and 2D range data. IFAC-PapersOnLine **51**(30), 210–215 (2018)
4. Espinace, P., Kollar, T., Roy, N., Soto, A.: Indoor scene recognition by a mobile robot through adaptive object detection. Robot. Auton. Syst. **61**(9), 932–947 (2013). https://doi.org/10.1016/j.robot.2013.05.002
5. Rahman, A., Jin, J., Rahman, A., Cricenti, A., Afrin, M., Dong, Y.: Energy-efficient optimal task offloading in cloud networked multi-robot systems. Comput. Netw. **160**, 11–32 (2019). https://doi.org/10.1016/j.comnet.2019.05.016
6. Bergamini, L., Sposato, M., Pellicciari, M.: Deep learning-based method for vision-guided robotic grasping of unknown objects. Adv. Eng. Inform. **44**, 101052 (2020). https://doi.org/10.1016/j.aei.2020.101052
7. Wanga, R., Xu, J., Hanb, T.X.: Object instance detection with pruned Alexnet and extended training data. Signal Process. Image Commun. **70**, 145–156 (2019). https://doi.org/10.1016/j.image.2018.09.013
8. Badawy, M., Khalifa, H., Arafat, H.: New approach to enhancing the performance of cloud-based vision system of mobile robots. Comput. Electr. Eng. **74**, 1–21 (2019). https://doi.org/10.1016/j.compeleceng.2019.01.001
9. Kabir, R., Jahan, S., Islam, M.R., Rahman, N., Rajibul, M.: Discriminant feature extraction using disease segmentation for automatic leaf disease diagnosis. In: ICCA 2020: Proceedings of the International Conference on Computing Advancements, vol. 32, pp. 1–7 (2020). https://doi.org/10.1145/3377049.3377100
10. Krizhevsky, A., Sutskever, I., Hinton, G.E.: Imagenet classification with deep convolutional neural networks. Commun. ACM **60**(6), 84–90 (2017). https://doi.org/10.1145/3065386
11. Islam, M.R., Mitu, U.K., Bhuiyan, R.A., Shin, J.: Hand gesture feature extraction using deep convolutional neural network for recognizing american sign language. In: 4th International Conference on Frontiers of Signal Processing (ICFSP), no. 18290482 (2018). https://doi.org/10.1109/ICFSP.2018.8552044
12. Tao, F., Cheng, Y., Xu, L.D., Zhang, L., Li, B.H.: CCIoT-CMfg: cloud computing and internet of things-based cloud manufacturing service system. IEEE Trans. Ind. Inf. **10**, 1435–1442 (2014)
13. Lin, T.-Y., et al.: Microsoft COCO: common objects in context. In: Fleet, D., Pajdla, T., Schiele, B., Tuytelaars, T. (eds.) ECCV 2014. LNCS, vol. 8693, pp. 740–755. Springer, Cham (2014). https://doi.org/10.1007/978-3-319-10602-1_48

Knowledge Based and Decision Support Systems

The Concept of Information Graphs as a Tool to Identify Vulnerabilities in the Information Map of an Organisation

Zygmunt Mazur[1]([⊠]) [iD] and Janusz Pec[2]

[1] Faculty of Computer Science and Management, Wroclaw University of Science and Technology, Wrocław, Poland
zygmunt.mazur@pwr.edu.pl
[2] Central Statistical Office, Warsaw, Poland

Abstract. This paper defines the information graph concept and proposes its use to describe information links, with particular emphasis on information security. The information graph is a certain extension of the concept of a graph known from graph theory. The introduction of the information graph concept makes it possible to describe and analyse processes taking place in any organisation as information streams. In terms of information security in information systems described by means of information graphs, graph structures such as information graphs with vertices with a large number of classifiers, Hamiltonian cycles, and cliques are of particular importance. The analysis of these types of graph structures make it possible to identify vulnerability in the topology of information links of an organisation, and consequently the possibility of exploiting this vulnerability by a relevant threat. The proposals presented in the paper concerning the description of information links in an organisation may serve as guidelines for the designers of information systems, including the definition of roles and relations between individual users of these systems, especially in terms of security. The paper also reviews the literature related to the discussed issue that has inspired the authors of this paper to define the concept of information graph and to work on the applications of such graphs.

Keywords: Information graph · Thematic graph · Graph reduction · Information classifier · Information channel · Catalogued information

1 Introduction

One of the methods of describing the information flow in any organisation is a process approach, consisting of identifying all processes taking place within the organisation, their classification in terms of information and creating a map of information links between these processes, i.e. the topology of information flow between them. The analysis of such a links map may prove useful not only for the optimisation of information flows between organisational units (e.g. removal of redundant/duplicated processes), but also for the simplification of the flow structure by replacing several processes with one (equivalent in terms of information and retaining all necessary information and recipients

© Springer Nature Switzerland AG 2021
H. Fujita et al. (Eds.): IEA/AIE 2021, LNAI 12799, pp. 215–226, 2021.
https://doi.org/10.1007/978-3-030-79463-7_18

of that information) by eliminating organisational units participating in the exchange of information.

An important aspect of the process approach to analysing an organisation from the point of view of information flows is the analysis of vulnerabilities inherent in the structure of information links between its individual units. Vulnerability is a kind of weakness of an organisation – it refers to a lack of resistance to the effects of a hostile action. Vulnerability means that there are hazards (internal or external) against which there are no adequate safeguards and losses may occur.

An organisation wishing to build its own comprehensive information security management system (ISMS) may use a process-based model rather than a classic functional model, which, despite its many advantages, also has many disadvantages. By the classical functional model of an organisation, we mean assigning tasks to individual organisational units.

In the case of a determined and described set of processes and their map of information links, it is possible to monitor the phenomena of process variability within the organisation (disappearance of processes, changes, or the emergence of new ones) with the use of appropriate tools (even with the use of slightly outdated Shewhart control charts). In the case of the classical functional model, due to ignorance of the process map, it is not known how many gaps there are and of what kind, and also which the trend is and direction of changes.

When developing an information model of an organisation, a properly performed risk analysis plays an important role. In the authors' opinion, the use of a process approach in risk analysis in this case also significantly improves its quality, compared to classical methods, such as qualitative, quantitative or hybrid one. This, of course, has a huge impact on the correct development of other documents, such as the hierarchical architecture of security policy – usually a three-tier one – and the remaining documents, such as operating procedures or other operating instructions of the information system. A poorly performed risk analysis affects the development of the remaining documents. It can also be a serious threat to organisations, because it distracts the attention of information security systems designers from the actual threats and diverts the effort of designing security measures onto the wrong track. The reference to the process approach to developing an information security system in institutions and companies was made in the foreword to paper [7]. According to the information obtained by the authors of this paper from the co-author of MEHARI (*MEthod for Harmonized Analysis of RIsk*) methodology [8], the next version of the methodology will be based on a process approach.

2 Information Security Problems

By information we mean any sequence of characters from a fixed alphabet which has the same semantic meaning for the sender and the recipient and is interpreted by them in a given period of time and with a fixed character processing technology, either equally or similarly. It would be desirable for the information to have the following characteristics:

- formal ones, such as: aggregation, unambiguity, communicativeness, redundancy, assimilability, comparability,

- factual ones, such as: purposefulness, decision-making aspect, accuracy, flexibility, quantity, completeness, validity, veracity, reliability, consistency, reliability, source of origin, usefulness, sensibility, prospectiveness, retrospectiveness.

There are currently many distributed organisations, virtual offices with a network structure, where data security and communication is of the utmost importance. Information is a strategic component of an organisation. The collection, processing and sharing of information, and anything that contributes to the increase in the amount of data, complicates the automation of IT processes, which require appropriate protection measures.

An intuitive and encyclopaedic notion of the term *information security* assumes it to be the degree of justified (e.g. by means of risk analysis and accepted risk management methods) confidence that no potential loss resulting from undesired (accidental or deliberate) disclosure, modification, destruction or prevention of processing of information stored, processed and transmitted within a specific information flow system will be incurred. The definition of the term information security combines the processing of information with the perception of an organisation's business activity seen from the angle of risk related to the use of information. Secure information is properly secured (well-protected) information, and methods of dealing with risk consists of providing appropriate security protections. However, security is not the same as safety, as the former concerns organisational and technical measures and the latter concerns subjective feelings. We do not formally define these concepts by adopting their common notion. The assessment and interpretation of the characteristics of information by a sender or a recipient lies within language pragmatics that is very difficult to define in formal terms, especially in the various environments in which the sender and recipient may be present [5]. One of the attempts to define the pragmatics of language in formal terms is presented in paper [9]. A description of these issues and their formalised discussion by means of lattice theory is presented in paper [12].

Controlling the flow of information between individual objects (e.g. organisational units) is one of the main requirements imposed on IT tools, including the Database Management System (DBMS) in terms of supporting the maintenance of security of the data collected and made available, as mentioned in paper [10] (chapter 6.1.2). This paper also mentions the use of "hidden channels" by unauthorised users as one of the threats to information security. A high risk results from poorly designed/implemented or underdeveloped IT systems.

After analysing the map of information links between individual processes, hidden processes can be identified (consciously – e.g. by the management or an organisation or the processes of which the organisation itself is unaware) and used as a channel for transforming information or eavesdropping on it by unauthorised persons. An example of how a Wireshark package can be used in practice to analyse network traffic and eavesdrop on a conversation between two persons is described in paper [17]. The methodology of the process approach and the process map have a great impact on the quality of data in IT systems. This is important for example for the insurance industry [11].

In paper [13], on the basis of the results obtained by SWOT analysis, the lack of process approach to the Information Security Management System (ISMS) operated in the Central Statistical Office (GUS) and public statistics in general was indicated.

The results of the weakness in SWOT analysis were a stimulus for the authors of this paper to formulate the concept of information graphs and their use in the area of ISMS. When analysing the requirements of PN-ISO/IEC 27001:2017–06 standard [18], we can observe that the risk analysis and the ISO 9001 quality management system [23] propose a process approach. Also in the TOGAF documentation (**T**he **O**pen **G**roup **A**rchitecture **F**ramework), a tool to facilitate the transformation of the organisation, in Phase B of the Architecture Development Method (ADM), which is its central part, attention is paid to services and business processes, including links between them [19].

An interesting issue related to the process map is the attempt to describe the infrastructure of a particular type of organisation, i.e. the state. This applies in particular to the critical information infrastructure of the state in terms of security of its operation in non-standard conditions, such as war, natural disaster, etc. The significance of this issue for the security of the state was discussed, among others, in Dorothy Denning's monograph [21]. In paper [20, pp. 305–306], an expert in the field of theory and practice, lists 15 interconnected layers, noting that *"The individual layers include standards, resources, processes or information systems with different functions within the entire information infrastructure"*.

The processes taking place in the organisation and their optimisation to increase information security are mentioned in paper [16]. In addition, Edward Yourdon, an authority in the field of object-based methodology, in his work [15] in the chapter devoted to "death march" projects mentions processes and their role in risk management. In paper [14] describing broadly the security protections engineering and various security protections models in information flow control, a simplified military model of Bell-LaPadula [25] is presented, which is more user-friendly and suitable for organisations.

3 Definition of Information Graph

We will begin the description of the term information graph by interpreting its vertices.

Vertex (node) $v(p_1, p_2, \ldots p_n) \in \mathbf{V}$ of $\mathbf{G}^{\text{infc}}(\mathbf{V}, \mathbf{E})$ graph may be interpreted as an organisational unit, a person, or a group of persons linked by formal or informal ties. The vertex can be described with the set parameters $p_1, \ldots p_n$ specifying, for example, the type of organisational unit or the type of personnel group, the degree of hierarchy in the organisational structure of a given organisation, the type of role performed, the types of information generated, transmitted or received, or the period of activity of the unit. These parameters may take alphanumeric, time and logical values.

Edge $e(p_1, p_2, \ldots, p_n) \in \mathbf{E}$ of $\mathbf{G}^{\text{infc}}(\mathbf{V}, \mathbf{E})$ graph may be interpreted as a means of transmitting information (information channel type) with channel parameters $p_1, \ldots, p_n$, which may specify, e.g. bandwidth, channel operation period, channel type (transmission medium), types of information transmitted by the channel, degree of resistance of the channel to interference. These parameters may take alphanumeric, time and logical values.

From among the parameters of $p_i \in \mathbf{P}$ ($1 \leq$ and $\leq n$) of the set of parameters of a given vertex (edge), we distinguish those which form a set $\mathbf{P}_{\mathbf{I}(v)}$ of ordered tuples with $j + 4$ values in the form $<\mathbf{I}, \mathbf{G}, \mathbf{T}, \mathbf{O}, \mathbf{K_1}, \ldots, \mathbf{K_j}>$, characterising a given type of information of a given vertex, the first four symbols of which denote:

- **I** – identifier – catalogued name of information (type of information) belonging to the information resources of an organisation, i.e. the **KT** catalogue being a collection of names, $I \in KT$.
- **G** – a dummy variable indicating whether information is generated or processed in the vertex or in the edge.
- **T** – a dummy variable that determines whether given information is transmitted from the vertex to the channel, and in the case of edges, whether given information is transmitted through the channel – that is, we determine the flow capacity of the channel.
- **O** – a dummy variable, indicating whether the information is received at the vertex or at the edge.
- **Kj** – j-th element belonging to the $K \subset P$ set of relevant parameters describing information **I**, with $j + 4 \leq n$. **K** being the smallest set of those information parameters which do not change or change only within the strictly defined limits (within acceptable tolerance ranges) during the flow in the channels (graph edges). However, these parameters allow for the identification of information **I** (unambiguous identification of information) even after modifications that may be made to the information network.

The set $P_{I(v)}$ is the collection of state catalogued (classified) information at vertex v $\in V$, and respectively the set $P_{I(e)}$ is the collection of information for edge $e \in E$. The information identifier **I** (the name in the directory) alone may not be sufficient to identify the information after it has been transformed within a network, which may later result in misclassification and assignment, e.g. a different degree of confidentiality. The minimum set **K** is defined by the designer of secure information systems for any information with identified **I** by creating a string of such sets $\{K^I\}$.

The appearance of a value for any of the symbols **G, T, O** or a combination of symbols in an ordered (j + 4) tuple briefly indicates the existence of information with the specified attributes. We also accept the existence of an **UNDEF** undefined value, other than logical values **0** and **1**, for the sole purpose of defining the concept of **an information classifier**. It may be interpreted as the absence of any information on the **G, T** or **O** process. Such an ordered (j + 4) tuple reduced by the symbols **G, T, O** which we omit (we do not analyse the **UNDEF,0** or **1** value for these symbols) is called the information classifier with the identifier **I** and we shall denote it as KL_I. By **classifying** information, we mean assigning a classifier to it.

Each $KL_I \in KL_{I(e)} \cup KL$ classifier, where $KL_{I(e)}$ is a set of edge classifiers and $KL_{I(v)}$ is a set of vertex classifiers.

For a channel (edge) we exclude two cases $<I, 1, 0, 0, ...>$ and $<I, 1, 0, 1, ...>$ in which the channel is an information generator but does not fulfil its basic natural function of transmitting information. As a result, the resulting information cannot be classified in any way, as it cannot get out of the channel. All other cases offer reasonable knowledge of the possibility of information classification or refraining from its classification due to its absence in the channel.

The set $KL_{I(e)}$ of edge e classifiers is a subset of classifiers of at least one of its adjacent vertices, i.e. $KL_{I(e)} \subset KL_{I(v)}$ and exactly one in case when an edge (channel) loses any of the **K** set parameters along the path (e.g. signal fading or distortion). The recipient then loses the classifier to the sender and channel. In the case of a two-way channel (two incident edges for the same vertices with opposite orientations in the directed graph), $KL_{I(e)}$ is a subset of a set of classifiers for both incident vertices.

Any subset of the set of all parameters of the vertex (edge) $\mathbf{P}$ set is called the vertex (edge) label. In further consideration, we will mainly deal with the subset $\mathbf{K} \subset \mathbf{P}$, treating the remaining parameters of the $\mathbf{P}$ set as additional information, supporting the operations carried out on the classifiers and subject (or not subject to) circulation, which is important for information security in the organisation.

Let us note that a given vertex may perform several roles, e.g. it may simultaneously be a generator, a relay (an intermediary) and a recipient of information. Any arrangement of dummy variables from the $\{\mathbf{G}, \mathbf{T}, \mathbf{O}\}$ set is possible. In the language of combinatorics, it is a variation with repetitions, so all possibilities correspond to $2^3 = 8$. For the edge, the number of role performance possibilities is reduced by two previously discussed cases ($2^3 - 2 = 6$), due to the assumption that information has to be classified (the two exclusions are <$\mathbf{I}$, 1, 0, 0, ...> and <$\mathbf{I}$, 1, 0, 1, ...>).

The channel can also perform all these roles simultaneously. Let us suppose, for example, that it is a messenger or a technical medium (a cable or a network device). Such a medium can receive disturbances from the outside (the role of the receiver), while interfering with the transmitted signal it will process it, so it will be a generator (the role of the generator) and it will pass it on (the role of the relay). Signal processing may be caused by objective factors or by natural impact. This also applies to an individual who, by generating a rumour, distorts the original source information and passes it on in the changed form.

Using the introduced concepts, we will now formally define the concept of an information graph $\mathbf{G}^{infc}(\mathbf{V}, \mathbf{E})$.

Definition 1. The information graph $\mathbf{G}^{infc}(\mathbf{V}, \mathbf{E})$ of an organisation is a simple graph (non-oriented graph, without loops and without multiple edges), which additionally meets the following conditions:

1. each vertex or edge is assigned a parameter vector $\mathbf{P}$,
2. the edge between two vertices exists when and only when there is any flow of information between the vertices; if so, we can the characterise the edge using the parameters available and known to us,
3. the transmitted information belongs to the essential information resources of the organisation, important for its business activity and security - catalogued information,
4. in the set of tuples $\mathbf{P}_{I(v)}$, $\mathbf{P}_{I(e)}$ there is exactly one information classifier that is the same for all vertices and edges where the information is recorded, i.e. generated, transmitted or received; it is indistinguishable by its vertex or edge,
5. a set of classifiers $KL_{I(e)}$ of the edge e is a subset of classifiers of at least one of its adjacent vertices, i.e. $KL_{I(e)} \subset KL_{I(v)}$.

As a reminder, we assume that by generating information we mean, in addition to creating completely new information at the vertex, also the processing of incoming information. Whether given information will change its classifier to another depends on the designer's choice of the $\mathbf{K}$ set, i.e. the selection of such a set of its elements (parameters) that determine the identity of such information. The designer may also set tolerance ranges for the values of individual parameters for which the classifier remains unchanged. We have already mentioned this when defining the information classifier.

In this paper we do not consider vertices with loops, i.e. edges of which both ends are in the same vertex. An example of such a vertex would be an organisational unit that generates information for itself, processes it and receives it, i.e. the one that 'consumes' its own information. We shall omit such a case in further deliberations.

In our deliberations to date, we have tacitly assumed that the information channel (edge) is bidirectional – information can be transmitted in both directions. Otherwise, it would be appropriate to consider targeted informational graphs and to modify the definition accordingly. We have not assumed the graph consistency condition in the definition due to the fact that for a given thematic graph (examples below), there may exist, e.g. an entity (organisational unit) that is not interested in specific information (an entity isolated with reference to this thematic issue) or there may exist parallel groups of units exchanging information on a given thematic issue, regardless of the others.

A **thematic graph** is an information graph in which the identifier $I \in \{P_{I(v)}, P_{I(e)}\}$ describes only one type of information catalogued in these sets.

Examples of thematic information graphs are as follows:

- financial information flow graph,
- HR information flow graph,
- technological information flow graph,
- management information flow graph,
- logistical information flow graph,
- marketing and trade information flow graph,
- defence information flow graph,
- organisational information graph,
- graph of information exchange with the environment.

The information graph of an organisation may consist of a number of **thematic sub-graphs,** which are informational graphs. The information graph $G^{infc}(V, E)$ of an organisation is the concatenation of some or all of the thematic graphs under consideration – in particular, it may be one thematic graph. The operation of concatenation (bonding) and reduction of information graphs and overlapping of graphs is described in paper [24].

The information graph $G^{infc}(V, E)$ is not a fixed structure graph, but a dynamic graph, i.e. the number of vertices and the number of edges change (may change) with time. This results both from the dynamics of transformations taking place in the organisation (e.g. as a result of restructuring), but also from the process of detailed analysis of the existing information graph. Thus, a string of graphs $\{G_t^{infc}(V, E)\}$ marked with the timestamp t is created. New information may appear (generation of new information on the basis of the analysis of other information – new information quality), which will require a new communication channel with new parameters, or the creation of new nodes (graph vertices). Also because of the desire to optimise the information structure within an organisation, it can be simplified. This task can be carried out through a so-called graph reduction operation.

The analysis of information processes (analysis of the organisation information graph) may serve to optimise the flow of information. The edges of the information graph may determine how the information channel is used (frequency of use, capacity, stability, lifetime). These features may be described by numerical parameters, time stamps, alphanumeric characters or logical values.

The depth and the way of breaking down the problem into thematic graphs determines the accuracy of description of the actual model of information flow in an organisation. Due to the labour intensity of such a method, a reasonable level of information graph analysis should be chosen, e.g. adapted to the selected level of information security within the organisation. If the designer of the information security system determines such a level and identifies elementary processes at this level, consideration may be given to using the Petri net to analyse business processes in a more precise manner. However, as the author of the paper suggests [9], using the Petri net to analyse business processes is not an easy task. In addition, the conditions for moving a process from one condition to another, in the case of security processes, are often hidden and classified, if only because of the desire to keep secret the private interests of individual users, including the management of the organisation, or because of unconscious relationships between organisational units within the organisation. These situations are adequately described by the words of Sławomir Mrożek: "Feelings depend on information, which means they may have nothing to do with the truth if the information is false".

There is a problem with the choice of method (criterion) for creating a list of thematic graphs. These methods could be divided as follows:

- a targeted method (task-oriented, e.g. information protection task),
- a usability method (usefulness of the information for a specific person or group of persons).
- a complete analysis method for the actual situation.

In the information or thematic graph of an organisation, structures such as cliques, Hamiltonian cycles or Eulerian cycles can be distinguished. With regards to information protection issues, such structures as Hamiltonian cycles and cliques are important if we consider them in terms of information links and security problems.

The existence of the Hamiltonian cycle (path) in the information graph, i.e. a path in the graph which does not repeat the vertices traversing all of them, is undesirable from the point of view of information security, because a possible hacking into the information system of an organisation makes it much easier for an intruder to recognise the entire company's information system. This is an important design guideline for the correct development of the company information system. When designing the information graph, it would be advisable to avoid creating such structures and instead create those that would reduce the risk of a possible intruder gaining control of the entire information system and would only allow for some part of it to be taken over.

Let us consider, for example, the behaviour of a potential hacker with a limited budget and time, having certain skills, who uses the Internet and intends to decode information links in the computer network of a global organisation. If there is a network of information links in the organisation in the form of a clique, then with one communication channel assigned (e.g. one frequency band), the intruder obtaining access to any node of the organisation can recognise the situation in one step by distributing the signal from the controlled vertex (e.g. through frequency multiplexing) to all other vertices. A hacker is in a worse situation if the Hamiltonian cycle is used in the information network of the organisation (the path on the graph passes through all the vertices without repeating them except for the first and last one). Then the hacker must have an effective algorithm to search for the Hamiltonian cycle (a difficult task), have the appropriate knowledge and have a lot of time, but using, for example, a few, a dozen or several dozen computers with the appropriate computing power, he can make the task much easier for himself (speed up computing) and also threaten the organisation. The same is true for the remaining structures. Their existence in the organisation information network is generally not perceived or realised, which makes it much easier for an intruder to penetrate the network. In general, neither the management of the organisation nor the relevant services are aware of the risks. The issue should be considered and analysed during the design stage of the information network in terms of security issues and the creation of the organisational structure of units within the organisation.

When developing a procedure for a secure information system, the vulnerability of both nodes and information channels must be considered. Nodes can provide an attractive 'information retrieval' point for an intruder, and channels can be technically easy to take control of and eavesdrop on them.

The structure of the information graph can be the basis for the selection of:

- vulnerable nodes,
- positions on information protection,
- defining functions for personnel in charge of security protections,
- protected areas,
- areas suitable for computerisation (creation of an IT subgraph),
- selection of security protection types for hardware and software,
- organisational matters, e.g. the formulation of a reporting structure in the field of information protection issues, relations between organisational units within a given organisation as well as procedures.

The general model of information protection of an organisation is shaped by the development strategy of the organisation and the existing legal standards created by the legislator, imposing certain obligations on the governing bodies of the company, e.g. the Management Board and the Supervisory Board. The main Information Security Policy Document (ISPD) adopted by the organisation's management and approved by the Supervisory Board should in turn be defined by a document describing the company's development strategy and a technical document describing the structure of the organisation information graph. On the basis of the ISPD, provided to the organisation management by a team of experts consisting of analysts, organisational and management specialists, IT specialists and system designers dealing with security matters, derivative documents should be generated, describing detailed information security plans with a thematic and geographical breakdown.

By the G^{inft} information graph we mean, in an informal way, the G^{infc} subgraph of the organisation information graph, where the edges of the G^{inft} graph define the method of data transmission through an electronic medium – a digital or an analogue channel – and the information is processed by any digital devices, including computers.

By having the organisation information graph G^{inft}, it is possible to define roles for administrators of individual IT systems operating in the organisation and for ordinary users of these systems.

The G^{infc} – G^{inft} difference defines a non-computerised area – an area to define the relationship between the personnel managing the security of information systems and personnel generally involved in information protection such as, for example, employees of the Information Protection Office, employees of the Secret Office, industrial guards.

Defining the relations between security administrators and the administrators of individual IT systems is an important task in creating a methodology for information security policy within a given organisation. Usually, guidelines are described in the ISPD (which is actually a set of documents). This document is a starting point for the creation of derivative documents – a policy of lower tiers defining the rules of conduct and relations between the administrators of individual IT systems and the administrators of information security of those systems.

According to the TISM (Total Information Security Management) methodology developed by ENSI (European Network Security Institute) [6], there are two subordinate structures: local information security administrators subordinate to the company's Chief Security Officer (a function usually performed by a proxy of the company Board of Directors) and local information system administrators (data processing systems) subordinate to the information administrator, e.g. Chief IT Specialist or Chief Information Technology Officer. The latter in turn reports to the Chief Information Administrator (CIA) – a function usually performed by the company Management Board or a Board Member.

The two divisions cooperate in this respect; however, the information protection division performs a control role over the processing division and has primary responsibility for information protection. Therefore, employees of the security division, often referred to as information security inspectors, who are involved in computer system security audits, are often IT specialists or persons with related education – provided that they have completed relevant courses organised by companies specialising in the above issues or by the relevant state services.

During the procedure of determining the tools for analysing and developing a security model, it is very important to label the nodes and edges of the information graph. The label could contain a number of parameters describing graph elements (vertices and edges), as we mentioned earlier. A label for a node would include, for example, the name of the node, the degree of attractiveness, the type of security, identifiers for belonging to the types of thematic graphs, types of legal regulation, the number of links to other nodes and other parameters referred to in the definition of the information graph. The label for the edge (channel) can contain, for example, the name of the edge, the type of transmission medium, the degree of vulnerability, the type of protection, the list of edge predecessors, the list of successors, bandwidth and other parameters.

The graph bonding and reduction operation determines the labelling process (creation and removal of edge and vertex labels) and changes the value of their parameters. Paper [2] describes a parallel programming language for such a task.

4 Conclusions and Future Work

In this paper the authors use the concept of information graph and operations on these graphs for the analysis of information flow in any organisation. The first idea of introducing the concept of information graph and the definition of two basic operations on information graphs was earlier indicated in paper [2]. A similar interpretation, however on a very general level, but not equivalent to the object of a defined information graph, has been applied in paper [22] to issues related to library science. Instead of an information graph, it considers multimodal, unimodal, and dynamic graphs as well as operations of reducing multimodal to unimodal graphs.

Research on information graphs in terms of information security should be developed in particular towards the identification of 'hazardous graph structures' such as Hamiltonian graphs or cliques. The presented approach to the information system in a given organisation in terms of security differs from the classical approach presented e.g. in paper [3] based on the process of risk assessment and management.

Without prejudging the superiority of any of the methodologies, it is worth noting in relation to every aspect of practical application that an approach based on the topology of processes taking place in an organisation by means of information graphs seems theoretically to be more precise from the point of view of information security. Information graphs containing such a structure as a Hamiltonian cycle can be analysed using the theory of finding and existence of Hamiltonian cycles – an important section of graph theory. Current issues of the existence and finding Hamiltonian cycles can be found in the review paper [4]. A certain algorithm of finding the Hamiltonian cycle in ordinary graphs (without loops and multiple edges) can be also found in paper [1].

The authors of this paper in their next paper [24] attempted to use information graphs for information security analysis by identifying vulnerabilities inherent in the organisational structure itself.

References

1. Pec, J.: O pewnym algorytmie znajdywania cykli Hamiltona w grafach skończonych). Prace Instytutu Badań Systemowych PAN, Zeszyt 96, Warszawa (1983)
2. Pec, J.: Bezpieczeństwo danych w systemach informatycznych przedsiębiorstwa – metody i narzędzia, rozprawa doktorska, WNE UW, Warszawa (2004)
3. EL Fray, I.: Metoda określająca zaufanie do systemu informacyjnego w oparciu o proces szacowania i postępowania z ryzykiem, rozprawa habilitacyjna, Wydział Informatyki, Zachodniopomorski Uniwersytet Technologiczny, Szczecin (2013)
4. Gould, R.J.: Updating the Hamiltonian problem – a survey. J. Graph Theory (1991)
5. Martin, R.M.: Toward a Systematic Pragmatics, Studies in Logic and the Foundations of Mathematics. North-Holland Publishing Company, Amsterdam (1959)
6. TISM ver. 1.4CL European Network Security Institute 2000–2002
7. Białas, A.: Bezpieczeństwo informacji i usług w nowoczesnej instytucji i firmie, WNT, Warszawa (2007)
8. MEHARI – Risk Analysis and Treatment Guide, Paris, France: Club de la Sécurité de l'Information Français (2010)
9. Walczak, M.: Zastosowanie sieci Petriego w modelowaniu procesów biznesowych, Zeszyty Naukowe nr 736, Akademia Ekonomiczna w Krakowie (2007)

10. Stokłosa, J., Bilski, T., Pankowski, T.: Bezpieczeństwo danych w systemach informatycznych. PWN, Warszawa (2001)

11. Jakość danych w systemach informatycznych zakładów ubezpieczeń, materiały z IX i X edycji seminariów Polskiej Izby Ubezpieczeń, Warszawa (2011)

12. Wolniewicz, B.: Ontologia sytuacji, Podstawy i zastosowania. PWN, Warszawa (1985)

13. Szczerba, A., et al.: Studium wykonalności Systemu Zarządzania Bezpieczeństwem Informacji dla GUS, InfoStrategia, Kraków (2015)

14. Anderson, R.: Security engineering: a guide to building dependable distributed systems. Wiley, New York (2008)

15. Yourdon, E.: Byte Wars: The Impact of September 11 on Information Technology, Prentice Hall (2002)

16. Pipkin, D.L.: Information Security – Protecting the Global Enterprise, Hewlett-Packard Company (2000)

17. Forshaw, J.: Attack on the network with the eye of a hacker, Helion (2019)

18. ISO/IEC 2700: 2005 Information technology – Security techniques – Information security management systems - Requirements (2005)

19. Szafrański, B., Sobczak, A. (eds.): Wstęp do architektury korporacyjnej, WAT, Warszawa (2008)

20. Oleński, J.: Infrastruktura informacyjna państwa w globalnej gospodarce, WNE Uniwersytet Warszawski, Warszawa (2006)

21. Denning, D.E.: Information Warfare and Security. Addison-Wesley-Longman, Singapore (1999)

22. Kamińska, A.M.: Zastosowanie struktur grafowych do analiz bibliometrycznych i webometrycznych, Modele i metody Nowa Biblioteka. Usługi, Technologie Informacyjne i Media 2(29), 47–63 (2018). ISSN 2451–2575

23. EN ISO 9001:2015 Quality management systems – Requirements (2016)

24. Mazur, Z., Pec, J.: Use of information graphs for security analysis (under preparation)

25. Liderman, K.: Podstawowe Twierdzenie Bezpieczeństwa, Biuletyn WAT, vol. lX, No. 4 (2011)

A Learning-Automata Based Solution for Non-equal Partitioning: Partitions with Common GCD Sizes

Rebekka Olsson Omslandseter[1]([⊠]), Lei Jiao[1], and B. John Oommen[1,2]

[1] University of Agder, Grimstad, Norway
{rebekka.o.omslandseter,lei.jiao}@uia.no
[2] Carleton University, Ottawa, Canada
oommen@scs.carleton.ca

Abstract. The Object Migration Automata (OMA) has been used as a powerful tool to resolve real-life partitioning problems in random Environments. The virgin OMA has also been enhanced by incorporating the latest strategies in Learning Automata (LA), namely the Pursuit and Transitivity phenomena. However, the single major handicap that it possesses is the fact that the number of objects in each partition must be equal. Obviously, one does not always encounter problems with equally-sized groups (When the true underlying problem has non-equally-sized groups, the OMA reports the best equally-sized solution as the recommended partition.). This paper is the pioneering attempt to relax this constraint. It proposes a novel solution that tackles partitioning problems where the partition sizes can be both equal and/or *unequal*, but when the cardinalities of the true partitions have a Greatest Common Divisor (GCD). However, on attempting to resolve this less-constrained version, we encounter a few problems that deal with implementing the inter-partition migration of the objects. To mitigate these, we invoke a strategy that has been earlier used in the theory of automata, namely that of mapping the machine's state space onto a larger space. This paper details how this strategy can be incorporated, and how such problems can be solved. In essence, it presents the design, implementation, and testing of a novel OMA-based method that can be implemented with the OMA itself, and also in all of its existing variants, including those incorporating the Pursuit and Transitivity phenomena. Numerical results demonstrate that the new approach can efficiently solve partitioning problems with partitions that have a common GCD.

Keywords: Learning Automata · Object Migration Automata · Object Partitioning with GCD

1 Introduction

Object Partitioning Problems (OPPs): OPPs, where the true data elements are represented as "abstract" objects, concern dividing a set of elements into subsets based on a certain underlying criterion. OPPs are NP-hard and have been studied since the 1970s. Within OPPs, the sub-field of Equi-Partitioning Problems (EPPs) [3], where all the partitions are of equal sizes, have been solved efficiently using Learning Automata (LA).

© Springer Nature Switzerland AG 2021
H. Fujita et al. (Eds.): IEA/AIE 2021, LNAI 12799, pp. 227–239, 2021.
https://doi.org/10.1007/978-3-030-79463-7_19

To solve EPPs, LA-based Object Migration Automata (OMA) algorithms, based on the semi-supervised Reinforcement Learning (RL) paradigm, have demonstrated a superior efficiency, when compared with former algorithms [8–11].

Observe that the nature of the "true" underlying partitioning problem is always unknown. However, the system presents a sequence of queries that are a realization of objects belonging together. The OMA uses this information to infer and converge to the near-optimal groupings. Essentially, OMA-based solutions are clustering algorithms, except that they do not require an imposed distance-based relation between the objects.

Existing OMA Algorithms: There are different types of OMA algorithms, namely the original OMA, the Enhanced OMA (EOMA), the Pursuit EOMA (PEOMA), and the Transitivity PEOMA (TPEOMA)[1]. Of these algorithms, the OMA is the original pioneering solution [3,4]. Later, an enhancement to the OMA, termed the EOMA, was proposed in [2], and this prevent the so-called *Deadlock Situation*. The authors of [11] and [8] proposed the improved PEOMA, which incorporated the Pursuit concept (already established in the LA literature) into the EOMA, reducing the levels of noise presented to the learning mechanism. Thereafter, the TPEOMA was introduced in [10], where the transitivity phenomenon was further augmented into the PEOMA algorithm, ensuring even better results in certain Environments and reducing the required number of queries before convergence [7]. Numerous applications of OMA-based algorithm have been in reported in different fields, including that of increasing the trustworthiness of reputation systems [12], and user grouping in mobile radio communications [6]. A detailed survey of OMA-based solutions for various applications is included in [7].

Limitations of Existing OMA Solutions: The developments in the field of OMA have considerably improved their respective performances. However, one salient issue remains unresolved, namely the restriction that the algorithms can only handle partitioning problems where the partitions are equally-sized. There are currently no solutions reported in the literature to address this prominent issue.

Relaxing the Limitations of OMA Solutions: We now state the main goal of this research. In this paper, we relax the equi-partitioning constraint needed for the existing OMA algorithms, by introducing the Greatest Common Divisor OMA (GCD-OMA) algorithm. The fascinating aspect of this novel concept is that it can be implemented in *all* of the current OMA variants. Our proposed solution can solve both Non-Equal Partitioning Problems (NEEPs) and EPPs, whenever the partition sizes possess a non-unity GCD between them. For example, the unknown state of nature may be a partitioning problem that has three objects in one group, six in the second and twelve in the third. However, it will not be able to handle partitions that have three objects in one group and thirteen in the second, since the partition sizes do not have a non-unity GCD.

---

[1] It is clearly, impossible to survey all these families in this short paper. Apart from those mentioned below, the Pursuit OMA (POMA) is another version of the OMA. The concepts motivating the POMA are similar to its PEOMA variant, and its details can be found in [9].

The Paper's Contributions: The contributions of this paper are as follows:

1. We present the novel GCD-OMA algorithm, whose fundamental paradigm can be incorporated in all the reported versions of OMA algorithms.
2. We formalize a new evaluation criterion for assessing the performance of OMA algorithms. This criterion can also be used for evaluating the accuracies of other algorithms that can solve similar partitioning problems.
3. By resorting to a rigorous experimental regime, we demonstrate the efficiency of the algorithms.

The structure of the paper is organized as follows. In Sect. 2, we formulate the nature of the set of partitioning problems studied in this paper, and analyze their complexities. Then, in Sect. 3, we present the GCD-OMA algorithm in detail, including its Reward and Penalty modules. The performance of the proposed algorithm is presented in Sect. 4, after which we conclude the paper in Sect. 5.

2   Problem Formulation

The partitioning problem is formalized as follows: We are dealing with an Environment containing O objects, where the set of objects is denoted by $O = \{o_1, o_2, ..., o_O\}$. Our goal is to partition these objects into K disjoint partitions, and the given set of partitions is indicated by $\mathcal{K}$, where $\mathcal{K} = \{\rho_1, \rho_2..., \rho_K\}$. For example, partition ρ_1 might consist of o_1, o_2 and o_3, denoted as $\rho_1 = \{o_1, o_2, o_3\}$. The problem, however, is that the identities of the objects that should be grouped together are unknown, but are based on a specific but hidden criterion, known only to an "Oracle", referred to as the "State of Nature". The Oracle *noisily* presents the objects that should be together in pairs, where the degree of noise specifies the difficulty of the problem.

We assume that there is an true partitioning of the objects, Δ^*, and the solution algorithm determines a partitioning, say Δ^+. The solution is optimal if $\Delta^+ = \Delta^*$. The initialization of the objects before partitioning starts is indicated by Δ^0.

2.1   Complexity

The complexity of the problems that can be solved using the existing OMA algorithms and the GCD-OMA algorithms is related to their respective combinatorics. We emphasize that, in reality, we cannot perform an exhaustive search to determine the optimal partitioning. This is because, in traditional OMA problems, we are only presented with queries encountered as time proceeds. Unfortunately, we do not have a performance parameter that directly indicates the fitness of a particular partitioning.

When we consider the objects and their group affiliations, the minimum number of possible partitions of the set of objects is given by an unordered Bell number[2]. Note that we consider the Bell number to be unordered because we do not care about the order of the objects. Rather, we are only concerned about whether the objects are grouped or not. In our problems, we want to partition O objects into K non-empty sets, where

---

[2] This is a count of the different partitions that can be established from a set with O elements.

we note that each object can only be assigned to a single group. Thus, we have B_O partitioning options, where B_O is the O-th Bell number, and the O-th Bell number is given by $B_O = \sum_{k=1}^{O} \left\{ {O \atop k} \right\}$. Here $\left\{ {O \atop k} \right\}$ is the Stirling numbers of the second kind [1], and $k \in \{1, ..., O\}$. For the O-th Bell number, it follows that $\left(\frac{O}{e \ln O} \right)^O < B_O < \left(\frac{O}{e^{1-\lambda} \ln O} \right)^O$, which has exponential behavior for O and $\lambda > 0$. However, in our case, the partitioning is pre-defined, independent of whether we have an EPP or an NEPP. Consequently, what we need to consider is the different combinations of objects in the various partitions.

In general, the number of possible combinations for partitioning problems, where the cardinalities are defined, is given by:

$$W = \frac{O!}{(u!)^x x! (v!)^y y! ... (w!)^z z!}, \tag{1}$$

where we have x groups of size u, y groups of size v, and so on for all groups and sizes. Note that, in this case, $ux + vy + ... + wz = O$. When all the groups are of equal size, we have the combination number W as:

$$W = \frac{O!}{\left(\frac{O}{K}! \right)^K K!}, \tag{2}$$

where $\frac{O}{K}$ is an integer, and consequently, such partitioning problems are also characterized by a combinatorial issue. However, this number is significantly smaller than the one given by the Bell numbers.

In addition to the combinatorial complexity of the problem, the interactions between the Environment and the algorithm is also contaminated by noise. In other words, the queries may include misleading messages. Due to the system's stochastic nature, the problem is more complicated than just finding an instantaneous optimal partitioning, because the optimal partitioning is defined *stochastically*.

2.2 Evaluation Criteria

We measure the efficiency of OMA algorithms by counting the required queries presented to the LA before convergence. The larger the number of queries needed, the less efficient is the algorithm. The number of queries presented to the LA is, in principle, equal to the number of responses from the Environment before convergence, which is a standard performance criterion in LA. But sometimes, these two indices differ.

For the OMA, the EOMA, and their proposed GCD variants, a generated query always results in a response from the Environment. Therefore, for the OMA and EOMA types, measuring the number of queries is equivalent to measuring the feedbacks from the Environment, as in the case of standard LA. We will denote the number of queries received before the LA has reached convergence by the parameter, Ψ. In the PEOMA, a query is only considered by the LA if the estimated joint probability of the accessed objects is greater than a threshold, τ. Thus, we filter out some queries before we send them to the LA, and so, a query will not always result in a response from the Environment. Thus, the number of queries, Ψ, indicates the number of queries that are let through the filtering process before the LA reaches convergence. For the number of queries required from the Query Generator before the automaton has converged, we will utilize the parameter, Ψ_Q. Note that for the OMA and the EOMA variants, $\Psi = \Psi_Q$.

The TPEOMA, similar to the PEOMA, also filters out queries before they are given to the LA. However, in the TPEOMA, artificially-generated queries are also presented to the automaton due to the transitivity phenomenon. Therefore, in the TPEOMA, Ψ, includes both the queries that "survive" the pursuit filtering, and the artificially gener- ated queries. Again, Ψ_Q indicates the number of queries made by the Query Generator. Besides, we introduce the parameter Ψ_T for counting the artificially-generated queries.

When the OMA algorithms and their pre-specified versions have reached conver- gence, we can analyze the partitioning that they have discovered. To be able to explain the discovered partitioning in a similar manner for different configurations, we need a parameter for indicating the similarity of the converged partitions, when compared with Δ^*. To achieve this, we introduce the parameter γ, which is referred to as the *accuracy* of the converged partitioning, defined as:

$$\gamma = \frac{\sum_{\forall i, \forall j, i \neq j} \Gamma_{o_i, o_j}}{\sum_{k=1}^{K} \frac{\eta_k!}{2!(\eta_k - 2)!}}, \tag{3}$$

where $i, j \in \{1, 2, ..., O\}$, $i \neq j$ and $k \in \{1, 2, ..., K\}$. Note that $\sum_{\forall i, \forall j, i \neq j} \Gamma_{o_i, o_j}$ indi- cates the number of queries that are correctly grouped, and that $\sum_{k=1}^{K} \frac{\eta_k!}{2!(\eta_k - 2)!}$ indi- cates the total number of potentially correct queries. Note that the η_k parameter, where $k \in \{1, ..., K\}$, is the number of objects in each partition. To determine γ, we need to check all possible query pairs, observe if the objects in a query are grouped both in Δ^+ and Δ^*, and divide this by the total of possible correct queries. More specifically, we define:

$$\Gamma_{o_i, o_j} = \Gamma_{o_j, o_i} = \begin{cases} 1, & \text{if } o_i \text{ and } o_j \text{ is grouped in } \Delta^* \text{ and } \Delta^+, \\ 0, & \text{otherwise.} \end{cases} \tag{4}$$

Clearly, when $\Delta^+ = \Delta^*$, we have 100% accuracy, which implies an optimal solution.

3   The Proposed GCD-OMA Scheme

3.1   The Novel Paradigm: State Expansion

The technique that we use to solve GCD-related OPPs is by invoking a fine, but estab- lished methodology that has been used in the theory of Finite State Machines (FSMs). In order to cite its importance, we mention two domains where it has been applied.

Firstly, when designing FSM Acceptors for Regular Languages, one first creates a Non-Deterministic FSM (NDFSM) by using elementary machines, and by including the operations of Concatenation, Union and Kleene-Star. In this way, one is able to obtain the NDFSM for the entire language. Subsequently to obtain the find the *Deterministic* FSM, one transforms the NDFSM into a deterministic one by increasing the number of states to be the power set of the original machine. In this way one can obtain a Deter- ministic machine with 2^N states, but that is totally equivalent to the N-state NDFSM.

An analogous technique is also used to create LA with *deterministic* Output Matri- ces, where the Output Matrix of the original LA is stochastic. Again, one transforms this into an equivalent LA, except that the states of the new machine increases. Every state in the new machine is specified by a *pair* which contains information about the state of the old machine *and* the output generated by the old machine. In this way, the output matrix of the new machine is rendered deterministic. The reader should observe that by expanding the number of states, the complexity of the machine does not change, although the *capability* of the machine changes.

This is exactly what we shall do in our particular case. We shall design new machines associated with a given GCD, and coalesce them to design the overall machine.

3.2   Designing the GCD-OMA

In traditional OMA, we handle pairs of objects and try to bring them together. Thus, when the query objects are in the same partition, they are rewarded. They are penalized when they are in different partitions. By intelligently replacing the object that changes its partition, we ensure that the number of objects in each partition always remains the same. In the proposed GCD scheme, all the partition sizes have a common GCD. In this way, we can link some of the "sub-partitions" together, and consider them as being associated with the same partition in terms of their behaviors when it concerns rewards and penalties. We refer to the proposed algorithm as the GCD-OMA. However, because it can be utilized together with any member of the OMA family, the nomenclature would be GCD-OMA, GCD-EOMA, GCD-POMA, GCD-PEOMA, and GCD-TPEOMA depending on the OMA type, where the latter suffix is the type of OMA involved.

To extend the OMA functionality to handle NEPPs with non-unity GCDs, we need to change two fundamental concepts in the OMA algorithms. Firstly, we need to change the initialization of objects to align with the GCD. Secondly, we need to link the required sub-partitions in the OMA together to fulfill the size requirement of the overall partitions. Observe that these links need to be a part of the Reward and Penalty functionalities. Additionally, the links also need to be implemented in checking which objects that are together in the final solution reported by the LA. Due to these changes, the new functionality affects many parts of the original OMA structure.

To make the partition links, we need to consider the GCD of the partitions. We will denote the GCD of the partitioning problem by $\Lambda > 1$, which can be trivially obtained. After we have determined Λ, we need to link the partitions together in the LA, and consider them as representing a single entity. When a certain partition size is not equal to Λ, we need to conceptually consider two or more partitions together as being a single overall partition. The number of partitions that need to be considered together for a given partition k is indicated by x_k given by $x_k = \frac{n_k}{\Lambda}$, where $x_k = 1$ for a partition size equal to Λ, indicating that this partition is single and is not part of any link. For indicating the links between partitions inside the LA, we can utilize the state space, and consider the set of states given in ranges for the overall partition k as follows:

$$\iota_k = \{\max(\iota_{k-1}) + 1, ..., \max(\iota_{k-1}) + x_k S\}, \quad \forall k, \tag{5}$$

where the state range $\{a, .., b\}$ indicates that the objects with states within a and b are inside partition k. Note that partition 1 ($\rho_1 = 1$), in reality, has no previous partition. Thus, for ρ_1, $\iota_0 = 0$ and $\max(\iota_0) = 0$, which leads to $\iota_k = \{1, ..., x_1 S\}$. The max function indicates that we use the highest value in the range of states from the previous partition to make the range of states of the next partition.

To clarify this, we consider an example where we have $\iota_1 = \{1, ..., 4\}$. Consequently, it follows that $\max(\iota_1) = 4$. One should also note that we have one state range for each of the K partitions in our problem. The Reward and Penalty responses from the Environment is thus based on whether the objects in the query are currently in the same state range or not. Note that in the LA, we have $R = \sum_{k=1}^{K} x_k$ partitions, and that S is the number of states per partition R.

Consider an example with the partitioning sizes of $\eta_1 = 3, \eta_2 = 9$ and $\eta_3 = 12$. Additionally, we have four states ($S = 4$) in the sub-partitions of the LA. The states of this example are visualized in Fig. 1. As indicated by the colors in the figure, to comply with the partition sizes, we need to consider ρ_1 as a partition in itself. In contrast, partition two to four is another overall partition, and partition five to eight constitute the last overall partition. Thus, if one object in a query is in state 17, and the other object is in state 30, we will reward them, and not penalize them, as we would have done in the original OMA for EPPs. Following Eq. (5), we have $\iota_1 = \{1, ..., 4\}$, $\iota_2 = \{5, ..., 16\}$ and $\iota_3 = \{17, ..., 32\}$, as the ranges for the states of our partitions ρ_1, ρ_2 and ρ_3 respectively.

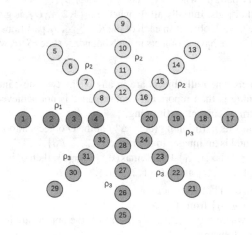

Fig. 1. Example of partition links in GCD with 3 partitions and 4 states as described in the text. (Color figure online)

To change the OMA functionality, we need to change both the original OMA and the EOMA. We emphasize that these changes also apply to the PEOMA and TPEOMA versions, but because these algorithms utilize the EOMA as a basis, we can directly invoke the same principles in their operations. The EOMA version of GCD is described in Algorithm 1. Observe that the GCD-OMA is easily extended to the existing OMA scheme, and is omitted to avoid repetition.

In the GCD schemes, the objects are still initialized in the same manner as before, but instead of placing $\frac{O}{K}$ objects in each partition, we put Λ objects in each partition initially. For the OMA, the objects are randomly distributed into the $\sum_{k=1}^{K} x_k S$ states, while they are distributed among the $\sum_{k=1}^{K} x_k$ boundary states in the EOMA version. We also utilize the existing Reward and Penalty functionalities. Because we fulfill the requirement of having equally-sized partitions, we do not need to make any changes to the existing transitions on being rewarded and penalized. Understandingly, when two objects are rewarded, they behave as if they were in the same partition even though they are in different sub-partitions within the LA. This is done by invoking "EOMA Process Reward" where the objects go deeper into their present action one step at a time, or stay in the same state if they are in the most internal state. Similarly, the objects in a query need to be in different state ranges to be penalized. Again, this is done by invoking "EOMA Process Penalty" where the objects go towards the central boundary states one step at a time, or switch actions when they reach the border.

Algorithm 1. GCD-EOMA

Input:

- The objects $O = \{o_1, ..., o_O\}$.
- S states per sub-partition.
- A sequence of query pairs Υ, where each entry $Q = \{o_i, o_j\}$.
- Initialized θ_i for all objects. Initially all θ_i, where $i \in \{1, 2, ..., O\}$, is given a random boundary state, where we have Λ objects in each of the $R = \sum_{k=1}^{K} x_k$ partitions. Thus, in each of the R partitions in the LA, we have Λ objects in each boundary state $rS \, \forall r$, where $r \in \{1, 2, ..., R\}$.

Output:

- Convergence happens when all objects are in any of the two most internal states, and the converged partitioning is then reported. If convergence is not achieved within $|\Upsilon|$ queries, the LA should return its current partitioning.
- The LA, thus, outputs its partitioning ($\mathcal{K} = \Delta^+$) of the O objects into K partitions.
- θ_i is the state of o_i and is an integer in the range $\{1, 2, ..., RS\}$.
- If $\theta_i \in \iota_k$, where $\iota_k = \{\max(\iota_{k-1}) + 1, ..., \max(\iota_{k-1}) + x_k S\}$, then o_i is assigned to ρ_k, which is done for all $i \in \{1, 2, ..., O\}$ and $k \in \{1, 2, ..., K\}$.

1: **while** not converged or $|\Upsilon|$ queries not read **do**
2:     Read query $Q = \{o_i, o_j\}$ from Υ
3:     **if** θ_i and $\theta_j \in \iota_k$, where $k \in \{1, 2, ..., K\}$ **then**   // If the objects are in the same state range
4:         EOMA Process Reward
5:     **else**   // If the objects are in different state ranges
6:         EOMA Process Penalty
7:     **end if**
8: **end while**
9: Output the final partitioning based on θ_i, $\forall i$.   // According to the state ranges

---

Algorithm 2. EOMA Process Reward

Input:
- The query $Q = \{o_i, o_j\}$.
- The states of the objects in Q ($\{\theta_i, \theta_j\}$).

Output:
- The next states of o_i and o_j.

1: **if** $\theta_i \bmod S \neq 1$ **then**
2:     $\theta_i = \theta_i - 1$ // Move o_i towards the innermost state
3: **end if**
4: **if** $\theta_j \bmod S \neq 1$ **then**
5:     $\theta_j = \theta_j - 1$ // Move o_j towards the innermost state
6: **end if**

---

4 Experimental Results

In this section[3], we demonstrate the performance of GCD-OMA types for various degrees of noise. Section 4.1 demonstrates results for EPPs compared with other existing OMA algorithms. Section 4.2 demonstrates the GCD's performance for NEPPs, which cannot be compared with any of the existing OMA algorithms, as they are unable to handle problems of these kinds. Furthermore, in this context, noise is referred to as queries of objects that are not together in Δ^* but are presented to the LA. A system with noisy queries might also yield a slower convergence rate than a system with fewer (or zero) noisy queries. Consequently, we use:

$$Noise = 1 - \Pi_{o_i, o_j} = 1 - \Pi_{o_j, o_i}, \quad \text{for } o_i, o_j \in \Delta^*, \forall i, j,$$

as the probability reference for LA being presented with a noisy query in the simulations. To clarify, Π_{o_i, o_j} is the probability of o_i and o_j being accessed together and being together in Δ^*. For all the simulations, we utilized 100,000 queries as the maximum number of queries. If the OMA algorithm had not converged within the consideration of $|\Upsilon| = 10^5$, we deemed that the algorithm *had not converged*.

4.1 Existing OMA and GCD-OMA for an EPP

Let us first consider the simulations for an EPP where we simulated a partitioning problem with 30 objects to be partitioned into three partitions, implying that $\frac{O}{K} = 10$. Table 1 show simulation results for different existing OMA types, and Table 2 presents results obtained for the GCD-OMA types. GCD-EOMA required approximately 307 and 422 queries before convergence for 0% and 10% noise, respectively. These convergence rate levels are almost equal to those of the existing EOMA algorithm given in Table 1. As the noise level increased, the number of iterations increased. As more noisy queries

---

[3] The results presented here are a brief summary of all the results obtained for numerous settings. The detailed set of results are found in the Masters Thesis of the First Author [5].

Algorithm 3. EOMA Process Penalty

Input:
  - The query $Q = \{o_i, o_j\}$.
  - The states of the objects in Q ($\{\theta_i, \theta_j\}$).

Output:
  - The next states of o_i and o_j.

1: **if** $\theta_i \bmod S \neq 0$ and $\theta_j \bmod S \neq 0$ **then**   // Neither are in boundary
2:     $\theta_i = \theta_i + 1$
3:     $\theta_j = \theta_j + 1$
4: **else if** $\theta_i \bmod S \neq 0$ and $\theta_j \bmod S = 0$ **then**   // o_j is in boundary
5:     $\theta_i = \theta_i + 1$
6:     $temp = \theta_j$ // Store the state of o_j
7:     $o_l = unaccessed$ object in group of $staying$ object (o_i) closest to boundary
8:     $\theta_j = \theta_i$
9:     $\theta_l = temp$
10: **else if** $\theta_i \bmod S = 0$ and $\theta_j \bmod S \neq 0$ **then**   // o_i is in boundary
11:     $\theta_j = \theta_j + 1$
12:     $temp = \theta_i$ // Store the state of o_i
13:     $o_l = unaccessed$ object in group of $staying$ object (o_j) closest to boundary
14:     $\theta_i = \theta_j$
15:     $\theta_l = temp$
16: **else**   // Both are in boundary states
17:     $temp = \theta_i$ or θ_j // Store the state of $moving$ object, o_i or o_j
18:     $\theta_i = \theta_j$ or $\theta_j = \theta_i$ // Put $moving$ object and $staying$ object together
19:     $o_l = unaccessed$ object in group of $staying$ object closest to boundary
20:     $\theta_l = temp$ // Move o_l to the old state of $moving$ object
21: **end if**

---

are presented to the LA, more objects are "misguided" to be together, even if the contrary represents reality. Clearly, the GCD-OMA types and the existing OMA algorithms had similar performance. This behavior is expected. When GCD-OMA types were presented with partitions of equal sizes, it would consider all partitions in the LA separately, which, in essence, yielded a similar operation to that of the existing OMAs.

Note that Ψ indicates the number of queries considered by the LA, Ψ_Q the total number of queries generated, and Ψ_T the queries made from the concept of transitivity in the TPEOMA. For PEOMA, we have to include the parameter κ, indicating the number of queries before we decide to start filtering the queries based on their likeliness before letting the LA process it (pursuit). Additionally, we have the parameter τ, indicating the threshold for whether a query should be considered or not [8, 10].

Table 1. Statistics of existing OMA types for a case involving 30 objects, 3 partitions and 10 states averaged over 1,000 experiments.

Type	Noise	γ	$\Delta^+ = \Delta^*$	Not Conv.	Ψ	Ψ_Q	Ψ_T	κ	τ
EOMA	0%	100%	100%	0%	305.36	305.36	-	-	-
EOMA	10%	100%	100%	0%	425.08	425.08	-	-	-
PEOMA	0%	100%	100%	0%	307.42	309.71	-	270	$\frac{0.1}{0}$
PEOMA	10%	100%	100%	0%	398.11	417.58	-	270	$\frac{0.1}{0}$
TPEOMA	0%	100%	100%	0%	369.55	275.46	96.28	270	$\frac{0.2}{0}$
TPEOMA	10%	100%	100%	0%	555.63	316.91	253.81	270	$\frac{0.2}{0}$

Table 2. Statistics of GCD-OMA types for a case involving 30 objects, 3 partitions and 10 states averaged over 1,000 experiments.

Type	Noise	γ	$\Delta^+ = \Delta^*$	Not Conv.	Ψ	Ψ_Q	Ψ_T	κ	τ
GCD-EOMA	0%	100%	100%	0%	307.04	307.04	-	-	-
GCD-EOMA	10%	100%	100%	0%	421.89	421.89	-	-	-
GCD-PEOMA	0%	100%	100%	0%	303.84	305.90	-	270	$\frac{0.1}{0}$
GCD-PEOMA	10%	100%	100%	0%	398.39	417.96	-	270	$\frac{0.1}{0}$
GCD-TPEOMA	0%	100%	100%	0%	371.59	275.37	98.54	270	$\frac{0.2}{0}$
GCD-TPEOMA	10%	100%	100%	0%	553.50	316.94	251.72	270	$\frac{0.2}{0}$

4.2 GCD-OMA Variants for NEPPs

This section presents the results for the GCD-OMA types' NEPPs with a non-unity GCD between the respective partition sizes. As demonstrated in Sect. 4.1, the PEOMA and the TPEOMA variants can enhance the convergence rate of the methods in different ways. The PEOMA is best for systems with higher noise levels, and the TPEOMA is preferred when we have less information (queries) from the system. However, as they are essential parts of the OMA paradigm, repeating the same methods' performance with the EOMA, PEOMA, and TPEOMA might not be necessary to analyze and discuss their performance for NEPPs. We thus present the results only for the GCD-EOMA.

The first problem that we considered had three partitions and 18 objects. The first partition had room for three objects ($\eta_1 = 3$), the second partition had room for six objects ($\eta_2 = 6$), and the last partition had room for nine objects ($\eta_3 = 9$). The second problem that we considered, had 20 objects, where $\eta_1 = 2, \eta_2 = 4, \eta_3 = 6$ and $\eta_5 = 8$. For this problem, the maximum number of queries was increased to $|\Upsilon| = 10^6$.

Let us first consider the 18-objects case, where the results are listed in Table 3. For 0% noise and three states, we can observe that the method had issues with obtaining the optimal solution. However, the accuracy was not at the same low level but was around 70% on average, which means that most of the objects that should have been grouped were grouped in the LA. The reason for simulating a noise-free problem that utilized only three states was because the method achieved convergence only for a minimum of the experiments, with six states.

Observing the results for 10% and 20% noise for GCD-EOMA in Table 3, we see that we were able to obtain a higher percentage of the experiments converging to the optimal solution with respectively 98.90% and 99.90% for the different noise levels. Additionally, the accuracy and the percentage of experiments converging to the optimal partitioning increased as the noise level became higher. However, when the system was noise-free or the noise level was lower, the algorithm, astonishingly, performed less accurately, and required more queries if one considered the state depth.

Table 3. Statistics of GCD-EOMA for the problem with 18 objects ($\eta_1 = 3, \eta_2 = 6, \eta_3 = 9$) with different noise levels, averaged over 1,000 experiments.

Noise	S	Accuracy	$\Delta^+ = \Delta^*$	Not Conv.	$\Psi = \Psi_Q$
0%	3	69.56%	14.49%	0%	3,168.04
10%	6	99.63%	98.90%	0%	7,880.37
20%	6	99.98%	99.90%	0%	24,864.40

In Table 4, we present the results for the second problem with GCD-EOMA for higher noise levels than for the first problem. The algorithm required more queries for the case of 5% noise compared with the case of 10% noise. Based on this observation, surprisingly, we confirm that a higher noise level is easier to manage than a lower one. In real-life, the noise levels are usually unknown, but they are seldom noise-free.

Table 4. Statistics of GCD-EOMA for the problem with 20 objects ($\eta_1 = 2, \eta_2 = 4, \eta_3 = 6, \eta_4 = 8$), with different noise levels and 6 states, averaged over 1,000 experiments.

Noise	Accuracy	$\Delta^+ = \Delta^*$	Not Conv.	$\Psi = \Psi_Q$
5%	99.73%	98.6%	0%	85,397.82
10%	99.93%	99.6%	0%	68,945.01
15%	99.98%	99.9%	0%	111,335.16
20%	100%	100%	2.8%	248,926.46

From the results, the performance of GCD-EOMA seemed to increase for higher noise levels. This behavior might seem counter-intuitive. However, one observes that a high level of noise causes more movement of the objects, which is a desirable phenomenon for the convergence rate, and mitigates problems of having objects "stuck" or locked into a configuration. If we consider the case of a noise-free Environment, the objects will only be accessed together and go deeper, with no ability to move out of a partition that they should not be in. Thus, the noise helps objects being moved out of "stuck" (or locked in) situations similar, to the Deadlock Situation [2].

5 Conclusions

The existing algorithms within the OMA paradigm can only solve partitioning problems with partitions of equal sizes. The constraint of having equally-sized partitions is a limitation to the algorithms' application to real-life issues. In this paper, we have relaxed the constraint of having equally-sized partitions in OMA schemes. We propose a novel solution that tackles partitioning problems, where the partition sizes can be both equal and/or *unequal*, but when the cardinalities of the true partitions have a GCD. We achieve this by invoking a strategy that has been earlier used in the theory of automata, namely that of mapping the machine's state space onto a larger space. In essence, we have presented the design, implementation, and testing of a novel OMA-based method that can be implemented with the OMA itself, and also in all of its existing variants. The scheme has also been rigorously tested. This paper is a novel contribution and constitutes the first reported OMA-based solution for NEPPs.

References

1. Berend, D., Tassa, T.: Improved bounds on bell numbers and on moments of sums of random variables. Probabil. Math. Stat. **30**(2), 185–205 (2010)
2. Gale, W., Das, S., Yu, C.T.: Improvements to an algorithm for equipartitioning. IEEE Trans. Comput. **39**(5), 706–710 (1990). https://doi.org/10.110912.53585
3. Oommen, B.J., Ma, D.C.Y.: Deterministic learning automata solutions to the equipartitioning problem. IEEE Trans. Comput. **37**(1), 2–13 (1988)
4. Oommen, B.J., Ma, D.C.Y.: Stochastic automata solutions to the object partitioning problem. Comput. J. **35**, A105–A120 (1992)
5. Omslandseter, R.O.: Learning automata-based object partitioning with pre-specified cardinalities. M.S. thesis, University of Agder, Norway (2020)
6. Omslandseter, R.O., Jiao, L., Liu, Y., Oommen, B.J.: User grouping and power allocation in NOMA systems: a reinforcement learning-based solution. In: Fujita, H., Fournier-Viger, P., Ali, M., Sasaki, J. (eds.) IEA/AIE 2020. LNCS (LNAI), vol. 12144, pp. 299–311. Springer, Cham (2020). https://doi.org/10.1007/978-3-030-55789-8_27
7. Shirvani, A.: Novel solutions and applications of the object partitioning problem. Ph.D. thesis, Carleton University, Ottawa (2018)
8. Shirvani, A., Oommen, B.J.: On utilizing the pursuit paradigm to enhance the deadlock-preventing object migration automaton. In: 2017 International Conference on New Trends in Computing Sciences (ICTCS), pp. 295–302, October 2017. https://doi.org/10.1109ICTCS.2017.40
9. Shirvani, A., Oommen, B.J.: On Enhancing the object migration automaton using the pursuit paradigm. J. Comput. Sci. **24**, 329–342 (2018). https://doi.org/10.1016/j.jocs.2017.08.008, http://www.sciencedirect.com/science/article/pii/S1877750317302259
10. Shirvani, A., Oommen, B.J.: On invoking transitivity to enhance the pursuit-oriented object migration automata. IEEE Access **6**, 21668–21681 (2018). https://doi.org/10.1109/ACCESS.2018.2827305
11. Shirvani, A., Oommen, B.J.: On enhancing the deadlock-preventing object migration automaton using the pursuit paradigm. Pattern Anal. Appl. (2019). https://doi.org/10.1007/s10044-019-00817-z
12. Yazidi, A., Granmo, O.C., Oommen, B.J.: Service selection in stochastic environments: a learning-automaton based solution. Appl. Intell. **36**(3), 617–637 (2012)

Building a Knowledge Graph
with Inference for a Production Machine
Using the Web of Things Standard

Sascha Meckler[1(✉)], Harald Steinmüller[1], and Andreas Harth[1,2]

[1] Fraunhofer IIS, Nuremberg, Germany
{sascha.meckler,andreas.harth}@iis.fraunhofer.de
[2] University of Erlangen, Nuremberg, Germany

Abstract. This paper presents an architecture for a knowledge-based
system (KBS) that consists of a Knowledge Graph, an inference engine
and services. The Web of Things standard is used to translate sensor data
from a production machine into an RDF graph. The KBS architecture
is implemented for a physical twin of a real machine using open-source
Semantic Web technologies. The performance evaluation of the system
reveals limitations for the application in production.

Keywords: Web of Things · Knowledge Graph · Digital Twin

1 Introduction

In modern factories, business decisions and intelligent control systems for production machines require the joint analysis of interconnected data from different
sources. Knowledge Graphs (KG) [1] are a new approach for an efficient enterprise data management that combines knowledge representation and data integration. By interlinking domain knowledge, enterprise data and external data
in a uniform graph representation, new possibilities for data management and
analysis arise. KGs are no longer only used by the large IT corporations such
as Google or Facebook, but also in industrial applications [2]. The standardized
W3C Semantic Web technologies are well suited for building KGs for industrial
applications such as in our use case:

In the automated production of control cabinets, new intelligent software systems shall be used to predict failures, recommend actions and prevent costly down
times. One source of error is the magazine tower used for part provisioning for the
robot-based assembly of top hat rails. There are slowly occurring malfunctions,
e.g. caused by wear, as well as instantaneous errors like jamming. A knowledge-
based system (KBS) is supposed to detect possible error states and impending
failures and create recommendations for actions. The KBS must support decisions
based on domain knowledge and the analysis of data from different sources.

Our main contribution is the application of a KG together with the Web of
Things (WoT) and inference techniques to a real production machine. We describe

© Springer Nature Switzerland AG 2021
H. Fujita et al. (Eds.): IEA/AIE 2021, LNAI 12799, pp. 240–251, 2021.
https://doi.org/10.1007/978-3-030-79463-7_20

how to combine a domain ontology, the WoT Thing Description and a WoT implementation to generate RDF graphs from machine sensor data. We start by presenting an architecture for a web-based KBS in Sect. 2. The KBS is implemented for a physical twin of the magazine tower for part provisioning from the production, described in Sect. 3. The proof of concept implementation is then evaluated regarding the requirements of the industry use case. The first evaluation criteria is the suitability for integrating heterogeneous data and providing a uniform interface for analysis components. The second criteria is the system performance regarding scalability and response times. Section 4 presents the result of the experiments and leads to the discussion in Sect. 5, which depicts possible improvements of the KBS and shows the connection to related work and the Digital Twin concept. Section 6 concludes the paper.

2   Conceptual System Overview

By definition[1], a KBS consists of two major components - the knowledge base and the inference engine. The knowledge base is the foundation of any KBS. While domain knowledge is typically generated from human input, factual knowledge is usually derived from concrete data. The domain knowledge is formalized in domain-specific ontologies using the Resource Description Framework (RDF), RDF Schema and the Web Ontology Language (OWL). Moreover, additional logical rules, e.g. if-then statements, are generated based on domain knowledge. The basic procedure for building the knowledge base is to translate all incoming data into the uniform, standardized RDF data format and store it inside a Knowledge Graph. During the transformation of the heterogeneous data into the RDF format, the factual knowledge is associated with the domain knowledge.

The W3C Web of Things (WoT) standard provides an abstraction layer for the communication with IoT devices and creates interoperability between different IoT platforms [3]. Therefore, IoT devices with different communication protocols from different vendors can be accessed in a uniform way. An implementation of WoT is used to retrieve data from IoT devices and map it to the RDF format. Besides that, the WoT Thing Description [4] embeds semantics which are used to translate incoming IoT data into the RDF format. (Semi-)structured data from relational databases or spreadsheets can be translated into the RDF format using the RDF Mapping Language [5], a superset of the W3C-recommended R2RML [6]. In the domain of control cabinets, the database may contain product data using industry standards like the IEC CDD[2] (IEC 61360) or e-Cl@ss[3]. If the database contains data about the loading of the magazine tower, the weight of the contained parts can be put into context with the drive sensor data in the Knowledge Graph.

Based on the KG, a two-step inference engine deducts new knowledge about the observed production machine. The first part of the inference engine is a

---

[1] https://en.wikipedia.org/wiki/Knowledge-based_systems.
[2] https://cdd.iec.ch/.
[3] https://www.eclass.eu/.

logical, ontology- and rule-based inference used for automatic data preprocessing. A reasoner applies the logic and rules, which are formalized in an ontology and domain rules, to the data stored in the RDF KG. The original and inferred data are the basis for the second part of the inference engine, a domain-specific, in-depth data analysis which uses AI methods such as machine learning.

Based on the interconnected data and the results of the inference engine, "knowledge-based" services are able to perform tasks that would not be possible without the KG. A data visualization service, a monitoring and notification service and a decision support system can provide deeper insight and generate recommendations for action.

3   Implemented System

3.1   Data Source: Physical Twin

The project partners Mangelberger Elektrotechnik[4], Schneider Electric[5] and E. Braun[6] built a physical twin of the magazine tower for part provisioning in order to prevent any interference with the running production. The electro-mechanical machine with control cabinet, which is shown in Fig. 1, uses a similar servomotor, programmable logic controller (PLC) and industrial PC (IPC) as the magazine tower. The workload is simulated with a pneumatic disc brake that is attached to the motor shaft. The brake force replaces the resistance and the inertia force during the rotation of the magazine tower. The brake pressure can be controlled by the PLC (SE PacDrive LMC 300) using a Web-based user interface. Via the interface, a constant or an alternating mode that imitates the load behavior in production is used to simulate different operating conditions and anomalies. The motor parameters of the servo drive (SE Lexium 32i) are transmitted to the PLC via CAN bus and are forwarded to the IPC (SE Green-Box) using the OPC-UA protocol. The IPC acts as an IoT Gateway by providing

Fig. 1. Physical twin machine

---

[4] https://www.mangelberger.com/.
[5] https://www.se.com/de/de/.
[6] https://www.e-braun.de.

internet access to the machine. The development tool NodeRED[7] was used to set up an HTTP server on the IPC. In the NodeRED flow, the OPC-UA data was processed and served over HTTP. The KBS is polling the HTTP server on the IPC for the motor data in JSON or CSV format. Overall, the physical twin reproduces the complete chain from the mechanics to IoT data. The communication between the twin components is illustrated in Fig. 2. In the experiments, a specific braking behavior was specified for each test and the parameters shown in Table 1 were recorded at the same time.

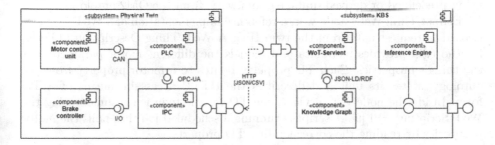

Fig. 2. Component diagram of the physical twin and the connected KBS

Table 1. Groups of motor and brake parameters selected for monitoring

Group	Description	Parameter CURIE	Unit CURIE
Temperature	Motor temperature	:MotorTemperature	om:degreeCelsius
	Output stage temperature	:OutputStageTemperature	om:degreeCelsius
Power	Electric current	:ElectricCurrent	om:ampere
	Power output	:PowerOutput	om:watt
	Mean power output	:MeanPowerOutput	om:watt
Rotation speed	Speed	:Speed	isb4wbs:rpm
	Reference speed	:RefSpeed	isb4wbs:rpm
Motor load	Motor torque	:Torque	om:percent
	Motor load	:MotorLoad	om:percent
	Motor overload	:MotorOverload	om:percent
Position deviations	load-induced speed variation	:LoadIndSpeedVariation	isb4wbs:rpm
	Trailing distance	:TrailingDistance	om:degree
	Load-induced trailing distance	:LoadIndTrailingDistance	om:degree
	Maximum load-induced	:MaxLoadInd	om:degree
	Trailing distance	TrailingDistance	
Status/error codes	Operation status code	:OperationStatusCode	
	Last error code	:LastErrorCode	
	Last warning code	:LastWarningCode	
Brake control	Brake valve input signal	:ValveInputSignal	om:millibar
	Brake valve output signal	:ValveOutputSignal	om:millibar

---

[7] https://nodered.org/.

3.2   Knowledge-Based System

Knowledge Graph. A domain-specific OWL ontology defines the physical twin and the measured motor properties from Table 1. The domain ontology adopts the Smart Appliances REFerence (SAREF) ontology [7] and the Ontology of units of measure (OM2) [8]. As shown in Listing 1.1, the twin is a device (saref:Device) that measures (saref:measuresProperty) different motor properties which are of the type saref:Property or subclasses such as saref:Temperature, saref:Power or saref:Motion. The units of the motor properties are expressed using predefined or derived units, e.g. om:watt, from the OM2 ontology.

Eclipse ThingWeb[8] node-wot, a reference implementation of a WoT servient, is used to request data from the twin IPC. A WoT Thing Description (TD) [4] for the twin provides metadata and models the different motor parameters as the thing's properties. Each TD property relates to a motor property from the ontology, states its unit and describes the HTTP access by means of a TD form. Inside the node-wot servient, the TD for the twin is consumed using the WoT Scripting API [9]. A script is running a scheduled job that polls the motor properties by reading the corresponding TD property.

```
@prefix rdfs: <http://www.w3.org/2000/01/rdf-schema#> .
@prefix xsd:  <http://www.w3.org/2001/XMLSchema#> .
@prefix saref: <https://w3id.org/saref#> .
@prefix om:
<http://www.ontology-of-units-of-measure.org/resource/om-2/>.
@prefix : <https://iis.fraunhofer.de/isb4wbs#> .

:MotorProperty a saref:Property .
:MotorTemperature a saref:Temperature ;
  rdfs:subClassOf :MotorProperty ;
  saref:isMeasuredByDevice :Servomotor .

:Twin a saref:Device ;
  saref:hasModel "ISB4WBS-Demonstrator 1.1" ;
  saref:hasManufacturer "SE, E.Braun, Mangelberger" ;
  saref:consistsOf :Brake, :PLC, :IPC, :Servomotor ;
  saref:measuresProperty
    :MotorTemperature, :ElectricCurrent, :TrailingDistance .

# example measurement
:Twin saref:makesMeasurement [
  a saref:Measurement ;
  saref:hasTimestamp "2020-11-25T14:40:10.10"^^xsd:dateTime ;
  saref:hasValue "40"^^xsd:integer ;
  saref:isMeasuredIn om:degreeCelsius ;
  saref:relatesToProperty :MotorTemperature ;
] .
```

Listing 1.1. Turtle serialization of a subset of the twin modelling with an example measurement

---

[8] https://www.thingweb.io/.

In the next step, the retrieved JSON response is transformed to RDF by automatically filling the value and the semantics from the TD into an RDF template, which describes a measurement (saref:Measurement). The RDF is finally sent to the KG using the SPARQL Graph Store protocol[9].

Apache Jena Fuseki[10], one of the top-ranked RDF databases[11] was chosen for implementing the KG. The Fuseki RDF store is configured to have one dataset with multiple named graphs for the raw data and a second dataset for the application of an ontology-based reasoner. The setup uses the Jena Fuseki SPARQL server and the TDB2 RDF database in version 3.14.

Inference Engine. The first part of the KBS inference engine are generic ontology-based RDFS or OWL reasoners. Different built-in reasoners from the Apache Jena framework (RDFS, OWL Mini, OWL-FB)[12] and Openllet[13], an OWL 2 DL reasoner, have been tested. Only Openllet was capable of assigning classes to measurements based on OWL restrictions for the measured value. Openllet is able to infer the class 'CriticalMotorTemperature' when a motor temperature measurement has a value greater than a threshold. Eiter et al. conclude that future inference engines of the Semantic Web have to integrate both ontology-based inference and rule-based inference [10]. Rule-based reasoning can be used for more complex, functional dependencies which exceed the capabilities of OWL-based reasoners. Well-known rule languages include FOL RuleML, the Semantic Web Rules Language (SWRL), the rule exchange format RIF and Notation3 (N3) [11,12]. Notation3 is a human-readable logic language which forms a superset of the RDF Turtle language [13]. In the experiment, Linked Data-Fu [14], a data processing system for Linked Data, was used to execute N3 rules, e.g. a temperature classification rule as shown in Listing 1.2. The second stage of the inference engine is an AI data analysis service that uses a neuro-fuzzy inference system for detecting unusual operation conditions.

```
@prefix math: <http://www.w3.org/2000/10/swap/math#> .
@prefix saref: <https://w3id.org/saref#> .
@prefix : <https://iis.fraunhofer.de/isb4wbs#> .
{
  ?measurement saref:relatesToProperty :MotorTemperature .
  ?measurement saref:hasValue ?value .
  ?value math:greaterThan "50" .
} => {
  ?measurement a :CriticalMeasurement .
} .
```

Listing 1.2. N3 rule for temperature classification

---

[9] https://www.w3.org/TR/sparql11-http-rdf-update/.
[10] https://jena.apache.org/documentation/fuseki2/.
[11] https://db-engines.com/en/ranking/rdf+store.
[12] https://jena.apache.org/documentation/inference/.
[13] https://github.com/Galigator/openllet.

The neuro-fuzzy approach uses a combination of a neural network and fuzzy logic to reason about error states of the physical twin. It takes into consideration domain-specific if-then rules which are defined by a human domain expert. After the training of the network, the analysis service was able to identify error states based on the data from the KG.

3.3   Knowledge-Based Services

Figure 3 shows two services that were implemented for the KBS. A SPARQL interpreter for Apache Zeppelin has been published[14] that allows to visualize the results of a SPARQL query in a notebook. With this interpreter, Zeppelin's various built-in charts can be used to visualize values queried from the Fuseki RDF store. A decision support service implements a simple decision tree for the generation of notifications and recommendations for action. SPARQL ASK and SELECT queries are used to retrieve the knowledge for the decisions and a job scheduler periodically queries the KG for the appearance of certain statements or domain-specific values, e.g. a measurement with the class :CriticalMeasurement.

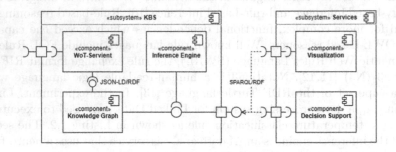

Fig. 3. Component diagram of the KBS and connected services

4   Performance Tests

The KBS solution for the magazine tower twin was examined regarding its functionality and performance. In the experiment, the Fuseki RDF store increased drastically in size when thousands of measurements are gradually added. However, Jena TDB2 offers a compaction functionality[15] that eliminates the over-proportional growth in case of many writes. Therefore, a regular compression of the TDB2 has to be installed. As shown in Fig. 4, the storage in the RDF store is still very voluminous and inefficient in comparison to other data formats.

---

[14] https://zeppelin.apache.org/docs/0.9.0-preview1/interpreter/sparql.html.
[15] https://jena.apache.org/documentation/tdb2/tdb2_admin.html.

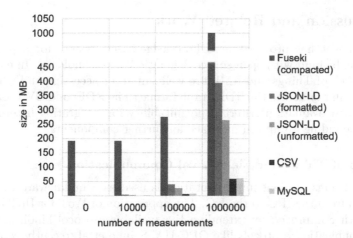

Fig. 4. Sizes of Fuseki TDB2, JSON-LD and CSV text files and a MySQL database for different numbers of saved measurements

The query performance of the Fuseki SPARQL server heavily depends on the number of triples and the installed reasoner. Figure 5 shows the query durations for increasing numbers of measurements with no reasoner, Jena's RDFS and OWL-Mini reasoner. The simple RDFS reasoner has little effect on the query duration. For both OWL 2 reasoners (OWL-Mini and Openllet), the JVM heap space must be increased from 4 GB to 16 GB in order to prevent out-of-memory errors in the case of one million measurements, which corresponds to 6 million triples. The queries with 10,000 and 100,000 measurements show a high standard deviation because the first queries take two to three times longer than the subsequent queries.

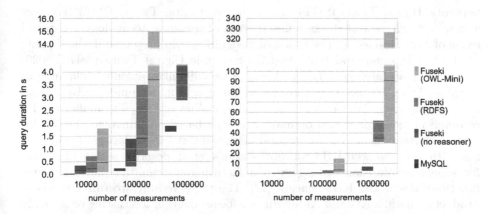

Fig. 5. Query durations for increasing numbers of measurements with no reasoner, Jena RDFS and OWL-Mini reasoner in comparison to a MySQL database. Mean and lower/upper bound of the first 5 queries. SELECT-WHERE-FILTER query that retrieves every measurement whose value is greater than a threshold.

5   Discussion and Related Work

The experiment has proven that a knowledge-based system for a production machine can be built with open-source Semantic Web technologies. In particular, the W3C Web of Things and RML are well suited for accessing and translating IoT and tabular data into the RDF graph format. The RDF- and OWL-based KG meets the first evaluation criteria, the suitability for integrating heterogeneous data and providing a uniform interface for further components.

5.1   Web of Things for Field-Level Communication

A Web of Things servient implementation is used as a middleware to pipeline sensor data from the IPC to the KG. The application of WoT for IIoT use cases can be further improved by extending the available protocol bindings to field-level communication protocols like OPC-UA. Sciullo et al. recently contributed a quality of service (QoS) vocabulary for the WoT Thing Description as well as a design and an open-source implementation of protocol bindings for OPC-UA and NETCONF [15]. With a WoT OPC-UA binding, the data flow from the PLC to the KG could be shortened. Instead of translating messages from OPC-UA to HTTP, a WoT servient could be deployed on the IPC (IoT gateway) that directly accesses the servomotor data from the PLC via OPC-UA and pushes the RDF to the KG. The OPC-UA support also simplifies the implementation of a bidirectional data flow. The WoT servient could be used to send control commands to the PLC. A "knowledge-based" service could not only recommend but also trigger actions at the machine. If actions are executed in a control loop fashion, the system could be seen as a digital twin of the magazine tower.

5.2   Relation to Digital Twin Concepts

Semantic Digital Twins (SDT) and Cognitive Digital Twins (CDT) represent a new research area that examines the use of semantic technology for digital twins of a physical asset. The vision of a cognitive twin presented in the keynote at the first International Workshop On Semantic Digital Twins (SeDiT 2020) [16] foresees an intelligent DT with cognitive skills like reasoning, planning or learning. The CDT not only recognizes, but deeply understands a given situation and supports the decision process and possible actions. The ability to give recommendations for action or make decisions based on formalized knowledge is characteristic for a KBS in general. Therefore, the CDT has many similarities with the presented KBS concept. Rozanec et al. describe actionable CDTs for supporting decision-making in manufacturing systems that have the same functionalities as the KBS concept [17]. The presented architecture consists of production data, a KG and AI algorithms for production forecasting or anomaly detection. We could find many similarities between our KBS concept and the CDT described in this publication. Whereas Rozanec et al. describe the CDT for a complete production line on a higher abstraction level, we focused on the implementation for a single machine. In the last years, several more studies investigated the use of knowledge graphs for DTs in industrial applications [18–22].

5.3   Query Performance of RDF Stores

The KBS implementation revealed performance limitations for possible industry applications. The query duration of the deployed Fuseki RDF store increases strongly with the number of triples in the dataset. This behavior matches with the findings in other research projects: Bellini & Nesi compared the performance of different RDF graph databases for smart city services with similarly high numbers of sensor records. In their tests, the Virtuoso RDF store performed significantly better than the Fuseki RDF store [23]. Nikolić et al. concluded in their study that Virtuoso is more efficient and faster than Fuseki for datasets with more than one million triples [24]. A similar observation was made by Kilintzis et al. when evaluating the performance of open-source triplestores for medical data. In contrast to Virtuoso and the RDBMS, Fuseki had a severe performance drop when the complete record was requested [25]. This matches with the high query duration for one million measurements in our experiment. The limiting factor for query execution is, however, the usage of complex OWL 2 reasoners.

5.4   Virtual Data Integration and Scalability

The materialization of sensor data and structured data in a KG consumes huge amounts of storage space. A more efficient data storage approach is the separation of static metadata and dynamic data. In this case, the KG only contains the information about the data, the relations, the data source and possible mapping rules. Chevallier et al. follow a similar approach for their architecture of smart building twins [26]. Building sensors, their communication protocol and database schemata are described in the RDF graph whereas the actual time series data is saved in separate databases. A well-known virtual data integration approach is Ontology-Based Data Access (OBDA) where a global ontology is used to provide an abstracted interface to many different data sources. When the user submits a query in the global vocabulary, the OBDA system rewrites the query into the vocabulary of the different data sources and delegates it to the query answering system, e.g. a relational database management system (RDBMS) [27,28]. On the one hand, a virtual ontology-based data integration approach prevents duplicate data, but on the other hand, it complicates the implementation of an inference engine. Distributed knowledge graphs are a solution for Big Data. Each virtual or materialized KG has a specific application focus and is easier to maintain by itself. The distributed architecture strongly improves the scaling capabilities in comparison to a single gigantic KG [29].

6   Conclusion and Future Work

In this paper, we described the building of a Knowledge Graph, a multi-stage inference engine and services for the physical twin of a magazine tower, a part of a real-world factory. The Web of Things Thing Description, Scripting API and servient implementation were used together with a domain ontology to retrieve sensor values from the physical twin and integrate them into the RDF Knowledge Graph. The performance evaluation of the KBS revealed limitations in terms of storage space consumption and query duration. Possible solutions by means of a virtual ontology-based data integration approach like OBDA or a network of distributed KGs have been discussed. We will examine the use of distributed KGs for industrial applications in future research.

Acknowledgment. This work was part of the project "Vernetzte industrielle Schaltschrankplanung, -Bau und -Service 4.0 (ISB4WBS)" which was supported by the Bavarian State Ministry of Economic Affairs, Regional Development and Energy within the research program "Information and Communication Technology".

References

1. Hogan, A., et al.: Knowledge graphs. arXiv:2003.02320 (2020)
2. Hubauer, T., Lamparter, S., Haase, P., Herzig, D.: Use cases of the industrial knowledge graph at Siemens. In: ISWC 2018, Monterey (2018)
3. Kovatsch, M., Matsukura, R., Lagally, M., Kawaguchi, T., Toumura, K., Kajimoto, K.: Web of Things (WoT) architecture. W3C Recommendation 9 April 2020 (2020). https://www.w3.org/TR/wot-architecture/
4. Käbisch, S., Kamiya, T., McCool, M., Charpenay, V., Kovatsch, M.: Web of Things (WoT) thing description. W3C Recommendation 9 April 2020 (2020). https://www.w3.org/TR/wot-thing-description/
5. Dimou, A., Vander Sande, M., Colpaert, P., Verborgh, R., Mannens, E., Van de Walle, R.: RML: a generic language for integrated RDF mappings of heterogeneous data. In: Proceedings of LDOW 2014, Seoul (2014)
6. Das, S., Sundara, S., Cyganiak, R.: R2RML: RDB to RDF mapping language. W3C Recommendation 27 September 2012 (2012). https://www.w3.org/TR/r2rml/
7. ETSI: SAREF: The Smart Appliances REFerence ontology (2015) . https://ontology.tno.nl/saref/. Accessed 9 Dec 2020
8. Rijgersberg, H., van Assem, M., Top, J.: Ontology of units of measure and related concepts. Semant. Web **4**(1), 3–13 (2013)
9. Kis, Z., Peintner, D., Aguzzi, C., Hund, J., Nimura, K.: Web of Things (WoT) scripting API. W3C Working Group Note 24 November 2020 (2020). https://www.w3.org/TR/wot-scripting-api/
10. Eiter, T., Ianni, G., Krennwallner, T., Polleres, A.: Rules and ontologies for the semantic web. In: Baroglio, C., Bonatti, P.A., Małuszyński, J., Marchiori, M., Polleres, A., Schaffert, S. (eds.) Reasoning Web. LNCS, vol. 5224, pp. 1–53. Springer, Heidelberg (2008). https://doi.org/10.1007/978-3-540-85658-0_1
11. Rattanasawad, T., Runapongsa Saikaew, K., Buranarach, M., Supnithi, T.: A review and comparison of rule languages and rule-based inference engines for the Semantic Web. In: ICSEC 2013. Bangkok (2013)
12. Mehla, S., Jain, S.: Rule languages for the semantic web. In: Proceedings of IEMIS 2018, vol. 3, pp. 825–834 (2019)
13. Berners-Lee, T., Connolly, D.: Notation 3 (N3). W3C Team Submission (2011). http://www.w3.org/TeamSubmission/n3/
14. Harth, A., Käfer, T.: Linked data techniques for the Web of Things. In: IoT 2018, Santa Barbara, California (2018)

15. Sciullo, L., Bhattacharjee, S., Kovatsch, M.: Bringing deterministic industrial networking to the W3C Web of Things with TSN and OPC-UA. In: Proceedings of IoT 2020, Malmö, Sweden (2020). https://doi.org/10.1145/3410992.3410997

16. Stojanovic, L.: Cognitive digital twins: challenges and opportunities for semantic technologies (keynote). In: Proceedings of SeDiT 2020 (ESWC 2020), Heraklion, Greece (2020)

17. Rožanec, J., et al.: Towards actionable cognitive digital twins for manufacturing. In: Proceedings of SeDiT 2020 (ESWC 2020), Heraklion, Greece (2020)

18. Banerjee, A., Dalal, R., Mittal, S., Pande Joshi, K.: Generating digital twin models using knowledge graphs for industrial production lines. In: Industrial Knowledge Graphs Workshop 2017, Troy, USA (2017)

19. Boschert, S., Heinrich, C., Rosen, R.: Next generation digital twin. In: Proceedings of 12th International Symposium TMCE 2018, Las Palmas de Gran Canaria, Spain (2018)

20. Ringsquandl, M., et al.: On event-driven knowledge graph completion in digital factories. In: IEEE Big Data 2017, Boston, USA, pp. 1676–1681 (2017)

21. Gómez-Berbís, J.M., de Amescua-Seco, A.: SEDIT: semantic digital twin based on industrial IoT data management and knowledge graphs. In: Valencia-García, R., Alcaraz-Mármol, G., Del Cioppo-Morstadt, J., Vera-Lucio, N., Bucaram-Leverone, M. (eds.) CITI 2019. CCIS, vol. 1124, pp. 178–188. Springer, Cham (2019). https://doi.org/10.1007/978-3-030-34989-9_14

22. Senington, R., Baumeister, F., Ng, A., Oscarsson, J.: A linked data approach for the connection of manufacturing processes with production simulation models. Proc. CIRP **70**, 440–445 (2018)

23. Bellini, P., Nesi, P.: Performance assessment of RDF graph databases for smart city services. JVLC **45**, 24–38 (2018)

24. Nikolić, N., Savić, G., Segedinac, M., Gostojić, S., Konjović, Z.: RDF stores performance test on servers with average specification. In: Proceedings of ICIST 2015, vol. 1, pp. 67–72 (2015)

25. Kilintzis, V., Beredimas, N., Chouvarda, I.: Evaluation of the performance of open-source RDBMS and triplestores for storing medical data over a web service. In: EMBC 2014, Chicago, USA (2014)

26. Chevallier, Z., Finance, B., Boulakia, B.C.: A reference architecture for smart building digital twin. In: Proceedings of SeDiT 2020 (ESWC 2020), Heraklion, Greece (2020)

27. Xiao, G., et al.: Ontology-based data access: a survey. In: Proceedings of IJCAI-ECAI-2018, Stockholm, pp. 5511–5519 (2018)

28. Kontchakov, R., Rodríguez-Muro, M., Zakharyaschev, M.: Ontology-based data access with databases: a short course. In: Rudolph, S., Gottlob, G., Horrocks, I., van Harmelen, F. (eds.) Reasoning Web 2013. LNCS, vol. 8067, pp. 194–229. Springer, Heidelberg (2013). https://doi.org/10.1007/978-3-642-39784-4_5

29. Zeng, K., Yang, J., Wang, H., Shao, B., Wang, Z.: A distributed graph engine for web scale RDF data. Proc. VLDB Endow. **2013**, 265–276 (2013)

Open-World Knowledge Graph Completion Benchmarks for Knowledge Discovery

Felix Hamann[1(✉)], Adrian Ulges[1], Dirk Krechel[1], and Ralph Bergmann[2]

[1] RheinMain University of Applied Sciences, Wiesbaden, Germany
{felix.hamann,adrian.ulges,dirk.krechel}@hs-rm.de
[2] University of Trier, Trier, Germany
bergmann@uni-trier.de
http://lavis.cs.hs-rm.de, http://www.wi2.uni-trier.de

Abstract. The construction and completion of knowledge graphs in industrial settings has gained traction over the past years. However, modelling a specific domain is often entailed with significant cost. This can be alleviated by including other knowledge sources such as text—a challenge known as open-world knowledge graph completion. Although knowledge graph completion has drawn significant attention from the research community over the past years, we argue that academic benchmarks fall short at two key characteristics of industrial conditions: (1) open-world entities are drawn randomly in benchmarks although in practice they are more volatile than closed-world entities, and (2) textual descriptions of entities are not concise.

This paper's mission is to bring academia and industry closer by proposing Inductive Reasoning with Text (IRT), an approach to create open-world evaluation benchmarks from given knowledge graphs. Two graphs, one based on Freebase and another derived from Wikidata, are created, analysed, and enhanced with textual descriptions according to the above assumptions. We evaluate a modular system that can tether any vector space knowledge graph completion model and a transformer-based text encoder to align sentence and entity representations. We show the difficulty of learning with such scattered text in contrast to text provided by other benchmarks and lay out a solid baseline study for future model benchmarking.

1 Introduction

Businesses' domain knowledge, claimed to be the "oil of the of the 21st century", is mostly digitized these days, but it rarely comes in structured form. Therefore, industrial knowledge management applications feature a knowledge engineering step in which a new domain with its entities and their properties, relations, problems and solutions is captured—often in form of a knowledge graph (KG). Here, a key challenge is **open-world knowledge graph completion (OW-KGC)**: As the knowledge engineer adds a new **open-world entity** e to the graph, the

© Springer Nature Switzerland AG 2021
H. Fujita et al. (Eds.): IEA/AIE 2021, LNAI 12799, pp. 252–264, 2021.
https://doi.org/10.1007/978-3-030-79463-7_21

system suggests/predicts facts about this entity. It does so by combining graph information (the current **closed-world** status of the KG) with a domain-specific text collection (such as reports, or documentation) featuring mentions of e.

Overall, knowledge engineering remains a time-consuming process and hand-engineered rules [5] are still the prevalent approach in practice. This is in contrast to recent developments in NLP research, where neural language models such as BERT [6] or the GPTs [4,13,14] are considered state-of-the-art. To bring these worlds closer together, better strategies are required to benchmark the applicability of neural methods for practical knowledge engineering. We argue that recent open-world KGC benchmarks in academia (e.g., [19–21,25]) fall short with respect to two aspects:

1. In current datasets such as FB15k237-OWE [20], open-world entities are drawn randomly. In practice, however, KGs feature a T-Box (with generic concepts such as VALVE) as opposed to an A-Box (with concrete instances such as AVENTICS 5342). We argue that T-Box knowledge is often acquired manually or transferred from other cases, but expanding a company's specific domain knowledge typically targets A-Box entities. Therefore, we propose an approach to create benchmarks in which we identify T-Box nodes using connectivity properties of the graph, and exclude such nodes from the open-world test set.
2. Current benchmarks feature high-quality encyclopaedic text, and entities (such as J.R.R. TOLKIEN) come with short and concise definitions (e.g. *"British philologist and author of classic high fantasy works"*) drawn from Wikipedia pages' introductions or Wikidata entity descriptions. In contrast, entities' mentions in industrial settings may be scattered throughout tickets and service logs, FAQs, and documentations, where usually the target entity is not even the subject of the sentence. To this end, our benchmark features incidental mentions rather than authored definitions.

To bridge the gap, we present a new benchmark coined Inductive Reasoning with Text (IRT), which features a clearer T-Box/A-Box separation for two knowledge bases (KBs) and more scattered text. We study how these two factors impact system performance, and present results for a neural approach as opposed to a keyword matching baseline. We show that constructing realistic OW-KGC benchmarks is greatly simplified by the proposed algorithm (Sect. 3) and our results indicate the difficulty of training with less focused text contexts (Sect. 5). We make our dataset[1] and trained models[2] publicly available as a reference for future research.

2 Related Work

Despite the current interest of the research community in developing closed-world knowledge graph completion (CW-KGC) models, relatively few works tackle the

---

[1] https://github.com/lavis-nlp/irt.
[2] https://github.com/lavis-nlp/irtm.

task of OW-KGC. These efforts tend to propose both their approaches and novel datasets in conjunction. As one of the earliest approaches, Xie et al. [25] present the FB20k benchmark as part of their work on DKRL. FB20k is based on FB15k, first introduced by Bordes et al. [3], a KG based on Freebase. As such it inherits the problem of test leakage introduced by inter-relation symmetry and redundancy first identified by Toutanova and Chen [22]. DKRL employs weighted CBOW representations of entity contexts to be encoded by a CNN. The encoded representation and structural embeddings are then trained jointly for knowledge graph completion (KGC).

Similar datasets are proposed by Shi and Weninger [21] with their Con-Mask model. These benchmarks are called DBPedia50k and DBPedia500k and are based on the DBPedia KB which is extracted from Wikipedia tables. All mentioned datasets use a single, concise textual description. We, however, are interested in a scenario, where quantitatively more but qualitatively less concise text is available. ConMask uses the names and descriptions of entities and relations to train a model that scores target entity plausibility. A recent adaption of this approach is named MIA [7].

Closely related to our work is FB15k237-OWE by Shah et al. [19,20]. Their dataset is based on FB15k237 and thus does not suffer from the aforementioned redundancy problem. The textual descriptions for the entities are sampled from Wikidata and as such there is only one rather short but quite concise sample of text assigned per entity. An important difference between their and our split lies in the idea of the concept entities: Whereas their scenario requires predictions for open-world entities such as BACHELOR OF SCIENCE or ATTORNEY GENERAL, we make sure that these non-volatile entities are found in the closed-world split. Also, our scenario does not limit itself to tail prediction but tackles both head- and tail-prediction and aims towards a scenario where *all* relevant facts for an unknown entity are to be retrieved. In their approach, a KGC model and a mapping of aggregated word embeddings to the KGC-embeddings is trained. A similar recent approach to OW-KGC includes WoWe [28], where the embedding aggregator is replaced with a weighted attention mechanism.

However, FB15k237 is challenged by Safavi and Koutra [18] who present CoDEx. This is a KG based on Wikidata and claims to mitigate problems with established benchmarks such as the aforementioned test leakage, unnaturally biased and hardly interpretable relations and exploitable peculiarities. The benchmark addresses CW-KGC and thus presents itself as a great candidate for our approach. We implement and try IRT-CDE as our open-world version of CoDEx.

Other datasets that combine graph and text can be found in scenarios geared towards relation extraction (RE) and are usually weakly supervised [15,23]. They, however, assume the whole triple to be expressed in one text passage—a constraint we are not subjected to. In short, no current dataset satisfies our requirements for scattered text and a purposeful open-world split.

3   Dataset

We define a knowledge graph (KG) as a tuple $G = (E, R, T)$, where R denotes a set of pre-defined relations, E is a set of entities forming the nodes of our graph, and $T \subset E \times R \times E$ is the set of *triples* (h, r, t), where h denotes the *head* (subject), r the *relation* (predicate), and t the *tail* (object).

KGC estimates the likelihood of new triples (h, r, t), typically by estimating a score $\varphi(h, r, t)$. We address an open-world scenario: The **closed-world part** of the graph $G^c = (E^c, R, T^c)$ is formed of closed-world entities E^c and the relations between them, i.e. $T^c = \{ (e, r, e') \mid e, e' \in E^c, r \subset R \}$. The remaining open-world entities $E^o = E \backslash E^c$ form a separate **open-world part** $G^o = (E^o, R, T^o)$ with $T^o = T \backslash T^c$. Besides the KG, we assume each entity $e \in E$ to come with a varying number of textual contexts in which e is mentioned (*"In a hole in the ground there lived a* HOBBIT*"*). This textual information is the only input describing open-world entities. The task at hand is now, given an open-world entity $e \in E^o$, to infer as many facts (i.e. triples) from T^c for e based on the associated text contexts.

In this section, we introduce two novel benchmark datasets (**IRT**) featuring (1) open-world entities sampled by identifying A-Box properties, and (2) less concise text data. Our first dataset (**IRT-FB**) is based on the FB15k237 graph dataset by Toutanova et al. [23], which is currently the de-facto standard benchmark for closed-world KGC. The second dataset (**IRT-CDE**) features CoDEx by Safavi and Koutra [18]. For both datasets, we identify **concept entities**, produce an **open-world/closed-world** partition of the triples, and sample **text contexts** for all entities. The approach can be applied to any existing knowledge base and we offer an implementation of our construction procedure as well as the datasets online in the aforementioned repositories.

Identifying Concept Entities. A key observation that can be made for real-world KBs is the different volatility of the modelled entities. For example, in politics **concept entities** such as political functions, bureaus and administrated territories remain relatively static, while **open-world entities** such as politicians will come and go.

We identify concept entities and reserve them for the closed-world split. Our key assumption is that concept entities are characterised by relations which exhibit a strong disproportion between their heads and tails. Specifically, we determine the ratio between a relation r's domain size (its number of heads) $\mathrm{dom}(r) := |\{h \mid \exists t : (h, r, t) \in T\}|$ and the range size (its number of tails) $\mathrm{rg}(r) := |\{t \mid \exists h : (h, r, t) \in T\}|$:

$$\mathrm{ratio}(r) := \frac{\min(\mathrm{dom}(r), \mathrm{rg}(r))}{\max(\mathrm{dom}(r), \mathrm{rg}(r))} \tag{1}$$

We assume relations with a low ratio to be indicators of concept entities: For example, in FB15k237, r_{18} (LOCATION:LOCATION:TIME_ZONES) features 1388 heads but only 13 tails (ratio(r_{18}) $\approx$ 0.00937). Obviously, these tail entities—the time zones—can be considered concept entities.

Therefore, our strategy is to traverse relations r with lowest ratio and—after a brief manual inspection of each relation—label their domain entities (or range entities, respectively) to be concepts if $dom(r) \gg rg(r)$ (or $rg(r) \gg dom(r)$, respectively). We found the ratio to be a suitable criterion for identifying concepts: when using the top 100 FB15k237 and top 27 CoDEx relations, only 7.1% of FB15k237 relations and 5.9% of CoDEx relations had to be corrected in a manual post-processing. Examples of the resulting concept entities are biological genders (FEMALE ORGANISM), countries (BRAZIL), professions (LAWYER), or academic degrees (BACHELOR OF ARTS).

Open-World and Closed-World. The triples are partitioned such that there is an open-world and a closed-world set with the constraints defined above. We divide the entity set E into E^c and E^o, where all concept entities form a subset of E^c and all other non-concept entities are distributed randomly between the two sets. The triple sets T^c and T^o emerge from this split by adding all triples connecting closed-world entities to the closed-world split and all other triples to the open-world split. We choose the split such that we retain around 75% of all triples for the closed-world partition.

	IRT-FB		IRT-CDE	
entities	14541		17050	
triples	310116		206205	
	Closed	Open	Closed	Open
concept entities	2389	0	2548	0
open-world entities	0	2377	0	4959
total entities	12164	10888	12091	9803
links to concepts	175316	37152	131486	60948
total triples	238190	71926	137388	68817

Text Contexts. For both closed-world and open-world entities, we sample textual contexts from Wikipedia. This emulates a use case where an upstream entity linking (EL) -System [8] identifies **mentions** of entities in documentation, reports, etc. As both FB15k237 and CoDEx are aligned with or based on Wikidata, each entity has its corresponding Wikipedia page assigned. The Wikipedia hyperlink structure is also employed borrowed from the work of [9,10] for context sampling: For a given entity, all its mentions (i.e. the link texts) from all backlinks to its Wikipedia page are aggregated. These mentions are then used to sample **entity contexts** from all such linked pages. Limiting to the close neighbourhood is a simple albeit effective heuristic to increase the probability that the text context actually refers to the entity, especially for highly ambiguous mentions such as PRINCE. Overall, however, these context sentences often discuss topics which feature the entity incidentally instead of offering a concise description. The set of text contexts for an entity e is denoted as $C(e) = \{c^1(e), c^2(e), \ldots c^{n(e)}(e)\}$ where each $c^j(e)$ is a free token sequence. In Wikipedia, the amount of text contexts sampled varies greatly from only a few mentions to up to tens of thousands. We randomly select up to 30 contexts per entity as we aim for a setting where text is scarce.

An Inference Example. Given the open-world entity TOLKIEN in IRT-CDE, relations both to open-world (ow), closed-world (cw) and concept entities are to be found. Some of the 37 triples to be identified include:

$$\text{C. S. LEWIS (ow)} \cdot \text{INFLUENCED BY} \cdot \text{TOLKIEN (ow)}$$
$$\text{TOLKIEN (ow)} \cdot \text{INFLUENCED BY} \cdot \text{GEORGE MACDONALD (cw)}$$
$$\text{TOLKIEN (ow)} \cdot \text{EDUCATED AT} \cdot \text{UNIVERSITY OF OXFORD (concept)}$$
$$\text{TOLKIEN (ow)} \cdot \text{RELIGION} \cdot \text{CATHOLIC CHURCH (concept)}$$

The context set of TOLKIEN includes, among others: *"MacDonald was a major influence on both J. R. R. Tolkien and C. S. Lewis."*, *"Particularly affecting for Tolkien was Edith's conversion to the Catholic Church from the Church of England for his sake upon their marriage (...)."*, and *"For example J. R. R. Tolkien, his friend C. S. Lewis and other members of the Oxford literary group were known as the Inklings."*. Note that both the hints towards TOLKIEN'S religion and education are merely described indirectly by the text samples. This differentiates our task from common relation extraction tasks [27].

4 Model

To assess the difficulty of the novel datasets, we adopt the current state-of-the-art approach by [20], where an independently trained KGC model and a pre-trained token embedding are combined to allow open-world link prediction. We extend this approach two-fold: (1) Our model studies how well the approach handles multiple contexts per entity, and (2) instead of static word embeddings we utilize contextualized embeddings encoded by a transformer model. An overview of the approach is given in Fig. 1.

Closed-World Knowledge Graph Completion. Our starting point is a compositional vector space model for KGC that uses learned latent features for entities and relations [3,11,12,24]. We employ DistMult by Yang et al. [26], a conceptionally rather simple albeit competitive model for KGC [17] (note, however, that our approach can be combined with any of the above models). Entities and relations are represented via dense d-dimensional vectors (i.e. embeddings) $\mathbf{g}(\cdot)$ learned during training. For each triple (h, r, t), a score is derived as the representations' inner product:

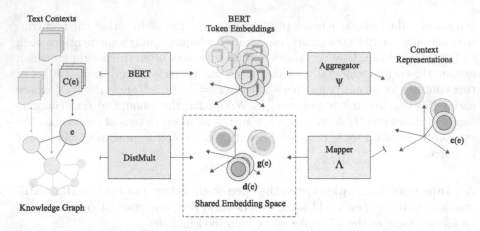

Fig. 1. High level overview of the proposed approach: BERT token embeddings (top) are aggregated to context representations (right) and projected into the KGC embedding space (bottom).

$$\text{score}(h, r, t) = \phi(\mathbf{g}(h), \mathbf{g}(r), \mathbf{g}(t)) := \sum_{i=1}^{d} \mathbf{g}_i(h) \cdot \mathbf{g}_i(r) \cdot \mathbf{g}_i(t) \tag{2}$$

Training is either conducted (1) pair-wise, where the model is trained to score true facts higher than random non-existing facts, or (2) list-wise, where all head or tail entity candidates are scored in a single step. Using the above scores, inference can be conducted, e.g. **head-prediction**—given a tuple (r, t)—or **tail-prediction**—given a tuple (h, r)):

$$h^* = \underset{h' \in E}{\text{argmax}} \ \text{score}(h', r, t) \qquad t^* = \underset{t' \in E}{\text{argmax}} \ \text{score}(h, r, t') \tag{3}$$

Text-Encoding. Text-based entity representations are derived using BERT [6], a popular state-of-the-art transformer encoder. BERT is pre-trained on a large text corpus using masked language modelling, and can be fine-tuned to the task at hand. An entity e's context sentence $c^j(e)$ is tokenized into m tokens using a byte-pair encoding and fed to BERT, which produces a $\mathbb{R}^{m \times d'}$ sentence representation. This matrix is then reduced by an **aggregator** $\psi : \mathbb{R}^{m \times d'} \mapsto \mathbb{R}^{d'}$ to obtain a single vector representation of the input sequence (e.g. by averaging the token representations or—following common practice—by selecting BERT's CLS-token): $\mathbf{c}^j(e) = \psi(\text{BERT}(c^j(e)))$.

Inference. Given an entity's representations (graph-based vs. text-based), we learn a projection Λ_Θ which maps the text representation to the graph-based one. To score facts involving open-world entities, we simply replace their (unknown) graph-based representation $\mathbf{g}$ with a representation $\mathbf{d}$ derived by mapping the text-based representations:

$$\text{score}(h, r, t) = \phi(\mathbf{f}(h), \mathbf{r}, \mathbf{f}(t)) \quad \text{with} \quad \mathbf{f}(e) = \begin{cases} \mathbf{g}(e) & \text{if } e \in E^c \\ \mathbf{d}(e) & \text{if } e \in E^o \end{cases} \quad (4)$$

To define $\mathbf{d}$, note that our scenario assumes *multiple* text contexts $c^1(e), ..., c^{n(e)}(e)$ per entity to be given, yielding multiple representations $\mathbf{c}^1(e), ..., \mathbf{c}^{n(e)}(e)$. We study two strategies to combine these contexts, which differ in their representation, but also—more importantly—in training: (1) The **single-instance** scenario, where the model operates only on single entity-context pairs without any explicit intra-context knowledge. Here, $\mathbf{d}$ is the average of the projected contexts: $\mathbf{d}(c) = \frac{1}{n(e)} \sum_j \Lambda_\Theta(\mathbf{c}^j(e))$. (2) The **multi-instance** scenario, where multiple contexts per entity are max-pooled to obtain a single vector representation of all context sentences prior to projection: $\mathbf{d}(e) = \Lambda_\Theta(\text{max\_pool}(\mathbf{c}^1(e), ..., \mathbf{c}^{n(e)}(e)))$.

Vector Space Alignment. We use a simple affine mapping $\Lambda_{W,\mathbf{b}} := W\mathbf{c}^j(e) + \mathbf{b}$. Overall, the model's parameters Θ include $W, \mathbf{b}$ and (when fine-tuning) the BERT parameters. They are optimized using stochastic gradient descent operating on a geometric loss function to reduce the distance of the projections from the reference KGC embedding.

$$\underset{\Theta}{\text{argmin}} \sum_{e \in E^c} \mathcal{L}(e) \quad \text{with} \quad \mathcal{L}(e) = \begin{cases} \sum_j \left\| \mathbf{g}(e) - \Lambda_\Theta(\mathbf{c}^j(e)) \right\|_2 & \text{(single)} \\ \left\| \mathbf{g}(e) - \mathbf{d}(e) \right\|_2 & \text{(multi)} \end{cases} \quad (5)$$

5   Experiments

We conduct a series of experiments on our novel dataset to create a comprehensive set of base metrics to be referenced by future research. Our objectives include to (1) determine the performance difference between the neural approach and a keyword-matching baseline (2) compare the single- and multi-instance scenarios to determine the impact of intra-context knowledge, (3) devise and try approaches to enhance the models' ability to generalise to unseen data, and (4) study the difference between our scattered texts and the concise texts offered by the upstream KBs.

Evaluation Protocol. We use the PyKEEN library [2] to run both the closed-world KGC training and open-world evaluation. For a given test triple $y = (h, r, t)$ both head- and tail-prediction (see Eq. 3) is performed. Target filtering is applied by PyKEEN. The key figures selected to determine model performance include hits@k and the mean reciprocal rank averaged over both head and tail prediction.

Data Split and Model Configuration. (1) We partition the closed-world triple set T^c into training (80%), validation (10%) and test (10%) for **kgc training**. We use the validation set to optimize hits@10 in a hyperparameter sweep using Optuna's Bayesian search [1]. The models with highest validation performance are evaluated on the test set. (2) For **projector training** all entities of the closed-world part are used. (3) To measure how well the projections are suited for **OW-KGC**, we use around 65% of the open-world entities for validation and 35% for testing. We again optimize hits@10 performance but now for the OW-KGC model based on this validation set. We apply gradient clipping (usually 1), accumulate batches (around 10 30-sentence context sets), and try drop-out (without discernable effect on stability or performance, however).

Bag-of-Words Baseline. A baseline is implemented that retrieves the most similar closed-world entity based on the bag-of-words representation of its contexts. The relations of that entity are used as a blueprint for the open-world entities' facts. To do so, all contexts describing an entity are concatenated and form $D(e)$, a **document** describing entity e. Now, for an unknown open-world entity e' the document $D(e')$ is used as a BM25 [16] query against an index containing all closed-world entity documents. The document with the highest score $D(e^*)$ is selected and all associated triples are used for prediction by replacing e^* with e'. It follows that relations between open-world entities cannot be found this way.

Text Modes. The text is preprocessed in three modes: (1) **clean** – the raw text, (2) **marked** – which introduces explicit marker tokens as indicators for the mention, and (3) **masked** – where all mentions are replaced with a mask token ([MASK]) and only the surrounding context remains. The aggregator ψ comes in two variants: **cls**, where only the classifier token ([CLS]) is used and **max**, the max-pooled context tokens. In some experiments, the text encoder is frozen (i.e. the BERT parameters are not fine-tuned).

Table 1. Test results for IRT-FB and IRT-CDE with 30 sentences per entity. The multi-instance configuration generally outperforms single-instance and masking reduces overfitting. Models where the text encoder is frozen are marked with †.

Mode	Inst.	Agg.	IRT-FB				IRT-CDE			
			H@1	H@5	H@10	MRR	H@1	H@5	H@10	MRR
baseline			9.14	15.86	17.08	12.44	10.86	15.40	16.11	13.04
marked	single	max†	9.44	16.38	19.75	13.08	12.35	21.57	26.22	16.90
marked	single	max	8.68	15.60	19.47	12.45	5.55	14.16	19.50	9.82
marked	single	cls	10.39	18.14	22.75	14.68	15.44	26.99	32.15	21.11
marked	multi	cls	11.20	21.19	26.86	16.55	17.74	30.43	36.18	24.07
clean	single	max†	9.64	16.57	20.29	13.31	11.90	21.60	25.88	16.65
clean	single	max	11.39	20.74	25.34	16.14	7.76	15.84	21.76	12.36
clean	single	cls	11.52	20.77	25.45	16.29	15.65	26.93	31.65	21.13
clean	multi	cls	12.19	23.54	29.60	18.07	15.33	26.47	31.39	20.82
masked	single	max†	8.65	15.18	18.61	12.09	11.38	20.37	25.00	15.82
masked	single	max	11.00	19.22	23.69	15.33	5.80	15.10	19.71	10.28
masked	single	cls	12.61	22.40	27.62	17.72	17.11	28.60	33.77	22.78
masked	multi	cls	**13.82**	**27.16**	**34.18**	**20.61**	**20.88**	**34.60**	**40.67**	**27.62**

Results. Table 1 compares the single- and multiple-instance scenarios on both IRT KG's with different model configurations. Generally, using the CLS-token as aggregator and fine-tuning the encoder outperforms other configurations. Masking the concrete entity mention proves useful for generalisation to unseen data. The multiple-instance approach works best for all modes with at least 4% margin to the next best single-instance configuration.

Figure 2 illustrates how the different modes and configurations affect model performance for different context sizes. We study three variations: 5, 15 and 30 sentences per entity. It can be observed that reducing the amount of context information also diminishes the influence of the text mode. We hypothesize that masking the mentions dissuades the model from focusing to excessively on the mention identity (which are the obvious intra-context connecting links). It is instead forced to rely more on contextual hints for classification—something that is only observable when enlarging the entity context.

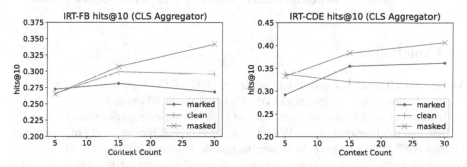

Fig. 2. Hits@10 measured on datasets with different context sizes (5, 15 and 30 sentences) when using the multi-instance variant of the model. While differences in text modes are not pronounced for small amounts of context sentences, masking helps with generalisation for larger contexts.

Table 2 enumerates performance figures when using only a single sentence as we argue that the texts provided in other OW-KGC benchmarks are unrealistically concise. A single sentence from our text contexts is randomly selected for training and we contrast this to (1) the Wikidata descriptions as used in the OWE approach by [19,20] and (2) the first sentence of the associated Wikipedia page as provided by [18] for CoDEx. The results reflect our assumption as can be seen by the large performance gap. In combination with Table 1 (where 30 sentences are used), we argue that working with realistic data requires different model approaches—in our case the multi-instance approach. This gives reason for confidence that from multiple sentences of lower quality the same amount of information can be derived as from a single concise one.

Table 2. Model performance when using only a single sentence. Overall, the models perform significantly better when using the provided Wikidata descriptions for IRT-FB and the first sentence of the associated Wikipedia page for IRT-FB (theirs) as opposed to a randomly assigned single sentence from our dataset (ours).

		IRT-FB				IRT-CDE			
		H@1	H@5	H@10	MRR	H@1	H@5	H@10	MRR
baseline	ours	4.24	6.78	7.22	5.47	5.75	7.83	8.09	6.74
	theirs	**8.74**	**13.22**	**14.51**	**11.06**	**10.19**	**14.39**	**15.14**	**12.20**
cls	ours	8.17	15.69	19.77	12.19	13.58	26.07	32.03	19.82
	theirs	**12.70**	**24.20**	**30.25**	**18.63**	**23.07**	**38.91**	**45.73**	**30.86**
max	ours	8.40	15.85	19.90	12.43	13.87	26.10	31.90	19.99
	theirs	**13.02**	**24.68**	**30.71**	**19.04**	**23.04**	**39.47**	**46.82**	**31.11**
max†	ours	7.73	13.31	15.94	10.66	12.22	22.43	27.14	17.19
	theirs	**10.49**	**18.00**	**22.21**	**14.52**	**14.46**	**25.41**	**30.44**	**19.83**

6   Conclusion

We present IRT, an approach to construct OW-KGC benchmarks for zero-shot link-prediction utilizing free text. We offer two novel KG splits, text sampled in the manner of an EL system, and a set of baseline experiments as the foundation for future model development. With these, we study different effects of model and dataset configurations and show how to enable learning for larger text contexts. We invite both industry practitioners and academia to utilize these datasets to evaluate and study approaches to infer symbolic knowledge from scattered textual data. All datasets, models and accompanying hyperparameter configurations can be obtained at https://github.com/lavis-nlp/irt & https://github.com/lavis-nlp/irtm.

References

1. Akiba, T., Sano, S., Yanase, T., Ohta, T., Koyama, M.: Optuna: a next-generation hyperparameter optimization framework. In: 25rd ACM SIGKDD (2019)
2. Ali, M., et al.: Pykeen 1.0: a Python library for training and evaluating knowledge graph emebddings. arXiv preprint arXiv:2007.14175 (2020)
3. Bordes, A., Usunier, N., Garcia-Duran, A., Weston, J., Yakhnenko, O.: Translating embeddings for modeling multi-relational data. In: Advances in NIPS, pp. 2787–2795 (2013)
4. Brown, T.B., et al.: Language models are few-shot learners. arXiv preprint arXiv:2005.14165 (2020)
5. Chiticariu, L., Li, Y., Reiss, F.: Rule-based information extraction is dead! long live rule-based information extraction systems! In: Proceedings of the 2013 EMNLP, pp. 827–832 (2013)

6. Devlin, J., Chang, M.W., Lee, K., Toutanova, K.: Bert: pre-training of deep bidirectional transformers for language understanding. arXiv preprint arXiv:1810.04805 (2018)
7. Fu, C., Li, Z., Yang, Q., Chen, Z., Fang, J., Zhao, P., Xu, J.: Multiple interaction attention model for open-world knowledge graph completion. In: Cheng, R., Mamoulis, N., Sun, Y., Huang, X. (eds.) WISE 2020. LNCS, vol. 11881, pp. 630–644. Springer, Cham (2019). https://doi.org/10.1007/978-3-030-34223-4_40
8. Logeswaran, L., Chang, M.W., Lee, K., Toutanova, K., Devlin, J., Lee, H.: Zero-shot entity linking by reading entity descriptions. arXiv preprint arXiv:1906.07348 (2019)
9. Mihalcea, R., Csomai, A.: Wikify! linking documents to encyclopedic knowledge. In: Proceedings of the 16th ACM CIKM, pp. 233–242 (2007)
10. Milne, D., Witten, I.H.: Learning to link with Wikipedia. In: Proceedings of the 17th ACM CIKM, pp. 509–518 (2008)
11. Nickel, M., Rosasco, L., Poggio, T.: Holographic embeddings of knowledge graphs. In: 30th AAAI (2016)
12. Nickel, M., Tresp, V., Kriegel, H.P.: A three-way model for collective learning on multi-relational data. In: ICML, vol. 11, pp. 809–816 (2011)
13. Radford, A., Narasimhan, K., Salimans, T., Sutskever, I.: Improving language understanding with unsupervised learning. OpenAI (2018)
14. Radford, A., Wu, J., Child, R., Luan, D., Amodei, D., Sutskever, I.: Language models are unsupervised multitask learners. OpenAI blog (2019)
15. Riedel, S., Yao, L., McCallum, A.: Modeling relations and their mentions without labeled text. In: Balcázar, J.L., Bonchi, F., Gionis, A., Sebag, M. (eds.) ECML PKDD 2010. LNCS (LNAI), vol. 6323, pp. 148–163. Springer, Heidelberg (2010). https://doi.org/10.1007/978-3-642-15939-8_10
16. Robertson, S.E., Walker, S.: Some simple effective approximations to the 2-Poisson model for probabilistic weighted retrieval. In: Croft, B.W., van Rijsbergen, C.J. (eds.) SIGIR 1994, pp. 232–241. Springer, London (1994). https://doi.org/10.1007/978-1-4471-2099-5_24
17. Ruffinelli, D., Broscheit, S., Gemulla, R.: You can teach an old dog new tricks! on training knowledge graph embeddings. In: ICLR (2019)
18. Safavi, T., Koutra, D.: CoDEx: a comprehensive knowledge graph completion benchmark. In: Proceedings of the 2020 EMNLP (2020)
19. Shah, H., Villmow, J., Ulges, A.: Relation specific transformations for open world knowledge graph completion. In: TextGraphs, pp. 79–84. ACL, December 2020. https://www.aclweb.org/anthology/2020.textgraphs-1.9
20. Shah, H., Villmow, J., Ulges, A., Schwanecke, U., Shafait, F.: An open-world extension to knowledge graph completion models. In: 33rd AAAI (2019)
21. Shi, B., Weninger, T.: Open-world knowledge graph completion. arXiv preprint arXiv:1711.03438 (2017)
22. Toutanova, K., Chen, D.: Observed versus latent features for knowledge base and text inference. In: Proceedings of the 3rd Workshop for IJCNLP, pp. 57–66. ACL, July 2015. https://doi.org/10.18653/v1/W15-4007
23. Toutanova, K., Chen, D., Pantel, P., Poon, H., Choudhury, P., Gamon, M.: Representing text for joint embedding of text and knowledge bases. In: Proceedings of the 2015 EMNLP, pp. 1499–1509 (2015)
24. Trouillon, T., Welbl, J., Riedel, S., Gaussier, É., Bouchard, G.: Complex embeddings for simple link prediction. In: ICML, pp. 2071–2080 (2016)
25. Xie, R., Liu, Z., Jia, J., Luan, H., Sun, M.: Representation learning of knowledge graphs with entity descriptions. In: 30th AAAI (2016)

26. Yang, B., Yih, W.t., He, X., Gao, J., Deng, L.: Embedding entities and relations for learning and inference in knowledge bases. arXiv preprint arXiv:1412.6575 (2014)
27. Yao, Y., et al.: DocRED: a large-scale document-level relation extraction dataset. In: Proceedings of ACL 2019 (2019)
28. Zhou, Y., Shi, S., Huang, H.: Weighted aggregator for the open-world knowledge graph completion. In: Zeng, J., Jing, W., Song, X., Lu, Z. (eds.) ICPCSEE 2020. CCIS, vol. 1257, pp. 283–291. Springer, Singapore (2020). https://doi.org/10.1007/978-981-15-7981-3_19

A Case-Based Reasoning Approach for a Decision Support System in Manufacturing

Sascha Lang[1]([✉]), Valentin Plenk[1], and Ute Schmid[2][iD]

[1] Institute of Information Systems, Hof University, Hof, Germany
{sascha.lang,valentin.plenk}@hof-university.de
[2] Cognitive Systems, University of Bamberg, Bamberg, Germany
ute.schmid@uni-bamberg.de

Abstract. We propose Case-based reasoning (CBR) as an approach to assist human operators who control special purpose production machines. Our support system automatically extracts knowledge from machine data and creates recommendations, which help the operators solve problems with a production machine. This support has to be comprehensive and maintainable by process experts, also the system has to be easy transferable to different machines. We present CBR as a suitable approach for a decision support system in an industrial production.

Keywords: Decision support system for industry ·
Case-based-reasoning · Case extraction · Reasoning on distance
measurements

1 Introduction

Workers have to control increasingly complex machines. Untrained employees have to rely on the experience of skilled ones to run the machines properly. This is obviously time consuming and a skilled worker is not available at any time, e.g. if he leaves the company. We propose a system which extracts knowledge stored in the machines and helps the operator to become a 'Smarter Operator' [12]. The idea of assisting the user is not new, in 1998 Park et al. [10] proposed an assistant systems for manufacturing CRT monitors. We want to address machines manufactured in a small quantity. To make this economical, we have to reduce the amount of background knowledge used for the system. As Kravis et al. [4] stated, gathering background knowledge is an expensive and complex process.

We can think about three groups of learning: Implicit learning, explicit rule learning and instance-based learning (Table 1). Artificial neural networks (ANN) are a widely employed family of instance-based learning approaches. The strength of ANNs is their high expressiveness, allowing the approximation of arbitrary non-linear functions. Current approaches such as convolutional networks allow end-to-end learning which overcomes the bottle neck of feature

© Springer Nature Switzerland AG 2021
H. Fujita et al. (Eds.): IEA/AIE 2021, LNAI 12799, pp. 265–271, 2021.
https://doi.org/10.1007/978-3-030-79463-7_22

Table 1. Comparison of different types of learning

	Implicit learning	Explicit learning	Instance-based learning
Class of algorithms	Artificial neural networks	Rule-based systems	Case based reasoning
Application example	Object recognition	Classification of Bact. infection	Vehicle fault diagnosis
Background knowledge	No	Yes	No
Data prerequisites	High amount /Balanced	Low amount/ Unbalanced	Low amount/ Unbalanced
Effort learning instances	Worst case: complete retraining	Recreation of the rule set	Simple addition

extraction from raw data [14]. Learning is data-driven and relies on the availability of a large number of training data [7]. An example for an explicit learning approach is a decision set [5], which allows the induction of explicit rules from data. Inductive logic programming approaches have an expressivity going beyond simple rules and provide a natural way to combine learning and reasoning [8]. The generated models are transparent and can be made comprehensible to humans [13].

As both approaches do not fulfill our requirements, we need a system being able to work with a limited amount of data, even if it is unbalanced, also we need to justify our results. New cases have to be learned instantly. The rules generated by an explicit learning approach have to be regenerated with every new case and an ANN has to be retrained in the worst case. We decided to use an instance-based method called of case-based reasoning (CBR) [1]. CBR is able to work with a few examples, but can also handle a large amount of data, learning a new case is simply adding them to the case base. CBR can handle every data type for which a distance or similarity measurement is definable. Although it seems the best choice, we have some drawbacks. The retrieved instance(s) depend on the selected distance measure and CBR is prone to the curse of dimensionality, so the overall similarity might be dominated by irrelevant features [9]. Also a CBR system is not as comprehensive as a rule based system. The data which is used to determine the similarity could also be used as an justification, but the effort has to be higher as extracting justification from rules.

In Sect. 2, we describe a rough proposal of our decision support system. Afterwards, in Sect. 3 we present first results in a real world scenario. The paper concludes with a short discussion and planned future work.

2   Method

In this Section, we briefly describe our system. Actually this includes the creation of our case base and the retrieval step. The revision step, which enables our system to learn new cases, is added in the future. Figure 1 shows the two steps and their sub steps, the usage of background knowledge is also illustrated. A case consists of a problem, which describes the machine state at the time the case occurred and also a solution containing the interactions the operator performed.

2.1 Extraction of the Solution

To extract the interactions between the operator and the machine, we have to analyze our data. The data has to be separated into two categories, the first category we call operator data (OP_Val) and the other is called process data (P_Val). We could possibly distinguish both by there properties, but we decided to use background knowledge. This knowledge is also necessary to create human understandable recommendations, we use it especially as we think it is easy to get, e.g. from the manual of the control system. After separating the data, we iterate through all OP_Vals, every change is denoted as an event. Figure 2 shows

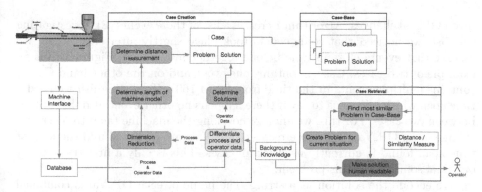

Fig. 1. The green steps need no background knowledge, the yellow step benefits from it, the red step needs it Extruder schematic: https://commons.wikimedia.org/wiki/File:Extruder_section.jpg. (Color figure online)

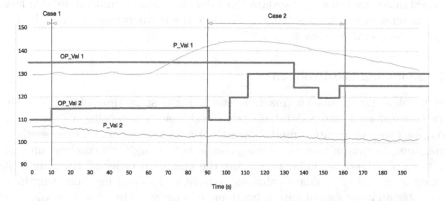

Fig. 2. Synthetic data to illustrate the case extraction

Algorithm 1: Solution extraction from data

Input   : Length of pause P, Data (in chronological order) D
Output: List of Solutions S
List of Events $E \leftarrow \{\}$
foreach $d_{n-1}, d_n \in D$ **do**
    foreach *Op-Value* $op_{n-1} \in d_{n-1}$ *and* $op_n \in d_n$ **do**
        if $op_{n-1} \neq op_n$ **then**
            $E \leftarrow E \cup e(d_n.time; op_{n-1} - op_n)$

foreach $e \in E$ **do**
    Solution $s \leftarrow \{\}$
    while $e_n.time - e_{n-1}.time < P$ **do**
        $s \leftarrow k \cup \{e_n, e_{n-1}\}$
    $S \leftarrow S \cup s$
return S

---

seven OP_Val changes. Algorithm 1 creates a list of these events (**E**). Investigating this list, we noticed that some events took place shortly after each other. We assume that events close in time belong together in one case. Figure 2 gives an example of two cases: Case 1 contains one event and on the other hand Case 2 contains multiple events in the time from 90 to 160 s. To distinguish we need a time span which allows us to say if there happens no other event, it differentiates between two cases. For this, we analyze how long the machine takes to react to a change in an OP_Val. Therefore respective P_Vals are analyzed and the longest time span found is currently used for all cases. This is only a first try and not our final solution for this problem.

We encode the solution as a string. The name of each OP_Val is combined with its value at the end time of its respective case. The OP_Vals are sorted alphabetical by name and separated by #. The solution for Case 1 results in `OP_Val_1_135#OP_Val_2_115#` and for Case 2 in `Op_Val_1_125#OP_Val_2_135`. As mentioned, we have to translate this later in a human understandable form by using background knowledge, e.g. "Reduce the temperature in zone 1 by 10°, raise the temperature zone 2 by 20°".

2.2   Modeling the Problem

The problem represents the machine state at the start time of its case. Our data is transferred into a database table, each row representing a time stamp. From each row we create a multidimensional point, each column representing a dimension. Assuming that one data point is not enough, we combine multiple points to a polygonal chain, preserving the temporal order of the points. As we cannot use all of the data columns we have and should limit our length, we use cluster analysis paired with a brute force approach. But this dimension and length estimation will not be our final method. Our dimensions have different value ranges, so we standardize them with z-score.

2.3 Retrieving a Case

To retrieve suitable cases from the case base, we need a distance measure for polygonal chains. A suitable measurement is the Frèchet-distance, which is hard to implement and therefore we approximate it with a discrete Variant [3]. As the underlying distance for the points itself, we use Minkowski Metric with $p = 1$ (Manhattan distance). As Aggarwal et al. [2] stated using a smaller p for the Minkowski distance will lead to better contrast if high dimensional data is used.

Table 2. Datasets for our application

Dataset	Duration (months)	Attributes	
		OP_Val	P_Val
5	12	11	103
6	11	29	196

Table 3. Resulting case bases

Dataset	Statistical		Machine reaction	
	All	Learnable	All	Learnable
5	565	55	225	14
6	743	103	331	23

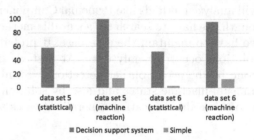

Fig. 3. Results compared to a simple benchmark

3 Results

The data we use for our test is gathered from two plastic extruders, the extruders and the general environment is described in our previous work [11]. Table 2 details the data sets, we have up to 29 operator attributes used in the solutions, and up to 196 process attributes used in the problem. In our previous work [6], we described a method creating the cases with a statistical method analyzing the pauses between events. We compare this method with the method described in this paper. The created case bases are detailed in Table 3. We distinguish between learnable and unlearnable solutions. Learnable solutions are solutions contained at least twice in the case base. As we use a leave-one-out evaluation even if a solution is used for test it is also contained in another case in the case base. If the solution of the test-case equals the solution of the retrieved case, it is a positive result. The percentage of correct to all learnable cases is the result. We compare our results with a simple algorithm, which returns always the most frequent solution contained in the case base. In all of our tests, we beat the simple algorithm, and notice an increase compared to the previous approach for creating the case base. The results are shown in Fig. 3.

4   Conclusion

In this work, we presented an idea of a decision support system for production machines. This system is able to extract case base from the machine data mostly automatically. The resulting case base is inspectable, and the problem of each case can be used to justify the created recommendations. We performed a first test on data gathered from two plastics extruder. The results seem promising, however our results have to be validated by process experts. Nevertheless our results support our assumption that equal solutions have similar problems.

We have to solve some issues, one is how to model the problem. We have to reduce the dimensionality and find a suitable length of our polygonal chain. Our current simple brute force algorithm is not suitable for a large amount of data, because the computing time will get very high. To reduce the dimensionality we will analyze methods like Principal Component Analysis. To determine a suitable length, we have to search for a suitable method or develop our own method. Also we have to maintain the case base: It probably contains bad cases and we have solutions occurring only once. At first we have to filter the case base, this is done by the use of outlier detection, we will either filter by problem to remove unusual machine states and also by solution to remove unusual operations. We also think about creating generalized cases to combine similar solutions.

References

1. Aamodt, A., Plaza, E.: Case-based reasoning: foundational issues, methodological variations, and system approaches. AI Commun. **7**(1), 39–59 (1994)
2. Aggarwal, C.C., Hinneburg, A., Keim, D.A.: On the surprising behavior of distance metrics in high dimensional space. In: Van den Bussche, J., Vianu, V. (eds.) ICDT 2001. LNCS, vol. 1973, pp. 420–434. Springer, Heidelberg (2001). https://doi.org/10.1007/3-540-44503-X_27
3. Eiter, T., Mannila, H.: Computing discrete frèchet distance. Technische Universität Wien, Technical report (1994)
4. Kravis, S., Irrgang, R.: A case based system for oil and gas well design with risk assessment. Appl. Intell. **23**(1), 39–53 (2005)
5. Lakkaraju, H., Bach, S.H., Leskovec, J.: Interpretable decision sets: a joint framework for description and prediction. In: Proceedings of the 22nd ACM SIGKDD International Conference on Knowledge Discovery and Data Mining, pp. 1675–1684. ACM (2016)
6. Lang, S., Plenk, V.: Preprocessing data for machine-learning algorithms to provide user guidance in special purpose machines. In: Proceedings of CENTRIC 2018: The Eleventh International Conference on Advances in Human-Oriented and Personalized Mechanisms, Technologies, and Services, pp. 32–41, October 2018
7. Marcus, G.: Deep learning: a critical appraisal. arXiv preprint arXiv:1801.00631 (2018)
8. Muggleton, S.H., Schmid, U., Zeller, C., Tamaddoni-Nezhad, A., Besold, T.: Ultrastrong machine learning: comprehensibility of programs learned with ILP. Mach. Learn. **107**(7), 1119–1140 (2018)
9. Park, C.H., Kim, S.B.: Sequential random k-nearest neighbor feature selection for high-dimensional data. Expert Syst. Appl. **42**(5), 2336–2342 (2015)

10. Park, M.K., Lee, I., Shon, K.M.: Using case based reasoning for problem solving in a complex production process. Expert Syst. Appl. **15**(1), 69–75 (1998)
11. Plenk, V.: Improving special purpose machine user-interfaces by machine-learning algorithms. In: Proceedings of CENTRIC 2016: The 9th International Conference on Advances in Human-Oriented & Personalized Mechanisms, Technologies & Services, pp. 24–28 (2016)
12. Romero, D., et al.: Towards an operator 4.0 typology: a human-centric perspective on the fourth industrial revolution technologies. In: International Conference on Computers and Industrial Engineering (CIE46) Proceedings (2016)
13. Schmid, U.: Inductive programming as approach to comprehensible machine learning. In: Proceedings of the 7th Workshop on Dynamics of Knowledge and Belief (DKB-2018) and the 6th Workshop KI & Kognition (KIK-2018), Co-located with 41st German Conference on Artificial Intelligence, vol. 2194 (2018)
14. Wang, J., Ma, Y., Zhang, L., Gao, R.X., Wu, D.: Deep learning for smart manufacturing: methods and applications. J. Manufact. Syst. **48**, 144–156 (2018)

Online Automatic Assessment System for Program Code: Architecture and Experiences

Yutaka Watanobe(✉), Md. Mostafizer Rahman, Uday Kiran Rage,
and Ravikumar Penugonda

The University of Aizu, Aizu-Wakamatsu, Fukushima, Japan
yutaka@u-aizu.ac.jp

Abstract. Online Automatic Assessment System (OAAS) is a vital component in Online Judge systems. It is used to assess the correctness of programs submitted by the users. Developing OAAS is a non-trivial and challenging task due to various functional and non-functional dependencies. Few OAAS architectures were reported in the literature; however, their stability in handling the voluminous data produced by millions of submissions over a long duration is unknown. In this paper, we present the internal architecture of our OAAS, which has assessed five million program codes and has been operating stably for more than 10 years. We will also share some of our real-world experiences related to the operation of this system.

Keywords: Automatic assessment system · Online judge · Programming education · Software engineering

1 Introduction

Executing and assessing the programs submitted by several users to a programming contest (or an assignment) is a challenging problem of great importance in the field of computer science programming [1]. Online Judge (OJ) systems were being explored to tackle this challenging problem. OJs are playing a key role in online learning, interviews, and software development process. The characteristics of OJ systems, in which the activities of programmers and their source codes accumulate, are also attractive to data science researchers [2].

Components of an OJ system include a set of problems (questions) and web clients as well as a number of servers to provide different services. Among them the core component of an OJ system is its Online Automatic Assessment System (OAAS), within which the verification and evaluation process is expected to be carried out rigorously and efficiently. In operation, an OAAS compiles and executes programs received from arbitrary users under a common environment, checks the program behavior via specified input/output data, and then reports the assessment results and resource consumption data to all related users.

H. Fujita et al. (Eds.): IEA/AIE 2021, LNAI 12799, pp. 272–283, 2021.
https://doi.org/10.1007/978-3-030-79463-7_23

In addition to these functional requirements, an OAAS should satisfy various non-functional requirements focusing on specific use cases. These include feedback on the performance, consistency, robustness, sustainability, and transparency of the evaluated code, as well as other tradeoff items including security, newness, reliability, portability, and scalability.

Most previous studies focused on improving the functionality and effectiveness of OAAS systems [3,4]. In general, most OAASs are implemented, constructed, and presented with client features oriented for specific uses. These include competitions, course management, and statistical visualization; technology adaptations and deployments such as docker containers, micro-services; and data science such as educational data mining for smart learning [5]. However, while some simplified architecture descriptions and flowcharts regarding such systems have been published, the technical details of major OAASs have not yet been discussed, and they do not always share the same architecture.

Consequently, we were motivated to present the architecture and implementation of our original OAAS, which is the core function of the Aizu Online Judge (AOJ) [6]. The AOJ, which is one of the longest-serving OJ systems, provides almost all of the commonly expected OJ functions. Herein, we present the architecture of its original OAAS, focusing on its primary components, the load balancer, broadcaster, and judge system. We also relate our experiences regarding this ten-year-long journey. The experiences demonstrate that our system with the presented architecture have operated successfully.

The rest of this paper is organized as follows. In Sect. 2, related work is presented, while OAAS requirements are provided in Sect. 3. The component and software architectures of the OAAS are presented in Sect. 4 and Sect. 5, respectively. Our experiences are discussed in Sect. 6, and we conclude this paper in Sect. 7.

2   Related Work

Although the aim of this paper is to introduce the internal features of our OAAS, we will also discuss related applications that have evolved over its history. However, first of all, we will review the most prominent OAASs deployed in OJ systems. These include University of Valladolid (UVa) Online Judge, which is a prominent OJ system, powered by its own OAAS, that has been providing user experiences for more than 10 years [7]. Another pioneering OJ system called Sphere Online Judge (SPOJ) is providing academic instruction services as well as judging competitions. The architecture and security measures taken by the SPOJ system in relation to malicious attacks (high and low-level language) are described in [8].

Although, as mentioned above, research aimed at developing services with OAASs is and has been fairly active, the important and proprietary components that are collectively referred to as Online Code Execution Systems (OCESs) are rarely discussed. Our investigations determined that the first OCES was developed as a commercial and closed-source product in the Sphere Engine [9], while another OCES is the camisole [10] system, which uses a sandbox approach. Currently, a wide variety of sandboxing techniques are available for managing untrusted source codes that work by allocating custom resources, such as Docker, Containers, Virtual Machines, among others. For example, sandbox isolation is a popular technique that is commonly used in judge systems to securely compile and execute source codes that may include malicious data.

Only recently have the internal structure features of online assessment systems been presented for discussion. For example, the architecture of a robust and scalable code execution system is presented in [11]. Judge0 is an advanced open-source code execution system that uses sandbox isolation techniques. Its application program interface (API) is an open-source OCES that is scalable, robust, and easy to integrate with web-based applications as well as OJ systems [12]. A Code Execution Engine (CEE) is an OJ system component that uses sandboxes to compile, generate various metadata, and then execute source codes. OCESs use CEEs for code compilation and execution.

As mentioned above, the OAASs that are used in OJ systems and online compilers/executors now perform a wide variety of functions. Generally speaking, the implementation of an OJ system and its OAAS is a very expensive undertaking because of the required hardware, software, maintenance, support, and other factors. Thus, current research trends are concentrating on security, portability, and maintainability among other non-functional requirements. Additionally, the complete internal architecture and implementation of OAASs have rarely been discussed, revealed, or presented in previous studies in spite of their complex technical mechanisms. In contrast, even though our OAAS is also oriented toward other non-functional requirements including performance, consistency, robustness, and sustainability, we also embrace transparency. Therefore, our goal in this paper is to highlight the architecture and functional activities of our system that are oriented towards those non-functional requirements.

3   Online Automatic Assessment System Requirements

In this section, the primary requirements of OAAS are described briefly. We also discuss non-functional requirements that differ depending on the use cases and development policies.

3.1   Requirements

The system assesses correctness and performance of programs submitted by novices, students, engineers, researchers, and any other programmers. Hackers must also be assumed to be among the users as all submitted programs are run with a degree of anonymity.

The system should be always available. Users can submit programs and receive corresponding verdicts at any time. It reports the assessment results not only to the user, but to all related online audiences as well.

For consistency and assessment fairness, the system is deployed in a centralized dedicated server cluster where computational resources are shared by the users. From the user's perspective, the program is executed and evaluated on the cloud, and not on his/her local machine.

3.2   Non-functional Requirements

Since there are various tradeoff items between the non-functional OAAS requirements, it is necessary for the service provider side to determine which of those requirements should be emphasized. This section presents some major non-functional OAAS requirements where tradeoffs may be made.

Performance. When an OAAS is requested to provide real-time feedback, it is necessary to shorten the time from when the request is given until the assessment is available. However, because resources are shared, individual processes can impact the latency of other requests.

Security. In the OAAS, the submitted program must not affect operations of the internal system such as file access or process operations. Most importantly, the system must prevent the submitted program from affecting the external world across the network.

Consistency. The system presupposes that the performance of a program for a task is compared with other programs (even for the same user). Therefore, in terms of performance and consistency, a legitimate, reproducible, and error-free evaluation must be performed.

Newness. Since the OJ system hardware affects the system's execution performance, it should be updated in a timely manner. It is also necessary to upgrade the compilers/environments for the supported programming languages in a timely manner.

Robustness. The system must be kept running 24 h a day, even if there is no manager. Therefore, it requires mechanisms that will allow it to recover from or compensate for failures. The system must also be capable of handling programs that consume excessive central processing unit (CPU) cycles, memory, and stack resources.

Reliability. The system must not make unfair evaluations, judge what is wrong as correct, nor judge what is correct as wrong. The measurements performed must be accurate and should not overestimate or underestimate.

Sustainability. A related service of OAAS persists data about users, submissions, verdicts, etc. Since solutions will be subjected to reevaluations and comparisons, as well as being shared as knowledge, the assessment system must stay current with the accompanying data.

Portability. A highly portable system can be easily installed and deployed by a third party to provide a service.

Transparency. The OAAS state should be widely disclosed to all users and be reported in detail in a timely manner. Such reports should not only cover the judgment results for submitted programs, but also the status of submissions in the queue (waiting, running, available, etc.).

Scalability. It must be possible to scale up the system by adding physical servers as the number of users and access increases.

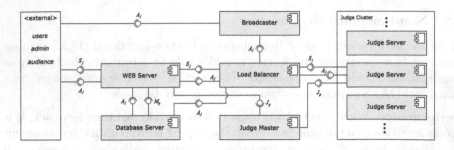

Fig. 1. Primary OAAS components and related services

The OAAS architecture featured in the AOJ system emphasizes, among other things, feedback performance, consistency, robustness, sustainability, and transparency.

4   Component Architecture

An OAAS should be implemented and deployed based on the theories of various architectures and algorithms while considering both its functional and emphasized non-functional requirements. This section describes the complete OAAS architecture features of the AOJ. Figure 1 shows a component diagram that overviews the architecture in which main components are communicating with data related to the assessment. (Note that the APIs, database schema, and user interfaces depend on their corresponding uses. In this paper, we focus on data related to assessments rather than other services.)

4.1   Webserver

A webserver is an interface between the external World Wide Web (WWW) and the OJ system. In an OAAS, upon receipt of a request via a public API, the webserver provides data based on the resource-oriented architecture without generating pages [2]. The submission S_j received by the webserver consists of source code and its parameters. A unique judge identifier j is assigned to the submission. The meta-data M_p, which is obtained from the database server by the problem identifier p in the parameters, is inserted into S_j. M_p includes parameters such as resource limitations which are needed for the assessment. Then S_j is sent to the load balancer and the assessment result A_j will become available after the judge.

4.2   Database Server

The database server cooperates with the webserver and the load balancer through private APIs and stores, provides, and manages all information related to the service, such as the problem set, registered users, and assessment result information. Solution codes and statistical data are also accumulated.

4.3 Judge Cluster

The judge cluster, which is the core of the OAAS, receives S_j, runs them, and returns the corresponding verdicts A_j based on judgment data J_p. The judge cluster should be isolated physically (or at least virtually) and only authorized processes should be allowed to connect to it via the closed API. This is necessary in order to prevent data leaks resulting from malicious and unintended operations. To improve the service quality of judgement processes as a whole, the judge cluster consists of multiple judge servers considering the following issues:

– Parallel machines where each server can use hardware resources exclusively to execute a given program (for feedback performance)
– Parallel machines that support each other (for robustness)
– Parallel machines that can be easily scaled up (for scalability)

4.4 Load Balancer

The load balancer, which is an intermediary between the webserver and the judge cluster, includes triggers for status updates and notifications. Internally, it is primarily responsible for balancing the load and scheduling submissions S_j received from the webserver. It allocates the submission S_j to the corresponding judge server via the private API. Another role of the load balancer is to manage A_j received from the judge cluster. It also provides status information of S_j in the queue and the corresponding A_j to all users.

4.5 Broadcaster

In the OAAS architecture, status change notifications (S_j and A_j) are performed through three different channels. The first channel is a public API that provides persisted status information from the database server in response to given query parameters from the webserver. The second channel, which is also from a public API, provides the status of all recent submissions in the queues (memory) managed by the load balancer. The third channel is based for asynchronous communication by the broadcaster and is specialized for real-time notifications.

The broadcaster is a server dedicated to transmitting judgment status reports to all users and audience in real-time. It is a relatively high-impedance component that provides information to all connected users by PUSH-type communications instead of ordinary PULL-type communications. Therefore, this component does not persist the data, but is dedicated instead to providing fast notifications.

4.6 Judge Master

One of the unique features of our OAAS architecture is that the payload between the load balancer and the judge cluster does not include judge data J_p, which is relatively heavy. Instead, the judge master manages a set of judge data for all problems, and their clones are deployed to all judge servers in advance. More specifically, when the administrator adds/updates any elements in J_p, a continuous integration mechanism is activated. Then, the judge master deploys the refined judge data to all of the judge servers.

5   Software Architecture

In this section, details of the software architecture of the main OAAS components are presented.

5.1   Load Balancer

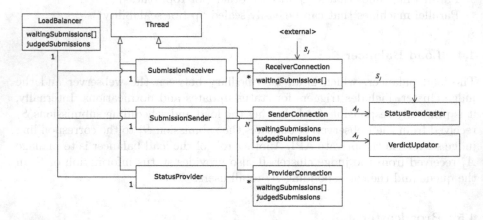

Fig. 2. Main load balancer classes

The load balancer is a core system that continuously receives submission requests from the webserver and distributes them to judge servers according to the specified criterion. It also reports the assessment results through different channels. Figure 2 is a class diagram of the load balancer. The main load balancer components are organized via a multi-threaded process consisting of the SubmissionReceiver that receives submissions, the SubmissionSender that sends them to the judge servers, and the StatusProvider that reports the status of the submissions. In the load balancer, submissions and assessments are managed by two different queue types shared by the threads. One type is for waiting for submissions S_j and the other is for judged submissions A_j.

When the load balancer is activated, SubmissionSender creates N threads named SenderConnection, each of which manages a waitingSubmissions queue of the corresponding judge server where N is the number of judge servers. So the load balancer manages N waitingSubmissions queues as a whole. When a SubmissionReceiver receives a submission S_j from the webserver, it creates a ReceiverConnection thread and adds S_j to the corresponding waitingSubmissions queue. The ReceiverConnection decides the judge server (SenderConnection) based on the criteria, which can be defined according to S_j and the status

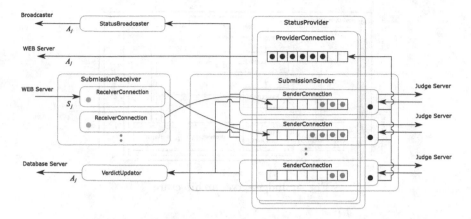

Fig. 3. Flow of submissions and assessments in load balancer

of the queues. Each SenderConnection sequentially sends the submissions in its queue and manages the assessments. The StatusProvider integrates the contents of the queues and provides them to the webserver upon request. The load balancer also has two other components, StatusBroadcaster and VerdictUpdator, which are used to connect with the broadcaster and database server, respectively.

Figure 3 shows the flow of S_j and A_j produced by the threads in the load balancer where a SenderConnection can be added by scaling up the judge cluster. A ReceiverConnection inserts a received submission S_j to the corresponding waitingSubmissions queue, after which a SenderConnection sends the pending submission waiting at the front of its queue to the corresponding judge server (if it is available). The SenderConnection waits for a reply from the judge server until the assessment A_j is available, after which the submission is added to the judgedSubmission queue.

As mentioned above, the status of S_j and A_j can be obtained from different channels. The A_j is persisted in the database server through the VerdictUpdator when it is available. The status of S_j and A_j are also provided through the StatusProvider based on the webserver request. This channel is used to quickly provide the most recent status without referring to the database server.

5.2   Judge Cluster

Figure 4 shows the configuration of the judge server that has a host operating system (OS) installed on a dedicated hardware machine. The OS system consists of four modules (processes): observer, controller, launcher, and executor. The observer, which is the process with the highest authority, monitors the process of the submission program, and kills it if there is a problem. The controller, which is responsible for the bridge between the load balancer and the judge server, receives a submission S_j and returns the assessment A_j. The launcher prepares for the given program for execution, after which the executor is launched from the launcher and executes and evaluates the program.

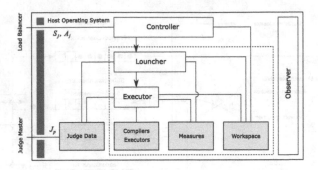

Fig. 4. Judge server architecture

Necessary programs and data are installed in the OS in advance (as shown in the lower part of the figure). Judge data is a set of J_p, each of which are deployed by the judge master. The compiler/executor is an environment for compiling and executing given programs in the available programming languages. Measures is a group of programs used by the judge server that includes available OS commands, while workspace refers to a designated location where files generated and read by the modules are managed. As outlined by the dotted box in Fig. 4, the core function can be virtualized within a dedicated container. The firewall is set so that it can only communicate with the load balancer and judge master. The host OS machines communicate with the load balancer through the controller. Judge data are deployed from the data manager through secure communications and all other communications are blocked.

Figure 5 shows a sequence diagram for a submission request in which the processes and data resources presented above are involved. In the beginning, the controller waits for a request from the JudgeConnection. When it receives a request, data for the solution code s in the given S_j are set as data files and the launcher is activated. Next, the launcher attempts to compile (if necessary) the source code. If this attempt fails, it generates error messages and the process returns to the controller and then to the JudgeConnection along with the failure message. If the launch process is successful, according to the number of test cases, the generated code is executed by the executor within the resource limitations. The executor generates a runtime signal and messages if errors occur. If no errors occur, it generates a program output file for each test case. When the resource limits for a user program process are exceeded, the executor terminates the process. After finishing each run, the executor determines the assessment A_j (along with the CPU time and memory usage) and sends the information to the controller. When the solution is rejected or all test cases are passed, control is returned back to the controller with a summary of the verdict.

6   Experiences

In this section, we discuss some real-world experiences involving the presented OAAS, which has assessed more than five million submissions and performed

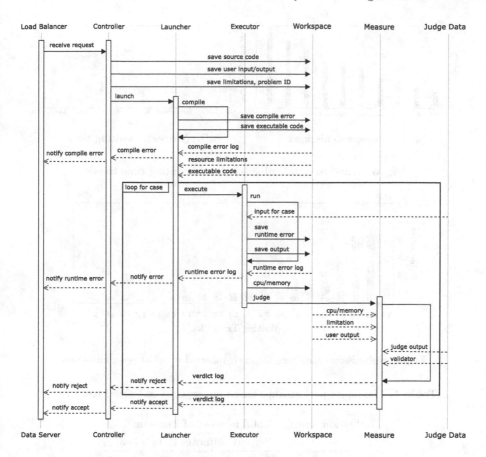

Fig. 5. Judge server sequence diagram

successfully for more than ten years. During this long journey, 105 contests and more than 3300 virtual contests/exercises have been conducted.

Figure 6 shows the submission numbers and average waiting times for each year. The waiting time for a submission is the difference between the time a ReceiverConnection received the submission from the webserver and the time a SenderConnection received the assessment from the corresponding judge server. Here, it can be seen that the chart shows a linear trend for the average waiting time in spite of the increasing number of submissions.

Figure 7 shows the number of submissions for each waiting time interval, as delimited by a tenth of a second. For example, there are around 200,000 submissions that were assessed within 0.1 s. Overall, even though there is a long tail of submissions that have longer waiting times, the chart shows that 77% of the submissions finished very quickly (within one second).

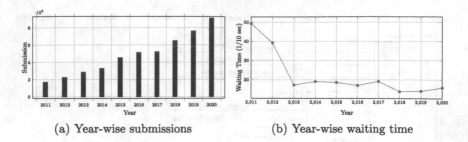

(a) Year-wise submissions   (b) Year-wise waiting time

Fig. 6. Year-wise total submissions and waiting time trends

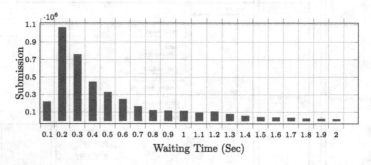

Fig. 7. Submission numbers for each interval of waiting submissions

Table 1. Maximum performance based on assessed codes and test cases

Evaluation items	Total number of items in:			
	Second	Minute	Hour	Day
Assessed codes	7	125	1600	6653
Assessed test cases	294	2535	19953	79729

Table 1 shows the maximum number of codes and test cases assessed per second, minute, and hour, respectively. The statistical values listed demonstrate the maximum practical performance of the OAAS over the course of ten years. However, we also need to measure the maximum possible performance through stress tests. Generally speaking, the maximum possible performance is much higher than that of the results presented in Table 1 because of the idling time that occurs during practical testing.

7   Conclusion

In spite of rising demands for the development of related applications, the technical details of OJ systems or online execution systems have not yet been thoroughly discussed. In this paper, the architecture of our OAAS and the experiences obtained through ten years of operation have been presented. We also discussed the non-functional requirements of the OAAS and the system architecture while examining tradeoffs among the issues of performance, consistency, robustness, sustainability, and transparency. The results presented herein demonstrate that our system and its presented architecture have operated successfully with acceptable performance for more than ten years.

Acknowledgement. This research was funded by the Japan Society for the Promotion of Science (JSPS) KAKENHI (Grant Number 19K12252).

References

1. Wasik, S., Antczak, M., Badura, J., Laskowski, A., Sternal, T.: A survey on online judge systems and their applications. ACM Comput. Surv. (CSUR) **51**(1), 1–34 (2018)
2. Watanobe, Y., Intisar, C.M., Cortez, R., Vazhenin, A.: Next-generation programming learning platform: architecture and challenges. In: SHS Web of Conferences, vol. 77, p. 01004 (2020)
3. Petit, J., et al.: Jutge.org: characteristics and experiences. IEEE Trans. Learn. Technol. **11**(3), 321–333 (2018). https://doi.org/10.1109/TLT.2017.2723389
4. Georgouli, K., Guerreiro, P.: Incorporating an automatic judge into blended learning programming activities. In: Luo, X., Spaniol, M., Wang, L., Li, Q., Nejdl, W., Zhang, W. (eds.) ICWL 2010. LNCS, vol. 6483, pp. 81–90. Springer, Heidelberg (2010). https://doi.org/10.1007/978-3-642-17407-0_9
5. Rahman, M.M., Watanobe, Y., Nakamura, K.: Source code assessment and classification based on estimated error probability using attentive LSTM language model and its application in programming education. Appl. Sci. **10**(8), 2973 (2020)
6. Watanobe, Y.: Aizu online judge. https://onlinejudge.u-aizu.ac.jp
7. Revilla, M.A., Manzoor, S., Liu, R.: Competitive learning in informatics: The UVa online judge experience. Olympiads Inf. **2**(10), 131–148 (2008)
8. Kosowski, A., Małafiejski, M., Noiński, T.: Application of an online judge & contester system in academic tuition. In: Leung, H., Li, F., Lau, R., Li, Q. (eds.) ICWL 2007. LNCS, vol. 4823, pp. 343–354. Springer, Heidelberg (2008). https://doi.org/10.1007/978-3-540-78139-4_31
9. Labs, S.R.: Online compilers and programming challenges APIs - sphere engine. https://sphere-engine.com. Accessed 7 June 2020
10. Prologin, A.: "camisole,". https://camisole.prologin.org. Accessed 7 June 2020
11. Došilović, H.Z., Mekterović, I.: Robust and scalable online code execution system. In: 43rd International Convention on Information, Communication and Electronic Technology (MIPRO). Opatija, Croatia **2020**, pp. 1627–1632 (2020)
12. Mekterović, I., Brkić, L., Milašinović, B., Baranović, M.: Building a comprehensive automated programming assessment system. IEEE Access **8**, 81154–81172 (2020). https://doi.org/10.1109/ACCESS.2020.2990980

A Multi-criteria Group Decision Making Procedure Based on a Multi-granular Linguistic Approach for Changeable Scenarios

José Ramón Trillo(ID), Enrique Herrera-Viedma(ID),
Francisco Javier Cabrerizo(✉)(ID), and Juan Antonio Morente-Molinera(ID)

Andalusian Research Institute in Data Science and Computational Intelligence,
Department of Computer Science and Artificial Intelligence, University of Granada,
18071 Granada, Spain
jrtrillo@ugr.es, {viedma,cabrerizo,jamoren}@decsai.ugr.es

Abstract. Nowadays, real world decision making environments are becoming more heterogeneous and flexible than ever. For this reason, we present in this study an innovative multi-criteria group decision making procedure whose main purpose is to be used in scenarios where the decision context is variable. First, the experts can provide their preferences on different moments. Second, by applying a multi-granular linguistic approach, the experts can express themselves more diversely because they select the linguistic label set that they prefer. Third, criteria, alternatives and experts in the course of the decision process. In addition, the procedure makes use of consensus measures to verify that the experts agree with the decision taken.

Keywords: Multi-criteria group decision making · Multi-granular linguistic modeling · Consensus

1   Introduction

With the development of new technologies, such as Web 2.0 [12], multi-criteria group decision making (McGDM) methods have become increasingly important [16]. The traditional methods aim to reunite a group of experts in an area to choose an alternative by giving their opinions or preferences [13]. Nevertheless, the real world has become more varied and heterogeneous, which means that decision making methods must evolve to adapt to the needs of human beings [18, 20]. Thanks to the new technologies provided by Web 2.0, the experts can provide their preferences, whenever and wherever they want. Moreover, they can express their opinions online and, therefore, they can generate a debate without being present in the same room [2].

In real-world problems, each person's needs are expressed differently, and not always at the same time. It may be the case that, once the decision process has

© Springer Nature Switzerland AG 2021
H. Fujita et al. (Eds.): IEA/AIE 2021, LNAI 12799, pp. 284–295, 2021.
https://doi.org/10.1007/978-3-030-79463-7_24

started, a new participant is added or, as individuals participate in the process, they come up with a new point of view that involves taking into account new evaluation criteria [24]. Consequently, the experts have to change their preferences during the decision process [8,24].

The criteria are characteristics of an alternative that can be assessed. The decision processes that use different criteria to allow a group of experts to choose an option or alternative are McGDM problems. In McGDM problems, the experts usually have to assess all the criteria. However, they could not be a specialist in all aspects that arise. For this reason, we must take into account that the participants only give their preferences on those criteria that they know. To rate these known criteria, the experts use the evaluation form that is most comfortable for them. Therefore, we must consider the problems as non-homogeneous [22]. Furthermore, there is another factor to take into account. This factor is that any feature of the problem can be altered at any time during the process. For example, an expert may drop out at a certain point in the time, a new option or alternative may appear or a new criterion may be added or removed [24].

Recent McGDM approaches can be found in literature, which study different aspects associated with the decision process. See, for example, [3,14,28]. Although the existing proposals analyze interesting aspects related to the decision process, none of them take into account a heterogeneous and variable scenario. Therefore, we present in this research a procedure that solves the issue just mentioned, since the existence of changeable characteristics is considered by our procedure. In this way, we can deal with problems in which there is a change in any of the parameters associated with the decision process, for instance, experts can give up the decision process or new criteria can be added.

In our proposal, initially the experts provide their opinions using the linguistic label set that is more familiar with each of them. This poses a first problem, designated as multi-granular linguistic problem. It means experts communicate their preferences or opinions using different linguistic label sets [19]. Afterwards, this diverse set of information must be homogenised using a multi-granular linguistic process. Once the opinions have been homogenised, we can produce the ranking of alternatives and check if the decision made by the experts is accepted by them. For this purpose, consensus measures [4] are used to find out whether the experts agree with the selection of the best alternative. Whether the process obtains a consensus higher than a limit established at the beginning of the decision process, we can assume that there is agreement among the experts, but if not, the procedure should be repeated in order to improve the consensus achieved.

This research is divided into six sections. In Sect. 2, some basic concepts, which are used by our procedure, are recalled. In Sect. 3, the proposed McGDM procedure based on a multi-granular linguistic approach for changeable scenarios is elaborated on. In particular, all their stages are described in detail. Then, in Sect. 4, an example of application is illustrated. In Sect. 5, advantages and disadvantages are discussed, and finally, in Sect. 6, conclusions are drawn.

2   Preliminaries

This section recalls some basic concepts to understand the proposed procedure. Concretely, Sect. 2.1 describes McGDM problems and Sect. 2.2 introduces the concepts related to multi-granular linguistic approaches.

2.1   McGDM Problems

In a group decision making process, a group of experts has to choose the best option or alternative between a set of them [15]. To do it, a ranking of the alternatives is generated using the experts' opinions or preferences. The experts usually use preference relations in order to provide their opinions [23]. In addition, each expert's preference is commonly provided by using a linguistic label set [21]. It means that to assess, for instance, that one wine is better than other one, we can have the following linguistic labels: "Much Better", "Better", "Equal", "Worse", and "Much Worse".

McGDM methods are an extension of traditional group decision making methods [13,16]. These procedures differ from group decision making approaches in that experts have to assess different characteristics (criteria) related to an alternative or option, which implies that there is no general evaluation of the alternatives.

To develop a McGDM procedure, we proceed to designate a group of m experts as $E = \{e_1, \ldots, e_m\}$, a set of n alternatives or options as $X = \{x_1, \ldots, x_n\}$, and a set of k criteria as $C = \{c_1, \ldots, c_k\}$. In addition, the criteria can have different levels of importance. Consequently, a vector $\Pi = \{\pi_1, \ldots, \pi_k\}$ is introduced to indicate the weight that should be assigned to each one of the criteria. Finally, in McGDM approaches using preference relations to model the experts' preferences, the preference relations are denoted as P and obtained from each expert belonging to the set E.

2.2   Multi-granular Linguistic Approaches

Human-machine interaction has always been a problem, because the machine works with numbers while humans use symbolic and natural language. To resolve it, linguistic modeling has been used to transform the human's opinion into something the machine can understand [11]. This procedure can be complex because the linguistic labels that an expert can have in mind could be very different from the linguistic labels that the approach allows to use. Therefore, an expert could neither provide a more specific nor a more general opinion.

A solution to this problem is that the experts can choose the linguistic label set when assessing alternatives. As a result, the use of a multi-granular linguistic approach is needed [19,21,25]. It presents the following stages:

– Obtaining information from experts by using a linguistic label set. The provided information can be represented using different linguistic label sets. This allows experts to provide their preferences more accurately than whether the experts would have an only one linguistic label set.

- Converting the information into the same representation format. Once the procedure has obtained all the information from the experts, the information must be homogenised and expressed in the same linguistic label set.
- Using the information to perform calculations. The procedure uses the previously transformed information to perform the required calculations. The information is transformed into the chosen linguistic label set again whether for some reason the information must be presented using a different linguistic label set than the one used for calculations.

Different multi-granular linguistic models can be found in the literature, such as [21], where the approach is used for supervised classification, or [26], which uses probabilistic linguistic terms.

3   A McGDM Procedure Based on a Multi-granular Linguistic Approach for Changeable Scenarios

In this section, we elaborate on in detail the new proposed procedure for McGDM problems, which is composed of the next five stages:

- Establishing parameters and providing preferences. In this first stage, the necessary parameters of the decision problem are established, such as the number of alternatives or the number of criteria. The experts also provide their preferences on the alternatives according to the criteria.
- Homogenisation of the information. Once all the preferences have been obtained, they are standardised to use the same linguistic label set. This allows the aggregation of the experts' preferences in the next stage.
- Aggregation of results. All the preferences provided are fused to obtain a collective preference containing the overall preference of all the experts.
- Calculating the ranking. Using the collective preference from the previous stage, a ranking of alternatives is generated to find out which alternative or option is the one chosen.
- Checking consensus and modifying the characteristics. Using the preferences given by the experts, the consensus among them is measured. Whether it is enough, the decision process is finished. Otherwise, the experts must modify their preferences in another decision round in order to increase the consensus. In addition, the set of criteria, experts and alternatives could be modified.

In the following subsections, these stages are elaborated on in a more detailed way.

3.1   Establishing Parameters and Providing Preferences

At the beginning of the decision process, the initial parameters for carrying out the McGDM process are defined. Concretely, we must establish the group of m experts, $E = \{e_1, \ldots, e_m\}$, the set of n alternatives, $X = \{x_1, \ldots, x_n\}$, and the set of k criteria, $C = \{c_1, \ldots, c_k\}$. We must also determine the maximum number of decision rounds, denoted by the variable $R \in \mathbb{N}$, since there are problems where the experts have a great difficulty to achieve consensus, and the minimum consensus threshold, designated by $\Omega \in [0, 1]$.

Once the initial parameters have been defined, each expert proceeds to select the linguistic label set that she or he wants to use to provide her or his preferences. Each expert e_i also chooses the criteria on which she or he wants to give her or his opinions. This set is denoted as $C^i = \{c_1^i, \ldots, c_{b_i}^i\}$. It verifies that $b_i \leq k$, $i = 1, \ldots, m$.

Next, for each criterion selected by the expert, she or he must provide a preference relation $P_{c_s^i}^{e_i}$, where c_s^i refers to the criterion and e_i refers to the expert. The preference relation can be characterized by a matrix as:

$$P_{c_s^i}^{e_i} = \begin{pmatrix} - & \cdots & p_{c_s^i}^{1n} \\ \vdots & \ddots & \vdots \\ p_{c_s^i}^{n1} & \cdots & - \end{pmatrix} \tag{1}$$

being each $p_{c_s^i}^{hl}$, $h = 1, \ldots, n$, $l = 1, \ldots, n$, a linguistic label belonging to the linguistic label set chosen by the expert to provide her or his preferences.

The set of preference relations for each expert, denoted as $\mathfrak{B}^i$, is defined as follows:

$$\mathfrak{B}^i = \{P_{c_s^i}^{e_i} \mid s = 1, \ldots, b_i\} \tag{2}$$

3.2 Homogenisation of the Information

In the second stage, the heterogeneous information is homogenised into an only one linguistic label set to perform the needed computations. Here, we make use of the 2-tuple fuzzy linguistic modeling [10]. A linguistic 2-tuple value is characterized via a pair of values (l_i, δ), where l_i is a linguistic label and δ in $[-0, 5, 0, 5)$ is the symbolic translation. From l_i and δ a numerical value can be calculated. This value is called α. The translation function that allows us to do it is defined as [10]:

$$\Delta : [0, d] \to L \times [-0.5, 0.5)$$
$$\Delta(\alpha) = (l_i, \delta) \text{ with } \begin{cases} l_i & i = round(\alpha) \\ \delta = \alpha - i & \delta \in [-0.5, 0.5) \end{cases} \tag{3}$$

We resolve the value of α using the function [10]:

$$\Delta^{-1} : L \times [-0.5, 0.5) \to [0, d]$$
$$\Delta^{-1}(l_i, \delta) = \alpha = i + \delta \tag{4}$$

Using the functions Δ and Δ^{-1}, we can define the function, $\mathcal{V}_{l_i}^{y_i}$, that converts a linguistic label l_i to a linguistic label y_i located in other linguistic label set:

$$\mathcal{V}_{l_i}^{y_i}(l_i, \delta) = \Delta \left(\frac{(\Delta^{-1}(l_i, \delta) - 1) \cdot (d_y - 1)}{d_l - 1} \right) + 1 \tag{5}$$

where d_y is the number of elements of the linguistic label set to which y_i belongs and d_l is the number of elements of the linguistic label set to which l_i belongs.

3.3 Aggregation of Results

Once the preferences have been homogenised, they must be aggregated to obtain the collective preference. This is carried out in two steps.

First, a collective preference is computed for each expert. To be able to calculate it, called Λ^{e_i}, each expert e_i defines a vector $\Pi^i = \{\pi_1^i, \ldots, \pi_{b_i}^i\}$ representing the importance that she or he gives to each selected criterion. Then, we can define Λ^{e_i} as:

$$\Lambda^{e_i} = \sum_{s=1}^{b_i} \pi_s^i \cdot P_{c_s^i}^{e_i} \tag{6}$$

Second, the collective preferences of the experts are aggregated with the aim of obtaining a global collective preference that contains all the preferences given by the experts on the criteria. Here, we can assign importance weights to the experts. That is, whether the vector $W = \{w_1, \ldots, w_m\}$ is used to assign importance weights to the experts, the global collective matrix, Λ, is computed as:

$$\Lambda = \sum_{i=1}^{m} w_i \cdot \Lambda^{e_i} \tag{7}$$

Once Λ has been calculated, we can proceed to produce the ranking of the alternatives.

3.4 Calculating the Ranking

This stage uses Λ to generate the ranking of the alternatives. To do it, different choice functions can be applied. Here, we make use of the quantifier guided dominance degree (QGDD) operator [9], even though other functions could also be used.

To generate the ranking of the alternatives, first, the information contained in Λ is transformed into numerical values via the α form of the 2-tuple representation using (4), and, second, the QGDD operator is applied for each alternative x_h, $h = 1, \ldots, n$, as follows:

$$QGDD_h = \phi(\Lambda^{hl}), \; l = 1, \ldots, n \wedge h \neq l \tag{8}$$

where ϕ is the mean operator and Λ^{hl} represents the value located in the entry (h, l) of Λ.

Finally, the ranking positions are determined in descending order according to the results returned by the QGDD operator.

3.5   Checking Consensus and Modifying the Characteristics

Measuring the consensus among experts serves to know if the preferences provided by the experts are similar to each other [4]. The expression that measures the similarity between two preference relations, P and O, can be determined as:

$$Simil_P^O = 1 - \frac{\sum_{h=1}^{n} \sum_{l=1;h \neq l}^{n} |p^{hl} - o^{hl}|}{n \cdot (n-1)} \tag{9}$$

Using (9), we can compute the consensus between two experts, e_i and e_j. To achieve this goal, we only need to calculate the similarity between the collective preferences of both experts. The expression is developed as:

$$SimilE_{e_i}^{e_j} = Simil_{A^{e_i}}^{A^{e_j}} \tag{10}$$

Then, we can obtain the global consensus achieved, $\mathcal{U}$, by aggregating all the $SimilE$ values as follows:

$$\mathcal{U} = \frac{\sum_{i=1}^{m} \sum_{j>i}^{m} SimilE_{e_i}^{e_j}}{\sum_{q=1}^{m-1} q} \tag{11}$$

As mentioned above, this value has to be greater than the value of Ω in order to finish the decision process. If not, the experts must modify their preferences in order to increase the consensus. However, if the maximum number of rounds, R, is reached, the final decision will be the one obtained when the ranking is calculated, independently of the consensus achieved.

In addition, it is possible that some initial parameters of the McGDM problem may change. For instance, new experts can be invited to the decision process, some experts could abandon the decision process, some alternatives can be added or removed, or some criteria can be added or deleted. Whether any of these events occur, the affected sets must be modified with the purpose of including or excluding the corresponding information.

4   Illustrative Example

In this section, we present an example that illustrates the application of the procedure proposed in this study. Let $E = \{e_1, e_2, e_3\}$ be the set of experts composed of three individuals. They have to select a computer for their company. Concretely, the experts must make their decision based on different criteria: the amount of RAM (c_1), the quality of the graphics card (c_2) and the quality of the processor (c_3). To determine the best computer, there exist five different options, $X = \{x_1, x_2, x_3, x_4, x_5\}$. To give the opinions, the participants e_1 and e_3 decide to use the linguistic label set L^5, defined as $L^5 = \{l_1^5, \ldots, l_5^5\}$ while the participant

e_2 decide to utilize the linguistic label set $L^9 = \{l^9_1, \ldots, l^9_9\}$. Moreover, e_2 only evaluates two criteria, while the rest evaluate all of the criteria.

The preferences communicated by the three experts for each criterion are the following:

$$
P^{e_1}_{c_1} =
\begin{pmatrix}
- & l^5_2 & l^5_3 & l^5_2 & l^5_3 \\
l^5_1 & - & l^5_3 & l^5_1 & l^5_2 \\
l^5_5 & l^5_4 & - & l^5_5 & l^5_4 \\
l^5_2 & l^5_1 & l^5_1 & - & l^5_1 \\
l^5_3 & l^5_2 & l^5_1 & l^5_3 & -
\end{pmatrix}
\quad
P^{e_1}_{c_2} =
\begin{pmatrix}
- & l^5_2 & l^5_1 & l^5_2 & l^5_1 \\
l^5_2 & - & l^5_2 & l^5_2 & l^5_2 \\
l^5_4 & l^5_4 & - & l^5_4 & l^5_4 \\
l^5_2 & l^5_1 & l^5_3 & - & l^5_2 \\
l^5_2 & l^5_3 & l^5_2 & l^5_2 & -
\end{pmatrix}
\quad
P^{e_1}_{c_3} =
\begin{pmatrix}
- & l^5_2 & l^5_1 & l^5_1 & l^5_2 \\
l^5_2 & - & l^5_2 & l^5_3 & l^5_2 \\
l^5_5 & l^5_5 & - & l^5_5 & l^5_4 \\
l^5_1 & l^5_1 & l^5_3 & - & l^5_3 \\
l^5_1 & l^5_1 & l^5_2 & l^5_1 & -
\end{pmatrix}
$$

$$
P^{e_2}_{c_1} =
\begin{pmatrix}
- & l^9_3 & l^9_4 & l^9_5 & l^9_4 \\
l^9_4 & - & l^9_6 & l^9_3 & l^9_2 \\
l^9_9 & l^9_8 & - & l^9_7 & l^9_8 \\
l^9_2 & l^9_1 & l^9_3 & - & l^9_4 \\
l^9_5 & l^9_4 & l^9_2 & l^9_3 & -
\end{pmatrix}
\quad
P^{e_2}_{c_2} =
\begin{pmatrix}
- & l^9_3 & l^9_2 & l^9_1 & l^9_4 \\
l^9_5 & - & l^9_2 & l^9_1 & l^9_1 \\
l^9_9 & l^9_8 & - & l^9_6 & l^9_9 \\
l^9_3 & l^9_2 & l^9_1 & - & l^9_3 \\
l^9_1 & l^9_1 & l^9_2 & l^9_1 & -
\end{pmatrix}
$$

$$
P^{e_3}_{c_1} =
\begin{pmatrix}
- & l^5_2 & l^5_1 & l^5_2 & l^5_3 \\
l^5_2 & - & l^5_3 & l^5_2 & l^5_2 \\
l^5_4 & l^5_5 & - & l^5_4 & l^5_5 \\
l^5_3 & l^5_2 & l^5_1 & - & l^5_1 \\
l^5_1 & l^5_1 & l^5_2 & l^5_3 & -
\end{pmatrix}
\quad
P^{e_3}_{c_2} =
\begin{pmatrix}
- & l^5_3 & l^5_2 & l^5_2 & l^5_1 \\
l^5_1 & - & l^5_3 & l^5_2 & l^5_1 \\
l^5_5 & l^5_5 & - & l^5_5 & l^5_5 \\
l^5_4 & l^5_3 & l^5_2 & - & l^5_1 \\
l^5_1 & l^5_1 & l^5_2 & l^5_3 & -
\end{pmatrix}
\quad
P^{e_3}_{c_3} =
\begin{pmatrix}
- & l^5_2 & l^5_2 & l^5_2 & l^5_1 \\
l^5_2 & - & l^5_3 & l^5_1 & l^5_1 \\
l^5_4 & l^5_4 & - & l^5_4 & l^5_4 \\
l^5_3 & l^5_2 & l^5_1 & - & l^5_1 \\
l^5_2 & l^5_1 & l^5_2 & l^5_1 & -
\end{pmatrix}
$$

Each expert decides, on a personal basis, the importance she or he gives to each criterion. In this way, each expert provides a weighting vector. The vectors are:

$$\Pi^1 = \{0.5,\ 0.25,\ 0.25\} \quad \Pi^2 = \{0.34,\ 0.66\} \quad \Pi^3 = \{0.25,\ 0.25,\ 0.5\}$$

Once all the preferences have been provided, we proceed to homogenise them by representing all preferences using L^5. Then, we can calculate the global collective matrix, designated as Λ. Here, we suppose the level of importance is the same for all the experts, that is, $W = \{0.33, 0.33, 0.33\}$. The global collective matrix Λ obtained, in which the values are modeled by using 2-tuples, is:

$$
\Lambda =
\begin{pmatrix}
- & (l^5_2, 0.08) & (l^5_2, -0.14) & (l^5_2, -0.19) & (l^5_2, 0.08) \\
(l^5_2, 0.03) & - & (l^5_3, -0.44) & (l^5_2, -0.47) & (l^5_1, 0.47) \\
(l^5_5, -0.33) & (l^5_4, 0.42) & - & (l^5_4, 0.22) & (l^5_4, 0.44) \\
(l^5_2, 0.28) & (l^5_2, -0.39) & (l^5_1, 0.45) & - & (l^5_2, -0.36) \\
(l^5_2, -0.19) & (l^5_2, -0.50) & (l^5_2, -0.33) & (l^5_2, -0.14) & -
\end{pmatrix}
$$

At this point, let us suppose that a new expert, e_4, is added to the group. She or he uses the linguistic label set L^5 and wants to evaluate the next three criteria $\{c_2, c_3, c_4\}$. That is, a new criterion, c_4, is also added, which represents the secondary memory capacity of the computer. The preferences of e_4 are:

$$
P^{e_4}_{c_2} =
\begin{pmatrix}
- & l^5_1 & l^5_1 & l^5_2 & l^5_1 \\
l^5_2 & - & l^5_2 & l^5_1 & l^5_2 \\
l^5_5 & l^5_5 & - & l^5_5 & l^5_5 \\
l^5_2 & l^5_2 & l^5_1 & - & l^5_1 \\
l^5_3 & l^5_2 & l^5_2 & l^5_3 & -
\end{pmatrix}
\quad
P^{e_4}_{c_3} =
\begin{pmatrix}
- & l^5_2 & l^5_1 & l^5_2 & l^5_1 \\
l^5_1 & - & l^5_2 & l^5_2 & l^5_1 \\
l^5_4 & l^5_5 & - & l^5_4 & l^5_5 \\
l^5_2 & l^5_2 & l^5_2 & - & l^5_1 \\
l^5_1 & l^5_1 & l^5_2 & l^5_2 & -
\end{pmatrix}
\quad
P^{e_4}_{c_4} =
\begin{pmatrix}
- & l^5_2 & l^5_2 & l^5_2 & l^5_1 \\
l^5_1 & - & l^5_3 & l^5_1 & l^5_1 \\
l^5_5 & l^5_4 & - & l^5_5 & l^5_5 \\
l^5_2 & l^5_2 & l^5_1 & - & l^5_2 \\
l^5_3 & l^5_1 & l^5_2 & l^5_1 & -
\end{pmatrix}
$$

Table 1. Consensus among experts.

Experts	Consensus
e_1, e_2	0.9126
e_1, e_3	0.8875
e_1, e_4	0.9125
e_2, e_3	0.8909
e_2, e_4	0.8943
e_3, e_4	0.9150
Avg. consensus	0.9022

To obtain the ranking of the alternatives, as a new expert has been added to the decision process, the global collective matrix must be recalculated. The new Λ, in which numerical values are now shown, is:

$$\Lambda = \begin{pmatrix} - & 1.9 & 1.7 & 1.9 & 1.8 \\ 1.9 & - & 2.5 & 1.5 & 1.5 \\ 4.7 & 4.5 & - & 4.4 & 4.6 \\ 2.2 & 1.7 & 1.4 & - & 1.5 \\ 2.0 & 1.5 & 1.8 & 2.0 & - \end{pmatrix}$$

Subsequently, the average consensus is calculated. In the case of being lower than a value of Ω, which for this example is chosen as $\Omega = 0.8$, the whole process has to be repeated. However, it can be observed that there is a consensus among the experts because the average value obtained (see Table 1) is higher than the minimum consensus threshold.

Finally, the ranking of alternatives among the experts is computed by means of the QGDD operator. The results of the ranking are:

$$QGDD = \{1.825,\ 1.85,\ 4.55,\ 1.7,\ 1.825\}$$
$$\text{Ranking} = \{x_3,\ x_2,\ \{x_1,\ x_5\},\ x_4\}$$

It is observed that choice x_3 is the one preferred by the experts. Furthermore, options x_1 and x_5 are equally preferred by them.

5   Discussion

This study has developed an innovative McGDM procedure applicable in changeable scenarios that has been built to be used in real situations. It presents the following advantages and drawbacks:

– Experts' experience. The developed procedure allows that each expert can use the linguistic label set that she or he prefers. As a consequence, even if the experts communicate their preferences in a heterogeneous way, the procedure takes care of homogenising the preferences provided. Moreover, unlike other approaches, whether an expert is not familiar with some criteria, she or he may not provide information about these criteria.

- Real-world decision problems. In recent literature, we can find methods that use a limited number of features that remain fixed, and therefore they cannot really be applied to everyday life. Nevertheless, with the appearance of new technologies, there is a need to create systems and algorithms that can be applied to everyday life [27]. Our procedure is applicable to Web 2.0 technologies [12], which allow that the model can be used in changeable contexts.
- Linguistic label sets. The linguistic label sets are a common way of defining human-machine communication, but these sets are limited by the use of a restricted set of linguistic values. Nonetheless, procedures allowing to provide preferences without any restriction, for example, using free text, should be designed [6].

McGDM is an active area in recent research. Nevertheless, there is not much research on McGDM procedures for changeable scenarios. In [16], extra information on the criteria is given by the experts. In [5], a concrete solution to a problem is proposed. In [1], the models are applied to renewable energies. In [7], the method uses type-2 fuzzy sets. In [17], a McGDM problem solving model is developed. The method creates groups of experts to give their opinions to each other. However, the participants can only use a single linguistic label set.

Finally, we claim that it is a method suitable for different types of scenarios. Therefore, an expert can participate whenever she or he thinks it is convenient. Some studies develop McGDM methods and work in fixed and unalterable scenarios, and do not take into account that experts may be unaware of a criterion. Nonetheless, this study does take into account that experts may not assess all the criteria and, moreover, for the criteria chosen for evaluation, the experts can select the linguistic label set they prefer.

6   Conclusions

This study has developed a McGDM procedure that works on changeable scenarios. Among its novelties, we find the following ones. First, it allows experts to participate in the process without having to assess all the criteria. Second, the experts can join or leave the decision process whenever they want. Third, as the preferences can be changed at any time during the process, a debate takes place during the whole process, that is, it allows an open debate, which is facilitated by means of Web 2.0 technologies.

In the current literature, the experts must evaluate all criteria. However, this is not the case in real-world scenarios. The participants in the decision process only asses the criteria they know. The procedure that has been developed in this study allows expert to select those criteria. Furthermore, in order to improve the human-machine communication, the expert is free to decide the linguistic label set with which she or he feels more familiar. Consequently, experts can communicate their opinions more accurately than whether they have an only one linguistic label set to give their preferences.

Acknowledgments. This research has been funded by the Spanish State Research Agency through the project PID2019-103880RB-I00/AEI/10.13039/501100011033. We would also like to thank the "Juan de la Cierva Incorporación" grant from the Spanish Ministry of Economy and Competitiveness.

References

1. Alizadeh, R., Soltanisehat, L., Lund, P.D., Zamanisabzi, H.: Improving renewable energy policy planning and decision-making through a hybrid MCDM method. Energy Policy **137** (2020)
2. Alonso, S., Pérez, I.J., Cabrerizo, F.J., Herrera-Viedma, E.: A linguistic consensus model for web 2.0 communities. Appl. Soft Comput. **13**(1), 149–157 (2012)
3. Baudry, G., Macharis, C., Vallee, T.: Range-based multi-actor multi-criteria analysis: a combined method of multi-actor multi-criteria analysis and Monte Carlo simulation to support participatory decision making under uncertainty. Eur. J. Oper. Res. **264**(1), 257–269 (2018)
4. Cabrerizo, F.J., Al-Hmouz, R., Morfeq, A., Balamash, A.S., Martínez, M., Herrera-Viedma, E.: Soft consensus measures in group decision making using unbalanced fuzzy linguistic information. Soft. Comput. **21**(11), 3037–3050 (2017)
5. Cadavid-Giraldo, N., Velez-Gallego, M.C., Restrepo-Boland, A.: Carbon emissions reduction and financial effects of a cap and tax system on an operating supply chain in the cement sector. J. Cleaner Prod. **275** (2020)
6. Cambria, E., Schuller, B., Xia, Y., Havasi, C.: New avenues in opinion mining and sentiment analysis. IEEE Intell. Syst. **28**(2), 15–21 (2013)
7. Deveci, M., Cali, U., Kucuksari, S., Erdogan, N.: Interval type-2 fuzzy sets based multi-criteria decision-making model for offshore wind farm development in Ireland. Energy **198** (2020)
8. Dong, Y., Zhao, S., Zhang, H., Chiclana, F., Herrera-Viedma, E.: A self-management mechanism for noncooperative behaviors in large-scale group consensus reaching processes. IEEE Trans. Fuzzy Syst. **26**(6), 3276–3288 (2018)
9. Herrera, F., Herrera-Viedma, E., Chiclana, F.: A study of the origin and uses of the ordered weighted geometric operator in multicriteria decision making. Int. J. Intell. Syst. **18**(6), 689–707 (2003)
10. Herrera, F., Martínez, L.: A 2-tuple fuzzy linguistic representation model for computing with words. IEEE Trans. Fuzzy Syst. **8**(6), 746–752 (2000)
11. Herrera, F., Alonso, S., Chiclana, F., Herrera-Viedma, E.: Computing with words in decision making: foundations, trends and prospects. Fuzzy Optim. Decis. Making **8**(4), 337–364 (2009)
12. Huffman, K.: Web 2.0: beyond the concept practical ways to implement RSS, podcasts, and wikis. Educ. Libr. **29**(1), 12–19 (2017)
13. Hwang, C.L., Lin, M.J.: Group Decision Making Under Multiple Criteria: Methods and Applications. Springer, Heidelberg (1987). https://doi.org/10.1007/978-3-642-61580-1
14. Joshi, D.K., Beg, I., Kumar, S.: Hesitant probabilistic fuzzy linguistic sets with applications in multi-criteria group decision making problems. Mathematics **6**(4), 47 (2018)

15. Kacprzyk, J.: Group decision making with a fuzzy linguistic majority. Fuzzy Sets Syst. **18**(2), 105–118 (1986)
16. Liang, R., Wang, J., Li, L.: Multi-criteria group decision-making method based on interdependent inputs of single-valued trapezoidal neutrosophic information. Neural Comput. Appl. **30**(1), 241–260 (2018)
17. Liao, H., Wu, X., Liang, X., Yang, J.B., Xu, D.L., Herrera, F.: A continuous interval-valued linguistic ORESTE method for multi-criteria group decision making. Knowl. Based Syst. **153**, 65–77 (2018)
18. Liu, W., Dong, Y., Chiclana, F., Cabrerizo, F.J., Herrera-Viedma, E.: Group decision-making based on heterogeneous preference relations with self-confidence. Fuzzy Optim. Decis. Making **16**(4), 429–447 (2017)
19. Morente-Molinera, J.A., Al-Hmouz, R., Morfeq, A., Balamash, A.S., Herrera-Viedma, E.: A decision support system for decision making in changeable and multi-granular fuzzy linguistic contexts. J. Multiple Valued Logic Soft Comput. **26**, 485–514 (2016)
20. Morente-Molinera, J.A., Cabrerizo, F.J., Mezei, J., Carlsson, C., Herrera-Viedma, E.: A dynamic group decision making process for high number of alternatives using hesitant fuzzy ontologies and sentiment analysis. Knowl. Based Syst. **195** (2020)
21. Morente-Molinera, J.A., Mezei, J., Carlsson, C., Herrera-Viedma, E.: Improving supervised learning classification methods using multi-granular linguistic modelling and fuzzy entropy. IEEE Trans. Fuzzy Syst. **25**(5), 1078–1089 (2017)
22. Morente-Molinera, J.A., Pérez, I.J., Ureña, M.R., Herrera-Viedma, E.: Building and managing fuzzy ontologies with heterogeneous linguistic information. Knowl. Based Syst. **88**, 154–164 (2015)
23. Orlovsky, S.: Decision-making with a fuzzy preference relation. Fuzzy Sets Syst. **1**(3), 155–167 (1978)
24. Pérez, I.J., Cabrerizo, F.J., Alonso, S., Dong, Y., Chiclana, F., Herrera-Viedma, E.: On dynamic consensus processes in group decision making problems. Inf. Sci. **459**, 20–35 (2018)
25. Seiti, H., Hafezalkotob, A., Herrera-Viedma, E.: A novel linguistic approach for multi-granular information fusion and decision-making using risk-based linguistic d numbers. Inf. Sci. **530**, 43–65 (2020)
26. Song, Y., Li, G.: A large-scale group decision-making with incomplete multi-granular probabilistic linguistic term sets and its application in sustainable supplier selection. J. Oper. Res. Soc., 1–15 (2018)
27. Trillo, J.R., Fernández, A., Herrera, F.: HFER: promoting explainability in fuzzy systems via hierarchical fuzzy exception rules. In: 2020 IEEE International Conference on Fuzzy Systems (FUZZ-IEEE), pp. 1–8. IEEE (2020)
28. Yu, S., Wang, J., Wang, J., Li, L.: A multi-criteria decision-making model for hotel selection with linguistic distribution assessments. Appl. Soft Comput. **67**, 741–755 (2018)

Multimedia Applications

Edge Based Method for Kidney Segmentation in MRI Scans

Ala'a R. Al-Shamasneh[1](✉), Hamid A. Jalab[1], and Hend Alkahtani[2]

[1] Department of Computer System and Technology,
Faculty of Computer Science and Information Technology, University of Malaya,
50603 Kuala Lumpur, Malaysia
shamasneh@siswa.um.edu.my, hamidjalab@um.edu.my
[2] Department of Information System, College of Computer and Information Sciences, Princess
Nourah Bint Abdulrahman University, Riyadh 84428, Saudi Arabia
Hkalqahtani@pnu.edu.sa

Abstract. The precise and proficient detection of the kidney boundary in low-contrast images is considered as the main difficulty in the detection of kidney boundary in MRI image. The exact identification of a kidney shape in medical images with decreased non-kidney components to acquire insignificant false edge detection is adequately vital for several applications in surgical planning and diagnosis. Low illumination, poor-contrast, image close to the non-uniform state of organs with missing lines, shapes, and edges are considered fundamental difficulties in kidney boundary detection in MRI images. Kidney image edge detection is a significant step in the segmentation procedure because the final appearance and nature of the segmented image depend greatly on the edge detection technique utilized. This study presented a new method of extracting kidney edges from low quality MRI images. The proposed method extracted the unique information of the pixels, which represent the contours of the kidney for segmenting the region. The experimental results on different low-quality kidney MR images showed that the proposed model be able to carry out the effective segmentation of kidney MRI images based on the use of kidney edge components while preserving kidney-segmented edge information from low-contrast MRI images.

Keywords: Kidney segmentation · Edge-based method · Medical imaging · MRI images

1 Introduction

The precise segmentation of medical images is significant but considered as a challenge because of pathological changes and large variations in renal shapes. As such, developing an automatic method to extract the region of interest (ROI) of a kidney is difficult because of image noise, inhomogeneity, discontinuous boundaries as well as the similar visual appearance of neighboring parts of various structures. During kidney segmentation, the precise and effective segmentation of kidney edges in medical images is important for many applications associated with surgical planning and diagnosis. Effective methods, including the use of a low-contrast agent for neighboring parts, have

© Springer Nature Switzerland AG 2021
H. Fujita et al. (Eds.): IEA/AIE 2021, LNAI 12799, pp. 299–309, 2021.
https://doi.org/10.1007/978-3-030-79463-7_25

been applied to overcome kidney MRI challenges such as the issue of partial volume, high artefacts and leakage gradient response, high signal-to-noise ratio, and intensity inhomogeneity [1–3]. The most edge recognition techniques require an image enhancement to improve the image contrast. Automated segmentation systems are essential for detecting abnormalities through medical imaging. Most of proposed edge-based methods for kidney segmentation are depended on Canny edge approach which is not working properly with low-contrast and degraded images. As such, it is necessary to develop a potentially practical approach for a kidney segmentation model in MRI based on the use of kidney edge components, while preserving kidney-segmented edge information from low-contrast MRI images. This study is prepared as follows: literature is being described in Sect. 2, while Sect. 3 details the proposed method. Section 4 describes the experimented result. Lastly, the paper concludes with Sect. 5.

2 Related Work

A representation of the edges of an image will reduce the amount of information to be handled, while holding the basic data about the shape of object in the scene. This explanation of an image is easy to incorporate into a lot of object recognition algorithms utilized in computer vision alongside other image processing applications. The significant characteristic of the edge identification strategy is its ability to extract a definite edge line with great orientation, as shown by the increased literature about edge detection that has been accessible over the past three decades. Edge detection is a basic tool for image segmentation. Edge detection techniques change the original images into edge images, which profit by the grey level progressions in the image. In the preparation of the images, particularly in PC visions, the edge recognition handles the restriction of critical varieties of a grey level image and the detection of the physical and geometrical properties of objects at the scene. It is a basic procedure that recognizes the frame of an object, its boundaries, and the background in the image. Edge detection is the most common methodology used for distinguishing critical discontinuities in intensity values. Edges are neighbourhood changes in the image intensity. Edges typically occur on the boundary between two regions. The main feature is that such intensities can be extracted from the edges of an image. Edge detection is considered as an active research area in which it facilitates a higher level of image analysis. There are three unique kinds of discontinuities in the grey level, namely, lines, edges and points. A spatial mask can be used to recognize all three kinds of discontinuities in an image. There are many edge detection techniques for image segmentation in the literature [4, 5]. Canny used as pre-processing step for proposed segmentation method, for this reason we considered Canny edge detection in literature review. A discontinuity-based edge detection procedure that is commonly used is the Canny edge detection technique. This is a standard edge detection strategy that was first introduced by John Canny in 1983, and it is still able to outperform many of the newer algorithms that have been created. Canny edge detection approach starts with removing the noise from the image before detecting the edges. The Canny edge detection [6], attempts to illuminate the edges of an image by distinguishing them from various areas. The advantage of this method is that it can be used to investigate images by reducing the proceed information, while saving essential auxiliary data about the boundary of the object [7]. However, the Canny edge detection may still fail to precisely meet the desired boundary if the noise level in an image is high because noise and edges include high-frequency components. The study in [8] adjusted a bilateral filter to perform edge recognition, which is the inverse of bilateral smoothing. The Gaussian domain kernel of a bilateral filter was replaced by an edge location mask, and a Gaussian range piece was replaced by an inverted Gaussian kernel. While the study in [9] presented a speckle-reducing anisotropic diffusion (SRAD) system in the image denoising portion of the Canny algorithm structure. The proposed technique removes speckle noise related to image details. A comparable methodology was exhibited by [10]. However, in this method, diverse procedures and distinctive phantom images are used, which means that a designed object is scanned or imaged in the field of medical imaging to analyse, evaluate, and tune the performance of different imaging devices. The study in, [10] proposed a change in the Canny main algorithm by replacing the Gaussian filter with an adjusted median filter. Those approaches do not segment the kidney accurately. Thus, the models that investigate the Canny edge by using various filters may not function well for low-contrast and degraded images. The [11] proposed a new method for kidney segmentation based on an active contour model driven by fractional-based energy minimization. Since the special characteristic of fractional calculus is its ability to deal with low contrast and degraded images by preserve high-frequency contours regardless of contrast variations and noise, the proposed work explored this characteristic for the segmentation of kidney images. However, it should be noted that this method is said to be computationally expensive. The motivation for using the active contour-based method is to develop a generalized method to obtain accurate results. As such, it is necessary to develop a potentially viable strategy for a kidney MRI segmentation model based on the use of kidney edge components, while preserving kidney-segmented edge information from low-contrast MRI images.

3 Proposed Method

Edge features is one of the most important features in image processing applications. The purpose is to detecting discontinuities of object boundary in the levels of brightness. The edge detection has been used extensively in many applications, so that it is important to design an efficient edge detector which influence the image analysis. This study presented a new method of extracting kidney edges from low quality MRI images. The proposed algorithm was designed to remove significant non-kidney elements while preserving kidney-segmented edge information from low-contrast MRI images. However, the Canny-based output does not provide segmentation results directly.

Therefore, to reduce the complexity of the background, Canny edge information is used as it eliminates background information and provides finely detailed images of the kidney region. The information given by the Canny for the kidney region is considered as input for the subsequent steps to segment the kidney region. In other words, the Canny information is used as a pre-processing result to segment the kidney region in the images. The proposed edge-based method for kidney image segmentation was applied to the MRI image-based Canny edge detection under three applicable conditions, namely:

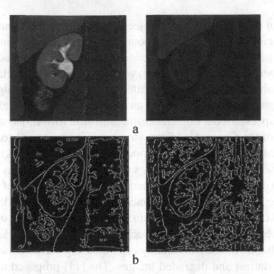

Fig. 1. Samples of kidney images

1. Angle from the centroid to boundaries.
2. Distance from the centroid to boundaries
3. Shape factor of the kidney.

The first step was to apply the Canny edge detection to the input image. The input images are shown in Fig. 1(a), and the Canny edge images are shown Fig. 1 (b). The connected-component labelling in 2-D binary images was used to label each blob. Some objects were chosen from both examples, as shown in Fig. 2 and Fig. 3.

The detailed steps for the proposed algorithm were as follows:

a) Input MRI image.
b) Apply Canny edge.
c) Label connected components (Fig. 2, and Fig. 3). The connected-component labelling (bwlabel) in 2-D binary images was used to label each blob, which is a fundamental process for computer vision systems, and several image processing applications. It used to find the individual connected component and labelling them in a binary image to segment those objects, so can searched shape, boundaries, etc. [12, 13].
d) Find the centroid for each object using the region props function (Fig. 4, and Fig. 5).
e) The function bwboundaries (BW) used to trace the region in the binary image, and to calculate (x, y) the boundaries points [14].
f) Calculate the distance from the centroid to the boundary by:

$$Distance = sqrt(x - xCentroid) \cdot \hat{2} \cdot (y - yCentroid) \cdot \hat{2} \qquad (1)$$

g) Calculate the angle from the centroid to the boundary by:

$$Angle = atan2d(y - yCentroid, x - xCentroid) \qquad (2)$$

The angle from the centroid to the boundary is calculated as the max angle and max distance found for each object hence the max angle and max distance represent the kidney components. The angle values for the kidney object is 180 and it is the maximum value. The Distance values for the kidney object bigger than 70 and it is the maximum values.

h) Find the minimum distance from the centroid to the boundary. Then, the object is removed or otherwise kept.

To extract the kidney edge without any non-kidney component, the following condition is checked. If the centroid is close to one of the white pixels, then remove this object. This happens by finding the minimum distance from the centroid to boundaries using the Eq. (1). If the minimum distance is less than 10 pixels then remove this object, otherwise keep the object.

i) Calculate the shape factor of the kidney to remove any non-kidney component and keep kidney edges to get final result by:

$$SF = \frac{4\pi A}{L^2} \tag{3}$$

where A is the area of region, L is the number of boundaries. [15].

For the kidney, the SF will be the min value. The final result extracted for the kidney edge is shown in Fig. 6.

Fig. 2. Label object sample image 1

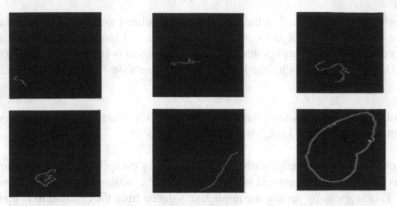

Fig. 3. Label object sample image 2.

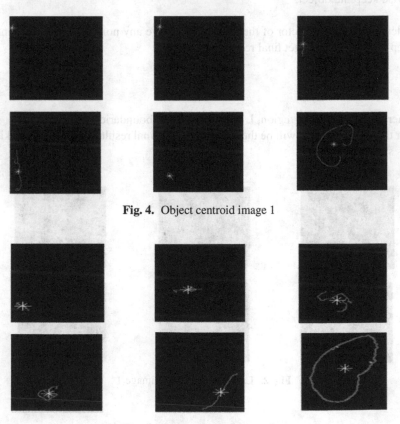

Fig. 4. Object centroid image 1

Fig. 5. Object centroid image 2

Fig. 6. The result of proposed segmentation model

4 Experimental Results

The datasets for this study were collected from two different sources to evaluate the performance of the proposed and existing methods. A dataset consisting of 230 images of different patients was collected from a hospital in Saudi Arabia. The dataset, called dataset1 for the experiment, included images with low contrast, low resolution, and noise. Images were also collected from Wikimedia Commons, which consisted of 20 images. This was considered as a standard dataset and was called dataset2 in this experiment. In total, 230 + 20 = 250 images were considered for the experiments.

The datasets were considered adequate enough to evaluate the proposed and existing methods for kidney image segmentation because the nature of the dataset varied in terms of low-quality characteristics that included the possible causes of kidney image segmentation. In order to measure whether the proposed model was able to segment kidney parts correctly or not, standard measures, namely, sensitivity, accuracy, Jaccard's similarity coefficient (JSC) [16], Dice's similarity coefficient (DSC) [17], and time were used. Kidney regions were segmented manually, and the segmented regions were further verified by a doctor who was an expert radiologist. The ground truth samples and segmentation results of the proposed edge-based method for kidney segmentation for the dataset are shown in Fig. 6. To show the effectiveness and usefulness of the proposed model, it was compared with the following state-of-the-art methods: Canny edge strategy [6], which uses Gaussian filtering for segmentation. However, the Canny edge detection may still fail to precisely meet the desired boundary if the noise level in the kidney MRI is high, because the noise and edges both include high frequency components. The execution of the Canny edge identification depends on Gaussian filtering. Gaussian filtering does not just remove image noise and smothers image subtleties, but also weakens the edge data. The study [8], adjusted the bilateral filter to do edge recognition, which is the inverse of bilateral smoothing. Moreover, [9] presented the speckle-reducing anisotropic diffusion (SRAD) system in the image denoising part of the Canny algorithm structure. The proposed technique is able to remove speckle noise while maintaining image subtleties. Finally, [11] proposed fractional Mittage-Leffler-minimization method for kidney segmentation offers the advantages of fractional calculus which can deal with low-contrast and degraded images, the active contour-based method is computationally expensive because it involves a large number of iterations. These approaches have not segmented the kidney accurately as the proposed approach which is successfully removed the non-kidney part from low-complexity MRI images as shown in Fig. 7.

4.1 Qualitative Results

The qualitative results of the proposed segmentation model for the dataset1 and dataset2 are shown in Fig. 7 and Fig. 8, respectively. It was observed that the input images were affected by multiple factors, such as poor quality (low contrast), degradations, and contrast variations, as shown in Fig. 7 (a) and Fig. 8(a). The proposed model was able to successfully segment the kidney regions, as shown in Fig. 7(c) and Fig. 8(c). This was evident from the comparison of the segmentation results of the proposed model and the ground truth, where the results of the proposed edge-based method for kidney segmentation were almost the same as the ground truth. This shows that the proposed model has the ability to handle complex situations (i.e., kidney diseases). This is the advantage of the proposed model for segmentation.

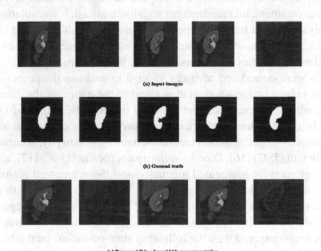

(a) Input images

(b) Ground truth

(c) Proposed Edge-based kidney segmentation

Fig. 7. Samples of kidney segmentation using proposed edge-based method on dataset1.

A qualitative evaluation comparative for recent paper [11] is provided using dataset1. The qualitative results of both segmentation models for dataset1 are shown in Fig. 9. It was observed that the input images were affected by multiple factors, as shown in Fig. 9(a). The machine learning-based segmentation approach not used in this study, due to the fact that the machine learning models need a huge number of images which is not easy task in case of medical imaging.

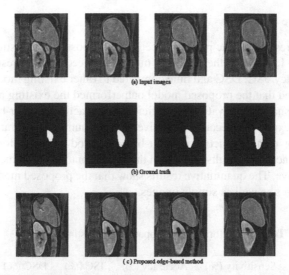

Fig. 8. Samples of kidney segmentation using proposed edge-based method on dataset2.

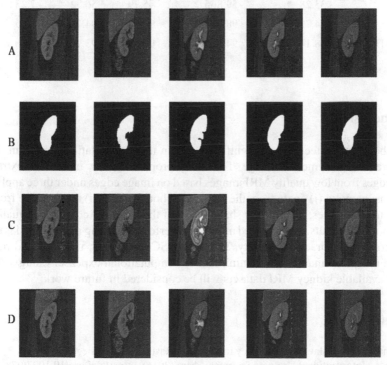

Fig. 9. The comparison results between the [11] and proposed segmentation methods using dataset1 (A) Input images, (B) Ground Truth, (C) [11] segmentation method, (D) Proposed segmentation 2

4.2 Quantitative Results

The quantitative results for the performance of the proposed and existing methods are reported in Table 1. It shown the proposed model produced the best results in terms of sensitivity, accuracy, JSC, DSC and time compared to other existing models. Therefore, it can be concluded that the proposed model outperformed the existing models in terms of segmentation, shape preservation and efficiency. The active contour-based method is computationally expensive because it involves a large number of iterations. However, the motivation for using the active contour-based method is to develop a generalized method to obtain accurate results. Although the active contour-based method is computationally expensive. The quantitative results show that the proposed model was suitable for complex images as well as simple images.

Table 1. Perform of the proposed and existing methods.

Method	Sensitivity (%)	Accuracy (%)	JSC (%)	DSC (%)	Time (Sec)
[8]	30.28	63.788	63.788	42.79	7.50
[9]	33.28	59.865	45.79	56.32	7.23
[11]	94.79	98.95	93.11	94.70	3.26
Proposed method	98.14	94.656	90.55	93.92	0.76

5 Conclusion

Kidney boundary detection is a significant step in the segmentation algorithm due to the nature of the segmented image. This study proposed a new method of extracting kidney edges from low quality MRI images based on image edges under three applicable conditions; namely: (i) angle from the centroid to boundaries; (ii) the distance from the centroid to boundaries, and (iii) the shape factor of the kidney. According to qualitative and quantitative results, the proposed method outperforms existing methods and is useful in the terms of accuracy, sensitivity, JSC, and DSC. Moreover, the proposed method achieved this performance with a minimum of computational expense. Using different publicly available kidney MRI datasets will be considered in future work.

References

1. Chehab, M., Bratslavsky, G.: Kidney imaging. In: Rastinehad, A., Siegel, D., Pinto, P., Wood, B. (eds.) Interventional Urology. Springer, Cham (2016). https://doi.org/10.1007/978-3-319-23464-9_17
2. Nikken, J.J., Krestin, G.P.: MRI of the kidney—state of the art. Eur. Radiol. 17(11), 2780–2793 (2007)
3. Huang, A.J., Lee, V.S., Rusinek, H.: Functional renal MR imaging. Magn. Reson. Imaging Clin. N. Am. 12(3), 469–486 (2004)

4. Thong, W., Kadoury, S., Piché, N., Pal, C.: Convolutional networks for kidney segmentation in contrast-enhanced CT scans. Computer Methods in Biomechanics **6**(3), 277–282 (2018)
5. Torres, H.R., Queiros, S., Morais, P.: Kidney segmentation in ultrasound, magnetic resonance and computed tomography images: a systematic review. Comput. Methods Programs Biomed. **157**, 49–67 (2018)
6. Canny, J.: A computational approach to edge detection. IEEE Trans. Pattern Anal. Mach. Intell. (6), 679–698 (1986)
7. Shrimali, V., Anand, R., Kumar, V.: Current trends in segmentation of medical ultrasound B-mode images: a review. IETE Tech. Rev. **26**(1), 8–17 (2009)
8. Tomasi, C., Manduchi, R.: Bilateral filtering for gray and color images. In: Sixth International Conference on Computer Vision (IEEE Cat. No. 98CH36271), pp. 839–846. IEEE (1998)
9. Chai, H.Y., Wee, L.K., Supriyanto, E.: Edge detection in ultrasound images using speckle reducing anisotropic diffusion in canny edge detector framework. In: Proceedings of the 15th WSEAS international conference on Systems, pp. 226–231. World Scientific and Engineering Academy and Society (WSEAS) (2011)
10. Nikolic, M., Tuba, E., Tuba, M.: Edge detection in medical ultrasound images using adjusted Canny edge detection algorithm. In: 2016 24th Telecommunications Forum (TELFOR), pp. 1–4. IEEE (2016)
11. Al-Shamasneh, A.R., Jalab, H.A., Shivakumara, P., Ibrahim, R.W., Obaidellah, U.H.: Kidney segmentation in MR images using active contour model driven by fractional-based energy minimization. Signal Image Video Process. 1–8 (2020)
12. Nassimi, D., Sahni, S.: Finding connected components and connected ones on a mesh-connected parallel computer. SIAM J. Comput. **9**(4), 744–757 (1980)
13. Ronse, C., Devijver, P.A.: Connected components in binary images: the detection problem (1984)
14. Gonzalez, R.C., Eddins, S.L., Woods, R.E.: Digital Image Publishing Using MATLAB. Prentice Hall, Hoboken (2004)
15. Danielson, P.-E.: A new shape factor. Comput. Graph. Image Process. **7**(2), 292–299 (1978)
16. Jaccard, P.: Étude comparative de la distribution florale dans une portion des Alpes et des Jura. Bull Soc Vaudoise Sci Nat **37**, 547–579 (1901)
17. Dice, L.: Measures of the amount of ecologic association between species. Ecology **26**(3), 297–302 (1945)

Using the HAAR Wavelet Transform and K-nearest Neighbour Algorithm to Improve ECG Detection and Classification of Arrhythmia

A. M. Khairuddin$^{(\boxtimes)}$ and K. N. F. Ku Azir

Centre of Excellence Advanced Computing (ADVCOMP),
Faculty of Electronic Engineering Technology (FTKEN), Universiti Malaysia Perlis,
Kampus Pauh, 02600 Ulu Pauh, Perlis, Malaysia
adamkhairuddin@studentmail.unimap.edu.my, fazira@unimap.edu.my

Abstract. This study attempted to enhance ECG detection and classification of arrhythmias by using ECG arrhythmia classification algorithm implemented from the Haar wavelet transform and the k-nearest neighbor (k-NN) classifier. The development of the ECG arrhythmia classification algorithm consisted of five essential phases which included pre-processing, R-peak detection, feature extraction, feature selection, and classification. The pre-processing phase involved the band-pass Butterworth filter and zero-phase digital filter. The Haar wavelet transform and thresholding process were used to detect the R-peaks of the ECG signals. The morphological features were extracted from the R-peak locations, whereas the statistical features were extracted from the wavelet decomposition of Haar wavelet transform in the feature extraction phase. The feature selection phase utilized the neighborhood component analysis (NCA) and hyper-parameter optimization to select relevant features for the classification model. The classification model was developed by using the k-nearest neighbor (k-NN) classifier. The ECG signals obtained from the MIT-BIH arrhythmia database were used to evaluate the performance of the classification algorithm as proposed in this study. The result of this study showed average accuracy (ACC) of 97.30%.

Keywords: Electrocardiography · Arrhythmia · Filter · Wavelet · R-peaks · Features · Classification · Neighborhood component analysis · k-nearest neighbor

1 Introduction

Cardiac arrhythmia is a disorder of the heart rhythm that occurs when the human heart beats too fast, too slow, or irregularly. The interruption to the electrical impulses of the heart can cause it to contract and result in arrhythmia [1, 2]. Although some arrhythmias may be considered as not dangerous, there are irregular heartbeats that are lethal and harmful to the extent that they can reduce cardiac output which can lead to sudden death. Nonetheless, since arrhythmias produce symptoms, they are commonly detected by using the electrocardiogram (ECG) [3]. The ECG is considered as one of the most effective ways to diagnose arrhythmias. The ECG records the electrical activity of the

© Springer Nature Switzerland AG 2021
H. Fujita et al. (Eds.): IEA/AIE 2021, LNAI 12799, pp. 310–322, 2021.
https://doi.org/10.1007/978-3-030-79463-7_26

heart to assess its rhythm, chamber size and thickness of the muscle. Life threatening arrhythmias are detected based on the information obtained from the ECG.

Given the dangerous nature of arrhythmias, it is vital to ensure that the ECG monitoring system can detect them early as well as classify them accurately. The literature and previous studies have emphasized on the importance of categorizing ECG arrhythmias accurately by using arrhythmia classification algorithms. The review of past studies indicates that several arrhythmia classification algorithms have been proposed. For instance, one of the earlier research by [4] recommended the ECG arrythmia classification algorithm that consisted of principal component analysis (PCA), kernel-independent discrete wavelet transform (DWT), and support vector machine (SVM) optimized with genetic algorithm (GA). The algorithm developed in the study was able to classify five classes of ECG beats that included normal, left bundle branch block (LBBB), right bundle branch block (RBBB), premature ventricular contraction (PVC) and atrial premature beat (APC). According to the results of the study, the proposed algorithm was able to achieve accuracy of 98.8% when evaluated with the MIT-BIH arrhythmia database.

A more recent study by [5] developed an arrhythmia classification algorithm that consisted of discrete wavelet transform (DWT), dynamic feature, morphological feature, independent component analysis (ICA), Teager energy operator, and neural network (NN) classifier. The algorithm adopted in the study was able to acquire accuracy of 99.75% and 99.84% when evaluated with the MIT-BIH arrhythmia database and the MIT-BIH supraventricular arrhythmia database, respectively.

The contemporary research by [6] developed another ECG arrhythmia diagnosis algorithm that adopted the discrete wavelet transform, the higher order statistic feature extraction and the entropy based feature selection. In the study, the neural network and support vector machine (SVM) classifiers were used to categorize the various arrhythmia classes. When tested with the MIT-BIH arrhythmia database, the proposed algorithm managed to obtain accuracy of 99.83% and 99.03% on the neural network (NN) and the support vector machine (SVM), respectively.

Although the literature reveals the need to use arrhythmia classification algorithm to improve the categorization of the various types of arrhythmia, the review of prior studies appears to indicate limitations in the focus and scope of the previous classifications algorithms, especially in terms of their ability to categorize the actual numbers of arrhythmia classes as well as limited use of the various types of features in the development of these algorithms. Hence, this study aims to develop an enhanced ECG arrhythmia classification algorithm by using the band-pass Butterworth filter, the zero-phase digital filter, the Haar wavelet transform, the thresholding process, the morphological features, the statistical features, the neighborhood component analysis (NCA), the hyper-parameter optimization, and the k-nearest neighbor (k-NN). Accordingly, the study reported in this paper is organized into the following sections. Section two below describes the detailed procedures of the proposed arrhythmia classifier. Section three discusses the experimental design of the study. Next, section four presents and discusses the experimental results of the study. Lastly, section five of the paper provides the conclusion of the paper.

2 Proposed Methodology

The ECG arrhythmia classification algorithm proposed in this study involved the following five major phases: (1) pre-processing; (2) R-peak detection; (3) feature extraction; (4) feature selection; and (5) classification. The proposed classifier is presented in Fig. 1.

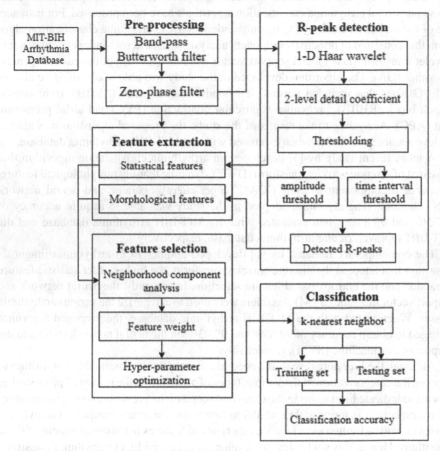

Fig. 1. The block diagram of the proposed ECG arrhythmia classification algorithm.

Accordingly, the following section briefly explains each of the five phases of the development of the algorithm as proposed in this study.

2.1 Pre-processing

In the pre-processing phase, the ECG signals contaminated with artifacts such as low frequency noises (baseline wander) and high frequency noises (power-line interference, muscle noise) acquired from the MIT-BIH arrhythmia database were filtered. The band-pass Butterworth filter was used to filter the contaminated signals as well as to facilitate the detection of the R-peaks of the ECG signals. The zero-phase digital filter was also used to reduce the noise in the original ECG signals, maintained the fiducial points of the R-peaks as well as prevented the signal delay.

2.2 R-peak Detection

The Haar 1-D wavelet transform was utilized to decompose the filtered ECG signals to level 9 wavelet decomposition. This level 9 wavelet decomposition contained the high-pass filter and the low-pass filter. The high-pass filter produced detail coefficients, $cD_1 - cD_9$, whereas the low-pass filter produced approximation coefficients cA_9. To detect the R-peaks of the ECG signals, 2-level detail coefficient (cD_2) produced from the wavelet decomposition was selected. In locating the R-peaks, the following two threshold coefficients were selected in the thresholding process: (1) amplitude threshold, T_{amp}; and (2) time interval threshold, T_{time}.

2.3 Feature Extraction

The purpose of feature extraction phase is to transform the original signals into the feature vector without losing the important information. More specifically, the two types of features extracted during the feature extraction phase in this study involved: (1) morphological features; and (2) statistical features. Seven morphological features were extracted from the R-peak locations of the ECG signals [7]. These morphological features included: (1) average heart rate; (2) mean RR interval distance; (3) root mean square distance of successive RR interval; (4) number of R peaks that differ more than 30 ms; (5) standard deviation of RR interval; (6) standard deviation of heart rate; and (7) power spectral entropy.

In addition, there were 80 statistical features extracted from the level 9 wavelet decomposition using the Haar 1-D wavelet transform. These statistical features were extracted from both detail coefficients, $cD_1 - cD_9$ and approximation coefficients cA_9 which included: (1) mean; (2) standard deviation; (3) skewness; (4) kurtosis; (5) root mean square; (6) mean ratio; (7) maximum; (8) minimum; and (9) energy. As a result, a total of 87 features were used to implement the proposed ECG arrhythmia classification algorithm.

2.4 Feature Selection

The objective of feature selection phase was to reduce the dimension of the extracted features by selecting only the relevant features that have the best predictive power. These relevant features were used to develop the classification model in this study. The two types of feature selection technique selected in the study involved: (1) the neighborhood component analysis (NCA); and (2) the hyper-parameter optimization. The hyper-parameter optimization function in the MATLAB was adopted to find the optimal parameters for the k-nearest neighbor (k-NN) classifier. The hyper-parameter optimization generated the optimal values for number of neighbors and the distance metric for the classification model.

2.5 Classification

The k-nearest neighbor (k-NN) classifier was chosen to implement the ECG arrhythmia classification algorithm. The classification model was developed by using the MATLAB function of 'fitcknn'. This function returns the k-nearest neighbor (k-NN) classification model based on the selected relevant features (predictors) and classes (responses). The two important parameters that were chosen for this classification model involved: (1) number of neighbors; and (2) distance metric.

3 Experimental Design

In the study, the ECG signals acquired from the MIT-BIH arrhythmia database were used to implement as well as to evaluate the performance of the proposed arrhythmia classifier. This database has 48 half-hour ECG records that were sampled at 360 Hz. The two types of leads for each record included modified limb lead II and modified lead V1. For the purpose of this study, only modified limb leads II were selected for the algorithm implementation and evaluation. The 10-s (3600 samples) fragments of the ECG signal were randomly selected [8].

A 10-fold cross validation method was used for the training of the classifier. This method was used to prevent overfitting of the data by partitioning the data set into respective folds and estimating the accuracy for each of these folds. The selected feature index for each feature weight was fed to the MATLAB classification learner application to train the k-nearest neighbor (k-NN) model.

The MIT-BIH arrhythmia database contained 17 classes of ECG heartbeats. These 17 classes consisted of: (1) normal sinus rhythm; (2) atrial premature beat; (3) atrial flutter; (4) atrial fibrillation; (5) supraventricular tachyarrhythmia; (6) pre-excitation; (7) premature ventricular contraction; (8) ventricular bigeminy; (9) ventricular trigeminy; (10) ventricular tachycardia; (11) idioventricular rhythm; (12) ventricular rhythm; (13) fusion of ventricular and normal beat; (14) left bundle branch block beat; (15) right bundle branch block beat; (16) second-degree heart block; and (17) pacemaker rhythm. Accordingly, the proposed ECG arrhythmia classification algorithm was implemented to classify these 17 classes of ECG beats.

4 Results and Discussions

In the study, the performance of the pre-processing technique which included the band-pass Butterworth filter and zero-phase digital filter was evaluated by using the mean square error (MSE). Table 1 indicates the MSE value for 2 records when using the pre-processing technique, whereas Table 2 shows the MSE value for 2 records without using the pre-processing technique.

Based on the results in Table 1, it appears that the value of MSE for the record 100 and the record 124 are higher as compared to the results in Table 2. The MSE value of 0 indicates that the use of pre-processing technique can filter the unwanted noises from the ECG signals. This finding suggested that the lower the value of MSE, the better the number of correctly detected R-peaks (true positive) in the ECG signals.

Table 1. MSE value without using the pre-processing technique.

Record	Actual beats	True positive	MSE
102	2187	2124	1.814815
124	1619	1618	0.000618

Table 2. MSE value when using the pre-processing technique.

Record	Actual beats	True positive	MSE
102	2187	2187	0
124	1619	1619	0

The record 108 was chosen to investigate the effect of the different value of the amplitude threshold, T_{amp} and the time interval threshold, T_{time} in detecting the R-peaks of the ECG signals. Table 3 presents the sensitivity (SEN), positive predictivity (+P), and accuracy (ACC) for the different value of amplitude threshold, T_{amp} and the time interval threshold, T_{time}, applied on record 108.

Table 3. Sensitivity, positive predictivity and sensitivity for record 108.

T_{amp}				
	T_{time}	0.10	0.15	0.20
SEN (%)	20	100.00	100.00	97.12
+P (%)		95.80	93.86	93.04
ACC (%)		95.80	93.86	90.42
SEN (%)	25	100.00	100.00	97.12
+P (%)		97.68	97.24	95.03
ACC (%)		97.68	97.24	92.43
SEN (%)	30	100.00	100.00	100.00
+P (%)		97.55	97.50	100.00
ACC (%)		97.55	97.50	100.00

Table 3 indicates that the optimal T_{amp} and T_{time} for record 108 are 0.20 and 30, respectively. These findings suggested that different values of amplitude threshold and time-interval threshold can affect the sensitivity, positive predictivity and sensitivity of the ECG signals. This may also be due to the ECG signals having different morphological properties (distance between peaks, height of the peaks) as well as the number of noises and artifacts.

There were 87 morphological features and statistical features extracted during the feature extraction phase. These 87 predictors were fed to the neighborhood component analysis (NCA) model. The feature weight, f_w were set to $0.1 \geq n \geq 0.5$. Predictors that had feature weight greater than n, $(f_w > n)$ we re selected. Table 4 presents the predictors analyzed with five different feature weights. Table 5 shows the feature index with their respective features.

Table 4. Predictors analyzed with five different feature weights.

Feature weight	Number of features	Selected feature index
>0.1	16	23, 31, 32, 34, 35, 58, 63, 65, 66, 76, 80, 81, 82, 83, 84, 85
>0.2	14	23, 31, 32, 34, 35, 58, 63, 65, 66, 76, 80, 81, 82, 84
>0.3	13	23, 31, 32, 34, 35, 58, 63, 65, 66, 76, 80, 81, 84
>0.4	12	23, 31, 32, 34, 35, 63, 65, 66, 76, 80, 81, 84
>0.5	8	23, 31, 35, 63, 65, 66, 76, 84

Table 5. Feature index with their respective features.

Feature index	Types of features	Features
23	S	Skewness of the 4th detail coefficient, cD_4
31	S	Kurtosis of the 1st detail coefficient, cD_1
32	S	Kurtosis of the 2nd detail coefficient, cD_2
34	S	Kurtosis of the 4th detail coefficient, cD_4
35	S	Kurtosis of the 5th detail coefficient, cD_5
58	S	Mean ratio of the 8th detail coefficient, cD_8 and 9th detail coefficient, cD_9
63	S	Maximum of the 4th detail coefficient, cD_4
65	S	Maximum of the 6th detail coefficient, cD_6
66	S	Maximum of the 7th detail coefficient, cD_7
76	S	Minimum of the 7th detail coefficient, scD_7
80	S	Energy
81	M	Average heart rate
82	M	Mean RR interval distance
83	M	Root mean square distance of successive RR interval
84	M	Number of R-peaks that differ more than 30ms
85	M	Standard deviation of RR interval

S - Statistical; M - Morphological

In order to find the optimal number of neighbors and distance metric for the k-nearest neighbor classification model, the hyper-parameter optimization technique was used and it was based on the selected feature index as well as determined by the neighborhood component analysis (NCA) as presented in Table 4. The following Table 6 shows the accuracy of the k-nearest classification model based on the optimal number of neighbors and distance metric returned by the hyper-parameter optimization.

Table 6. Accuracy of classification model based on optimal number of neighbors and distance metric.

Feature weight	Num. of neighbors	Distance metric	Accuracy (%)
>0.1	1	seuclidean	96.66
>0.2	1	cityblock	97.30
>0.3	1	cityblock	96.30
>0.4	1	cityblock	95.30
>0.5	1	cityblock	96.00

As shown in Table 6, the feature weight >0.2 that has number of neighbors of 1 and distance metric of cityblock achieved the highest accuracy (ACC) rate of 97.30%. These results appear to indicate that the classification accuracy of the ECG arrhythmia classification algorithm can be affected by the feature weight and distance metric. Although the feature weight of >0.1 has more features as compared to the feature weight >0.2, the feature weight >0.2 was able to achieve accuracy of 0.30% higher than the feature weight >0.1. This suggests that higher number of features do not necessary affect the accuracy of the classification. In addition, the use of both morphological and statistical features can affect the accuracy of the classification. For example, the 14 features (11 statistical features, 3 morphological features) selected by the feature weight >0.2 have the most predictive power as compared to the other four feature weights.

The training and the testing set were formed by using the 301 fragments with their respective 17 arrhythmia classes. The cross validation of 10-fold was used for the validation of the classification. The 301 fragments were split into training sets and testing sets in 80:20 ratio. This resulted in producing 241 training sets and 60 test sets. The classification results by using the k-NN classifier is summarized in Table 7.

The results in Table 7 shows that at least 12 classes of arrhythmias achieved accuracy of 100.00%, whereas the other five classes of arrhythmias achieved accuracy of less than 100.00%. In order to determine the performance of the k-nearest neighbor (k-NN) in each class, the confusion matrix was plotted. Figure 2 illustrates the confusion matrix plot.

Table 7. Classification performance of the ECG arrhythmia classification algorithm.

Class	Correctly classified	Misclassified	Accuracy (%)
Normal sinus rhythm	12	0	100.00
Atrial premature beat	29	0	100.00
Atrial flutter	11	0	100.00
Atrial fibrillation	38	1	97.00
Supraventricular tachyarrhythmia	4	1	80.00
Pre-excitation	18	0	100.00
Premature ventricular contraction	25	1	100.00
Ventricular bigeminy	19	6	84.00
Ventricular trigeminy	5	0	100.00
Ventricular tachycardia	7	0	100.00
Idioventricular rhythm	7	1	88.00
Ventricular flutter	7	1	88.00
Fusion of ventricular and normal beat	5	0	100.00
Left bundle branch block beat	44	0	100.00
Right bundle branch block beat	25	0	100.00
Second-degree heart block	9	0	100.00
Pacemaker rhythm	25	0	100.00
Average accuracy			**97.30**

The performance of the ECG arrhythmia classification algorithm in this study was also compared to the other previously published classification algorithms. The comparison of the performance of the classification algorithms is shown in Table 8.

The results in Table 8 indicate that the different number of arrhythmia classes, features, and classifiers selected for the development of ECG arrhythmia classification algorithm can influence the performance of the algorithm in terms of its average accuracy (ACC). The difference in the average accuracy (ACC) may be due to several of the following factors. First, in addition to the number of arrhythmia classes, selection of extracted features, and classifiers, the use of different types of filters to eliminate unwanted noises and artifacts can also affect the number of correctly detected true positive (TP) in the ECG signals. Second, the optimal values of amplitude threshold, T_{amp} and time interval threshold, T_{time} used in the thresholding process can also influence the sensitivity (SEN), positive predictivity (+P) and accuracy (ACC) of the R-peaks detection. Third, the higher the number of correctly detected true positive (TP) can result in extracting more morphological features from the ECG signals. This can impact the accuracy of the algorithm. Fourth, the combination and the selection of relevant morphological and statistical features can also enhance the accuracy (ACC) of the ECG arrhythmia classification algorithm. Fifth, appropriate feature selection techniques can help to select the relevant features that have high predictive power. This is because features with high

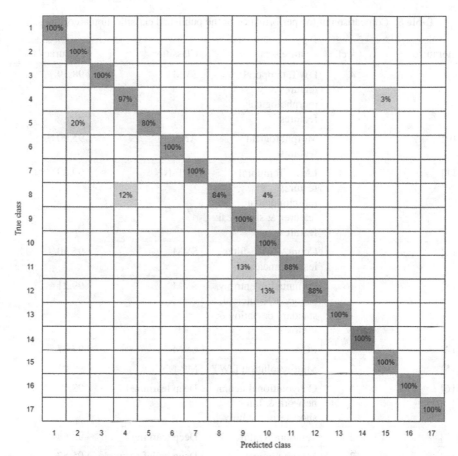

Fig. 2. The confusion matrix plot. 1 – normal sinus rhythm; 2 – atrial premature beat; 3 – atrial flutter; 4 – atrial fibrillation; 5 – supraventricular tachyarrhythmia; 6 – pre-excitation; 7 – premature ventricular contraction; 8 – ventricular bigeminy; 9 – ventricular trigeminy; 10 – ventricular tachycardia; 11 – idioventricular rhythm; 12 – ventricular flutter; 13 – fusion of ventricular and normal beat; 14 – left bundle branch block beat; 15 – right bundle branch block beat; 16 – second-degree heart block; 17 – pacemaker rhythm

predictive power can increase the average accuracy (ACC) of the algorithm. Sixth, the parameters of the k-NN classifier such as number of neighbors and distance metric need to be adjusted correctly so that they can increase the average accuracy (ACC) of the algorithm. Finally, the results in Table 8 also seem to suggest that different feature sets may be suitable for adopting different kinds of machine learning classifiers. Although the proposed ECG arrhythmia classification algorithm has a slightly low average accuracy (ACC) as compared to the previous studies, the algorithm developed in this study was able to not only improve the detection of the R-peaks but also successfully classify all the 17 classes of arrythmias as recorded in the MIT-BIH arrhythmia database.

Table 8. Comparison of the performance of the published classification algorithms.

Literature	# cl.	Feature sets	Classifier	Accuracy (%)
[9]	4	DWT, temporal features & morphological features	SVM	98.39
[10]	5	Morphological features	ANN	95.00
[11]	5	EMD, Temporal features, morphological features & statistical features	RBF-NN	99.89
[12]	3	Count2 & VF-filter leakage measure	SVM	95.90
[13]	16	Permutation entropy, energy, RR-interval, standard deviation & kurtosis	SVM	99.21
[14]	5	PCA	SVM	97.77
[15]	2	Multiresolution DWT	MP-NN	99.07
[16]	5	Convolutional neural network & long short-term memory	Deep learning	98.10
[17]	2	Temporal features	Deep learning	99.68
[18]	2	Morphological features & statistical features	Deep belief network	95.57
[19]	5	Coupled-convolution layer structure	CNN	99.43
[20]	15	Parametric & visual pattern of ECG morphology	KNN	97.70
[21]	2	Wave & Gabor features	CNN	93.19
Proposed method	**17**	**Haar wavelet transform, thresholding, NCA, hyper-parameter optimization**	**k-NN**	**97.30**

5 Conclusion

The ECG arrhythmia classification algorithm developed in this study was used to improve the ECG detection and classification of arrhythmias. The classification algorithm consisted of band-pass Butterworth filter, zero-phase digital filter, Haar wavelet transform, thresholding, morphological features, statistical features, neighborhood component analysis (NCA), hyper-parameter optimization, and k-nearest neighbor (k-NN). The performance of the proposed classification algorithm was evaluated by using the MIT-BIH arrhythmia database. The results of this study showed that the proposed classification algorithm was able to achieve average accuracy (ACC) of 97.30%. Based on the result of this study, it can be concluded that the performance of the classification algorithm as proposed in this study is compatible with the previously published algorithms.

References

1. WebMD: When Your Heart Rhythm Isn't Normal. WebMD (2020). https://www.webmd.com/heart-disease/atrial-fibrillation/heart-disease-abnormal-heart-rhythm#1-2. Accessed 12 Mar 2020
2. Heart Foundation: Arrhythmias. Heart Foundation (2020). https://www.heartfoundation.org.au/your-heart/heart-conditions/arrhythmias. Accessed 13 Mar 2020
3. Stanford Medicine: What is an electrocardiogram? Stanford Medicine (2020). https://stanfordhealthcare.org/medical-tests/e/ekg.html. Accessed 12 Mar 2020
4. Das, M.K., Ari, S.: ECG beats classification using mixture of features. Int. Sch. Res. Not. **2014**, 1–12 (2014)
5. Anwar, S.M., Gul, M., Majid, M., Alnowami, M.: Arrhythmia classification of ECG signals using hybrid features. Comput. Math. Methods Med. **2018** (2018)
6. Chashmi, A.J., Amirani, M.C.: An efficient and automatic ECG arrhythmia diagnosis system using DWT and HOS features and entropy-based feature selection procedure. J. Electr. Bioimpedance **10**(1), 47–54 (2019)
7. Deshmukh, S.: ECG Feature Extractor. MathWorks (2017)
8. Plawiak, P.: ECG signals (1000 fragments). Mendeley Data (2017)
9. Sahoo, S., Kanungo, B., Bchera, S., Sabut, S.: Multiresolution wavelet transform based feature extraction and ECG classification to detect cardiac abnormalities. Meas. J. Int. Meas. Confed. **108**, 55–66 (2017)
10. Li, P., et al.: High-performance personalized heartbeat classification model for long-term ECG signal. IEEE Trans. Biomed. Eng. **64**(1), 78–86 (2017)
11. Sahoo, S., Mohanty, M., Behera, S., Sabut, S.K.: ECG beat classification using empirical mode decomposition and mixture of features. J. Med. Eng. Technol. **41**(8), 652–661 (2017)
12. Nguyen, M.T., Shahzad, A., Van Nguyen, B., Kim, K.: Diagnosis of shockable rhythms for automated external defibrillators using a reliable support vector machine classifier. Biomed. Signal Process. Control **44**, 258–269 (2018)
13. Raj, S., Ray, K.C.: Automated recognition of cardiac arrhythmias using sparse decomposition over composite dictionary. Comput. Methods Programs Biomed. **165**, 175–186 (2018)
14. Yang, W., Si, Y., Wang, D., Guo, B.: Automatic recognition of arrhythmia based on principal component analysis network and linear support vector machine. Comput. Biol. Med. **101**, 22–32 (2018)
15. Rai, H.M., Chatterjee, K.: A novel adaptive feature extraction for detection of cardiac arrhythmias using hybrid technique MRDWT & MPNN classifier from ECG big data. Big Data Res. **12**, 13–22 (2018)

16. Oh, S.L., Ng, E.Y.K., Tan, R.S., Acharya, U.R.: Automated diagnosis of arrhythmia using combination of CNN and LSTM techniques with variable length heart beats. Comput. Biol. Med. **102**, 278–287 (2018)
17. Sannino, G., De. Pietro, G.: A deep learning approach for ECG-based heartbeat classification for arrhythmia detection. Futur. Gener. Comput. Syst. **86**, 446–455 (2018)
18. Mathews, S.M., Kambhamettu, C., Barner, K.E.: A novel application of deep learning for single-lead ECG classification. Comput. Biol. Med. **99**, 53–62 (2018)
19. Xu, X., Liu, H.: ECG heartbeat classification using convolutional neural networks. IEEE Access **8**, 8614–8619 (2020)
20. Yang, H., Wei, Z.: Arrhythmia recognition and classification using combined parametric and visual pattern features of ECG morphology. IEEE Access **8**, 47103–47117 (2020)
21. Atal, D.K., Singh, M.: Arrhythmia classification with ECG signals based on the optimization-enabled deep convolutional neural network. Comput. Methods Programs Biomed. **196**, 105607 (2020)

Query by Humming for Song Identification Using Voice Isolation

Edwin Alfaro-Paredes(iD), Leonardo Alfaro-Carrasco(iD), and Willy Ugarte(✉)(iD)

Universidad Peruana de Ciencias Aplicadas, Lima, Peru
{u201611810,u201212551}@upc.edu.pe, willy.ugarte@upc.edu.pe

Abstract. There are some methods for searching in large music databases, like searching by song name or artist name. However, in some cases these methods are not enough. For instance, a person might not remember the name of a song, but might remember its melody. In Music Information Retrieval, there is a task called Query-By-Humming, which allows retrieving a rank of songs that are similar to an audio humming. In this research, we propose the use of vocal isolation methods to improve query-by-humming systems. To achieve this, different configurations of Query-by-Humming systems were tested to analyze the results and determine in which cases our proposal works better. The results showed that vocal isolation improves the performance of Query-by-Humming systems when the music collection consists of modern songs.

Keywords: Query-by-Humming · Music similarity · Melody extraction · Music information retrieval

1 Introduction

In today's world, there is an ever-growing content of music available to the public and an equally growing access to information. An example of this is the number of songs that are indexed in digital databases like Spotify, where 40,000 new songs are added each day[1]. Although parts of this information are structured and organized, other parts are difficult to find or retrieve. Due to the latter, there is a need for searching methods in large amounts of music data. For example, one way of searching for a song is by its name or artist. However, this isn't helpful if the user doesn't know or doesn't remember the name of a song or any identifying information other than the song's melody. For this reason, the investigation area of Music Information Retrieval has an approach called Query-By-Humming/Singing, where new methods for music recognition, using the user's hum or voice, are studied.

A Query-By-Humming System is composed by two main parts, as described by [20] in their proposed diagram. First, a descriptor extractor, which processes the songs and returns a descriptor of each song. This is an important task,

---

[1] Music Business Worldwide - https://bit.ly/37TQNE4.

H. Fujita et al. (Eds.): IEA/AIE 2021, LNAI 12799, pp. 323–334, 2021.
https://doi.org/10.1007/978-3-030-79463-7_27

because the database is constructed with the extracted descriptors. Also, the user's hum or voice needs to be processed to extract a descriptor that represents similar information of the hummed song as the one in the system's database. The second part consists of a method to measure the similarity between a song and the user's interpretation (e.g., correlation). The ranking results use these scores to retrieve the songs in similarity order. Therefore, the user can recognize the song only by their interpretation.

Recognizing a song by a user's hum or voice is a difficult task, because the user does not necessarily have good singing/humming abilities, as a research affirms that 62% of non musicians were poor singers [9]. This might lead to significant differences between the user's interpretation and the original song [10]. Furthermore, the process of searching in a large database is likely a time consuming task, thus the solution mitigates all the mentioned problems.

Our main motivation for this research project is the relatively small amount of proposals in the state of art related to the direct analysis of frequencies in an audio file. Starting from this, our contributions are as follows:

- We want to demonstrate that vocal isolation could improve results for Query-By-Humming systems, because the user is more likely to hum the voice part from a given song.
- To obtain the best performance on our Query-By-Humming system, we have made an exhaustive comparison between different configurations, which includes descriptors and alignment methods.
- Two different datasets were used to find in which cases our contribution could improve the performance of Query-By-Humming systems.

This paper is organized as follows. In Sect. 2, we define the main concepts of Query-By-Humming systems. In Sect. 3, we present our contribution. Section 4 contains several works that we have reviewed. Our experiments and results are shown in Sect. 5. Finally, in Sect. 6, we analyze our results and give some recomendations for future works.

2   Background

In this section, we define all those concepts and methods that are related with the Query-By-Humming task. These concepts are important to understand this research and how these systems are constructed using different approaches.

2.1   Cover Song Identification

This task consists of identifying all the possible covers from a database given a song [21]. Similarly to Query-By-Humming, this approach is composed of two main parts, descriptor extraction and similarity computation. Usually, for this task, the descriptor is constructed from melody and harmony, like this research project [20]. There are some clear similarities between Cover Song Identification and Query-By-Humming. For this reason, the latter task can be considered as a general case from the other, where hummings and songs could be related to the concept of cover [20]. The main difference is noted in the descriptor extraction process, where only the melody is used, because the user's hum is a monophonic audio and represents the main melody of a song [20].

2.2 Melody Extraction Process

The purpose of this process is the automatic extraction of the main melody from a polyphonic audio, and it's worth noting its importance in many music information retrieval tasks [19]. In Query-By-Humming systems, the output of this process is used to compute the descriptor of a song or hum.

There are mainly two kinds of melody extraction methods in the literature:

- First, the database is created from midi files, where the melody is extracted based on channel elimination like [15], or based on a main salience function that constructs a route of the melody between all the available channels [8].
- Second, the database is created from wav files, where frequency analysis is applied to recognize the main melody [18,19,27].

2.3 Descriptor Computation Process

As mentioned earlier, to construct a Query-By-Humming database, it's necessary to compute the descriptors from the songs and hummings. These descriptors should have some important properties: compactness, expressiveness and portability [6]. Thus, the descriptors can be stored efficiently, they can represent the most outstanding melody expressions and the system can be more resistant to different types of inputs (key and tempo variation) [6].

The most basic form to represent the melody is with the UDS descriptor (see Fig. 1a), which uses the letter "U" to represent an increase between two consecutive notes, the letter "D" to represent a decrease between two consecutive notes, and the letter "S" to represent no change between two consecutive notes [4]. Another descriptor is the melody contour string (see Fig. 1b), which uses the pitch difference between two consecutive notes [11]. There are some descriptors that are usually used in Cover Song Identification task, like chromagrams, which represent the frequencies from an audio in twelve different pitch classes. Some of these chromagrams can be used in Query-By-Humming [20].

The Harmonic Pitch Class Profile (HPCP) (see Fig. 1c) is a type of chromagram used to represent the chords of an audio. We use HPCP in this research for our experiments and test a method for Cover Song Identification in Query-By-Humming. Another chromagram we used is the proposed by [20], a Semitone-band Based Chromagram (henceforth denoted as SBBC) (see Fig. 1d). To obtain this descriptor, the cents and semitones are computed from the fundamental frequency of the melody. Then, the results are mapped into a single octave. Finally, a pitch class histogram is computed and a normalization is applied.

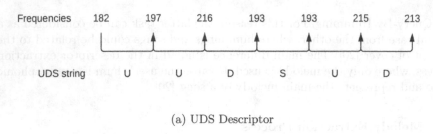

(a) UDS Descriptor

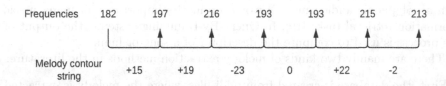

(b) Melody Contour Descriptor

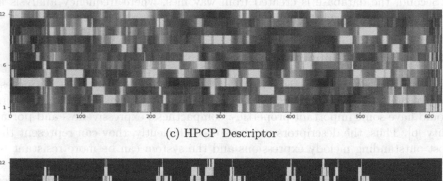

(c) HPCP Descriptor

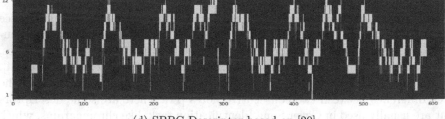

(d) SBBC Descriptor based on [20]

Fig. 1. Melody descriptors

2.4   Alignment Methods

These methods allow us to compute a similarity score between a query (humming) and a reference (songs from database). Thus, it is possible to obtain a similarity ranking, ordered from the most similar song to the least one.

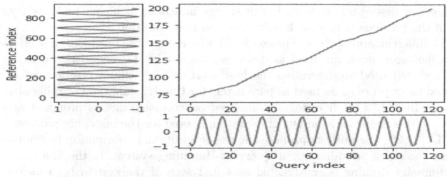

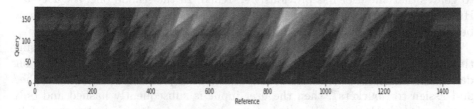

(a) DTW Alignment (dtw-python package)

(b) Qmax Alignment (Essentia Package)

Fig. 2. Alignment methods

Now, we are going to define two methods that have shown a good performance in many music information retrieval tasks:

- First, Dynamic Time Warping (DTW) (see Fig. 2a), defined from [23]: *"this algorithm allows finding the optimal scaling of the time axis of the compared sequences by minimizing the cost of matching one of them to the other"*.
- Second, Qmax algorithm (see Fig. 2b), proposed by [22], which computes a similarity score between two time series, based on local alignment [20].

This method receives a similarity matrix as an input, which is computed from the query and the reference into their form of descriptor (chroma). For this research, we used both DTW and the Qmax algorithm in order to test different configurations and find out which one gives better results.

3 Related Works

To the best of our knowledge, the earliest work on Query-by-Humming systems is [4], where a simple but robust UDS descriptor is used and a fuzzy matching algorithm is applied to account for errors in the user input when comparing it to a database of MIDI song descriptors. Another work is [13] in which a more expressive descriptor is created with strings indicating a higher or lower note than the previous one, a pitch difference and note duration.

A different approach is explored in [3] where n-grams, fixed-length overlapping sub-sequences, are used as descriptors, while in [17] neural networks are trained and used to determine the best starting and ending positions of the stored descriptors to be used as parameters for the dynamic time warping algorithm. In [20], a pitch histogram, inspired on chromagrams, is proposed as a melody descriptor and the Qmax algorithm is used for the matching process.

In [11,25], the authors propose the use of additional information to complement the results obtained by a Query-by-Humming system. In the first one, a preliminary ranking is constructed as a first step of the system by a melody matching algorithm, then it is reordered by giving priority to results that belong to genres that the user has previously searched. In the second one, a Query-by-Humming/Singing system is proposed, where an additional comparison is done between any lyrics obtained from the user (singing) query and the lyrics.

Finally, other works have taken an approach to tackle the high processing time problem that a Query-by-Humming system inevitably faces with a big database of song descriptors. In [5], the song descriptors are repeatedly hashed and assign to "buckets", then the user input is subsequently hashed and only compared with the songs that belong to the same bucket that the query falls into, effectively reducing the number of matching candidates and thus search time. In [26], a Piecewise Aggregate Approximation transformation is applied to create a much shorter and simpler pitch sequence of the user query that is then used to filter out descriptors that are less likely to match.

All these works have focused on common steps of Query-by-Humming system but, to the best of our knowledge, none of them have added any pre-processing steps to the data used to build the descriptors database. We noticed there is room for improvement that may significantly improve the results of Query-by-Humming systems by filtering the raw data that is then processed and used as a database to look for matches. Our proposal applies a voice extraction process to the music tracks which eases up the following descriptor extraction step by reducing the amount of noise that the algorithm has to detect and filter.

4   Main Contribution

Our main interest is to find out if separating the vocals and the accompaniment of each music track may improve the descriptor extraction process that is an inherent part of Query-by-Humming systems. This separation will be made as a preprocessing step, thus, instead of using directly songs to compare, using the separated vocals and the accompaniment of each song as an input.

Isolating the vocals from a music track should reduce the amount of noise a melody extraction algorithm must detect and remove, allowing for better descriptors and an overall higher precision in the final results. This isolation was done by pretrained machine learning models, Spleeter [7] and Demucs [2], to create derived datasets that contain only the vocals of the original songs. They were selected since they have the best results in the literature to our knowledge [2, 7], and because are provided by serious companies like Deezer (specialized in music related products) and Facebook Research.

Furthermore, algorithms for both descriptor extraction and melody matching have a huge impact on the precision of the results. Thus, we compare and setup different combinations of these algorithms, which includes HPCP and SBBC for descriptor extraction process, and for the matching similarity task Qmax and Dynamic Time Warping. Additionally, musical collections that differ in their "oldness" (i.e., the average release year of their songs) might influence the behavior of the algorithms and its results. Thus, we compare and setup different experiments on two musical collections that differ on their "oldness".

Our test planification included experiments to verify how the different configurations for Query-by-Humming systems behave in a real situation with popular music. However, we noticed that the MTG-QBH collection[2] is composed by old songs. For this reason we had to create our own collection, which is composed by "modern" popular songs (i.e., on average, from the last 20 years). This collection also includes 24 humming queries of 16 songs.

5   Experiments

5.1   Experimental Protocol

Data:

- *Musical Collections:* To evaluate our method, we used two musical collections.
  - The first one is a subset of the MTG-QBH (See footnote 2) dataset, which consists of 481 canonical songs and 118 humming queries. Because our method works by extracting the vocals from an audio file, 78 tracks that contain no lyrics were excluded from the original collection for a total of 403 songs used for our experiments.
  - The second dataset was constructed for this research, and consists of 50 songs and 24 humming queries.

  Both datasets differ from each other in their songs' release dates: the first one contains music released between 1926 and 2004, with an average of 1972, while the second one consists of music from 1965 to 2018 with an average of 2004.
- *Dataset Partition:* Since the aforementioned datasets do not have the same amount of songs and hummings, and if we want to compare both collections, it is important to create samples of the first one to make it as similar as possible in size and distribution terms to the second one.

  For this reason, during our experiments, we grouped the queries from each dataset by their target songs and then randomly selected hummings from the first collection's groups to mirror the second query distribution. Thus, we made 24 queries (10 queries where each one targets a different song, 8 queries

---

[2] Music Technology Group - https://bit.ly/2IdElnG.

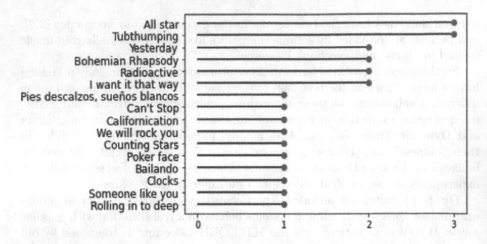

Fig. 3. Distribution of hummings from music collection 2

where each pair targets the same song, and 6 queries where each half has the same target song) for collection 1. Finally, 34 songs were randomly selected (in addition to the 16 songs targeted by the previous queries) (Fig. 3).

Equipment:

- The computer we used for the experiments has the followings characteristics: AMD Ryzen 7 3700X 8-Core Processor 3.60 GHz, 16 GB RAM 3200 MHz, and NVIDIA GeForce RTX 2060 SUPER.
- The programming language used was Python 3.7.
- The code and datasets are publicly available at https://bit.ly/3ngQh7o.

Experiment Configurations: For our experiments:

- We use two types of descriptors, HPCP from the Essentia package [1] and SBBC based on [20].
- For the alignment methods: we use the DTW and Qmax algorithms.
- For comparing full melody from songs against the vocal part from songs for both collections: we use vocal isolation techniques Spleeter [7] and Demucs [2] (two pre-trained models for separating vocals and accompaniments).
- For measuring the performance of these configurations, we use Mean Reciprocal Rank (MRR) (Eq. 1) and Top-X Hit Rate (Eq. 2) from [14].

$$MRR = \frac{1}{|Q|} \sum_{i=1}^{|Q|} \frac{1}{r_i} \tag{1}$$

$$Top\text{-}X = \frac{|\{c \in Q \mid r_c \leq X\}|}{|Q|} \tag{2}$$

where r_i = result position of i-th query and Q = Query set

Each configuration used a unique combination of a dataset, a melody descriptor, and a matching algorithm and all configurations were run against three different versions of the musical collections: the full songs (vocals + accompaniment), vocal isolation processed by Spleeter, and processed by Demucs. The Query-by-Humming framework used by each configuration is as follows: For each song on the database and the query (user's humming), its main melody is extracted with Melodia algorithm, which is based on frequency analysis [19]. Then, a descriptor is calculated from each extracted melody. Finally, the query in its form of descriptor is compared with each song's descriptor using an alignment method, and the ranking is elaborated from the scores of each alignment.

Each experiment with the collection 1 was run five times, generating different samples, and the average was calculated.

5.2 Discussion

Quantitative Results: In Table 1 shows our results of experiments. For instance, 0.14 is the MRR for collection 2 using SBBC as descriptor, which is constructed with the melody of the voice part of a song extracted with Spleeter, and Qmax as the alignment method.

We could bring another example, 7.50% is the Top 5 for collection 1 using HPCP as descriptor, which is constructed with the melody of the full song, and DTW as the alignment method. Also, there are some numbers in bold, which means the best result for that configuration. For instance, 0.26 is the MRR obtained for the best configuration (SBBC as descriptor and Qmax as alignment method) for the first collection using the melody of the full song.

On one hand, in Table 1 that, for both music collections, the SBBC descriptor has generally the best performance for all metrics (most of the bold values are in columns 4, 5, 8, 9, 12, 13, 16 and 17). This descriptor obtains the best result for the combination of melody extracted from the full song (first line for collection 1) and Qmax alignment, obtaining an MRR of 0.26 (numbers in bold for column 5), a Top 1 of 15.83% (numbers in bold for column 9), a Top 5 of 35% (numbers in bold for column 13), and a Top 10 of 50% (numbers in bold for column 17).

Table 1. Comparison of the descriptor extraction methods, alignment methods, and Collections 1 and 2 with MRR and Top-X hit rate metrics.

	MRR				Top 1				Top 5				Top 10			
	HPCP		SBBC		HPCP		SBBC		HPCP		SBBC		HPCP		SBBC	
	DTW	Qmax	DTW	Qmax	DTW	Qmax	DTW	Qmax	DTW	Qmax	DTW	Qmax	DTW	Qmax	DTW	Qmax
Collection 1																
Full	0.08	0.10	0.17	**0.26**	2.50	2.50	9.17	**15.83**	7.50	10.83	20.83	**35.00**	13.33	25.00	30.83	**50.00**
Spleeter	0.10	0.09	**0.14**	0.13	2.50	4.18	**6.67**	4.17	8.33	5.83	13.33	**17.50**	21.67	15.83	**27.50**	25.83
Demucs	0.13	0.06	0.13	**0.16**	5.00	0.83	5.00	**8.33**	15.83	5.00	14.17	**20.00**	33.33	8.30	24.17	**49.17**
Collection 2																
Full	0.16	0.06	**0.17**	0.13	**8.33**	0.00	**8.33**	4.17	16.67	4.17	**20.83**	12.50	**29.17**	12.50	20.83	25.00
Spleeter	0.11	0.10	**0.23**	0.14	0.00	4.17	**16.67**	8.33	20.83	12.50	**25.00**	16.67	**29.17**	16.67	**29.17**	20.83
Demucs	0.10	0.06	**0.24**	0.11	4.17	0.00	**16.67**	4.17	4.17	4.17	**25.00**	12.50	25.00	20.83	**37.50**	16.67

On the other hand, in Table 1, the DTW algorithm combined with the vocal isolation approaches obtain better results for the collection 2, being 0.24 its highest value for MRR (number in bold for Demucs in column 4), 16.67% for Top 1 (numbers in bold for Spleeter/Demucs in column 8), 25% for Top 5 (numbers in bold for Spleeter/Demucs in column 12), and 37.5% for Top 10 (number in bold for Demucs in column 16).

Qualitative Results: First, Fig. 4a shows that SBBC descriptor [20] mostly has a much better performance than the HPCP descriptor (most of the points are located in the upper triangle/SBBC side). HPCP was developed to store harmonic information, even if the melody is used to construct it. Thus, HPCP might not be suitable for the Query-By-Humming task. Contrarily SBBC descriptor is suitable for it because they are based on semitone and octave abstraction, which makes the descriptor more robust to octave changes and local expressions [20].

After, Fig. 4b shows that DTW algorithm has a better performance for the Collection 2 (i.e., modern songs). Contrarily, the Qmax algorithm is more suitable for the Collection 1 (i.e., older songs). All of (resp. some of) the blue (resp. red) points are displayed below (resp. above) and relatively far from (resp. close to) the diagonal line for Collection 2 (resp. Collection 1). This is similar to [20], where the authors have obtained good results for the same collection.

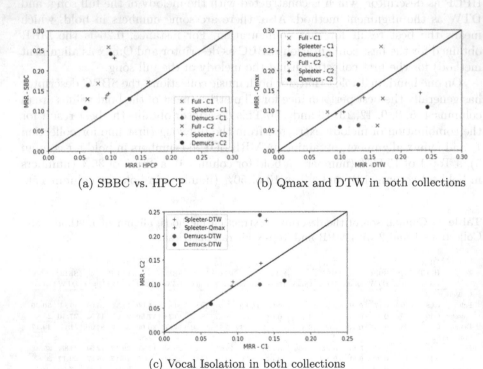

(a) SBBC vs. HPCP   (b) Qmax and DTW in both collections

(c) Vocal Isolation in both collections

Fig. 4. Results graphics

Finally, Fig. 4c shows that vocal isolation improves the performance mostly for collection 2 (most of the points are displayed above the diagonal line). This might indicate that there are some important differences between current music and old music that explain this behaviour. For instance, according to [16], there is a decrease in terms of loudness and rythm complexity, and an increase about timbre complexity.

6 Conclusion

In this paper, we have experimented with different configurations for Query-by-Humming systems, which includes two alignment algorithms (DTW and Qmax), two methods for constructing a song descriptor (HPCP and SBBC), and with (or without) an extra pre-processing step for vocal isolation.

Our results show that SBBC descriptor mostly performs much better than the HPCP descriptor, on one hand, the DTW algorithm performs better for modern songs (i.e., Collection 2), on the other hand, the Qmax algorithm is more suitable for older songs (i.e., Collection 1) and the vocal isolation mainly improves the performance only for collection 2.

Our results point to a clear distinction between Collection 1 (older songs) and Collection 2 (modern songs), nevertheless deeper studies need to be performed to confirm this insight. Furthermore, developing a recommender system that automatically adapts the retrieval parameters (e.g., descriptors, alignment metrics, ...) according to the type (or genre) of the hummed song to improve the quality of the results, seems a promising research prospect. These improvements to the Query-by-Humming task may be integrated into a song recognition system that could implement other solutions, e.g. simple tasks like Query-by-Text by asking the user to input genres or artists to reduce the search space, or reading music sheets [12]. Finally, softness may be a key element for fine tunning the parameters [24].

References

1. Bogdanov, D., et al.: Essentia: an audio analysis library for music information retrieval. In: ISMIR (2013)
2. Défossez, A., Usunier, N., Bottou, L., Bach, F.R.: Music source separation in the waveform domain. CoRR abs/1911.13254 (2019)
3. Doraisamy, S., Rüger, S.M.: Robust polyphonic music retrieval with n-grams. J. Intell. Inf. Syst. **21**(1), 53–70 (2003)
4. Ghias, A., Logan, J., Chamberlin, D., Smith, B.C.: Query by humming: musical information retrieval in an audio database. In: ACM Multimedia (1995)
5. Guo, Z., Wang, Q., Liu, G., Guo, J.: A query by humming system based on locality sensitive hashing indexes. Signal Process. **93**(8), 2229–2243 (2013)
6. Gómez, E., Klapuri, A., Meudic, B.: Melody description and extraction in the context of music content processing. J. New Music Res. **32**, 23–40 (2003)
7. Hennequin, R., Khlif, A., Voituret, F., Moussallam, M.: Spleeter: a fast and efficient music source separation tool with pre-trained models. J. Open Source Softw. **5**(50), 2154 (2020)

8. Huang, Y., Lai, S., Sandnes, F.E.: A repeating pattern based query-by-humming fuzzy system for polyphonic melody retrieval. Appl. Soft Comput. **33**, 197–206 (2015)
9. Hutchins, S., Peretz, I.: A frog in your throat or in your ear? searching for the causes of poor singing. J. Expe. Psychol. General **141**, 76 (2011)
10. Khan, N.A., Mushtaq, M.: Open issues on query by humming. In: ICADIWT (2011)
11. Liu, N.: Effective results ranking for mobile query by singing/humming using a hybrid recommendation mechanism. IEEE Trans. Multim. **16**(5), 1407–1420 (2014)
12. Lozano-Mejía, D.J., Vega-Uribe, E.P., Ugarte, W.: Content-based image classification for sheet music books recognition. In: 2020 IEEE Engineering International Research Conference (EIRCON) (2020)
13. Lu, L., You, H., Zhang, H.J.: A new approach to query by humming in music retrieval. In: IEEE ICME (2001)
14. Manning, C.D., Raghavan, P., Schütze, H.: Introduction to Information Retrieval. Cambridge University Press, Cambridge (2008)
15. Ozcan, G., Isikhan, C., Alpkocak, A.: Melody extraction on MIDI music files. In: IEEE ISM (2005)
16. Parmer, T., Ahn, Y.: Evolution of the informational complexity of contemporary western music. In: ISMIR (2019)
17. Pham, T.D., Nam, G.P., Shin, K.Y., Park, K.R.: A novel query-by-singing/humming method by estimating matching positions based on multi-layered perceptron. KSII Trans. Internet Inf. Syst. **7**(7), 1657–1670 (2013)
18. Rocamora, M., Cancela, P., Pardo, A.: Query by humming: automatically building the database from music recordings. Pattern Recognit. Lett. **36**, 272–280 (2014)
19. Salamon, J., Gómez, E.: Melody extraction from polyphonic music signals using pitch contour characteristics. IEEE Trans. Speech Audio Process. **20**(6), 1759–1770 (2012)
20. Salamon, J., Serrà, J., Gómez, E.: Tonal representations for music retrieval: from version identification to query-by-humming. Int. J. Multim. Inf. Retr. **2**(1), 45–58 (2013)
21. Serrà, J., Gómez, E., Herrera, P.: Audio cover song identification and similarity: Background, approaches, evaluation, and beyond. In: Raś, Z.W., Wieczorkowska, A.A. (eds.) Advances in Music Information Retrieval. SCI, vol. 274, pp. 307–332. Springer, Heidelberg (2010). https://doi.org/10.1007/978-3-642-11674-2_14
22. Serrà, J., Serra, X., Andrzejak, R.: Cross recurrence quantification for cover song identification. New J. Phys. **11**, 09307 (2009)
23. Stasiak, B., Skiba, M., Niedzielski, A.: FlatDTW - dynamic time warping optimization for piecewise constant templates. Digit. Signal Process. **85**, 86–98 (2019)
24. Ugarte, W., Boizumault, P., Loudni, S., Crémilleux, B., Lepailleur, A.: Soft constraints for pattern mining. J. Intell. Inf. Syst. **44**(2), 193–221 (2013). https://doi.org/10.1007/s10844-013-0281-4
25. Wang, C., Jang, J.R.: Improving query-by-singing/humming by combining melody and lyric information. IEEE ACM Trans. Audio Speech Lang. Process. **23**(4), 798–806 (2015)
26. Wang, L., Huang, S., Hu, S., Liang, J., Xu, B.: Improving searching speed and accuracy of query by humming system based on three methods: feature fusion, candidates set reduction and multiple similarity measurement rescoring. In: INTER-SPEECH. ISCA (2008)
27. Zhang, W., Chen, Z., Yin, F.: Main melody extraction from polyphonic music based on modified Euclidean algorithm. Appl. Acoust. **112**, 70–78 (2016)

IMAGE-2-AQI: Aware of the Surrounding Air Qualification by a Few Images

Minh-Son Dao[1(✉)], Koji Zettsu[1], and Uday Kiran Rage[2]

[1] National Institute of Information and Telecommunications Technology,
Tokyo, Japan
{dao,zettsu}@nict.go.jp
[2] The University of Aizu, Fukushima, Japan
udayrage@u-aizu.ac.jp

Abstract. It is no doubt that air pollution influences human health. The report of diseases related to and numbers of patients suffered from air pollution increase rapidly over time. Hence, the requirement of measuring the air quality index (AQI) precisely and economically becomes the utmost purpose of communities. Although the most precise AQI comes from high-end stations, there is a problem with deploying such stations to cover all corners of particular areas. Some replacement methods are used to measure AQI using other data sources than from stations such as satellite, UAV, google street views, SNS, and open data from the Internet. This paper introduces a method that can predict AQI at a local and individual scale with a few images captured from smartphones and open AQI and weather datasets by utilizing lifelog data and urban nature similarity. Image retrieval and prediction model approaches are developed and evaluated on different open datasets of air pollution, weather, and images. The results confirm our hypothesis about the high correlation between the AQI and the surrounding environment's snapshots.

Keywords: AQI · Image retrieval · Prediction model · Open data · Healthcare

1 Introduction

Subject well-being (SWB) has become a significant factor that attracts researchers and policymakers when considering planning or making policy decisions that will impact society. The study on air pollution shows that air pollution negatively correlates to SWB [1]. Hence, being aware of air pollution can alleviate the burdens of loss on individual and social scales. The traditional approach to know air pollution is to use stations or high-tech devices that are expensive and difficult to install on a granular scale. Hence, measuring and predicting air pollution without relying heavily on standard stations becomes the utmost need to deal with SWB.

One of the replacement solutions to increase air pollution awareness is to predict or interpolate air pollution from historical data collected by standard stations.

© Springer Nature Switzerland AG 2021
H. Fujita et al. (Eds.): IEA/AIE 2021, LNAI 12799, pp. 335–346, 2021.
https://doi.org/10.1007/978-3-030-79463-7_28

It will help decrease the number of stations while still getting valuable and precise air pollution data at a granular scale [2]. Nevertheless, this approach still relies on data coming from existing stations. Hence changing existing stations (both in positions and number of stations) becomes a big obstacle for improving the accuracy of prediction models.

Another solution is to combine images taken by UAV and air pollution data recorded by on-ground wireless devices to predict air pollution data and manage the system economically, as introduced in [3]. First, images captured from UAVs are utilized to predict the air quality index (AQI) level. If this AQI level satisfies some predefined conditions, on-ground devices are wakened up to measure AQI value. This approach can increase the number of stations economically and flexibly by having UAVs get more data from locations that on-ground devices cannot reach.

Along with the significant development in computer vision and deep learning domains, people start thinking of using only images to approximate AQI [4]. This approach could probably be the most economical solution since it does not rely much on air pollution stations. This approach's further step is to use street view images to understand the relation between urban natures (e.g., green zone, building zone), seasons (e.g., summertime), and AQI levels [5]. This approach tries to point out the high-semantic features of images that can probably enhance the accuracy of AQI prediction.

Although the approaches mentioned above have benefited communities, a simple application that an ordinary person can use to get the awareness of AQI around him/her is still an open demand. When people capture images using their smartphone, the ideal application is that the approximate AQI value or precise AQI level can immediately display on the smartphone. In [6], the authors introduced a method that can turn to be an ideal application mentioned above. This method relied on Fukuoka dataset [7], a personal data archive where smartphone-taken images are associated with sensor-box-recorded AQI value.

In general, the vital role of images as the replacement factor to predict AQI is no doubt. Nevertheless, very few researchers pay attention to building reasonable hypotheses by which both training data collection and prediction model/method can be constructed productively and reciprocally. Hence, building hypotheses that support creating an explainable AQI prediction model and pointing out which semantic features of images correlate tightly to AQI is the utmost requirement.

In light of the discussion mentioned above, we introduce our research that contributes to the image-based AQI prediction problem as follows:

- We introduce hypotheses to clarify which image factors can enhance prediction models/methods' productivity and explain these models/methods' architecture and strategy.
- We utilize these hypotheses to build the Image-2-AQI system to predict AQI using images with one straight and straightforward approach and one complicated deep-learning approach.
- We evaluate different images and AQI datasets with different perspectives and point out the necessary factors when creating such datasets.

The paper is organized as follows: Sect. 1 introduced the problem statement and motivation, Sect. 2 describes the proposed methodology, Sect. 3 discusses evaluation and comparison, and Sect. 4 gives conclusions and future works of the proposed method.

2   Methodology

In this section, the methodology is introduced, described, and discussed in detail.

2.1   Hypotheses

First, we introduce our hypotheses on the correlation between the surrounding landscapes and AQI.

Hypothesis 1: *If a set of surrounding environment images, which were captured repeatedly and continuously in the same place and the same period, share the typical AQI level for a significant ratio, a few images captured in the same place and period but in the short future could probably share the same typical AQI level.*

Example 1: Figure 1 illustrates the AQI level distributed on the same route and the same period for one week. The average AQI level for this route is almost the same except for some abnormal spots.

Hypothesis 2: *The fluctuation of AQI level at a particular place (i.e., anomaly AQI level compared to the average AQI level) could probably correlate to abnormal activities (by humans) or events (by nature) happen at that place within a particular time length (e.g., one hour, one day).*

Example 2: Figure 2 shows the difference between images captured when we got the abnormally high AQI level and others with average AQI level. Naked eyes could see the (potential) reason that a construction site could cause a high AQI level.

Hypothesis 3: *There could probably be a set of visual features (both raw and high-semantic level) extracted from images correlated to urban nature (e.g., park, street, lake) and surrounding environmental sensing data (e.g., AQI level, weather) where such images are captured.*

Example 3: Figure 3 denotes an example of hypothesis 3 applied to the Fukuoka city dataset. The route passes by three different urban nature spots, from a park, streets to a shrine. The diagram on the left-hand side shows the correlation between the surrounding environment sensing data. The high-semantic features on the right-hand side are extracted from images captured by lifelog cameras (e.g., Chinon camera) mixed with urban nature annotated by people. There exists a robust correlation among these data sources.

Relying on these hypotheses, we propose two approaches to predict AQI level/value using images, surrounding environment sensing data, and urban nature: (1) image retrieval and (2) prediction model. Inversely, by evaluating these approaches on the real dataset, we confirm our hypotheses' righteousness towards applying them for further developments.

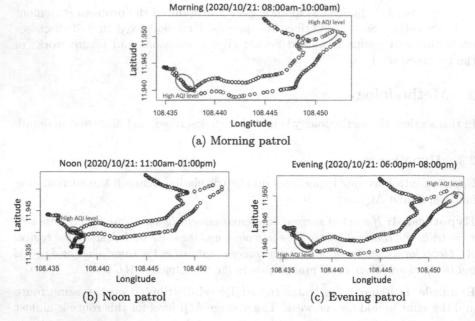

Fig. 1. Example of Hypothesis 1: AQI levels measured repeatedly and continuously on the same route at the same period tend to be stable.

2.2 Image Retrieval Approach

We design our first approach as follows:

1. with each image in the dataset, we extract predefined features that later are vectorized and indexed using FAISS index [8]. We assume that all images in our dataset have their AQI level/value by synchronizing surrounding environmental sensing data using time and location.
2. with the querying image, we first extract its predefined features and then send this feature vector to the FAISS index to find the most similar one.
3. the AQI level/value assigned to the queried image is assigned as the AQI level/value of the querying image.

This approach relies on hypothesis 1, where similar images captured in the same place at the same period could probably bear the same AQI level/value. It also takes a part of hypothesis 2, where the images sharing the same high-semantic features that tightly correlate to AQI levels can have the same AQI level/value with looser conditions of location and time.

We decide to select three different models to extract features from images. The list of these models and the reason why to utilize them in our paper are described as follows:

1. **FixRes** [9]: This model aims to increase classification accuracy by fixing the train-test resolution discrepancy. It helps build a classifier working on

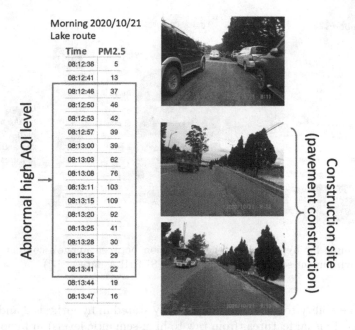

Fig. 2. Example of Hypothesis 2: abnormal AQI levels caused by humans or nature

the datasets whose content contains many diverse-resolution images captured from crowdsourcing (e.g., CCTV, smartphone, lifelog camera, street view images).

2. **SwAV** [10]: This unsupervised learning model can learn more robust representations, not just high-level features, and achieve a certain level of invariance to image transformations. Hence, it is useful when applying this method on evolving datasets where new images from new places frequently come with lots of images that have never appeared before.

3. **FasterCRNN** [11]: This model aims to enhance object detection. Hence, it is suitable for capturing semantic meaning that enhances the correlation between urban natures (e.g., building, vehicle, trees, sky, clouds) and AQI level/value from images.

2.3   Prediction Model Approach

We design our prediction model as a Conditional-LSTM-NN model, as illustrated in Fig. 4. The architecture of our model inherits from the three hypotheses we introduced. Our model's conditional component comes from hypothesis 1, where the constraint of the same location and period plays an essential role in clustering the same images sharing the same AQI level/level. The LSTM component reflects hypothesis 1 in the role of historical data, where we can look back at the history at the same place and period to predict the next one. The NN component

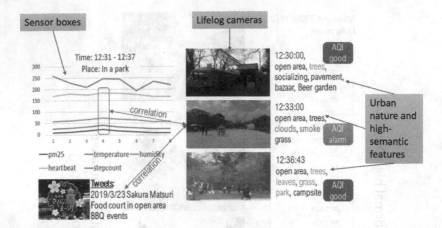

Fig. 3. Example for hypothesis 3: the correlation between image's content and surrounding environment sensing data (Data from SEPHLA dataset [7])

enhances the ability to detect an abnormality stated in hypothesis 2 and utilizes multi-levels of visual features (from raw to high-semantic levels) in hypothesis 3.

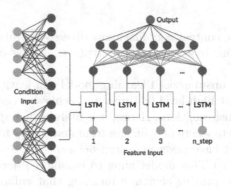

Fig. 4. The conditional LSTM NN model architecture

3   Experimental Results

3.1   Datasets and Metrics

In this section, we introduce datasets and metrics we use for evaluating our proposed solutions. We use three different datasets collected from three different countries (Vietnam, Japan, and India). All these datasets are published and easy to gather. Part of these datasets is denoted in Table 1. We only list out those data items we use for evaluating our method.

Table 1. Datasets

Name	Public data	Personal data	#Images
Tokyo [12]	PM2.5, NO2, O3, GPS, time, Meteorology	PM2.5, O3, NO2, image GPS, time	119,928
MNR-HCM [13]	PM2.5, GPS, Meteorology Time	PM2.5, O3, NO2, image GPS, time	6,566
Vision-Air [14]	PM2.5, time Meteorology, GPS	GPS, time Image, PM2.5	6,067

The **VisionAir** project publishes its dataset on its website [14]. The data has three parts (1) images continuously captured at the same place every 5 min with both HDR and non-HDR formats. There are several spots for image capturing (10 at the moment), (2) PM2.5 data are collected from less-than-one-km stations nearby; otherwise, the personal device, namely AirVeda, is utilized measuring the PM2.5. These PM2.5 values are assigned to an associated image as a label, (3) weather crawled from government sources.

The **MNR-HCM** [13] dataset has two parts: (1) public data included PM2.5, and meteorological data are crawled from open data websites, (2) personal data are collected using sensor boxes and smartphones. Volunteers carried these boxes and patrol around the fixed route every day.

The **Tokyo** [12] dataset was established with the same procedure as the MNR-HCM dataset. It also has two parts: (1) public data are crawled from the Japanese government open dataset, and (2) personal data are collected using sensor boxes and GoPro camera.

The most significant difference between VisionAir and the two rest datasets is that locations of images of VisionAir are fixed while others patrol around a fixed route. It means that with MNR-HCM and Tokyo datasets, it is seldom to find two images sharing the same GPS.

We use metrics *Precision* and *MAE (Mean Absolute Error)* to evaluate the accuracy of Image Retrieval and Prediction Model approaches.

3.2 Image Retrieval Approach

For each dataset, we randomly select 2/3 dataset to build the FAISS index and 1/3 for querying. It should be noted that each vector has its format as <features, label> where features are extracted by using a predefined pre-trained model, and labels are PM2.5 values from a personal dataset (i.e., PM2.5 measured by a personal device). Every querying vector is initialized with its label set as "unknown." After the query finishes, the related ground-truth is compared to a predicted value. Here, we do not use the absolute value of PM2.5 but use the level of PM2.5, described in Fig. 5, instead. Table 2 denotes the results of Image Retrieval approach.

PM$_{2.5}$	Air Quality Index	PM$_{2.5}$ Health Effects	Precautionary Actions
0 to 12.0	Good 0 to 50	Little to no risk.	None.
12.1 to 35.4	Moderate 51 to 100	Unusually sensitive individuals may experience respiratory symptoms.	Unusually sensitive people should consider reducing prolonged or heavy exertion.
35.5 to 55.4	Unhealthy for Sensitive Groups 101 to 150	Increasing likelihood of respiratory symptoms in sensitive individuals, aggravation of heart or lung disease and premature mortality in persons with cardiopulmonary disease and the elderly.	People with respiratory or heart disease, the elderly and children should limit prolonged exertion.
55.5 to 150.4	Unhealthy 151 to 200	Increased aggravation of heart or lung disease and premature mortality in persons with cardiopulmonary disease and the elderly; increased respiratory effects in general population.	People with respiratory or heart disease, the elderly and children should avoid prolonged exertion; everyone else should limit prolonged exertion.
150.5 to 250.4	Very Unhealthy 201 to 300	Significant aggravation of heart or lung disease and premature mortality in persons with cardiopulmonary disease and the elderly; significant increase in respiratory effects in general population.	People with respiratory or heart disease, the elderly and children should avoid any outdoor activity; everyone else should avoid prolonged exertion.

Fig. 5. PM2.5 levels (source: www.epa.gov)

Table 2 shows that the constraints of time and location brought the best accuracy regardless of dataset or feature types. The time constraint gives the second rank of accuracy while the location constraint posses the third rank. The worst is to have no constraints at all.

These results can confirm the righteousness of hypothesis 1 for the role of historical data taken in the same place at the same period. Nevertheless, using only time constraints is acceptable when we want to use historical images of one place as the reference to predict AQI at a new place (i.e., never collect data before). In this case, the 'same location' terminology can be replaced by the 'same surrounding environment' concept from hypothesis 3. Using only location constraint gives better results of no constraint since it holds hypothesis 3 (same surrounding environment). Hypothesis 2 (i.e., anomaly) can be applied to acknowledge why using only location constraint gives worse results than a time constraint: the same location, but at different periods it could be different human activities or natural events that change AQI value.

For feature types, the FasterRCNN gives the best result; even when combined with others, it still dominates. It should be noted that FasterRCNN is designed

Table 2. Image retrieval approach evaluation (metrics: accuracy)

Constraints	FixRes	Faster RCNN	SwAV	FixRes, SwAV	FixRes, Faster-RCNN	SwAV, Faster-RCNN	All
Tokyo Dataset [12]							
Time and location	0,778	**0,830**	0,795	0,778	0,830	0,818	0,830
Time (same period)	0,795	0,824	0,727	0,795	0,824	0,818	0,824
Location (same route)	0,625	0,756	0,756	0,625	0,756	0,75	0,756
No restriction	0,557	0,727	0,670	0,557	0,727	0,722	0,727
MNR-HCM Dataset [13]							
Time and location	0,835	**0,860**	0,848	0,835	0,860	0,860	0,860
Time (same period)	0,700	0,775	0,745	0.7	0,775	0,775	0,775
Location (same route)	0,658	0,725	0,745	0,658	0,725	0,725	0,725
No restriction	0,660	0,738	0,770	0,668	0,738	0,738	0,738
VisionAir India Dataset [14]							
Time and location	0,770	**0,840**	0,825	0,770	0,840	0,840	0,840
Time (same period)	0,768	0,815	0,780	0,768	0,815	0,808	0,815
Location (same place)	0,662	0,763	0,762	0,662	0,763	0,763	0,763
No restriction	0,610	0,726	0,680	0,617	0,726	0,733	0,726

to detect objects, so it conveys high-semantic features. Hence, it confirms the reasonability of hypothesis 3.

3.3 Prediction Model Approach

For each dataset, we also randomly select 2/3 datasets for training the model and 1/3 for testing. Table 3 shows the results of the Conditional-LSTM-NN model running on the Tokyo dataset with different constraints. In this case, we use the absolute value of PM2.5 with MAE function to evaluate accuracy. The column MAE of the Table expresses the average of MAEs of the testing set.

In this evaluation, we use a different combination of input data to see whether we can use only images or images plus open PM2.5 data (i.e., PM2.5 measured by stations nearby) to predict PM2.5 at the place the images are captured.

Table 3 shows that using only open PM2.5 data to predict the local PM2.5 gives the worst results regardless of all constraints. It could be explained by the influence of the distance d(station, local) between the nearest air pollution station and the place the image is captured. The density of stations could play an important role when using open PM2.5 data to predict local PM2.5 data. The more stations installed in the same area, the more precise the predicted PM2.5 is.

We can recognize that using open PM2.5, images, and weather data also does not produce a good result. The instability of weather data compared to other factors could reason for not good results.

Table 3. Conditional-LSTM-NN model - 7 d look back - Input: public sensing data + personal images - ground truth: sensor box (PM2.5) - Predict PM2.5

Input	Constraints	MAE		
		Tokyo [12]	MNR-HCM [13]	VisionAir [14]
Image	Both	4.089	21.28	7.19
PM25, image, weather		16.928	12.06	12.42
PM25, Image		**4.064**	**9.23**	9.55
PM25		21.741	29.34	24.80
Image	Time	4.111	19.51	9.84
PM25, image, weather		17.664	14.21	19.39
PM25, image		4.107	10.81	7.11
PM25		22.485	28.90	28.42
Image	Location	4.117	19.48	13.73
PM25, image, weather		16.916	10.34	11.50
PM25, Image		4.076	9.48	**5.82**
PM25		21.771	20.00	21.89
Image	None	4.120	18.53	10.86
PM25, image, weather		17.136	10.06	14.22
PM25, image		19.573	10.24	18.17
PM25		21.892	27.35	24.33

The results of using only images to predict local PM2.5 give a satisfactory conclusion for our hypotheses 1 and 3. Hence, we could say that the historical images of the same place (e.g., route, location) and high-semantic features extracted from these images could predict PM2.5.

Finally, the combination of images and open PM2.5 values gets the best results. It could be reasoned by hypothesis 2, the anomaly. While images can help predict the most common PM2.5 of a particular place and period, the open PM2.5 value can support adjusting the predicted PM2.5 if there is any abnormal in that area. Theoretically, the sudden change of PM2.5 value (up high or goes down) could be measured by the nearest station or by abnormal features in images (e.g., sudden-high number of vehicles, smokes).

Time and location constraints on different datasets can give new insights into each place's air pollution situation. The VisionAir dataset gives the best results on only location constraints. This result can be understood since the VisionAir collects images using a tripod camera with a regular shuttle. So images taken from the same place can logically share the same AQI level. Nevertheless, the constraint of location and time gives worse results comparing the constraint of location only. This observation can lead to the assumption that there must be an anomaly in the air pollution situation. For example, the images captured on the morning of day one and day two could reflect different AQI level (i.e., location and time constraint), but the images captured on the morning of day one and evening of day two (or day one) can share the same AQI level (only location constraint). We will investigate more of this discovery to see whether we can extract the pattern or anomaly of air pollution.

3.4 Hypotheses' Righteousness

Images of three datasets contain differently exciting information. VisionAir images focus on capturing 'sky' instances. The hypothesis is that the higher the AQI level, the more fog the sky is (i.e., due to smoke). Tokyo images focus on snapshotting 'urban nature' instances. The hypothesis here is that a particular urban nature type could relate to a certain AQI level (e.g., AQI level is low at a green zone such as parks). The MNR-HCM images record 'on-street' instances. The hypothesis here is that there is a relation between traffic, construction site, and AQI level. Although three datasets focus on the different semantic meanings of images, our two approaches still get a good result. That confirms our hypotheses' righteousness that can cover different cognition of people who define the procedure of collecting image data. This confirmation also supports people in creating an explainable (deep-learning) model for predicting AQI.

4   Conclusions

We introduced hypotheses by which the Image-2-AQI solution using only images (captured by personal devices) and/or open AQI dataset can predict a local AQI value/level. The research also contributes to answering the question "Can the personal air quality be predicted by using other data that is easy to obtain?" raised in MediaEval2020 Insights for wellbeing task. Moreover, the research gives a reasonable explanation for the success of existing methods that have tried to predict local AQI by using images. Different input data factors are evaluated thoroughly towards having a lighthouse for creating a new dataset for the same research problem. In the future, we will investigate more on building a new prediction model, features extractor, and taking into account the annotation of people that could give more cues for improving the accuracy of Image-2-AQI.

Acknowledgement. We appreciate the contribution of our students Anh-Vu Mai-Nguyen and Trong-Dat Phan for running experimental results.

References

1. Li, Y., et al.: A psycho-physical measurement on subjective well-being and air pollution. Nat. Commun. **10**(1), 1–8 (2019)
2. Xu, Y., Liu, H., Duan, Z.: A novel hybrid model for multi-step daily AQI forecasting driven by air pollution big data. Air Qual. Atmos. Health **13**(2), 197–207 (2020)

3. Yang, Y., Hu, Z., Bian, K., Song, L.: ImgSensingNet: UAV vision guided aerial-ground air quality sensing system. In: IEEE INFOCOM 2019 - IEEE Conference on Computer Communications, pp. 1207–1215 (2019)
4. Zhang, Q., Fu, F., Tian, R.: A deep learning and image-based model for air quality estimation. Sci. Total Environ. **724**(1), 138178 (2020)
5. Dong, W., Gong, J., Liang, J., Sun, J., Zhang, G.: Analyzing the influence of urban street greening and street buildings on summertime air pollution based on street view image data. IS- PRS Int. J. Geo-Inf. **9**(9), 500 (2020)
6. Vo, P., Phan, T., Dao, M., Zettsu, K.: Association model between visual feature and AQI rank using Lifelog Data. In: IEEE International Conference on Big Data (Big Data), pp. 4197–4200 (2019)
7. Sato, T., Dao, M.-S., Kuribayashi, K., Zettsu, K.: SEPHLA: challenges and opportunities within environment - personal health archives. In: Kompatsiaris, I., Huet, B., Mezaris, V., Gurrin, C., Cheng, W.-H., Vrochidis, S. (eds.) MMM 2019. LNCS, vol. 11295, pp. 325–337. Springer, Cham (2019). https://doi.org/10.1007/978-3-030-05710-7_27
8. Johnson, J., Douze, M., Jegou, H.: Billion-scale similarity search with GPUs. arXiv preprint arXiv:1702.08734 (2017)
9. Touvron, H., Vedaldi, A., Douze, M., Jegou, H.: Fixing the train-test resolution discrepancy. In: Advances in Neural Information Processing Systems (NeurIPS) (2019)
10. Caron, M., Misra, I., Mairal, J., Goyal, P., Bojanowski, P., Joulin, A.: Unsupervised learning of visual features by contrasting cluster assignments. arXiv preprint arXiv:2006.09882 (2020)
11. Yang, J., Lu, J., Batra, D., Parikh, D.: A faster Pytorch implementation of faster R-CNN. https://github.com/jwyang/faster-rcnn.pytorch (2017)
12. Zhao, P., Dao, M.-S., Nguyen, N.-T., Nguyen, T.-B., Dang-Nguyen, D.-T., Gurrin, C.: Overview of MediaEval 2020: insights for wellbeing task - multimodal personal health Lifelog Data analysis. In: MediaEval Benchmarking Initiative for Multimedia Evaluation, CEUR Workshop Proceedings, December 2020
13. Nguyen-Tai, T.-L., Nguyen, D.-H., Nguyen, M.-T., Dang, T.-H., Dao, M.-S.: MNR-HCM Data: a personal Lifelog and surrounding environment dataset in Ho-Chi-Minh City, Vietnam. In: ICMR-ICDAR 2020: Proceedings on Intelligent Cross-Data Analysis and Retrieval Workshop, pp. 21–26, June 2020
14. VisionAir (2020). https://vision-air.github.io/

Advances in Sports Video Summarization – A Review Based on Cricket Videos

Vani Vasudevan ⓘ and Mohan Sellappa Gounder[(✉)] ⓘ

STEMP, University of the South Pacific, Suva, Fiji
{vani.vasudevan,mohan.gounder}@usp.ac.fj

Abstract. Watching sports videos over streaming sites and television network is one of the most entertaining ways to engage with sports activities. Sports videos like cricket has been viewed by larger audiences than viewing in person. The pandemic since 2020 has changed the world of sports viewing to a larger extent. Some of the sports events are even streamed live through YouTube. The most interesting part of any sports videos is watching the highlights or events of great interest. This is because of the lack of time to watch the entire length of the game. Automatic video summarization is the solution to this. Some of the day long sports like cricket needs the summarization to be very precise and bring the content within few minutes to the audience. There are several attempts in the literature to automatically summarize the sports videos, particularly the game of cricket. In this paper, an attempt has been made to review some of the latest developments in creating the video summary of cricket sports. A brief review of existing methods of video summarization that addresses many sports including soccer, cricket, tennis, and basketball are reviewed at the beginning. Later, the methods that are developed based on latest machine learning and high-performance algorithms are discussed in detail. Towards the end of this paper, a comparison of these methods is presented. The goal is to lead the prospective researchers in the direction where the methods have open avenues and scope to strengthen.

Keywords: Video summarization · Machine learning · Deep learning · Sports video classification · Cricket video summarization · Sports video highlights

1 Introduction

Sports video summarization is one of the interesting fields of research as it tends to generate a highlight of the broadcast video. Usually, the sports broadcast videos are longer, and the audiences may not have enough time to watch the entire duration of the game. Some of the sports like cricket are even longer for the entire day or series of days. Hence, creating a summarization that contains only events of interest is an intense human task. There are several approaches in the literature that attempts to automate the process of creating such highlight or summarization video. Some of them are specific to certain games like cricket, soccer, tennis, etc. In this paper, an attempt has been made to review some of the latest developments in the sports video summarization, particularly the game of cricket. The reason behind choosing the cricket sport is that,

© Springer Nature Switzerland AG 2021
H. Fujita et al. (Eds.): IEA/AIE 2021, LNAI 12799, pp. 347–359, 2021.
https://doi.org/10.1007/978-3-030-79463-7_29

it is the only game that is played for several days. Test cricket matches are played for 5 full days. The most common format of cricket is One-day International (ODI). As the name reveals, the match is played for the whole day. Creating the summarization automatically from such longer videos will lead to research challenges and scope for further research. With the advances in computer architecture like GPU, TPU computing and the development of deep learning algorithms, it is much more interesting to solve the challenges in automating the video summarization process.

2   Relevant Works on Sports Video Summarization

The focus of this survey is to identify the approaches published in recent years on video summarization of cricket videos. Some of the highly cited papers are considered for a brief review. Rest of them are reviewed critically. One of the earliest works is found to be authored by Tang et al. [1]. They propose a novel method for detecting highlights in sports video. It is based on an unsupervised event detection framework which further leads to video clip representation comprising of unigram and bigram statistics of the events detected. It is stated that they trained with 7000 clips and 7000 test clips and achieved a low error rate of 12.1%. The method has been extensively tested on cricket videos. Kolekar et al. [2] presented an approach based on extracted events and semantic concepts. With about 90 min of recorded videos of a ODI, they came out with a hierarchical feature-based classifier extracted concepts that are ranked as various moments. In [3] and [4], the events and audio energy are used to generate highlights. In [4], a Bayesian Network based highlights are generated for soccer videos. The scenes are classified into events such as replay, player, referee, spectator, and players gathering. A method proposed by Namuduri [5], segments the video into shots, then extracting low level features from key frames leads to views or states. The states and their transitions are represented by Hidden Markov Model (HMM). This work is one of the major references in the approach proposed by Kumar et al. [6].

An automatic video analysis and summarization of soccer video has been proposed by Ekin et al. [7], using cinematic and object-based features. They applied dominant color region detection, robust shot boundary detection and shot classification, goal detection, referee detection and penalty-box detection. The summary is generated as three classes: all slow-motion, all goals and slow motion according to object-based features. Sports video summarization in general, as discussed by several authors [8–14], deals with common approaches that could be applied on all types of sports. Majority of the works [8–14] addresses the sports of soccer or football or basketball. Some of the works like [15] intended to generate video datasets for cricket stroke extraction. The work proposed by Kumar R et al. [16], classifies the outcome of cricket videos to create automatic commentary. Each ball delivered is classified into an outcome such as run, dot, boundary, and wicket. Other than the summarization and classification, few works are proposed for classifying cricket shot [17], cricket stroke extraction [18] [19], classify bowlers based on their actions [20], detection of no balls in cricket [21], and Crowd event classification [22].

In this paper, a detailed review of some of the key research works [6, 23–27] that are proposed to address the video summarization of cricket sports videos are discussed. Most of the methods discussed here use the machine learning and deep learning approaches to automate the task of highlight generation. We have also tried to find how these methods have used the latest computing advances in terms of GPU computing. At the end of detailed review, we have tabulated a comparison of these methods in terms of some common characteristics like approaches, use of GPU computing, etc.

2.1 Scene Classification for Sports Video Summarization [23]

The authors of this paper have proposed a technique to classify the scenes in the sports video. For the case study, the authors have taken Cricket sports video and classified the scenes into five categories: batting, bowling, boundary, crowd, and close-up. The pre-trained AlexNet Convolutional Neural Network (CNN) has been deployed to classify the scenes into five categories. The authors have claimed an accuracy of 99.26%. It is compared with other deep-learning models like Inception V3, VGGNet16, VGGNet19, ResNet50 and AlexNet. The framework of the proposed model is depicted in Fig. 1.

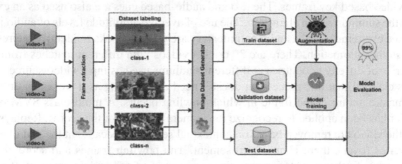

Fig. 1. Proposed model for Scene Classification (Source: Rafiq et al. [23])

For performance evaluation, the authors claimed that they compared the model with other deep CNN as in Table 1 which outperforms other state-of-the-art methods.

Table 1. Classification F1-score comparison with state-of-the-art models [23].

Model names	Epoch	Batting	Boundary	Bowling	Close-ups	Crowd	Mean
Minhas et al	1000	88%	96%	90%	96%	88%	92%
Inception v3	50	96%	99%	988%	100%	97%	98%
ResNet50	50	94%	100%	97%	100%	99%	98%
VGGNET16	50	90%	98%	95%	98%	96%	955
VGGNET19	50	91%	98%	96%	98%	95%	96%
SVM	NA	84%	90%	95%	92%	88%	90%
Proposed method [23]	50	96%	100%	98%	100%	100%	99%

The authors have claimed that the same approach can be used for other fields like medical imaging, agriculture, biological organism, and self-driving vehicles classification. The method has not addressed: Duration and efforts needed for data augmentation and preprocessing, real time scene classification, testing samples from other video sources, total length of the input video vs the length of output video summary produced out of this approach and performance evaluation of the model under non-GPU based computing. Nevertheless, the proposed method is a strong reference and benchmark for researchers looking forward to pursuing the video summarization of cricket sports.

2.2 Automatic Summarization of Broadcast Cricket Videos [6]

The paper proposes a novel technique for summarizing the cricket videos based on contextual semantics. The approach is based on each delivery that is categorized into events of interesting or non-interesting segments. The events are boundaries and wickets. Key frames are extracted using finite state automation-based modeling of temporal segments. Further, a hierarchical summary has been produced to provide access to different parts of the video based key frames. The text and audio-based cues are also used as an extension to the summarization algorithm. The use of average amplitude levels of audio input and voice excitement in the audio commentary are used as hooks to identify interesting events in the automation. There are 30 cricket videos with different matches from various series of different countries at different stadiums used as input video sources. The authors claimed that this processing doesn't need any training as it works on utilizing the semantic nature of the frame in which bowling occurs. A multi-class SVM based classifier has been applied to recognize the numerals to extract the scores. Replays and ads in the video are removed based on contextual semantic, because at the end of every 6 deliveries (over), there is an advertisement. The bowling frames and score change detections are further used to improve the accuracy of ad and replays removal. Replays are also identified based on the transitions, like strip-wipe transition and motion-wipe. It is mentioned that the important frames are extracted based on an event that has a specific state transition. State transition diagram is given in Fig. 2.

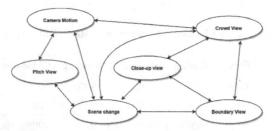

Fig. 2. State Transition Diagram to model the dynamics of video segment and extract important key frames and example transitions (Source: Kumar et al. [6])

The transition is to find pitch, camera motion, scene change, crowd view and boundary view. To sum up, this paper claims to produce summarization of cricket videos based on contextual semantics. The strength of the paper is that it covers most of the classes that contributes to the summarization of the cricket videos. The authors have claimed the accuracy results based on the input samples from three matches. The paper does not compare the proposed results with any bench-marking results or datasets. The paper neither tried on experimenting with any real time videos nor attempted to experiment on GPU based architecture. Some of the key ideas like types of transition may fail in new cricket series if the broadcasting companies change the transition methods.

2.3   Content-Aware Summarization – An Audio-Visual Feature Extraction Approach [24]

In this paper, a method to generate sports highlights by extracting features from audio and visual contents using SIFT features has been proposed. A deep neural network-based approach is applied to extract the information from text regions. These are then converted to key frame representation to generate highlights based on user preferences. The audio features are considered as an indicator of an exciting event and the visual features are used to detect the type of exciting moments. The overall architecture of the method is given in Fig. 3.

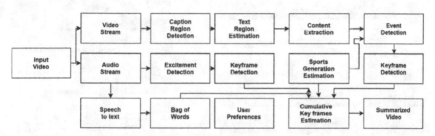

Fig. 3. Architecture of Content-aware summarization (Source: Khan et al. [24])

The authors have experimented using self-created and annotated dataset as they claim that there are no standard datasets available. For the training process, it is stated that the method does not require any training, rather it learns features from sports video automatically. The dataset contains 104 videos of 12 categories of sports including cricket and football. They also have compared briefly with other datasets. It is claimed that a non-machine learning approach, namely, Maximally Stable External Regions (MSER) is applied to find the text regions in scorebox after enhancing the text region to remove the non-text features like texture. Further, deep CNN proposed to recognize the characters and numbers in the scorebox text region. The convolution network is trained from the dataset that contains 15,000 samples from 52 videos. The audio feature is one of the evidences of exciting events in the sports videos. The key frames are extracted whenever the high energy feature is obtained because of crowd cheering. A butter-worth band pass filter is applied to only allow human speech frequencies that falls approximately between 300–3.4 kHz. Change in camera viewpoint is a challenge in identifying start and end frames. A speech to text using google API has been added as an additional level of confidence in detecting key-events. To conclude, the method claims to be a comprehensive approach for most common sports video summarization. However, the source of samples used for cricket sports is not clearly indicated. A detailed analysis of the outcome of each of the sports videos and the challenges in them could have revealed more insights into the work. The performance evaluation is not by comparing the state-of-the art methods. Overall, the paper has opened lot of avenues for sports video highlight generation. Applying this to the cricket sports and resolving the challenges specific to the game would lead to further research work.

2.4   A Hybrid Approach for Summarization of Cricket Videos [25]

In this paper, an attempt is made to combine both learning and non-learning-based methods to generate summarization of cricket video. Figure 4 shows the block diagram of this approach. The research work has considered four events from the cricket video to form event detection framework which include: four (boundary), six, wicket and replays. Furthermore, this research work had overcome the drawbacks of earlier approaches such as: dependency on score-caption design, camera variations, replay speed, logo design size and placement.

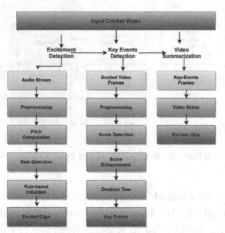

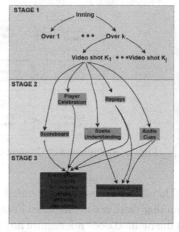

Fig. 4. Hybrid Approach for Cricket video summarization (Source: Javed et al. [25])

Fig. 5. Stages of automatic cricket highlight generation from event and excitement highlights (Source: Shukla et al. [26])

Excitement detection framework is considered for extracting the clips. Here, rule-based induction technique is deployed to detect excited audio clips. Then, these excited clips are given as an input to key-events detection framework where the score caption region is processed. An OCR algorithm is used to recognize the characters. A decision tree classifier [32, 34] is used for classifying key-events from score caption. Finally, a video skim against each detected key event is generated and the video is summarized by obtaining the required length from the user. The performance of this hybrid approach is measured using four qualitative measures namely Precision, Recall, Accuracy and Error. Authors have claimed that on an average, 91.87% precision, 89.85% Recall, 95.01% Accuracy and 4.99% Error for the detection of four events in the chosen 20 cricket videos. In addition to these experimental results, authors have compared the performance achieved with three other cricket video summarization systems namely Kolekar et al. [2], Namuduri et al. [5] and Tang et al. [1]. To sum up, this paper claims to have adapted a unique hybridized approach for cricket video summarization. The approach finds correlation between audio and video frames. Simple and well proven, machine learning techniques such as rule-based induction and decision tree are used to generate video skims and then video summary from the long duration cricket videos. However, authors have not clearly discussed the hybridization of excitement and event detection frameworks to generate video skims. Use of GPU and other high-performance computing is not experimented on the proposed approach.

2.5 Automatic Cricket Highlight Generation Using Event-Driven/Excitement-Based Features [26]

This paper attempts to automatically generate cricket highlights from long duration video based on event and excitement features. Three stages are considered to generate cricket highlights/summary as in Fig. 5. Stage 1: extract important video shots. Stage 2: detect in parallel, player celebration, scoreboard, scene understanding, replays and audio queues. Stage 3: Generate event-driven and excitement driven highlights. In Stage 1, the cricket video is divided into video shots. In Stage 2, replay detection is given importance as it provides vital cues for important events. Convolutional Neural Network (CNN) with Support Vector Machine (SVM) framework is used to classify the video shot as an on-going event or replay/advertisement. The framework relies on 4096 representations extracted from Fully Connected 7 layer of the AlexNet which are fed to a trained Linear SVM. The SVM is trained on representation of 2000 images of both on-going and as a replay/advertisement classes. Then, to detect the score board, a two-step methodology was employed to identify runs and wickets in the scoreboard. The positions of the digits are located using text location in complex images proposed by A.Gonzalez et al. [28]. Then, OCR classifier is trained to recognize limited set of characters including hyphen used to distinguish runs from wickets. The model is trained on 1100 images with 100 images for each class (0–9 & hyphen). Then, playfield scenes detections were achieved by using CNN and SVM methodology which distinguish key frames/starting frame from other frames. A binary linear SVM is trained on 500 images of each class to classify a given video frame as a starting frame or not. Then, by utilizing loudness as an audio feature, important events like milestones and boundaries are detected. Then, the player celebration is another important cue to detect the milestone event. The model is trained on a CNN + bilinear SVM framework with two classes (positive and negative) of gray scale images that relied on representations extracted by fc7 layer of the AlexNet model. Positive class images comprise of batsman who has completed the milestone whereas negative class images comprise of other images from the cricket match. In Stage 3, event-driven highlights are generated by considering the top 4 events based on the cricket fans survey result. The top 4 events are milestones, wickets, fours and sixes. Score board detection technique was used to detect the boundary, six and wickets. On the other hand, excitement-based highlights are generated by considering replays and audio intensity. If there are more than three replays associated with the event, then it is regarded as a secondary event related to excitement. For experimentation, a dataset over 15 h of video footage of T-20 matches of 2010's Indian Premier League (IPL) has been considered. The chosen dataset is preprocessed over by over to ensure an over comprised of six legal deliveries only. The dataset is annotated manually and all the important events, such as boundaries, sixes, wickets and milestones are associated to corresponding video shots. Intersection of Union (IOU) metric is used to capture the overlap between official and generated highlights for given innings. Average IOU of 73.1% is achieved for all the innings considered in the dataset. Another metric called Mean Average Precision (MAP) is used to analyze the performance of the model based on the 4 major events considered in this paper. MAP of greater than 85% is achieved for boundaries, sixes and wickets, while MAP of 72.31% for milestones.

To conclude, this paper has adapted a staged approach to generate event and excitement highlights from important video shots. In every stage, different deep learning frameworks are used. However, the approach used for combining excitement and event highlights are not discussed. Certainly, this paper can be considered as one of the benchmark papers to further investigate and develop cricket video summarization system using various enriched deep learning frameworks.

2.6 Shot Classification of Field Sports Videos Using AlexNet Convolutional Neural Network (CNN) [27]

This paper proposes an effective shot classification method based on AlexNet CNN to achieve better accuracy in field sport video summarization. Figure 6 shows the block diagram for shot classification. The proposed method classifies the shots into 1. Medium, 2. Long, 3. Close-up, and 4. Out-of-the-field shot. Compared to other existing shot classification approaches, the model in this paper focuses not only on in-field segments but also out-of-the-field or crowd shots. This was due to the crowd shots that also contain few exciting segments.

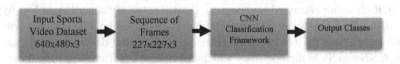

Fig. 6. Block diagram for shot classification

For performance evaluation, diverse dataset comprising of both soccer and cricket videos from YouTube were selected. The dataset includes 10 videos of 13 h from six major broadcasters. The dataset videos comprised of different shot types. 70% of frames were used for training and rest 30% for validation. Unfortunately, dataset which is provided as one of the references is not accessible currently. Also, during training, authors do mention that, the network takes four epochs. Each epoch has 500 iterations. A Stochastic approximation of gradient descent is used to perform training iterations on the dataset in four to five days to train on two GTX 580 GPUs. However, during the discussion, authors said that they have used CPU for training of sports videos and their system is not integrated with GPU. Therefore, it is a mere observation made during their experimentation about GPUs. It is given that training can be carried out in a faster pace with the help of CUDA enabled GPUs. Precision, Recall, F-1 score, Accuracy and Error Rate are the five objective measures considered to evaluate the performance of the shot classification model. The method achieves an average Precision of 94.8%, Recall of 96.24%, F1-score of 96.49% Accuracy of 94.07% and Error Rate of 5.93 on 10 sets of videos that were considered in the dataset. Also, the model's performance is compared with SVM, Extreme Learning Machine (ELM), K-Nearest Neighbors (KNN), and standard CNN with the same set of 10 videos. In addition to it, the model performance is compared against baseline state-of-art shot classification [9–11, 25] [29–31] approaches. In conclusion, authors have claimed that the proposed model outperforms all other considered models as well as state-of-art shot classification approaches proposed by others. Also, based on the obtained results, it is concluded that proposed method as a reliable approach for shot classification of the sport videos which is robust to camera variation, scene change, action speed and lighting conditions. The accomplished results and performance in this approach could be considered as a benchmark to assess the performance of the upcoming cricket video highlight systems as well as to increase its prediction accuracy as in [33].

3 Summary of Methods

From the detailed critical analysis of research works in Sect. 2, Table 2 compares those works under some features like the types of machine learning algorithms, GPU computing, the type of dataset, and performance evaluation metrics used to evaluate the systems. In addition to it, the scope for further research is also highlighted. Though it is unfair to compare all the methods under some common criteria, the intention is to find the open avenues where further research on enhancing the methods is possible.

The works that applies machine learning and advanced deep learning approaches like [6, 23–27] are much capable to cater to the needs of processing high volume of videos and classes. It is also interesting to note that only one method [23] applied GPU computing on the video summarization and classification. Looking at the dataset, there is no standardized or benchmarked dataset is available for the research community, particularly for cricket video summarization. Creating authorized dataset and benchmarking would add a significant contribution. Among the methods reviewed, the maximum frame size processed is 640 × 480 [23, 25–27]. Though, the algorithms will be processing the frames and classifying them correctly, the results produced may not be of high resolution. A real time processing on streaming videos would certainly need to process higher resolution frames. The metrics of evaluation is interesting to observe as the way to find the accuracy of proposed methods. Any researchers who would like to enhance the existing methods and propose some novel ideas can compare with these results.

Finally, the suggested improvements of each of the methods is given as a scope for further research. It is clearer that improving the methods listed using high performance computing architectures would result in engaging research work.

Table 2. Comparison of the reviewed methods

Reviewed systems	Approaches/methods	Dataset/sample details	Performance metrics	Scope for further research
[6]	K-Means clustering Multi-class SVM Classifier Velocity Hough Transformation	Dataset not specified Videos: 30	Accuracy	Applying more ML or DL approaches for event detection and audio highlights Use of GPUs to improve performance
[23]	Transfer Learning AlexNet CNN Imagenet with 100 classes Adam optimizer Data Augmentation	Youtube videos (2014 series) 6800 frames extracted	Accuracy, Error, Precision, recall, F1-Score	Advanced GPU computing, Different transfer learning approaches
[24]	Deep CNN (convNet) Binary Map hole filling	Self-created and annotated 11 videos (42 h duration)	Precision, Recall, F1-Score	Evaluate the method on standard dataset Apply GPU to test the performance
[25]	Rule based induction and Decision Tree classifier	20 videos (6 h duration)	Accuracy, Error, Precision, Recall	Evaluate the method on standard data set and apply GPU to test the performance
[26]	AlexNet CNN + Linear/bilinear SVM OCR	2020 IPL match videos Manually processed and annotated(15 h)	IOU, MAP	Generate automatic caption for sports videos, Generate highlight clips of individual players
[27]	AlexNet CNN, No pretrained data, Adam optimizer	Cricket and Soccer Videos from YouTube (13 h)	Accuracy, Error, Precision, Recall, F1-score	Evaluate the method on CUDA GPU GTX 580. Apply the method to more diverse and larger dataset

4 Conclusion

The purpose of this paper is to review and compare the latest developments on video summarization of sports video. The paper summarized some of the key methods in detail by analyzing the strength and scope for further research. It is believed that the challenges posed by each of the papers can potentially lead to open problems that can be solved by the researchers of this domain. Though, most of the papers, focused on resolving the problem of highlight generation, each of the method has its own merits and demerits. Another major investigation on these methods is to find the exploitation of latest machine learning methods and high-performance computing. Very few methods have deployed the GPU computing to resolve the methods. This throws avenues for the prospective researchers to experiment the potential of GPUs for processing such high volume of data like sports video. The results of such summarization can be instantly compared with highlights generated by broad casting channels at the end of every match. Going further, the results of cricket highlights should also include some key events and drama, not just the fours, sixes and wickets. Some of other elements like pre- and post-match ceremony, player's entry, injuries to players, etc. should also be captured. Eventually the machine learning based methods should learn to include audio smoothening, scene transition and smooth commentary cuts that will reduce human editors' work. It is believed that our review on the recent developments of sports video summarization will strongly help the ongoing research to strengthen the results and outcomes.

References

1. Tang, H., Kwatra, V., Sargin, M., Gargi, U.: Detecting highlights in sports videos: cricket as a test case. In: IEEE International Conference on Multimedia and Expo, Barcelona (2011)
2. Kolekar, M.H., Sengupta, S.: Event-importance based customized and automatic cricket highlight generation. In: IEEE International Conference on Multimedia and Expo, Toronto, Ont. (2006)
3. Kolekar, M.H., Sengupta, S.: Caption content analysis based automated cricket highlight generation. In: National Communications Conference (NCC), Mumbai (2008)
4. Kolekar, M.H., Sengupta, S.: Bayesian network-based customized highlight generation for broadcast soccer videos. IEEE Trans. Broadcast. 2, 195–209 (2015)
5. Namuduri, K.: Automatic extraction of highlights from a cricket video using MPEG-7 descriptors. In: First International Communication Systems and Networks and Workshops, Bangalore (2009)
6. Kumar, Y., Gupta, S., Kiran, B., Ramakrishnan, K., Bhattacharyya, C.: Automatic summarization of broadcast cricket videos. In: IEEE 15th International Symposium on Consumer Electronics (ISCE), Singapore (2011)
7. Ekin, A., Tekalp, A., Mehrotra, R.: Automatic soccer video analysis and summarization. IEEE Trans. Image Process. 12(7), 796–807 (2003)
8. Shih, H.: A survey of content-aware video analysis for sports. IEEE Trans. Circuits Syst. Video Technol. 28(5), 1212–1231 (2018)
9. Tavassolipour, M., Karimian, M., Kasaei, S.: Event detection and summarization in soccer videos using Bayesian network and copula. IEEE Trans. Circuits Syst. Video Technol. 24, 291–304 (2014)

10. Bagheri-Khaligh, A., Raziperchikolaei, R., Moghaddam, M.: A new method for shot classi-fication in soccer sports video based on SVM classifier. In: Proceedings of the 2012 IEEE Southwest Symposium on Image Analysis and Interpretation (SSIAI), Santa Fe, NM (2012)
11. Kapela, R., McGuinness, K., O'Connor, N.E.: Real-time field sports scene classification using colour and frequency space decompositions. J. Real-Time Image Process. , 1–13 (2014). https://doi.org/10.1007/s11554-014-0437-7
12. Fani, M., Yazdi, M., Clausi, D., Wong, A.: Soccer video structure analysis by parallel feature fusion network and hidden-to-observable transferring markov model. IEEE Access 5, 27322–27336 (2017)
13. Tien, M.-C., Chen, H.-T., Chen, Y.-W., Hsiao, M.-H., Lee, S.-Y.: Shot classification of bas-ketball videos and its application in shooting position extraction. In: Proceedings of the IEEE International Conference on Acoustics, Speech and Signal Processing (ICASSP 2007), Honolulu, HI, USA (2007)
14. Raventos, A., Quijada, R., Torres, L., Tarrés, F.: Automatic summarization of soccer highlights using audio-visual descriptors. Springer Plus (2015)
15. Gupta, A., Muthaiah, S.: Cricket stroke extraction: Towards creation of a large-scale cricket actions dataset arXiv:1901.03107 [cs.CV] (2019)
16. Kumar, R., Santhadevi, D., Janet, B.: Outcome classification in cricket using deep learning. In: IEEE International Conference on Cloud Computing in Emerging Markets CCEM, Bengaluru (2019)
17. Foysal, M.F., Islam, M., Karim, A., Neehal, N.: Shot-net: a convolutional neural network for classifying different cricket shots. In: Santosh, K., Hegadi, R. (eds.) Recent Trends in Image Processing and Pattern Recognition, Springer Singapore (2018). https://doi.org/10.1007/978-981-13-9181-1_10
18. Gupta, A.: Cricket stroke extraction: towards creation of a large-scale cricket. CoRR, vol. abs/1901.03107 (2019)
19. Gupta, A., Muthiah, S.: Viewpoint constrained and unconstrained Cricket stroke localization from untrimmed videos. Image Vis. Comput. 100 (2020)
20. Islam, M., Hassan, T., Khan, S.: A CNN-based approach to classify cricket bowlers based on their bowling actions, Dhaka, Bangladesh (2019)
21. Harun-Ur-Rashid, M., Khatun, S., Trisha, Z., Neehal, N., Hasan, M.: Crick-net: A Convolu-tional Neural Network based Classification Approach for Detecting Waist High No Balls in Cricket (2018)
22. Jothi Shri, S., Jothilakshmi, S.: Crowd video event classification using convolutional neural network. Comput. Commun. 147, 35–39 (2019)
23. Rafiq, M., Rafiq, G., Agyeman, R., Choi, G., Jin, S.-I.: Scene classification for sports video summarization using transfer learning. Sensors (2020)
24. Khan, A., Shao, J., Ali, W., Tumrani, S.: Content-aware summarization of broadcast sports videos: an audio–visual feature extraction approach. Neural Process Letter, 1945–1968 (2020)
25. Javed, A., Bajwa, K., Malik, H., Irtaza, A., Mahmood, M.: A hybrid approach for sum-marization of cricket videos. In: IEEE International Conference on Consumer Electronics-Asia(ICCE-Asia), Seoul (2016)
26. Shukla, P., Sadana, H., Verma, D., Elmadjian, C., Ramana, B., Turk, M.: Automatic cricket highlight generation using event-driven and excitement-based features. In: IEEE/CVF Con-ference on Computer Vision and Pattern Recognition Workshops (CVPRW), Salt Lake City, UT (2018)
27. Minhas, R., Javed, A., Irtaza, A., Mahmood, M., Joo, Y.: Shot classification of field sports videos using AlexNet Convolutional Neural Network. Appl. Sci. 9(3) (2019)
28. Gonzalez, A., Bergasa, L., Yebes, J., Bronte, S.: Text location in complex images. In: IEEE ICPR (2012)

29. Sharma, R., Sankar, K., Jawahar, C.: Fine-grain annotation of cricket videos. In: Proceedings of the 3rd IAPR Asian Conference on Pattern Recognition (ACPR), Kuala Lumpur, Malaysia (2015)

30. Krizhevsky, A., Sutskever, I., Hinton, G.: Imagenet classification with deep convolutional neural networks. In: Advances in Neural Information Processing Systems;Neural Information Processing System Foundations Inc. 1097–1105 (2012)

31. Murala, S., Maheshwari, R., Balasubramanian, R.: Local tetra patterns: a new feature descriptor for. IEEE Trans. Image Process **21**, 2874–2886 (2012)

32. Vadhanam, B.R.J., Mohan, S., Ramalingam, V., Sugumaran, V.: Performance comparison of various decision tree algorithms for classification of advertisement and non-advertisement videos. Indian J. Sci. Technol. **9**(1), 48–65

33. Vani, V., Kumar, R.P., Mohan, S.: Profiling user interactions of 3D complex meshes for predictive streaming and rendering. In: Kumar, S. (ed.) Proceedings of the Fourth International Conference on Signal and Image Processing 2012 (ICSIP 2012). Lecture Notes in Electrical Engineering, vol 221, pp. 457–467, Springer, India (2012). https://doi.org/10.1007/978-81-322-0997-3_41

34. Rahman, A.A., Saleem, W., Iyer, V.V.: Driving behavior profiling and prediction in KSA using smart phone sensors and MLAs. In: IEEE Jordan International Joint Conference on Electrical Engineering and Information Technology (JEEIT), pp. 34–39 (2019)

Augmented Audio Data in Improving Speech Emotion Classification Tasks

Nusrat J. Shoumy[1]($\boxtimes$), Li-Minn Ang[2], D. M. Motiur Rahaman[1], Tanveer Zia[1], Kah Phooi Seng[3], and Sabira Khatun[4]

[1] School of Computing and Mathematics, Charles Sturt University, Bathurst, NSW, Australia
nshoumy@csu.edu.au
[2] School of Science and Engineering, University of the Sunshine Coast, Sunshine Coast, QLD, Australia
[3] School of Engineering and IT, University of New South Wales, Canberra, Australia
[4] Faculty of Electrical and Electronics Engineering, Universiti Malaysia Pahang, Pahang, Malaysia

Abstract. To achieve high performance and classification accuracy, classification of emotions from audio or speech signals requires large quantities of data. Big datasets, however, are not always readily accessible. A good solution to this issue is to increase the data and augment it to construct a larger dataset for the classifier's training. This paper proposes a unimodal approach that focuses on two main concepts: (1) augmenting speech signals to generate additional data samples; and (2) constructing classification models to identify emotion expressed through speech. In addition, three classifiers (Convolutional Neural Network (CNN), Naïve Bayes (NB) and K-Nearest Neighbor (kNN)) were further tested in order to decide which of the classifiers had the best results. We used augmented audio data from a dataset (SAVEE) in the proposed method to conduct training (50%), and testing (50%) was executed using the original data. The best performance of approximately 83% was found to be a mixture of augmentation strategies using the CNN classifier. Our proposed augmentation approach together with appropriate classification model enhances the efficiency of voice emotion recognition.

Keywords: Audio data · Emotion recognition · Data augmentation · Data classification · Neural Network

1 Introduction

The emotional state of human beings plays a key role in human computer experiences. Therefore, automated methods for understanding and recognizing human emotions are increasingly in demand. Emotion recognition is the ability to consistently recognize other people's feelings at each moment within a time period and to recognize the relation between their feelings and related expressions [1].

Audio mining is a method used to search and analyze audio files from spoken words or phrases. It is usually used to save audio files in databases, then search required specific data in terms of keywords within the huge and heterogeneous database. Here, keywords

© Springer Nature Switzerland AG 2021
H. Fujita et al. (Eds.): IEA/AIE 2021, LNAI 12799, pp. 360–365, 2021.
https://doi.org/10.1007/978-3-030-79463-7_30

of interest are determined based on their occurrence frequency in spoken words. This method is used to obtain valuable information from high volume of recorded speech.

The audio data of spoken human language is also considered as speech data. These types of data are widely available from a variety of sources such as, webcasts, conversations, music, meetings, voice messages, lectures, television, and radio. Research done by authors in [2–4] focuses on sentiment analysis using audio data from EMODB, IEMOCAP and FAU AIBO database, Multiple Features Database (MFD) and Spoken Reviews (manual collection) respectively.

Research on emotional recognition is primarily divided into two areas: (i) single modality for the classification of emotions, such as facial expressions in images or video, or speech or electroencephalogram (EEG) signals; and (ii) multimodal approaches for the classification of emotions by integrating different modalities of emotion. Audio data (unimodal) is analyzed for the proposed work in this paper, whereas multimodal systems are left for future works.

One of the major drawbacks of any recognition method is the lack of data for the training of the classifier. When large datasets are used for training, the more likely it is that there will be a similarly matched example of training during testing. As a consequence, output accuracy is likely to improve when more training data are available. However, there are inadequate data in many of the databases currently available. One way to solve this issue is to perform data augmentation (DA) in order to increase the number of data samples. There are several ways to increase the data. A few examples are using audio-specific augmentation techniques like pitch shifting, time-scale modification, time shifting, noise addition, and volume control. In addition, the DA often overcomes the system's over-fitting problems [5]. New DA phases are employed in our proposed emotion recognition method to resolve the problems created by the lack of data for classifier training.

The classification of data is an integral part of the emotion recognition system. Neural networks (NN), naïve-bayes (NB), linear discriminant analysis (LDA), support vector machine (SVM), fuzzy logic, decision trees (DT) and genetic algorithm classifiers comprise of some state-of-the-art classifiers [6]. Convolutional neural networks (CNN) have especially provided outstanding success in terms of performance accuracy in the field of emotion recognition in speech signals [7], while classifiers such as NB [8] and kNN [9] have also shown great promise. In order to compare the output accuracy, three different classifiers (CNN, NB and kNN) were used separately for audio data classification for this experiment.

In this paper, we analyze and compare the influence of various well-established DA techniques and classifiers on an emotion recognition model's output accuracy. This was carried out in three stages: augmentation of data, extraction of features and, finally, classification. In order to identify the six fundamental expressions along with a neutral state, the experiments were performed on the publicly accessible and well-established Surrey Audio-Visual Expressed Emotion (SAVEE) dataset.

The rest of this paper is organized as follows. The proposed approaches are discussed in Sect. 2. This is followed by results and analysis along with their comparison in Sect. 3, and finally conclusion for the proposed works with future directions in Sect. 4.

2 Proposed Framework

The main aim of the proposed work is to research the efficacy of data augmentation strategies in conjunction with various emotion processing classifiers in speech signals. Each part of the proposed framework is discussed in detail in the rest of the section.

2.1 Dataset

Firstly, a suitable dataset was selected. The Surrey Audio-Visual Expressed Emotion (SAVEE) dataset which has 120 spoken sentences from 4 native English male actors was chosen for this experiment. Each sentence represents one emotion. Speech signals containing seven different emotions (happiness, sadness, surprise, fear, anger, disgust and neutral) were extracted from the dataset for further analysis.

2.2 Audio Data Augmentation

To create the training set, 50% of the speech signals from each of the seven different emotion categories were separated. Then, various augmentation techniques were implemented to increase these training images, which were shift pitch (SP), control volume (CV) and add noise (AN). These techniques are described in detail below:

- Shift pitch (SP): Pitch shifting technique changes the original pitch of a sound by raising or lowering the pitch of the speech signal.
- Control volume (CV): Volume control technique increases or lowers the volume of the speech signal according to specifications.
- Add noise (AN): This technique adds white noise to the original speech signal.

By creating new copies of the original speech signals for the emotion model training phase, these approaches aim to increase the size of the training set.

2.3 Audio Feature Extraction

The audio features that were extracted were mel frequency cepstrum coefficients (MFCC). The MFCC are a small collection of features that concisely define the overall form of a spectral envelope. In order to obtain the MFCC with a 40 ms hanning window and a 10 ms overlapping, 94 Mel-filter banks were used for each speech signal. The MFCC were extracted from speech signals of all four speakers in seven different emotions presented.

2.4 Speech Signal Classification

To train the various classifiers to construct the prediction model for each classifier, the emotion labels associated with each speech data and the augmented audio were used. Then, the proposed system was assessed with three classifiers, CNN, NB and kNN. Each classifier is briefly described below:

- CNN: Convolutional neural network or CNN is a deep learning neural network which recognize patterns in data by understanding and remembering the features of training data.
- NB: Naïve Bayes or NB is a probabilistic machine learning model which assumes that there is no relation between the existence of a specific feature in a class and the presence of any other feature.
- kNN: The k-nearest neighbors or kNN is a supervised machine learning algorithm that can be used to solve both classification and regression problems. kNN functions in classification problems by defining the distances between a test sample and the given training examples, choosing the specified number of examples (k) nearest to the test sample, then voting for the most frequent class or name.

Emotion prediction models can then process audio data from the research and predict one of the seven human emotions (anger, sadness, surprise, happiness, disgust, fear or neutral). The goal of this experiment is to determine the impact on the output of the emotion prediction model of each DA technique and classifier, which is measured using 50% audio test data from the dataset that does not contain any audio data used to train the model for unbiased evaluation purposes.

3 Experimental Results

In the following sections, the experimental results for each DA and classifier are compared.

3.1 GDA Comparison

By training the proposed system with augmented SAVEE audio data data and testing with the original audio data from the dataset, the emotion recognition model evaluation procedure was conducted. With the considered DA techniques, the SAVEE dataset augmented audio data was as follows: (1) 180 audio augmentation created with SP; (2) 180 audio augmentation produced with CV (3) 180 audio augmentation created with AN. The training database size was set to 540 audio features when both 3 SP, CV and AN techniques were used. With CNN, NB and kNN classifiers, the DA techniques were processed to be grouped into particular emotion labels. Test data consisting of 50% of the un-augmented, original data from the SAVEE dataset was entered into the individual classifier prediction models and the output accuracy of each classifier was obtained.

The performance accuracy was calculated using the following equation:

$$P = \frac{TP}{TP + FP} \tag{1}$$

Where TP stands for true positive and FP stands for false positive.

Considering the different geometric augmentation techniques and classifiers, Table 1 summarizes the values of the overall accuracy of emotion recognition achieved. A combination of SP, CV, and AN was 83.3% of the highest output accuracy obtained with the CNN classifier, and an accuracy rate of 82.4% was achieved when no DA technique was applied. With an accuracy of 82.0% and 81.6% respectively, SP and CV techniques created no improvement compared to no DA, while AN had a significantly decreased accuracy of 81.6%. The addition of noise (AN) causes this slight decrease in performance due to classification difficulty. For each classifier, this pattern is replicated, with the best accuracy for NB and kNN being 77.3% and 76.9% respectively by using a combination of DA techniques.

It can be shown that the strategy that incorporates all the augmented techniques outperforms the rest and the best result was obtained by the CNN classifier. The output is likely to improve by providing additional audio data and modalities to the training database, which will be the goal for our future experiments.

Table 1. Performance accuracy achieved with the SAVEE dataset using different DA techniques and classifiers.

Data augmentations	Performance accuracy		
	CNN	NB	kNN
No DA	82.4%	76.1%	76.0%
SP	82.0%	76.5%	75.9%
CV	81.6%	76.6%	75.4%
AN	82.1%	75.1%	75.0%
SP, CV and AN	83.3%	77.3%	76.9%

4 Conclusion

Using DA techniques (SP, CV and AN) to augment the obtained dataset, this paper presented an emotion recognition model and tested it with three well-known classifiers: CNN, NB and KNN. The results show that DA transformations, specifically SP, CV and AN combinations, provide performance improvements of up to 10% in the case where DA is not used. Through this experiment, it can be shown that a large amount of data is needed in speech signals for more precise emotion detection and that augmented audio offers an option to compensate for lack of data in place of small datasets or small numbers of audio data. The result of the experiment in this paper underlines the value of training data for emotional recognition tasks and the efficacy of the correct DA technique when large datasets are not available. The use of GAN on audio datasets to create a synthetic novel dataset for emotion recognition system from audio data with better accuracy and precision is a future work to be considered. The use of EEG modalities with other GDA techniques will also be taken into consideration.

References

1. Shoumy, N.J., Ang, L.-M., Seng, K.P., Rahaman, D.M.M., Zia, T.: Multimodal big data affective analytics: a comprehensive survey using text, audio, visual and physiological signals. J. Netw. Comput. Appl. **149**, 102447 (2020). https://doi.org/10.1016/j.jnca.2019.102447

2. Deb, S., Dandapat, S.: Emotion Classification using Segmentation of Vowel-Like and Non-Vowel-Like Regions. http://ieeexplore.ieee.org/document/7987785/ (2017). https://doi.org/10.1109/TAFFC.2017.2730187

3. Mairesse, F., Polifroni, J., Di Fabbrizio, G.: Can prosody inform sentiment analysis? experiments on short spoken reviews. In: ICASSP, IEEE International Conference on Acoustics, Speech and Signal Processing – Proceedings, pp. 5093–5096 (2012). https://doi.org/10.1109/ICASSP.2012.6289066

4. Sawata, R., Ogawa, T., Haseyama, M.: Novel audio feature projection using KDLPCCA-based correlation with EEG features for favorite music classification. IEEE Trans. Affect. Comput. 1–1 (2017). https://doi.org/10.1109/TAFFC.2017.2729540

5. Shorten, C., Khoshgoftaar, T.M.: A survey on image data augmentation for deep learning. J. Big Data **6**(1), 1–48 (2019). https://doi.org/10.1186/s40537-019-0197-0

6. Gavali, P., Banu, J.S.: Deep convolutional Neural Network for image classification on CUDA platform. In: Deep Learning and Parallel Computing Environment for Bioengineering Systems, pp. 99–122. Elsevier (2019). https://doi.org/10.1016/B978-0-12-816718-2.00013-0

7. Padi, S., Manocha, D., Sriram, R.D.: Multi-Window Data Augmentation Approach for Speech Emotion Recognition. Presented at the (2020)

8. Bhakre, S.K., Bang, A.: Emotion recognition on the basis of audio signal using Naive Bayes classifier. In: 2016 International Conference on Advances in Computing, Communications and Informatics (ICACCI), pp. 2363–2367 (2016). https://doi.org/10.1109/ICACCI.2016.7732408

9. Meftah, I.T., Le. Thanh, N., Ben Amar, C.: Emotion recognition using KNN classification for user modeling and sharing of affect states. In: Huang, T., Zeng, Z., Li, C., Leung, C.S. (eds.) ICONIP 2012. LNCS, vol. 7663, pp. 234–242. Springer, Heidelberg (2012). https://doi.org/10.1007/978-3-642-34475-6_29

Innovative Applications of Intelligent Systems

Intelligent System of Mooring Planning, Based on Deep Q-Learning

B. V. Gurenko and M. A. Vasileva[✉]

Research and Development Institute of Robotics and Control System, Taganrog, Russia
marv@sfedu.ru

Abstract. During processes of globalization, the flow of ships in large marinas is increasing, and parking becomes more difficult for the ship's captains. Mooring is one of the most complex elements of the control of a ship. This is one of the most dangerous maneuvers requiring analysis of many changing parameters and fast decision-making on the use of various methods of controlling the ship.

Given the modern development of methods for controlling moving objects, these tasks can be solved with the help of intelligent technologies. This article discusses a method for controlling the position of the rudder, speed, and direction of rotation of the ship's propeller to solve the problem of mooring automation. Of the possible principles used to build control systems, a system based on machine learning algorithms is more suitable. Because it gives the system the ability to make decisions in situations that cannot be described by the algorithm, or its description would be very large. Deep reinforcement learning was chosen as the machine learning algorithm. The article presents the modeling of the proposed method's functioning. There is given an example of the creation and training of two software agents that form an intelligent scheduler, at their output the required speed and course of a moving sea object is given. The developed control system can be used to automate the mooring of both autonomous and crewed marine moving objects.

Keywords: Artificial neural networks · Mooring automation · Movement planning · Q-learning

1 Introduction

The flow of ships in large marinas becomes denser every year [1], this process makes the task of maneuvering more difficult and leads to the need for automation of ship control: the main cause of emergencies is the human factor.

One of the biggest difficulties in ship handling is the process of maneuvering to the mooring point. Often in ports during performing a maneuver, there is no possibility to reinsure with a margin of distance traveled and speed and making a wrong decision leads to much greater negative consequences than during maneuvering in free water conditions [2].

The problem of automation of ship control on free water is solved by several methods [3–8]. The development of modern technologies makes it possible to implement and

© Springer Nature Switzerland AG 2021
H. Fujita et al. (Eds.): IEA/AIE 2021, LNAI 12799, pp. 369–378, 2021.
https://doi.org/10.1007/978-3-030-79463-7_31

automate a more complex process such a controlling a marine mobile object in the mooring mode. The most promising are methods based on the use of intellectual approaches [9–16]. Among technologies that are currently considered in the literature, the state-of-art of intellectual approaches are fuzzy systems and neural network technologies.

Thus, the review [10] presents methods and approaches to the control of unmanned vessels using fuzzy logic. The options for tuning the coefficients of the PID controller by a fuzzy algorithm, a combination of fuzzy controllers with sliding modes, and neuro-fuzzy control are considered. This paper said, usually, a fuzzy system is used to adapt a traditional controller, i.e., its independent use is limited. It is also noted that the methods of using fuzzy logic to control unmanned boats require their development in terms of solving the problems of traffic planning.

In [12], a fuzzy controller is also considered, in combination with a traditional controller it solves the problem of controlling an unmanned vessel by considering the wind speed and direction. In this work, a fuzzy regulator is used to correct the operation of a traditional regulator and to solve part of the motion planning problems.

In [16], a neural network traffic control system is considered, it implements tracking a given trajectory of an unmanned ship under conditions of uncertain dynamics and external disturbances. In this work, a disturbance identifier is implemented based on a neural network. Also, like in the case of a fuzzy system, a neural network is used in an indirect adaptive control scheme.

It should be noted that neural network methods of movement planning have recently gained popularity [21, 22, 25]. The use of deep learning networks for solving this problem allows us to impart robustness to the planning process and consider the dynamics of the environment.

Therefore, in this article, to solve the problem of autonomous planning of the docking process a neural network system is used.

2   Formulation of the Problem

The task is to develop a block of a marine vessel control system that performs planning of maneuvering to the docking point.

The operability of the proposed system was verified by performing of simulation of the marine vessel's model control process (Fig. 1), the mathematical model of its movement [5] has the form (1,2).

$$y = Ryx \tag{1}$$

$$x = M - 1Bu + Fd + Fv, \tag{2}$$

$$R = \begin{bmatrix} \cos y_3 & \sin y_3 & 0 \\ -\sin y_3 & \cos y_3 & 0 \\ 0 & 0 & 1 \end{bmatrix}, F_d = \begin{bmatrix} -mx_2x_3 - c_{x1}x_1 \\ -mx_1x_3 - c_{x2}x_2 \\ -m_{x3}x_3 \end{bmatrix},$$

$$B_u = \begin{bmatrix} 1 & 0 \\ 0 & 0 \\ 0 & 1 \end{bmatrix}, M = \begin{bmatrix} m & 0 & 0 \\ 0 & m & 0 \\ 0 & 0 & J \end{bmatrix}.$$

Here $y = [y_1 y_2 y_3]$ T; y_1, y_2 – these are the linear coordinates of the ship in a stationary system O $Y_1 Y_2$; y_2 – yaw angle; $x = [x_1 x_2 x_3]$ T; x_1, x_2 – the projection of the ship's linear velocities in the moving coordinate system O $X_1 X_2$; x_3 – angular velocity; Fv – vector of unmeasured disturbances; u – vector of control actions; m – is the mass of the vessel; J – is the moment of inertia about the vertical axis; c_{x1}, c_{x2}, m_{x2} – positive movement resistance coefficients.

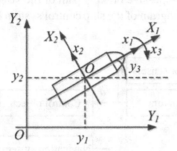

Fig. 1. Marine vessel

The marine vessel model can be characterized by three parameters: coordinates on the map, course relative to the north, and speed. The work involves the implementation of control by changing the course and speed of the marine vessel.

The environment in this work is described by the coordinates of static and dynamic obstacles, presented in the form of a mapped image (Fig. 2).

Thus, the input data for the developed block are the current and final coordinates of the marine vessel, a map of static and dynamic obstacles. At the output of the block, the course and speed of the marine vessel for the current moment should be generated.

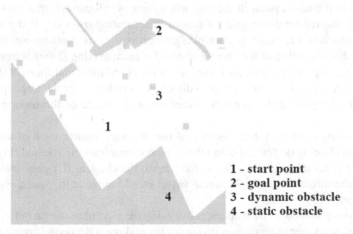

1 - **start point**
2 - **goal point**
3 - **dynamic obstacle**
4 - **static obstacle**

Fig. 2. An example of a port map with randomly plotted dynamic obstacles, the initial and final coordinates of the vessel trajectory

3   Development of the Control Block for Maneuvering During Mooring

The mooring maneuvering system is a part of the general marine vessel's control system. The beginning of the use of the system is conditioned by the fulfillment of the requirement: the object must approach the mooring place to a distance that no more than a radius which is equal to the passive braking path of the vessel.

The general functional diagram of the ship control system [16, 17] is shown in Fig. 3.

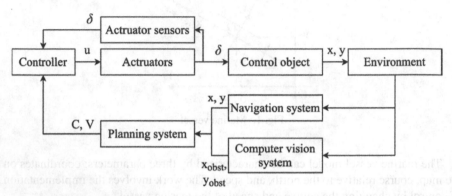

Fig. 3. Functional diagram of the marine vessel maneuvering system

Here, the following data comes from the environment to the planning system: target coordinates, current coordinates of the control object, and its speed. In the planning system (block diagram is shown in Fig. 4), considering the current speed and position relative to the final coordinate, is calculated the maximum distance that can be approached to the target point in the way when there is still enough space for reducing the speed to the required one and for maneuvering during mooring. If the maximum distance is reached, the mooring control algorithm is triggered; otherwise, the marine vessel operates according to the control system for maneuvering in free water.

Upon reaching the specified radius ($r_{barking}$), the coordinates and speed of the marine vessel, its course relative to the northern direction, coordinates of the target point, data about approaching obstacles are transmitted to the entrance of the mooring control system.

The mooring control system consists of two software agents, each of which is an artificial neural network, trained using the reinforcement learning method (Fig. 5). The Q-agent (V) generates a speed value at the output, the Q-agent (C) generates a course that shows the direction in which marine vessel should move at the speed specified by the first agent.

The mooring control system operates following the algorithm shown in Fig. 5. At the beginning of work, the information necessary for making a decision is read: the initial and final coordinates of the trajectory, a map of obstacles, all the information received is formed into an image, which is then transmitted to the input of Q-agents. Q-agents form the values of the speed and course, which the vessel should adhere to at the moment.

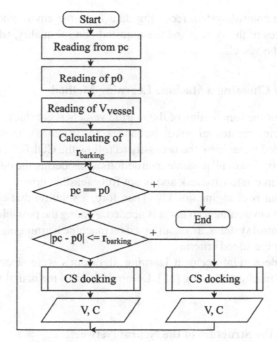

Fig. 4. Block diagram of the control system selection algorithm

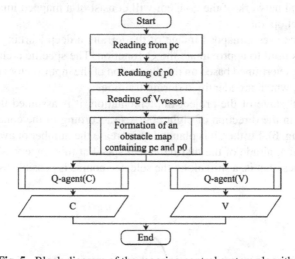

Fig. 5. Block diagram of the mooring control system algorithm

According to the diagram shown in Fig. 3, the block of the planning system transmits the output values as a reference to the controller, there they are converted into a control signal for the actuators.

The rate of the control system receiving data from the environment is set by the technical capabilities of the system and the required control quality, which depends on the parameters of the vessel.

3.1 Rationale for Choosing a Machine Learning Method

The environment for the functioning of the marine vessels is complex: it includes static and dynamic obstacles, creates various disturbances, and in a case when the marine vessel operates in a crowded water area, the necessity to follow the COLREGs is an additional difficulty. The description of all possible instructions, considering the possible branching of events, is a resource-intensive task and is not fully feasible now.

The environment is changing quickly. Therefore, a solution that allows to quickly respond to dynamic environment changes is needed. Among the possible principles used for constructing control systems, a system based on machine learning algorithms [18–24] is most suitable for the stated criteria.

In this paper, deep reinforcement learning algorithms were selected as the most perspective area of machine learning [18]. Determination of the neural network training algorithm.

3.2 Determining the Structure of the Neural Network

Since the functioning environment is not of the same type all the time, the input data set entering the neural network of the Q-agent will consist of a mapped image of the port where the Q-agent operates.

Since the work uses a mapped image of the terrain, a deep learning convolutional neural network is used to approximate the Q-function. The specific architecture of the neural network is determined based on the dimension of the input vector and the features of a specific task, which are identified during training.

At the current stage of the project implementation, it is assumed that the control object can move in the direction of eight courses (according to the concept of 8-wind compass rose) (Fig. 6). Further, it is planned to increase the number of available courses to 360. And the magnitude of the marine vessel speed at this stage was discretized to five possible values, that is, a shift along the selected course is possible by no more than five units.

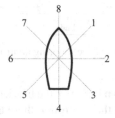

Fig. 6. Numeration of courses

The set of the neural network's output values of each of the Q-agents will contains values that indicate how rational each of the available actions will be in the current situation.

To train neural networks, which are the basis of the planning system, it is necessary to create a set of training examples. This set was obtained in the environment simulator.

In this work to create a training sample used strategy that differs from the classical ones. The strategy is a subspecies of the epsilon-greedy strategy, where initially the Q-agent uses only the most profitable actions, and over time the number of situations when the Q-agent chooses to study the environment increases. In the strategy used in the work, the study of the environment is carried out programmatically, and at the first stage, the Q-agent learns using situations that lead at the end of the route to the maximum reward (at first stages Q-agent does not explore the environment to find situations with the biggest profit - it gets only that kind of situations as a training set). Then previously got skill is used to explore the environment by Q-agent and generate a new training set. At the next stages of creating the set, the correlation between exploration and expectation depends on how the Q-agent learns in the previous stages. This strategy allows to speed up the learning process in the early stages.

The learning process proceeds following the algorithm described below.

At the first stages of training, the D-star algorithm was used as a teacher. At further stages of the development of the system, the D-star algorithm is planned to be replaced by the experience of real navigation.

At the first stage, a situation with randomly given initial and final coordinates is generated. Then D-star plots a route, and an image with this situation is saved to the corresponding folder as an example of choosing a course (number of directions, that D-star built the first step) and speed (how many steps within 5 moves you can move in the direction of the first step made by the D-star algorithm without changing the direction of movement). These steps perform a lot of times until the training set would not have enough samples.

At the second stage, the Q-agent collects a new training sample by passing the route, using the experience that already obtained at the first stage. That is, it performs steps based on the solution of the neural networks trained at the first stage. Next, the network learns in those situations where, in comparison to the D-star solution, the agent made a mistake.

Then these stages are repeated. The number of repetitions of stages is established empirically.

3.3   Training and Research of the Maneuvering System

The training of two neural networks was carried out using the Matlab environment.

For the initial training 2500 images per each class were generated using only D-star algorithm. Then Q-agent's networks were retrained on updated with images filtered by previously learned network. The accuracy of neural networks on the validation set and on test sample for first and last learning iterations presented at Table 1.

Additional training of networks was performed 7 times while increasing the number of training sets until the test sample presented a satisfactory accuracy of 93%.

Table 1. Q-agent's neural networks learning statistic

Iteration, №	Q-agent index	Images number	Validation accuracy, %	Test accuracy, %
1	1	2500 × 8	57	47
	2	2500 × 8	41	38
7	1	42500 × 8	92	89
	2	42500 × 8	96	93

4   Research Results

To explore developed system previously trained Q-agents were used in the mooring control system at the marine vessel maneuvering system (Fig. 3, Fig. 5). Modeling of the agent's functioning was carried out in a software simulator developed in the MATLAB application package.

The results obtained during the study are shown in Fig. 7.

Here are examples of the passage of the vessel's model under control of Q-agents in various, additionally generated, situations. The star in the figures denotes the endpoint, the circle denotes the starting point, the green dotted line shows the path calculated by the D-star algorithm, black - the path calculated by the intelligent planner, red shapes - static and dynamic obstacles. Dynamic obstacles were generated at random place of map during all simulation time.

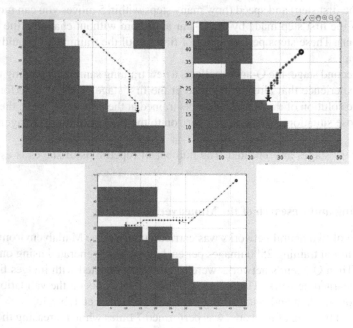

Fig. 7. Simulation results

In 100% of simulated passages motion control system based on Q-agents showed sevenfold speed advantage according to D-star algorithm. And Q-agents path length was replicated in 68% of cases.

5   Conclusion

The results obtained in the framework of the study confirm the suitability of the system for solving problems of dynamic path planning and make the prospect of further work on the project of the maneuvering system expedient.

The modeling examples presented in the work showed that the marine vessels control system in most cases repeats the path built by the D-star algorithm, and it is also a dynamic path planning system, but it compares favorably with it in speed: each next step is calculated individually and based on the state of the environment, there is no need to calculate the entire route at every moment.

Further work with the project involves carrying out tests using a scale model of the vessel, replacing the usage of the D-star algorithm with human experience (operator control sessions), and adapting software Q-agents for use on real vessels.

The development can be applied in any category of shipping since the proposed system is flexible enough to make it possible to customize its parameters for operation on various types of marine vessels.

Acknowledgement. The materials of the article were prepared as part of the work on the grant of the Russian Science Foundation No. 16-19-00001 at the Research and Development Institute of Robotics and Control System.

References

1. Zhang, Z.-G., Yin, J.-C., Wang, N., Hui, Z.-G.: Vessel traffic flow analysis and prediction by an improved PSO-BP mechanism based on AIS data. Evol. Syst. **10**(3), 397–407 (2018). https://doi.org/10.1007/s12530-018-9243
2. Information on: http://pro-arctic.ru/13/12/2016/technology/24519
3. Liu, Z., Zhang, Y., Yu, X., Yuan, C.: Unmanned surface vehicles: an overview of developments and challenges. Ann. Rev. Control **41**, 71–93 (2016)
4. Klinger, W.B., Bertaska, I.R., Ellenrieder, K.D., Dhanak, M.R.: Control of an unmanned surface vehicle with uncertain displacement and drag. IEEE J. Ocean. Eng. **42**(2), 458–476 (2017)
5. Kostukov, V., Gurenko, B., Maevskiy, A.: Mathematical model of the surface mini vessel. In: Proceedings of the 5th International Conference on Mechatronics and Control Engineering, pp. 57–60. ACM, New York (2016)
6. Pshikhopov, V., Gurenko, B.: Development and research of a terminal controller for marine robots. In: Fujita, H., Fournier-Viger, P., Ali, M., Sasaki, J. (eds.) IEA/AIE 2020. LNCS (LNAI), vol. 12144, pp. 899-906. Springer, Cham (2020). https://doi.org/10.1007/978-3-030-55789-8_76
7. Liu, Y., Bucknall, R.: Path planning algorithm for unmanned surface vehicle formations in a practical maritime environment. Ocean Eng. **97**, 126–144 (2015)

8. Naeem, W., Irwin, G., Yang, A.: Colregs-based collision avoidance strategies for unmanned surface vehicles. Mechatronics **22**, 669–678 (2012)
9. Lyu, H., Yin, Y.: Fast path planning for autonomous ships in restricted waters. Appl. Sci. **8**(12), 2592 (2018)
10. Xiang, X., Yu, C., Lapierre, L., Zhang, J., Zhang, Q.: Survey on fuzzy-logic-based guidance and control of marine surface vehicles and underwater vehicles. Int. J. Fuzzy Syst. **20**(2), 572–586 (2017). https://doi.org/10.1007/s40815-017-0401-3
11. Im, N., Lee, S.K., Hyung, D.B.: An application of ANN to automatic ship berthing using selective controller. Int. J. Marine Navig. Saf. Sea Transp. **1**(1) (2007)
12. Lebkowski, A., Smierzchalski, R., Gierusz, W., Dziedzicki, K.: Intelligent ship control system. Int. J. Marine Navig. Saf. Sea Transp. **2**(1), 63–68 (2008)
13. Lazarowska, A.: Swarm intelligence approach to safe ship control. Polish Marit. Res. **22**(4), 34–40 (2015)
14. Lee, T., Kim, H., Chung, H., Bang, Y., Myung, H.: Energy efficient path planning for a marine surface vehicle considering heading angle. Ocean Eng. **107**, 118–131 (2015)
15. Hong, Y.-H., Kim, J.-Y., Oh, J.-H., Lee, P.-M., Jeon, B.-H., Oh, K.-H.: Development of homing and docking algorithm for AUV. In: ISOPE 2003, International Offshore and Polar Engineering Conference, 23–30 May 2003, pp. 205–212 (2003)
16. Wang, N., Sun, J.-C., Er, M.J., Liu, Y.-C.: A novel extreme learning control framework of unmanned surface vehicles. IEEE Trans. Cybern. **46**(5), 1106–1117 (2016)
17. Pshikhopov, V., Medvedev, M.: Position-Path Control of a Vehicle. Path Planning for Vehicles Operating in Uncertain 2D Environments, pp. 1–23 (2017)
18. Medvedev, M., Gurenko, B.: Development of AUV path planner based on unstable mode. In: IOP Conference Series: Materials Science and Engineering, vol. 533, pp. 2–9 (2019)
19. Ravichandiran, S.: Hands-On Reinforcement Learning with Python. Packt Publishing Ltd, First published, June 2018
20. Information on: https://missinglink.ai/guides/neural-network-concepts/7-types-neural-network-activation-functions-right/
21. Gaiduk, A.R., Martyanov, O.V., Medvedev, M.Yu., Pshikhopov, V.Kh., Hamdan, N., Farhud, A.: Neural network control system for a group of robots in an undefined two-dimensional environment. Mechatron. Autom. Control **21**(8), 470–479 (2020)
22. Medvedev, M., Pshikhopov, V.: Path planning of mobile robot group based on neural networks. In: Fujita, H., Fournier-Viger, P., Ali, M., Sasaki, J. (eds.) IEA/AIE 2020. LNCS (LNAI), vol. 12144, pp. 51–62. Springer, Cham (2020). https://doi.org/10.1007/978-3-030-55789-8_5
23. Russell, S., Norvig, P.: Artificial Intelligence: A Modern Approach. Per. from English, 2nd edn, 1408 p. House "Williams" (2006)
24. Simon, H.: Neural Networks. Complete Course, 1104 p. Williams (2006)
25. Pshikhopov, V., Medvedev, M., Vasileva, M.: Neural network control system of motion of the robot in the environment with obstacles. In: Wotawa, F., Friedrich, G., Pill, I., Koitz-Hristov, R., Ali, M. (eds.) Advances and Trends in Artificial Intelligence, vol. 11606, pp. 173–181. Springer, Cham (2019). https://doi.org/10.1007/978-3-030-22999-3_16

Experimental Study on Predictive Modeling in the Gamification Marketing Application

Zhou-Yi Lim, Lee-Yeng Ong[✉], and Meng-Chew Leow

Faculty of Information Science and Technology, Multimedia University, Melaka, Malaysia
lyong@mmu.edu.my

Abstract. Nowadays, many companies are using the gamification approach to promote their products in digital marketing. A gamification marketing approach can only be more effective if the companies can understand their customers' behaviors through their navigation patterns. Once their behaviors are known by the companies, the appropriate enhancements can be made to improve the marketing strategy. This paper aims to analyze the navigation patterns of the customers based on customer engagement metrics of *the time spent on page* and *visit frequency of each page*. Based on these engagement metrics, the action sequences of customers are generated and then evaluated. A sequence model is created to predict the subsequent actions of the customers and to determine the likelihood of using the gamification marketing application. The sequence algorithms, Markov model, and Recurrent Neural Network (RNN) are applied to the sequence models to analyze the customer's navigation pattern when they are accessing the gamification marketing application.

Keywords: Navigation pattern · Action prediction · Markov model · Recurrent neural network

1 Introduction

Gamification marketing involves combining gaming elements into a non-gaming context to enhance digital marketing [1]. Gaming elements refer to the design elements for gamification such as rewarded points, virtual badges, leaderboard, and other motivational ways [15]. Games are incorporated into marketing to attract customer's attention towards the company's product. Older marketing strategies such as advertisements on billboards are too passive. In contrast, the gamification strategy gives a sense of control to the customers, allowing the customers to feel more motivated and engaged when using the marketing application. Hence, gamification as a marketing tool can improve customer engagement, enhance brand identification and build customer loyalty.

Gamification marketing applications have similar concepts in terms of their general processes. The common processes include login, play the game, collect points from the game and redeem a gift, as shown in Fig. 1. The Starbucks Rewards program is a good example of a gamification strategy, which lets the members achieve simple challenges to gain reward [2]. Starbucks customers first need to register a Starbucks account. As part

© Springer Nature Switzerland AG 2021
H. Fujita et al. (Eds.): IEA/AIE 2021, LNAI 12799, pp. 379–390, 2021.
https://doi.org/10.1007/978-3-030-79463-7_32

of their membership benefits, customers can collect 'stars' on every purchase. Members can get extra 'stars' if they play other games in the Starbucks application. Members can then redeem free food and drinks with the collected 'stars'. On the other hand, the online shopping platform Shopee is also implementing the gamification approach [3]. Shopee uses the 'coin' system to promote the customer's participation in their application. The 'coins' can be obtained in a few ways such as entering the application daily to get free 'coins' or purchasing any products in Shopee, where the amount of 'coins' is collected based on the price of the product. The 'coins' can be redeemed for vouchers to purchase products in the application. Another example is the Nike+ application, which helps to monitor the customer's running distance, speed, and time [4, 5]. Nike implements gamification marketing differently from Starbucks and Shopee. To use the Nike+ application, customers need to purchase Nike shoes and a Nike+ sensor. This sensor must be placed under the insole of a Nike shoe to be compatible with Nike+. This Nike+ sensor will then track the customer's activity. This process can be considered synonymous with the 'login' process in other applications. The 'play game' process happens when the customers perform the running activity. The reward that the customers can get is in the form of a leaderboard and virtual badges. If the customer is one of the top runners, the player's profile will be shown on the leaderboard. Also, the customer can get badges if they unlock significant achievements such as the longest run and farthest run.

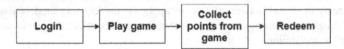

Fig. 1. General processes of gamification marketing applications

There are several types of customer engagement metrics available in the existing literature but two commonly used metrics, such as time on page and visit frequency can reveal the navigation patterns of the customers in the marketing application [6, 7]. Time on page is the total amount of time spent by a customer on a particular page. Visit frequency determines how often a customer returns to a particular page. Normally, both of these metrics are used to measure customer engagement to investigate the engagement level of the customer. For example, if a customer only spends 2 s on the game page or does not return to the application after 2 visits, it might be an indication that the customer is not interested in the gamification marketing application. Both metrics are used to generate the action sequences of the customers. from the moment the customers logged into the application until they exit from it. For example, a customer who visits the game page followed by logging out is interpreted as an action sequence. Different customers will navigate the application differently. The action sequences indirectly disclose the customer's preference and interactions in the marketing application. Once their action sequences are known, the appropriate enhancements can be made to improve the gamification approach and marketing strategy.

In this paper, experiments are conducted to investigate if predictive modeling can assist in the understanding of customer's behavior in the gamification marketing application. Since the gamification marketing application is still newly developed, it is still unknown if the gamification approach can improve customer's engagement towards the company's product. This is important as highly engaged customers are more likely to purchase more products and share their feedback with others. Pages that are often visited by customers would be good candidates for adding more marketing elements while pages that are less visited by customers would need improvement to increase customer engagement. Therefore, this paper aims to present a preliminary experimental study using past and predicted action sequences to evaluate the customers' navigation patterns in a newly developed gamification marketing application. Other than analyzing the customer's past action sequences, this paper aims to predict the customer's future actions. Based on the combination of past and future action sequences, the company can better evaluate the strengths and weaknesses of the gamification marketing application. Two sequence models, the Markov model and Recurrent Neural Network (RNN), are tested to observe the action sequences from customers and to perform action prediction. Both models are tested for their suitability to perform action prediction for Web pages.

The rest of this paper is organized as follows. Section 2 presents the related applications that use Markov model and RNN. Section 3 presents a detailed description of the experiment setup to test the sequence models. Section 4 presents the experimental result and discussion. Finally, the experimental study is concluded with a discussion on the contribution and future work in Sect. 5.

2 Related Works

2.1 Markov Model

A Markov chain is defined as a collection of random variables, with the transition from one state to another according to certain probabilistic rules. In [8], Markov models are used for studying and understanding the stochastic processes and are shown to be well-suited for predicting a user's browsing behavior in a website. The simplest Markov model, 1st order Markov model predicts the next action by only observing the last action performed. A more complicated Markov model, which is generalized as K^{th}-order Markov model, predicts the next action by looking at the last K actions performed by the user. The Markov model consists of web sessions, with the sequences of pages that are accessed by different users. When the Markov model is built, the state transition probability matrix is computed. This matrix will be used to make a prediction for the web sessions. The next action predicted by the model is the action that has the highest probability in the state transition probability matrix.

Markov model is also used in marketing channel attribution [9]. The marketing channels in this context refers to the platforms that are used to market products, such as E-mail, social media, and company website. Companies usually use multiple marketing channels to market their products. Marketing attribution is the practice of evaluating the marketing touchpoints, which a consumer used to purchase a product. In [9], the Markov model is used to analyze the multichannel path of a selected company. Before analyzing the customer's path, the authors firstly determined the set of states, $S = \{Direct,$ *Organic search, Paid search, Email, Referral, Social network, Display advertising}*. The contents of set S are showing different marketing channels used by the company. Another two additional states are added, *Start* (representing the start of the customer journey) and *Conversion* (representing purchase). Markov model can statistically model the customer's journey and how each channel affects another channel.

2.2 Recurrent Neural Network (RNN)

RNN is a deep learning model that requires high computational power. RNN can remember the past actions of a sequence and the past actions that influence future predictions. This characteristic enables RNN to be used for processing sequential data like handwriting, speech, and language translation. Nevertheless, RNN has a known problem of leaving out important information at the beginning of the sequence if the sequence is too long. During backpropagation, RNN suffers from the vanishing gradient problem. Meanwhile, LSTM, an improved version of RNN, has cell states that can keep information from the earlier time steps to the later time steps.

In [10], a dataset that consists of resident's actions events, j, in an apartment with annotated activities such as "LeaveHouse" and "UseFreezer" is collected to train the RNN. The researchers used n actions as the input to predict the next action, where n is the different sequence length. Word2Vec algorithm is used to provide semantic embeddings for each action in the dataset. This embedding layer will be the input to the deep learning model. After embedding the list of actions in the dataset, the embedded list is fed to the deep learning model of LSTM layers, fully connected layer, and dropout regularization. This idea has proven the suitability of RNN in using the action sequence to predict the next action in a gamification marketing application.

3 Methodology

This section briefly describes the preparation processes of the dataset before evaluating the predicted actions with both models. The dataset is obtained from a ready gamification marketing application. After preparing the dataset into a suitable format, the dataset is then applied separately into the Markov model and the RNN. The customers that participated in the gamification marketing application are termed as 'user' for the rest of this article. The raw dataset obtained from the application is stored in the form of a.csv file. The dataset contains the sequence of actions from a total number of 148 users. The dataset is collected for 8 days and accumulated a total of 8669 records of actions. Figure 2 shows the snippet of the dataset. There are 8 pages that the user can visit, which are the main page, shop page, scoreboard, redeem history page, two game access pages, and two game score pages. The two games that are offered in the gamification marketing application are Flappy Bird and Brick Breaker. In the dataset, the Flappy Bird is stated as 'game_4' and can be completed within 5 s. The Brick Breaker is stated as 'game_6' and can be completed within 30 s.

The gamification marketing application follows similar general processes as illustrated in Fig. 1. The main purpose of the gamification marketing application is to play the game to redeem the voucher. The user firstly logs into the application using their Gmail account. After that, the user is directed to the main page which displays two available games. Selecting any of the games will lead to the respective game page. After completing the game, the user is led to the game score page which displays the game score and

log_id	page	user_id	log_time ▲ 1	device
443	main_page	71	2020-08-17 01:28:38	desktop
444	game_4	71	2020-08-17 01:28:40	desktop
445	create_game_score_4	71	2020-08-17 01:28:53	desktop
446	main_page	86	2020-08-17 11:45:44	desktop
447	shop	86	2020-08-17 11:45:49	desktop
448	redeem_history	86	2020-08-17 11:45:56	desktop
449	score_board	86	2020-08-17 11:46:01	desktop
450	main_page	86	2020-08-17 11:46:37	desktop
451	game_4	86	2020-08-17 11:46:39	desktop
452	create_game_score_4	86	2020-08-17 11:46:55	desktop

Fig. 2. A snippet of the dataset

number of points earned from the game. Then, the application will direct the user back to the main page to continue playing another game or to navigate to the shop page for voucher redemption. The redeem history page and scoreboard page are optional pages to display the voucher redemption history and the leaderboard. When the user decides to log out, they will be led to the log out page. Based on the flow of the gamification marketing application, the processes have a structure that is fixed for a certain logical sequence of actions. For instance, the log out page will never appear at the beginning or in the middle of the sequence. Likewise, the game score page will only appear after the game is completed.

Figure 3 shows the processes for the data preparation. The dataset is first cleaned to remove unnecessary data and to perform the necessary conversion of data type. When the dataset is first read, the data type of *log_time* is a string. Hence it has to be converted into datetime format for the time on page calculation. After that, the cleaned dataset will be stored in a table named 'Log'. The 'Log' table is inserted into the database, named 'Gamification'. From this 'Log' table, the two customer engagement metrics, which are time on page and visit frequency are calculated. The time on page of each log record is calculated and inserted into the new table called 'Engagement_metrics' along with the *user_id* and *page*. The time on page is calculated by subtracting the datetime for the future page from the datetime of the current page. According to the time on page, a user is determined as idle by either the time on page is more than 1800 s (30 min) or the page is a 'log_out' page. If the user is indeed idle, then 'True' is recorded in the new table and vice versa. After that, the page visit frequency is calculated and inserted inside the table.

During the creation of the action sequence, the data from the 'Engagement_metrics' table is grouped by *user_id* and *visit_frequency*. After that, based on the *visit_frequency* of each user, the pages from the same *visit_frequency* are concluded as an action sequence. Each of the action sequences is added with one extra action, which is the 'Start' label at the beginning of an action sequence. This addition of the 'Start' label is used to indicate the beginning of the action sequence. Then, the action sequences are used for testing with the Markov model and RNN. Both sequence models can be used to analyze, either based on the general navigation patterns of all the users or individual's navigation patterns. If the individual's navigation pattern is analyzed, only the action sequences of the particular individual are concerned.

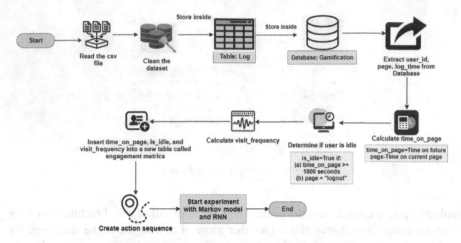

Fig. 3. The processes of the data preparation

Figure 4 illustrates the steps to build a Markov model. Based on the action sequences that are created in the data preparation process, the transition states between the pages are determined and calculated. According to the calculated transition states, the transition probabilities of each transition state are calculated. The transition probabilities are then converted into a matrix according to 1st order Markov model.

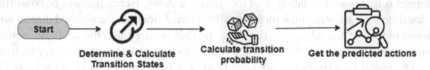

Fig. 4. Process of building Markov model

Figure 5 shows the process of building an RNN. Traditionally, the inputs are represented as one-hot vectors [10]. The disadvantage of using this vectors is that it does not contain any meaningful information towards the actions itself. Thus, word embedding is used to convert the word into numerical representation but also maintaining the semantic of the word [11]. Two types of word embeddings implementation that are widely used, which are CBOW and Skip-gram. CBOW model predicts a word based on its neighboring words, meanwhile, the Skip-gram model predicts the neighboring words based on the current word.

In the RNN model, the Word2Vec algorithm with CBOW architecture that was proposed by Mikolov et al. is used to calculate the embeddings [12]. Since the Word2Vec algorithm requires the 'list of lists' format, the action sequences are first converted into the required format [13]. The Word2Vec implementation from the Gensim library is selected to calculate the embedding values for each of the pages in the dataset. The dimensionality of word vectors used is 30. The deep neural network of RNN consists of four layers, which are the Embedding layer, LSTM layer, Dense layer, and Softmax

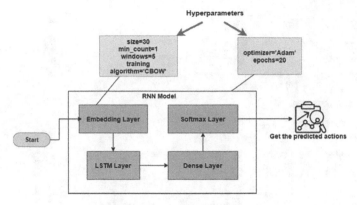

Fig. 5. Process of building RNN

layer. Instead of putting the words directly into the model, the Embedding layer acts as an input to store the procedural information on how to transform an action to its embedding. After the LSTM layer, it will be processed in the Dense layer with 10 network units as there are 10 actions in total (including the addition of the 'Start' label at the beginning of each action sequence). Finally, it will be processed in a Softmax layer to obtain the next action predictions. The model is trained for only 20 epochs as the size of the dataset and number of pages are small. The hyperparameters used in the RNN model are depicted in the yellow boxes of Fig. 5.

4 Experiment and Results

For both the Markov model and RNN, the action sequences are divided into training set and testing set, each having 80% and 20% of the original action sequences respectively [14]. In this section, the result of the Markov model is firstly presented, followed by RNN. The result analysis is further discussed after presenting the result of each model.

In the first experiment, 1st order Markov model is used to obtain action prediction. Table 1 shows the performance of the Markov model in different situations, considering

Table 1. Performance of Markov model

User ID	Prediction			
	Number of action sequences	Number of correct predictions	Total number of predictions	Accuracy (%)
All	727	1011	1641	61.61
145	21	16	27	59.26
153	19	4	13	30.77
132	12	19	19	100.00
178	8	7	12	58.33

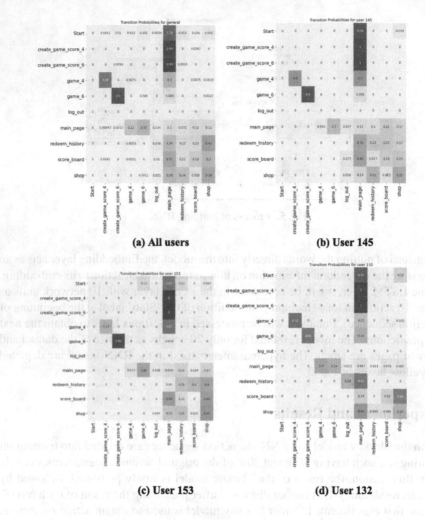

(a) All users

(b) User 145

(c) User 153

(d) User 132

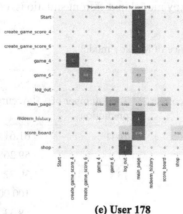

(e) User 178

Fig. 6. Heatmap of Markov model for (a) all users, (b) user 145, (c) user 153, (d) user 132 and (e) user 178

all of the action sequences in the dataset and also action sequences based on user ID. To guarantee that the accuracy of the Markov model of an individual is not biased, a total of four users that have a different number of action sequences are selected, namely user 145, 153, 132, and 178. The total number of predictions depends on the number of actions in the action sequences. The accuracy of Markov model is defined as the total number of correct predictions per total number of predictions. For each action sequence in the testing set, every action is used to predict the next action in the action sequence.

To visualize the model, a heatmap is used. Figure 6 shows the heatmaps of the transition probability matrix for all users and 4 individual users, namely user 145, user 153, user 132, and user 178. The current action and the future action are indicated in the row and column respectively. The color intensity of the box represents the probability of the transition. The darker color of the box represents a higher state transition probability. The Markov model predicts the next action by analyzing the highest state transition probability. As shown in Fig. 6(a), the Markov model predicts the next action of 'Start' is the 'main_page' because 'main_page' has the highest state transition probability of 0.78 in the 'Start' row.

In Table 1 which depicts the performance of several Markov models, it can be seen that the number of action sequences does not affect the accuracy of the model. Although the number of action sequences used in the Markov model of user 178 is less than user 153, the accuracy of user 178 is higher than user 153. A similar situation can be observed for user 145, which has a higher number of action sequences compared to the user 132. In the end, the accuracy of the Markov model for user 132 is higher than user 145. This shows that the accuracy highly relies on the type of action sequences that are passed into the model.

The type of action sequences determines the navigation patterns of the users. There are two types of navigation patterns that can be observed using the Markov model, which are consistent and randomized patterns. Based on the state transition probability of user 178 in Fig. 6(e), most of the state transition probabilities are more than 0.7. This indicates that the action sequences made by user 178 are consistent in all the transitions. Moreover, when the testing set is passed into the Markov model, the model predicts the future action with fairly high accuracy of 58.33% in Table 1. This pattern also applies to user 145, who similarly has a relatively more consistent sequence.

On the other hand, the navigation patterns of user 153 in Fig. 6(c) are often changing. Based on the observed state transition probability matrix, there are only 3 cells of state transition probabilities that are more than 0.7. Meanwhile, user 178 exhibits 8 cells of state transition probabilities that are more than 0.7. For instance, if the current action made by user 153 is the 'redeem_history' page, there are four possible actions that will most likely take place, namely 'main_page', 'redeem_history', 'score_board', and 'shop'. Two of the four possible transitional paths have almost equal probability of getting selected, namely the 'score_board' and 'shop' that has only a probability difference of 0.1. Although the probability difference is low, it is clearly shown that the user has a higher chance of visiting either of the pages. This creates difficulties for the Markov model to predict as it will only choose the next action that has the highest state transition probability from the matrix. Unlike user 178, it is quite certain that the user is most likely to visit the 'main_page' after the 'redeem_history' page, by referring to the state transition probability of 1.0.

In the second experiment, RNN is used for predictive modeling. Table 2 shows the performance of RNN in different situations, similar to the Markov model. The RNN is trained to predict the last action based on the action sequences from the training set. The model is then evaluated by using the testing set. Figure 7 shows a sample action sequence predicted by RNN.

Table 2. Performance of RNN

User ID	Prediction		
	Number of action sequences	Training accuracy (%)	Testing accuracy (%)
All	727	30.58	22.76
145	21	58.82	25.00
153	19	40.00	25.00
132	12	45.45	33.33
178	8	33.00	0.00

```
Generating text after epoch: 19
start... -> start shop score_board create_game_score_4 create_game_score_4 log_out log_out log_out redeem_history log_out gam
e_6 game_6 main_page start log_out score_board game_6 score_board shop main_page redeem_history
```

Fig. 7. Predicted action sequence for all users

In comparison to the performance of the Markov model, the number of action sequences affects the training accuracy of the RNN model. This can be observed from the performance of RNN in Table 2. By using the same 4 sample users (145, 153, 132, and 178), the training accuracy decreases as the number of action sequences is reduced. The testing accuracy also decreases drastically from user 132 to user 178. This is probably because the RNN is a deep learning model that requires a large amount of data to perform better. Although all 727 sequences from all the users are utilized for predictions, the data is still insufficient because the training and testing accuracy are relatively low.

Figure 7 shows the incorrectly predicted action sequence highlighted in yellow. The 'create_game_score_4' page should appear if the user navigates to the 'game_4' page. However, it is clearly shown that the model does not predict the 'game_4' page before the 'create_game_score_4' page. The predicted action sequence does not follow the logical structure of the actions (mentioned in Methodology) as it can be seen that the 'log_out' page is predicted thrice at the same time. The weak performance might be due to the lack of data quantity for training and the lack of variation in the dataset. In most cases that use RNN, the dataset contains more words or actions to give more possibilities. In this dataset, there are only 9 pages, giving only a few variations.

5 Conclusion and Future Work

As more applications are using the gamification approach, companies often find different ways to enhance their gamification marketing applications. In this paper, experiments are carried out to find out if predictive modeling can be used to understand customer's behavior in gamification marketing applications. This experiment uses past and predicted action sequences to understand customers' navigation patterns. A comparison of performance between the Markov model and RNN in predicting the future action sequences in the gamification marketing application is performed. After performing experiments using both models for this specific application, the Markov model showed a more promising result than RNN. The overall accuracy achieved by the Markov model is higher than RNN, with RNN performing considerably good in itself. In this situation of pages' access prediction, the Markov model is more suitable as it will predict the page that has the highest state transition probability. RNN is most likely to perform better if there are more variations of actions involved in a larger dataset. To improve the current experiment with RNN, the dependency of some actions (like 'game_4' and 'create_game_score_4') has to be manually configured in the experiment setup, instead of separating both actions as two individual actions.

In the future, this work may involve clustering users to learn specific models for each cluster. To achieve this, more user information such as age can be collected to understand the navigation behavior of the specific user groups. To improve this experiment further, adding more customer engagement metrics such as bounce rate and session time would be useful in providing a more accurate prediction result.

Acknowledgments. This work is supported in part by Telekom Malaysia Research & Development Grant No. RDTC/191001 (MMUE/190086) and Multimedia University.

References

1. Lu, H.P., Ho, H.C.: Exploring the impact of gamification on users' engagement for sustainable development: a case study in brand applications. Sustainability **12**(10), 4169 (2020). https://doi.org/10.3390/su12104169
2. Palanitkar, S.: Starbucks rewards case study – what makes it work? (2019). https://zinrelo.com/loyalty-rewards-case-study-new-starbucks-rewards-program.html. Accessed 1 Nov 2020
3. Yeo, S.: The new phase of user engagement (2020). https://www.techinasia.com/phase-user-engagement. Accessed 1 Nov 2020
4. Christians, G.: The origins and future of gamification. Senior Theses **254**, 46–47 (2018)
5. Lin, C.W., Mao, T.Y., Huang, Y.C., et al.: Exploring the adoption of nike + run club app: an application of the theory of reasoned action. Math. Probl. Eng. (2020). https://doi.org/10.1155/2020/8568629
6. Atkins, A., Wanick, V., Wills, G.: Metrics feedback cycle: measuring and improving user engagement in gamified eLearning systems. Int. J. Serious Games **4**(4), 3–19 (2017). https://doi.org/10.17083/ijsg.v4i4.192
7. Baltierra, N.B., Muessig, K.E., Pike, E.C., et al.: More than just tracking time: complex measures of user engagement with an internet-based health promotion intervention. J. Biomed. Informat. **59**, 299–307 (2016). https://doi.org/10.1016/j.jbi.2015.12.015

8. Deshpande, M., Karypis, G.: Selective Markov models for predicting web-page accesses. ACM Trans. Internet Technol. **4**(2), 163–184 (2004). https://doi.org/10.1145/990301.990304

9. Kakalejč, L., Bucko, G., Resende, P.A., et al.: Multichannel marketing attribution using Markov chains. J. Appl. Manage. Invest. **7**(1), 49–60 (2018)

10. Almeida, A., Azkune, G.: Predicting human behaviour with recurrent neural networks. Appl. Sci. **8**(2), 305 (2018). https://doi.org/10.3390/app8020305

11. Ghannay, S., Favre, B., Esteve, Y., et al.: Word embeddings evaluation and combination. In: Proceedings of the Tenth International Conference on Language Resources and Evaluation (LREC 2016), pp. 300–305 (2016)

12. Mikolov, T., Sutskever, I., Chen, K., et al.: Distributed representations of words and phrases and their compositionality. In: Advances in Neural Information Processing Systems, pp. 3111–3119 (2013)

13. Li, Z.: A beginner's guide to word embedding with gensim Word2Vec model (2019). https://towardsdatascience.com/a-beginners-guide-to-word-embedding-with-gensim-word2vec-model-5970fa56cc92#b513. Accessed 9 Nov 2020

14. Sekaran, K., Ramalingam, S.R., Chandra Mouli, P.V.S.S.R.: Breast cancer classification using deep neural networks. In: Knowledge Computing and Its Applications, pp. 227–241 (2018). https://doi.org/10.1007/978-981-10-6680-1_12

15. Kankanhalli, A., Taher, M., Cavusoglu, H., et al.: Gamification: a new paradigm for online user engagement. In: Thirty Third International Conference on Information Systems, pp. 1–10 (2012)

Pivot Point Based Intelligent System to Associate Creative Textual Artefacts

Hrishikesh Kulkarni[1]([⊠]) and Bradly Alicea[2]

[1] Georgetown University, Washington, DC 20057, USA
hpk8@georgetown.edu
[2] Orthogonal Research and Educational Laboratory, Champaign, IL, USA

Abstract. Readers many times look for similar books, similar movies or creative artefacts with reference to a particular creative artefact of their interest. This similarity is not simply about the subject but also about overall presentation and the way overall plot in a creative artefact evolves. Most of the systems generally consider meta-data, authors, titles and genres for recommending book(s) to readers or movie(s) to viewers. But they miss on a few crucial aspects of similarity including progression of sentiment or that of overall theme. Similarity is a holistic concept and not confined to the title or topic. In narratives, progression of emotions across the key events could prove to be the key for similarity. In this paper, we establish similarity among narratives based on computational relationships among sentiment progression using intelligent text analysis. For reference we have used database http://www.cs.cmu.edu/~dbamman/booksummaries.html with 16559 books. We have proposed Sentiment Progression Association Model (SP-AM) based on pivot points to derive and map similarities. Further, analysis of changes in sentiments is used to derive book clusters of interest to readers. The promising analytical findings endorse the scientific approach of deriving similarity based on sentiment progression. This pivot point based intelligent system can address numerous real-life problems related to recommendation, association and retrieval of creative artefacts.

Keywords: Intelligent system · Natural language processing · Text analysis · Machine learning · Information retrieval · Sentiment mining · Pivot point

1 Introduction and Related Work

1.1 Going Beyond Similarity

Recommending book(s) or creative textual artefact(s) is generally driven by names of authors, topics and keywords. Similarity measures based on topics may work very well for research papers but do not work that well in the case of creative textual artefacts like books, movie scripts and fictions. When one refers to similarity among books, the similarity is not confined to genre, topic or author but it is more about theme, progression of emotional upheavals and at times exuberance of relationships among characters. Though titles may sometimes lead to selection, but it has very little to do with overall similarity. In the ocean of books where more than 2 million books are published every year, finding out books similar to the particular book of your choice is very challenging.

© Springer Nature Switzerland AG 2021
H. Fujita et al. (Eds.): IEA/AIE 2021, LNAI 12799, pp. 391–398, 2021.
https://doi.org/10.1007/978-3-030-79463-7_33

1.2 Related Work

Linguistic perspective is very important for narrative assessment. Surprises bring unexpected changes in relationships and concepts, differentiating adorable events [1]. The overall narrative can be viewed as an emotional journey. It can also be viewed as a concept journey along the core theme. Here different concepts are battling for existence and key concept proved to be the ultimate winner. Emotional aspects blended in very personalized culture are at the helm of this journey. These emotional aspects are associated with part of stories or creative textual artefacts depicted through different impacting sentences [2]. While dealing with multiple stories, sentence similarity and word mapping can lead to initiation of analysis [3]. At later stage we need to deal with sentiment composition and progression from linguistic point of view [4].

Creative artefacts irrespective of genre need to be analyzed from different perspectives [5]. In any of such scenarios decoding personality and cultural analysis with personality vector analysis prove to be effective for mapping [6, 7]. Researchers also used text-based analysis for clustering books [8].

The progression of relationships among characters in a narrative can be used for decoding similarity. To make it possible, this paper focuses on core character identification and pivot point determination. The emotional progression in a way portrays subtle aspects of the message delivered through the narratives. Sentiment progressions along with these relationships among themes evolve as the story progresses and end up in generally delivering a message along one or more prominent themes at emotional climax. This paper proposes 'Sentiment Progression Association Model' (SP-AM) based on pivot points to derive and map association. Themes, sentiments and culturally relevant touchstones form the basis for any story. There could be strong and weak emotions in the story and as the book progresses the sentiment progression takes place with emotional revelations. The relationships among sentiment progressions and thematic happenings are proposed in this paper to derive similarities among creative artefacts. The proposed approach in this paper captures abrupt interest elevation points those can prove to be contextual similarity indicators for narratives.

2 Sentiment Progression Association Model (SP-AM)

The proposed method is divided into four important phases:

1. Identifying core word and building word clusters around it.
2. Pivot points determination algorithm and association
3. Sentiment Progression Analysis
4. Use of 'Sentiment Affinity Index' to derive similarity.

3 Data Analysis

A database of 1076 books from different genre is prepared and used for testing and learning. Another database used is http://www.cs.cmu.edu/~dbamman/booksummaries. html. One of the sample books we used as an example - titled "*Rage of Angels*" is a part of both of these datasets. The analysis on this data is preformed using SP-AM to find book pairs those are similar ones.

4 Mathematical Model

4.1 Identifying Core Characters

Core characters are identified based on frequency of their presence and their relationships with other characters. Core characters are generally very well connected to different key events and other characters across the narrative. This process is performed after word sense disambiguation and co-reference resolution. Similarly, core themes are identified based on longevity and impact of theme across the book.

To explain the concept, we have chosen two interesting fictions those were read by 50 out of 150+ book lovers from the BDB book club[1]: First one is the fiction published in 1980 titled '*Rage of Angels*'[2] by Sidney Sheldon & the second one is Marathi Classic '*KraunchVadh*'[3] by Gyanpeeth awardee writer V.S. Khandekar.

The algorithm is developed around core words and pivot points. Here core word is defined as a word belonging to keywords occurring with highest frequency across the text space of interest. This highest occurring word is kept at the center while high frequency key words occurring in proximity of that word are used to form a word cluster.

Representative Core Character (RCC) is the key character in narrative and is defined from association of two or more characters. When more characters get associated with the character of interest, the weight associated with it increases.

Equation 1 gives mathematical definition of RCC.

$$\forall c \in c | C \in [CC] \ and \ c \rightarrow [CC] \ where \ [CC] \neq \Phi \tag{1}$$

where $[CC] \neq 0$. Going through narrative in an iterative fashion, the core characters are identified. The characters Jenifer, Michael and Adam are identified as core characters in *Rage of Angels*.

4.2 Pivot Points Determination and Association

Pivot point is one where major occurrence and interactions among core characters take place. They are points of intense interaction associated with the presence of core characters or themes. The text artefact or book is divided into logical blocks where logical blocks are typically sets of paragraphs with predefined length measured in terms of tokens. The relationship at a pivot point along with core expressive word distribution are used to derive sentiment index. Thus, analyzing relationships lead to overall sentiment index. The progression of sentiment across these pivot points is used to detect similarity. The detail algorithm for pivot point determination from the creative textual artefacts and sentiment association is given in Algorithm 1.

---

[1] A major book club run by BDB India Pvt Ltd in Pune https://bdbipl.com/index.php/bdb-book-club/.

[2] https://en.wikipedia.org/wiki/Rage_of_Angels.

[3] https://en.wikipedia.org/wiki/Vishnu_Sakharam_Khandekar.

Algorithm 1 Algorithm for determination of the pivot points in Text Artifacts

```
 1: function DETPIVOTPOINTS(TA)
 2:     n ← COUNTARTIFACTS(TA)
 3:     for TAᵢ in [TA] do
 4:         Wᵢ ← EXTRACTTOKENS(TAᵢ)
 5:     for i = 0 to n do
 6:         for w in Wᵢ do
 7:             w ← LOWERCASE(w)
 8:             if w ∉ [stopWords] then
 9:                 [TAᵢ.wlist] ← [TAᵢ.wlist] ∪ LEMMATIZE(w)
10:     for i=0 to n do
11:         for w in [TAᵢ.wlist] do
12:             if w ∈ [wordCorpus] then
13:                 [specialChar] ← [specialChar] ∪ w
14:     for ch in [specialChar] do
15:         for TAᵢ in [TA] do
16:             ch.freq ← ch.freq + GETFREQ(ch, TAᵢ)
17:             distributionᵢ ← GETFREQ(ch, TAᵢ)
18:             if ch.freq > GETTHRESHOLD(distribution) and δ_base <
    GETSD(distribution) then
19:                 [coreSet] ← [coreSet] ∪ ch
20:     for TAᵢ in [TA] do
21:         TAᵢ ← COREFERENCERESOLUTION(TAᵢ)
22:         TAᵢ ← WORDSENSEDISAMBIGUATION(TAᵢ)
23:         for ch in [coreSet] do
24:             coreDistributionⱼ ← GETFREQ(ch, TAᵢ)
25:         if threshold_{TA} < GETMAX(coreDistribution) then
26:             [pivotSet] ← [pivotSet] ∪ TAᵢ
        return [pivotSet]
```

4.3 Sentiment Affinity Index (SAI)

Statistically, Sentiment Affinity Index (SAI) gives similarity between sentiment progression patterns. Here sentiment progression is represented as a series. Hence, we get representative sentiment progression series for each book or text artefact. We will consider two creative artifacts at a time; hence we will get two sentiment progression series. Along with prominent pivot points, supporting points are added so that both series have equal number of elements. Hence series will look like:

$$R \ni R(i) = P_1(i) + P_2(i) \tag{2}$$

Here, R is representative series which is derived by summing corresponding pivot point sentiment values. Thus, probable sentiment value (PS) in accordance with representative sentiment progression is determined using Eq. 3.

$$PS = \frac{\sum_{i=1}^{n} P_1(i)}{\sum_{i=1}^{n} T(i)} \tag{3}$$

PS is used to derive expected sentiment value with assumption that sentiment progression in second series is same. It is used to calculate correction factor CF.

$$CF(i) = \frac{PS \times R(i) - P_1(i)}{\sqrt{R(i) \times PS \times (1 - PS)}} \tag{4}$$

The sentiment distance SD between two text artefacts is given by Eq. 5.

$$SD = \frac{\sum_{i=1}^{n} CF(i)^2 \times N(i)}{\sum_{i=1}^{n} N(i)} \tag{5}$$

Here N is normalization factor $N(i) = \sqrt{R(i)}$.

Further, the Affinity Index (AI) is calculated using Eq. 6

$$AI = \frac{1}{(1 + ln(1 + x))} \tag{6}$$

It makes sure that 'Sentiment Affinity Index' will drop slowly with increase in sentiment distance. Value of 'Sentiment Affinity Index' is close to 1 for similar patterns while it approaches zero for dis-similar ones. For exactly identical patterns it is exactly 1. Thus, Pivot point-based sentiment analysis makes it sure that you are capturing sentiment at crucial point and not in general across the creative artefact.

4.4 Handling Unequal Length Pivot Point Data Sets

Handling unequal length data series is one of the most challenging aspects of this method. To deal with this, we distributed pivot points based on its distribution across the book for the shorter length data series. The biggest gap is filled with intrapolation first. This process is continued till the length of two data series becomes same. The 30% length difference can be handled with this method but the method fails for more than 30% length difference between two series. In this case the secondary pivot points are used while extrapolating. A secondary pivot point between two primary pivot points is selected and the values are adjusted with reference to primary adjacent pivot point.

5 Experimentation

5.1 Baselines

Creative artifacts are generally clustered based on textual similarity. This association in the past, is performed using two different approaches [8]. In the first approach books are clustered based on metadata, author names, genre, keywords and titles. In the second approach textual similarity is used across the complete text or on summary of the books. The first approach is developed as the baseline-1 while the second one is developed as baseline-2. The results of these baselines are compared with SP-AM to validate suitability of the proposed approach.

5.2 Results

Books from database (http://www.cs.cmu.edu/~dbamman/booksummaries.html) are used for experimentation. We needed complete text of the book, hence the number of samples used for experimentation is kept limited. The feedback from 150 book lovers is compiled for analysis of outcome. Total 100 top book pairs are formed using SP-AM. This outcome is compared with results from baseline algorithm and assessment by 4 book lovers. Out of 100 identified similar pairs, for 92 all the book lovers were in agreement with experimental results. On the other side baseline-1 algorithm based on TFIDF using author names and metadata found only 61 of these 100 titles similar. Baseline-2 uses text similarity algorithm based on book summaries which could find

66 of the given sample book pairs textually similar. Sample 10 book pairs identified as similar based on SP-AM are given in Table 1. The response of 4 book lovers for these 10 sample book pairs is also shown in Table 1. It is even compared with baseline-1 and baseline-2. Around 31% improvement could be obtained for the given set of data using SP-AM over the baseline-1 and 25% over baseline-2.

This sample response endorses that readers look for sentiment progression rather than metadata related to book. Though the sample size is small one, it is representative of overall similarity. When we applied the same algorithms of pivot point identification, we found relationships in *Rage of Angels* are more distributed. Thus, the impact of evolution for another relationship on the original one is minimal in case of *Rage of Angels*. To examine this, we have also identified pivot points for the relationship between Jenifer & Adam and additional pivot points for the relationship between Jenifer & Michael. The sentiment progression between pivot points for the Jenifer-Adam & Jenifer-Michael relationships is shown in Fig. 1. As there is no overlap between these sets of relationship pivot points, there is a need for additional pivot point association outside of the dyadic relationships presented here. Table 2 gives sentiment indices at normalized pivot points for fictions *Rage of Angels* and *KraunchVadh*. The Sentiment Affinity Index (SAI) between these two fictions is 0.649149. Figure 2 depicts sentiment progression for them across pivot points.

Table 1. Pivot point mapping and ranking.

Book pairs (SP-AM)	Author, title, metadata-based algo (baseline-1)	Text similarity algorithm (baseline -2)	Book lover 1	Book lover 2	Book lover 3	Book lover 4
1	Y	Y	Y	Y	Y	Y
2	N	Y	Y	Y	Y	Y
3	N	N	Y	Y	Y	Y
4	Y	Y	Y	Y	Y	Y
5	Y	Y	Y	Y	Y	Y
6	N	N	Y	Y	Y	Y
7	N	N	N	Y	Y	N
8	Y	N	Y	Y	Y	Y
9	Y	Y	Y	Y	Y	Y
10	N	N	Y	N	N	Y

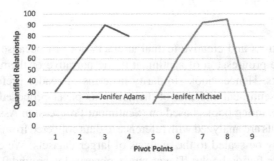

Fig. 1. Sentiment progression in *Rage of Angels*: Jenifer & Adam and Jenifer & Michael

Table 2. Pivot point mapping and ranking across the fiction (normalized values)

Pivot points	Sentiment index: *Rage of Angels*	Sentiment index: *KraunchVadh*
1	0.73	0.62
2	0.5	0.71
3	0.6	0.75
4	0.82	0.65
5	0.89	0.82
6	0.5	0.85
7	0.53	0.9
8	0.3	0.3
9	0.71	0.4
10	0.77	0.42
11	0.6	0.42
12	0.6	0.42

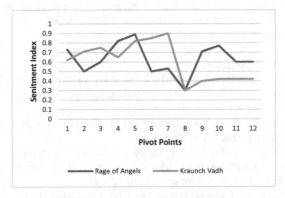

Fig. 2. Comparison of sentiment progression

6   Conclusion

Readers like narratives and creative textual artefacts not just because of the story but also because of the progression of sentiment in the narrative or theme progression in case of other books. Hence, book similarity in terms of reader preferences depends on progression of sentiment and that of themes. This paper proposed an approach of finding similarities among books based on 'Sentiment Progression Association Model' (SP-AM). The results are analyzed with reference to data collected from 150 book lovers, but the method may be scaled to the analysis of larger datasets. We considered 50 of them for two classic fiction books. The accuracy observed is around 92 percent, which is consistent with verification by expert readers. Multiple characters are also considered in calculating this progression. The proposed algorithm gives around 31% improvement over the base line algorithm based on Topic Modelling, keyword-based method that uses TFIDF and word similarity. The algorithm SP-AM can further be improved with multi-level graph clustering. The promising results and myriad applications of text artefact association with literary inclination definitely help in taking new pathways for building intelligent systems dealing with creative artifacts. This method can find its applications in identifying the best narrative for readers, calculating possible prospects of a particular movie or a book. It can even evolve to application that can help publishing houses to classify and rank submitted manuscripts before those are sent to evaluators. Further research on thematic relationships in case of strategy and self-help books can prove very interesting and equally challenging. Also, extending this idea for movies and news could be an interesting extension to this research.

References

1. Oard, D.W., Carpuat, M., et al.: Surprise languages: rapid-response cross-language IR. In: ACM NTCIR-14 Conference, 10 June 2019, Tokyo, Japan (2019)
2. Quan, C., Ren, F.: Selecting clause emotion for sentence emotion recognition. In: International Conference on Natural Language Processing and Knowledge Engineering, Tokushima, Japan (2011)
3. Saad, S.M., Kamarudin, S.S.: Comparative analysis of similarity measures for sentence level semantic measurement of text. In: IEEE International Conference on Control System, Computing and Engineering, pp. 90–94 (2013)
4. Mitchell, J., Lapata, M.: Vector-based models of semantic composition. In: Proceedings of the ACL Conference, Columbus, Ohio (2008)
5. Berendt, B.: Text mining for news and blogs analysis. In: Sammut, C., Webb, G.I. (eds.) Encyclopedia of Machine Learning and Data Mining. Springer, Berlin (2017). https://doi.org/10.1007/978-1-4899-7687-1_833
6. Kulkarni, H., Alicea, B.: Cultural association based on machine learning for team formation. arXiv preprint arXiv:1908.00234 (2019)
7. Kulkarni, H., Marathe, M.: Machine learning based Cultural Suitability Index (CSI) for right task allocation. In: IEEE International Conference on Electrical, Computer and Communication Technologies (IEEE ICECCT), Coimbatore, India (2019)
8. Spasojevic, N., Poncin, G.: Large scale page-based book similarity clustering. In: International Conference on Document Analysis and Recognition, Beijing, pp. 119–125 (2011). https://doi.org/10.1109/ICDAR.2011.33

Mood Support: A Personalized Intelligent Support Assignment System Using an Agent-Based Dynamic Configuration Model

Azizi Ab Aziz[✉], Roqia Rateb, and Arya Muhammad Bimo

Relational Machines Group, Human-Centred Computing Lab, School of Computing, Universiti Utara Malaysia, 06010 Sintok, Kedah, Malaysia
aziziaziz@uum.edu.my

Abstract. Social support is often labelled as a critical component of solid relationships and vital psychological health. It involves having a network of family and friends that persons can turn to in times of need. Scientific study has also shown the link between social relationships and several health and wellness aspects where poor social support has been linked to depression. However, many conditions can make seeking help hard for various reasons. Also, assigning incorrect support will create a burden for both support providers and recipients. This paper addresses how a social support network can be formed, taking the support recipient's needs and potential support providers' possibilities into account. To do so, previous work on agent-based computational models about support preferences and provision was used as a basis in a dynamic configuration support assignment.

Keywords: Cognitive modelling · Configuration approach · Ambient systems · Computational cognitive science

1 Introduction

Psychological stress has been identified by The World Health Organization (WHO) report as one of the modern-day killer epidemics and leading worldwide sources of years of well-being lost to illness in both women and men. It has also substantially contributed to the global burden of illness and connected to the loss of around 750,000 lives each year [1]. Without control and proper intervention, stress yields great economic costs, in terms of both the budgets of well-being and social consideration and different costs like the loss of workdays. There is a range of methods to help individuals to manage their stress. These include pharmacological treatment (medication), psychological techniques, and social support. Social support can be defined as the care or help from others that individuals can feel, notice, or accept and give mutual support or self-help for people facing various health-related problems [2]. From this spectrum, social support has become an immensely widely held and highly significant concept in the research literature of cognitive psychology, mental health, social development and psychological well-being [3].

© Springer Nature Switzerland AG 2021
H. Fujita et al. (Eds.): IEA/AIE 2021, LNAI 12799, pp. 399–411, 2021.
https://doi.org/10.1007/978-3-030-79463-7_34

In this paper, the foundation of the agent-based dynamic configuration support assignment model is presented. This paper is organized as follows; Sect. 2 describes several theoretical constructs of social support networks and their relation to stress management. Some ideas in a previous agent-based support provision and recipient model are discussed (Sect. 3). Later in Sect. 4, we describe some fundamental aspects of the configuration approach. In Sect. 5, the prototype's main components are covered, later followed by two experiments using pilot study and user experience evaluation (Sect. 6). Finally, Sect. 7 concludes the paper.

2 Fundamental Concepts in Social Support

According to the Attachment Theory [2, 4], social support is conceptualized as an interpersonal process that requires one partner's support-seeking endeavours and the other partner's caregiving reactions. There are many theoretical explanations for the relationship between social support and perceived stress. Most prominent is the buffering hypothesis, which asserts that social support protects individuals from adverse effects of extended stress following a calamity event. Buffering is described as any social support effect that intervenes between stressors and health. Additionally, previous researchers look at social support more structurally. They have defined social support as a system where individuals get care, respect, support and valued participation in a network of individuals for mutual benefit. These individuals offering support could be spouses, relatives, friends, colleagues, or other community members, as seen in Table 1 [3–6].

Table 1. Types of social support

Support types	Description	Ties	Examples
Emotional	• Provisions of confident support, attachment to enhance self-esteem and functions as close support	Strong	• Listening and offering sympathy after they had bad news
Instrumental	• Provision of tangible support, material aid (e.g. monetary, time, skills)	Strong/Weak	• Support in term of cash or excellent cook meals for disabled people
Informational	• Provision of advice, guidance, appraisal, and problem-solving	Weak	• Offer information, guidance, and advice
Companionship	• Refers to social activities that help people recognize that they are essential	Strong	• Engaging in activities with others, such as seeing a movie

Social ties relate to the individual connections maintained by people in their social circle contained by which they interact and exchange varied kinds of activities. These ties can be categorized into strong (spouse, close friends, family) and weak (colleagues, professionals) [3]. Besides, social ties play vital roles in requesting/providing types of support. For example, emotional support (sharing sadness or personal problems) are more likely to be solved by strong ties members [3, 6].

3 Agent-Based Computational Model for Social Support Dynamics

The agent-based computational model provides simulated (quantitative or qualitative) demonstrations that a specific micro-specification that is, in fact, sufficient to produce a macrostructure of interest. The modellers may use probabilistic approaches or data analytics to measure a given micro-specification's generative sufficiency—to test the agreement between real-world and generated macro structures. Each agent has a clear limit between its environment and other agents. Besides, it can be differentiated from other agents by their unique characteristics. As agents co-operate with other agents and their environment, it creates feasible judgments and emergent actions. Throughout this paper, two types of agents were represented, namely 1) support-recipient agent and 2) support-provision agent. These two agents are interacting through the dynamics of informal support activities.

3.1 Support Request and Provision Models

Figure 1 provides a visual outline of the model set out in [7, 8], based on the major theories about informal social support recipient and provision behaviours. The individual receipt and provision attributes were the first components that reflect an individual's personality characteristic for both support recipients and providers. Then, network ties determine a social support network's strength, either strong ties or weak ties. Similarly, this generated information will be directed to the social network ties part, which acts to determine an individual's tie in looking for support. After the social support-tie preference is selected, then the support generation is regulated. Support preference generation refers to the types of social support requested and provided during the process [6]. In this model, a stress component has been represented by adverse events, which act as an external factor stimulus that triggers short-term stress [3]. Such a stress condition is intensified by individual receipt traits such as neurotic personality, which later accrues in specific periods to develop a long-term stress illness [4]. Short-term stress also plays an imperative role to evoke support preference related to the receipt characteristics. Finally, the support provision attributes will establish the level of support feedbacks regarding the support recipient. As illustrated in Fig. 1, many variables represent key elements with social support networks members. These variables can be distinguished according to their behaviour, either instantaneous or temporal relations. For example, the instantaneous relationship happens without any temporal delay, in contrast to the temporal relationship.

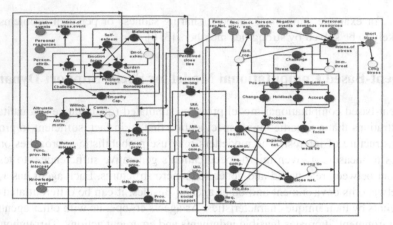

Fig. 1 Graphical representation of the connection between support provision and recipient agent-based models.

First, the instantaneous relationship explains the direct impact on states and their connections. For example, in a *Support Recipient Model*, the *challenge (Ch)* is related to *personality attributes (Pa)*, while negatively with the *intensity of stressful events (Ie)* through the proportional factor (β_c). In contrast, the *level of threat (Th)* can be defined by the proportional contribution (γ_h) on the *imminence of threat (Im)* and the *intensity of stressful events*. In this case of a *threat*, a negative relation is established with *personality attributes*. Therefore, the formal specifications for challenge and threat within an agent support recipient *r* can be written as;

$$Ch_r(t) = [(\beta_c.Pa_r(t) + (1-\beta_c).(1-Ie_r(t))].(1-Pa_r(t)) \tag{1}$$

$$Th_r(t) = [\gamma_h.Im_r(t) + (1-\gamma_h).Ie_r(t)].(1-Pa_r(t)) \tag{2}$$

where $r = \{n \mid n \in Z^+ \text{ and } n > 0\}$

Second, the temporal relationship often related to the accumulated effect from previous contribution of the same function. This form of contribution can be considered as a "delay condition" (regardless accumulating or decaying contributions). A description of temporal representation of y function can be presented as:

$$y(t+\Delta t) = y(t) + \tau.<total\_change>.\Delta t$$

assuming $\tau > 0$, this is equivalent to $<total\_change> = 0$ for all variables y.

Moreover, as; $<total\_change> = (1-y(t)).Pos(<change>)-y(t).Pos(-<change>)$, where $Pos(x) = 0 \text{ or } Pos(-x) = 0$. In this agent-based model, several concepts implemented the temporal relations to represent the accumulative impacts throughout time. One of them is *emotional exhaustion* (from the *Support Provision Model*). Emotional exhaustion *(Eh)* is an unsatisfactory outcome that individuals feel after experiencing the effect of *maladaptation (Ma)*. Repeated maladaptation over a long period will trigger an exhaustion phase [5]. Later, this condition will increase the perceived burden level for providers. Emotional exhaustion increases and decreases over time, depending on the current level of maladaptation [4, 5].

$$Eh_r(t+\Delta t) = Eh_r(t) + \psi_e[Ma_r(t)-Eh_r(t)].(1-Eh_r(t)).Eh_r(t).\Delta t \qquad (3)$$

where ψ_e is the change rate factor, $0 \leq \psi_e \leq 1$, and $0 \leq \Delta t \leq 1$.

From Eq. 3, the parameter ψ_e is used to determine the changing rate of temporal relationship, which reflects a considerable presence of maladaptation, the amount of emotional exhaustion will increase. The details of these formal specifications can be found in [7, 8].

3.2 Support Utilization Evaluation

The utilized social support concept reflects the actual use of social support that the support provider can offer to help recipients meet their requests based on two scenarios [5] (as depicted in Fig. 2). First, if the support provider can offer support more than or equal to the requested support, then the provided support was wholly covered the fundamental needs of the requested support. Second, if the support provider can offer support less than requested support, then the provided support has partially covered the needs of any requested support.

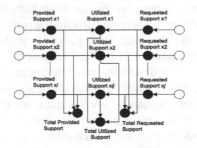

Fig. 2 Conceptualization of the support utilization.

In general, the support utilization US specification can be summarized as;

$$US_x(t) = min\left[1, \frac{PS_x(t)}{RS_x(t)}\right] \qquad (4)$$

where $x = \{informational, companionship, instrumental, emotional\}$, $RS_x(t) \neq 0$, and $min(.)$ is defined by $min(x,y) = 1$ if $x > = y$ or otherwise $min(x,y) = x/y$. The utilized x support (US_x) describes the actual use of support based on the current provided support PS_x to help support recipients (requested support, RS_x) their need. If the emotional provided support is higher or equal than requested emotional support, this means it completely covers an individual's needs. Otherwise, it is partially covered ($PS_x(t)/RS_x$ (t)).

4 Dynamic Configuration for Support Assignment

The provision of informal support is depicted as a dynamic process by which individual, relational and contextual factors of both care recipient and caregiver are interlinked. Compared to the previous static configuration support assignment in [8], our proposed model introduces the temporal dynamic approach to suit the constant changes in support provision and recipient tasks, especially on social networks [9].

4.1 Configuration Approach

The dynamic support assignment is based on a configuration algorithm approach. This approach's focal idea is that it expects every individual can be seen as "resource providers" as required in the model. The construction of connections among requested and provided support is not viewed in terms of one-to-one pairing but on choices and preferences. This configuration task is executed for a set of parameters by a target algorithm with a given configuration space and a collection of instances. To apply a configuration model in a computational social support domain, three elements are needed [10, 11]; i) a functional requirement, ii) a sub-model for choosing parts and regulating their mutual requirements, iii) a sub-model for arranging parts. First, a functional requirement for a configuration task defines the requirements that the configuration must satisfy. Secondly, a sub-model for parts specifies the parts selected for a configuration and other parts' requirements. Some parts require other parts for their correct functioning or use [12]. For example, social support parts for the recipient include all requested support. Thirdly, a sub-model for spatial arrangement describes parts' placement and specifies parts' possible arrangement [13, 14]. Together, the arrangement model and the requirement form a basis for describing which arrangement is acceptable and preferred. These resources are limited and consumed differently by different arrangements [11, 15]. Finally, those resources can be used in the configuration process to utilize support recipient information to choose support members obtainable for support provision. The crucial information (requirements) needed for a configure process are; i) *tie's preferences*, ii) *long-term stress*, iii) *support receipt preferences*, iv) *function in social networks*, and v) *support provision preferences*. Using this information with a set of configuration rules, an algorithm to generate a set of social support members to provide support was developed. Before the algorithm's execution, a set of constraints, like preference number of providers, the level of acceptance requested and provided support, and a level of acceptance burden must be initialized first [5, 7, 9].

4.2 Dynamic Configuration Algorithm

The configured selection model (as shown in Fig. 3) offers social provision tasks based on individuals within their unique preferences and resources based on a configuration approach. For example, a member with a high network tie (strong tie) P_{se} will be chosen first and followed by a member with a high support provision and so forth. For example, if companionship support is needed, then a support provider within a strong tie network is preferred over a weak tie. The support assignment model starts with check support receipt long term stress and required help to start the process. Simultaneously, it checks the intensity of stressful event for the provider and checks the provider's burden level (Bl). Later it determines the provider's proportion of support and checks perceived close tie and need of help from a strong tie network, and addressed the support. Based on this, the matching process between recipient and provider will begin. As a result, a configured support recipient-provider combination will be produced.

Input: *social ties, types of support, stress threshold, support assignment parameters, parameters in social support & provision model*
Output: *assign support*
Start:
    Initialization: provider i, such that $1 \leq i \leq n$; timestep t, such that $t \leftarrow 1 \leq t \leq t_{max}$
    While *($t <= numStep$ & $i \neq 0$ & ($Sr \neq 0$ || $Sp \neq 0$))*
        If *($Ls_{sr} >= stressTh_{sr}$)*   // evaluate the long term stress level
            $P_{se} \leftarrow [Se /\Sigma support\_tie].100$ // percentage of strong tie
            $P_{we} \leftarrow [We/\Sigma support\_tie].100$ // percentage of weak tie
            $Pc \leftarrow (func\_provision + func\_recipient)/\Sigma cs$ // perceived close tie
      Else
            Exit ( )
      End If
      If *($Pc >= priorityTh$ & $SupportBurden < BurdenLimit$ & $Ps > 0$)*
            assign_InfoSup(Ir, Ip, Bl)   // assign informational support
            assign_EmoSup(Er, Ep, Bl)   // assign emotional support
            assign_InsSup (Nr, Np, Bl) // assign instrumental support
            assign_ComSup (Cr, Cp, Bl) // assign companionship support
        Else
            select_next_provider(i, n)
      End If
        Select *provider i*
        Remove *provider i from the provider's list*
      Update *Ls_{sr}, SuportBurden, Sr & Sp, i*
      $t \leftarrow t + 1$
End

Fig. 3 The Main dynamic configuration algorithm

The support assignment function (based on a related support request, *ReqSup* and provided support, *ProvSup*) will evaluate the assigned support based on available support, burden and request. For this part, the generic support assignment for all support types will be shown as *assignSupport*).

From Fig. 4, this algorithm evaluates the provider's stress (including intensity of cognitive threat and burden). It is essential to ensure the providers will not be overwhelmed by repetitive support providing tasks [5, 9]. The assigned support will be based on two primary conditions, 1) the support provider has adequate preferences and resources to deliver the assigned support and 2) the support proportion should be lesser than an experienced burden.

```
assign_Support (ReqSup, ProvSupp, Bl )
      If (ReqSup>supportTh) & (Ie<=intensityTh) & (Bl<=burdenTh)
             provider_proportion ← (1-Bl)
             requestSupport (providerSupport)
         Else
             select_next_provider(i, n)
      End
requestSupport(providerSupport)
      If (providerSupport>supportTh)
             assignSupport ←providerSupport . provider_proportion
             neededSupport ← (providerSupport/Σn)    // n = total providers
      End
      If (providerSupport >= neededSupport)
             requestedSupport ← (requestedSupport - assignedSupport )
             providerSupport ← (providerSupport - assignedSupport)
             Bl ← (Bl+ assignedSupport)
      Else
             Select_Next_Provider(i,n)
      End
End
```

Fig. 4 Support assignment and request algorithm

5 Prototype

Our prototype is composed of the main modules shown in Fig. 5(a). In short, during any interaction, the user's input (selected questions) are processed by the *Support Provision /Recipient Interface* modules, which directs the sessions and elicits information from the user in an attempt to assess the user's most probable needed/provided support via related questions (as directed by the *Questions/Psychometric Bank*). The *Support Provision /Recipient Models* will generate types of support needed or provided by the users.

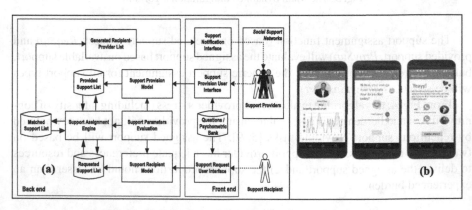

Fig. 5 (a) Software architecture and (b) user interfaces

Later, both agent-based models (*Support Provision* and *Recipient*) will compute needed and provided support. Also, the *Support Parameters Evaluation* module will provide some important parameter settings based on each individual. Later, the *Support Assignment Engine* will arrange for support providers-recipient lists based on a dynamic configuration algorithm. The generated list will be channelled to the Support Notification Interface as a pop-up notification for respective support providers. Figure 5(b) provides an example of the prototype interfaces. This prototype was developed using an Android Development Studio as a programming platform and SQLite as a database and activities repository.

6   Results

We experimented with evaluating our proposed approach in providing support to the recipient. For this pilot study, 30 graduate students at Universiti Utara Malaysia were selected based on their social support networks (minimum three persons for each social support group). The experiment was a within-subjects design to eliminate inter-subject variation to boost our study's power and conducted in two weeks.

6.1   Pilot Study (Qualitative Results)

In this paper, we use a fictional representation to maintain the anonymity of the participants. For brevity, we select one of the cases where the support recipient X required informational support from his/her social support networks. The details of the parameters and attributes for social support receipt and provision, as presented in Table 2. These values were extracted based on selected questionnaires related to the concepts.

Table 2. Parameter settings for support provider members

Concept/Provider	A	B	C	D	E	F
Personal resources (Prp)	0.6	0.1	0.6	0.7	0.5	0.9
Negative event (Nvp)	0.3	0.8	0.7	0.3	0.1	0.1
Altruistic attitudes (Al)	0.8	0.4	0.8	0.9	0.8	0.7
Recipient interests (Rs)	0.2	0.4	0.2	0.2	0.1	0.1
Provider interests (Ps)	0.1	0.5	0.4	0.1	0.3	0.2
Knowledge level (Kl)	0.3	0.1	0.6	0.9	0.8	0.7
Personal attributes (Pap)	0.7	0.2	0.5	0.7	0.8	0.3
Agreeableness (Ag)	0.4	0.4	0.3	0.1	0.2	0.1
Extraversion (Evp)	0.3	0.1	0.1	0.2	0.1	0.3
Function provider in social network (Fp)	0.9	0.8	0.4	0.1	0.2	0.3

With these parameter's values, consider this description:

"Individual X experiences stress and seeks help. The support recipient model generated results, and it shows that he needs more informational support (0.8).

Also, he prefers members from a weak tie network (0.7) to a strong tie network (0.1)."

From these members, the computational agent model generated the support provision availability for each individual and presented as in the following (tie network, informational support); A(strong, 0.3), B(strong, 0.1), C(weak, 0.5), D(weak, 0.7), E(weak, 0.6), and F(weak, 0.4). Using a support tie preference, individual X prefers 88% from weak tie support members and 12% from strong tie members. The algorithm assigns each provider to provide at least an informational support level at 0.13.

Thus, in this case, all providers can provide informational support to X (except B as his/her support provision level < 0.13). However, as the support provided is not adequate, the support assignment was computed again, and the support model re-generated a list that contains potential members to provide needed support. Figure 6 shows a summary of the dynamics ($t_1 \rightarrow t_2$) in utilized support based on simulated cases in this case study. Note that requested support (informational support) reduces at time t_2 as it receives adequate support from his social support network members. It explains the increment in a utilized support level.

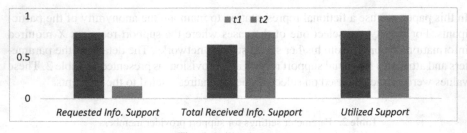

Fig. 6 Utilized support

Besides, using *Depression, Anxiety and Stress Scale*-21 Items (DASS-21) [16], an individual X's stress level is measured twice a week. As can be seen from Fig. 7, the stress level is declining from "severe stress" to "normal" during the observation period. The respondent was interviewed, and he/she acknowledged the assigned support providers did help him/her reduce the stress level. Also, at the end of each session, we conducted semi-structured interviews to elicit individuals experience of the interaction and suggestions for improvement. Participants commented positively on the support members' function and perceived the system as "knowing what it should do".

X: *"I like how the system suggested a list of members that can help me, especially with the type of support I need. Although not 100 per cent correct but it surprises me with the suggested names. It is like the system to know what I need. Quite a mixed feeling."*

B: *"When the system suggested my name to help X. What I found interesting, at first, I was surprised, and the recommended type of support to be given was quite accurate as I am the one who loves to advise on something."*

Fig. 7 Level of stress (Individual X) during the experimental period

6.2 User Experience Experiment

The user experience experiment's objective is to allow a quick assessment done by end-users covering a preferably comprehensive impression of user experience. There are two evaluation constructs used, namely, 1) hedonistic and pragmatic qualities. *Pragmatic qualities* refer to the perceived usefulness, efficiency, and ease of use (utility and usability aspects). In contrast, the *hedonic qualities* consider the "joy of use" and emphasize stimulation, identification and evocation generated using a system. This study used the short- user experience questions (S-UEQ) with Likert-scale 1–7 item. The S-UEQ measures related constructs such as supportiveness, easiness, efficiency, and clarity for pragmatic quality, while excitement, interestingness, inventiveness and novelty (leading edge) for hedonic quality [17]. Later, the obtained results will be converted into a range of the scales between −3 (horribly bad) and +3 (extremely good). Participants from the pilot study were required to fill in the S-UEQ at the end of the experiment timeframe. Table 3 shows the results obtained from this experiment.

Table 3. The user experience results

Scale	Mean (SD)	Confidence interval ($p = 0.05$)
Pragmatic quality	1.48 (0.42)	CI[1.27,1.69]
Hedonic quality	1.40 (0.35)	CI[1.22,1.58]
Overall	1.44 (0.33)	CI[1.27,1.61]

By comparison, this prototype scores "above average" evaluation based on the benchmark dataset collected from 452 product evaluation studies concerning different digital products/applications (https://www.ueq-online.org) [17] (Fig. 8).

The "above average" describes that 25% of the benchmark outcomes are better than the result for the evaluated product; 50% of the results are worse [18]. Through a questionnaire like the UEQ, it is possible to make an informed decision regarding the areas in which improvements will have the highest impact. The measured user experience qualities provide some assumptions about where to look for improvements.

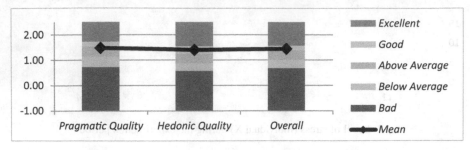

Fig. 8 Comparison of the results based on the UEQ benchmark

7 Conclusion

We have developed an intelligent support provision assignment to be deployed on a smartphone/tablet. The challenge addressed in this paper is to design a computational entity capable of assigning the most suitable support provider(s) based on related requested support. This computational entity covers two aspects; 1) generating support provision and recipient behaviours and 2) configuring social support pair. The resulting solution can help understand how certain concepts at a societal level (e.g. personality attributes) may influence other individuals while asking and providing informal support. Additionally, we demonstrate the potential of such a system through our pilot study in which stressed participants managed to reduce their stress based on the suggested type of support and providers. The work is ongoing, and the most critical future step is to conduct a quantitative study for wider randomized sample sizes and finalize it for deployment in public settings.

References

1. James, S.L., et al.: Global, regional, and national incidence, prevalence, and years lived with disability for 354 diseases and injuries for 195 countries and territories, 1990–2017: a systematic analysis for the Global Burden of Disease Study 2017. Lancet **392**(10159), 1789–1858 (2018)
2. Feeney, B.C., Collins, N.L.: A new look at social support: a theoretical perspective on thriving through relationships. Pers. Soc. Psychol. Rev. Off. J. Soc. Pers. Soc. Psychol. Inc **19**(2), 113–147 (2015)
3. Harandi, T.F., Taghinasab, M.M., Nayeri, T.D.: The correlation of social support with mental health: a meta-analysis. Electron. Phys. **9**(9), 5212–5222 (2017)
4. Riley, S.G., Pettus, K.I, Abel, J.: The buddy group—peer support for the bereaved. Lond. J. Prim. Care (Abingdon) **10**(3), 68–70 (2018)
5. Kondrat, D.C., Sullivan, W.P., Wilkins, B., Barrett, B.J., Beerbower, E.: The mediating effect of social support on the relationship between the impact of experienced stigma and mental health. Stigma Health **3**(4), 305–314 (2018)
6. Wang, J., Mann, F., Lloyd-Evans, B.: Associations between loneliness and perceived social support and outcomes of mental health problems: a systematic review. BMC Psychiat. **18**, 156 (2018)
7. Rateb, R., Aziz, A.A., Ahmad, R.: Formal modeling and analysis of social support recipient preferences. J. Telecommun. Electron. Comput. Eng. **9**, 69–75 (2017)

8. Aziz, Azizi A., Klein, Michel C.A., Treur, J.: Intelligent configuration of social support networks around depressed persons. In: Peleg, M., Lavrač, N., Combi, C. (eds.) AIME 2011. LNCS (LNAI), vol. 6747, pp. 24–34. Springer, Heidelberg (2011). https://doi.org/10.1007/978-3-642-22218-4_4

9. Choi, M,J., et al.: Toward predicting social support needs in online health social networks. J. Med. Internet Res. **19**(8), e272 (2017)

10. Felfernig, A., Reiterer, S., Stettinger, M., Tiihonen, J.: Intelligent techniques for configuration knowledge evolution. In: Proceedings of the Ninth International Workshop on Variability Modelling of Software-intensive Systems (VaMoS 2015), pp. 51–58 (2015)

11. Hanafy, M., El Maraghy, H.: A modular product multi-platform configuration model. Int. J. Comput. Integrat. Manufact. **28**(9), 999–1014 (2015)

12. Gönnheimer, P., Kimmig, P., Ehrmann, C., Schlechtendahl, J., Güth, J., Fleischer, J.: Concept for the configuration of turnkey production systems. Procedia CIRP **86**, 234–238 (2019)

13. Jaworski, W., Wilk, P., Juszczak, M., Wysoczańska, M., Lee A.Y.: Towards automatic configuration of floorplans for indoor positioning system. In: International Conference on Indoor Positioning and Indoor Navigation (IPIN), pp. 1–7 (2019)

14. Monticolo, D., Badin, J., Gomes, S., Bonjour, E., Chamoret, D.: A meta-model for knowledge configuration management to support collaborative engineering. Comput. Indus. **66**, 11–20 (2015)

15. Qiao, H., Feng, F., Qi, J.: A scalable product configuration model and algorithm. Cluster Comput. **22**, 6405–6415 (2019)

16. DASS 21 Scale website. http://www2.psy.unsw.edu.au/dass/. Accessed 13 Jan 2021

17. Schrepp, M., Hinderks, A., Thomaschewski, J.: Design and evaluation of a short version of the user experience questionnaire (UEQ-S). IJIMAI **4**(6), 103–108 (2017)

18. Schrepp, M., Hinderks, A., Thomaschewski, J.: Construction of a benchmark for the User Experience Questionnaire (UEQ). Int. J. Interact. Multimed. Artif. Intell. **4**(4), 40–44 (2017)

Continuous Build Outcome Prediction: A Small-N Experiment in Settings of a Real Software Project

Marcin Kawalerowicz[1]([✉])(iD) and Lech Madeyski[2](iD)

[1] CODEFUSION Sp. z o.o. and Faculty of Electrical Engineering, Automatic Control and Informatics, Opole University of Technology, Opole, Poland
marcin@kawalerowicz.net
[2] Department of Applied Informatics, Wroclaw University of Science and Technology, Wrocław, Poland
Lech.Madeyski@pwr.edu.pl

Abstract. We explain the idea of Continuous Build Outcome Prediction (CBOP) practice that uses classification to label the possible build results (success or failure) based on historical data and metrics (features) derived from the software repository. Additionally, we present a preliminary empirical evaluation of CBOP in a real live software project. In a small-n repeated-measure with two conditions and replicates experiment, we study whether CBOP will reduce the Failed Build Ratio (FBR). Surprisingly, the result of the study indicates a slight increase in FBR while using the CBOP, although the effect size is very small. A plausible explanation of the revealed phenomenon may come from the authority principle, which is rarely discussed in the software engineering context in general, and AI-supported software development practices in particular.

Keywords: Software defect prediction · Agile experimentation · Continuous integration · Machine learning

1 Introduction

While the raise of the complexity of software systems poses challenges that need to be addressed by Software Engineering processes, techniques and tools, the proposed novel approaches need to be evaluated against the earlier adopted ones. Software defect prediction (SDP) is an existing technique used to identify error-prone software modules. It is a cost-effective [1], software engineering assisting activity used to mitigate the problems that could arise if a software defect occurs. In our previous paper [2], we coined the idea of a lightweight version of Continuous Defect Prediction (CDP), named here Continuous Build Outcome Prediction (CBOP), that uses classification to label the possible build result (success or failure) based on historical data and metrics (features) derived from the software repository. In this paper, we build upon this idea and describe how we instantiated the CBOP practice in a real software project, as well as provide an empirical evaluation of the practice in real settings.

© Springer Nature Switzerland AG 2021
H. Fujita et al. (Eds.): IEA/AIE 2021, LNAI 12799, pp. 412–425, 2021.
https://doi.org/10.1007/978-3-030-79463-7_35

In CBOP, we use machine learning (ML) models that predict the continuous integration (CI) build results on the basis of historical CI results (success or failure) combined with metrics harvested from the software repository. A software developer is equipped with a set of tools that deliver continuous feedback by overseeing his actions. Metrics are calculated on the fly and sent to the prediction model that checks if the changes developer is currently making in the source code might lead to a problem during the integration performed on the CI server. If a possible problem is detected, the feedback might lead the developer to be more cautious and to fix the problem before it manifests itself as a failing build.

In this article, we discuss the current state of knowledge and technology in the area of SDP (Sect. 2). We describe how the experiment aimed to evaluate the usefulness of CBOP in real-world, industrial settings was planned (Sect. 3) and executed (Sect. 4). We present the experiment results (Sect. 4.3).

Discussion is presented in Sect. 5. Conclusions are presented in Sect. 6.

2   Background

It is not easy to automatically detect a software defect. That is why using machine learning to aid software defect prediction fascinated researchers for a long time (see, e.g., [3–5]). The idea was refined later in [6–8] and called just-in-time quality assurance or just-in-time defect prediction.

From one side, we build on top of a described and prototyped tool [3,9] that performs defect prediction directly in the Integrated Development Environment (IDE). From the other side, we are using the unambiguous data from CI [10] server as a source of buggy/clean information and synthesizing it with the code metrics mined from the software repository.

Until now, the defect prediction approaches were based mainly on lexical examination of the commit message or the information from the bug tracking software [11]. We are classifying the change as buggy or not based on the result of the build on the CI server. We are using the build server as a definite source of information (oracle) about the "bug". If the build fails, we can presume the introduced change was buggy. This information is then fed into the model to improve it further. Finally, the effect we get is a constantly learning model based on unambiguous data derived from the build server.

Having the model ready, we are able to give the developer continuous real-time feedback in the form of build outcome prediction. Using this feedback, the developer can assess if the changes, he is working on, are likely to introduce a bug into the project or not. We are achieving this by exposing the build outcome prediction model to the IDE the developer is working with. We have an IDE extension (add-on) that continuously communicates with the model sending the project measurements and receiving prediction in exchange. The prediction then is displayed in the developer IDE. This could make him aware that the changes he is introducing to the project might result in a build fail. Consequently, that might lead to a more careful examination of the changes and rule out the defect(s) that would lead to a failing build.

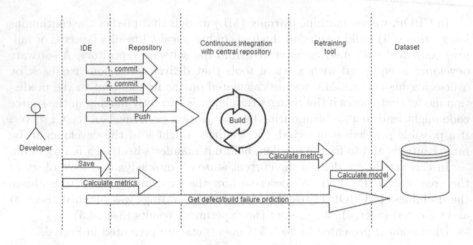

Fig. 1. Continuous build outcome prediction diagram

The idea of the technique we are proposing is presented in Fig. 1. The discrete process of repeatedly building the software, training the model and obtaining the predictions is enclosed in an uninterrupted feedback loop. Deriving the analogy from CI the continuous nomenclature was used for CDP and CBOP.

3   Experiment Plan

3.1   Scoping

We define the goal of our experiment as follows [12]: *Analyze* continuous build outcome prediction (CBOP) practice *for the purpose of* evaluation of the practice *with respect to* its effectiveness to reduce the build failure rate (BFR) *from the point of view of the* researcher and project manager *in the context of* a small group of professional software developers (subjects) working in an industrial-grade software project (object).

In other words, we want to conduct the experiment to get the answer whether the new CBOP practice will reduce the rate of failing builds in a day-to-day work on an industrial-grade software project. We will have one object (a software project) and multiple subjects/participants (a software development team). According to the terminology used by Wohlin et al. [12], we will conduct "Multi-test within object study". Technically, it will be a quasi-experiment as the object, the software project, and the subjects (i.e., the software developers) will not be chosen randomly. Nevertheless, we will use randomization techniques in our quasi-experiment.

3.2   Context Selection

The experiment will be conducted in vivo on an ongoing real business driven software project. Technically, it is a project consisting of two subprojects. One is a Microsoft .NET based project (ProjDotNet) in its 4th year of development, while the second project is a web-based Angular client (ProjWeb) that uses the ProjDotNet as an application programming interface (API). It is a software for banks and leasing companies. It is used in some large financial organizations on the German-speaking market. The software covers the complete loan and leasing contract lifetime from calculation, through offer creation to contract and contract recalculation, including after-contract object management and resell. The software was originally written in Clarion (fourth-generation programming language). New software features are now added to the software using Microsoft .NET and the C# language. They contain Windows Communication Foundation(WCF)-based Web services and interoperability managed code calls using Component Object Model (COM). The other part of the software is an Angular based Web client that uses the .NET services as an API layer. Table 1 shows some data about the ProjDotNet and ProjWeb projects derived from it at the end of June 2018. According to the classification by Wohlin et al. [12], we have an on-line project, involving professional developers, specific, and real problem.

Table 1. Project details

Number of distinct committers	18
Actively working in project	6–8 developers/week
The total number of commits	Over 10 000
Total number of files	Over 9 000
Total lines of code	Over 4 500 000
Average build commits per active week	Approx. 60

The CBOP practice was not introduced to the project before the start of the experiment. There was neither defect prediction nor build failure prediction used in this project from its beginning. The build results recording was started on 2018-06-20 and lasted until 2018-10-02.

3.3 Hypothesis Formulation

We formulate the following hypotheses:

H0 (null hypothesis): Using the CBOP practice (aka CBOPon) does not influence the Failed Build Ratio (FBR).
H1: Using CBOP reduces FBR.

3.4 Variables Selection

In the experiment we will control the time when we apply CBOP or not (independent variable in our experimental design). We will make the predictions available to the developers only in certain times through the toolset we provide. The idea is to turn the prediction on (i.e., use CBOP) and off, labelled as A and B, on a workday basis using a randomization schema. We will have days where the prediction is available to the developer and days where it is not. The experiment will be conducted during 4 weeks of real development.

The build failure count will be used to calculate FBR. Every push to the central repository ends with the build on the CI server. The possible results one may observe on Jenkins CI are: SUCCESS, FAILURE, UNSTABLE, ABORTED, NOT_BUILD[1]. Only the results of type FAILURE are counted as failed builds. We do not count UNSTABLE builds as failures as they are not necessarily associated with failures but, e.g., bad smells in production code or tests. The ABORTED and NOT_BUILD are not counted as failures as well. As a result, we calculate the failed build ratio (FBR) as follows: $FBR = \frac{\#FAILURE}{(\#UNSTABLE+\#ABORTED+\#NOT\_BUILD+\#SUCCESS+\#FAILURE)}$.

3.5 Selection of Subjects

The experiment will be conducted on a sample of the population of software developers. The company we are conducting the experiment in is a subcontractor of a larger software development company. The subcontractor leases 4 resources to its partner. One resource is 160 h of work in one calendar month. It amounts to 640 h of work (all of them not necessarily working full hours on that specific project). The work is conducted by 5–7 people. 4 to 5 software developers, software tester and a user experience specialist. All developers involved in the project are professionals with masters or bachelors degree in computer science with various experience levels: from 1 to 5 years of industrial experience as a software developer. The main task of all developers described here is the work in the subcontracted project described in detail in Sect. 3.2.

On the contractor side, there are 4 to 5 developers and one intern involved in that project. The developers are working full time on that project, while the intern is working only part time. One of the developers on the contractor is a software architect with 5+ years of experience and the three remaining developers are juniors with 1 to 3 years of experience.

Because we are interested in the largest possible sample of subjects, we used a convenience sampling technique to select the subjects – we selected all available subjects involved in the project. For the planing phase of the experiment we used the sample size of 4 for all the calculations. We were sure that we will be able to conduct the experiment with at least 4 developers (working in the project on the subcontractor side). During the execution of the experiment we were able to incorporate additional developers on the contractor side (the number of participants amounted 9).

---

[1] Jenkins CI Build results: http://javadoc.jenkins-ci.org/hudson/model/Result.html.

3.6 Choosing Experiment Design Type

In essence, we have here an experiment with one factor (the use of CBOP) and two treatments (presence or absence of the prediction). The participation of four developers from the contractor side in the experiment was certain. This rather small number of participants led us to use a small-n experimental design to study the effect of CBOP.

Dugard et al. [13] provided a list of experimental designs for single-case and small-experiments. Careful examination of the conditions for those experiments enabled us to find a proper design for our situation: "A small-n repeated-measures design with two conditions and replicates". We have at least two participants and two conditions to compare (A - No build outcome prediction available for the developer, B - build outcome prediction available for the developer). Each participant will receive each of the conditions on at least two occasions and it is possible to assign the conditions randomly.

Because we have expected at least 4 participants, we have not considered any of the "single-case" designs provided by Dugard et al. [13]. Other designs (Small-n one-way design, A small-n repeated-measures design, Two-way factorial small-n design) have been considered and were rejected as we knew that we will be able to measure the participants multiple times, but we will not have multiple levels of factors.

Because we will be able to change the condition multiple times, we have not considered the phase AB or ABA designs. They have their limitations making them more suitable for drug trials or medical experiments. Such trials need to have a clear distinction between the "intervention" (B after A) or even "withdrawal" (A after AB) and the baseline (A). Where we do have a distinction between the phases, we do not need to be that careful about the negative outcomes of our experiment. Thus, we will not conduct "The multiple baseline AB design" or "Multiple baseline ABA design" although technically possible in our case but too limited. In our case, a frequent succession of different conditions will be possible, thus an "Alternate design" will be a better choice according to Bulte and Onghena [14].

We will be able to apply each treatment multiple times using a randomization schema, giving us the possibility to perform several observations (replicates) on each condition.

Choosing the right period to alternate between the phases was not an easy task. We have gathered some actual data from 6 weeks preceding the start of the experiments on the rate of the various build results. We have come up with an average of 54 builds per week with six failed builds per week. Having this data, we decided that a day will be a good choice for the period to alternate between the phases in our experiment. It should give us enough data to draw meaningful conclusions.

Next, we have proceeded to calculate the possible power of the experiment. We expected to have a least 4 participants in our team and 4 weeks to perform the experiment, giving us 20 observation days (assuming 5 working days per week).

4   Execution

4.1   Experimental Setup

We have a working experimental CBOP setup in a commercial software project. The CBOP deployment in the project was possible thanks to our own dedicated tool called Jaskier [15]. Detailed information about the experiment instrumentation including the model prediction model creation is available in an online appendix [16].

4.2   Validity Evaluation

In accordance with Wohlin et al. [12], we discuss threats to validity of our research.

The threat to the internal validity that applies to our research is that a subject may react differently as time passes (maturation). We think this threat is to a large extent addressed by the CBOP on (aka CBOPon)/off (aka CBOPoff) randomized assignment, see Table 2.

The threats concerning the problems to generalize the results of the research to a wider population of software developers are threats to external validity. The threat of "interaction of selection and treatment" is addressed to some extent by the fact that in both teams there is a wide distribution of experience and knowledge (from juniors to seniors), good diversity in culture and educational background (two countries, different education paths). The threat of "interaction of setting and treatment" is mitigated through the use of two technically different projects (.NET and Angular), the usage of industry standard tools (Visual Studio, VSCode) and a real, not toy-like, project. However, this threat needs to be considered because the technical differences between other types of projects might impact the ability to generalize the results. We conduct the experiment during the period of several days what mitigates the threat of "interaction of history and treatment". The time of day should not impede the observations. The research was conducted solely in a real-life software development project, what makes the external validity considerations much less critical.

Another type of threats we have considered are construct validity threats. They concern generalizing the results of the experiment to the ideas behind it. To address "inadequate preoperational explication of constructs" we have defined, as clearly as possible, what we are looking for - less failing builds. We hope to widen the generalization to a broader concept of defect (not only failing build) prediction, but we decided to start with a problem of broken builds that developers have to deal with most often. Other threat that we think needs to be considered is the "restricted generalizability across constructs". It is important to check if the approach we are proposing will not effect the project in a negative way. For example, whether the usage of the prediction will not give the developers false beliefs and thus result in more careless committing. We have similar concerns regarding the social threats to the experiment. It is possible that the behavior of the software developers will change due to the usage of our

CBOP tools. It might be that they will feel more secure while receiving positive predictions and thus they will more boldly commit insecure changes to the repository.

The last type of threats we have considered are the threats to conclusion validity. In our case, it is the ability to draw a correct conclusion about the influence of CBOP on FBR in a software development project. Important threat is a potentially low statistical power of the experiment (because of the limits in the number of participants involved in the study). We tried to mitigate it by involving as many developers as we could. Finally, we were able to use data from 9 individual developers.

4.3   Analysis

In the experiment, we have analyzed 310 project days worth of data coming from a total of 9 developers. Table 2 shows the assignments for individual developers. The experiment assignments were prepared 40 days in advance. Different developers worked different number of days in the project under investigation (because of sick days, vacations, different project assignments etc.). Some days the developers did not make any commit resulting in a build. Those days were omitted from the results. Although in those days the developers were assigned a phase. If a developer participated in the experiment longer than 40 days, the sequence started from the beginning. If a developer participated in less than 40 days then only the days in which she or he participated were taken into account. The developers were working simultaneously in Visual Studio on the back-end .NET services and in VSCode working on the Angular front web client for the services. The results were aggregated for both projects separately.

Table 2. CBOPoff (A)/CBOPon (B) assignments for individual developers

Developer no.	Assignments plan	Days in exp.	Obs. count	Failure build count	Total build count
Developer 1	AAAAAABBBBBBBBBBBBBB BBBBAAAAABBBBBBBBBBBB	44	33	16	63
Developer 2	AAAAAAABBBBBBBBBBBBBB BBBBAAAAAAAAABBBBBBBB	27	20	3	32
Developer 3	AAAAAAAABBBBBBBBBBBBB BBBBAAAAAAAAABBBBBBBB	37	27	1	47
Developer 4	AAAAAAAAAABBBBBBBBAAA AAAAAAABBBBBBBBBBBBBB	60	84	58	227
Developer 5	AAAAAAAAAAABBBBBBBBBB BBBAAAAAABBBBBBBBBBBB	43	29	1	65
Developer 6	AAAAAAAAAAAABBBBBBBBB BBAAAAAAAABBBBBBBBBBB	54	61	39	134
Developer 7	AAAAABBBBBBBAAAAAAAAA AAAAABBBBBBBBBBBBBBBB	35	50	27	124
Developer 8	AAAAAAAAABBBBBBBBBAAA AAAABBBBBBBBBBBBBBBBB	40	55	59	239
Developer 9	AAAAABBBBBBBBBBBBBBBB BBBAAAAAAAABBBBBBBBBB	46	51	26	139

Analysis of Descriptive Statistics. In total, CBOP was turned off during 173 days and turned on during 237 days of the experiment. FBR dependent variable, calculated as described in the Sect. 3.4, is plotted in Fig. 2.

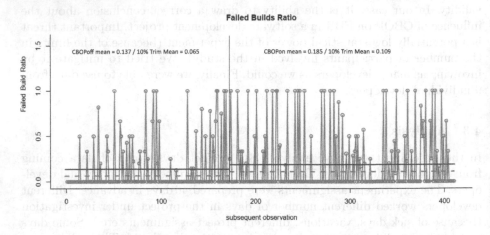

Fig. 2. Failed Build Ratio (FBR)

We see a slight increase in the mean of FBR when the CBOP was turned on, from 0.137 (CBOPoff) to 0.185 (CBOPon). Figure 3 shows the box plot for the same data. The median in both phases was 0.

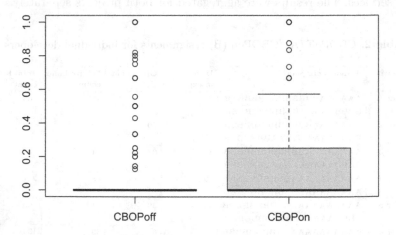

Fig. 3. Failed build ratio (Y-axis) box plot

As variances are not equal ($F = 0.70099$, $df1 = 172$, $df2 = 236$, $p - value = 0.01366$), we may use Welch's t-test, but the null hypothesis can not be rejected

($t = -1.5579$, $df = 400.34$, $p - value = 0.12$). Unfortunately, the data are auto-correlated in the CBOPon phase and have a visible trend in the CBOPoff phase. In such situation, transformation using differencing is recommended. Unfortunately, it does not remove autocorrelation. Hence, the Welch's t-test may not be reliable and we proceed further analyzing a robust measure of central location and effect sizes.

Mean is not a robust measure of the central location and can be strongly influenced by outliers, especially when the number of observations is small. However, the 10% trimmed mean (which is a more robust measure of the central tendency) also increased from 0.065 (when CBOPoff) to 0.109 (when CBOPon). Standard deviation increased in a similar manner from 0.281 (when CBOPoff) to 0.335 (when CBOPon). We will discuss possible explanations of such behaviour in Sect. 5, but now we focus on the size of the observed effect. Table 3 contains descriptive statistics for all phases and developers.

Effect Size. It has become a recommended practice to assess the magnitude of a treatment effect (CBOPon vs CBOPoff in our case) using effect size measures as it gives a sense of practical importance [17–19]. To grasp the effect of CBOPon vs CBOPoff, we report the most common effect size measures:

- ES calculated as the difference between the intervention CBOPon and baseline CBOPoff means divided by the standard deviation of the baseline ($ES = \frac{M_{CBOPon} - M_{CBOPoff}}{SD_{CBOPoff}}$),
- $d - index$ uses a pooled standard deviation and thus may be more appropriate when the variation between the phases differs ($d - index = \frac{M_{CBOPon} - M_{CBOPoff}}{SD_{pool(CBOPoff, CBOPon)}}$).

Table 3. Descriptive statistics for each developer for CBOPoff (off)/CBOPon (on)

	Obs. count		Mean		10% trim mean		Median		SD	
	Off	On	Off	On	Off	On	Off	On	Off	On
Developer 1	12	21	0.194	0.337	0.133	0.298	0.000	0.000	0.388	0.447
Developer 2	5	15	0.000	0.133	0.000	0.077	0.000	0.000	0.123	0.352
Developer 3	15	12	0.000	0.021	0.000	0.000	0.000	0.000	0.000	0.072
Developer 4	43	41	0.216	0.118	0.168	0.069	0.000	0.000	0.290	0.233
Developer 5	12	17	0.000	0.020	0.000	0.000	0.000	0.000	0.000	0.081
Developer 6	29	32	0.254	0.269	0.215	0.216	0.000	0.000	0.380	0.414
Developer 7	22	28	0.102	0.221	0.032	0.175	0.000	0.000	0.257	0.364
Developer 8	24	31	0.044	0.214	0.013	0.146	0.000	0.000	0.123	0.350
Developer 9	11	40	0.136	0.197	0.056	0.121	0.000	0.000	0.323	0.325

Both values ($ES = 0.16923$, $d - index = 0.15156$) are below 0.87 and indicate "small effect size". However, when there is a trend in any phase, then both measures are not appropriate and we need to use more sophisticated effect size measures. In our case, there is a visible trend in the baseline CBOPoff, see Fig. 4.

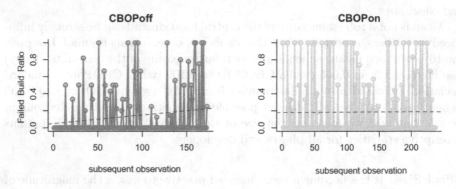

Fig. 4. Visualisation of trend

Hence, we report and rely on the following effect size measures:

- *PEM* (the percentage of the data points in intervention phase (CBOPon) exceeding the median of the baseline phase (CBOPoff)) [20],
- *PAND* (the percentage of all non-overlapping data) [21].

$PEM = 0$ (i.e., lower than 0.5) can be interpreted as "not effective" according to Ma [20]. $PAND = 0.578$ (i.e., lower than 0.69) can be interpreted as "debatable effectiveness" according to Parker et al. [21].

This indicates that CBOP is "not effective" or even its effectiveness is, contrary to the expectation, slightly in the opposite direction, i.e., may lead to a tiny increase in FBR.

5   Discussion

The experiment results indicate that our hypothesis that by using CBOP (CBO-Pon) one can positively influence the failing builds ratio was not reflected in results. By using our CBOP setup, developers were causing slightly more failing builds than without the CBOP in place (CBOPoff). The effect size was very small, but it prompted us to elaborate on plausible explanations. One of the possible reasons (we have considered as a threat before the experiment) is that developers equipped with a tool that was supposed to shelter them from the problems of failing builds became more careless. They start to commit a code of lesser quality because they had positive feedback about it.

This effect could be caused by the human tendency to use judgement heuristics while making decisions. It is generally easier for a human being to use simple strategies while finding solutions for a complex problem. One of those judgement heuristics is an authority principle. This principle was catalogued by Cialdini among "Six Principles of Influence" [22]. Authority principle says that humans tend to comply with the people they see to be in a position of authority (like shown in [23]). The authority principle applies also to non-human authorities like a law or legal precedent [24]. Our software tool Jaskier can be seen as a form of non-human authority. It is prominently visible in IDE and gives informed predictions about the coming build result. What if the software shows a false positive (it informs the developer that everything will be fine, but in fact there is a problem in the code base)? It might be the case that in such situations developers use a simple judgement heuristic and do not review the code sufficiently but check it in.

The authority principle explanation needs a rigorous test in order to fully explain the observed phenomena. It might also be interesting to look on the result from another analysis level and analyze the developer cognitive functioning (learning, thinking, reasoning, remembering, problem solving, decision making, and attention) [25].

6   Conclusions and Future Work

We have demonstrated the effect of employing the new CBOP practice (for predicting failures on the CI server) in a real software project. Based on historical CI data (build success vs. failure information) and metrics calculated from the software repository, we are able to create a prediction model for a build failure. We are matching the historical CI results with the commits that led to the CI build and based on that data we create the classification model. This model is used to predict how dangerous the changes the developer introduced to the project are in respect to the build outcome.

We have build a set of tools that form a practical implementation of the CBOP idea. We used CBOP in order to evaluate it in a commercial software project.

We are working to improve the prediction models, although using random forests we are currently reaching 95% of prediction accuracy (based on k-fold cross-validation). According to developers, the acceptance of the new practice and the supporting toolset is beyond doubt if the performance of the prediction model is high.

Although we were not able to support our hypothesis that "Using CBOP reduces FBR" by the obtained results, we plan to extend the toolset to capture brother plateau of defects and reevaluate brother CDP practice. The social behavioral explanation (impact of non-human authority) of the results might also to be narrowed to cognitive functioning of a single developer in its environment. More rigorous testing of the explanation is needed in order to fully explain the phenomenon.

The more sophisticated effect size measures had to be used because of the trend in the CBOPoff baseline. They indicate that CBOP is "not effective" (according to the PEM measure) or its effectiveness is "debatable" (according to the PAND measure). Descriptive statistics also suggest that the effectiveness of CBOP is low and slightly in the opposite direction than expected (i.e., CBOP may in fact lead to increase in FBR) but increasing FBR in the CBOPoff baseline (see Fig. 4) does not allow to come to strong conclusions.

The data obtained for this experiment is available though a download[2].

We reached a plausible explanation of the reveled phenomenon building upon the authority principle, which is rarely discussed in the software engineering context in general, and AI/ML-supported software development practices in particular, but we think deserves attention and should be taken into account with accelerating use of AI/ML techniques.

References

1. Arora, I., Tetarwal, V., Saha, A.: Open issues in software defect prediction. Proc. Comput. Sci. **46**, 906–912 (2015). https://doi.org/10.1016/j.procs.2015.02.161
2. Madeyski, L., Kawalerowicz, M.: Continuous defect prediction: the idea and a related dataset. In: 14th International Conference on Mining Software Repositories, Buenos Aires, Argentina, 20–21 May 2017, pp. 515–518 (2017). doi: 10.1109/MSR.2017.46
3. Kim, S., Whitehead, E.J., Jr., Zhang, Y.: Classifying software changes: clean or buggy? IEEE Trans. Softw. Eng. **34**(2), 181–196 (2008)
4. Menzies, T., Milton, Z., Turhan, B., Cukic, B., Jiang, Y., Bener, A.: Defect prediction from static code features: current results, limitations, new approaches. Autom. Softw. Eng. **17**(4), 375–407 (2010). https://doi.org/10.1007/s10515-010-0069-5
5. D'Ambros, M., Lanza, M., Robbes, R.: Evaluating defect prediction approaches: a benchmark and an extensive comparison. Empirical Softw. Eng. **17**(4–5), 531–577 (2012). https://doi.org/10.1007/s10664-011-9173-9
6. Kamei, Y., et al.: A large-scale empirical study of just-in-time quality assurance. IEEE Trans. Softw. Eng. **39**(6), 757–773 (2013)
7. Yang, X., Lo, D., Xia, X., Zhang, Y., Sun, J.: Deep learning for just-in-time defect prediction. In: IEEE International Conference on Software Quality, Reliability and Security (QRS), pp. 17–26 (2015)
8. Yang, X., Lo, D., Xia, X., Sun, J.: TLEL: a two-layer ensemble learning approach for just-in-time defect prediction. Inf. Softw. Technol. **87**, 206–220 (2017)
9. Madhavan, J.T., Whitehead Jr., E.J.: Predicting buggy changes inside an integrated development environment. In: Proceedings of the 2007 OOPSLA Workshop on Eclipse Technology eXchange, eclipse 2007, pp. 36–40. ACM, New York (2007)
10. Finlay, J., Pears, R., Connor, A.M.: Data stream mining for predicting software build outcomes using source code metrics. Inf. Softw. Technol. **56**(2), 183–198 (2014). https://doi.org/10.1016/j.infsof.2013.09.001
11. Antoniol, G., Ayari, K., Di Penta, M., Khomh, F., Guéhéneuc, Y.G.: Is it a bug or an enhancement?: a text-based approach to classify change requests. In: Proceedings of the 2008 Conference of the Center for Advanced Studies on Collaborative Research: Meeting of Minds, CASCON 2008, pp. 23:304–23:318. ACM, New York (2008)

---

[2] https://doi.org/10.6084/m9.figshare.14222273.

12. Wohlin, C., Runeson, P., Höst, M., Ohlsson, M., Regnell, B., Wesslén, A.: Experimentation in Software Engineering. Springer, Berlin (2012). doi: 10.1007/978-3-642-29044-2

13. Dugard, P., File, P., Todman, J.: Single-Case and Small-n Experimental Designs: A Practical Guide to Randomization Tests, 2nd edn. Routledge, Abingdon (2012)

14. Bulté, I., Onghena, P.: An R package for single-case randomization tests. Behav. Res. Methods **40**, 467–478 (2008). https://doi.org/10.3758/BRM.40.2.467

15. Kawalerowicz, M., Madeyski, L.: Jaskier: A Supporting Software Tool for Continuous Build Outcome Prediction Practice In: Fujita, H., et al. (eds.) IEA/AIE. LNCS (LNAI), vol. 12799, pp. 426–438. Springer, Cham (2021). https://doi.org/10.1007/978-3-030-79463-7

16. Kawalerowicz, M., Madeyski, L.: Appendix to "continuous build outcome prediction: a small-N experiment in settings of a real software project". https://madeyski.e-informatyka.pl/download/KawalerowiczMadeyski21CBOPApp.pdf

17. Ferguson, C.J.: An effect size primer: a guide for clinicians and researchers. Prof. Psychol. Res. Pract. **40**(5), 532–538 (2009)

18. Kitchenham, B., Madeyski, L., Budgen, D., Keung, J., Brereton, P., Charters, S., Gibbs, S., Pohthong, A.: Robust Statistical Methods for Empirical Software Engineering. Empirical Software Engineering **22**(2), 579–630 (2016). https://doi.org/10.1007/s10664-016-9437-5

19. Madeyski, L.: Test-Driven Development: An Empirical Evaluation of Agile Practice. Springer, Heidelberg, London, New York) (2010). doi: 10.1007/978-3-642-04288-1

20. Ma, H.H.: An alternative method for quantitative synthesis of single-subject researches. Behav. Modif. **30**(5), 598–617 (2006)

21. Parker, R.I., Hagan-Burke, S., Vannest, K.: Percentage of All Non-Overlapping Data (PAND): an alternative to PND. J. Spec. Educ. **40**, 194–204 (2007)

22. Cialdini, R.: Influence: The Psychology of Persuasion. HarperCollins e-books, Collins Business Essentials (2009)

23. Bickman, L.: The social power of a uniform. J. Appl. Soc. Psychol. **4**, 47–61 (1974). https://doi.org/10.1111/j.1559-1816.1974.tb02807.x

24. Schneider, A., Honeyman, C.: The Negotiator's Fieldbook. American Bar Association, Section of Dispute Resolution, Chicago (2006)

25. Fisher, G.G., Chacon, M., Chaffee, D.S.: Chapter 2 - theories of cognitive aging and work. In: Baltes, B.B., Rudolph, C.W., Zacher, H. (eds.) Work Across the Lifespan, pp. 17–45. Academic Press (2019). doi: 10.1016/B978-0-12-812756-8.00002-5

Jaskier: A Supporting Software Tool for Continuous Build Outcome Prediction Practice

Marcin Kawalerowicz[1]([✉]) [iD] and Lech Madeyski[2] [iD]

[1] CODEFUSION Sp. z o.o. and Faculty of Electrical Engineering,
Automatic Control and Informatics, Opole University of Technology, Opole, Poland
marcin@kawalerowicz.net
[2] Faculty of Computer Science and Management,
Wroclaw University of Science and Technology, Wrocław, Poland
Lech.Madeyski@pwr.edu.pl

Abstract. Continuous Defect Prediction (CDP) is an assisting software development practice that combines Software Defect Prediction (SDP) with machine learning aided modelling and continuous developer feedback. Jaskier is a set of software tools developed under the supervision and with the participation of the authors of the article that implements a lightweight version of CDP called Continuous Build Outcome Prediction (CBOP). CBOP uses classification to label the possible build results based on historical data and metrics derived from the software repository. This paper contains a detailed description of the tool that was already started to be used in the production environment of a real software project where the CBOP practice is being evaluated.

Keywords: Software defect prediction · Continuous integration

1 Introduction

Jaskier[1] is a software infrastructure aimed to support the Continuous Defect Prediction (CDP) practice proposed earlier by the authors [1]. CDP combines the unambiguous results of continuous integration (CI) like proposed in [2] with machine learning (ML) aided just-in-time quality assurance [3] and continuous feedback directly in the developer Integrated Development Environment (IDE) [4] and [5]. It implements the lightweight version of CDP called Continuous Build Outcome Prediction (CBOP). The basic idea of this practice is to combine the defect prediction techniques with the notion of continuous, just-in-time developer feedback on possible defects in their code. To implement CDP/CBOP, we needed to develop a set of client and server tools. Clients run on the software developer

---

[1] Jaskier is a code name we have used to develop the software at a company one of the authors is running. Jaskier in Polish means buttercup – a small yellow flower common in Poland.

© Springer Nature Switzerland AG 2021
H. Fujita et al. (Eds.): IEA/AIE 2021, LNAI 12799, pp. 426–438, 2021.
https://doi.org/10.1007/978-3-030-79463-7_36

machine where code is written. The clients need to watch what a developer is doing and gather metrics related to the changes he is making before the source code gets to the software repository. On the server side, we need a self-learning prediction model that was made accessible to the client tools to get the prediction and show it to the developer. The key objective of this paper it to present Jaskier, a practical implementation of CBOP. We will look closely at the problem Jaskier is trying to solve amid related work. We will provide the rationale behind developing the tool and provide a detailed description of the software architecture together with implementation details. We will throw a short look at an experiment where we have used Jaskier to evaluate the CDP/CBOP practice.

2   Problem Statement and Related Work

Continuous integration (CI) is "an automated process that builds [...] the software after each change in source code, to ensure its health [and ...] provides immediate feedback [...]" [6]. CI is very broadly used in the software engineering industry. There are a few rules that need to be obeyed while using CI, that might interrupt the flow of the process of software development. If the build fails, no one is allowed to pull the faulty code from the repository. Furthermore, pushes to the repository are banned until the failing build is fixed (preferably by the person that broke the build). This fix needs to be done as soon as possible, because it interrupts the whole development process. Other team members need to wait with necessary actions on the repository (like pushing or merging). Sometimes, if the build problems are more severe, fixing them may take substantial amount of time and have a greater impact on the project. This needs to be avoided.

There are techniques and rules that help deal with such situation. For example, builds need to be fast and if necessary, they shall fail fast. Maximum of 10 min is often taken as a rule of thumb for the maximal build duration. The tests in the CI process are often sorted from the ones that are the fastest, to the ones that take longer to execute. The rationale is that if the build needs to fail, it should fail sooner than later. Another technique is gated check-ins or pre-commit tests. In this technique, the CI process is started using the code prepared to be passed to the repository before it is actually checked-in. Regardless of countermeasures: the builds are sometimes failing, and it causes additional work and delays.

In order to mitigate this problem we are proposing to use CBOP, a lightweight implementation of CDP [1]. This technique is based on the years of research in the area of Software Defect Prediction (SDP) [3,5,7–12] that was implemented as software tools in [4,5]. Our approach is based rather on CI data [2] than lexical examination of the commit message or the bug tracking software entries [13].

Continuous Defect Prediction (CDP) is a practice we proposed that relays on machine learning and data form bug tracking software or build server. The goal of this practice is to detect possible software defects before they manifest themselves. Continuous Build Outcome Prediction (CBOP) is a subset of CDP that deals specifically with failing builds. Jaskier is the first attempt to put the idea into production. Build fail prediction model is calculated based on the build results in correlation with the software changes that triggered that build. The goal is to give the developer a tool that can run in the background of their IDE and, in real-time, gather the intelligence about the changes developer applies to the project and its possible outcomes. Based on these changes, the tool calculates the metrics and uses them to estimate the possibility that the changes can disrupt the build server or cause a bug. By doing so, we hope to give the software developer additional insight into the outcomes of his work. Maybe if the developer knows that the changes, he made are predicted to be risky, he can mitigate the problem before it occurs and disrupt the development flow.

3   Software Framework and Architecture

To give a comprehensive view of the tool and depict it as accurate as possible, we will use the "4+1" model view of architecture provided by Philippe Kruchten [14]. We use the "4+1" model because it was designed to describe software intensive/complex system like Jaskier. Furthermore is not bound to any notation or tool. It will allow us to show our system from the point of view of various stakeholder. Figure 1 shows the "4+1" view model divided into five views:

1. Logical View provides a logical design of the software.
2. Process View describes the integration aspects of the software.
3. Physical View provides an overview of how the software is mapped to hardware.
4. Development View describes the organization of the software project in a development environment.
5. Use Case View which describes usage scenarios of the software form the point of view of the end-users.

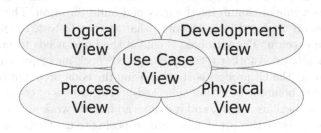

Fig. 1. "4+1" view model of software architecture

3.1   Logical View

Jaskier is a set of tools that address the problem described in Sect. 2. The software's logical design can be described in terms of the static structure and dynamic behaviour. In terms of the structure, it consists of independent and autonomous components:

1. IDE plugins for Microsoft Visual Studio and Microsoft VSCode used to gather just-in-time data and present predictions to the developer based on that data,
2. Web Service prediction interface that abstracts the access to a prediction model,
3. Model that can live in the cloud or on-premises and is used to generate predictions over a Web Service,
4. Model training module - Azure ML Training Experiment for the cloud-based model or R script for the on-premises model,
5. Statistics Harvester - a simple .NET Framework tool for gathering the statistics to be used for training (it is using the same mechanisms as the IDE plugin to do so),
6. Jaskier Database – a place where the statistics together with the build results are stored.

3.2   Process View

Figure 2 shows the integration of the tools described in Sect. 3.1. IDE plugins reside inside Visual Studio or VSCode and are constantly monitoring the work of the developer. If the developer changes something in the project (e.g., saves a file), the plugins are comparing local repository with the changes developer made to the source code to calculate current statistics. These statistics then are sent to the Web Service. The web service relays the statistics to the Prediction Model. Based on the model, a prediction of build failure is sent back through the Web Service. The prediction then is presented to the developer inside IDE using the plugin.

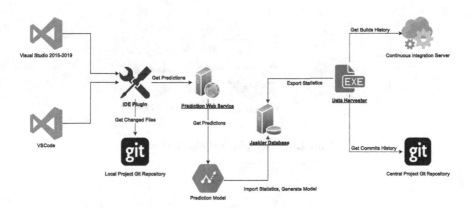

Fig. 2. Jaskier logical view

On the build server side, a new commit to a central repository triggers a build. After the build Data Harvester is started, it goes over the repository and gathers the statistics knowing whether those changes broke the build. The data is stored in Jaskier Database and then used to train the model once again.

3.3 Physical View

The IDE plugins run solely on the developer machine. It is a machine running on Microsoft Windows in case of Visual Studio 2015–2019 or macOS, Linux or Windows machine in case of VSCode. The Prediction Web Service needs a web server to run. For example, a standalone Microsoft IIS or Azure Cloud-based web server. The prediction model can live on a standalone Microsoft R Server or in Azure ML. Jaskier Database is a Microsoft SQL Server database. It also needs a standalone SQL Server engine to run or can be hosted in Azure Cloud. The Data Harvester resides on the Continuous Integration server.

Figure 3 shows the on-premises setup and Fig. 4 depicts the Azure Cloud setup of Jaskier.

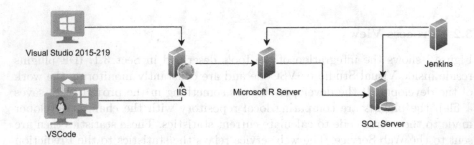

Fig. 3. Jaskier physical view

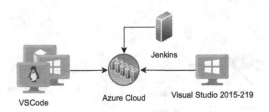

Fig. 4. Jaskier physical cloud view

3.4 Development View

From the development point of view, the Jaskier toolchain consists of the following modules:

1. Codefusion.Jaskier.API – interfaces and DTOs (Data Transfer Objects),
2. Codefusion.Jaskier.Common – common functionalities (database definition, requests and responses, helper classes, services),

3. Codefusion.Jaskier.Client.CLI – command line Jaskier client,
4. Codefusion.Jaskier.Client.VS2015 – Visual Studio 2015–2019 extension,
5. Codefusion.Jaskier.Client.VSCode – VSCode extension,
6. Codefusion.Jaskier.Export.CLI – Data Harvester code,
7. Codefusion.Jaskier.Web – Prediction Web Service,
8. R scripts – R scripts used on Microsoft R Server for training and prediction.

Figure 5 shows the project references and implementations in Jaskier Visual Studio solution.

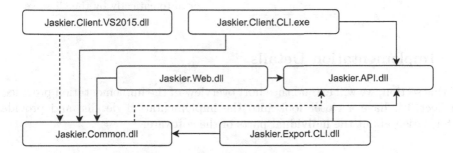

Fig. 5. Jaskier project references and implementations (stripped line).

3.5   Use Case View

The use case view gives a good perspective on how the system is being used by its users. Figure 6 shows the Use Case Diagram for Jaskier. We have two actors. A software developer is a primary actor. Software developers get predictions from the system. The second actor is someone (or sometimes an automated process) that prepares prediction models. Table 1 describes the use cases in more detail.

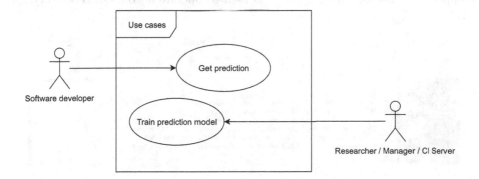

Fig. 6. Jaskier use case view

Table 1. Jaskier use cases

Use case	Actor	Basic flow
Get predictions	Software developer	While software developer writes his source code the just-in-time prediction of the build result is provided in his IDE
Train prediction model	Manager/Researcher/CI Server	Prediction model is created (trained or retrained) by software development manager, researcher or automatically by the CI server

4   Implementation Details

In this section, we will extend the short overview of the implementation provided in Sect. 3.4, have a closer look into the implementation details, and provide information about the individual parts of the software.

4.1   Clients

Jaskier has (at the moment of writing this text) three clients: Visual Studio and VSCode Extensions and a CLI tool.

Visual Studio Extension and the CLI tool are written in C# and use Microsoft .NET Framework. The VSCode Extension is written in TypeScript.

Visual Studio Extension is shown in Fig. 7. The core functionality of the C# client is defined in the IChangeTrackerService interface placed in Codefusion.Jaskier.API project. GitChangesTrackerService is an implementation of this interface in Codefusion.Jaskier.Common project. As the name suggests, this implementation uses Git to determine the changes. It knows the repository path, and based on that repository, it can determine which files changed since the last commit. The library LibGit2Sharp[2] is used to operate on the Git repository.

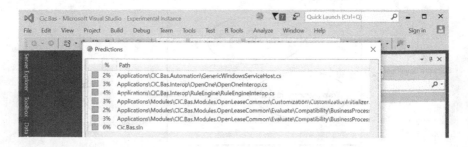

Fig. 7. Prediction extension results in Microsoft Visual Studio

---

[2] https://github.com/libgit2/libgit2sharp.

If any other source code management system needs to be used, the IChange-TrackerService needs to be implemented for that system.

To determine if a prediction is needed and to retrieve the prediction for any given change, implementation of IPredictionService is used. The implementation of this service is used in C# client applications.

VSCode Extension is shown in Fig. 8.

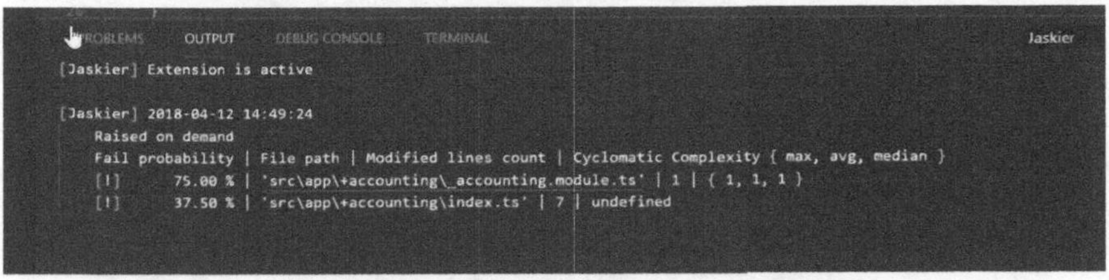

Fig. 8. Prediction extension results in Microsoft VSCode

Because of the nature of VSCode, which is an HTML5 application, our Jaskier extension is written entirely in TypeScript. The architecture of this extension roughly resembles the architecture of the Visuals Studio extension. It is also service-based and loosely coupled. We have the PredictionsService class that corresponds to the IPredictionService interface from the C# version and GitChangesTracker, which corresponds to the IChangeTrackerService interface.

4.2   Data Harvester and Database

Another important interface in Jaskier is IBuildInfoServie. This interface defines the methods used to harvest the build information from a CI system. At the moment of writing this article, two implementations of this interface exist–one for Bitbucket and one for TravisTorrent. Bitbucket implementation was used in the performed preliminary empirical evaluation of CBOP in real project, while TravisTorrent implementation was used to create a data mining package for [1].

To harvest the statistics (metrics) from a repository, IBuildStatisticsService needs to be implemented. In Jaskier, GitBuildStatisticsService is implemented. It uses Git repository to calculate the code metrics for any given branch. To determine the changes that need the statistics calculated, it uses the before mentioned GitChangesTrackerService.

The whole configuration of the dependencies in the Harvester project (Code-fusion.Jaskier.Export.CLI) is done using the Simple Injector[3] inversion of control library. By using the Dependency Injection (DI) pattern, it is possible to configure the needed libraries on runtime in app.config.

The Harvester runs as a standalone Windows executable. It needs a direct connection to the database to store the statistics and commit information.

---

[3] https://simpleinjector.org/.

The database used in Jaskier runs on Microsoft SQL Server engine. It is a simple relational database. Figure 9 shows the database diagram with the tables that Jaskier needs to run. There are also other tables in the database that were added to facilitate Agile Experimentation [15] within the tool.

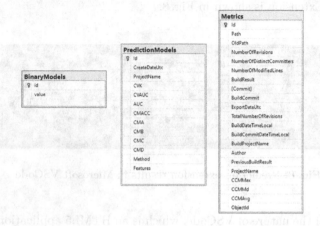

Fig. 9. Part of the Jaskier database

The central table in Jaskier is the Metrics table. This table stores the data gathered by the Data Harvester. For every changed file in any given commit, a set of metrics together with the build status is stored. Data from this table is used to train and retrain the prediction models.

Those prediction models can also be stored in the database in the Binary-Models table. This table is only used for an on-premises installation of Jaskier. In a cloud base setup, the models are stored on Azure Storage. Details on that will be provided in Sect. 4.3.

The table Prediction Requests stores all the build result inquiries from the Jaskier clients together with the resulting prediction.

4.3   Prediction Model

The Prediction Web Service serves as a communication mean between the Clients and the Prediction Model. The Prediction Model can be calculated, stored, and used in two different ways:

1. By using an on-premises Microsoft Machine Learning Server,
2. By using Microsoft Azure ML cloud infrastructure.

At the time of writing Jaskier, the Microsoft Machine Learning Server official name was Microsoft R Server. This server's history dates to the time when R was maintained and developed by Revolution Analytics, which was bought by Microsoft in 2015.

The setup of a standalone ML server is aimed at the enterprise level. At that level, all aspects of the software need to be controlled and under the strict supervision of the software company, which is using it. In such an environment, no cloud or multi-tenant setup is possible or wanted. In that setup, the Prediction Model is calculated using the R scripts and stored in the database.

Alternatively, to an on-premises R usage within Microsoft Machine Learning Server, Jaskier is prepared to work with Microsoft Azure ML as a provider of Prediction Models. In that case, the training, retraining, and prediction are done using Experiments in Microsoft Azure cloud. Experiments in Azure are configured using a diagramming tool. The basic steps of a Training Experiment are to read the data (Import Data) from the database and select the proper columns for the experiment (Select Columns in Dataset). Then to split the data into training and scoring set (Split Data). The training part of the data goes to model training (Train Model) which takes the input from a training algorithm (e.g., Two-Class Boosted Decision Tree). The scoring set plus the model's output goes to scoring (Score Model) and evaluation (Evaluate Model). The Training Experiment can be published as a web service to facilitate retraining functionality. In that case, input and output knots are created: Web Service Input for new data and two Web Service Outputs for the model and for the scoring output. The Training Experiment, when ready, can be transformed using Azure ML functionalities into Prediction Experiment. The Prediction Experiment has a similar structure but gets the output model from the Training Experiment as input for scoring. It can also be published as a Web Service to provide a prediction for external data sources.

4.4 Prediction Web Service

In order to abstract the cloud and on-premises installation of the prediction service, a Prediction Web Service was built. It was placed in the solution as Jaskier.Web project. It is an ASP.NET which hosts three endpoints:

1. Training endpoint,
2. Prediction endpoint,
3. Telemetry endpoint.

The training endpoint abstracts the Azure ML Training Experiment Web Service and the Microsoft Machine Learning Server training R script. If called, it will retrain the model using current data from the database. As an input, it gets the project name for which the prediction model should be retrained.

The prediction endpoint abstracts the Azure ML Prediction Experiment and the Microsoft Machine Learning Server prediction R script. If called, it will provide the prediction for a given (in the request) set of changes. As an input, it gets the list of PredictionRequestFile objects for a given project. As an output, it delivers a list of PredictionResponse objects that contain the calculated probabilities.

The prediction endpoint in the case of Microsoft Machine Learning Server saves the requested data into the PredictionRequests table in the database and generates unique Guid for every request. This Guid is then passed as a command-line parameter to the R script. In the case of Azure ML Prediction Experiment, the Rest API call is made to Azure ML. The call contains all the input data. It triggers a synchronous prediction execution in the cloud.

The telemetry endpoint gets the information in form of a PutTelemetryRequest object. It contains a set of telemetry information like the username, machine name, user IP address, plugin version, Visual Studio version, an action and action payload. Action contains the name of the action the developer took during the Jaskier usage, and the payload contains additional information to the action. At the time of writing the article, the telemetry service gathered information about the user opening or closing the Jaskier pane in Visual Studio. This feature was introduced to Jaskier to be able to tell if the user was potentially seeing the provided prediction.

5   Experiment Using Jaskier

The first evaluation of Jaskier was conducted in real software development settings during an experiment aimed to "analyze continuous build outcome prediction (CBOP) practice for the purpose of evaluation with respect to its effectiveness to reduce the build failure rate (BFR) from the point of view of the researcher and project manager in the context of a small group of professional software developers (subjects) working in an industrial-grade software project (object)".

In order to achieve this goal, we have modified Jaskier to facilitate "A small-n repeated-measure design with two conditions and replicates" experiment design. The experiment is described in detail in [16]. Here we will provide brief overview of the results. We gathered from 27 to 60 days of data from 9 developers in a professional setup. Contrary to our expectation, we have registered a "small effect size" indicating that getting the prediction results while using Jaskier was negatively affecting BFR. The drop was very slight but noticeable. During the phase with CDP/CBOP turned off we measured the mean of BFR to be 0.137. While the CDP/CBOP prediction was turned on the measured the mean BFR to be 0.185. The working hypothesis to explaining the situation is either: (1) the model quality was insufficient and got the developers false believe they are on the road to successful build while there were in fact rendering the build failure; (2) or the developers merely seeing the build prediction were more restless, and that caused their commits to fail the build more often.

6   Conclusion and Future Work

Jaskier was created to be the first practical implementation of the CDP/CBOP practice. A set of tools was developed under the supervision and with the participation of the authors of the article by a professional software development company. The set of tools consists of three developer clients (for Visual Studio, VSCode and command line), a web service to facilitate the data exchange between the clients and prediction model living in the cloud or on on-premises machine learning server. A set of scripts to train and retrain the model together with the scripts to provide predictions was developed. Jaskier was made available as an open source on GitHub[4].

In order to facilitate the evaluation of the CDP/CBOP practice, Jaskier was extended with the ability to support an experiment devised by the authors of this article.

Jaskier, with its cloud-based prediction system, was used to examine the BFR in a professional software development project. The result was contrary to the desired outcome. It showed that the use of our tool was impacting BFR in a slightly negative way. Nevertheless, Continuous Build Outcome Prediction (CBOP) is only a part of CDP practice. Failing build is one type of issue CDP aims to fight. It would be very interesting to see how the prediction of other types of issues (e.g., real post-release software defects) performs in Jaskier. Next steps would be to build prediction models based on the bug reports in a bug tracking system and use them in Jaskier. It would examine if this kind of prediction, if provided to the developer, would perform better in a software development project.

References

1. Madeyski, L., Kawalerowicz, M.: Continuous defect prediction: the idea and a related dataset. In: 14th International Conference on Mining Software Repositories, 20–21 May 2017, Buenos Aires, Argentina, pp. 515–518 (2017). https://doi.org/10.1109/MSR.2017.46
2. Finlay, J., Pears, R., Connor, A.M.: Data stream mining for predicting software build outcomes using source code metrics. Inf. Softw. Technol. **56**(2), 183–198 (2014). https://doi.org/10.1016/j.infsof.2013.09.001
3. Menzies, T., Milton, Z., Turhan, B., Cukic, B., Jiang, Y., Bener, A.: Defect prediction from static code features: current results, limitations, new approaches. Autom. Softw. Eng. **17**(4), 375–407 (2010). https://doi.org/10.1007/s10515-010-0069-5
4. Madhavan, J.T., Whitehead Jr., E.J.: Predicting buggy changes inside an integrated development environment. In: Proceedings of the 2007 OOPSLA Workshop on Eclipse Technology eXchange, eclipse 2007, pp. 36–40. ACM, New York (2007). https://doi.org/10.1145/1328279.1328287
5. Kim, S., Whitehead, E.J., Jr., Zhang, Y.: Classifying software changes: clean or buggy? IEEE Trans. Softw. Eng. **34**(2), 181–196 (2008). https://doi.org/10.1109/TSE.2007.70773
6. Kawalerowicz, M., Berntson, C.: Continuous Integration in .NET. Manning Pubs Co Series. Manning (2011)
7. Turhan, B., Menzies, T., Bener, A.B., Di Stefano, J.: On the relative value of cross-company and within-company data for defect prediction. Empirical Softw. Eng. **14**(5), 540–578 (2009). https://doi.org/10.1007/s10664-008-9103-7
8. D'Ambros, M., Lanza, M., Robbes, R.: Evaluating defect prediction approaches: a benchmark and an extensive comparison. Empirical Softw. Eng. **17**(4–5), 531–577 (2012)
9. Kamei, Y., et al.: A large-scale empirical study of just-in-time quality assurance. IEEE Trans. Softw. Eng. **39**(6), 757–773 (2013). https://doi.org/10.1109/TSE.2012.70

---

[4] https://github.com/ImpressiveCode/ic-jaskier.

10. Jureczko, M., Madeyski, L.: Cross-project defect prediction with respect to code ownership model: an empirical study. e-Inf. Softw. Eng. J. **9**(1), 21–35 (2015). https://doi.org/10.5277/e-Inf150102
11. Yang, X., Lo, D., Xia, X., Zhang, Y., Sun, J.: Deep learning for just-in-time defect prediction. In: IEEE International Conference on Software Quality, Reliability and Security (QRS), pp. 17–26 (2015)
12. Yang, X., Lo, D., Xia, X., Sun, J.: TLEL: a two-layer ensemble learning approach for just-in-time defect prediction. Inf. Softw. Technol. **87**, 206–220 (2017)
13. Antoniol, G., Ayari, K., Di Penta, M., Khomh, F., Guéhéneuc, Y.G.: Is it a bug or an enhancement?: a text-based approach to classify change requests. In: Proceedings of the 2008 Conference of the Center for Advanced Studies on Collaborative Research: Meeting of Minds, CASCON 2008, pp. 23:304–23:318. ACM, New York (2008). https://doi.org/10.1145/1463788.1463819
14. Kruchten, P.: The 4+1 view model of architecture. IEEE Softw. **12**(6), 42–50 (1995). https://doi.org/10.1109/52.469759
15. Madeyski, L., Kawalerowicz, M.: Software engineering needs agile experimentation: a new practice and supporting tool. In: Madeyski, L., Śmiałek, M., Hnatkowska, B., Huzar, Z. (eds.) Software Engineering: Challenges and Solutions. AISC, vol. 504, pp. 149–162. Springer, Cham (2017). https://doi.org/10.1007/978-3-319-43606-7_11
16. Kawalerowicz, M., Madeyski, L.: Continuous build outcome prediction: a small-N experiment in settings of a real software project. n: Fujita, H., et al. (eds.) IEA/AIE. LNCS (LNAI), vol. 12799, pp. 412–425. Springer, Cham (2021). https://doi.org/10.1007/978-3-030-79463-7

CPS and Industrial Applications

Automated Diagnosis of Cyber-Physical Systems

Franz Wotawa(✉) ⓘ, Oliver Tazl, and David Kaufmann

Institute for Software Technology, Graz University of Technology,
Inffeldgasse 16b/2, 8010 Graz, Austria
{wotawa,oliver.tazl,david.kaufmann}@ist.tugraz.at

Abstract. Research on cyber-physical systems has gained importance
and we see an increasing number of applications ranging from ordinary
cars to autonomous systems. The latter are of increasing interest requiring
additional functionality like self-healing capabilities for improving availability. For autonomous systems, it is not only important to detect failures
during operation, but also to come up with their causes. In this paper, we
contribute to the foundations of diagnosis. We introduce a method for
modeling cyber-physical systems considering behavior over time, in order
to make use of model-based reasoning for computing diagnosis candidates.
In particular, we discuss a thermal model coupled with a controller for
keeping temperature within pre-defined values and show how this contributes to the computation of diagnoses given an unexpected behavior.
The discussed modeling principles can be used as a blueprint for similar
systems where controllers are coupled with a physical system. Diagnosis
results obtained when using the thermal model and the observed diagnosis
time, which was a fraction of a second, seem to indicate the applicability
of the presented approach for industrial applications.

Keywords: Model-based diagnosis · Answer set programming ·
Cyber-physical system diagnosis

1 Introduction

The detection of failures and finding out the reasons behind for being able
to bring a running system back to its operational state is of great practical
importance especially for autonomous cyber-physical systems. In today's cyber-
physical systems like cars a detected failure causes a warning or error message
and brings a system into a safe state, e.g., stopping operation, to assure preventing harm. The identification of the corresponding faults and repair actions
are carried out afterwards in separation where the system is not available for
operation. In order to increase the system's availability it would be necessary to
integrate diagnosis procedures allowing to detect failures, to locate and potentially repair corresponding faults. In this paper, we contribute to this idea and
present a diagnosis approach for systems interacting with their cyber-physical
environment.

© Springer Nature Switzerland AG 2021
H. Fujita et al. (Eds.): IEA/AIE 2021, LNAI 12799, pp. 441–452, 2021.
https://doi.org/10.1007/978-3-030-79463-7_37

The two application areas automotive and space, where we have been carrying out projects, motivated the research we are discussing in this paper. In all these areas we have to deal with control loops coupling a physical system with software in order to keep a pre-defined behavior. For example, we may have a heater that should keep the temperature of a water tank within a certain temperature range. The controller implemented in the heater takes the measured temperature, compares it with a given boundary value, and starts heating if the temperature is too low. Otherwise, the controller stops heating causing the water temperature to decrease. Such at least similar systems we do not only find in our homes, but also in many different technical systems. Now assume that the heater never stops heating, which is unexpected. Such a saturation needs to be explained. Appropriate repair steps have to be carried out after the identification of the root cause. In this paper, we make use of the heater example, to illustrate a model-based diagnosis approach.

Model-based diagnosis has a long history dating back to the 80th of the last century. [2] and later [8,10] provided the underlying foundations, which have mainly been based on the use of logic or similar reasoning systems. Most recently [16] discussed the use of model-based reasoning in the domain of autonomous systems. However, in any case making use of model-based diagnosis for systems interacting with a physical world remains an issue worth being further elaborated. In particular, we have to be able to represent physical processes that are continuous over time in a way, such that we can use it for diagnosis based on logic.

In this paper, we tackle this challenge and present a model that makes use of time in the context of model-based diagnosis based on logic representations of models. In particular, we make use of answer set programming for diagnosis, which has been discussed in detail before [6,17]. In contrast to precious work, which only captured modeling for combinatorial circuits not considering time, we present a model that deals with time. When generalizing the basic concepts, it is possible to come up with different models capturing the physics behind cyber-physical systems. It is worth noting that we do not consider continuous time but discrete time instead. This is an abstraction but allows to model state changes and their consequences. In order to show that the approach can be used in practice, we present a model for the simplified heating system as discussed before. Modeling itself provides an abstract representation of the system's behavior, which is sufficient for generating diagnoses within a very short runtime.

This paper is organized as follows. We first discuss the basic foundations. Afterwards, we introduce the thermal model used for diagnosis and its underlying principles. We further carry out a case study using a simplified controller for controlling the temperature around a pre-defined value. We present the results obtained and show how diagnosis results can be improved using a more sophisticated model. Finally, we discuss related research, summarize the paper, and provide information regarding future research activities.

2   Basic Foundations

In this section, we briefly summarize the concepts and definition of model-based reasoning and the computation of diagnoses. For the definitions as well as diagnosis we follow previous work [6] where we also capture fault models. To illustrate the approach, we make use of a circuit comprising a power supply, a switch and a heater having the purpose to keep the temperature in some given space constant. In Fig. 1 we present the schematics of the circuit, where a controller, i.e., a program turning the switch on and off as required to keep temperature constant. The temperature as well as the current flowing through the heater are expected to be measured using sensors. We depict the expected behavior in terms of temperature over time and the state of the switch in the picture on the top right of Fig. 1.

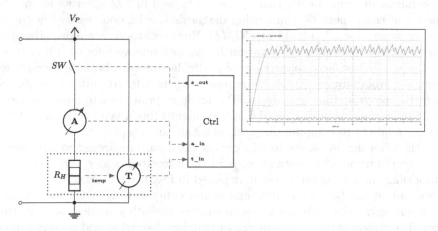

Fig. 1. Schematics of a controller comprising a heater and its on/off switch for keeping a temperature within given boundaries. The figure at the right shows the expected behavior of the temperature controlled using the switch.

Model-based diagnosis is used to identify the causes behind an observed behavior. In case of a failure, i.e., a behavior that contradicts our expectations, we want to identify the components that are responsible. In this paper, we make use of a special kind of diagnosis, i.e., consistency-based diagnosis [2,8,10], that makes use of a model of the correct behavior of the system and its components directly in order to compute diagnoses. For our heater control example, we may observe that the temperature is never reaching the expected maximum value, and we want to know why this is the case? An answer to this question would be the identification of components to behave faulty. As already said, we need a model of the system for diagnosis. In model-based diagnosis this model is referred to as system description SD. In addition, we need to know the components of the system, which we assume to be given in the set $COMP$, as well as the observations OBS.

Note that diagnostic reasoning in case of model-based diagnosis deals with the identification of those components that have to be faulty, or which are said to be in the health state abnormal, such that the underlying model is not contradicting the given observations. Formally, we define a diagnosis as a subset of the set of components as follows:

Definition 1 (Diagnosis (see [10])). *Given a diagnosis problem* $(SD, COMP, OBS)$. *A set* $\Delta \subseteq COMP$ *is a diagnosis, if and only if the following logical sentence is satisfiable (or not a contradiction):* $SD \cup OBS \cup \{ab(C)|C \in \Delta\} \cup \{\neg ab(C)|C \in COMP \setminus \Delta\}$.

It is worth noting that the predicate $ab(C)$ indicates the health state of component C. If C is faulty $ab(C)$ is true, and otherwise false. Moreover, any model taken for diagnosis makes use of the negated ab predicate to specify the correct behavior of components. Hence, $\neg ab(C)$ is used in SD when we define the behavior of component C. Computing diagnosis can be done easily via checking consistency for all subsets of $COMP$. However, there are more advanced algorithms. For more information regarding algorithms we refer to [10] or more recently [6, 17]. The latter papers are of particular interest, because they utilize answer set programming (ASP) for representing models. Accordingly to [6] the declarative programming language ASP is an appropriate tool to represent models and to implement model-based diagnosis algorithms. Even for larger systems the time required to compute diagnosis is within an acceptable range.

In the following, we do not further outline the details regarding how diagnoses are computed using ASP. Instead, we refer the interested reader to [6] and focus on modeling the heat control system depicted in Fig. 1. In the first part, we only have a look at the battery, switch, and heater component ignoring the thermal model and controller. We are going to discuss the other models later in this paper. The reason is that the behavior of switches, batteries, and heaters can be explained without considering time, which we cannot do for the other parts. For all these components, we define an input output behavior for any point in time. Note that time is presented in the model being a natural number starting from 0, representing the initial state, to a given pre-defined value. When we want to know which time points are defined, we can use the predicate time(T) that is true if time T is considered in our model.

Let us start modeling the more simple components. Note that all the models use the nab(.) predicate stating that the component is working not abnormal, i.e., is healthy not comprising a faulty behavior. For the switch model we have to consider two states on and off, where the state will be external controlled (e.g., by the controller). If the state is on the switch is closed, and opened otherwise. In case of an open switch, the current flowing in the switch is propagated to its output and vice versa. This can be formulated using the ASP solver clingo, which basically follows Prolog syntax, as follows:

```
tuple(switch, max, max).
tuple(switch, half, half).
tuple(switch, null, null).
val(out(S), W, T) :- type(S, switch), nab(S), on(S,T), val
    (in(S), V, T), tuple(switch, V, W).
val(in(S), W, T) :- type(S, switch), nab(S), on(S,T), val(
    out(S), V, T), T>0, tuple(switch, V, W).
val(out(S), null, T) :- type(S, switch), nab(S), off(S,T).
:- on(S,T), off(S,T).
```

Note, that in the switch model, we also added a constraint, which is in the last line, stating that a switch cannot be in different states at the same time. Next, we take a closer look at the heater. The model is very much similar to the switch. If there is a current at the input, the heater is producing heat depending on the amount of current. The maximum current causes maximum heating t_max, medium current low heating t_low, and no current no heating null.

```
tuple(heater, max, t_max).
tuple(heater, half, t_low).
tuple(heater, null, null).
val(out(H), W, T) :- type(H, heater), nab(H), val(in(H), V
    ,T), tuple(heater, V, W).
val(out(H),null,T) :- type(H,heater), ab(H), time(T).
```

The battery model is kept simple only delivering the maximum current in case it is in the not abnormal health state.

```
val(out(B),max,T) :- type(B,battery), nab(B), time(T).
```

In addition, to these models, we also have to specify the structure of the circuit. Using the predicate type we are able to set a particular component, and with conn, we connect two component ports. Later they are represented as in and out in the component models. For our circuit, we have the following structural definition:

```
type(sw, switch).
type(h, heater).
type(bat, battery).
conn(out(bat),in(sw)).
conn(out(sw),in(h)).
```

It is worth noting that the predicate conn is defined in a way allowing to propagate given values. Values are again represented using a predicate val that specifies a particular value for a given port at a specific time.

```
val(Y,V,T) :- conn(X,Y), val(X,V,T).
val(X,V,T) :- conn(X,Y), val(Y,V,T).
:- val(Y,V,T), val(Y,W,T), W!=V.
```

The last line is for stating that we only allow one value for any port at any time.

We now are able to use an algorithm like the one described in [6] for diagnosis. We only need to specify observations using the `val` predicate. Let us assume that the heater is not heating but the battery is delivering current at time 10 and the switch is closed.

```
on(sw,10).
val(out(bat),max,10).
val(out(h, null,10).
```

In this case, the diagnosis algorithm coupled with the ASP system would give us back two single fault diagnoses $\{h\}$ and $\{sw\}$ stating that either the heater or the switch must be faulty. This result can be further refined if we would observe whether there is a current at the output of the switch, which is connected with the input of the heater. In the next sections, we discuss the thermal model where we have to consider time more carefully, and, afterwards, the controller model.

3   Modeling Heating

After describing the basic foundations behind model-based diagnosis, we further elaborate how to come up with a cyber-physical system using the framework. For this purpose, we have to model a system with a continuous behavior over time using a formal representation. We illustrate the underlying ideas behind making use of our heater control example. The first idea is not to handle the continuous behavior but to introduce a certain type of abstraction. Instead of using the whole temperature domain, we use its qualitative abstraction. In qualitative reasoning [15] many concepts of how to come up with abstract models of physical systems to allow reasoning has been proposed. For the case of diagnosis, we consider the mapping of continuous values to their abstract domain, as well as operations (or functions) that map one qualitative value into another. In particular, for the given circuit, we are interested to come up with an abstract domain that allows handling control. Hence, we introduce some boundary values of temperature the heat controller is allowed to handle. In Fig. 2 we depict the quantitative and its corresponding qualitative domain.

For handling operations, that bring the physical system from one state to another, we make use of discrete time. An operator takes an input and computes an output that is valid at the immediate next time step. We allow that time advances starting from an initial time 0. This handling of time allows to specify changes. Note that this abstract time is not necessarily directly connected with real time. We may see that in practice (depending on the chosen level of abstraction), the time passing from one (abstract) state to another vary. However, the abstract behavior should represent how the system behavior is going to advance over time, e.g., that the temperature is increasing until it decreases again after reaching an upper bound etc.

For the abstract model of the particular space where we want to control temperature, we assume that the heating temperature directly comes from the

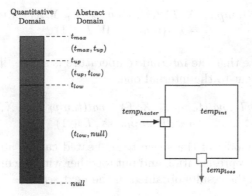

Fig. 2. From the quantitative temperature domain to its qualitative (abstract) one. The component on the right depicts the thermal component having one input temperature $temp_{heater}$, on output $temp_{loss}$, and the internal temperature $temp_{int}$, which we want to control to be always within given boundaries.

heater. We further assume that each temperature adaptation takes one time step. If the heating temperature is reached, no further increase of internal temperature can happen. To simulate the heating process in a more realistic way, we consider a constant heat flow loss, observed as a temperature loss in the heat model. Thus the temperature decreases to harmonize with the ambient temperature whenever the heating is off or at least not high enough. The first part of modeling is to establish a total order on the qualitative state of temperature. This can be done using the following equation:

$$t_{max} < (t_{max}, t_{up}) < t_{up} < (t_{up}, t_{low}) < t_{low} < (t_{low}, null) < null \qquad (1)$$

We furthermore formally define the heating and cooling process over time where we use a predicate dec and inc for stating the previous respectively next temperature for a given one. For example, $dec((t_{up}, t_{low}), t_{low})$ and $inc((t_{max}, t_{up}), t_{max})$ hold. In addition, we assume that the increment of the highest value is equivalent to the highest value, and the decrement of the lowest value is also equivalent to the lowest value.

The first logic formula states that the new internal temperature has to decrease if the heating temperature is lower than the internal temperature.

$$\forall X \forall Y \forall W \forall T : val(temp_{int}, X, T) \wedge val(temp_{heater}, Y, T) \wedge dec(X, W) \wedge X > Y$$
$$\rightarrow val(temp_{int}, W, T + 1)$$
$$(2)$$

The second formula is for stating a similar one but this time specifying a temperature increase internally, whenever heating temperature is higher.

$$\forall X \forall Y \forall W \forall T : val(temp_{int}, X, T) \land val(temp_{heater}, Y, T) \land inc(X, W) \land X < Y$$
$$\rightarrow val(temp_{int}, W, T + 1)$$

$$(3)$$

Finally, we state that the internal temperature is stable, if the heating temperature is equivalent to the internal one.

$$\forall X \forall T : val(temp_{int}, X, T) \land val(temp_{heater}, X, T)$$
$$\rightarrow val(temp_{int}, X, T + 1)$$

$$(4)$$

The described model of the space to be heated can be almost directly converted into an ASP representation and put together with the model of the control circuit. We discuss the results obtained in the next section.

4   Case Study

In order to show that model-based diagnosis using ASP is able to solve the diagnosis problem of the heating controller circuit (see Fig. 1), we implemented the controller in addition to the previously introduced models for switches, the batteries, heater, and the space to be heated up to a given temperature. The controller itself is assumed to turn on and off the switch whenever the current temperature is lower or higher than the given value. This control mechanism is known as a two-point controller without a hysteresis. Similar to the qualitative thermal model provided in the previous section, the controller has a time delay. The effect, i.e., turning on or off the switch, will be visible at the next time step. In the following ASP program, we set the respective values considering the current temperature to be smaller, or higher or equivalent to t_{up} (t_up) in the first three lines. In the forth line, we provide an initialization value for the switch, where we start with the "off" state.

```
on(sw,T+1)  :- val(int(tm),V,T), smaller(V,t_up).
off(sw,T+1) :- val(int(tm),V,T), greater(V,t_up).
off(sw,T+1) :- val(int(tm),t_up,T).
off(sw,0).
```

It is worth noting that for this case study we assume the controller to work correctly. Therefore, we have not introduced the controller as specific component using the type predicate. This can be done if needed as well. If we add now this partial model to the other models, we are able to use the resulting model for diagnosis. For diagnosis we need information about the observed values. In our case study, we want to explain why the switch is always on during operation, which is different to the expected behavior. Both behaviors are given in Fig. 3. For the wrong behavior the temperature is reaching but never exceeding the value t_{low} (t_low).

For diagnosis we represent this behavior using ASP and add the following facts to our model:

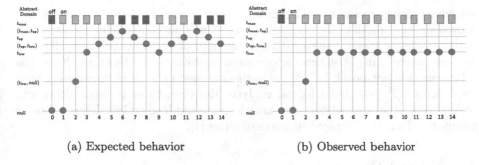

(a) Expected behavior   (b) Observed behavior

Fig. 3. The expected and observed behavior of the heating circuit from Fig. 1 showing the state of the switch and the obtained temperature over time.

```
val(int(tm),null,0).
val(int(tm),null,1).
val(int(tm),between(t_low,null),2).
val(int(tm),t_low,3).
...
val(int(tm),t_low,14).
```

When running the diagnosis algorithm based on the ASP solver `clingo` using the described model and observations, we obtain 3 single diagnosis $\{bat\}$, $\{sw\}$, and $\{h\}$ with a fraction of a second[1]. The reason is that when the structure of the circuit resembles a sequence of components where one faulty component lead to a situation where no input value for the immediately following component is available. In order to solve this problem, we further introduce a fault model for the components. For the battery, we state that it may supply half or none current. For switches, we assume that if broken, they will not let a current through, and finally for the heater, we state a similar idea. A faulty heater is not producing any heat. These extensions can be easily formulated using ASP:

```
val(out(B), half, T); val(out(B), null,T) :-
        type(B,battery), ab(B), time(T).
val(out(S), null, T) :- type(S, switch),ab(S), time(T).
val(out(H), null, T) :- type(H, heater),ab(H), time(T).
```

Running diagnosis using the extended model delivers one single fault $\{bat\}$ stating the battery to be the cause of the observed behavior. Diagnosis time again was within a fraction of a second. From the experiments we carried out, we see that model-based diagnosis is able to provide explanations for given observations. At least for smaller systems like our heating controller, diagnosis time can be neglected. The handling of time using logic is also possible to the extent needed,

---

[1] We used a MacBook Pro (15-inch, 2016), 2.9 GHz Quad-Core Intel Core i7, with 16 GB 2133 MHz LPDDR3 ram, and macOS Big Sur Version 11.1 for carrying out the experiments.

allowing to apply model-based diagnosis to the domain of cyber-physical systems. Moreover, fault models, i.e., explicit rules stating how components behave when being in a faulty state, help to reduce the number of diagnoses substantially even in cases where using structural information only would not be of any help. The latter result is not novel. In [14] the authors argued in favor of introducing fault models, and [7] provided a formal analysis. However, there is also another way of handling situations where more knowledge would lead to less diagnoses to be computed, i.e., stating physical impossibilities [4].

5   Related Research

In [9], the authors introduce a framework for MBD of CPS, which supports a designer in developing corresponding diagnostic solutions to detect and localize faults at runtime using either abductive or consistency-based diagnosis.

In [3], the authors present an approach to leverage methods from the fault detection and isolation community and model-based diagnosis to diagnose faults. Given a model of the production system a state-space model of its dynamic behavior is captured. Then there is a translation of the state-space model into satisfiability theory modulo linear arithmetic over reals. This process translates numerical information in symbolic logic. Relying on Reiter's diagnosis algorithm, these symbols can be used to diagnose faults. The demonstrating use case is a four-tank model. If the use-case is fully-observable (i.e. all components except the water tanks can be observed) this methodology detects all injected faults.

[18] propose a hybrid Model-Based and Data-Driven approach profiling the flight surface control systems, which they developed for the Airbus A380. They noted that fault signatures are often challenging to detect. This applies especially when an aircraft is in parking position or taxiing or when the data rates from sensors are low. Their approach calculates residuals, the result obtained by comparing the current servo positions with the estimated position predicted by the model. They tune the Kalman filters' sensitivity to build a trade-off between reliably detecting signals and robustness to normal environmental variations. [1] take a similar approach applying neural networks to dynamically model and monitor fifty flight parameters.

[5,11–13] propose a detailed procedure of the hybrid fault monitoring system. This is certified by NASA for operations at the International Space Station (ISS) and for the launch pre-diagnostics of Ares I-X. The Inductive Monitoring System (IMS) is a ground-based ICPS. This system processes in near real-time the telemetry from the ISS. It is based on several algorithms. They are rule-based, Model-Based and Data Driven in three distinct subsystems of the IMS. They employ a clustering approach from a fixed number of training points. This approach allows them to reconfigure IMS for new situations fast. In [11], the authors also note that there is a need for mission-critical systems like these to be flight-certified, because ground controllers rely on them to make go/no go decisions about launches. They also note that many Space Shuttle launches were delayed due to unreliable fault diagnoses. When launch faults can be evaluated more rapidly, redundant or hot-swappable modules can be deployed to reactivate launch sequences to meet critical time windows.

6   Conclusion

In this paper, we discussed how cyber-physical systems can be modeled for diagnosis. In particular, we introduced a model for a heating circuit comprising a controller, which is intended to keep the temperature within given limits. Besides the controller, we also introduced a thermal model, both requiring to handle time. Instead of considering quantitative values and continuous time, our model makes use of qualitative values and discrete time. The mapping of qualitative values to their corresponding qualitative representation has to be adapted for particular applications. The general concepts of how changes propagate over time, can be used in many applications of diagnosis dealing with cyber-physical systems.

Moreover, we carried out a case study showing that the approach provides valuable results. This holds especially, when introducing fault models, i.e., models that state how a component behaves when being in a fault state. When using fault models, we are able to come up with only one diagnosis as an explanation for given observations. Diagnosis time needed can be neglected for the case study due the small size of the underlying model (and circuit). It is worth noting that in this paper, we focus on permanent faults only.

In future research, we want to extend the model to be also able copying with temporal or transient faults. In addition, we want to apply the method for different cyber-physical systems, e.g., autonomous vehicles. Furthermore, we want to clarify whether constraints specifying physical impossibilities can also be used in the presented diagnosis framework for reducing the number of diagnoses. This is not a question of how to represent them, but whether they are capable to contribute to reductions as well as investigating on their impact on diagnosis time.

Acknowledgement. The research was supported by ECSEL JU under the project H2020 826060 AI4DI - Artificial Intelligence for Digitising Industry. AI4DI is funded by the Austrian Federal Ministry of Transport, Innovation and Technology (BMVIT) under the program "ICT of the Future" between May 2019 and April 2022. More information can be retrieved from https://iktderzukunft.at/en/.

References

1. Azam, M., Pattipati, K., Allanach, J., Poll, S., Patterson-Hine, A.: In-flight fault detection and isolation in aircraft flight control systems. In: IEEE Aerospace Conference Proceedings, vol. 2005, pp. 3555–3565 (2005). https://doi.org/10.1109/AERO.2005.1559659
2. Davis, R.: Diagnostic reasoning based on structure and behavior. Artif. Intell. **24**, 347–410 (1984)
3. Diedrich, A., Niggemann, O.: Diagnosing hybrid cyber-physical systems using state-space models and satisfiability modulo theory. In: Trave-Massuyes, L., S.A. (ed.) CEUR Workshop Proceedings, vol. 2289. CEUR-WS (2018)

4. Friedrich, G., Gottlob, G., Nejdl, W.: Physical impossibility instead of fault models. In: Proceedings of the National Conference on Artificial Intelligence (AAAI), Boston, pp. 331–336, August 1990. also appears in Readings in Model-Based Diagnosis (Morgan Kaufmann, 1992)

5. Iverson, D., et al.: General purpose data-driven system monitoring for space operations. J. Aerosp. Comput. Inf. Commun. **9**(2), 26–44 (2012). https://doi.org/10.2514/1.54964

6. Kaufmann, D., Nica, I., Wotawa, F.: Intelligent agents diagnostics - enhancing cyber-physical systems with self-diagnostic capabilities. Adv. Intell. Syst. **3**(5), 2000218 (2021). https://doi.org/10.1002/aisy.202000218

7. de Kleer, J., Mackworth, A.K., Reiter, R.: Characterizing diagnosis and systems. Artif. Intell. **56**, 197–222 (1992)

8. de Kleer, J., Williams, B.C.: Diagnosing multiple faults. Artif. Intell. **32**(1), 97–130 (1987)

9. Muškardin, E., Pill, I., Wotawa, F.: CatIO - a framework for model-based diagnosis of cyber-physical systems. In: Helic, D., Leitner, G., Stettinger, M., Felfernig, A., Raś, Z.W. (eds.) ISMIS 2020. LNCS (LNAI), vol. 12117, pp. 267–276. Springer, Cham (2020). https://doi.org/10.1007/978-3-030-59491-6_25

10. Reiter, R.: A theory of diagnosis from first principles. Artif. Intell. **32**(1), 57–95 (1987)

11. Schwabacher, M., Aguilar, R., Figueroa, F.: Using decision trees to detect and isolate simulated leaks in the J-2X rocket engine. In: IEEE Aerospace Conference Proceedings (2009). https://doi.org/10.1109/AERO.2009.4839691

12. Schwabacher, M., Goebel, K.: A survey of artificial intelligence for prognostics. In: AAAI Fall Symposium - Technical Report, pp. 107–114 (2007)

13. Schwabacher, M., Waterman, R.: Pre-launch diagnostics for launch vehicles. In: IEEE Aerospace Conference Proceedings (2008). https://doi.org/10.1109/AERO.2008.4526645

14. Struss, P., Dressler, O.: Physical negation – integrating fault models into the general diagnostic engine. In: Proceedings 11th International Joint Conference on Artificial Intelligence, Detroit, pp. 1318–1323, August 1989

15. Weld, D., de Kleer, J. (eds.): Readings in Qualitative Reasoning about Physical Systems. Morgan Kaufmann, Burlington (1989)

16. Lughofer, E., Sayed-Mouchaweh, M. (eds.): Predictive Maintenance in Dynamic Systems. Springer, Cham (2019). https://doi.org/10.1007/978-3-030-05645-2

17. Wotawa, F.: On the use of answer set programming for model-based diagnosis. In: Fujita, H., Fournier-Viger, P., Ali, M., Sasaki, J. (eds.) IEA/AIE 2020. LNCS (LNAI), vol. 12144, pp. 518–529. Springer, Cham (2020). https://doi.org/10.1007/978-3-030-55789-8_45

18. Zolghadri, A., et al.: Signal and model-based fault detection for aircraft systems. IFAC-PapersOnLine **28**(21), 1096–1101 (2015). https://doi.org/10.1016/j.ifacol.2015.09.673

Quick Start and Adaptive
New Server Monitor

Wei Zhang[✉]

Adobe Inc., McLean, USA
wzhang@adobe.com

Abstract. Customer Service Outage (CSO) in data centers can cost significant damage to technology companies, both financially and reputation-wise. CSOs can be detected early by checking anomalies in servers metrics, memory usage and latency, etc. We developed a data-driven solution for monitoring system metrics, so we can automatically notify responsible person to address the problem. Note system monitoring is especially important at the time of changes such as when new server being added to a data center, because system change is a major cause of service disruption. However, new servers do not have any usage history which is indispensable for data driven-approach to work. We propose to use data center statistics to jump start the monitoring service for new servers, then keep adapting to changes that the new server brings to the data center. The proposed solution can greatly reduce human burden of system monitoring, as well as giving companies time to fix problems before they become catastrophic.

1 Introduction

Nowadays technology companies use multiple data centers for data processing and storage. The configurations of data centers are changing from time to time: e.g., new servers being added to a data center; or a group of servers are taken off for software/hardware upgrading then put back. The changing of configuration is a major source of service disruption, for reasons such as bugs introduced during software upgrading, or system misconfiguration. Service disruptions can be extremely costly to every company, both in terms of direct financial impact and long term reputation damage.

Before service disruption happens, there are usually anomalies occurring in system metrics, e.g. exceptional high memory/CPU/disk usage or low number of hits from clients. Timely detecting anomalies in system metrics is critical for addressing potential problems before they become severe. It takes anywhere between minutes to hours or days for troubles to emerge after system changes, so it is impractical for Site Reliability Engineering (SRE) teams to constantly watch all kinds of system metrics for problems. Currently, they use manual thresholds for detecting anomalies. However, manual threshold has several disadvantages: Firstly, it requires deep understanding about system behaviors. Without in-depth domain knowledge, it's virtually impossible to set proper thresholds. Secondly, it cannot handle natural data variations, e.g. seasonality. See Fig. 1 for an

© Springer Nature Switzerland AG 2021
H. Fujita et al. (Eds.): IEA/AIE 2021, LNAI 12799, pp. 453–461, 2021.
https://doi.org/10.1007/978-3-030-79463-7_38

example. Last but not the least, the environments are dynamic and continuously evolving, with all kinds of changes: customer base, system load/configuration, etc. Thus, a perfect threshold for now might not work for the future.

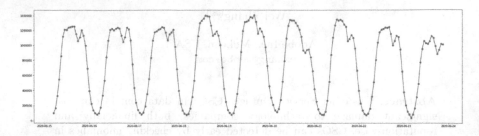

Fig. 1. The number of hits over time for a client. It exhibits strong daily seasonality: up and down in similar way every day. Setting one alerting threshold (e.g. alert when the number of hits falls below 20000) will either miss a significant drop during peak time, or gives false alarms during the down time.

Rather than manual threshold, we developed a machine learning and data-driven approach to determine if any exception happens. The solution is to build a time-series model based on historical data and check how the observed value deviated from the expected value. As Fig. 2 illustrates, for each timestamp, we can build a model based on previous data points, then predict the expected value (denoted as red) and the upper/lower alerting bound (black curve) for that time. In this particular case, the actual usage (blue) always fluctuated but was within the normal range most of the time. If the value is outside of the range, we send an alert to the responsible team.

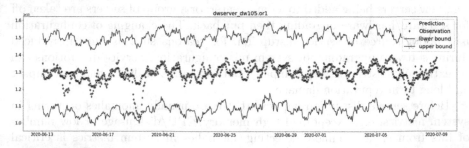

Fig. 2. The memory usage (blue) vs. the predicted value (red) as well as the normal range (black)of a server across time. (Color figure online)

Note however, when a new server is put into a data center, whether it is a newly added server or old one after upgrading, it starts fresh and has no

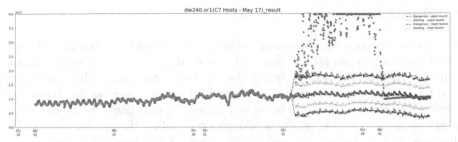

(a) A server was put into a data center on May. 17th, then exhibited problem due to a bug. Its memory usage went way above the normal range. Later when the problem was resolved, the predicted values are consistent with the real value.

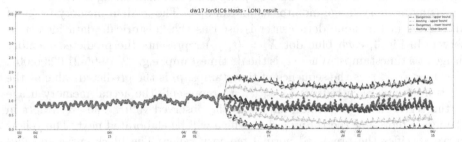

(b) Another server joined the another data center on May. 8th without any problem. Its actual memory usage was close to the prediction.

Fig. 3. Examples of using *standard data* to jump start memory monitoring of new servers, which were put into different data centers within a month period. Before joining a data center, a server has no history of memory usage, so there is no prediction (expected value/range) either. Thus there is only one curve (the *standard data*) in that time period. (Color figure online)

historical data at all.[1] One solution would be let it run for a week or two so we can collect enough "historical" data then start to detect exceptions. However, it is the first couple of hours or days that is critical for watching, since that is when problems are likely to occur. Moreover, the idea of waiting for data accumulation might not work. Because the initial data might be anomalous by themselves if there is something wrong with the server or the load balancer. See Fig. 3(a) for an example. In turn, we cannot build a reliable model. This is a problem of *new comer*, which is somewhat similar to the cold start problem [4] in recommendation system. However, it has its own unique property as the *new comer* will also affect the group behavior: the load will be redistributed across the group eventually. Therefore, we need to make sure that subsequent time-series model be updated continuously to adapt to the behavior change.

---

[1] More precisely, the old (rejoined) server may has some trace of history data, but they are sporadic and broken like random noise. After testing with the broken data, we found it more appropriate to eliminate them.

2   Our Solution

To address the *new comer* problem, we keep track of the median values of monitored metrics (memory/CPU usage, disk wait time, etc.) of all servers in the same data center. For each metric in the jth data center, its median value over time form a time series, we call it the "standard data", denote as $\bar{X}_j$. We do not need to keep the entire history of median values. $\bar{X}_j$ only contains the latest two month of median values, which is enough for building time-series models. We also tried to use the mean value over all servers, but found it less stable, as it can be affected by extreme values from a small number of servers. When a server is added into the jth data center, for each system metric to track, we retrieve its "standard data" and use the data to jump start the monitoring service.

Using memory usage monitor as an example. The median memory usage of all servers in the same data center is used as the "historical" data for a new server. In Fig. 3, each blue dot $X_i = (t_i, p_i)$ represents the predicted memory usage at a timestamps. Where t_i is the ith timestamp, e.g. "2019-05-21 02:00:00". $t_0 < t_1 < \cdots < t_i$ is the sequence of timestamps. p_i is the predicted value at the ith timestamp. Each red dot $O_i = (t_i, v_i)$ represents the actual memory usage of the server at the ith timestamp. v_i is the observed value. The green dots in the figure represent the *training data* which will be elaborated next. The yellow curve specifies the predicted normal memory range. The black curve specifies the predicted dangerous level of memory usage for this server, an alert will be sent if the observed value is above the black curve.

Each prediction X_i is estimated based on the model built using the *training data* before its timestamp. Currently, we use the Prophet library [8] for building time-series model and forecasting future values. For a blue dot $X_i = (t_i, p_i)$, p_i is forecasted based on the model built using $\tilde{X} = \{\tilde{X}_0, \tilde{X}_1, \ldots, \tilde{X}_{i-1}\}$. $\tilde{X}_k = (t_k, m_k)$ represents the *training data* at the t_k timestamp, m_k is our believed value of **normal** data at the kth timestamp. Note the training data at each timestamp is $\tilde{X}_i$, not X_i nor O_i. $\tilde{X}$ is an internally maintained time-series data. It is obtained using Algorithm 1.

Algorithm 1 describes the training data updating process with each new observation. i starts from L, the length of the initial training data. During this process, we set $\tilde{X}_i = O_i$ if v_i is within the predicted normal range defined by $p_i \pm 3 * \sigma_i$. Because we believe this is the nature variation with the data. By using the observed value, the updated training data can adapt to moderate trend changing in the observations. If the observed value is out of the predicted range, we use $p_i + \text{sign}(v_i - p_i) * \frac{1}{i-L+1} * \sigma_i$ to update the training data. Because in this case, O_i is an exception based on our estimate; using it for building model will likely hurt the model accuracy. Note $\tilde{X}_i \neq p_i$, since we cannot totally rely on the predicted value and range: they may not always be accurate. When $v_i > p_i$, $\text{sign}(v_i - p_i)$ is positive; otherwise it is negative. As a result, $\tilde{X}_i$ will be pulled slightly toward v_i. The pulled distance is determined by σ and γ. γ shrinks as time goes on, reflecting our assumption that metric value might be volatile when a server just joined but eventually stabilizing. Therefore, we allow $\tilde{X}_i$ to drift more at the beginning so it has more flexibility for adaptation.

Algorithm 1. Training data initialization and updating for new servers

1. When the server join the jth data center, $\tilde{X} \leftarrow \bar{X}_j$.
2. $L = \text{len}(\tilde{X})$
3. For a new observation $O_i = (t_i, v_i)$:
    (a) Build a time-series model using $\tilde{X}$ and forecast the expected value p_i and standard deviation σ_i.
    (b)   **if** $v_i \in [p_i \pm 3 * \sigma_i]$ **then**
    $$\tilde{X}_i = (t_i, v_i)$$
    else
    $$\gamma = \frac{1}{i-L+1}$$
    $$\tilde{X}_i = (t_i, \ p_i + \sigma_i * \text{sign}(v_i - p_i) * \gamma)$$
    if $v_i \notin [p_i \pm 6 * \sigma_i]$ **then**
    Send alert.
    (c) Append $\tilde{X}_i$ to $\tilde{X}$

Although each time $\tilde{X}_i$ is only pulled a little bit toward O_i, it will converge over time. γ helps to regularize the converging process so it will not oscillate. Figure 4 shows a typical example of how $\tilde{X}$ eventually converges to the real usage. The memory usage of this server is fairly stable after joining the cluster, but quite far away from the "standard data". Initially the observed values are identified as exceptions (outside of the yellow curve). If there is no adaptation, say we just set $\tilde{X}_i = (t_i, p_i)$, $\tilde{X}$ and the subsequent predictions will always be roughly the same as the proceeding training data, consequently never converge to the real value.

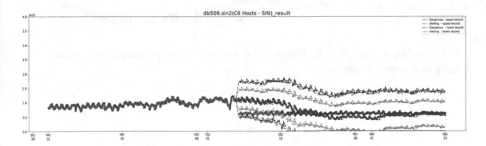

Fig. 4. The training data and predictions eventually converged to the real value. (Color figure online)

In Fig. 3(a), when the memory usage went way outside of the normal range, the observed values are excluded from the *training data*. So green dots (*training data*) are close to the blue dots (prediction) in that time period, only shifted a little toward the observed value. Because we want to adapt to the observed value for eventual convergence. In Fig. 3(b) when the server runs normally, the predicted values converge to the actual memory usage pattern of this server quite nicely. Note $\bar{X}_j$ will also be updated with data coming in from the new server. This is necessary since there might be more new servers joining later and they need the updated *standard data*.

3 More Experiments Results

See Fig. 5 and 6 for more examples of memory usage and CPU utility monitoring for servers added back to data center after being upgraded.

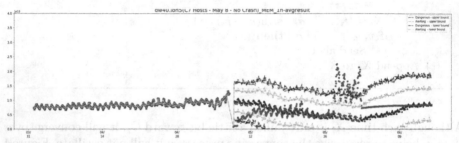

(a) Predicted usage adapts to the real usage. Then we detected exception after 2 weeks (when another round of server reconfiguration happened).

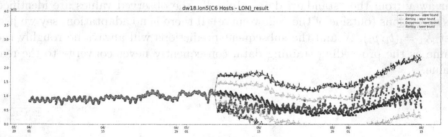

(b) Ater being added into the cluster, this server had no problem and memory was always in acceptable range.

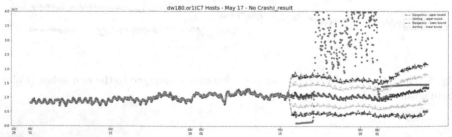

(c) Another server developed problem after joining in. Once the probem was solved, predictions started to get closer to the real value so no more alerts.

Fig. 5. More examples of monitoring newly joined servers.

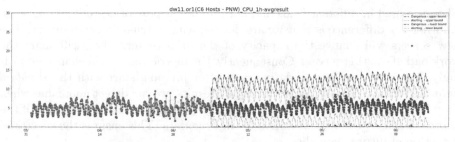

(a) After joining Oregon data center on 05/07, this server ran smoothly.

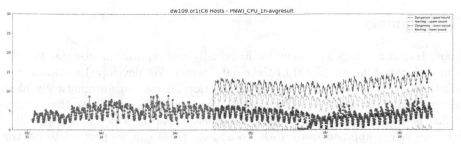

(b) Another server joined on 05/07 with some rough time, but didn't cause an trouble.

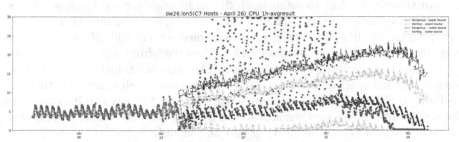

(c) Ater joining in on 04/27, this server demonstrated exceptional CPU usage due to a load balancer problem.

Fig. 6. CPU usage monitoring for newly joined servers.

4   Related Work

The cold start problem with recommendation system has been well studied [5–7]. When a new user joining the system, the solution is usually asking the user to provide some preferences so to build an initial user profile, then refine the profile with more interactions. In fields such as political science [2] and economics [3], people has been using the Synthetic Control Method [1] for the purpose of comparative case studies.

Both the solution to the cold-start recommendation and the Synthetic Control Method bear some resemblance to our approach, in the sense that they both use some similar entities to predict how it should be for the new entity.

They are used in different fields and not for the purpose of detecting anomalies. Another key difference is that we are dealing with a dynamic environment. The new servers will change the capacity of the data center. They will share the workload of existing servers. Consequently, the metric values will change accordingly. Therefore, we keep updating data after jumping start with the *standard data*. As we have demonstrated with many results, we can detect anomalies when they happen at the very beginning, while converging to the real data even if the *standard data* is not representative of the true data. This ensures the successful detection of future anomalies.

5   Summary

Many tech companies have been hit financially and reputation-wise due to Customer Service Outage (CSO) in their data center. We developed a data-driven solution for monitoring system health metrics, so we can automatically alert responsible team so they can fix potential problem. One challenge that we are facing is that new servers do not have any usage history which is indispensable for data driven approaches to work. To address this issue, we propose to use the "standard data" over the data center to fill in the blank history, and use it as the initial *training data* to jump start the monitoring service for new servers. Then we keep updating the *training data* to adapt to changes that the new server brings to the data center, as adding new servers will affect the system load distribution of the entire data center. Real data from our data centers are used to illustrate how our approach works. The proposed solution is expected to reduce human burden of monitoring, as well as giving tech companies the edge for fixing problems before they become catastrophic. So they can improve both the quality of our service (less service disruption) and the quality of employee life (less stressful manual monitoring and bug fixing).

References

1. Abadie, A., Diamond, A., Hainmueller, J.: Synthetic control methods for comparative case studies: estimating the effect of California's tobacco control program. J. Am. Stat. Assoc. **105**(490), 493–505 (2010)
2. Abadie, A., Diamond, A., Hainmueller, J.: Comparative politics and the synthetic control method. Am. J. Polit. Sci. **59**(2), 495–510 (2015)
3. Billmeier, A., Nannicini, T.: Assessing economic liberalization episodes: a synthetic control approach. Rev. Econ. Stat. **95**(3), 983–1001 (2013)
4. Bobadilla, J., Ortega, F., Hernando, A., Bernal, J.: A collaborative filtering approach to mitigate the new user cold start problem. Knowl.-based Syst. **26**, 225–238 (2012)
5. Chen, H.H., Chen, P.: Differentiating regularization weights-a simple mechanism to alleviate cold start in recommender systems. ACM Trans. Knowl. Discov. Data (TKDD) **13**(1), 1–22 (2019)
6. Elahi, M., Ricci, F., Rubens, N.: A survey of active learning in collaborative filtering recommender systems. Comput. Sci. Rev. **20**, 29–50 (2016)

7. Rubens, N., Elahi, M., Sugiyama, M., Kaplan, D.: Active learning in recommender systems. In: Ricci, F., Rokach, L., Shapira, B. (eds.) Recommender Systems Handbook, pp. 809–846. Springer, Boston, MA (2015). https://doi.org/10.1007/978-1-4899-7637-6_24
8. Taylor, S.J., Letham, B.: Forecasting at scale. Am. Stat. **72**(1), 37–45 (2018)

Map-Matching Based on HMM
for Urban Traffic

Dongzi Chen[1], Xinzheng Niu[2](✉), Philippe Fournier-Viger[3], Wenxin Wu[2], and Bing Wang[4]

[1] School of Information and Software Engineering, University of Electronic Science and Technology of China, Chengdu, Sichuan, China
[2] School of Computer Science and Engineering, University of Electronic Science and Technology of China, Chengdu, Sichuan, China
[3] Harbin Institute of Technology (Shenzhen), Shenzhen, China
[4] Southwest Petroleum University, Chengdu, China

Abstract. Map-matching for urban traffic is the process of matching geographical coordinates recorded by GPS devices to an electronic road network. However, the complexity of urban environments brings great challenges to map-matching. In urban areas, GPS data is usually sampled at a higher rate than in rural areas, and in poor conditions, low-speed vehicle driving will result in redundant GPS points. A large number of redundant points can cause mismatches, resulting in paths containing repeated u-turns and loops. Hence, to address this problem, this paper presents a novel method named HLI (Map-matching of **H**igh frequency and **L**ow-speed points at **I**dentification Area). The method first identifies low-speed segments of a trajectory to reduce redundancy in those segments. Next, map-matching is done by two processes: Normal map-matching and RLIA (**R**ule based **L**ocal matching at **I**dentification **A**rea). Then, matching rules are created to accurately match low-speed GPS trajectory points entering an identification area. Finally, both results are combined. Experimental results show that the proposed HLI method can effectively solve the problem and improve the accuracy of both local and global map-matching.

Keywords: Map-matching · Urban traffic · GPS trajectory

1 Introduction

In recent years, with the popularity of mobile positioning equipment, a large number of GPS trajectories data of moving vehicles has been generated. Map-matching consists of matching GPS trajectories to road networks, providing a basis for subsequent applications, e.g. real-time navigation, path design and planning [1], and urban area division [2]. Recent map-matching algorithms can be divided into four categories: geometric algorithms [3,4], topological algorithms [5,6], probabilistic algorithms [7,8], and advanced algorithms [9]. Most of the existing map-matching algorithms are designed for low-frequency GPS data,

© Springer Nature Switzerland AG 2021
H. Fujita et al. (Eds.): IEA/AIE 2021, LNAI 12799, pp. 462–473, 2021.
https://doi.org/10.1007/978-3-030-79463-7_39

and in particular to deal with the lack of low-frequency information [8]. However, with the development of GPS equipment and technology, high-frequency GPS data gradually becomes more common. Map-matching algorithms for low-frequency data can handle missing points and the high sparsity of trajectories, but they offer no solutions for data redundancy and low accuracy caused by high-frequency GPS data. These problems are common in urban areas. The GPS data generated by urban vehicles are mostly high-frequency data, acquired at short intervals (e.g. 1 s). Therefore, when traffic is congested and vehicles move slowly or at a standstill, many redundant points are generated. Because of the existence of errors, these redundant points scattered in the road network can be matched to adjacent road sections, resulting in repeated u-turns, loops and other mismatches that do not reflect the real situation. In addition, due to large urban road intersections, the matching complexity of GPS trajectory points is high, and the matching accuracy of high-frequency GPS trajectories is low.

This paper proposes a map-matching method for High-frequency and Low-speed points at Identification area (HLI method) based on HMM. The method first divides a GPS trajectory's points into low-speed and high speed, while applying a local filtering strategy to eliminate redundant data points. Then, an identification area is established for intersections. Based on a series of rules and assisted by normal speed points, the low-speed GPS trajectory points in the identification area are matched. Experimental result shows that this method is suitable for urban high-frequency GPS trajectory map-matching, and the accuracy of both global and local matching is improved.

The rest of this paper is organized as follows. Problem definition is presented in Sect. 2. Section 3 introduces the proposed HLI method. Section 4 describes experiments. Finally, we conclude the paper with Sect. 5.

2   Problem Statement

This section first introduces important definitions related to map-matching. Then, the problem of map-matching is described in detail.

Definition 1. *GPS trajectory point set. A GPS trajectory point set is a set of GPS points. $L = \{p_1, p_2, p_3.., p_n\}$. For GPS trajectory point $p_i \in L$, the longitude is $p_i.lat$, the latitude is $p_i.lng$, the timestamp is $p_i.t$, and the speed is $p_i.v$.*

Definition 2. *GPS trajectory. A GPS trajectory is a time-ordered sequence of GPS points, $T \subseteq L$, the time interval between each two points is less than a threshold $\triangle t$, that is $0 < p_{i+1}.t - p_i.t \leq \triangle t, 1 \leq i < n$.*

Definition 3. *Low-speed GPS point. For a GPS point $p_i, p_i \in L, 1 \leq i < n$, if the speed is less than s% of the average speed of all GPS points, $p_i.v < \frac{s\%}{n}(p_1.v + p_2.v+, .., +p_n.v)$, p_i is called as "low speed GPS point".*

Definition 4. *Low-speed trajectory fragment. A low speed trajectory fragment S is a low speed fragment of a GPS trajectory T, $S \subseteq T$, when there is a continuous low speed GPS trajectory and its number of continuous low speed GPS points exceeds a window size ω.*

Definition 5. *Road segment. A road segment is a directed edge. The length of a road segment is e.l, the starting point is e.start, and the ending point is e.end.*

Definition 6. *Road network. A road network is represented by a directed graph $G(V, E)$, where V is a set of vertices representing intersections and terminal points, and E is a set of edges.*

Definition 7. *Path. Let there be two vertices v_i and v_j of a road network, such that a path P starts at v_i and ends at v_j. The path is denoted as $P = \{e_1, e_2, ..., e_n\}$, where $e_1.start = v_i$ and $e_n.end = v_j$.*

The goal of map-matching is to use methods to reduce and eliminate the effects of errors in the raw road network and trajectory information, infer the real ground positions of the moving object corresponding to the trajectory and map it to the road network. The map-matching problem is defined as follows.

Definition 8. *Problem statement. Given a group of raw GPS trajectories T and road network $G(V, E)$, find the path P from G that can match GPS trajectories T with its real path.*

In this paper, the following approach is used to evaluate a map-matching algorithm. First, the global matching accuracy of all GPS trajectory points is calculated using the metrics presented in Eq. (1) and Eq. (2). These metrics have been used in other studies [9] but with different names.

$$CMP_{global} = \frac{N_{gcmp}}{N_{gap}} \tag{1}$$

$$CML = \frac{N_{cml}}{N_l} \tag{2}$$

In Eq. (1) and Eq. (2), CMP_{global} (**C**orrectly **M**atched **P**oint) and CML (**C**orrectly **M**atched **L**ength) are used to evaluate the global matching accuracy for matching a GPS trajectory to a road network. N_{gcmp} is the number of GPS trajectory points correctly matched, N_{gap} is the total number of GPS trajectory points, N_{cml} is the length of the trajectory segments correctly matched to the road network, and N_l is the total length of the trajectory.

In addition, this paper also evaluates the accuracy of local matching at intersections. The accuracy metric is expressed by Eq. (3):

$$CMP_{local} = \frac{N_{lcmp}}{N_{lap}} \tag{3}$$

In Eq. (3), CMP_{local} is the local matching accuracy in intersections, N_{lcmp} is the number of correctly matched GPS trajectory points in intersections, and N_{lap} is the total number of GPS trajectory points in intersections.

3   Method

An overview of the proposed HLI method is shown in Fig. 1. GPS trajectory points are first pre-processed to eliminate redundancy found in high frequency and low-speed trajectory data. Next low-speed GPS trajectory points are partitioned into different types based on whether they are within an identification area or not. Then, a dynamic identification area related to road types is established. Finally, the RLIA method is used locally, combined with a hidden Markov model to process GPS trajectory points and the result of map-matching is obtained.

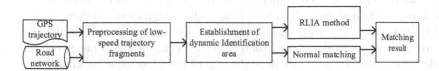

Fig. 1. Overview of the HLI method

GPS Trajectory Pre-processing. In the trajectory preprocessing stage, the low-speed GPS trajectory points are filtered out to reduce redundancy and smooth the trajectory.

First, the space filling curve is used to map the 2-D GPS points in the low-speed trajectory fragment into 1-D vectors. Then, the α-trimmed mean filter is used to process low-speed segments (see Fig. 2). A certain proportion of trajectory points in the starting part and ending part are removed. The proportion is determined by window size ω. The mean of the remaining points is calculated and the remaining original points are replaced.

Fig. 2. α-trimmed mean filter

Space filling curves are widely used as a scheme to map multidimensional space into 1-D space [10]. In this paper, space filling curves are used to map 2-D GPS trajectory points in low-speed trajectory segments into 1-D vectors and arrange them in a proper order. Through experiments on different space filling curves, it is found that sweep curve can meet the requirements of both accuracy and computing efficiency [11]. Hence, considering the large amount of low-speed GPS trajectory points, we use sweep curve to map 2-D points.

After 1-D vectors of low-speed trajectory segments $T = \{p_1, p_2, p_3, ..., pn\}$ are generated, the output of α-trimmed mean filter on sorted low-speed segments is:

$$p_i' = \frac{\Sigma p_i}{\omega - 2\lceil \alpha\omega \rceil}, i = \{i|i \in N^+, \lceil \alpha\omega \rceil + 1 \leq i \leq \omega - \lceil \alpha\omega \rceil\} \qquad (4)$$

Parameter ω is the window size. For parameter α, based on prior studies [11], we considered setting α to 0.2 as it provided better results.

Establishment of Dynamic Identification Area. First, road width and error should be considered to decide the radius of the identification area. Electronic road network data often lack road width but include road types, such as trunk road, secondary road and branch road. Therefore, we classify urban roads according to road types. Then a road width inference method based on the road grade is proposed to help calculate the size of the identification area.

Table 1. Type-grade-width correspondence Table

Road type	Road grade	Road width (m)
Express way	1	40–50
Trunk road	2	30–40
Secondary road	3	20–30
Branch road	4	10–20
Sidewalk	5	5–10

Urban roads are divided into five grades, where road width and grade are related. Based on the survey of road widths in the United States, Australia, Japan, China and other countries [12], the correlation between urban road type-grade-width is established according to the urban road grade and type in combination with the actual situation (see Table 1). The radius of Identification area is defined as:

$$r = f(l) + error(t) \qquad (5)$$

As shown in Fig. 3 (a), two types of errors should be considered when a vehicle reaches an intersection [13]. The first type of error is caused by the electronic road network. We use solid lines to represent real road positions and dotted lines to represent the road positions in the electronic road network. The error between e_1 and e_1' is caused by measurement errors. The second type of error is caused by the accuracy of GPS trajectory points. GPS trajectory point p_1 is the location of vehicle A recorded by the GPS device. And the error between the

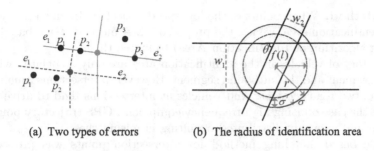

(a) Two types of errors   (b) The radius of identification area

Fig. 3. Establishing a dynamic identification area

real position p_1' of vehicle A and p_1 is caused by the accuracy of GPS trajectory points. Suppose that the error caused by the electronic road network data is σ', and the error caused by the accuracy of GPS trajectory points is $error\,(t)$, then the positioning error E at the intersection at time t of the GPS trajectory point is:

$$E = \sigma' + error\,(t) \tag{6}$$

Since the error caused by the electronic road network data does not change with time, the error caused by the accuracy of GPS trajectory points can be expressed by GPS accuracy. Therefore, Eq. (6) can be written as:

$$r = f\,(l) + \sigma' + \sigma \tag{7}$$

The radius of identification area is not related to time but only related to the road connecting to it. By finding the value of $f\,(l)$ in the Eq. (7), the identification area radius can be calculated.

First, we estimate road width w according to the relationship between road type and width in Table 1:

$$w = \frac{w_{max} + w_{min}}{2} \tag{8}$$

As shown in Fig. 3 (b), the radius of an identification area are only related to the angle, width and number of connecting roads. The size of the dynamic identification area changes according to the above factors. When there are only two roads connected at an intersection, $f\,(l)$ can be calculated by Eq. (9):

$$f\,(l) = \sqrt{\frac{w_1^2 + w_2^2 + 2w_1w_2cos\theta}{4sin^2\theta}} \tag{9}$$

When an intersection connects more than two roads, $f\,(l)$ is calculated for each of the roads, and the maximum $f\,(l)$ is calculated, as shown in Eq. (10):

$$f\,(l) = max\,(f_1\,(l), f_2\,(l), ..., f_3\,(l)) \tag{10}$$

RLIA Method. When points of the low-speed trajectory fragment are located in the identification area, we use the proposed RLIA method (**R**ule based **L**ocal matching algorithm at **I**dentification **A**rea) to match them.

Trajectory of vehicles in the identification area are only associated with the inbound segment and the outbound segment. However, intersections usually have more than two road sections. And vehicles at intersections tend to drive at low speed. In the case of using high-frequency equipment, GPS trajectory points are numerous and unevenly distributed, resulting in mismatches.

A rule based matching method for intersection points was proposed in another study [14]. But authors did not preprocess the low-speed points and underestimated the amount of redundancy in high frequency trajectory points at intersections. We improve the rules in the identification area. According to the characteristics of the trajectory, the trusted region is divided to match the GPS trajectory points more accurately (Fig. 4).

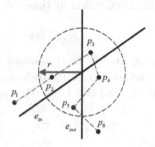

Fig. 4. Inbound section and outbound section of identification area

First, the inbound section e_{in} and outbound section e_{out} of the identification area must be obtained. The inbound section is matched before the vehicle enters the identification area. Considering the actual situation, vehicles often decelerate before entering the identification area, and the points of a low-speed GPS trajectory are prone to mismatching. Therefore, the last point of the last normal point that is the closest to the low-speed segment of the identification area is selected to match the inbound section. The inbound section is matched by using the LookAhead method [15].

Next, the identification area is partitioned (see Fig. 5). The entire circle shaped identification area is partitioned into trusted region C_1 and untrusted region C_0. The arc length L of untrusted region is calculated by the angle θ formed by the inbound segment e_{in} and outbound segment e_{out} in Eq. (11).

$$L = \pi r \left(1 - \frac{\theta}{180°}\right) \tag{11}$$

Then, the untrusted region is located according to the angle bisector. The untrusted region is the fan-shaped C_0 having the intersection's center as center,

r is the radius, the center line is the angle bisector extension line formed by the inbound section E_{in} and outbound section E_{out}, and L is the arc length.

After the trusted region and untrusted region are obtained, the following two matching rules are formulated to match the points in the identification area: (1) GPS trajectory points in the trusted region: Based on the hidden Markov model, the transition probability matrix and the emission probability matrix are calculated. The probability graph is constructed and the highest probability path is found by applying the Viterbi algorithm [16] as the matching result path. (2) The first GPS trajectory point in the untrusted region: The position of this point is relocated to the center of the identification area for matching. (3) Other GPS trajectory points in the untrusted region: Relocation is only performed once in a single map-matching of the identification area. After a GPS trajectory point has been relocated, other points in the trusted region are removed.

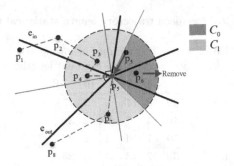

Fig. 5. Trusted region partitioning and matching rules

4 Experiments

This section presents the experiment that was carried out to evaluate the proposed HLI method. The section first describes the experimental setup, including the two datasets that were used, and the experiment's parameters. The results obtained by the proposed algorithm were compared with those of the ST-matching [9] and the junction decision domain model [13]. Finally, a discussion of the main results is presented.

Dataset Description. The method presented in this paper was tested on two real datasets.

DS1: The data in DS1 is from Melbourne, Australia. It contains GPS trajectory data, road network data and ground truth. The GPS trajectory dataset contains 2,512 GPS data points with a sampling interval of 1 s. The network map covers the longitude of Melbourne from 144.81800 to 145.11600, and the latitude from −37.91800 to −37.71000, including 107,315 vertices and 208,626 road segments.

DS2: The data in DS2 is from Seattle, Washington, USA. It contains GPS trajectory data, road network data and ground truth. The GPS trajectory dataset contains 7,531 GPS sampling points, and the sampling interval is 1 s. The network data covers an area of about 40 km radius of Seattle, Washington, USA, including 423,240 vertices and 158,167 road sections.

Parameter Settings. The parameters used for GPS trajectory preprocessing are: $s\%$, α and ω. The first parameter s is used to find low-speed trajectory points. Based on the survey of the actual vehicle speed, we set s to 30, 40 and 50 for the experiments. Referring to the selection in paper [11], we set the second parameter α to 0.2. The third parameter ω is used in the preprocessing step to control the window size, to find a suitable value for ω. Moreover, we calculate the length of the low-speed trajectory segment under the three values of s.

Table 2. Low-speed trajectory length statistical table

Dataset	s	The number of low-speed trajectory segment lengths				
		4	6	8	10	>10
DS1	30	8	17	6	3	17
	40	4	7	2	2	31
	50	1	4	1	2	29
DS2	30	12	13	4	3	23
	40	8	11	9	7	22
	50	3	5	2	13	40

We can see that most low-speed trajectory segments are longer than 10. However, the number of low-speed trajectories is already large when the length is equal to 4 in shorter parts, particularly in DS1, $s = 30$ (see Table 2). Thus, the minimum value was set to 4, $\omega \in \{4, 6, 8\}$, and tests were done for each of these values. The parameters required to calculate the transition probability matrix and the emission probability matrix of normal matching are as in [9]. Parameter σ and σ' are used in calculation of the identification area size. We set them both to 4.06 [13,17,18]. Therefore, the radius of the dynamic identification area, $r = f(l) + 8.12$, and $f(l)$ changes with the road grade.

Experimental Results. For $s = 30, 40$, and 50, $\omega = 6, 8$, and 10, the experimental results are shown in Fig. 6. For DS1, when $\omega = 10$ and $s = 50$, the global matching accuracy of the number of GPS trajectory points is the highest with 97.9%. When $\omega = 8$ and $s = 50$, the global matching accuracy of the length of the GPS trajectory is the highest, 97.5%. And when parameters $\omega = 6$ and $s = 50$, the local matching accuracy is the highest, at 98.7%. For DS2, when

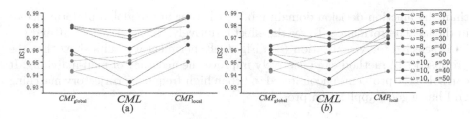

Fig. 6. Results for different parameter settings

$\omega = 8$ and $s = 50$, the global matching accuracy of the number of GPS trajectory points is the highest at 97.5%. When parameters $\omega = 10$ and $s = 40$, the global matching accuracy of the length of the GPS trajectory is the highest, at 97.3%. And when parameters $\omega = 6$ and $s = 50$, the local matching accuracy is the highest, at 98.8%.

In conclusion, we consider that the window size has no significant effect on the results. And when $s = 50$, the matching accuracy is basically the highest. Therefore, we set ω to 6, 8 and 10, and set s to 50 respectively.

The proposed HLI method is compared with other methods. We first compared it with the ST-matching [9], which is a classic of map-matching method. In ST-matching, the spatial and temporal information are used to construct hidden Markov model, and then the maximum likelihood path in the probability graph is found as the result. We then compared it to the junction decision domain model [13]. In that model a local matching strategy is added to improve the accuracy, and the main matching method is still based on the hidden Markov model. The comparison between the proposed HLI algorithm and the above two methods is shown in Fig. 7.

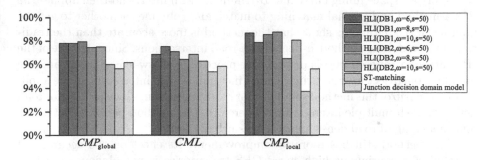

Fig. 7. Comparison of the proposed HLI method and other methods

It can be seen that the proposed HLI method has better results than ST-matching for the three indexes. In particular, the local matching accuracy of this method is excellent. The junction decision domain model also greatly improved the performance for local segments. However, the HLI method had a better effect than the junction decision domain model, whether in the global performance or in the local performance. To see the effect intuitively, the result of $\omega = 10$ and $s = 50$ is selected for visualization (See Fig. 8). Experimental results show that the proposed HLI method can effectively improve the accuracy of map-matching. It can solve the problems encountered in urban high-frequency trajectory matching and has a good application prospect.

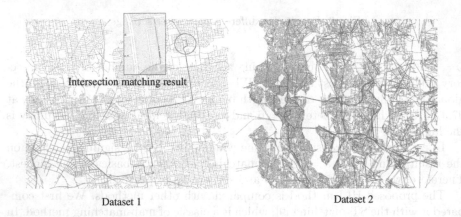

Dataset 1   Dataset 2

Fig. 8. Visualization of matching result

5   Conclusion

This paper proposed a novel HLI method based on HMM that is suitable for high frequency urban GPS data. This method can handle redundancy and distribution deviation of high-frequency GPS data. The method preprocesses a low-speed GPS trajectory by space filling curve and α-trimmed mean filter, and then applies the RLIA method and normal matching to match and combine each other to get the final result. Experiments show that the method is more accurate than the traditional ST-matching method, especially for road intersections. Since the core of the HLI method proposed in this paper is the processing of low-speed points and the matching of trajectory points in the identification area of intersections, the application scenario of this method should be for road congestion, slow-speed or for road networks with multiple intersections. Therefore, this method performs better for map-matching of road dense areas such as urban roads.

This method still has room for improvement. Its effect on the accuracy of matching for continuous high-speed GPS trajectories is not obvious, and it is more suitable for matching a trajectory which contains some low-speed segments. In the future, we will study how to use the features of a trajectory to intelligently select matching methods to improve the accuracy of map-matching.

Acknowledgements. This research is sponsored by the Science and Technology Planning Project of Sichuan Province under Grant No. 2020YFG0054, and the Joint Funds of the Ministry of Education of China.

References

1. Qu, B., Yang, W., Cui, G., Wang, X.: Profitable taxi travel route recommendation based on big taxi trajectory data. IEEE Trans. Intell. Transp. Syst. **PP**(99), 1–16 (2019)
2. Gao, Q., Fu, J., Yu, Y., Tang, X.: Identification of urban regions' functions in Chengdu, China, based on vehicle trajectory data. PLOS ONE **14**(4), 1–17 (2019)
3. Srinivasan, D., Cheu, R.L., Tan, C.W.: Development of an improved ERP system using GPS and AI techniques. In: Proceedings of the 2003 IEEE International Conference on Intelligent Transportation Systems. vol. 1, pp. 554–559 (2003)
4. Brakatsoulas, S., Pfoser, D., Salas, R., Wenk, C.: On map-matching vehicle tracking data. In: Proceedings of the 31st International Conference on Very Large Data Bases, Trondheim, Norway (2005)
5. Tang, J., Zhang, S., Zou, Y., Liu, F.: An adaptive map-matching algorithm based on hierarchical fuzzy system from vehicular GPS data. PLoS ONE **12**(12) (2017)
6. Zhao, X., et al.: Advanced topological map matching algorithm based on d-s theory. Arab. J. Sci. Eng. **43**(8), 3863–3874 (2018)
7. Wang, G., Zimmermann, R.: Eddy: an error-bounded delay-bounded real-time map matching algorithm using hmm and online Viterbi decoder. In: Proceedings of the 22nd ACM SIGSPATIAL International Conference on Advances in Geographic Information Systems (2014)
8. Yuan, L., Li, D., Hu, S.: A map-matching algorithm with low-frequency floating car data based on matching path. EURASIP J. Wirel. Commun. Netw. **2018**(1), 1–14 (2018). https://doi.org/10.1186/s13638-018-1154-x
9. Lou, Y., Zhang, C., Xie, X., Zheng, Y., Wang, W., Huang, Y.: Map-matching for low-sampling-rate GPS trajectories. In: Proceedings of the 17th ACM SIGSPA-TIAL International Conference on Advances in Geographic Information Systems, pp. 352–361 (2009)
10. Mokbel, M.F., Aref, W.G., Kamel, I.: Analysis of multi-dimensional space-filling curves. GeoInformatica **7**(3), 179–209 (2003)
11. Mohamed, R., Aly, H., Youssef, M.: Accurate real-time map matching for challenging environments. IEEE Trans. Intell. Transp. Syst. **18**(4), 847–857 (2017)
12. Han, S., Chen, X.: Research on width of urban streets in China. J. Tongji Univ. (Natl. Sci.) **34** (2006)
13. Xiaoqiang, H.: Jinqing: map-matching algorithm based on the junction decision domain and the hidden Markov model. PloS One **14**(5), e0216476 (2019)
14. Liu, M., Zhang, L., Ge, J., Long, Y., Che, W.: Map matching for urban high-sampling-frequency GPS trajectories. ISPRS Int. J. Geo-Inf. **9**, 31 (2020)
15. Brakatsoulas, S., Pfoser, D., Salas, R., Wenk, C.: On map-matching vehicle tracking data. In: Proceedings of the 31st International Conference on Very Large Data Bases, pp. 853–864 (2005)
16. Viterbi, A.J.: Error bounds for convolutional codes and an asymptotically optimum decoding algorithm. IEEE Trans. Inf. Theory **13**(2), 260–269 (1967)
17. Newson, P., Krumm, J.: Hidden Markov map matching through noise and sparseness. In: Proceedings of the 17th ACM SIGSPATIAL International Conference on Advances in Geographic Information Systems, pp. 336–343 (2009)
18. Raymond, R., Morimura, T., Osogami, T., Hirosue, N.: Map matching with hidden Markov model on sampled road network. In: Proceedings of the 21st International Conference on Pattern Recognition (ICPR2012), pp. 2242–2245 (2012)

The Choice of AI Matters: Alternative Machine Learning Approaches for CPS Anomalies

Uraz Odyurt[✉], Dolly Sapra, and Andy D. Pimentel

Informatics Institute (IvI), University of Amsterdam, Amsterdam, The Netherlands
{u.odyurt,d.sapra,a.d.pimentel}@uva.nl

Abstract. We compare the pros and cons of two Artificial Intelligence (AI) solutions, addressing the anomaly detection and identification challenge in industrial Cyber-Physical Systems (CPS). We demonstrate how our current approach, *Advanced DL*, based on Convolutional Neural Networks (CNN) differs from a previous one, *Classic ML*. Though both workflows prove to result in highly accurate classification of anomalies, Classic ML is superior in this regard with 99.23% accuracy against 94.85%. This comes at a cost, as Classic ML requires total insight and expertise regarding the system under scrutiny and heavy amounts of feature engineering, while Advanced DL treats the data as a black box, minimising the effort. At the same time, we show that finding the best performing CNN model design is not trivial. We present a quantitative comparison of both workflows in terms of elapsed times for training, validation and preprocessing, alongside discussions on qualitative aspects. Such a comparison, involving analysis of workflows for the given use-case, is of independent interest. We find the choice of AI solution to be use-case dependent.

Keywords: Machine learning · Convolutional neural network · Behavioural passports · Anomaly identification · Industrial cyber-physical systems

1 Introduction

We have witnessed the emergence of solutions based on classic Machine Learning (ML) and more advanced models, i.e., Deep Learning (DL) with Convolutional Neural Networks (CNN), for a plethora of problems for quite some time now. These techniques have become an integral part of any method of choice. The industry in particular, reaps the benefits of such solutions in production systems. As ML and DL provide more than just one way to solve a given problem, it is of utmost importance to pick the right solution and to employ the right workflow. For industrial systems, the extent of resource consumption and timely operation could very well mean the difference between success and failure, depending on the relevant requirements. In other words, it is not just about the accuracy of answers to problems, but also how fast and how efficiently they can be found.

© Springer Nature Switzerland AG 2021
H. Fujita et al. (Eds.): IEA/AIE 2021, LNAI 12799, pp. 474–484, 2021.
https://doi.org/10.1007/978-3-030-79463-7_40

We explore the balance between these factors for a given problem, which is a simplified version of an industrial use-case. We deal with an industrial Cyber-Physical System (CPS) with embedded computing nodes, for which we actively detect and identify anomalies. Anomalies can manifest themselves as diminished performance or other harmful behaviour. Anomaly detection and identification are open challenges for industrial CPS. As such systems evolve and become more complex, mainly as a result of software complexity, not every operational corner case can be covered at design time. Considering deployment in critical applications, anomalies are often very costly to rectify and leave costly effects behind when they occur. We aim to solve this challenge in a ML-based workflow, monitoring the system behaviour and identifying anomalies online.

We will be comparing two of these ML-based solutions, namely, *Classic ML* workflow developed earlier and *Advanced DL*, developed as an alternative in this paper. The Classic ML workflow incorporates regression modelling and classic algorithms, i.e., decision tree and random forest. Our Advanced DL workflow incorporates limited data preprocessing steps and takes advantage of CNNs. The main aspect driving us towards the Advanced DL workflow is the amount of domain specific knowledge, expertise and understanding of the system that is necessary for the Classic ML workflow. Our Advanced DL approach is a truly black box one, requiring no insight into the data or the internals of the system, but at the same time, has its own shortcomings.

Contribution. We have developed an alternative approach based on advanced DL to detect and identify anomalies in industrial CPS. We perform quantitative and qualitative comparisons between this approach and a previous one, utilising classic ML. Though we are dealing with a specific use-case, our comparison addresses the characteristics of the general methodology (depicted in Fig. 1) and the use-case is a demonstrator to generate data for it. We argue that there is no absolute winner and the choice of the workflow depends on the expected classification accuracy, the ability to explain the outcome based on the input data, the amount of internal knowledge, workflow development time and preference of a white box versus a black box approach towards data.

This introduction is followed by core concepts of our workflows for industrial CPS. Section 3 details our overall methodology, including the two approaches for its realisation, while Sect. 4 elaborates the implementation of the second approach, based on CNNs. Results and comparisons are given in Sect. 5, followed by the related work and concluding remarks in Sects. 6 and 7, respectively.

2   Machine Learning for Industrial CPS

When it comes to the industrial applications of CPS, there are high-value use-cases for the deployment of ML algorithms. One such use-case is the detection and classification of anomalies. Figure 1 showcases the high-level view of a methodology to address such a challenge. Different flavours of ML, whether classic ML or DL algorithms, are good fits when dealing with large amounts of data.

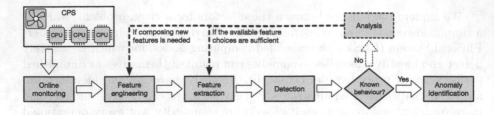

Fig. 1. Our reference analytics-based pipeline, provisioning the presence of feature engineering and anomaly identification steps, alongside anomaly detection and an optional analysis step, upon discovery of unseen anomalies.

Given that modern industrial CPS provide this large amount of monitoring data generation capability through software and hardware probes, the use of ML is not a preference, but a necessity. As such, the *analytics-based* pipeline shown in Fig. 1 is designed with data-centricity in mind [9].

Depending on the type of ML algorithm, certain amount of preprocessing is needed to transform the data into consumable forms. As it will be shown in Sect. 3, major parts of this preprocessing will be implemented rather differently, resulting in alternative characteristics and performance. Our anomaly detection is based on monitoring the system's Extra-Functional Behaviour (EFB), representing the behavioural traits of a system beyond its functional definitions and semantics. EFB is generated from different performance and operational metrics, e.g., execution time, latencies, power and energy consumption. EFB representations composed from such metrics can uniquely identify a specific system, under specific operational conditions [9].

3   One Challenge, Two Approaches

We have chosen the high-level methodology given in [9,11], aiming at detection and classification of anomalies in industrial CPS, as our reference. Since its implementation is based on classical ML algorithms [11], requiring much feature engineering effort, intimate knowledge of system internals and the data itself, we have devised a competing workflow, based on deep learning with CNNs.

3.1   Classic ML Workflow

Figures 2a and 2b visualise data set generation and anomaly classification flows for the Classic ML workflow, respectively. Here, we interpret and realise our reference workflow with classic ML classifiers, e.g., decision tree.

The Classic ML workflow involves the concept of *execution phases*, i.e., repetitive units of execution during the operational timeline of a system. Industrial CPS in particular, reveal the presence of such repetitions, as they are purpose-built systems with limited operational variety [10]. In other words, these are repeated smaller tasks, making up the complete execution.

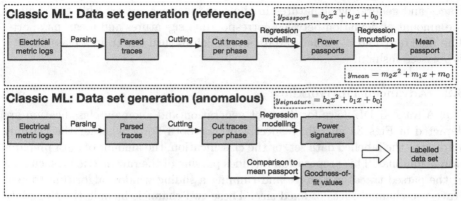

(a) Data set generation (preprocessing)

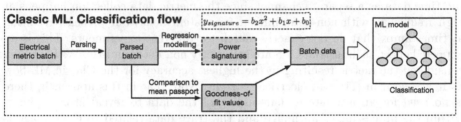

(b) Anomaly classification

Fig. 2. The two flows involved with the Classic ML approach, (a) data set generation flow from large amounts of trace data, leading to a training data set and (b) an anomaly identification flow, using much smaller trace batches with a previously trained classifier.

During data set generation, EFB metric logs, e.g., electrical current, are collected and parsed. What follows involves cutting parsed traces into parts corresponding to desired executional phases, i.e., tasks from the actual operation of the CPS, reflecting its behaviour. For instance, a CPS collecting imagery and processing them could perform load_image and process_image tasks, leaving us with three possible execution phases. These are *image load atomic phase*, *image processing atomic phase* and the combination, *image combo phase*. It is yet unknown to a designer which phase is the best to choose from and cut the traces based on, at solution design time.

For a collection of recorded readings over time for any EFB, it is possible to generate a regression function, which will serve as a unified representation of the readings. We call this a behavioural signature and when generated for a reference execution, we call it a behavioural passport [10]. Accordingly, data points from the log, including timestamps and metric readings, are used to generate a regression function as a representation. Passports are generated per metric and per phase. Numerous inputs to the CPS under reference circumstances result in numerous passports. To simplify future comparisons, we generate *mean passports* out of many passports, again per metric and per phase. By collecting anomalous traces and generating signatures in the same manner, we are able to calculate the amount of deviation between corresponding signatures and mean passports. The final outcome is a labelled data set, which in turn can train a classifier in a supervised fashion.

3.2 Advanced DL Workflow

Our Advanced DL flows for data set generation and anomaly classification are depicted in Figs. 3a and 3b, respectively. For both flows, whether the learning leading to the labelled data set, or the classification, the amount of data preparation is minimal. This preparation includes parsing of the raw metric logs, cutting of the parsed traces per image and running a sliding window algorithm to generate two-channel slices of fixed size. These two channels include the time data (timestamps) and the metric data (metric readings). It is necessary to consider the time data as a separate channel since the metric data collection happens at high frequency, with non-determinism for system behaviour present, resulting in timestamps that do not exactly match for different experiments. This is an expected effect as industrial CPS are inherently non-deterministic. We have only considered the metric resulting in the highest accuracy for the Classic ML flow as it was seen in [11], i.e., electrical current. Note that in this approach, there is no need for an intimate understanding of the data to reveal atomic phases within the processing of an image and the trace data related to each image is considered as a whole.

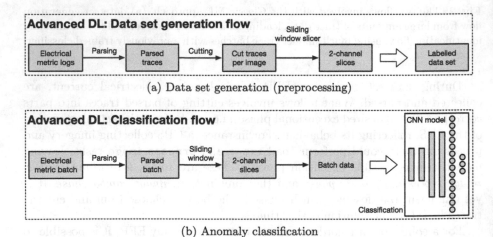

(a) Data set generation (preprocessing)

(b) Anomaly classification

Fig. 3. The two flows involved with the Advanced DL approach, (a) data set generation flow from large amounts of trace data, leading to a training data set (note the reduction in number of steps and their complexity) and (b) an anomaly identification flow, using much smaller trace batches with a previously trained classifier.

The Classic ML flow already has a rather high accuracy [11]. To push the classification accuracy of our Advanced DL flow to similar levels, we have performed a grid search for hyperparameter optimisation. The three groups of considered hyperparameters are data preparation, learning and CNN model parameters, further elaborated in Sect. 4.2.

4 Implementation

Regarding notable details of the Classic ML flow, in our experiments, polynomial regression functions of degree two provide sufficient interpolation accuracy. We transform the time-series data from traces into cumulative data for the metric part to make the regression function a monotonically increasing one. For goodness-of-fit tests, we use both coefficient of determination (R^2) and Root-Mean-Square-Deviation ($RMSD$) to compare a sample signature to a reference passport. The identification step uses Decision Tree (DT) [13] and Random Forest (RF) [2] classifiers. Considering the Classic ML implementation from [11], we focus on the Advanced DL elements, as it involves the bulk of this work.

4.1 Data Set

Our data sets are generated from the same raw electrical metric readings, collected via an external power data logger unit, Otii Arc [12], connected to an ODROID-XU4 computing device. These traces are in the form of time-series and every data point has a timestamp and a metric value. The data set for the Classic ML flow has many columns, such as execution time, regression function coefficients and intercept, goodness-of-fit test values and labels [11]. The Advanced DL data set on the other hand is rather simple, only including two separate time and metric data channels and corresponding labels.

For both workflows, we are considering three labels, i.e., Normal, NoFan and UnderVolt. The methodology can be implemented with any number of labels. Our demonstrator involves these labels corresponding to, normal circumstances for reference executions, faulty cooling fan for the system-on-chip, and unstable power supply, respectively. Both data sets are balanced as we have performed equal number of experiments for all scenarios (labels). For Advanced DL, the data is normalised at preprocessing. Training set and test set ratios to the whole data set are 80% and 20% for the Advanced DL trainings, respectively and 70% and 30% for the Classic ML trainings, respectively.

4.2 CNN Structure and Search Space

To arrive at an acceptable CNN design, we have performed a grid search for the hyperparameter variations listed in Table 1.

The most optimised model we arrived at consists of six convolutional layers with sizes 64, 64, 128, 128, 256, 256, a Fully Connected (FC) layer of size 4096, all kernel sizes 5×1, ReLU activation for each convolutional layer and the FC layer, and MaxPool layers after even convolutional layers. Our data analysis pipelines have been written in Python 3.8 and we use the Scikit-learn 0.23.2 package for

Table 1. Hyperparameters considered during the grid search and their variations

Parameter type	Parameter	Variations
Data preparation	Slice sizes	50, 100
	Slice shifts	10, 20
Learning	LR at start	0.01, 0.001, 0.0001, 0.00005
	Epochs	10, 20, 30, 40, 45, 50, 60
	Batch sizes	10, 20, 50, 100
	LR decay	present (mul. factor 0.1), absent
	Decay periods	8, 10, 20
CNN model	Conv. layers	2, 4, 6
	Conv. layer size	8, 16, 32, 64, 128
	Kernel size	3, 5
	FC layer size	512, 1024, 2048, 4096

regression and classical ML classification, as well as the PyTorch 1.6.0 package
for CNN implementations. The hardware infrastructure for our experiments is a
machine with a 2.20 GHz Intel® Xeon® E5-2650 v4 CPU, 64 GB of RAM and
a GeForce RTX 2080 Ti graphics card, with CUDA release 10.0, v10.0.130.

5   Results: Classic ML Vs Advanced DL

Considering the hyperparameters listed in Table 1, Fig. 4 displays an overview
of our grid search for paths achieving higher accuracies.

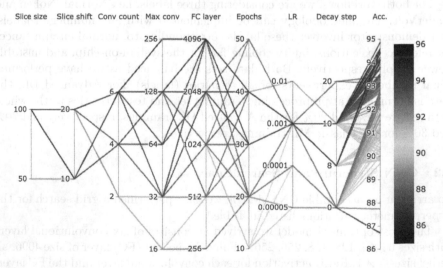

Fig. 4. The set of higher accuracies from our grid search, visualised in a parallel coordinates plot (decay step 0 denotes absence of decay)

To be able to quantitatively compare the two workflows, we consider *elapsed time* for different operations, collected with the `time.perf_counter()` call, providing a high-accuracy monotonic clock. Timing results are given in Table 2. Note that the Classic ML preprocessing is highly parallelised. Model training has to be considered for our industrial use-cases, since upon the introduction of a new anomaly, i.e., a new label, retraining will be necessary.

Table 2. Elapsed times in seconds during different stages of the two approaches

Workflow	Preprocessing	Training	Validation
Classic ML - DT (CPU)	204648 (~57 h)	0.02	0.001
Classic ML - RF (CPU)	204648 (~57 h)	0.32	0.021
Advanced DL (CPU)	2576	239976 (~67 h)	125
Advanced DL (GPU)	2576	18535 (~5 h)	25.5

It is evident from our observations during the CNN training that there is a limit to the Advanced DL workflow's achievable accuracy. This is considering the fact that minimal amount of preprocessing has been applied for this particular workflow on purpose. We also see that this achievable accuracy is an effective one, up to 94.85%, depending on hyperparameters. The accuracies for our Classic ML workflow using DT and RF classifiers are 99.15% and 99.23%, respectively. However, the high accuracy provided by the Classic ML workflow comes at a cost and arguably, a high one. The amount of analysis, design effort, experimentation and in short, feature engineering required for the Classic ML workflow is rather vast. Accordingly, there is much need for domain specific knowledge and understanding of the internals of the system under scrutiny. The workflow designer has to know beforehand, or explore, to understand which phases best reflect the overall behaviour of the system for the specific set of anomalies.

One of the capabilities missing in our Advanced DL workflow is the possibility to detect unknown behaviour, i.e., unseen anomalies. Though the CNN model itself can be retrained upon the addition of a new anomaly, the workflow does not include steps facilitating new anomaly discoveries. The reference methodology from Fig. 1 provisions this possibility, for we can use goodness-of-fit tests and detect unseen levels of deviation from a passport. Following this detection, further analysis will result in a new class of anomaly, which can be added and considered for feature engineering in future data sets. This addition of unknown anomalies is achievable in the Classic ML workflow. However, it does require the designer to go through the whole process again, as the new anomaly may or may not be easily detectable using the same phase data.

We would like to emphasise the fact that our Advanced DL workflow is a truly black box approach, requiring no insight into the data or the system internals. In this fashion, the Advanced DL flow cuts through the data processing complexities of the Classical ML flow. Though optimising hyperparameters is a time-consuming process, it does not depend on the internals of the system and is reusable in the future for more anomalies. We just have to retrain the network. On top of that, neural network frameworks are highly optimised for GPU acceleration, requiring minimal changes to the implementation code.

Stability and maturity of frameworks, in the sense that how much code transformation is enforced from one version to the next is another aspect. In our experience, the change is rapid and substantial with deep learning frameworks, as the field is constantly changing and evolving. This could very well be a factor in a business environment striving for long-term deployment.

Last but not least, with Classic ML workflow, we are able to explain why the classification has resulted in a certain label. Models such as decision trees can be traversed and every processing block in the Classic ML flow can be backtracked to initial trace values, directly connecting the outcome to the input.

6 Related Work

Anomaly detection for industrial CPS and relevant methodologies work upon various input sources, e.g., power signals, sensor data, network traffic data and system calls. Kim et al. [7] were among the first to highlight that power consumption can be used for anomaly detection. Caviglione et al. [4] detected attacks related to covert channels using the power consumption of the running processes. Covert channels occur when malicious applications exploit different assigned permissions and are able to exchange information. Liu et al. [8] developed a strategy using power side-channel data to detect anomalous behaviour in control flow execution applied to IoT microcontrollers. Similarly, Xu et al. [14] used power channels to detect attacks on the Distribution Terminal Unit.

In the last few years, the complexity of CPS has led to elusive and indiscernible faults. Conventional anomaly detection methods are increasingly substituted with state of the art deep learning techniques [5]. Moreover, CNNs have proven to be well suited for analysis of power signals and other similar time-series data for fault detection and classification [6]. Albasir et al. [1] proposed a CNN-based approach to detect malware activity, utilising the power consumption behaviour of smartphones. Canizo et al. [3] deployed CNNs together with recurrent cells to detect anomalies in time-series data from multiple sensors.

7 Conclusion and Future Work

We have developed an alternative AI workflow to a previously devised one, to detect and classify anomalies in industrial CPS. Both workflows, the earlier Classic ML and the new Advanced DL, show high classification accuracies, 99.23% and 94.85%, respectively. While achieving the high accuracy of the Classic ML required extensive design, feature engineering effort and costly computations, the Advanced DL also required extensive optimisation effort. We have discussed different qualitative aspects of both workflows, such as dependence on the inti-mate knowledge of the system and the data, stability AI frameworks, efficient GPU implementation and root-cause analysis.

In our opinion, there is no clear winner between these workflows. Critical applications and use-cases can benefit from highest accuracies and analytical capabilities provided by the Classic ML workflow, allowing the study of root-causes behind anomalies, while ease of extension with different anomalies is best served by the Advanced DL workflow. It is totally use-case dependent.

Acknowledgements. This paper is composed as a collaboration between the research project 14208, titled *"iDAPT"*, funded by The Netherlands Organisation for Scientific Research (NWO); and the research project titled *"ALOHA"*, supported and partly funded by the European Union Horizon-2020 research and innovation programme under grant agreement No. 780788.

References

1. Albasir, A., Manzano, R., Naik, K.: Deep learning based approach for classifying power signals and detecting anomalous behavior of wireless devices. In: 2019 IEEE World Congress on Services (SERVICES) (2019)
2. Breiman, L.: Random forests. Mach. Learn (2001)
3. Canizo, M., Triguero, I., Conde, A., Onieva, E.: Multi-head CNN-RNN for multi-time series anomaly detection: an industrial case study. Neurocomputing **363**, 246–260 (2019)
4. Caviglione, L., Gaggero, M., Lalande, J., Mazurczyk, W., Urbański, M.: Seeing the unseen: revealing mobile malware hidden communications via energy consumption and artificial intelligence. IEEE Trans. Inf. Forensics Secur. **11**(4), 799–810(2016)
5. Chalapathy, R., Chawla, S.: Deep learning for anomaly detection: a survey (2019)
6. Ismail Fawaz, H., Forestier, G., Weber, J., Idoumghar, L., Muller, P.-A.: Deep learning for time series classification: a review. Data Min. Knowl. Discov. **33**(4), 917–963 (2019). https://doi.org/10.1007/s10618-019-00619-1
7. Kim, H., Smith, J., Shin, K.G.: Detecting energy-greedy anomalies and mobile malware variants. In: Proceedings of the 6th International Conference on Mobile Systems, Applications, and Services (2008)
8. Liu, Y., Wei, L., Zhou, Z., Zhang, K., Xu, W., Xu, Q.: On code execution tracking via power side-channel. In: Proceedings of the 2016 ACM SIGSAC Conference on Computer and Communications Security (2016)
9. Meyer, H., Odyurt, U., Pimentel, A.D., Paradas, E., Alonso, I.G.: An analytics-based method for performance anomaly classification in cyber-physical systems. In: Proceedings of the 35th Annual ACM Symposium on Applied Computing (2020)
10. Odyurt, U., Meyer, H., Pimentel, A.D., Paradas, E., Alonso, I.G.: Software pass-ports for automated performance anomaly detection of cyber-physical systems. In: Pnevmatikatos, D.N., Pelcat, M., Jung, M. (eds.) SAMOS 2019. LNCS, vol. 11733, pp. 255–268. Springer, Cham (2019). https://doi.org/10.1007/978-3-030-27562-4_18
11. Odyurt, U., Roeder, J., Pimentel, A.D., Gonzalez Alonso, I., de Laat, C.: Power passports for fault tolerance: anomaly detection in industrial CPS using electrical EFB. In: 2021 IEEE Conference on Industrial Cyberphysical Systems (2021)

12. Qoitech AB: Otii arc - otii by qoitech (2020). https://www.qoitech.com/otii/
13. Rokach, L., Maimon, O.: Decision Trees (2005)
14. Xu, A., Jiang, Y., Cao, Y., Zhang, G., Ji, X., Xu, W.: ADDP: anomaly detection for DTU based on power consumption side-channel. In: 2019 IEEE 3rd Conference on Energy Internet and Energy System Integration (EI2) (2019)

On-demand Knowledge Graphs
for Standards-Based Power Grid Data
Provisioning

Vijay S. Kumar[✉], Sharad Dixit, Kareem S. Aggour,
Jenny Weisenberg Williams, and Paul Cuddihy

GE Research, 1 Research Circle, Niskayuna, NY 12309, USA
{v.kumar1,sharad.dixit,aggour,weisenje,cuddihy}@ge.com

Abstract. The evolution of the energy and utilities industry, comprising smart power grids and myriad distributed energy resources, bears parallels to Industry 4.0 digitalization. Replete with diverse data modalities, the grid industry has traditionally been steeped in standards defined to primarily govern information interchange between data systems and applications. We explore the practical application of Knowledge Graph technology to make these standards more actionable. This work-in-progress paper proposes and demonstrates the idea of *on-demand* knowledge graphs to provision clean, integrated power grid data, in accordance with IEC CIM standards, for an enterprise ML-based analytic solution targeting better response to storm-induced power outages.

Keywords: Knowledge graphs · Semantics · Power grid · Standards

1   Introduction

The electric power and energy sector is a fast-evolving exemplar of the Industrial Internet of Things (IIoT, a core aspect of Industry 4.0). Today's Smart Grids are equipped with sensors and networks capable of measuring and transmitting operational data at high speeds. Utility enterprises look to integrate this bulk data with other valuable pertinent information, and then leverage advanced ML-based analysis techniques in order to extract insights and provide new market solutions aimed at safe, efficient, reliable and sustainable grid operation.

A broader trend in the Grid industry has utilities consolidating their IT/OT environments into converged cloud-based digital technology platforms and ecosystems, whereby they can have greater access to analytics software-as-a-service offerings, both those developed in-house and externally by 3rd-party entities. While service-oriented architectures amplify the need for standards-based interoperability, the Grid industry has existing standards that, in theory, are designed to enable information exchange among relevant IT/OT systems and applications looking to consume this information. These include the IEC 61970-301 that specifies a Common Information Model (**CIM**) to accommodate

© Springer Nature Switzerland AG 2021
H. Fujita et al. (Eds.): IEA/AIE 2021, LNAI 12799, pp. 485–492, 2021.
https://doi.org/10.1007/978-3-030-79463-7_41

network modeling scenarios, and IEC 61968-11 that extends the CIM for electrical distribution systems [1]. Utilities tend to use these standards primarily to define interface specifications that streamline Grid operations [2,3]. The potential benefits of IEC CIM standards in enriching the process(es) of assembling relevant data from multiple IT/OT systems, and feeding harmonized, 'AI-ready' datasets to analytics services and solutions remains vastly unexplored, partly because the CIM is maintained as a relatively stagnant UML model. While subsequent extensions to the standards (IEC 61970-501, 61970-452 and 61968-13) define the CIM using RDF/XML artifacts, considerable challenges still remain in making these model standards more actionable, leading to unacceptable time-to-value and adversely impacting utilities' digital transformation initiatives.

This work explores the use of Knowledge Graph technology, in particular, ontology-based data access [4] and rule-based reasoning, as a foundational layer upon which Grid data can be democratized in accordance with IEC CIM standards. Our knowledge graph here is a semantic representation of the IEC CIM, grounded in W3C recommendations (RDF/S, OWL), that additionally includes model extensions for: (1) enabling extraction of instance data from multiple Grid OT systems, (2) aligning extracted data with concepts and relationships defined in the CIM, (3) refining aligned data to accommodate utility- or customer-centric interpretations, and (4) querying linked data to serve multiple applications. Traditional knowledge graph approaches seek to create and maintain a single persistent, centralized repository of knowledge [5] where instance data is incrementally added and linked to all previously assembled data in the graph. In contrast, we seek to (1) construct transient, standards-compliant knowledge graphs (i.e., targeted CIM *profiles*) in an on-demand manner, and (2) to further refine these linked data artifacts in accordance with custom interpretations of the instance data to easily and unambiguously serve *ad hoc* data requests from enterprise Grid analytics applications. We describe a proof-of-concept application of our system, along with its supporting data services, to automate the process of constructing, refining and querying CIM-compliant knowledge graphs to serve the data needs of an ML-based analytic that helps utilities better respond to weather events.

2   Motivation: Power Grid Data Harmonization

Utilities amass extremely large amounts of data typically locked away in an ever-increasing number of OT systems of record such as EMS/SCADA (transmission data), DMS (distribution data), GIS (network models), OMS (outage data), DERMS (distributed energy resource data), to name a few. There is limited standardization in data formats and representations adopted by OT software vendors, and incompatible variations even across software versions from the same vendor. With the Industry 4.0 emphasis on lean operation, breaking down these OT data silos is critical to reducing delivery time for solutions in the Smart Grid market. However, the time-to-value in trialling new solutions is far from optimal, with ~60–80% of the cost of a utility's engagements with enterprise software providers reportedly being devoted to data integration and harmonization. The value proposition of solving this broader data sourcing problem in the Grid context motivated our quest to democratize this raw siloed data to various B2B consumers using the IEC CIM as an intermediary common, shared data model.

In such engagements, utilities traditionally bear the responsibility of providing clean, consistent data as per formal application-specific requirements. Our goal is to replace this error-prone process with an automated one wherein an information broker, informed by a standards-compliant knowledge graph can reliably deliver this data. Potential uses of this harmonized data could range from closed-loop Grid controls (e.g., ADMS [3], that relies on accurate power flow network models to optimize Grid operations) to open-loop analytics solutions that generate predictive insights leading to valuable outcomes such as reduced downtime/outages, improved customer satisfaction and crew safety, better wildfire management, etc. Our initial focus is on enabling Grid analytics solutions, and this paper specifically addresses the input requirements of an analytic service that uses predictive ML models to help utilities mount an efficient outage response to storms. The analytic in question takes GIS data (e.g., the location and orientation of power system components such as transformers and cables) and historical outage information combined with weather forecast data to assess the impact of a storm within a utility's geographical regions of service. To this end, we developed a proof-of-concept solution to demonstrate that instance data obtained from multiple GIS and OMS vendor software can be integrated into a knowledge graph based on our semantic representation of the IEC CIM, and then be queried to generate appropriate input artifacts for the analytic service.

3   The Case for an Extended Semantic CIM

The IEC standard CIM expresses physical, electrical and data elements in typical power system networks (e.g., *transformers*, *switch/breakers*, *wires*) in UML, organizes them into one or more meaningful hierarchies (e.g., a *busbar* is a component within a *substation*), and specifies other possible relationships amongst these components (e.g., certain assets like *transformers* can be attached to *pole* structures). We build on the CIM-15 schema developed and maintained by the IEC TC57 working group and converted the CIM model to RDFS/OWL concepts and relationships [8]. Targeted CIM *profiles* were then extracted from this ontology and imported into an open-source semantic application development tool called SADL [9] that provides a controlled vocabulary for creation and maintenance of domain-specific knowledge bases. While CIM primarily serves well-identified needs of closed-loop distribution applications native to the power systems domain, application-driven CIM extension methodologies exist [6,7]. We propose the following extensions to the semantic CIM to automate the transformation of siloed raw data into clean input datasets for Grid analytics services:

1. **Metamodels** of common Grid data sources (e.g., GIS, OMS, EMS/SCADA) to enable extraction of instance data from these systems. A metamodel for GIS, for example, would define all concepts and relationships one could expect

```
import "http://www.iec.ch/TC57/CIM" as cim.

MountingType is a type of cim:PSRType,
  must be one of {Overhead, Underground}.
mounting describes cim:Equipment
  with values of type MountingType.
mounting is a type of cim:PSRType.PowerSystemResource.

{PSRType_Substation, PSRType_Unknown}
  are instances of cim:PSRType.
```

(a) Extending CIM for Grid analytic

```
Rule CableMounting (note "Rule to assign Underground
                    as value of mounting to any instance
                    of Equipment with 'cable' in its URI"):
  if psr is an cim:Equipment and
     uristr is strConcat(psr) and
     regex(uristr, ".*cable.*")
  then psr has mounting Underground.

Rule WireMounting (note "Rule to assign Overhead as
                    value of mounting to any instance
                    of Equipment with 'wire' in its URI"):
  if psr is an cim:Equipment and
     uristr is strConcat(psr) and
     regex(uristr, ".*wire.*")
  then psr has mounting Overhead.
```

(b) Inference Rules for Grid analytic

Fig. 1. Sample extensions to semantic CIM model

any typical GIS dataset to contain, irrespective of the vendor-specific data representation methods used. Developing individual data parsers for every vendor/version–application combination is infeasible. ML-based approaches, informed by such metamodels can partly automate instance data extraction, even in cases where instance data schemas have not been encountered *a priori*. As of the time of writing, the metamodels are an aspirational vision, and have not yet been implemented in practice.

2. In scenarios where information derived from Grid OT systems are not adequately expressible using the core CIM alone, the semantic CIM can be extended by defining **new concepts, properties and relationships**. For example, an outage prediction analytic may be 10x more accurate if data about the 'mounting type' of specific power system equipment is available (Overhead wires are more susceptible to damage from downed trees than are underground cables). However, we were unable to unambiguously map mounting type to any existing concept in the core semantic CIM. Such scenarios are reflective of a bigger issue, namely, that progress in CIM standards is often too slow to accommodate advances in Grid data capture and fast-evolving requirements that Grid analytics impose on them. Figure 1a shows one of our extensions to the semantic CIM expressed in SADL syntax. Here, we define MountingType as a sub-class of the CIM-defined PSRType, as an object property of Equipment, and constrain the values that it can take.

3. Extracted Grid data aligned with our extended semantic CIM concepts constitutes our initial knowledge graph. **Rule-based reasoning** is used to infer additional knowledge to further refine this graph. Figure 1b shows two simple rules we authored using SADL Rules syntax [10] to infer the mounting type of power system Equipment from their URIs. Inference rules need to be customized on a per-application basis – e.g., an outage prediction analytic may need to infer only the mounting type for Equipments, whereas an electrical network validation analytic may need to infer network connectivity information at a much finer granularity. Inference rules also need to account for custom interpretations of the instance data – e.g., one utility may universally interpret all their transformers as single-phase transformers, while another TSO may interpret their transformers within European service regions as three-phase transformers.

Figure 2 shows the process of transforming raw GIS data for a *switch* (as stored in a vendor system) into its extended semantic CIM representation. In step 1, data is mapped to standard CIM concepts. Step 2 involves rule-based inference of additional knowledge about the switch (including standard concepts like its equipment container and extended concepts like its mounting type).

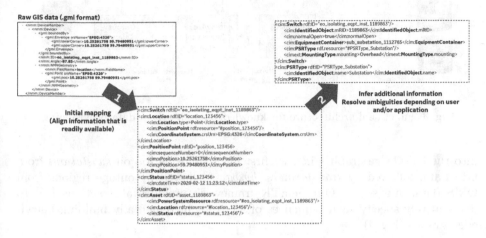

Fig. 2. Transformation and alignment of GIS data to extended semantic CIM

4 On-demand Knowledge Graph Framework

To facilitate automated transformation of raw Grid data into clean CIM-compliant information for consumption by Grid analytics applications, we build on SemTK [11,12], our open-sourced framework for on-demand construction and management of transient knowledge graphs from multiple data sources.

Figure 3 shows our high-level services-based functional architecture, where each service in our end-to-end pipeline (with the current exception of data extraction/parsing services) is informed by our extended semantic CIM model. First, raw Grid data stored in native formats like GML and CSV are extracted via parsing services. Futher, these services also derive additional information using common mathematical calculations – for a *cable*, this includes computing the total length from multiple, contiguous connected line segments in GIS; for other equipment, this could include using the Euclidean distance to determine the nearest substation for that equipment.

The next set of services instantiate the knowledge graph from the data extracted by the parsing services. This instantiation of the knowledge graph from raw data is facilitated via SemTK's developer and querying abstractions such as ingestion templates and *nodegroups* [13]. Instance data is aligned with concepts and relationships defined in our extended semantic CIM, and also incrementally linked, as a sequence of steps, to existing information previously ingested

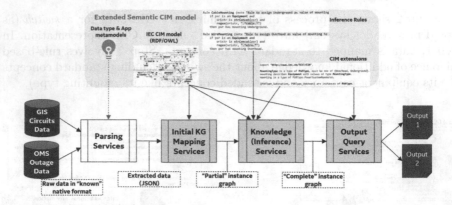

Fig. 3. Functional architecture for knowledge graph-driven data provisioning

into the knowledge graph – i.e., we first ingest information on *substations* from GIS data, followed by *transformers*, *busbars*, followed by outage regions from OMS data, and so on. Our SemTK framework provides abstractions [12] to declaratively specify such sequences of steps for incrementally building knowledge graphs (Fig. 4).

```
CIMSpec is a OnDemandKGSpec,
    with id "cim",

    with step ( a KGStep
        with retrieval( a Retrieval
            with inputNodegroupId "no-bootstrap",
            with serviceURL "http://server.com:48250/gis/initialize",
            with ingestNodeGroupId "SCIM - IngestPSRType"
        )
        with sequence 1
    )

    with step ( a KGStep
        with retrieval( a Retrieval
            with inputNodegroupId "SCIM - IngestPSRType",
            with serviceURL "http://server.com:48250/gis/equipmentContainer/substation"
            with ingestNodeGroupId "SCIM - StormReadiness - IngestSubstation"
        )
        with sequence 2
    )

    with step ( a KGStep
        with retrieval( a Retrieval
            with inputNodegroupId "SCIM - QuerySubstation",
            with serviceURL "http://server.com:48250/gis/equipment/powertransformer",
            with ingestNodeGroupId "SCIM - StormReadiness - IngestPowerTransformer"
        )
        with sequence 3
    )

    with step ( a KGStep
```

Fig. 4. Snippet of on-demand Knowledge Graph specification in SemTK

Next, inference services apply application-specific rules (such as the ones in Fig. 1b) on the initial knowledge graph to create a complete knowledge graph. In our running example, the application of rules (specified using SADL rules and executed via Jena rule engine) result in the generation of new inferred triples in the knowledge graph – such as the ones that associate the mounting type with an equipment (e.g., <*ACLineSegment*, MountingType.mounting, *Overhead*>). Finally, output query services leverage SemTK's pathfinding and automated SPARQL query generation [11] capabilities to run queries against this refined knowledge graph and to transform the query output into a form that meets the input requirements specification of the analytic – for the outage response analytic in question, this service produced two CSV files with pre-defined schemas specified in the formal application requirements.

5   Discussion

The Grid industry is witnessing the emergence of analytics applications with promising value-add prospects. These applications are characterized by ad hoc input data requirements that need to be fulfilled in traditionally siloed environments. While knowledge graphs, aided by governing IEC standards, are a useful catalyst for data interoperability, many analytics applications primarily need only short-term access to the integrated data. This is especially the case with ML-based analytics, where a model-based prediction is time-bound in terms of its usefulness. As a result, cost and security concerns aside, utility enterprises see little value in maintaining an exact replica of the entire collection of data across all their systems of record within a separate, persistent, all-encompassing knowledge graph [5]. Based on these considerations, we pursue the approach of generating multiple independent, CIM-compliant knowledge graphs on-demand via a framework of lightweight brokering services to meet the (potentially conflicting) data needs of these applications. Apart from completing the automation of our pipeline and supporting more source/application combinations, in future work, we will look to support more standards besides the IEC CIM. In addition, we will look to generate recurring value for these knowledge graphs by developing higher-order value-added services for domain-specific data harmonization, quality checking, imputation and normalization.

Acknowledgements. The authors would like to thank Andy Crapo for his technical contributions and Chris Bowman for the domain expertise and insights that motivated this work.

References

1. McMorran, A.W.: An Introduction to IEC 61970-301 & 61968-11: The Common Information Model. University of Strathclyde (2007)
2. The Common Information Model for Distribution: An Introduction to the CIM for Integrating Distribution Applications and Systems. Rep.#1016058, EPRI (2008)
3. Singh, A., Fisher, A., Allwardt, C., Melton, R.B.: A data exchange interface for a standards based data integration platform. In: Proceedings of the IEEE PES Innovative Smart Grid Technologies (ISGT) Conference (2020)
4. Xiao, G., et al.: Ontology-based data access: a survey. In: Proceedings of 27th International Joint Conference on AI (IJCAI), pp. 5511–5519 (2018)

5. Wang, J., Wang, X., Ma, C., Kou, L.: A survey on the development status and application prospects of knowledge graph in smart grids. IET Gener. Transm. Distrib. **15**, 383–407 (2021)
6. Kim, H.J., et al.: A comprehensive review of practical issues for interoperability using the common information model in smart grids. Energies **13**(6), 1435 (2020)
7. Nielsen, T.D., Neumann, S.A., King, T.L.: A methodology for managing model extensions when using the common information model for systems integration. In: Proceedings of IEEE PES GM (2009)
8. IEC CIM Ontology. https://ontology.tno.nl/IEC_CIM/. Accessed Apr 2021
9. Semantic Application Design Language (SADL). http://semanticapplication designlanguage.github.io/sadl/. Accessed Apr 2021
10. SADL Rules and Built-in Functions. http://sadl.sourceforge.net/sadl3/SadlConstructs.html#Rules. Accessed Apr 2021
11. Cuddihy, P., McHugh, J., Williams, J.W., Mulwad, V., Aggour, K.: SemTK: a semantics toolkit for user-friendly SPARQL generation and semantic data management. In: Proceedings of International Semantic Web Conference (ISWC) (2018). https://github.com/ge-semtk/semtk
12. Cuddihy, P., Williams, J.W., Kumar, V.S., Aggour, K.S., Crapo, A., Dixit, S.: FDC cache: semantics-driven federated caching and querying for big data. In: Proceedings of the IEEE International Conference on Big Data (2020)
13. Kumar, V.S., Cuddihy, P., Aggour, K.S.: NodeGroup: a knowledge-driven data management abstraction for industrial machine learning. In: Proceedings of 3rd International Workshop on Data Management for End-to-End Machine Learning (2019)

Defect, Anomaly and Intrusion Detection

Intrusion Detection Algorithm Based on SDA-ELM

Xiaotao Wei[✉], Shuyu Ren, Yinglong Li, Xi-Xi Wang, and Mengxia Jin

School of Software, Beijing Jiaotong University, Beijing, China
{weixt,20126327,17121710,20126351,18140653}@bjtu.edu.cn

Abstract. A deep learning intrusion detection algorithm based on stacked denoising autoencoder and extreme learning machine (SDA-ELM) is proposed to solve the problem that the traditional machine learning algorithm can't cope with the classification of multisource heterogeneous network intrusion data. The algorithm use Dropout regularization to improve the SDA deep learning model, and the integration features of low dimensionality and high robustness are extracted. Then the model use ELM to carry out a supervised learning for the low dimension data to recognize the network attack. The algorithm combines the abstract feature extraction capability of SDA and the fast learning ability of ELM. The experimental results show that the SDA-ELM algorithm improves the accuracy of classification and the detection rate of small sample attacks, reduces the false alarm rate.

Keywords: Intrusion detection · Stacked denoising autoencoder · Extreme learning machine

1 Introduction

With the development of Internet technology, a large amount of information is widely spread through the Internet, which brings speed and convenience to people's life, and at the same time, the network security problems caused by it are increasingly serious. The issue of network security has a great impact on individuals, society and even countries. How to effectively detect the types of intrusion attacks and how to warn and protect the security of the system has become one of the research directions of network security.

Intrusion Detection System (IDS) is generally used to protect network systems from malicious software attacks [1]. As a network security device, IDS can determine whether the current data is suspicious and can automatically alarm the system by tracking the data and users in the network. According to the monitoring method, intrusion detection technologies are generally divided into two types. One is behavior-based intrusion detection called anomaly detection, which detects attacks by comparing normal behaviors with abnormal behaviors. Another detection technique based on misuse is to identify intrusion attacks by comparing with known attack behaviors [2]. According to the source of the data,

© Springer Nature Switzerland AG 2021
H. Fujita et al. (Eds.): IEA/AIE 2021, LNAI 12799, pp. 495–505, 2021.
https://doi.org/10.1007/978-3-030-79463-7_42

it can be divided into two types. One is intrusion detection based on the host system. This intrusion detection is to install the agent software on a monitored server, and the agent software tracks malicious behaviors on the server in real time. The other is network-based intrusion detection, which is to install agent software on the local area network segment to monitor and analyze the data transmitted by the network.

This article proposes corresponding algorithms and models for intrusion detection. The second part mainly introduces the current research status of network intrusion detection. In the third part we propose an intrusion detection model based on the SDA-ELM algorithm. The fourth part introduces the SDA-ELM algorithm proposed in this paper. The fifth part conducts experiments on the proposed model to test the proposed algorithm. The sixth part summarizes the model and algorithm proposed in this article.

2   Current Research on Intrusion Detection

Due to the continuous development of artificial intelligence technology, machine learning algorithms have the advantages of high detection rate and false alarm rate compared with traditional intrusion detection algorithms, and have been widely used in the field of intrusion detection. Shen Shaoyu [3] et al. proposed an intrusion detection algorithm based on LFKPCA-DWELM, using an improved fruit fly algorithm (LFOA) to optimize the kernel principal component analysis algorithm (KPCA), and extract features from the data, and train the processed data, And finally use the trained model for classification experiment. Andrew H [4] et al. proposed the use of support vector machine (SVM) and artificial neural network (ANN) to identify important features of network intrusion data.

Sabhnani [5] et al. used multi-layer perceptron, k-means and decision tree algorithm to learn machine learning algorithms, and proposed a multi-classifier model. The detection effect is better than single classifier. However, the traditional machine learning method needs to construct the sample characteristics manually, which has obvious dependence, so it can't deal with the massive multisource heterogeneous network intrusion data in the context of the Internet of things. The deep neural network can fit arbitrary complex functions, use the deep neural network model to process the high-dimensional network attack data, and extract the low-dimensional data features, so as to obtain the classification result with higher detection effect.

In recent years, scholars in the field of intrusion detection research have proposed a variety of detection models based on deep learning. Liu Jingmei [6] et al. proposed an adaptive box feature selection algorithm based on information gain, and combined this algorithm with LightGBM to design a fast network intrusion detection system. On the basis of kDD-CUP 1999 data set, Dong Ning [7] et al. conducted data standardization and normalization, processed the data set with random forest, and extracted the importance of each feature. Liu Wenjun [8] et al. proposed a new intrusion detection system for wireless communication network of distribution network, which is composed of a circulating neural network with gated circulation unit, multi-layer perceptor and Softmax.

If the dimensionality of the network data is too high, the model will be over-fitting, and the generalization of the model will be poor, which will reduce the detection rate. The autoencoder can extract high-dimensional data out of the main features, which can effectively solve this problem. Hinton [9] et al. proposed using a autoencoder to reduce the dimension of high-dimensional data to avoid curse of dimensionality in high-dimensional data. Bengio [10] et al. imitated RBM to build a DBN method, using a autoencoder to implement stacked autoencoder. Based on the deep learning model of the conditional variational autoencoder, Luo Zhiyu [11] et al. built an intrusion detection system using the Tensorflow framework to effectively classify intrusions.

Vincent [12] et al. proposed a stacked denoising autoencoder. This model is based on a denoising autoencoder, and the denoising autoencoder hidden layer is used as the input of the next layer of denoising autoencoder to form a stacked denoising autoencoder. The denoising autoencoder has stronger learning feature capabilities than the autoencoder. Guan bin Huang [13] et al. put forward the extreme learning machine (ELM), whose hidden layer node parameters do not need to be adjusted by an iterative algorithm, and only need to set the number of hidden layer nodes to obtain the a unique optimal value through one-time learning. Srivastave [14] et al. proposed adjusting the hyperparameters p in the Dropout regularization to prevent over-fitting problems in the DBN.

In this paper, the autoencoder and extreme learning machine are intensively studied, and a hybrid deep learning intrusion detection algorithm based on stacked denoising autoencoder (SDA) and extreme learning machine (ELM) is proposed. This algorithm combines the ability of feature extraction from the encoder with the advantages of fast learning speed and good generalization performance of ELM. The effective evaluation of the SDA-ELM model by the NSL-KDD data set shows that the SDA-ELM algorithm has the advantages of high detection rate and low false alarm rate compared with the traditional methods.

3   SDA-ELM Intrusion Detection Model

The overall architecture of the intrusion detection algorithm based on SDA-ELM is shown in Fig. 1 in this paper. It mainly includes three steps:

- Data processing: In the first step, separate data and labels from a single instance of a dataset. In the second step, convert character feature to numeric feature. In the third step, the average value of the data be normlized to between [0, 1].
- Feature extraction: The first step, using the Dropout regularization to improve the neural network, designs the number of hidden layers and the number of nodes. And the second step, the pre-training of the neural network model and the fine adjustment of the weight. And the third step, SDA is used to extract the integrated features of preprocessed data sets.
- Intrusion detection: The dataset of low dimensionality and high robustness generated by SDA model is input to ELM classifiers to complete the recognition of four attack types.

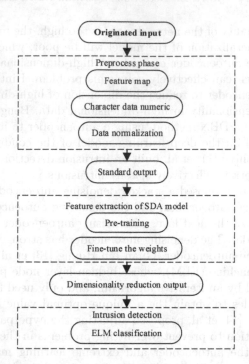

Fig. 1. SDA-ELM intrusion detection model.

4   Intrusion Detection Algorithm Based on SDA-ELM

4.1   AutoEncoder

AE(AutoEncoder) belongs to unsupervised model and is also a simple neural network discriminant model. It mainly captures the most embodying factors of data feature from the original data and can be used as an abstract feature representation of the original data. AE can be divided into shallow autoencoder and stacked autoencoder according to the number of hidden layers. The principle of AE is shown in Fig. 2.

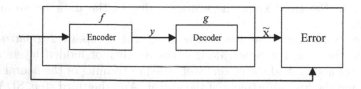

Fig. 2. The principle of AE.

The training processing of AE as follows:

- The calculation process from input layer to hidden layer: The input raw data is processed by weighted and biased $theta_1 = (W_1, b_1)$ between neurons, encoding of activation function f in Encoder, and finally the encoded data y are obtained.

$$y = f_{\theta_1}(W_1 x + b_1) \tag{1}$$

- The calculation process from hidden layer to input layer: The encoded data y is processed by $theta_2 = (W_2, b_2)$, encoding of function g in Decoder, and then the encode reconstruction $\tilde{x}$ are obtained.

$$\tilde{x} = g_{\theta_2}(W_2 y + b_2) \tag{2}$$

- Weight matrix W_1 of encoder usually with the weight matrix W_2 of the Decoder are transposed each other, we can use this $W_1^T = W_2 formula$ to express. The activation function of hidden layer neurons(HLN) usually uses Sigmod function to find the feature representation of input data through non-linear transformation. In order to minimize the encode reconstruction error L_{loss}, the iterative optimization of the parameters θ is needed.

$$L_{loss} = \|x - \tilde{x}\|^2 \tag{3}$$

4.2 Stacked Denoising Autoencoder (SDA)

For AE, for the complete reserved data input, the feature representation of the original data can be learned by simple reconstruction, and then the data-noise can be added to the original data to damage dataset, so as to realize the restoration of the damaged data set to the normal data set, and then the error reconstruction of the noise dataset can be carried out by using denoising autoencoder (DAE), thus the integration features of high robustness are obtained. The principle of DAE is shown in Fig. 3. On the basis of AE, DAE adds a stochastic mapping of Gaussian noise $x \sim q_D\left(x^{'}|x\right)$ with probability distribution q_D to the initial input and sets some of the features in the x to zero. Finally, the "disturbed" noise input data $x^{'}$ is obtained then it is possible to define a joint distribution function:

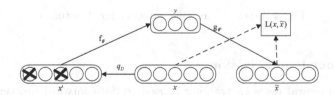

Fig. 3. Denoising autoencoder.

$$q^0\left(X, X', Y\right) = q^0(X)q_D\left(X'|X\right)\delta_{f_0(X')}(Y) \tag{4}$$

In the function, Y is the mapping function of X' and θ is the parameter. The gradient descent algorithm is used to minimize the objective function:

$$arg_{\theta_1\theta'}min = E_{q(X,X')}\left[L_H\left(X, g_{\theta'}\left(f_\theta\left(X'\right)\right)\right)\right] \tag{5}$$

Unlike shallow autoencoder, which are difficult to perform in large-scale, high dimensionality datasets, stacked autoencoder can extract more effective integration features by using deep models. SDA initializes the neural network in the same way as the Deep Belief Network (DBN) proposed by Hinton in 2006. In order to learn effective feature extraction, noise input is only used in the training of initialization single layer noise data.

Denoising autoencoder is composed of three-layer neural network. The objective function f_θ is obtained by inputting "noise data" x' into the first layer autoencoder DA_1, and using it to learn the original data x then the output of the original data of DA_1 is taken as the input of the second layer autoencoder, the second layer input is damaged again. And, like the training process of the first layer of autoencoder, repeat the training. Then layer by layer connection, the stacked denoising autoencoder structure is realized, as shown in Fig. 4. The noise input realizes the process of feature transformation through the training of layer by layer autoencoder. The stacked denoising autoencoder model outputs the data of denoising and dimension reduction, and then uses softmax processing in the last layer, and then uses BP algorithm to fine-tune the weights and adjust neural network parameters in order to classification function of the dataset.

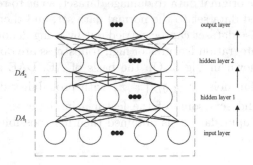

Fig. 4. Stacked denoising autoencoder structure.

4.3 Dropout Regularization

The classical neural network training is used to data forward propagation and error back-propagation. For this process, dropout randomly removes the hidden (layer) units. Since the deletion of the hidden layer units is a stochastic process, and a certain batch of training sets are randomly taken for training, Finally, it is guaranteed that each model is used with the equally-weighted, so that the effect similar to the boosting algorithm is realized. Ensures that every two hidden nodes can not occur at the same time, so that the full-connection network has a certain sparse property, and the synergistic effect of different characteristics is reduced, so that the neural network is more robustness. Dropout can effectively reduce the occurrence of over-fitting, to a certain extent the effect of regularization is achieved, and the convergence time of the neural network is reduced. The Dropout principle is shown in Fig. 5.

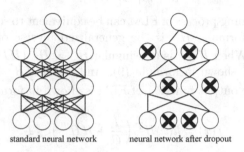

standard neural network   neural network after dropout

Fig. 5. The principle of dropout.

4.4 ELM Classification Algorithm

As shown in Fig. 6, the extreme learning machine (ELM) is a single-hidden layer feedforward neural network. Its hidden layer node parameters do not need to be adjusted by iterative algorithm, and the unique optimal value can be obtained by setting the number of hidden layer nodes. The output function is defined as follows:

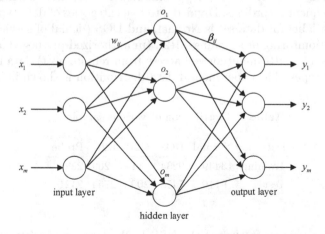

Fig. 6. Single-hidden layer feedforward neural network.

$$f_L(x) = \sum \beta_i h_i(x) = h(x)\beta = H\beta \tag{6}$$

In formula (6), β is the output vector between the hidden layer nodes and the output nodes, and $h(x)$ is the output vector of the hidden layer nodes:

$$H = h(x) = \begin{bmatrix} h_1(x_1) & \cdots & h_L(x_1) \\ \cdots & \cdots & \cdots \\ h_1(x_N) & \cdots & h_L(x_N) \end{bmatrix} \tag{7}$$

$$\beta = [\beta_1 \ \beta_2 \ \beta_3 \ \beta_4]^T \tag{8}$$

Therefore, The training process of ELM can be equivalent to solving the equation $H\beta = T$. In this formula, H^+ is the generalized inverse of the hidden layer output matrix H. When HH^T is nonsingular, $H^+ = H^T (HH^T)^{-1}$. The output function of ELM is shown in formula (9). And when HH^T is singular, $H^+ = (H^T H)^{-1} H^T$. The output function of ELM is shown in formula (10).

$$f(x) = h(x)H^T \left(\frac{I}{C} + HH^T \right)^{-1} T \tag{9}$$

$$f(x) = h(x) \left(\frac{I}{C} + HH^T \right)^{-1} H^T T \tag{10}$$

5   Experiment

5.1   Dataset Preprocessing

The NSL-KDD data set has been used in the experimental dataset as the training set and test set for the intrusion detection experiment. The NSL-KDD data set does not contain redundant records compared to the KDDCUP99 data set, which improves classifier detection performance because the classifier does not favor more frequent recordings. Divided into five categories of data types, normal category data label for data set is Normal, and DOS (denial of service attacks), Probe (port monitoring or scanning), R2L (unauthorized privileged access from local super user), U2R (unauthorized access from remote host) data labels for 4 major attack types. The experimental data distribution is shown in Table 1.

Table 1. Distribution of various samples.

Data	Normal	DOS	U2R	R2L	Probe
Training	13449	9234	11	209	2289
Test	9710	7458	200	2754	2421

The 41-dimensional feature of the NSL-KDD data set consists of 38 digital features and 3 character features. Before training, the character data is converted into a binary vector at first, that means the protocol types of tcp, udp, and icmp are represented respectively as $[0, 0, 1]$, $[0, 1, 0]$, $[1, 0, 0]$. Data labels of five character types are One-Hot encoding, tag types of Normal, DOS, R2L, U2R, and Probe are expressed as $[0, 0, 0, 0, 1]$, $[0, 0, 0, 1, 0]$, $[0, 0, 1, 0, 0]$, $[0, 1, 0, 0, 0]$, and $[1, 0, 0, 0, 0]$. After the character data mapping is completed, the data is averaged, and the data of each bit is normalized to between 0 and 1. Preventing big data from covering small data and improving the detection performance of the model in order to facilitate data processing.

The characteristic of a single data instance x, the maximum value of the feature x_{max}, the minimum value of the feature x_{min}, $x^{'}$ is the normalized data feature of x.

$$x^{'} = \frac{x - x_{max}}{x_{max} - x_{min}} \tag{11}$$

5.2 Experimental Evaluation Criteria

High accuracy rate, high detection rate, and low error rate are required typically in intrusion detection systems. In this paper, accuracy rate, detection rate and error rate are used as evaluation criteria for intrusion detection, as shown in the formulas:

$$Accuracy = \frac{T_p + T_N}{T_p + T_N + F_p + F_N} \tag{12}$$

$$Detection = \frac{T_N}{T_N + F_N} \tag{13}$$

$$Error = \frac{F_P}{T_N + F_P} \tag{14}$$

In the formulas, T_N indicates the number of correctly classified normal samples, T_P indicates the number of correct classifications of the attack samples, F_P indicates that the normal samples are falsely reported as samples of the attack, F_N indicates that the attack samples are falsely reported as normal.

5.3 Experimental Parameter Settings

The total number of layers of the autoencoder network is set to 5 layers, and the number of hidden layers is 3 layers. Among that, the number of input layer nodes is 122 nodes with high-dimensional mapping, the number of 3 hidden layers' nodes is 90-60-30, and the number of hidden layer nodes in the output layer is set to 5. The number of autoencoder iterations per layer is set to 100, and the number of fine-tuning iterations of the network weight BP back propagation algorithm is set to 100. Dropout regularized parameters is set to 0.5. The parameters of each network layer node are initialized by the training layer by layer, and the noise values with a certain probability added layer by layer are 0.6, 0.4, 0.4 and 0.2 respectively.

The NSL-KDD data is pre-trained using SDA during the experiment, conducting supervision training together with label data after training.

Table 2. Four model experimental results.

Model	Accuracy	Detection rate	False alarm rate
SDA	97.54	90.36	0.95
ELM	93.89	85.13	1.21
AE-DNN	94.47	88.01	1.09
SDA-ELM	98.85	96.53	0.44

Table 2 shows the recognition rates of four kinds of algorithms, SDA, ELM, AE-DNN and SDA-ELM, for all kinds of samples. Table 2 shows that compared with SDA, ELM, and AE-DNN, SDA-ELM model's accuracy rate is increased by 1.31%, 4.96%, 4.38%, the detection rate is increased by 6.17%, 11.40%, 8.42%, the error rate is decreased by 0.51%, 0.77%, 0.65%. It can be seen that the SDA-ELM model is superior to the SDA, ELM and AE-DNN in terms of accuracy rate, detection rate and error rate. Therefore, the SDA-ELM model has obvious advantages in detection performance.

6   Conclusion

For massive high dimensionality and heterogeneous data, the traditional intrusion detection model is less effective. In this paper, the algorithm of combining stacked denoising autoencoder (SDA) and extreme learning machine (ELM) is proposed. Adding a certain probability Dropout regularization to the SDA model can alleviate the over-fitting phenomenon in the deep neural network model. The preprocessed data set is used to extract the features in the SDA model, and then the extreme learning machine (ELM) is used to replace the softmax classifier for intrusion detection. Experimental results show that, relative to the comparison model, the SDA-ELM model has improvement in the accuracy rate, detection rate and error rate of the three indicators. In the future work, we will consider applying this model to the actual intrusion detection environment to solve practical problems.

References

1. Ning, D., Xiaorong, C.: Intrusion detection system based on deep learning. Netw. Secur. Technol. Appl. **10**, 30–32 (2020)
2. Depren, O., et al.: An intelligent intrusion detection system (IDS) for anomaly and misuse detection in computer networks. Expert Syst. Appl. **29**(4), 713–722 (2005)
3. Shen, S., Cai, M., Lu, T., Zhao, Q.: Intrusion detection scheme based on LFKPCA-DWELM [J/OL]. Comput. Eng. Appl. 1–13 (2020)
4. Sung, A.H., Mukkamala, S.: Identifying important features for intrusion detection using support vector machines and neural networks. Appl. Internet (2003)
5. Sabhnani, M., Serpen, G.: Application of machine learning algorithms to KDD intrusion detection dataset within misuse detection context. MLMTA (2003)

6. Liu, J., Gao, Y.: A fast network intrusion detection system based on adaptive binning feature selection[J/OL]. J. Xidian Univ. 1–8 (2020)
7. Ning, D., Cheng, X.: Intrusion detection system based on deep learning. Netw. Secur. Technol. Appl. **2020**(10), 30–32 (2020)
8. Wenjun, L., Guo Zhimin, W., Chunming, R.W., Boyang, Z., Ning, Z., Zhuo, L.: Intrusion detection system for wireless communication in distribution network based on deep learning. Chinese J. Electron. **48**(08), 1538–1544 (2020)
9. Hinton, G.E., Salakhutdinov, R.R.: Reducing the dimensionality of data with neural networks. Science **313**(5786), 504–507 (2006)
10. Bengio, Y., Lamblin, P., Popovici, D., Larochelle, H.: greedy layer-wise training of deep networks. In: International Conference on Neural Information Processing System, vol. 19, pp. 153–160 (2006)
11. Zhiyu, L., Liqun, H.: Design and implementation of intrusion detection system based on variational autoencoder. Comput. Knowl. Technol. **16**(13), 22–24 (2020)
12. Vincent, P., Larochelle, H., Lajoie, I., et al.: Stacked denoising autoencoders: learning useful representations in a deep network with a local denoising criterion. J. Mach. Learn. Res. **11**(6), 3371–3408 (2010)
13. Huang, G.-B., Zhou, H., Ding, X., Zhang, R.: Extreme learning machine for regression and multiclass classification. IEEE Trans. Syst. Man Cybern. Part B. **42**(2), 513–29 (2012)
14. Srivastava, N., Hinton, G., Krizhevsky, A., et al.: Dropout: a simple way to prevent neural networks from overfitting. J. Mach. Learn. Res. **15**(1), 1929–1958 (2014)

Explaining Defect Detection
with Saliency Maps

Joe Lorentz[1,2](✉)(iD), Thomas Hartmann[1](iD), Assaad Moawad[1](iD),
Francois Fouquet[1](iD), and Djamila Aouada[2](iD)

[1] DataThings S.A., 5 rue de l'industrie, 1811 Luxembourg, Luxembourg
{joe.lorentz,thomas.hartmann,assaad.moawad,
francois.fouquet}@datathings.com
[2] University of Luxembourg, 29 Avenue John F. Kennedy,
1855 Luxembourg, Luxembourg
joe.lorentz@ext.uni.lu, djamila.aouada@uni.lu

Abstract. The rising quality and throughput demands of the manufacturing domain require flexible, accurate and explainable computer-vision solutions for defect detection. Deep Neural Networks (DNNs) reach state-of-the-art performance on various computer-vision tasks but wide-spread application in the industrial domain is blocked by the lacking explainability of DNN decisions. A promising, human-readable solution is given by saliency maps, heatmaps highlighting the image areas that influence the classifier's decision. This work evaluates a selection of saliency methods in the area of industrial quality assurance. To this end we propose the distance pointing game, a new metric to quantify the meaningfulness of saliency maps for defect detection. We provide steps to prepare a publicly available dataset on defective steel plates for the proposed metric. Additionally, the computational complexity is investigated to determine which methods could be integrated on industrial edge devices. Our results show that DeepLift, GradCAM and GradCAM++ outperform the alternatives while the computational cost is feasible for real time applications even on edge devices. This indicates that the respective methods could be used as an additional, autonomous post-classification step to explain decisions taken by intelligent quality assurance systems.

Keywords: XAI · Saliency · Defect detection · Edge AI

1   Introduction

The ever-growing throughput and quality demands of modern manufacturing make it increasingly difficult to rely on the human eye for a rising number of quality assessment procedures. This development led to the introduction of computer vision algorithms, which are now widely used in different fields such as the

The present project is supported by the National Research Fund Luxembourg, under the industrial fellowship scheme (grant 14297122).

H. Fujita et al. (Eds.): IEA/AIE 2021, LNAI 12799, pp. 506–518, 2021.
https://doi.org/10.1007/978-3-030-79463-7_43

food industry [3] or the production of printed board-circuits [22]. Most of these approaches rely on handcrafted algorithms to recognize domain specific faults. The downside of these algorithms is that the development requires domain knowledge. Furthermore, the specific nature of handcrafted solutions makes them susceptible to changes on the production side and unsuitable for varying product types. The current evolution of the manufacturing domain towards the so-called Industry 4.0 demands for more flexible solutions, which can be introduced without extensive prior study of domain characteristics. Deep Neural Networks (DNNs) provide this by automatically learning high level features [9]. DNNs reach state-of-the-art performance on various computer vision tasks like object recognition or segmentation [10,13]. A major blocking point for the wide-spread application of this emerging technology in industry is the lacking explainability of classification decisions [24]. This drawback is a direct consequence of the end-to-end feature learning. Neural networks tend to rely heavily on features which are unintuitive for human perception [16,24]. This makes it difficult to justify decisions without profound knowledge of the technology. Additionally, DNN-based defect detection requires considerable computational effort and outsourcing costly computations to cloud services is not always an option. Therefore, any additional effort linked to providing explanations should be as low as possible.

The research field of explainable artificial intelligence (XAI) aims to provide human-understandable explanations for DNN decisions. The field is split in two main directions, explainable modeling and post-modeling explainability. Explainable modeling investigates ways to develop inherently more interpretable machine learning models. This methodology involves a trade-off between explainability and model performance [12]. Post-modeling explainability proposes additional algorithms to map existing models in a way that is easier to understand for humans. The drawback is the additional computational effort linked to the post processing. The goal of this work is to investigate suitable XAI methods to explain DNN decisions in the context of industrial defect detection and how to optimize them for this task. We consider this task as an image classification problem where each class represents either a defect-free product or a product with a defined defect type. We argue that XAI methods for this task should:

1. be compatible with existing models for maximum performance and flexibility
2. provide meaningful insights to human operators
3. have low computational cost to enable computation on the edge

Explainable modeling contradicts our first proposition by design, as the development of inherently interpretable models limits the usage of existing models. Hence, we focus on post-modeling explainability in our work and investigate the computational cost of available methods to find suitable candidates that provide the best trade-off between propositions 2 and 3. To measure the *meaningfulness* of explanations, we propose to train a model for classification of a defect dataset with available segmentation of the defects in question. We use a dataset[1] of flat steel plates that provides annotated areas of four defect classes. We then

---

[1] https://www.kaggle.com/c/severstal-steel-defect-detection/overview.

compute the correlation between areas of the image deemed important by XAI methods and the ground-truth defect location. We suggest that an explainable quality assurance AI should be able to focus attention on the image areas that contain a defect. Furthermore, XAI methods that succeed to do so could be used as weakly supervised defect segmentation systems with drastically reduced effort in data acquisition. It is easier, less time-consuming and less error-prone for human experts to provide a single label per image instead of precisely extracting defect areas. Benchmarks on explainable AI exist already but only for the analysis of natural images or handwritten digits [21]. To the best of our knowledge, we are the first to provide a benchmark of XAI for the domain of industrial defect detection. The computational cost of post-modeling XAI is an important factor, especially when cloud computing is unwanted or not realizable. A relatively powerful GPU is used to enable the extensive benchmark. With the rising interest and availability of edge-GPUs like *Nvidia's Jetson family* [20], we argue that the reported computational costs, can guide industry practitioners to decide which methods are suitable for integration in production. The contributions of this work can be summarized as follows:

1. extensive benchmark of XAI for industrial defect detection
2. new metric to evaluate the meaningfulness of saliency maps
3. tools to prepare a datset for the benchmark and metric

The remainder of this work is organized as follows. Section 2 introduces the dataset as well as preprocessing steps necessary for our experiments. The investigated methods are presented in Sect. 3. Section 4 introduces the experiments conducted and presents our results. Conclusions and proposed future work are given in Sect. 5. The code used for our experiments is publicly available[2].

2   Steel Patch Dataset

Our study requires a dataset linked to industrial defect detection with ground truth segmentation labels available. Furthermore, as to train a model on defect classification, samples should clearly belong to one class only. Datasets satisfying our requirements as well as quality demands are scarce, presumably due to the high effort linked to labeling. We use a dataset of flat steel sheets, provided by Severstal[3], a steel mining and manufacturing company. The set was originally used for a defect localization competition launched by Severstal and is now publicly available[4]. The set provides 12.6k grayscale training images and a file indicating defect locations for roughly half of them. Each image can contain a multitude of defects of any class. As we require samples that can be labeled as one class only, we split the original 1600×256 pixel images into 6 patches of 256×256 pixels. With no overlap among patches, we have a surplus of 64 pixels horizontally

---

[2] https://hub.datathings.com/papers/2021-ieaaie.

[3] https://www.severstal.com.

[4] https://www.kaggle.com/c/severstal-steel-defect-detection/overview.

which we remove by cropping 34 pixels at the left and right borders each. The original pictures seem to have been taken on a running production line with a fixed camera. Hence, some images feature large black background areas. We remove image patches from our data which contain more than 95% background pixels to avoid classifying pure background patches while still capturing defects on the edges of sample steel plates. We end up with a total of 35k image patches. Table 1 gives an overview of how many images per class the resulting steel patch dataset contains. A large portion (54%) of the patches show no defects, while a negligible amount (0.8%) features more than one defect class. We use the defect-free images during training as we argue that learning the patterns of defect-free steel plates will help the model to spot defects. We exclude the patches with multiple classes to avoid confusing the classifier. Note that the remaining patches can show more than one defect area, however, all areas belong to the same class. Figure 1 shows some examples of the steel patch datatset, with defect locations indicated by a boundary.

Table 1. Steel patch sample count

Class	# Samples	%
Defect 1	1473	4.2
Defect 2	221	0.6
Defect 3	12245	34.9
Defect 4	1871	5.3
No defect	18942	54.0
Multiple	289	0.8

(a) Defect class 3   (b) Defect class 4

Fig. 1. Steel patch samples; defects indicated by red boundary

3 Review of Saliency Maps for Defect Detection

Saliency maps are heatmaps showing the salient (i.e. important) areas of a picture. In XAI they are used to visualize the importance of every input image pixel in relation to the output of a DNN. In the case of image classification, the output of a DNN is usually a vector of length n, where each value indicates the probability of the input belonging to each of the n classes the model knows.

Methods that compute saliency maps for DNNs can roughly be divided into four groups: pertubation-based [5,6], deconvolution [18,24], gradient-based [2,15–17,19] and class activation map based [4,14,23,25]. Table 2 gives an overview of these categories and their features as exposed by the respective literature and existing reviews [1,21]. Pertubation methods achieve impressive results at the cost of high computational cost which contradicts our third proposition (see Sect. 1) as it makes them unsuitable for applications on the edge. Simonyan et al. [16] show that gradient-based methods generalize deconvolution, while the implementation of the latter is more challenging and restrictive.

Therefore, we choose to exclude pertubation and deconvolution based approaches from our study. The following sections introduce the gradient based and class activation based methods selected for investigation. Figure 2 shows the saliency maps computed for one sample from the steel patch dataset according to the selected methods.

Table 2. Overview of saliency method categories and the features according to the respective literature and reviews [1,21].

Category	Meaningfulness	Computation cost	Implementation
Pertubation [5,6]	Very high	Very high	Easy, flexible
Deconvolution [18,24]	Low-high	Low	Difficult, unflexible
Gradient [2,15–17,19]	Low-high	Low-high	Easy, flexible
CAM [4,14,23,25]	High	Low-high	Easy, flexible

3.1 Gradient-Based

Simonyan et al. [16] were among the first to introduce the idea of using the gradient of the model output w.r.t. the input as a measure of importance. For a given input image, the authors use the model's output class score vector (before softmax) and set all values to zero except for the value that corresponds to the class that should be visualized (e.g. the class with the highest score). Next they use the backpropagation algorithm to compute the partial derivatives of the one-hot vector w.r.t the input image pixels. Intuitively, the result indicates how small changes at any pixel would affect the confidence of classifying the image as the class in question. The method is fast as it can rely on efficient GPU-implementations of backpropagation which are widely available with most deep learning frameworks. In our study we refer to this procedure as *VanillaGrad*. The outputs of *VanillaGrad* tend to be very noisy.

Subsequent works tried to identify the reasons and counteract this behavior. In [17], meaningless local variations of the partial derivatives are framed as the main cause. The authors suggest *SmoothGrad* as a solution. They smooth the gradient by running several iterations of *VanillaGrad* while adding noise to the input image and calculating the average over the resulting saliency maps. Other works [15,19] suggest that the noise is mainly caused by saturated nonlinearities for which *VanillaGrad* fails to backpropagate values. To counteract, Sundararajan et al. [19] let the user choose a reference input (e.g. all zero) and integrate the gradient while the input varies along a linear path from the reference to the original input image. The integral is approximated by taking the average over a predefined number of discrete steps. Shrikumar et al. [15] also make use of a reference input. They propose *DeepLift*, a method to compute the saliency in terms of difference from reference in a single backpropagation-like step. As a reference input, [15] suggests either an all zero image or blurring the original input. In [1], it is shown that *DeepLift* (without the RevealCance rule) can be

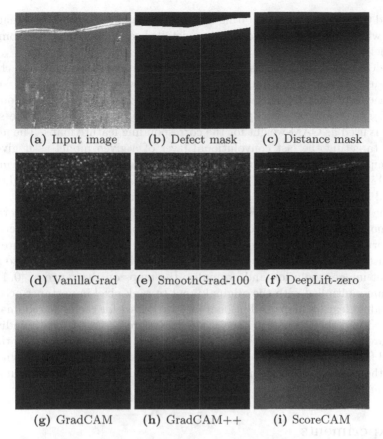

(a) Input image   (b) Defect mask   (c) Distance mask

(d) VanillaGrad   (e) SmoothGrad-100   (f) DeepLift-zero

(g) GradCAM   (h) GradCAM++   (i) ScoreCAM

Fig. 2. (a) Input image; (b) segmentation mask; (c) distance mask and saliency maps using gradient (**d–f**) and CAM (**g–i**) approaches respectively

implemented via the standard backpropagation algorithm and is most often a good approximation of integrated gradients. *Layer-wise Relevance Propagation (LRP)* [2], also shares some similarities with DeepLift, and is even identical to the latter under certain circumstances [1].

3.2 CAM-Based

The basic idea of class activation maps (CAM) is to compute a weighted average over convolutional feature maps (i.e. output of hidden convolution layers). Convolutional feature maps give a notion of learned features being present at spatial locations. Zhou et al. [25] use a fully convolutional model, compute the spatial average of each feature map of the last layer and use these values as input for a fully connected layer that produces the desired output (e.g. class scores). The weights of this classifier layer are first trained on the target data and later used as weights for the corresponding feature maps to compute the averaged CAM. Lastly, the resulting CAM is up-sampled to the input image resolution which leads to smoother but less detailed saliency maps when compared to gradient-based approaches.

GradCAM [14] generalizes this procedure. To avoid the need for changes on existing models and prior training of CAM-weights, the authors suggest to instead rely on the gradient similarly to the gradient-based methods (see Sect. 3.1). Gradients are backpropagated until the target layer and the spatial average is used as CAM-weight for the corresponding feature maps. The authors suggest targeting the last convolutional layer of a given model as it gives the best compromise between high-level semantics and detailed spatial information. *GradCAM++* [4] extends on *GradCAM* by computing the CAM-weights as a weighted average instead of a global average with identical weights.

Wang et al. [23] propose *ScoreCAM* to compute CAM without alternation of the model and without dependence on gradients. The authors first perform a single forward computation with the input image to retrieve the feature maps of the last convolutional layer. Next, they up-sample each feature map to match the input image resolution and normalize the maps on the range of $[0, 1]$. The results are multiplied with the original input to rank pixel importance according to individual feature maps. Additional forward passes for each masked image are performed and the changes in the target class score observed. Lastly individual scores are used as weights for the average CAM computation using the up-sampled feature maps retrieved during the initial forward step. The downside of this method is that the computational complexity increases with the number of feature maps used at the target layer.

4   Experiments

For our investigations, we used a ResNet-18 [7] pretrained on ImageNet [13], as available with PyTorch [11]. The fully connected layer and the later half of the convolution layers were unfrozen and fine-tuned for 50 epochs on the steel patch data presented in Sect. 2. We randomly selected one fourth of the images to validate the performance and reached an accuracy of 89%. For the benchmark we only used samples classified with high confidence ($\geq$90%). Low confidence decisions lead to fuzzy explanations which would negatively impact our benchmark. This left us with 1984 samples for which saliency maps were computed using VanillaGrad [16], SmoothGrad [17], DeepLift [15], GradCAM [14], GradCAM++ [4] and ScoreCAM [23]. For DeepLift we experimented with two reference variants. We either used a zero-image or blurred the input image with a Gaussian kernel. The authors of SmoothGrad propose to smooth gradients over 50 iterations and setting the standard deviation of the added noise to 0.2 times the range of the input image. Initial tests proofed that this noise scale is not suitable for our data. Instead, the noise was scaled with 0.02 and smoothing over 10, 50 and 100 iterations was investigated.

The computation time of methods that require more than 1 forward and backward pass on the model can be optimized via batched execution, in case the memory capacity of the used hardware allows for it. The implementation of batched execution is straightforward for ScoreCAM and SmoothGrad and does not differ much from the unbatched variant; hence, the computation times of both variants was compared. For SmoothGrad, we set the batch size to the number of iterations (i.e. 10, 50, 100) which we were able to fit on our *Nvidia GTX 1060*. For ScoreCAM we experimented with batch sizes of 1, 25 and 50. There was no need to further increase the batch size as the speedup between the latter two turned out to be negligible. In the case of DeepLift, PyTorch implementations, with and without batching differ substantially. We suggest that a batch size of 2, required for parallelized execution, is feasible even for edge computation. Hence, only the batched variant of DeepLift was investigated.

The raw saliency maps usually feature a wide spread with extreme outliers and negative values. The authors of the original methods propose various normalization schemes to produce more insightful explanations. Propositions from the original papers were gathered and an ablation study was conducted to determine the impact of normalization. We investigated taking the absolute values and using a rectified linear unit (ReLU) to reduce the spread potentially caused by large negative values. Afterwards a min-max-nomalization was performed to map the values on the range of $[0, 1]$:

$$\hat{x} = \frac{x - min(x)}{max(x) - min(x)}, \tag{1}$$

where x and $\hat{x}$ denote the saliency maps before and after normalization respectively. Additionally, we investigated capping the normalization at the 99th percentile instead of the maximum to remove outliers.

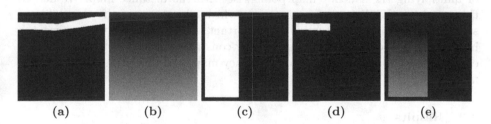

Fig. 3. Illustration of distance metric: (**a**) defect mask, (**b**) distance mask, (**c**) saliency map, (**d**) defect mask * saliency, (**e**) distance mask * saliency

4.1 Metrics

We report two metrics for our benchmark. We timed the individual saliency map generation over our 2k samples to determine the computational complexity. The median frames per second that the GPU could handle is reported. This should allow practitioners to decide which method could be feasible to use on the hardware available to them. For example, using *Nvidia*'s edge-GPU module *Jetson Nano*, fps are expected to be roughly 10 times lower than the reported numbers on the *GTX 1060* [8].

The quality of the saliency maps is investigated by comparing them with the ground-truth defect areas. Wang et al. [23] propose the *energy-based pointing game* in their work. For a given sample they first binarized the ground-truth, where pixels inside segmented areas were assigned a 1 and 0 otherwise. They computed the normalized saliency map, multiplied it point-wise with the binary mask and determined the sum of the saliency map values that fell inside the important areas. Lastly they divided this value by the sum over the full saliency map and reported the fraction. A score of 1 means that the whole saliency energy is displayed inside actually important regions and 0 indicates a map that fails to provide any meaningful highlights. We note one major flaw with this metric in that it does not matter how far away salient pixels are from the labeled areas. This is especially problematic for defect detection. Highlights in the near surroundings of defects are indeed helpful with the goal of focusing a human's attention. The samples depicted by Fig. 2 showcase this intuition. We therefore propose the following changes to the metric. In addition to the binary segmentation mask, a distance mask is determined. For every pixel the euclidean distance to the closest point labeled as a defect is computed. This distance is later used to penalize salient pixels that are far away from the defect areas and distract attention. We min-max-normalized (see Eq. 1) the distance mask by setting the maximum to the length of the diagonal of the input image and the minimum to 0 (i.e. inside defect areas). We did not change the computation of the fraction's numerator (inside-energy). For the denominator we took the sum of the inside-energy and the outside-energy. We define the latter as the sum over the result of multiplying the saliency map point-wise with the distance map. We denote this metric as the *distance pointing game* which allows to quantify the ability of saliency maps to focus attention on important image areas. Figure 3 shows the inside- and outside-maps for an artificially constructed example to illustrate the effect of point-wise multiplication of saliency maps and defect masks or distance masks.

4.2   Results

Figure 4 shows the results of the *distance pointing game*. For each method we report the values with the normalization setup that resulted in the highest median score respectively. Figure 4a plots the median score in relation to the median frames per second (fps) over the 2k samples. Lines connect points resulting from batched and unbatched variants of SmoothGrad and ScoreCAM. Additionally, the score distribution of the best hyperparameter setup per method, is reported at Fig. 4b. We record beyond 50 fps on methods that only require a single forward and backward pass. The more advanced weight computations of GradCAM++ in relation to GradCAM lead to a drop in median fps and a small increase in distance score. The batched DeepLift computation reached beyond 30 fps. The additional cost for computing a blurred image has negligible impact.

However, we report substantially higher distance score when using a zero reference instead. DeepLift-zero reached the highest median score in our experiment and also features a low spread when compared with the remaining methods. We report the lowest score for VanillaGrad. Smoothing the gradient over 10 iterations results in an increase of 0.097. Raising the number of iteration to 50 and 100 leads to a median score of 0.7991 and 0.8063 at the cost of drastically lowered fps. Computing all smoothing iterations within one batch increases the fps substantially for both SmoothGrad and ScoreCAM. The latter reaches lower distance scores compared to the other CAM methods while requiring substantially more computation time. Moreover, the batched implementations require memory capacities beyond 2 GB on the target hardware. This, paired with the low fps for unbatched SmoothGrad and ScoreCAM may rule out these methods for application on the edge.

Table 3 compares the median distance score of the various normalization schemes. We note that for all methods the scores are generally higher when capping at 100 percentile (true maximum) instead of the 99th percentile. Discarding negative values with a ReLU leads to slightly better results than using the absolute values. These observations indicate that saliency maps on the proposed dataset did not lead to extreme positive outliers and only a small amount of negative outliers. The score of GradCAM without ReLU or ABS before the normalization is only slightly lower. For ScoreCAM and GradCAM++ the scores do not vary at all, which indicates that no negative saliency values were computed. Allowing negative values has a more substantial impact on the gradient-based methods.

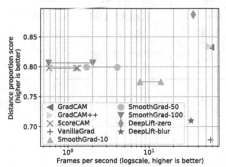
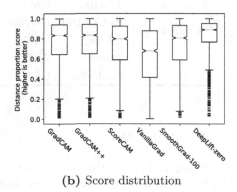

(a) Median score and median fps, lines connect batched and unbatched method variants

(b) Score distribution

Fig. 4. Distance pointing game results

Table 3. Median distance score for various normalization, best setups in bold

Method	Norm	Median	Method	Norm	Median
GradCAM	All-100	0.8240	SmoothGrad 100	All-100	0.5718
	Abs-100	0.8303		Abs-100	0.8055
	ReLU-100	**0.8325**		**ReLU-100**	**0.8063**
	All-99	0.8235		All-99	0.5680
	Abs-99	0.8298		Abs-99	0.7971
	ReLU-99	0.8318		ReLU-99	0.7971
GradCAM++	**All-100**	**0.8338**	SmoothGrad 10	All-100	0.5925
	Abs-100	**0.8338**		Abs-100	0.7752
	ReLU-100	**0.8338**		**ReLU-100**	**0.775**
	All-99	0.8333		All-99	0.5886
	Abs-99	0.8333		Abs-99	0.766
	ReLU-99	0.8333		ReLU-99	0.766
ScoreCAM	**All-100**	**0.7977**	DeepLift zero	All-100	0.4611
	Abs-100	**0.7977**		Abs-100	0.7658
	ReLU-100	**0.7977**		**ReLU-100**	**0.7660**
	All-99	0.7971		All-99	0.4176
	Abs-99	0.7971		Abs-99	0.7156
	ReLU-99	0.7971		ReLU-99	0.7156
VanillaGrad	All-100	0.6014	DeepLift blur	All-100	0.3255
	Abs-100	0.6778		**Abs-100**	**0.4555**
	ReLU-100	**0.6780**		**ReLU-100**	**0.4555**
	All-99	0.5971		All-99	0.3123
	Abs-99	0.6717		Abs-99	0.4198
	ReLU-99	0.6715		ReLU-99	0.4199

5   Conclusion

The rising quality and throughput demands of the manufacturing domain require flexible, accurate and explainable computer-vision solutions for defect detection. Deep Neural Networks coupled with saliency maps to highlight important image areas provide a promising alternative, suitable for computation on the edge. We provide an extensive benchmark of recent saliency methods for the use-case of defect detection on flat steel plates. For this we propose a new metric to quantify the ability of saliency maps to focus attention on defect areas. Our results show that DeepLift, GradCAM and GradCAM++ outperform the alternatives while the computational cost is feasible for real time applications even on edge devices. Furthermore, we show the importance of suitable normalization. This work is an important step in the direction of explainable, automated defect detection on the edge. Future work could extend our benchmark on additional DNN architectures and investigate the relation between saliency maps and model decision confidence. Additionally, the substantial performance difference between DeepLift-zero and DeepLift-blur expose the selection of good reference inputs as a potential research area.

References

1. Ancona, M., Ceolini, E., Öztireli, C., Gross, M.: Towards better understanding of gradient-based attribution methods for Deep Neural Networks, arXiv:1711.06104 [cs.LG] (2017)
2. Bach, S., Binder, A., Montavon, G., Klauschen, F., Müller, K.R., Samek, W.: On pixel-wise explanations for non-linear classifier decisions by layer-wise relevance propagation. PLoS ONE **10**(7) (2015). https://doi.org/10.1371/journal.pone.0130140
3. Brosnan, T., Sun, D.W.: Improving quality inspection of food products by computer vision–a review. J. Food Eng. **61**(1), 3–16 (2014). https://doi.org/10.1016/S0260-8774(03)00183-3
4. Chattopadhay, A., Sarkar, A., Howlader, P., Balasubramanian, V.N.: Grad-CAM++: generalized gradient-based visual explanations for deep convolutional networks. In: 2018 IEEE Winter Conference on Applications of Computer Vision (WACV), pp. 839–847. IEEE (2018). https://doi.org/10.1109/WACV.2018.00097
5. Fong, R., Patrick, M., Vedaldi, A.: Understanding deep networks via extremal perturbations and smooth masks. In: Proceedings of the IEEE/CVF International Conference on Computer Vision (ICCV), pp. 2950–2958 (2019)
6. Fong, R.C., Vedaldi, A.: Interpretable explanations of black boxes by meaningful perturbation. In: 2017 IEEE International Conference on Computer Vision (ICCV), pp. 3449–3457. IEEE (2017). https://doi.org/10.1109/ICCV.2017.371
7. He, K., Zhang, X., Ren, S., Sun, J.: Deep residual learning for image recognition. In: 2016 IEEE Conference on Computer Vision and Pattern Recognition (CVPR), pp. 770–778. IEEE (2016). https://doi.org/10.1109/CVPR.2016.90
8. Jo, J., Jeong, S., Kang, P.: Benchmarking GPU-accelerated edge devices. In: 2020 IEEE International Conference on Big Data and Smart Computing (BigComp), pp. 117–120. IEEE (2020). https://doi.org/10.1109/BigComp48618.2020.00-89
9. Li, H., Ota, K., Dong, M.: Learning IoT in edge: deep learning for the internet of things with edge computing. IEEE Network **32**(1), 96–101 (2018). https://doi.org/10.1109/MNET.2018.1700202
10. Lin, T.-Y., et al.: Microsoft COCO: common objects in context. In: Fleet, D., Pajdla, T., Schiele, B., Tuytelaars, T. (eds.) ECCV 2014. LNCS, vol. 8693, pp. 740–755. Springer, Cham (2014). https://doi.org/10.1007/978-3-319-10602-1_48
11. Paszke, A., et al.: PyTorch: an imperative style, high-performance deep learning library. In: Advances in Neural Information Processing Systems 32, pp. 8024–8035. Curran Associates, Inc. (2019)
12. Rai, A.: Explainable AI: from black box to glass box. J. Acad. Mark. Sci. **48**(1), 137–141 (2020). https://doi.org/10.1007/s11747-019-00710-5
13. Russakovsky, O., et al.: ImageNet large scale visual recognition challenge. Int. J. Comput. Vis. **115**(3), 211–252 (2015). https://doi.org/10.1007/s11263-015-0816-y

14. Selvaraju, R.R., Cogswell, M., Das, A., Vedantam, R., Parikh, D., Batra, D.: Grad-CAM: visual explanations from deep networks via gradient-based localization. In: Proceedings of the IEEE International Conference on Computer Vision (ICCV), pp. 618–626 (2017)
15. Shrikumar, A., Greenside, P., Kundaje, A.: Learning important features through propagating activation differences. In: Proceedings of the 34th International Conference on Machine Learning, ICML 2017, vol. 70, pp. 3145–3153. JMLR.org (2017)
16. Simonyan, K., Vedaldi, A., Zisserman, A.: Deep Inside Convolutional Networks: Visualising Image Classification Models and Saliency Maps, arXiv:1312.6034 [cs.CV] (2013)
17. Smilkov, D., Thorat, N., Kim, B., Viégas, F., Wattenberg, M.: SmoothGrad: Removing noise by adding noise, arXiv:1706.03825 [cs.LG] (2017)
18. Springenberg, J.T., Dosovitskiy, A., Brox, T., Riedmiller, M.: Striving for Simplicity: The All Convolutional Net, arXiv:1412.6806 [cs.LG] (2015)
19. Sundararajan, M., Taly, A., Yan, Q.: Axiomatic attribution for deep networks. In: Precup, D., Teh, Y.W. (eds.) Proceedings of the 34th International Conference on Machine Learning. Proceedings of Machine Learning Research, vol. 70, pp. 3319–3328. PMLR (2017)
20. Suzen, A.A., Duman, B., Sen, B.: Benchmark analysis of Jetson TX2, Jetson Nano and raspberry PI using deep-CNN. In: 2020 International Congress on Human-Computer Interaction, Optimization and Robotic Applications (HORA), pp. 1–5. IEEE (2020). https://doi.org/10.1109/HORA49412.2020.9152915
21. Tomsett, R., Harborne, D., Chakraborty, S., Gurram, P., Preece, A.: Sanity checks for saliency metrics. In: Proceedings of the AAAI Conference on Artificial Intelligence, vol. 34, pp. 6021–6029 (2020)
22. Tsai, D.M., Lin, C.T.: Fast normalized cross correlation for defect detection. Pattern Recogn. Lett. **24**(15), 2625–2631 (2003). https://doi.org/10.1016/S0167-8655(03)00106-5
23. Wang, H., et al.: Score-CAM: score-weighted visual explanations for convolutional neural networks. In: 2020 IEEE/CVF Conference on Computer Vision and Pattern Recognition Workshops (CVPRW), pp. 111–119. IEEE (2020). https://doi.org/10.1109/CVPRW50498.2020.00020
24. Zeiler, M.D., Fergus, R.: Visualizing and understanding convolutional networks. In: Fleet, D., Pajdla, T., Schiele, B., Tuytelaars, T. (eds.) ECCV 2014. LNCS, vol. 8689, pp. 818–833. Springer, Cham (2014). https://doi.org/10.1007/978-3-319-10590-1_53
25. Zhou, B., Khosla, A., Lapedriza, A., Oliva, A., Torralba, A.: Learning deep features for discriminative localization. In: 2016 IEEE Conference on Computer Vision and Pattern Recognition (CVPR), pp. 2921–2929. IEEE (2016). https://doi.org/10.1109/CVPR.2016.319

d-BTAI: The Dynamic-Binary Tree Based Anomaly Identification Algorithm for Industrial Systems

Jyotirmoy Sarkar[1]($^{\boxtimes}$), Santonu Sarkar[1], Snehanshu Saha[1], and Swagatam Das[2]

[1] BITS-Pilani KK Birla Goa Campus, Sancoale, Goa, India
[2] Indian Statistical Institute, Kolkata, India

Abstract. Many of the existing approaches to anomaly detection are based upon supervised learning and heavily dependent on training datasets. However, anomalies rarely occur in most industrial systems. Hence it is challenging to retrieve a training dataset labeled with true anomalies. Therefore, this motivates us to investigate such scenarios where it is arduous to get labeled data for anomalies. This paper has proposed a clustering-based recursive anomaly detection algorithm; dynamic-Binary Tree Anomaly Identifier (d-BTAI). d-BTAI has been applied on industrial devices since anomalies in large industrial devices can incur massive losses. The algorithm has experimented on various publicly available industrial datasets such as Cloudwatch, Yahoo, and Backblaze. d-BTAI has attained a higher Area under the ROC curve (AUC) in comparison with Isolation Forest (iForest), One Class Support Vector Machine (OCSVM), and Elliptic Envelope. The higher Negative Predictive Value (NPV) and specificity value demonstrate the algorithm's efficacy on multiple datasets.

Keywords: Dynamic Binary Tree · Unsupervised learning · Anomaly · Anomaly score

1 Introduction

Mission critical industrial systems do not fail frequently. When they do, the impact is catastrophic [6]. Proactive maintenance of such an industrial system is essential to reduce its downtime. According to a market research report [3], the medical equipment maintenance market is expected to generate $26.4 billion in revenue by 2024. One way to reduce downtime is to predict an operational device's anomalous behavior through continuous monitoring. A common problem with every anomaly prediction approach aims to reduce the false positivity [14]. If an anomaly prediction based monitoring system generates an alarm, the manufacturer needs to spend time and effort to check for any impending failure. A high amount of false-positive alarms results in massive wastage of the organization's maintenance cost.

Recently, deep-learning based models such as auto-encoders, CNN, long-short term memory (LSTM) [9,18,20] are gaining attention for anomaly detection.

© Springer Nature Switzerland AG 2021
H. Fujita et al. (Eds.): IEA/AIE 2021, LNAI 12799, pp. 519–532, 2021.
https://doi.org/10.1007/978-3-030-79463-7_44

Unsupervised Deep Learning-based models [13,20] have also been explored for anomaly detection. A Profile-based approach that combines Particle Swarm Optimization (PSO) and OCSVM have been applied for detecting anomalies which can potentially lead to intrusions in industrial control systems [17]. Several other approaches such as adaptive kernel density-based approach [19], invariant mining based approach [16], isolation forest (iForest) based approach [11] have been attempted to detect anomalous behavior of industrial and cloud-based systems. These approaches have several drawbacks. For instance, profile-based approaches generate too many false alarms. The unsupervised deep learning techniques also require retraining when the datatype changes. Isolation-forest based approaches require a large amount of memory when the number of trees grows. Random selection of a feature and a split value at a time for partitioning makes this approach computationally expensive for a higher dimensional dataset. It also suffers from a high amount of false alarms if the training sample is incorrect. Invariant based anomaly detection requires a proper training set in order to be effective.

In this paper, a novel algorithm called the dynamic-Binary Tree Anomaly Identifier (d-BTAI) for anomaly detection is proposed. d-BTAI uses a new data structure called Binary Anomaly Tree (BAT) in order to identify anomalous data points, and it does not need any training data for this purpose. The very nature of d-BTAI algorithm is such that it can be plugged with any standard clustering algorithm to produce the tree. Here, it has been shown that a single binary tree is capable of identifying several anomalies present in the dataset instead of creating a forest-like iForest. As a result, d-BTAI significantly reduces memory consumption and d-BTAI has better run time complexity in comparison to iForest.

The remainder of the paper is organized as follows. Section 5 discusses the various literature in the anomaly identification field. Section 2 discusses on the characterises of the BAT. Next Sect. 3 discusses on the anomaly detection methodology of the d-BTAI. The d-BTAI empirically evaluated in the Sect. 4. The paper is concluded in Sect. 6.

2 Charateristics of Binary Anomaly Tree (BAT)

The d-BTAI algorithm constructs a Binary Anomaly Tree (BAT) from the dataset by clustering the datapoint where one or more leaf nodes can have anomalous datapoints. The idea is similar to the isolation forest based approach. The number of leaves of a BAT directly impacts the memory requirement of the d-BTAI algorithm while internal nodes indicates the number of clustering performed to produce the tree.

Definition 1. *BAT is a binary tree* T *with the following properties:*

1. *A non-leaf node including the root node of* T *has exactly two children*
2. *The smallest Anomaly tree has three nodes with one root node*

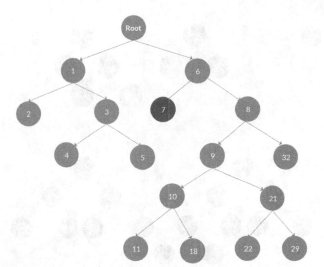

Fig. 1. A binary anomaly tree (BAT) generated by the d-BTAI algorithm on AWS cloudwatch anomaly dataset.

Example 1. Figure 1 shows a partial BAT generated from AWS cloudwatch dataset by our proposed d-BTAI algorithm. The root node represents the entire AWS dataset and the number associated with a node indicates the (depth-first) order in which the algorithm has generated it. For instance, node 1 generated first and 32 is the last node in the figure. From the root node, the algorithm has produced two children, 1 and 6. The leaf nodes 2, 4, 5, 7 participate in anomaly identification. The red color node 7 in level 2 contains an anomaly.

2.1 BAT Construction

Algorithm 1: BAT(D, θ, L, *ClusteringFunc*)

$v \leftarrow$ **new Node**()
$v.level \leftarrow L$
$v.cluster \leftarrow D$
if $(|D| \geq \theta \vee L == 0)$ **then**
    $(D_L, D_R) \leftarrow ClusteringFunc(D,2)$ ▷ D_L, D_R **are two clusters generated**
    by clustering function
    $v.left \leftarrow BAT(D_L, \theta, L+1$, *ClusteringFunc*)
    $v.right \leftarrow BAT(D_R, \theta, L+1$, *ClusteringFunc*)
end
return v

The BAT algorithm is invoked on a dataset D, with level $L = 0$. The algorithm recursively generates the Anomaly Tree based on the minimum clustering threshold θ. If the dataset size is less than the minimum clustering threshold, the

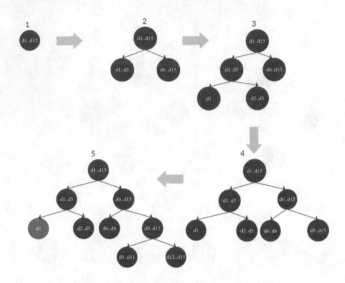

Fig. 2. Anomaly Tree construction by Algorithm 1

algorithm does not cluster further. The algorithm does not verify the minimum clustering threshold for the root node, which allows at least two clusters to be formed, since, without any cluster, the d-BTAI can not apply Enhanced Cluster Based Local Outlier Factor (ECBLOF) metric.

Example 2. Figure 2 explains a step by step construction of the entire tree for a hypothetical dataset $D = \{d_1, d_2, d_3 \ldots \ldots d_{15}\}$ where d_1 is the only anomalous data point. When Algorithm 1 is invoked externally with D and $L = 0$, it creates one root node and at least two children (tree 2 in the figure) since it does not check for the threshold condition. In this example, the minimum clustering threshold is 5, and let us use the K-means clustering function. Therefore, the entire dataset D is divided into two clusters in Tree 2. Assume that $\{d_1..d_5\}$ go to the left node, whereas $\{d_6..d_{15}\}$ move to the right node. Since both these nodes are still above the threshold, the algorithm is recursively applied on the left node to create Tree 3. Suppose that $\{d_1..d_5\}$ is further divided into two clusters $\{d_1\}$ and $\{d_2..d_5\}$. These two clusters are not divided any further. Next, $\{d_6..d_{15}\}$ (the right subtree of the root node) is divided into $d_6..d_8$ and $d_9..d_{15}$ as shown in Tree 4. In Tree 5, $\{d_9..d_{15}\}$ is further divided into $(d_9..d_{11})$ and $(d_{12}..d_{15})$ and the algorithm terminates with level = 3.

2.2   Properties of BAT

Lemma 1. *If $\mathcal{T}$ has $\mathcal{L}$ leaves, the number of internal nodes is $\mathcal{I} = \mathcal{L}-1$*

Proof. It can be proved by induction as follows.
Basis: By definition, $\mathcal{T}$ can have $\mathcal{L} = 2$ leaves and one root.
Step: Assume that the property holds for any $\mathcal{K} > 2$ leaves. The only way $\mathcal{T}$

can grow is by adding new leaf nodes to an existing leaf node. In such a case, an existing leaf node becomes an internal node, and the total internal nodes $\mathcal{I} = K$ and the new leaf node count becomes $\mathcal{K} - 1 + 2 = \mathcal{K} + 1$

Property 1: From Lemma 1 it can be easily derived that if Anomaly Tree (AT) $\mathcal{T}$ has $\mathcal{I}$ internal nodes, *the total number of nodes is* $\mathcal{N} = 2\mathcal{I} + 1$

Property 2: For a dataset D with $|D| = n$, and a minimum clustering threshold θ, the height of BAT H is bound within

$$[(\log \frac{n}{\theta}), (n - \theta)]$$

This can be easily observed from Algorithm 1. The minimum height is possible when D_L and D_R are identical and tree generation continues till the cluster size becomes θ, resulting in a balanced tree. The number of leaves $k = \frac{n}{\theta}$ and each leaf has exactly θ data points. In such a case, the height of the balanced BAT is $\log k = \log \frac{n}{\theta}$. Similarly, the worst case scenario happens when $ClusteringFunc()$ always partitions the input dataset in such way that the left partition $|D_L| = 1$ without any loss of generality. When ClusteringFunc is called with D_R as the input, D_R is split again with a singleton left cluster and this process continues till $|D_R| \leq \theta$. The height of the tree in this pathological case is $n - \theta$.

3   Anomaly Detection Using d-BTAI

Entire anomaly detection process can be divided into two phases. The first phase constructs the Binary Anomaly Tree (BAT) and the second phase tries to find the anomalies from the tree using the ECBLOF metric.

3.1   Enhanced Cluster Based Local Outlier Factor (ECBLOF)

To evaluate the efficacy of a clustering-based anomaly detector, the Cluster Based Local Outlier Factor (CBLOF) metric proposed by He et al. [10] has been used extensively. The CBLOF metric has been modified to avoid the multiplication with the cluster size since such a score can bias towards the large clusters. The following example explains the rationale

Example 3. Suppose that a small cluster C_1 has only one datapoint a which is an anomaly. Consider another large cluster C_2 with a non-anomalous datapoint $b \in C_2$. Suppose that the distance between a and centroid of C_2 cluster is 10 $(d(a, C_2) = 10)$. Since C_2 is the nearest larger cluster, as per the definition of the CBLOF, the anomaly score of $a = 10 \times 1$, whereas that of $b = 1 * |C_2|$ (since $b \in C_2$, its distance from the centroid of C_2 will be 1). If $|C_2| > 10$, then a will not be identified as an anomaly based on the CBLOF score and a normal datapoint b will be considered as anomaly because of the higher anomaly score.

The modified metric called ECBLOF is defined below: Let D be the dataset which has been partitioned into n clusters $C_1, \cdots, C_i \cdots, C_n$. The set of clusters have been categorized into two categories, namely Small Cluster (SC) and Large Cluster (LC). For a predefined threshold α, $C_i \in SC$ if $|C_i| < \alpha|D|$, otherwise it is in LC. For a datapoint $p \in D$, $ECBLOF(p)$ is defined as

$$ECBLOF(p) \begin{cases} = min(d(p,C_j)) \text{ if } C_i \in SC \text{ where} \\ p \in C_i, \ C_j \in LC \ \forall j = 1 \cdots b \\ = d(p,C_i) \text{ if } C_i \in LC \text{ where } p \in C_i \end{cases} \tag{1}$$

$d(p,C) = \sqrt{(x_p - x_c)^2 + (y_p - y_c)^2}$ computes the Euclidean distance between a datapoint p and the cluster center c of the cluster C.

3.2   Anomaly Identification

Algorithm 2: d-BTAI(D, $\theta, A_t, ClusteringFunc$)

Input: D- input data, θ - minimum clustering threshold, A_t- normalized
    anomaly threshold, *ClusteringFunc* is the clustering algorithm

$anomaly\_pt \leftarrow \emptyset$

$score \leftarrow \emptyset \ \triangleright$ *Hashtable of datapoints and their ECBLOF scores*

$AT\_root \leftarrow BAT(D,\theta,0,ClusteringFunc)$

$leaf\_nodes \leftarrow find\_leaves(AT\_root)$

$L_t \leftarrow \lceil \delta \cdot Height(AT\_root)\rceil \ \triangleright 0 < \delta < 1$

foreach $leaf \in leaf\_nodes$ **do**
  if $(|leaf.cluster| == 1) \wedge (leaf.level \leq L_t)$ **then**
  | $anomaly\_pt \leftarrow anomaly\_pt \cup leaf.cluster$
  end
end

$score[d] \leftarrow ECBLOF(leaf\_nodes)$

$score[d] \leftarrow score[d] \div max\{score\} \ \triangleright$ *normalization*

Let $score_{top} \subset score$ be datapoints whose normalized scores are in the top
  quartile of *score*

Let σ_{top} be the standard deviation of $score_{top}$

if $\sigma_{top} \geq S_t$ **then**
  foreach $d \in score_{top}$ **do**
    if $scores_{top}[d] \geq A_t$ **then**
    | $anomaly\_pt = anomaly\_pt \cup d$
    end
  end
end

return $anomaly\_pt$

The d-BTAI algorithm described in Algorithm 2 computes the anomaly score and finds out the anomalies. The algorithm considers any leaf node with a single data instance as an anomaly provided the node is within the tree level threshold (L_t). For example, in Fig. 2, tree 5 is the final AT with height $H = 3$. Say, $\delta = 0.5$ and $L_t = \lceil 0.5 * 3\rceil = 2$ are considered. The red colored leaf contains only d_1 and the level of the red node is 2. Therefore, d_1 is considered to be an anomaly by the d-BTAI.

Apart from single instance nodes, Algorithm 2 computes normalized ECBLOF for data points of all leaf nodes. Next, only those data points whose normalized scores are in the top quartile are selected, and the standard deviation σ of these selected data points is computed. If σ is low, it is assumed that these data points belong to the common population, and there is no anomaly. However, if σ is high, then any datapoint from the top quartile with normalized score higher than a predefined threshold is considered to be an anomaly.

While there are similarities between d-BTAI and other tree based anomaly identifies such as Isolation Forest (iForest), [12], our approach has the following unique characteristics.

- Unlike iForest, d-BTAI does not need any training set.
- Our approach creates a single tree, unlike the iForest, which creates 100 trees in a default setup.
- As shown in Algorithm 1, the dataset is split based on a clustering algorithm, rather than splitting randomly as in iForest.
- There is a different evaluation phase for anomaly identification in the case of iForest.

Time and Space Complexities. d-BTAI forms a single full binary tree. The time complexity to construct such a tree is $O(f(n)log(f(n)))$. $f(n)$ is the time complexity of the clustering algorithm. In contrast, the time complexity reported for iForest [12] is $O(tmlogm) + O(tnlogm)$ (m is the size of subsample involve in the training phase, t is the number of trees in the forest). The time complexity for OCSVM is $O(n^3)$.

Next, let us consider the memory consumption. For a dataset $|D| = n$, d-BTAI generates a single binary tree in a recursive manner. Hence it is required to consider the depth of the tree. Therefore the space complexity is $O(df(n))$, where d is the depth of the BAT, and $f(n)$ is the space complexity of the clustering algorithm. iForest takes a single feature and starts random partitioning, where s datapoints participate. It creates t number of such iTrees for this feature. Since all the n data elements needs to participate in tree construction, the space complexity is $O(t * n)$. The space requirement for OCSVM is $O(n^2)$. *Hence d-BTAI has lower time and space complexity. However, it is dependent on the external clustering algorithm* (Table 1).

Table 1. Time and space complexity of d-BTAI on various clustering algorithms

Algorithm	Time complexity	Space complexity
d-BTAI(K-means)	$O(nmIlogn)$[a]	$O((n+2)md)$
d-BTAI(Birch)	$O(nlogn)$	–
d-BTAI(Agglomerative)	$O(n^2logn)$	$O(n^2d)$
d-BTAI(DBSCAN)	$O(nlogn(logn + loglogn))$	$O(nd)$

[a] I is the iteration number, and m represents the attribute number.

4   Experimental Results

This section reports the performance of the d-BTAI on multiple datasets namely, 4 sets of AWS cloudwatch data [4], 4 sets of Yahoo webscope S5 data [1], and 5 sets of Backblaze [2] hard drive failure data published in Q3, 2019. For AWS as well as Yahoo, one day long operational data is considered. For Backblaze datasets, only the significant features identified by Apiletti et al. [5] have been considered in the anomaly identification process. These datasets have labeled anomalous datapoints. For unsupervised approaches, all the labels have been removed while applying the algorithms and then verified the result with the labels.

In order to evaluate the efficacy of d-BTAI, a two-pronged approach has been taken. First, three different clustering functions are plugged in d-BTAI to establish loose coupling with any specific clustering technique. The d-BTAI (K-means) version uses a K-means for clustering, whereas the d-BTAI (Agglomerative) version uses Agglomerative clustering algorithm. The d-BTAI (Birch) version invokes the Birch clustering approach. Second, d-BTAI has been compared with other popular algorithms that are 1. Ensemble based 2. Profile based and 3. Unsupervised. For Ensembled based, the well-known unsupervised binary tree ensemble algorithm iForest [12] has been selected. As discussed earlier iForest constructs an ensemble of binary trees for anomaly detection. For profile based, OCSVM is considered. Elliptic Envelope, which assumes that the normal data follow a known distribution, is selected in the unsupervised category. Table 2 shows the parameters used for each algorithm. The experiments are conducted on a dual-core Intel i3 CPU with 4 GB RAM.

Table 2. Parameters of each of the algorithm

Algorithm	Parameter description
d-BTAI	$\theta = 0.1 * (|D|)$, $A_t = 0.2$, $L_t = 0.5 *$ (tree height), $S_t = 0.2$, ClusteringFunc is K-means/Agglomerative/Birch
iForest [12]	All the parameters are default value of the sklearn package (Python)
OCSVM [17]	Training set $= 0.7 * (|D|)$. All the parameters are default value of the sklearn package (Python)
Elliptic envelope [15]	Training set $= 0.7 * (|D|)$. All the parameters are default value of the sklearn package (Python)

4.1   Quality Parameters

To evaluate the efficacy, **True Positive (TP)**, **False Positive (FP)**, **False Negative (FN)**, and **False Negative (FN)** are considered.

Sensitivity measures the proportion of the actual anomalies that are correctly identified. It is computed as $\dfrac{TP}{TP + FN}$

Specificity measures the proportion of actual non-anomalous data points that are correctly identified and it is expressed as $\frac{TN}{TN+FP}$

Positive Predictive Value (PPV) decides the probability that a detected anomalous datapoint is indeed a real one and it is computed as $PPV = \frac{TP}{TP+FP}$

Likewise, **NPV** is computed as $NPV = \frac{TN}{TN+FN}$

4.2 Analysis and Discussion

Table 3 shows a side-by-side performance comparison of the three versions of d-BTAI algorithm (using three different clustering functions) in terms of Sensitivity, Specificity, PPV and NPV. The results clearly show that for all the clustering algorithms, and for all the datasets, d-BTAI algorithm performed very well. In particular, the Specificity and NPV values, which have been consistently above 99%.

Table 4 compares the performance of d-BTAI with other algorithms using AUC (Area under the ROC curve). Figure 3 shows the AUC comparison between the d-BTAI (K-means) and the other algorithms, such as iForest, OCSVM. From Table 4 and Fig. 3 it is evident that d-BTAI has achieved higher AUC. In most of the cases, d-BTAI, irrespective of the underlying clustering algorithm, has achieved more than 0.9 AUC, whereas the iForest has garnered an average of 0.8 AUC across the datasets. The other algorithms can not achieve a higher AUC value like d-BTAI because of the higher FP rate. A noteworthy point about d-BTAI is that it attempts to identify anomalies in Small Cluster Single Data Instance (SCSD). In addition, ECBLOF helps to identify the remaining anomalies by computing the anomaly score. For example, there are 8 anomalies in the Yahoo dataset$_4$. SCSD corners 4 anomalies, whereas ECBLOF identifies the remaining 4 anomalies. d-BTAI has reported a lower value in Yahoo dataset$_2$ because it could not identify one anomaly even though it's anomaly score was very close to the normalized anomaly threshold.

Table 3. Statistical analysis of the d-BTAI (K-means), d-BTAI (Agglomerative) and d-BTAI (Birch) on different parameters

Dataset	d-BTAI (K-means)				d-BTAI (Agglomerative)				d-BTAI (Birch)			
	Sensitivity	Specificity	PPV	NPV	Sensitivity	Specificity	PPV	NPV	Sensitivity	Specificity	PPV	NPV
AWS1	100%	100%	100%	100%	100%	100%	100%	100%	100%	100%	100%	100%
AWS2	100%	98.9%	25%	100%	100%	98.58%	20%	100%	100%	98.58%	20%	100%
AWS3	100%	99.6%	50%	100%	100%	99.37%	33%	100%	100%	99.37%	33%	100%
AWS4	100%	99.09%	25%	100%	100%	97.5%	33%	100%	100%	97.5%	33%	100%
Backblaze1	100%	99.56%	50%	100%	100%	99.12%	33%	100%	100%	99.12%	33%	100%
Backblaze2	100%	100%	100%	100%	100%	100%	100%	100%	100%	100%	100%	100%
Backblaze3	100%	100%	100%	100%	100%	100%	100%	100%	100%	100%	100%	100%
Backblaze4	100%	99.14%	33%	100%	100%	99.14%	33%	100%	100%	99.14%	33%	100%
Backblaze5	100%	98.43%	20%	100%	100%	98.43%	20%	100%	100%	98.43%	20%	100%
Yahoo1	100%	100%	100%	100%	100%	100%	100%	100%	100%	100%	100%	100%
Yahoo2	87.5%	99.99%	87.5%	99.99%	87.5%	99.99%	87.5%	99.99%	87.5%	99.99%	87.5%	99.99%
Yahoo3	100%	100%	100%	100%	100%	100%	100%	100%	100%	100%	100%	100%
Yahoo4	100%	100%	100%	100%	100%	100%	100%	100%	100%	100%	100%	100%

Table 4. AUC of 1. d-BTAI (K-means), 2. Elliptic Envelope, 3. iForest, 4. d-BTAI (Agglomerative), 5. OCSVM and 6. d-BTAI (Birch)

Dataset	AUC_1	AUC_2	AUC_3	AUC_4	AUC_5	AUC_6
AWS_1	1	0.96	0.92	1	0.71	1
AWS_2	**0.98**	0.46	0.48	0.97	0.76	0.97
AWS_3	**0.99**	0.97	0.46	**0.99**	0.77	**0.99**
AWS_4	0.98	0.93	0.46	**0.99**	0.71	**0.99**
$Backblaze_1$	1	0.94	0.95	1	0.71	1
$Backblaze_2$	1	0.94	0.95	1	0.71	1
$Backblaze_3$	1	0.94	0.95	1	0.65	1
$Backblaze_4$	1	0.94	0.95	1	0.60	1
$Backblaze_5$	**0.99**	0.95	0.95	**0.99**	0.69	**0.99**
$Yahoo_1$	1	0.89	0.89	1	0.75	1
$Yahoo_2$	0.90	**0.96**	**0.96**	0.90	0.78	0.90
$Yahoo_3$	1	0.86	0.82	1	0.5	1
$Yahoo_4$	1	0.96	0.95	1	0.70	1

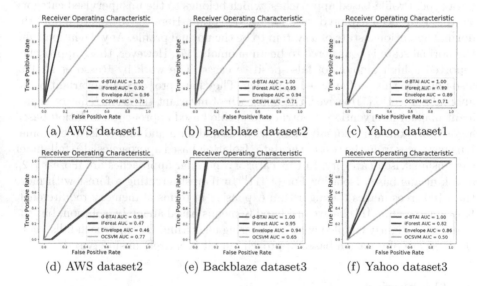

(a) AWS dataset1   (b) Backblaze dataset2   (c) Yahoo dataset1

(d) AWS dataset2   (e) Backblaze dataset3   (f) Yahoo dataset3

Fig. 3. ROC comparison between d-BTAI (K-means) and other algorithms for various datasets

5   Related Work

An early survey by Chandola et al. [7] has reported extensive usage of various supervised algorithms for anomaly detection. These algorithms assume the availability of good training data. A SVM based approach has been developed for

Google's self-driving car [8] where a monitoring system aims to raise the alarm at least 5 min before an impending communication failure. Along with supervised approaches, researchers have explored self-supervised approaches based on Deep Learning (DL) for anomaly detection. For instance, models based on auto-encoders, long-short term memory [9,20] are increasingly gaining attention for anomaly detection. Yin et al. [18] have proposed an integrated model of Convolutional Neural Network (CNN) and Long Short Term Memory networks (LSTM) based auto-encoder for Yahoo Webscope time-series anomaly detection. For reasons unknown, [18] have taken only one Yahoo Webscope data to demonstrate their approach's efficacy. Supervised approaches require labeled data for training the model. These approaches' efficacy relies on the availability of appropriate training data with a good sample of anomalous scenarios. Moreover, a supervised algorithm, trained for one class of machines, may not be extendable. Unsupervised approaches, on the contrary, do not assume the presence of labels in data. Therefore, unsupervised approaches can be a good alternative, specifically when required to focus on anomaly detection of industrial systems. The DeepAnT [13] approach employs DL methods, but it uses unlabeled data for training. However, the approach is meant for time-series data set such as Yahoo Webscope, Real traffic, AWS cloudwatch, and the method requires *retraining* for a different kind of data type. Profile-based approaches, which belongs to the unsupervised category as well, have been explored for anomaly detection. Here the idea is to model the normal operational state of a system to be the normal profile. Any deviation from the normal state is considered to be an anomaly [17]. However, these approaches reported a high amount of false-positive cases. The work by Russo et al. [16] also falls into this profile-based approach. They have proposed an invariant based anomaly detection. However, the approach of invariant selection requires significant manual intervention. Contrary to profile based approaches, isolation based algorithms consider anomaly along with normal data and aim to isolate anomalous instances from the rest of the data. Isolation based approaches also fall under the unsupervised category. In this category, popular approaches are iForest [12], and k-means based Isolation Forest [11]. In iForest, creating a forest with more than 100 trees makes the algorithm expensive in terms of memory requirement. Karczmarek et al. [11] have considered K-means based anomaly isolation, but the approach is tightly coupled with a clustering algorithm. Our approach falls under the category of isolation based approach, and it is entirely unsupervised.

6   Conclusion

In this paper, a novel binary tree-based algorithm (d-BTAI), which has been used to detect anomalies present in various industrial systems is introduced. It has been shown that the algorithm has high specificity values with negligible false negatives. Such a result is undoubtedly quite promising in the context of industrial systems. As for future work, it is required to reduce the dependency of the d-BTAI on the multiple thresholds and explore other metrics, such as path length [12].

References

1. https://webscope.sandbox.yahoo.com/catalog.php?datatype=s&did=70 . Accessed 15 Jan 2019
2. Backblaze failure data. https://www.backblaze.com/b2/hard-drive-test-data.htm. Accessed 2 Mar 2019
3. Globenewswire. https://www.globenewswire.com/news-release/2019/05/13/1822194/0/en/Medical-Equipment-Maintenance-Market-to-Reach-26-4-Billion-by-2024-P-S-Intelligence.html. Accessed 15 Feb 2020
4. Nab. https://github.com/numenta/NAB/tree/master/data. Accessed 15 Jan 2019
5. Apiletti, D., et al.: istep, an integrated self-tuning engine for predictive maintenance in industry 4.0. In: IEEE International Conference on ISPA-IUCC-BDCloud-SocialCom-SustainCom (2018)
6. Bruke, R.: Hazmat studies: Nmr and mri medical scanners: Surviving the ïnvisible force (2012). https://www.firehouse.com/rescue/article/10684588/firefighter-hazmat-situations. Accessed 15 Feb 2019
7. Chandola, V., Banerjee, A., Kumar, V.: Anomaly detection. ACM Comput. Surv. **41**(3), 1–58 (2009). https://doi.org/10.1145/1541880.1541882
8. Chigurupati, A., Thibaux, R., Lassar, N.: Predicting hardware failure using machine learning. In: 2016 Annual Reliability and Maintainability Symposium (RAMS), Tucson, AZ, USA, January 2016. https://doi.org/10.1109/RAMS.2016.7448033
9. Erfani, S., Rajasegarar, S., Karunasekera, S., Leckie, C.: High-dimensional and large-scale anomaly detection using a linear one-class SVM with deep learning. Pattern Recogn. **58**, 121–134 (2016)
10. He, Z., Xu, X., Deng, S.: Discovering cluster-based local outliers. Pattern Recogn. Lett. **24**, 1641–1650 (2003)
11. Karczmarek, P., Kiersztyn, A., Pedrycz, W., Al, E.: K-means-based isolation forest. Knowl. Syst. **195** (2020)
12. Liu, T.F., Ting, M.K., Zhou, Z.H.: Isolation forest. In: 2008 Eighth IEEE International Conference on Data Mining, pp. 273–280 (2008). https://doi.org/10.1109/ICDMW.2016.0046
13. Munir, M., Siddiqui, A.S., Dengel, A., Ahmed, S.: Deepant: a deep learning approach for unsupervised anomaly detection in time series. IEEE Access **1**(1), 1085–1100 (2018). https://doi.org/10.1109/access.2018.2886457
14. Narsingyani, D., Kale, O.: Optimizing false positive in anomaly based intrusion detection using genetic algorithm. In: 2015 IEEE 3rd International Conference on MOOCs, Innovation and Technology in Education (MITE) (2015)
15. Rousseeuw, P.J., Driessen, K.V.: A fast algorithm for the minimum covariance determinant estimator. Technometrics **41**(3), 212–223 (1999). https://doi.org/10.1080/00401706.1999.10485670
16. Russo, A., Sarkar, S., Pecchia, S.: Assessing invariant mining techniques for cloud-based utility computing systems. IEEE Trans. Serv. Comput. (2017)
17. Shang, W., Li, L., Wan, M., Zeng, P.: Industrial communication intrusion detection algorithm based on improved one-class SVM. In: 2015 World Congress on Industrial Control Systems Security (WCICSS) (2015). https://doi.org/10.1109/wcicss.2015.7420317
18. Yin, C., S. Zhang, J.W., Xiong, N.N.: Anomaly detection based on convolutional recurrent autoencoder for IoT time series. IEEE Trans. Syst. Man Cybern. Syst. 1–11 (2020). https://doi.org/10.1109/tsmc.2020.2968516

19. Zhang, L., Lin, J., Karim, R.: Adaptive kernel density-based anomaly detection for nonlinear systems. Knowl. Based Syst. **41**(3), 50–63 (2018)
20. Zhou, C., Paffenroth, R.C.: Anomaly detection with robust deep autoencoders. In: Proceedings of the 23rd ACM SIGKDD International Conference on Knowledge Discovery and Data Mining - KDD (2017). https://doi.org/10.1145/3097983.3098052

Identifying Anomaly Work in Intralogistics Using BLE and LPWA

Masahiro Yamaguchi[1]([⊠])(iD), Noriko Yuasa[1], Yuki Yoshimura[1],
and Takanobu Otsuka[2]([⊠])

[1] Computer Science Program, Graduate School of Engineering,
Nagoya Institute of Technology, Nagoya, Japan
yamaguchi.masahiro@otsukalab.nitech.ac.jp
[2] Department of Computer Science, Graduate School of Engineering,
Nagoya Institute of Technology, Nagoya, Japan
otsuka.takanobu@nitech.ac.jp

Abstract. Due to recent increased competition in the automobile industry, many studies have optimized manufacturing models to reduce costs. However, such studies have produced scant benefits because these models have matured due to the long-term improvements in the automobile industry. Therefore, we propose a way to identify anomaly work in intralogistics. Anomaly work means inefficient work whose efficiency is worse than the normal work in this paper. As a concrete method, workers and forklifts are given BLE beacons, and the radio waves transmitted by them are collected by a sensor network using LPWA. Next the collected BLE beacon data continuously estimate the positions of workers and forklifts and are converted into intralogistics data. Regression analysis is performed on these intralogistics data to identify anomaly work. This proposed method identifies the locations and the times when anomaly work occurs in a factory, and with such data, logistics will be improved and manufacturing costs will be reduced.

Keywords: Intralogistics · BLE · LPWA · Identifying anomaly work

1 Introduction

Competition in the automobile industry has become fiercer. Many studies have addressed the reduction of manufacturing costs, for instance, optimizing manufacturing models. Unfortunately, such studies have produced few benefits, because the models have already matured due to the automobile industry's long-term development [1]. Against that the industrial models are richly researched, the intralogstics admits of more studies. An IoT-based system for improving factory processes was recently proposed [2]. It first installed Bluetooth Low Energy (BLE) beacons in a factory to get the positions of the workers whom it tracks

Supported by the FUTABA INDUSTRIAL CO.

with smart tags. Next it created a heat map from the obtained data and displayed it on a visualization system. The system identified (in processes) problems whose solutions led to improved processes. However, that study's analysis method seems insufficient to actually improve the processes, because it creates a heat map, which is simply based on the amounts of time spent and activity. Such an analysis method is appropriate only if we assume that the staying times and amount of activity of each process are generally constant. But such assumptions do not hold in many factories. Therefore, a method is required that evaluates whether each process's efficiency was better or worse than usual.

We propose a system that identifies anomaly work in intralogistics. In this paper, anomaly work means inefficient work whose efficiency is worse than the normal work, and intrologistics denotes the logistics among manufacturing processes. Our proposed system identifies anomaly work and makes intralogistics efficient using the identified anomaly work data.

This paper is organized as follows: Sect. 2 presents a method for identifying anomaly work in intralogistics. Section 3 evaluates our proposed method, and Finally, Sect. 4 presents the conclusion of this study.

2   Approach to Identify Anomaly Work in Intralogistics

For identifying anomaly work in intralogistics, this section presents an approach that consists of three main technical elements: a sensor network that obtains intralogistics data; a position estimation algorithm that gets the location information of factory workers; an analysis method that identifies anomaly work.

2.1   Sensor Network for Obtaining Intralogistics Data

We constructed a sensor network using Bluetooth Low Energy (BLE) and Low Power Wide Area (LPWA) to obtain intralogistics data. Its outline is shown in Fig. 1. The network collects intralogistics data by the following processes. First, workers and such equipment as forklifts are tagged by BLE beacons, which emit (every three seconds) radio waves, which are received by ESP32 Developers mounted at each base station. The ESP32 Developer acquires BLE beacon identification numbers and the received signal strength indication (RSSI) values from these radio waves and saves the acquired data in an ATSAMD mounted at each base station also. The BLE beacon identification numbers including universally unique identifier(UUID), Major and Minor are used to identify the BLE beacon. Additionally, mentioned below, RSSI values are used to estimate the position where the BLE beacons are. The ATSAMD stores the data for a certain period of time, a minute in this study, and sends them to the ES920LR2 mounted at each base station when the time elapses. When the ES920LR2 receives the data, it sends them to a gateway by LoRa communication. Finally, the gateway stores the data in a data base by Ethernet communication.

In this study, we analyzed and visualized intralogistics by utilizing the BLE beacon data collected by this network.

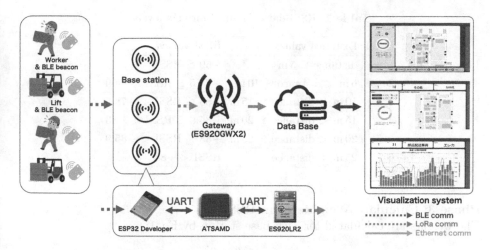

Fig. 1. Sensor network using BLE beacon and LPWA

2.2   Position Estimation Algorithm

We estimated the positions of the BLE beacons to understand their intralogistics. Such information is also crucial for identifying anomaly work. Although the position estimation accuracy is important, based on introducing a hundred, in future more for expanding system, of BLE beacons to a factory, implementing an algorithm that reduces the burden of calculation processing has greater importance. Therefore, we implemented an algorithm that has sufficient accuracy to determine the actual factory routes the BLE beacons are located in and with a small computational load.

Many studies have addressed position estimation using BLE beacons [3–7]. Unfortunately, our study struggled to implement these algorithms due to installation or calculation costs, position estimation accuracy, for example. Thus, we propose a position estimation algorithm that is comprised of the following phases.

Phase 1: Capturing BLE Beacon Data
As described in Sect. 2.1, the ESP32 Developer receives the radio waves transmitted by the BLE beacons attached to workers and forklifts.

Phase 2: Classifying and Storing the RSSI Data
The received signal strength indication (RSSI) values fluctuate due to the effects of radio wave absorption and reflections [3]. This fluctuation must be smoothed to improve the position estimation accuracy. Therefore, the ESP32 Developer classifies the RSSI values into six levels (Table 1). At this time, the thresholds of the six levels are based on the RSSI data calculated from a relationship between the RSSI and distance [6]. In addition, the ESP32 Developer temporarily stores the BLE beacon data, including the classified RSSI data, in the ATSAMD to compress the BLE beacon data. These classification and compression average the RSSI's fluctuate and make computational load at server be small.

Table 1. RSSI data classified into six levels

Level	Distance values	RSSI values
1	distance $\leq 5\,\mathrm{m}$	$-69 \leq$ RSSI
2	$5\,\mathrm{m} <$ distance $\leq 10\,\mathrm{m}$	$-78.5 \leq$ RSSI < -69
3	$10\,\mathrm{m} <$ distance $\leq 15\,\mathrm{m}$	$-83 \leq$ RSSI < -78.5
4	$15\,\mathrm{m} <$ distance $\leq 20\,\mathrm{m}$	$-85.9 \leq$ RSSI < -83
5	$20\,\mathrm{m} <$ distance $\leq 25\,\mathrm{m}$	$-88 \leq$ RSSI < -85.9
6	$25\,\mathrm{m} <$ distance	RSSI < -88

Phase 3: Calculate Weights from RSSI

The weights are calculated for each base station by Eq. 1:

$$W_{result} = \sum_{i=1}^{6} W_i C_i, \tag{1}$$

where

W_{result} is the result of the weight,

W_i is the weight of RSSI level i (1 to 6), and

C_i is the count of RSSI level i (1 to 6) that has been observed for a minute.

Phase 4: Estimate the Positions of the BLE Beacons

In this phase, first, the top two weights are identified from each base station. Next the BLE beacon position is estimated by Eq. 2 based on a weighted centroid localization algorithm [8]:

$$(x, y) = \left(\frac{\omega_1 x_1 + \omega_2 x_2}{\omega_1 + \omega_2}, \frac{\omega_1 y_1 + \omega_2 y_2}{\omega_1 + \omega_2} \right), \tag{2}$$

where

(x, y) is the coordinate of the position estimation result,

(x_i, y_i) is the coordinate of the base station that has the ith highest weight, and

ω_i is the ith highest weight.

Phase 5: Modify the Estimated Position

In this study, we assumed that workers and forklifts can pass only on a path, which denotes a factory route through which both workers and forklifts can navigate. If the estimated position coordinates calculated before the prior phase are not on the path, this estimated coordinates must be modified to the nearest point on the path.

2.3   Analysis Method of Identifying Anomaly Work

Recall that our study's objective is identifying anomaly work in intralogistics. In this section, continuous location information is considered intralogistics data, and anomaly works are identified by analyzing these data. Intralogistics data consist of three parameters: "X," which is the longitude estimated in Sect. 2.2; "Y," which is the latitude estimated in Sect. 2.2; and "Distance," which is the shortest distance on paths from one estimated coordinate to the next estimated coordinate. The Distance is calculated by Dijksta's algorithm [9] and Eq. 3.

$$d = r \cos^{-1} \left(\sin y_1 \sin y_2 + \cos y_1 \cos y_2 \cos(x_2 - x_1) \right), \qquad (3)$$

where

d is the Distance result,

r $(= 6378.137\,\text{km})$ is the radius of the equator,

x_i is the longitude of the ith coordinate, and

y_i is the latitude of the ith coordinate.

Regression analysis is performed on these intralogistics data to identify anomaly work. An analysis flow for intralogistics data is shown in Fig. 2. It is mentioned above, we assumed that workers and forklifts can pass only on a path in this paper. Therefore, intralogistics data can be conducted regression analysis for each cross-sectional in scatter plot of intralogistics data since intralogstics data always exists on a path. In addition, here regression analysis is conducted three times: first it conducts regression analysis for raw intralogistics data; second it conducts regression analysis for intralogistics data whose Distance is halved; third it conducts regression analysis for intralogistics data whose Distance is 1/8. For this analysis, we obtain three regression curves whose color is green, yellow and red represented in Fig. 2. Starting from the curve with the largest Distance value, the following four regions are obtained with these three curves as boundaries: "Better Work," "Good Work," "Caution Work," and the "Alert Work" areas. We define the intralogistics data found in the "Alert Work" area as anomaly work in this paper.

This analysis can assess how much activity workers or forklifts normally perform at a given coordinate. In addition, a type of work whose Distance is much smaller than the normal work at a certain coordinate can be regarded as anomaly work. Thereby, we assume anomaly work will be identified by these approach. In the next section, we will verify whether this analysis method can be used to identify anomaly work in an actual factory.

3 Verification Experiment

In this section, we verify the identification of our anomaly work approach. We describe the experiment setting and our result and analysis.

3.1 Experiment Setting

The sensor network described in Sect. 2.1 was constructed at Factory of the FUTABA INDUSTRIAL CO. With our proposed method, we divided the Factory into nine paths and evaluated the paths where and the time periods during which anomaly work is likely to occur. The nine paths in the Factory are defined as Path0 to Path8.

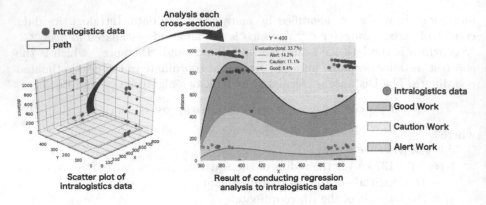

Fig. 2. Analysis flow for intralogistics data (Color figure online)

3.2 Experiment Result and Analysis

Table 2 shows the analysis result of the intralogistics data obtained on 2020/01/08 for each path. In the Anomaly column, Path8 represents the largest value with the highest occurrence of anomaly work during the experiment day; Path2 represents the largest Better value, meaning that the workers and fork-lifts functioned smoothly on this path on the experiment day. In this way, the proposed method evaluated which path was prone to anomaly work.

We also analyzed the intralogistics data not only for each path but also for the time shown in Table 3. The Anomaly column shows the largest value from 06:00 to 08:00. According to this result, Path8 had the highest occurrence of anomaly work from 06:00 to 08:00 on this day. This was probably due to the fact that the shift change between the day and night shifts at this factory took place at 08:00, during which time the work could not be done smoothly. In this

Table 2. Result of analyzing intralogistics data for each path on experiment day

Path	Anomaly (%)	Somewhat (%)	Good (%)	Better (%)
Path0	15.3	5.1	18.5	61.1
Path1	21.7	34.2	11.3	32.8
Path2	15.9	7.7	7.7	**68.7**
Path3	10.9	5.5	28.8	54.8
Path4	22.0	31.6	5.9	40.5
Path5	24.6	17.7	12.0	45.7
Path6	15.3	5.1	18.5	61.1
Path7	9.7	23.2	34.7	32.4
Path8	**29.8**	23.7	11.9	34.6

Table 3. Result of analyzing intralogistics data of path: 8 for time

Time (hh-hh)	Anomaly (%)	Somewhat (%)	Good (%)	Better (%)
00–02	17.9	27.6	6.7	47.8
02–04	25.2	18.7	2.9	53.2
04–06	16.8	29.4	11.8	42.0
06–08	**32.7**	24.2	11.8	31.3
08–10	11.2	15.0	16.2	57.6
10–12	10.6	10.6	21.3	57.5
12–14	18.3	27.5	14.7	39.5
14–16	15.6	17.7	9.4	57.3
16–18	18.3	17.4	10.1	54.2
18–20	18.3	28.0	12.2	41.5
20–22	16.1	28.8	13.6	41.5
22–24	7.8	27.8	10.0	54.4

way, the proposed method evaluated the time period when anomaly work was likely to occur on a certain path.

4   Conclusion

We proposed a system for identifying anomaly work in intralogistics by constructing a sensor network using BLE and LPWA and classifying the intralogistics data acquired by it by regression analysis. Our proposed method identifies the locations and times when anomaly work occurs. With such information, the logistics can be improved and manufacturing costs reduced.

Although not mentioned in this paper for example, at the FUTABA INDUSTRIAL CO factory where proposed system was used, they actually identified areas where the layout of the factory made forklift traffic difficult. Furthermore, modifying such layout, they improved intralogistics at these areas. In the future, we plan to evaluate these case studies quantitatively.

References

1. Zhou, Y., Chen, G.: Research on an automobile company's factory logistics optimization. In: 2020 International Conference on Artificial Intelligence and Electromechanical Automation (AIEA), Tianjin, China, pp. 168–171 (2020). https://doi.org/10.1109/AIEA51086.2020.00042
2. Nakata, S., Okamoto, A., Horikawa, M., Sato, Y.: Proposal of Utilization Method for Process Improvement Using Smart Tags, Information Processing Society of Japan (IPSJ), pp. 205–206 (2020)
3. Sano, H., Tsukamoto, M., Katagiri, M., Ikeda, D., Ohta, K.: Improving robustness against BLE beacon failures in indoor position system. Inf. Process. Soc. Japan (IPSJ) **58**(5), 1138–1150 (2017)
4. Torteeka, P., Chundi, X., Dongkai, Y.: Hybrid technique for indoor positioning system based on Wi-Fi received signal strength indication. In: 2014 International Conference on Indoor Positioning and Indoor Navigation (IPIN), Busan, pp. 48–57 (2014). https://doi.org/10.1109/IPIN.2014.7275467
5. Baniukevic, A., Sabonis, D., Jensen, C.S., Lu, H.: Improving Wi-Fi based indoor positioning using bluetooth add-ons. In: 2011 IEEE 12th International Conference on Mobile Data Management, Lulea, pp. 246–255 (2011). https://doi.org/10.1109/MDM.2011.50
6. Liu, H., Darabi, H., Banerjee, P., Liu, J.: Survey of wireless indoor positioning techniques and systems. IEEE Trans. Syst. Man Cybern. Part C (Appl. Rev.) **37**(6), 1067–1080 (2007). https://doi.org/10.1109/TSMCC.2007.905750
7. Figueira, B., Goncalves, B., Folgado, H., Masiulis, N., Calleja-Gonzalez, J., Sampaio, J.: Accuracy of a basketball indoor tracking system based on standard bluetooth low energy channels (NBN23R). Sensors (2018)
8. Ru, L., Zhang, L.: A weighted centroid localization algorithm for wireless sensor networks based on weight correction. In: 2017 9th International Conference on Advanced Infocomm Technology (ICAIT), Chengdu, pp. 165–169 (2017). https://doi.org/10.1109/ICAIT.2017.8388908
9. Johnson, D.B.: A note on Dijksta's shortest path algorithm. J. ACM (1973). https://doi.org/10.1145/321765.321768

Financial and Supply Chain
Applications

Impact Analysis of Proactive and Reactive Inventory Disruption Management on Supply Chain Performance

Maroua Kessentini[✉] and Narjes Bellamine Ben Saoud

University Manouba, ENSI, RIADI LR99ES26 Campus Universitaire Manouba 2010, Manouba, Tunisie

Abstract. An inventory management system is a complex network of worldwide components that produce, handle and distribute specific products. This heterogeneous components as well as distributed decision making across such components, make this system a complex network that needs a special kind of activities management. These activities allows company to prevent and react more quickly to the dynamic events. For this purpose, an appropriate modeling and simulation tools that allows system performance analysis under various conditions is required. Agent-based technology has been proven as a suitable approach for modeling such complex networks with distributed actors. This paper illustrates the utility of agent-based modeling to evaluate the impact of disruptions on system performance. The model can be useful to prevent and react against the effects of disruption events. The inventory system's behavior, as well as the effects of handling strategies during disruption situations, is studied. As an illustrative case, agent-based simulation models of distribution chain that buys and distributes final products are introduced. The major observation from the simulation experiments is that our model can be applied to quantify the impacts of key strategies on system performance compared to the non-use of action.

Keywords: Agent-based modeling · Inventory management system · Disruption management · Performance analysis · Decision support

1 Introduction

A supply chain is composed of interrelated components in different geographical locations structured to acquire raw materials, convert them to finished products, and deliver these products to the end customers [1]. The actors involved in this network form an interconnected complex system. Each entity in this complex network has its own goals and responsibilities for various internal activities (such as planning, scheduling, inventory management) that are sometimes in conflict with others. Further, the complex behavior is not only due to system's

© Springer Nature Switzerland AG 2021
H. Fujita et al. (Eds.): IEA/AIE 2021, LNAI 12799, pp. 543–553, 2021.
https://doi.org/10.1007/978-3-030-79463-7_46

heterogeneous components but also the distributed decision making across various actors involved in this network. The interaction between these entities is added to the complexity. Therefore, this complex network needs a special kind of activities management to study the dynamic of the system and to examine the effects of alternative solutions and policies in system performance. Thus, developing appropriate models to study and support the supply network components' behaviors and effects on system performance are called for. A model should have a deep understanding of the whole system and reflect all these complexities. It aims to help decision makers to study alternative designs and also to improve the operation with respect to some important performance indicators.

Appropriate activities management enables company to react more quickly to the dynamic events, reduce its operating costs and increase customer satisfaction in the normal cases. Moreover, it can be more resilient and recover from disruption more rapidly during disruption cases [2]. To manage disruptions, a trail from risk identification to disruption handling is needed to follow. Many key trends and practices need to be orchestrated during a disruption management process, e.g. multi or dual sourcing, internal and external safety stocks, flexibility, information sharing and partners' collaboration, and supplier contracting [3–5].

Analytical models to deals with inventory disruptions problems in supply chain have received much attention in literature [6]. Most of them are based on operations research approaches and mathematical programming. Despite their potential, it's hard to deal with uncertain problems taking into account the inter-organizational complexity of inventory network problem. In such situations, agent-based models can provide an alternative approach to constructing an artificial environment within which the dynamicity of disruptions can be assessed. The disruptive events and uncertainties as risk sources can be modeled in agent's behaviors considering their ability to incorporate discrete-event simulation mechanisms. These systems provide a very comprehensive simulation and analysis environment for comparing alternative risk mitigation solutions with various constraints based on multiple performance measures. Nevertheless, compared with many efforts on optimization-based methods, research works on agent-based models for inventory disruption problem in supply chain are very limited.

This paper considers a distribution chain and its performance analysis in pre and post disruption situations using an agent-based model. The model allows to analyze the dynamicity of inventory system and to examine different experiments with realistic policies by referring to different decision-making levels.

2   Agent-Based Modeling and Inventory Disruption Management Problem

Agent-based modeling and simulation is considered as a promising approach to modeling complex systems comprised of interacting autonomous agents. Given that, agents have the following main characteristics enabling them to model distributed and decentralized problems. First of the all, the autonomy behavior of agents make able take decisions without a central controller by a collection of rules that determine their behavior. Likewise, the proactive behavior authorizes not only to act in response to changes that have occurred in their environments but also to have their own goals. Another characteristic of agents is that they have social-ability to communicate amongst each [7].

By analogies, inventory system can be presented as a modular, decentralized, adaptive and complex system composed of many heterogeneous and dynamic components. These components are customers, the focal firm and suppliers. The overall behavior of the system emerges from the interaction of these components. Each component can be located in different locations and has some level of autonomy to control its own actions and states. Decision making is also distributed across the different components or maybe across various departments in the same component. They interact amongst each other and through material and information flows. Each component or department has a specific role and perform certain tasks/activities by its own policies. Accordingly, agent-based modeling conveys the concepts needed to describe more precisely how the methods could be undertaken in domain dependent models focused on the notion of an agent. Agent-based models permit the simulation of involved actor's decisional processes and the evaluation of solution pertinence. Moreover, it also allows describing how help enacting disruption management policies by referring to the cooperative processes.

It is then evident that the components of the inventory system have the same basic characteristics as an agent namely autonomy, social-ability, pro-activeness and dynamicity. The dynamic behavior emerges from the individual behavior of different actors and their interactions. In addition the flexible behavior of agent can be easily used to conceive many experiments related to the structure of actors and to study their effects on the desired performance of the system. Thus, agent-based modeling looks like an appropriate approach that allows the modeling and the analyzing of inventory system performance as decentralized and complex system.

The next section illustrates the usage of agent-based modeling for inventory disruptions management problem.

3 Agent-Based Model for Handling Disruptions

Solving disruption in each inventory system might include different kinds of activities. Although some activities are taken to minimize the exposure to potential disruptions, disruptive events might happen and influence firm's performances. Therefore, these activities can be divided in two major categories: pre-disruption (before) as proactive view and post-disruption (after) as reactive view.

Despite the role of investing in risk prevention to reduce disruptions, prevent each disruption is not possible. So, when disruptions cannot be prevented, the attention will be given to the response side. Therefore to enhance the efficiency of disruption management, what firms do before and after the occurrence of the disruption are both important and should be implemented and coordinated. Thus, in order to manage disruptions effectively, both perspectives must be addressed. Thereby, these two perspectives are coupled and an integrated and interconnected view of both cycles is proposed with strong mutual feedback as delineated Fig. 1.

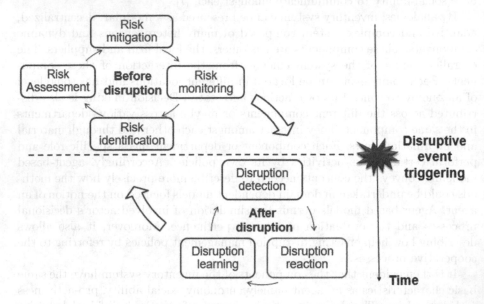

Fig. 1. An integrated and interconnected cycle for solving disruptions.

As this paper will focus only in evaluating the impact of disruptions as well as the effect of risk mitigation and disruption reaction strategies on system performance, identifying the boundary of our chain are being essential. The chain studied here comprises three main actors: Customers, suppliers, and the distribution center itself. The distribution center has multiple suppliers at different locations. All suppliers can provide various types of products in order to fulfill a set of customer orders. The actors in this chain can be viewed in two levels as shown in Fig. 2:

- Global level: we propose to assign three agents for each identified actor in the supply chain who will help the smooth running of the exchanges of physical and information flows: the supplier agents, the customer agents and the distribution center agent.
- Distribution center level: The distribution center can be seen as a multi-agent system constitute of three main agents namely the monitoring agent that allows the detection of disruptions, the management agent that allows perform management tasks in the pre and post disruption cases and the interface Agent who receives the order from the customers, responds to their requests and places orders to the supplier based on stock policy used.

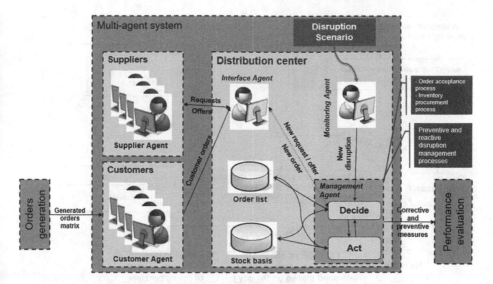

Fig. 2. Proposed multi-agent organization.

3.1 Order Generation

The order generation process is presented in Fig. 3. It is adapted form [8]. This procedure consists firstly in determining an estimated demand curve $DD_{p,d}$ where p represents the product and d represents the index for each day. The next step is to translate the demand curve into discrete orders by firstly determine the cumulative monthly demand $MD_{p,m}$ where m represents the index for each month. After that, for each customer, a uniform [0, 1] random variable $\mu_{p,d}$ is generated every day in the month. This variable is compared to the order frequency index f_p to capture the uncertainty of order occurrence $ratd_{p,d}$. We assume that, on each day, each customer can send at most one order for each product type. For each month m, the portion of monthly demand $DR_{p,d}$ that is placed on the day d following an order occurrence is next generated. Given that the calculated demand amount might be unreasonably low or high, we generate the actual demand after accounting for the minimum and maximum order size limits, D_{min} and D_{max}, respectively. $AD_{p,d}$ represents one customer order that will be created if $AD_{p,d} > 0$.

3.2 Inventory Management

For inventory management, the reorder point policy is used in this paper. Using this policy, the product will be purchased when its inventory level IR_p falls below the reorder point RR_p. The amount of the product p purchased $RP_p(d)$ is then calculated. $RP_p(d) = RT_p - IR_p(d) + \sum RW_p(d)$ if $IR_p(d) + \sum RW_p(d) < RR_p$. Otherwise $RP_p(d) = 0$. RT_p represents the maximum capacity of storage tanks and RW_p is the amount of the product p that has been ordered but not yet arrived.

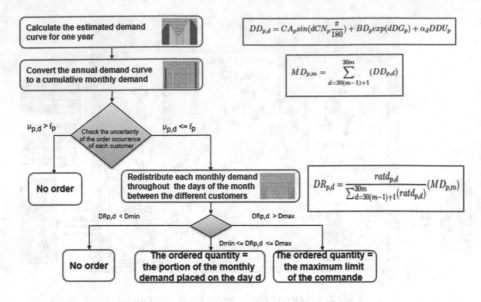

Fig. 3. Order generation process (adapted from [8]).

3.3 Order Acceptance

Each day, the customers' orders are stored in a list. Accordingly, acceptance/rejection/negotiation decisions are taken for each order in the list. The top order in the list is considered for evaluation, the decision is taken and again the new top order is considered until the list is empty. First, the profitability level of the order is checked. The order is considered profitable when it revenue is equal or larger than 20% of it incurred costs. Accordingly, six possible cases can be taken into account as presented in Fig. 4.

3.4 Disruption Management

The first step in disruption management is generating a disruption scenario. Accordingly, the occurrence of a disruption is firstly checked by generating a uniform $[0, 1]$ random number and comparing it with the probability of a disruption to occur D_p. If the random number is less than D_p, so there is a disruption in that day (the disruption start time (DST) = d). Next, the disruption duration DD is defined according to triangular distribution. Finally, the disruption end time DET = DST + DD can be calculated.

Once disruption scenario is generated, handling strategies can be defined and implemented. In this work, we consider two prevention strategies and three reactive strategies for experimentation. As prevention strategies, we consider the inventory mitigation (carries some excess inventory) and the sourcing mitigation (sources from two suppliers kinds i.e. one global supplier and one backup high-cost supplier). As reactive strategies, we consider the emergency procurement

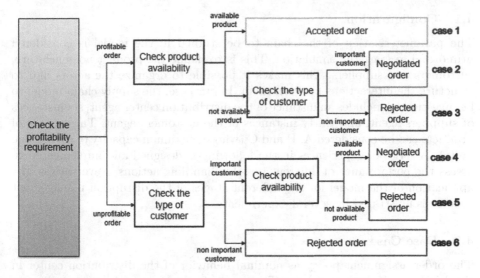

Fig. 4. Possible case for order acceptance process.

(placing an emergency order to alternative suppliers and assigns the request to the supplier(s) with the nearest delivery time), the customer negotiation (re-negotiate with some customers to extend their orders' due date if the orders affected by the disruption are accepted before the announcement of the disruption or adjusts the order acceptance strategy else) and orders re-allocation (exchange the orders affected by the disruption between the different resources currently available).

3.5 Performance Measuring

The performance can be measured through various key performance indicators: logistics and financial performances. As logistics performances, we consider customer satisfaction (the percentage of on time deliveries out of the number of accepted orders), the number of late orders (the number of accepted orders less the number of on-time deliveries orders) and the total tardiness. And as financial performances, we consider the profit that is measured as the revenue minus the various Costs (the transportation cost, the late delivery penalty, the purchasing cost, the storage cost and the fixed operating cost).

4 Experiments

The developed model will be used in some experimental configurations for decision making support in the management of pre and post disruptions at different stages in the supply chain.

4.1   Configuration

The parameterization of the chain to be studied in the model is considered primordial to start the simulation. This is to define the product nomenclature, customers and suppliers. This makes it possible to organize the actors and to structure the interactions between them. In our case, the supply chain model to be investigated includes an instance of the distribution center agent, six instances of suppliers agent, and thirty instances of the customers agent. Three types of products can be considered A, B and C (whose maximum capacity of each is 800 units). A series of experiences in the following is designed and implemented to assess the performance of different possible handling actions. Nevertheless, the application of the model for the different stages of the disruption management process is illustrated by several experiments.

4.2   Base Case

The order assignment policy as nominal behavior of the distribution center in the base case is presented here. Three specific cases on order acceptance are experimented. The first case concerns the no-negotiation case in which customer orders will be accepted as long as the product is available before the due date. The second case is about the order selectivity case in which the level of profitability of the order is checked. In the third case (the negotiation case), an order that cannot be accepted will not be immediately rejected but will be negotiated to reach an agreement on the due date. The results of simulation are presented in Fig. 5.

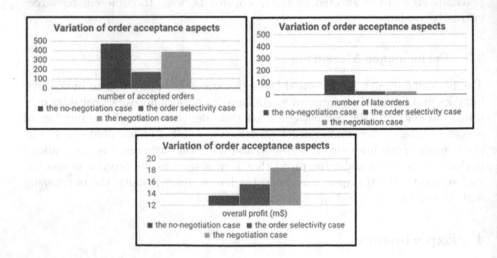

Fig. 5. Simulation results of the order acceptance process cases.

The results shows that the number of accepted orders in the no-negotiation case is considerably higher than in the other two cases. This can be explained by the fact that the only criterion of orders acceptance is the availability of the products. However, the number of late orders in this case is much higher than in the other two cases. On the other hand, the overall profit in the case of negotiation is greatly increased compared to the two other cases. As a conclusion, the negotiation allows to improve company' profit.

The other nominal behavior of the distribution center is the inventory assignment policy. Two category of supplier are experimented: a global supplier with delivery time of 7 days and a local supplier with delivery time of 4 days but with 25% higher unit product price. As the reorder point policy is used, we assume that the reorder point can be on 25% or 40% of the capacity of storage and that the inventory top-up-to level S is set as the maximum capacity of storage. The simulation results are presented in Fig. 6.

Fig. 6. Simulation results of the Inventory Management Process.

The results shows that the delivery time can not generally be considered as an important factor in comparing it to the inventory management policy. The second obvious conclusion is that the policy (s, S) with s = 40% gives better results and can be considered as a point of reference. The implementation of an appropriate inventory management policy should therefore be considered as the main factor for improving the inventory management process. However, selecting a higher control point can increase the cost of storage and subsequently decrease the profit.

4.3   Pre-disruption Situation (Proactive Manner)

The disruption considered for experimentation is the supplier disruption. The probability of this disruption is $D_p = 0,005$ (or the expected frequency of once per 200 days). And the duration is sampled from a triangular distribution with a minimum value of 5 days, a most likely value of 10 days and a maximum value of 20 days. The results comparing the inventory mitigation, the sourcing mitigation and the case of no mitigation action are presented in Fig. 7.

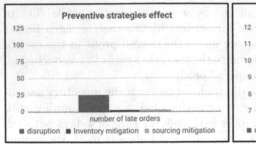 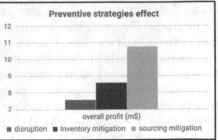

Fig. 7. Effect of preventive strategies on the chain performance.

As can be seen, by defining a prevention strategy, profit can be improved up to 13–42%. The average profit for sourcing mitigation strategy however is higher in comparison with the other two options. It can be concluded that this strategy is the appropriate strategy to manage supplier disruptions.

4.4 Post-disruption Situation (Reactive Manner)

In this experiment, we considers that supplier disruption is occurs on day 148 of the simulation horizon. The abnormal event will result in 25 late orders with 46 late days. As mentioned before, three possible actions to react to this disruption: emergency demand, re-assignment of orders and customer negotiation. For customer negotiation action, we run the simulation with two possible parameters. The probability of the customer agreeing to extend the delivery date is estimated at 35% for the optimistic case and 15% for the pessimistic case. The result is presented in Fig. 8.

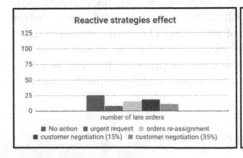 

Fig. 8. Effect of reactive policies on the chain performance.

As we can be shown, the emergency demand results in a considerable improvement in logistic performance. However, the other two policies can also improve the logistic performance of 25 late orders to an average of 15 late orders. On the other hand, in terms of financial performance, negotiation with the client is the most attractive policy. This is explained by this policy does not entail additional costs for its implementation. Of course, many other alternative policies and different combinations of the aforementioned policies can be tested with the model. Nevertheless, the experiences mentioned here fulfil our purpose of showing that our model can support more informed decision-making before and after disruption.

5   Concluding Remarks

The main objective of this paper is to capitalize the knowhow handling strategies of supply chain in order to model inventory disruption management problem. According to this, we present how agent-based modeling can be used as a decision making support in inventory network during pre and post disruption situations. The model allows evaluating and analyzing different policies to handle the effects of disruption and their effect on system performance. The results of the experiments highlight the applicability of agent-based models to identify key strategies for handling inventory disruptions and to quantify their impacts on system performance compared to the non-use of action. In the future, the model can be extended by having more suppliers and customers with different geographical locations and by providing current agents with more complex decision making capabilities. Also, applying the model to real cases can be another important direction for future research. We will also explore means to choose the appropriate handling strategy to the disruptive problem based on the overall system performance by coupling logistic and financial performance indicators.

References

1. Garcia, D.J., You, F.: Supply chain design and optimization: challenges and opportunities. Comput. Chem. Eng. **81**, 153–170 (2015)
2. Scheibe, K.P., Blackhurst, J.: Supply chain disruption propagation: a systemic risk and normal accident theory perspective. Int. J. Prod. Res. **56**(1–2), 43–59 (2018)
3. Narayanan, S., Narasimhan, R., Schoenherr, T.: Assessing the contingent effects of collaboration on agility performance in buyer-supplier relationships. J. Oper. Manage. **33**, 140–154 (2015)
4. Palmer, C., Urwin, E.N., Niknejad, A., Petrovic, D., Popplewell, K., Young, R.I.M.: An ontology supported risk assessment approach for the intelligent configuration of supply networks. J. Intell. Manuf. **29**(5), 1005–1030 (2016). https://doi.org/10.1007/s10845-016-1252-8
5. Tsai, W.C.: A dynamic sourcing strategy considering supply disruption risks. Int. J. Prod. Res. **54**(7), 2170–2184 (2016)
6. Hassini, E., Surti, C., Searcy, C.: A literature review and a case study of sustainable supply chains with a focus on metrics. Int. J. Prod. Econ. **140**(1), 69–82 (2012)
7. Kumar, V., Srinivasan, S.: A review of supply chain management using multi-agent system. Int. J. Comput. Sci. Issues (IJCSI) **7**(5), 198 (2010)
8. Adhitya, A., Srinivasan, R.: Dynamic simulation and decision support for multisite specialty chemicals supply chain. Ind. Eng. Chem. Res. **49**(20), 9917–9931 (2010)

A ML-Based Stock Trading Model for Profit Predication

Jimmy Ming-Tai Wu[1], Lingyun Sun[1], Gautam Srivastava[2],
and Jerry Chun-Wei Lin[3(✉)]

[1] College of Computer Science and Engineering, Shandong University of Science
and Technology, Qingdao, China
wmt@wmt35.idv.tw, 201983060020@sdust.edu.cn
[2] Department of Mathematics and Computer Science, Brandon University,
Brandon, Canada
SRIVASTAVAG@brandonu.ca
[3] Department of Computer Science, Electrical Engineering and Mathematical
Science, Western Norway University of Applied Sciences, Bergen, Norway
jerrylin@ieee.org

Abstract. This paper uses a new convolutional neural network framework to collect data on leading indicators including historical prices and their futures and options, and use arrays as the input map of the CNN framework for stock prices trend prediction. Experiments are then conducted by the stock markets of the United States and Taiwan using historical data, futures and options as data sets to predict the stock prices. After that, genetic algorithm is then utilized to find trading signals. Results showed that the designed model achieves good return of the investments.

Keywords: Convolutional neural network · Genetic algorithm · Trading signals · Leading indicators

1 Introduction

The financial market [19] is a mechanism for determining the price of financial funds and trading financial assets. It is a market that enables the financing of securities and the trading of securities. The capital market is also called "long-term financial market", which mainly includes the stock market, fund market, and bond market. Its volatility can reflect the degree of risk of assets. The fluctuation of stock prices plays a considerable role in the appropriate timing of buying and selling stocks [13]. For investors, the true meaning of investing in the stock market is to obtain extraordinary returns by buying low and selling high, so the prediction of stock price fluctuations has become a special focus of private investors and investment companies [16].

Investors are not completely rational, for example, people may have positive or negative emotions at certain moments [2,6,10,11,14]. Therefore, after this

© Springer Nature Switzerland AG 2021
H. Fujita et al. (Eds.): IEA/AIE 2021, LNAI 12799, pp. 554–563, 2021.
https://doi.org/10.1007/978-3-030-79463-7_47

hypothesis was raised, there were both support and opposition, thus becoming one of the most controversial investment theories [4,8]. Some researchers believe that if the trading signals [3] of the stocks can be found, the stocks can be bought and sold at the appropriate time to obtain relatively high profits.

Deep learning is based on traditional neural networks, including convolutional neural networks, recurrent neural networks, etc., and has good results in image recognition, text classification, machine translation and other fields. It forms the consistency of specific data and the consistency of goals on the basis of specific data, especially the rise of convolutional neural networks in deep learning research. At present, many researchers have applied convolutional neural networks to the prediction of the stock market [9,18].

The main contributions of this article are as follows. First, this study uses a two-dimensional tensor as the input of the SSACNN framework, and divides the output into three categories: rising, falling and unchanged. Also, the SSACNN framework and genetic algorithm are combined to propose a stock trading system. This system can find stock trading signals relatively well, so that investors can get a certain amount of income.

2 Related Work

The prediction of stock prices is mainly the analysis of historical behaviors, such as people's historical emotions, historical market information, etc., and then useful features are extracted from them to train better predictive models. The value of stock prices is a time series. Revealing the development and changes of stock prices is an objective record of stock historical behavior. In the early days of the stock market, a host of investors relied on their own experience to judge stock price movements, which seemed too subjective and lacked scientific basis. In addition, stock prices are also affected by many other factors. For instance, Zheng et al. [21] studied the relationship between exchange rates and stock prices on the Hong Kong stock market.

Intelligent optimization algorithms are used to find the optimal solution. In recent years, researchers have been more enthusiastic about using genetic algorithms to solve problems. In the financial market, many researchers also use genetic algorithms to find stock trading signals. Allen et al. [1] used the genetic algorithm to learn a technical trading rule based on the daily prices of the S&P 500 index from 1928 to 1995. Based on a series of technical indicators that generate buying and selling signals [17], a genetic algorithm is used to propose a trading strategy. Hirabayashi et al. [12] proposed a genetic algorithm system to find suitable trading signals and automatically generate trading rules based on technical indicators. The focus of this system is not to predict the price of the transaction, but to find the right trading opportunity. Lin et al. [15] used genetic algorithms to set optimal values for the parameters of the problem, and bought or sold stocks at the appropriate trading time.

3 Methodology

3.1 Designed Optimization Framework

The stock market has always been the focus of investors' attention. As the stock market is affected in many ways, finding trading signals for stocks is always a big problem. In the past, investors generally used trading strategies to obtain stock trading signals, which were generated by technical indicators or fundamentals [5,7]. CNN has been proven to have good image recognition capabilities, and many researchers have also used CNN for stock price prediction.

CNN includes convolutional layer, pooling layer and fully connected layer. The convolution layer mainly extracts local features of the input data. The researcher defines a convolution kernel inside the convolution layer. Its shape is a square matrix that is used to extract a certain feature. The convolution kernel is multiplied by the corresponding bits of the digital input matrix and then added to obtain the output value of a convolution layer. The calculation process is shown in Eq. 1.

$$V_{a,b}^L = \imath \left(\sum_{m=0}^{K-1} \sum_{n=0}^{K-1} w_{m,n} V_{a+m,b+n}^{L-1} + biase^{L-1} \right) \tag{1}$$

In the Eq. 1, $V_{a,b}^L$ is the value of layer L at row a, column b, $\imath$ is a activation function. $bias^{L-1}$ is represent the bias of $L-1$. $w_{m,n}$ is the weight of convolution filter at row m, column n. The formula for calculating the output image size of the convolutional layer is shown in Eq. 2.

$$w' = \frac{w + 2p - k}{s} + 1 \tag{2}$$

Among them, the size of the convolution kernel is k, the size of the input matrix is w, the number of zero-filling layers is p, and the step size is s. Give an example for this progress, the input layer $L-1$ is set as a 5×5 matrix and use the 3×3 convolutional filter. The layer of input L is calculated by Eq. 1, which is set as 3×3. Because one convolution kernel recognizes one feature, and the input data may have multiple features, there may be numerous convolution kernels in one convolution layer to extract multiple features. We then use the output of the obtained convolution layer as the input of the pooling layer.

However, before entering the value into the pooling layer, an activation function is usually added to solve the nonlinear problem. At present, the activation function Relu (Rectified Linear Unit) is commonly used, which is shown in Eq. 3.

$$f(x) = \begin{cases} 0, x \leq 0 \\ x, x > 0 \end{cases} \tag{3}$$

The pooling layer is mainly used to reduce the number of training parameters and reduce the dimension of the feature vector output by the convolution layer. The most common pooling layers are maximum pooling and mean pooling.

In this article, we choose maximum pooling; that is, the maximum value in a specified area is selected to represent the entire area. The output value of the pooling layer is then expanded as the input of the fully connected layer to generate the final output.

After several times of convolution, excitation, and pooling, the model will learn a high-quality feature map, and then input the feature map to the fully connected layer to get the final output. The calculation process is shown in Eq. 4.

$$V_a^b = \imath \left(\sum_K V_K^{b-1} w_{K,a}^{b-1} + biase^{b-1} \right) \tag{4}$$

In this formula, V_a^b is the value of layer b in neuron a, $\imath$ is an activation function, and $w_{K,a}^{b-1}$ is a weight which connects between neuron K from layer $b\text{-}1$ and neuron a from layer b. $bias^{b-1}$ represents the bias of $b-1$. The pseudo-code of this process is shown in Algorithm 1.

Algorithm 1. Designed model

Require: d is the data of training; K is the data of testing; Z is the number of iteration; A is batch size; Algorithm SGD is named *Adam*.
Ensure: the train model m; evaluation result *accuracy*
1: Initialize algorithm
2: $d \leftarrow Initializealgorithm$
3: $S \leftarrow$ (split d in equal parts of A)
4: **for** each round $t = 1, 2, ..., z$ **do**
5:     $\{verify, train\} \leftarrow \{S_t, S - S_t\}$
6:     $(tf, vf) \leftarrow$ (generate feature of $train$ and $verify$)
7:     $m_t \leftarrow$ modelFit($Adam, tf$)
8:     $r_t \leftarrow$ modelEvaluate(m_t, vf)
9: **end for**
10: $m \leftarrow$ bestModel
11: $K \leftarrow m$
12: $accuracy \leftarrow$ modelEvaluate($m, test$)

In this study, the stock data for a period of time is converted into an image, and this image is used as the input of the CNN framework. The input here is 30-day stock data, and the generated "input image" is input to the convolutional layer, pooling layer, dropout layer, and norm layer. Then, loop this process three times. After a series of experiments, it is concluded that when the convolutional neural network is used for image recognition, the size of the convolution kernel is 3×3 and the size of the pooling layer is 2×2, the experimental effect obtained is the best it is good. Therefore, in order to achieve better results for this research, the size of the convolutional layer and pooling layer are set to 3×3 and 2×2, respectively. The specific structure of this framework is shown in Fig. 1.

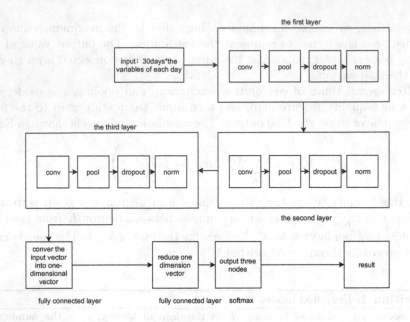

Fig. 1. The designed framework for stock trading prediction.

3.2   Genetic Algorithm

In this section, the components of the GA-based method are described as follows.

Chromosome Representation: The main goal of this method is to find trading signals for stocks, namely buy signals and sell signals. Therefore, in this method, the chromosome is composed of two parts, as shown in Fig. 2.

Fig. 2. Representation of chromosome.

The first part represents the threshold when the stock has a buy signal, and the second part represents the threshold when the stock has a sell signal.

Fitness Evaluation: The fitness function is used to evaluate the quality of chromosomes, that is, to evaluate whether the threshold value of the generated buying and selling signals is the optimal solution. In this method, the fitness function is defined as the cumulative return over a period of time, which is shown in Eq. 5.

$$fitness = \sum_{i=0}^{n}(SClose_i - BClose_i) \tag{5}$$

Among them, n indicates that there have been n buying and selling signals in total during this period. $SClose_i$ represents the closing price of the stock when the i-th sell signal appears, and $BClose_i$ represents the closing price of the stock when the i-th buy signal appears.

Crossover: The genetic algorithm performs crossover and mutation operations to generate new solutions. The crossover operation needs to find two chromosomes from the chromosomes of the previous generation, one as the father and one as the mother. Then the two chromosomes are cut and spliced together at a certain position to generate a new chromosome. Part of the new chromosome is the father's genes, and the remaining part is the mother's genes.

Mutation: The crossover operation is only to operate on the original chromosomes, only to exchange their gene order. This can only guarantee a local optimal solution after multiple evolutions. In order to achieve the global optimal solution, a mutation operation is added. Introduce new genes into existing chromosomes by randomly modifying genes.

4 Proposed a Stock Trading System Combining SSACNN and GA

4.1 Dataset

Futures trading, as a special trading method, has undergone two complex evolutionary processes from the beginning of spot trading to forward trading, and then from forwarding trading to futures trading. To put it simply, futures are not a spot, but a standardized contract. The purpose of futures trading is generally not to obtain physical objects at maturity, but to buy and sell futures contracts. Time, quantity, and quality are the three elements of this standardization, that is, a contract that delivers a fixed quantity and a certain quality of a certain quality at a specific time. Futures contracts are uniformly formulated by the futures exchange. The delivery period of futures is placed in the future.

Options are similar to futures and are also a contract. The option is generated on the basis of futures. When the option is traded, the party who buys the option is called the buyer, the assignee of the right, and the party who sells the option is called the seller, the obliger who must perform the buyer's exercise of the right. The difference between futures and options is that options give the buyer of the contract the right to buy or sell a predetermined number of commodities at the agreed price within the agreed period of the parties. It is a right to choose whether to execute or not in the future.

Five important indicators of historical price are often used: *opening price, lowest price, highest price, closing price* and *volume* for stock price analysis. The futures indicators uses in our experiments include *opening price, highest value, lowest value, closing price* and *volume*. The indicators of the options the test uses include *volume, open interest, closing price* and *settlement price*.

First, let's look at a dataset of two stocks in the Taiwan market. The two stocks are: *DJO* and *DVO* Table 1, Table 2, and Table 3 are the historical data, futures data, and option data of the two Taiwan stocks, respectively.

Table 1. The historical prices of the two stocks

	d_{i1}	d_{i2}	d_{i3}	d_{i4}	$d_{i.}$
DJO	260	264	259	264	...
DVO	244.5	246.5	243	246.5	...

Table 2. Futures data of the two stocks

	t_{i1}	t_{i2}	t_{i3}	t_{i4}	$t_{i.}$
DJO	163.5	262	263.5	258	...
DVO	246	244	246.5	243.5	...

Table 3. Option data of the two stocks

	z_{i1}	z_{i2}	z_{i3}	z_{i4}	$z_{i.}$
DJO	14.85	1	0.27	1	...
DVO	3.4	2	6.85	2	...

The d_i, t_i, z_i are the various factors that affect the stock price. d_i represents the open, high, low, close or volatility attributes of the stock. t_i represents the current price, the opening price, the highest price, and the closing price of the futures. z_i represents the attributes of open interest and settlement price of options. Among them, options include buy options and sell options.

4.2 Data Initialization

Before the experiment, input data needs to be further processed, that is, to standardize the data. Because the experiment may be affected by the size of the data and the results are not ideal. First, standardize the original data to make the range of all data consistent. The processed data conforms to the standard normal distribution and helps improve the accuracy of the prediction, which is shown in Eq. 6.

$$x^* = (x - \mu)/\sigma, \tag{6}$$

where μ is the mean of all sample data and σ is the standard deviation of all sample data.

4.3 Proposed Stock Trading System

In this section, the proposed stock trading system is introduced in detail. This system consists of SSACNN framework and GA. In order to make the predicted stock price closer to the actual value, we uses three data sets, including historical prices, futures and options. First, input three data sets into the SSACNN framework to get the values of three nodes. These three nodes represent three meanings: the first node represents a buy signal, the second node represents a hold signal, and the third node represents a sell signal. Here, only the first node and the third node are used. In the designed model, you only need to know the buy signal and sell signal of the stock. Next, use two nodes to find the optimal threshold of stock trading signals. The nodes are input into the genetic algorithm, and the thresholds of the two buying and selling signals can be obtained through operations such as crossover, mutation and iteration. Finally, the value of the node obtained through the test data set is compared with the threshold to obtain a more correct buying and selling point, and this rule is used to calculate the cumulative income over a period of time.

5 Experimental Results

In this study, a new SSACNN framework with leading indicators is used. Combining this framework with genetic algorithms can find a pair of trading signals. Using this trading signal for stock trading can get a certain amount of income. In the experimental part, a total of two stocks were used, including International Business Machines (IBM) and Facebook, Inc. (FB) in the US market. Two stocks including MediaTek (DVO) and Asustek (DJO) in the Taiwan market. In the experiment, three data sets are used, which are historical stock prices, futures and options. The data set is divided into two parts, one part is used for training and the other part is used for testing. This research compares the proposed stock trading system with another trading strategy (Deep Q-Learning combined with Technical Index). The specific experimental process is shown below.

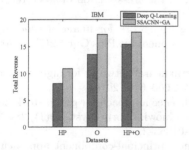   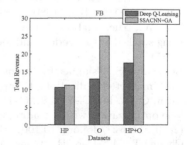

Fig. 3. The total income of IBM stock.   **Fig. 4.** The total income of FB stock.

First, conduct a study on two stocks in the US stock market shown in Fig. 3 and Fig. 4. Among them, the abscissa represents the data set, "HP" represents historical prices, "O" represents options, and "HP+O" represents historical prices and options. Because there is no leading indicator of futures in the US stock market, only two data sets, historical prices and options, are used. In addition, the two data sets of historical price and option rights are combined to form a third data set, namely "HP+O". The ordinate represents the cumulative income during the test period. The experimental results show that the stock trading system we proposed is better than the trading strategy composed of Deep Q-Learning and technical index. The benefits of training with the "HP+O" and "O" data sets are better than the benefits of training with the "HP" data sets. The benefits of training with the "HP+O" data set are better than the benefits of training with the "O" data set.

6 Conclusion

This paper mainly proposes a stock trading system by CNN and GA algorithms for obtaining stock price prediction. Genetic algorithms are used to find the optimal value of stock trading signals. This paper integrates the data into a matrix, and then uses the matrix as input instead of inputting it into the model one by one. In addition, the output of the model adopts a classification method to divide the stock price into three categories of the predicted stock price. The output of the designed model is three nodes. In this study, only the first node and the third node are concerned, that is, only the buy signal and the sell signal are concerned. The experimental results show that the proposed stock trading system can help investors obtain certain returns within a period of time.

References

1. Allen, F., Karjalainen, R.: Using genetic algorithms to find technical trading rules. J. Financ. Econ. **51**(2), 245–271 (1999)
2. Baker, M., Wurgler, J.: Investor sentiment and the cross-section of stock returns. J. Financ. **61**(4), 1645–1680 (2006)
3. Bao, W., Yue, J., Rao, Y.: A deep learning framework for financial time series using stacked autoencoders and long-short term memory. Plos One **12**(7), 0180944 (2017)
4. Borovkova, S., Tsiamas, I.: An ensemble of lstm neural networks for high-frequency stock market classification. J. Forecast. **38**(6), 600–619 (2019)
5. Chen, C.-H., Lu, C.-Y., Lin, C.-B.: An intelligence approach for group stock portfolio optimization with a trading mechanism. Knowl. Inform. Syst. **62**(1), 287–316 (2019). https://doi.org/10.1007/s10115-019-01353-2
6. Chong, T.T.L., Cao, B., Wong, W.K.: A new principal-component approach to measure the investor sentiment (2014)
7. Chou, Y.H., Kuo, S.Y., Chen, C.Y., Chao, H.C.: A rule-based dynamic decision-making stock trading system based on quantum-inspired tabu search algorithm. IEEE Access **2**, 883–896 (2014)

8. Cowles 3rd, A.: Can stock market forecasters forecast? Econometrica: Journal of the Econometric Society, pp. 309–324 (1933)
9. Gunduz, H., Yaslan, Y., Cataltepe, Z.: Intraday prediction of borsa istanbul using convolutional neural networks and feature correlations. Knowl.-Based Syst. **137**, 138–148 (2017)
10. Han, B.: Investor sentiment and option prices. Rev. Financ. Stud. **21**(1), 387–414 (2008)
11. Hiew, J.Z.G., Huang, X., Mou, H., Li, D., Wu, Q., Xu, Y.: Bert-based financial sentiment index and lstm-based stock return predictability. arXiv preprint arXiv:1906.09024 (2019)
12. Hirabayashi, A., Aranha, C., Iba, H.: Optimization of the trading rule in foreign exchange using genetic algorithm. In: Proceedings of the 11th Annual Conference on Genetic and Evolutionary Computation, pp. 1529–1536 (2009)
13. Kim, T., Kim, H.Y.: Forecasting stock prices with a feature fusion lstm-cnn model using different representations of the same data. PloS One **14**(2), e0212320 (2019)
14. Lee, C.M., Shleifer, A., Thaler, R.H.: Investor sentiment and the closed-end fund puzzle. J. Finan. **46**(1), 75–109 (1991)
15. Lin, L., Cao, L., Wang, J., Zhang, C.: The applications of genetic algorithms in stock market data mining optimisation. Management Information Systems (2004)
16. Samuelson, P.A.: Lifetime portfolio selection by dynamic stochastic programming. In: Stochastic Optimization Models in Finance, pp. 517–524. Elsevier (1975)
17. Schoreels, C., Logan, B., Garibaldi, J.M.: Agent based genetic algorithm employing financial technical analysis for making trading decisions using historical equity market data. In: Proceedings. IEEE/WIC/ACM International Conference on Intelligent Agent Technology, 2004. (IAT 2004), pp. 421–424 (2004)
18. Siripurapu, A.: Convolutional networks for stock trading. Stanford Univ. Dep. Comput. Sci. **1**(2), 1–6 (2014)
19. Tsai, H.H., Wu, M.E., Wu, W.H.: The information content of implied volatility skew: evidence on Taiwan stock index options. Data Sci. Pattern Recogn. **1**(1), 48–53 (2017)
20. Wu, J.M.T., Li, Z., Srivastava, G., Tasi, M.H., Lin, J.C.W.: A graph-based convolutional neural network stock price prediction with leading indicators. Pract. Experience Softw. **51**(3), 628–644 (2020)
21. Zheng, L., Jiang, Y., Long, H.: Exchange rates change, asset-denominated currency difference and stock price fluctuation. Appl. Econ. **51**(60), 6517–6534 (2019)

Machine Learning-Based Empirical Investigation for Credit Scoring in Vietnam's Banking

Khanh Quoc Tran[1,2], Binh Van Duong[1,2], Linh Quang Tran[1,2],
An Le-Hoai Tran[1,2], An Trong Nguyen[1,2], and Kiet Van Nguyen[1,2(✉)]

[1] University of Information Technology, Ho Chi Minh City, Vietnam
{18520908,18520505,18520997,18520426,18520434}@gm.uit.edu.vn,
kietnv@uit.edu.vn
[2] Vietnam National University, Ho Chi Minh City, Vietnam

Abstract. In thons for credit scoring in Vietnam with machine learning models based on our submissions for the Kalapa Credit Score Challenge. We conduct experiments with modern machine learning methods based on ensemble learning models: LightGBM, CatBoost, and Random Forest. Our experimental results are better than single-model algorithms such as Support Vector Machine (SVM) or Logistic Regression. As a result, we achieve the F1-Score of 0.83 (Random Forest) with the sixth place on the leaderboard. Subsequently, we analyze the advantages and disadvantages of the used models, propose suitable measures to use for similar problems in the future, and evaluate the results to select the best model. To the best of our knowledge, this is the first work of the field in Vietnamese banking.

Keywords: Credit scoring · Prediction · Machine learning · Ensemble models · Data mining

1 Introduction

Machine learning plays an essential role in all areas of human lives in Industry 4.0. The finance-banking sector is potential, having many aspects of applying machine learning such as: predicting the stock market, classifying customers for banks. In particular, credit scoring is a real problem, which machine learning can effectively solve it.

The latest Fitch Ratings report said The COVID-19 pandemic led to an increase in overdue debts. These debts threaten Vietnamese banks[1] income and capital growth - leading many banks to face a shortage of capital if economic conditions continue to weaken. In the banking and finance sector, bad debt is always a problem. Bad debt affects financial resources and reduces profits,

---

[1] Vietnam Credit Fitch Ratings - https://www.fitchratings.com/entity/vietnam-80442269.

© Springer Nature Switzerland AG 2021
H. Fujita et al. (Eds.): IEA/AIE 2021, LNAI 12799, pp. 564–574, 2021.
https://doi.org/10.1007/978-3-030-79463-7_48

and consequently, it hinders economic growth. Therefore, minimizing the bad debt ratio is an urgent problem for banks and credit institutions, especially the potential risk of bad debt increased due to the effects of the COVID-19 epidemic.

Credit scoring is a procedure that every credit institution or bank always conducts when customers want to open a new credit card or loan. This is an indicator of whether a borrower can receive a loan or open a credit card. This is an essential step in opening a credit card or loan because it affects the lender's ability to recover the debt and helps reduce the risks of bad debt [1].

Nearly all banks have their method of credit scoring. However, thanks to data science and machine learning development, measuring consumers' credit scores by applying artificial intelligence is an efficient method. This method is a big step in helping banks to evaluate customers accurately, effectively, and economically.

Machine learning is a subfield of artificial intelligence involved in researching and building techniques that allow systems to learn from data to solve problems. In credit scoring, the specific issue is to predict the credit score of customers. A research dataset which we use is realistic data from Kalapa Credit Scoring Challenge For Students (a competition organized by a technical company), so this dataset is valuable for credit scoring in Vietnam.

Our research aims to build an optimal solution for credit scoring in Vietnam and find an appropriate metric to evaluate our results. With the provided dataset, we conduct processing, building, and evaluating a machine learning tool for labeling good/bad corresponding to the customer's credit score. From the obtained results, we can provide suggestions to assist banks in deciding whether or not to open a credit card or loan for a customer.

This paper focuses on introducing related information about credit scoring problems in the Kalapa Credit Score dataset. In Sect. 2, we represent some related works. We describe the processing of the dataset in detail in Sect. 3. In Sect. 4, the solutions and models are represented. Our experiments and results are presented in Sect. 5. Finally, we conclude the paper in Sect. 6.

2 Related Works

In 2007, Cheng-Lung Huang et al. [8] proposed a solution to use the Support Vector Machines (SVM) model to evaluate a customer's credit score based on two datasets of Australian and German Credit. SVM achieved relatively positive classification accuracy (accuracy of GP, BPN and C4.5 is 88.27%, 87.93% and 87.06% for Australian Credit dataset; 77.34%, 75.51% and 73.17% for the German Credit). Experimental results showed that SVM is a promising addition to existing data mining methods. Although SVM has proven to perform well in the classification process, some still have some inductive deviation.

One effective way to reduce predictive bias is to use ensemble models. Ligang Zhou et al. built synthetic models based on the Least Squares Support Vector Machines (LSSVM) method with an AUC score of 63.95% on UK Credit dataset

[13]. The experiment proved to be no significant difference in accuracy and different measurements. Banks can mainly use this model to determine the value of a customer's credit.

Currently, along with the vibrant development of the consumer finance market is the introduction of many personal credit scoring services. There are many factors to consider an individual's credit score, such as income (financial score), loan history (debt score), personal reputation (social score), and identity (who the borrower is, identity card, household registration). Moreover, one of the specific tools built to support solving the above problem is FPT.AI Credit Scoring[2]. FPT.AI Credit Scoring integrates big data and machine learning technology, it can analyze and evaluate credit scores based on data sources on social networks in Vietnam, with more than 60 million accounts. Another organization that is also very interested in credit scoring in Vietnam, with high applicability topics, is Kalapa. Kalapa has launched the contest Credit Scoring Challenge For Students to create a competition for students to solve real problems. At the same time, this is also an opportunity for Kalapa to find the most feasible credit scoring model to support bank partners and credit institutions.

3   Dataset

This section presents the basics information of the dataset and the challenges we faced on the Kalapa Credit Score dataset[3].

3.1   Overview

The original dataset contains customer information including 73,411 data points. There are two labels represent the credit score of customer: 0 for the low credit and 1 for the high credit. Labels are design to facilitate the study of the corelation between information fileds of a user with there credit score.

Table 1. Overview statistics of the Kalapa Credit Score Challenge dataset

	Sample size	#Goods	#Bads	#Features
Training	53,030	36, 834	16,196	195
Test	20,381	10,508	9,873	193

---

[2] FPT.AI Credit Scoring - https://fpt.ai/vi/fptai-credit-scoring-dich-vu-danh-gia-diem-tin-dung-khach-hang-ca-nhan.

[3] Kalapa Credit Scoring Challenge - https://challenge.kalapa.vn/home#gioi-thieu.

3.2   The Challenges

This personal credit scoring topic based on this Kalapa Credit dataset is difficult in the initial data processing. The fact that data fields tend to be encrypted to secure customer information is one of the significant challenges to understand and process on the dataset. Therefore, we carry out detailed observations on the dataset to find important information, the basic rules, and the relationship between independent and dependent attributes.

By surveying on the data, we conclude that the challenges posed in the dataset is to find the best solution to this credit scoring problem.

– Imbalanced data: 53,030 data used for training, but only 16,196 bad labels.
– Missing data: up to 117 attributes have a missing data rate> 50%.
– Noise data: several attributes are not normalized (Examples maCv and diaChi), the content contains ambiguous characters/strings (Field_45, 49, 68), the value None accounts for the majority.
– In addition, we also face specific challenges of credit data in Vietnam, such as data is inconsistent, has not been given adequate attention, and database systems are limited, leading to the data is not really big and quality enough. Various properties are encrypted for security reasons, leading to a situation that can make it difficult to understand for our experiment.

4   The Methodologies

4.1   Preprocessing

We work with a relatively complex dataset with many properties, many data types, and many missing data fields, causing a lack of meaning noise. Therefore, we implement separate data preprocessing methods for each of the above challenges.

First, we remove the attributes with low impact because, after the research, we assess that these are insignificant components in the process of solving the problem, such as: calculating only one uniform value on all data points (Field_13, Field_14, Field_16) has no categorical significance. Some independent attributes have high correlation coefficients, keeping only one attribute in each pair of high correlation attributes (correlation > 0.8 or correlation < -0.8).

Next, we deal with the missing data, divide the attributes of the dataset into three sub-sets based on its data type: categorical, numerical, datetime, and replace the missing data such as 'NaN', 'None', 'NULL' equal to mean values (for numerical fields) or by mode values (for categorical, datetime fields).

For attributes with a datetime data type, we progress to: standardize attributes Field_34, ngaySinH and do delta calculation of attributes x_startDate, x_endDate (where x: A, C, E, F, G).

For attributes with a categorical data type, we advance to standardize data in some attributes: Field_38, Field_47, Field_62, and try the Count Encoding method.

For attributes with a numerical data type, the Maximum Normalization method is applied to normalize data. Then, K-mean clustering is used to cluster consumer data into different groups. Once the data has been grouped in K-zoning, analytic hierarchy is used to assign credit ratings. Using these credit ratings, employees are classified as very important, important, normal, or bad customers. We calculate delta for some property pairs and compute the mean and standard deviation of the partner_X attributes. Moreover, we create and compare some 'auto columns' from original numerical fields.

We create some meaningful new attributes from the original ones. By researching and extracting information from the original attributes, we create new attributes to serve more information for the classification process. For instance, we create an age attribute from the available birth attribute, the gender attribute from the gioiTinh and info_social_sex attributes,...

As a result, after the pre-processing, we obtain a new dataset with 173 properties (22 properties removed). We find out that while the tuple complexity is reduced, we can still deal with the lack of context created by this normalization. Although the extraneous attributes and confusing data points are most removed to avoid confusing the prediction, the rest may still noise the data.

4.2 Models

In this paper, we choose to experiment on the dataset provided with machine learning methods LightGBM Classifier, CatBoost Classifier, and Random Forest. These models have the advantages in training time (very suitable for the competitive challenge where we have to deliver the result fast). They are easy to apply, and the SOTA and popular models. Then, statistically, we compare results on models to make conclusions and choose the most suitable machine learning model for the Kalapa Credit Score dataset.

4.2.1 LightGBM Classifier: LightGBM stands for Light Gradient Boosting Machine [6], it is a free and open-source distributed gradient boosting system for AI at first created by Microsoft. It depends on choice tree calculations and is utilized for positioning, order, and other AI assignments. Its features are the presentation and adaptability.

LGBM was used extensively in many winning solutions in machine learning competitions. Comparative tests on public datasets show that LGBM outperforms existing gradient boosting frameworks in both efficiency and accuracy, with significantly lower memory consumption. [10].

4.2.2 CatBoost Classifier: is YanDex's open source and machine learning algorithm[4]. It can operate on various data types such as audio, text, video. The algorithm's strength is that it produces good results without the need for large

---

[4] CatBoost-https://catboost.ai/.

amounts of data and the strong support for descriptive data types that lead to business problems.

CatBoost controls an automatic classification of features based on various statistics. We can use CatBoost without explicit preprocessors to convert categories to numbers.

Besides, CatBoost also supports the ability to fine-tune the hyper-parameters to reduce the overfitting risk which makes the model more general [5].

4.2.3 Random Forest: Random Forest is a machine learning algorithm built on multiple sets of **Decision Tree**. The model's output is based on the aggregate decision on the decision trees it generates with the voting method. **Random Forest** is a **Supervised Learning** method to handle classification and regression problems. Random Forest gives us a very accurate result with such a mechanism, but the trade-off is that we cannot understand how this algorithm works due to the complicated structure of this model. This is one of the Black Box methods - that is, we put our hands inside and get the results, but cannot explain the mechanism of the model [7,11].

4.3 Features Selection

In this works, we apply a procedure for feature selecture using target permutation [3]. Feature selection process using target permutation tests actual importance significance against the distribution of feature importances when fitted to noise (shuffled target). We implements the following steps:

1. We create the null importances distributions: these are created to fit the model over several runs on a shuffled version of the target. This shows how the model can make sense of a feature irrespective of the target.
2. We fit the model on the original target and gather the feature importances. This gives us a benchmark whose significance can be tested against the Null Importances Distribution.
3. For each feature test, the actual importance:
    - We compute the probability of the actual importance with the null distribution. We use a very simple estimation using occurrences while the article proposes to fit the known distribution to the gathered data. In fact that we compute 1 - the probability so that things are in the right order.
    - We compare the actual importance to the mean and max of the null importances. This gives a sort of feature importance that allows seeing major features in the dataset. Indeed, the previous method may provide us with lots of ones.

Finally, we decide to select the 33 features that have the most impact (Information Values > 0.2) on prediction. We use them as key attributes to training the machine learning models. The results obtained from the experimental process are presented in the Fig. 1, Table 2 and Sect. 5.3.

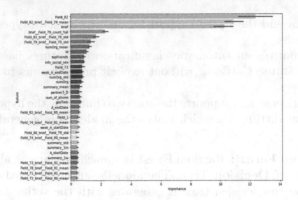

Fig. 1. The top 33 features most influence the dependent variable.

Table 2. Experimental results on Kalapa Credit dataset.

Model	Original		Processed	
	AUC	F1-score	AUC	F1-score
LightGBM Classifier	0.71	0.69	0.75	0.71
CatBoost Classifier	**0.77**	0.73	**0.82**	0.78
Random Forest	0.74	**0.78**	0.81	**0.83**

5   Experiments

5.1   Data Preparation

We implement data preprocessing, as mentioned in Sect. 4. Subsequently, the dataset is split into training and test sets. We also take advantage of the Cross-validation method on the training set while training the models. This technical method helps us train the models on some subsets from the training set to directly evaluate the models on the training phase to find out the best models to apply on the test set.

5.2   Models Implementation and the Parameters Refinement

The models are all trained on the training set and assessed on the test set. In this paper, we evaluate experiments through three given models: LightGBMClassifier, CatBoostClassifier, and Random Forest. Then, we can also make comparisons of their performances on the dataset.

- **LightGBM**: We refine 3 parameters with specific values num_leaves = 128, learning_rate = 0.02, and max_depth = 8.
- **CatBoost**: With Catboost model we use these parameters: iteractions = 1000, learning_rate = 0.1, and random_seed = 42.
- **Random Forest**: We implement a Random Forest model with max_depth = 17, max_features = 'auto', seed = 2020, and n_trees = 767.

5.3   Experimental Results

In this Session, the achievements that we obtained from the Kalapa Credit Challenge For Students 2020 contest are visualized. The contest results are based on the Gini score (with Gini = 2 * AUC - 1). Besides, we add one more measure: the F1-score with an effort to find out the appropriate measure for classification problems in general and credit scoring problems in particular [9]. The experiment results on the Kalapa Credit Score dataset are revealed in Table 3. We draw a conclusion that the Random Forest model has the best performance.

Table 3. Experimental evaluation on the Kalapa Credit Score dataset.

Model	AUC-score	F1-score
LightGBM Classifier	0.75	0.71
CatBoost Classifier	**0.82**	0.78
Random Forest	0.81	**0.83**

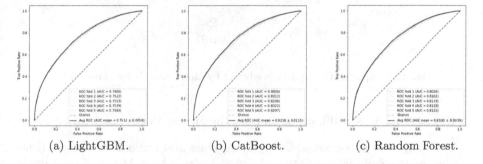

(a) LightGBM.	(b) CatBoost.	(c) Random Forest.

Fig. 2. Plot of ROC Curve - AUC.

Table 4 shows the top 5/760 high-performance solutions on public test data from the Kalapa Credit Challenge For Students 2020 contest. As a result, we ranked 5th on the individual standings with a Gini score of 0.50013. The score was not far different from the rest. Nevertheless, in the final ranking table, we were ranked 6th place (the_cook_of_the_king) on the team standings.

Table 4. The results of the top 5 on private-test set - Kalapa Credit Challenge.

Rank	Team	Gini-score	F1-score
1	bker_team_-_khanh_vu_duy	0.46028	0.75
2	iu_boys	0.45295	0.74
3	ai_beginner	0.44732	0.74
4	carl_friedrich_gauss	0.44455	0.73
5	cainaychoisao	0.44250	0.72
6	**the_cook_of_the_king**	0.44183	0.83

5.4   Results Analysis and Discussion

5.4.1   ROC Curve and AUC. ROC Curve and AUC in this particular problem (or binary classification problems) are usually the crucial measures chosen as a criterion for finding out the best model [12].

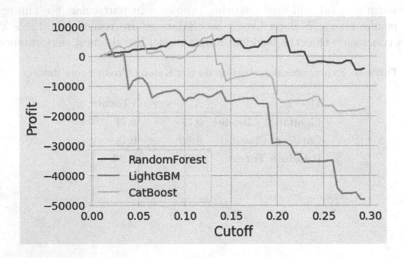

Fig. 3. Comparison of profits predicted by three models by threshold.

Despite this, it is still hard to find out the answer to the practical problem:

- The thing that is concerned by credit agencies and banks is the profit. However, no one can make sure that the model with a high AUC will be suitable in practice. As shown in Table 3, the CatBoost model and Random Forest model's AUC scores are 0.82 and 0.81, respectively. Despite having a higher AUC score, the interest predicted by the Catboost model is less than that of the Random Forest model (Fig. 3).
- Regardless of profit increment, the banks also take care of financial risks, or profit volatility [4]. Figure 3 shows that the revenue predicted by the CatBoost model starts to fall dramatically (the orange line) with a little bit of different amount from the optimal threshold, even though it has the highest predicted profit. Meanwhile, the value predicted by the Random Forest model is less than that of the CatBoost model, but there is no similar volatility around the optimal threshold. In other words, profit volatility from the CatBoost model is larger, so that the usage of this model raises potential financial risks.

A consequence can be obtained from the above: Though CatBoost results in the highest AUC score, banks or Kalapa companies will not deploy this model for credit scoring problems in practice. It is possible that they can take other models that have less AUC score into account.

5.4.2 Classification Results on Each Label. Each class from the Kalapa Credit Score dataset (training set) is immensely imbalanced (class 0: 36,234/53,030 samples, class 1: 16,796/53,030 samples). In order to handle this threat, Recall and F1-score are recommended as the most common and efficient measures.

Table 5. The classification result in each class on the test set.

Label	Model					
	LightGBM		CatBoost		Random Forest	
	Recall	F1-score	Recall	F1-score	Recall	F1-score
0	0.95	0.86	0.95	0.87	0.97	0.90
1	0.44	0.57	0.57	0.69	0.66	0.77
Average	0.70	0.71	0.76	0.78	0.81	0.83

As can be seen from the metric records in Table 3, we can figure out that the three models all classified relatively well on class 0 (good). On the other hand, we see a contrary result in class 1 (bad). This can be explained by the imbalance of the dataset (the class 1 just accounts for 30.54%).

According to the experiment results above, the classification accuracy is effective in general because the F1-scores are greater than 70%. Moreover, the Random Forest model has slightly higher accuracy than the rest (83%). In conclusion, Random Forest is an acceptable and flexible solution to optimize the features subset and parameters for credit scoring problems in practice.

6 Conclusion and Future Works

In this paper, we introduce scoring credit methods in the Vietnamese market by applying some machine learning algorithms. These methods are useful in evaluating customers' credit scores and help save time and money compared to traditional methods. We analyzed essential information about credit scoring and evaluated several ensembles learning experimental results on the Kalapa CreditScore dataset. As we can see, the solution of applying machine learning for credit scoring is good. The best algorithm is Random Forest with AUC, Recall, and F1-score is 0.81, 0.81, and 0.83, respectively.

The LightGBM model can process a large amount of data with little memory, parallel computing, and GPU learning, and this obtains better accuracy, less training time, and is more effective. The CatBoost Classifier performs the best AUC performance with 0.82. This is because Catboost effectively handles categorical features and allows to tune hyperparameters. However, when CatBoost is not optimal, it shows significant volatility, and low-performance [2]. Finally, Random Forest gains a valuable model with optical performance and stability, but its drawback is needing much time and memory to train and process.

For credit score datasets in general and Kalapa CreditScore in particular, data preprocessing, exploratory data analysis, and important feature selection are significant for developing models. They are factors that affect the performance of models. The good handling of essential features can increase the model's results and make the model more accurate and reliable.

We plan to apply deep learning algorithms to find out better performances for credit scoring in the future. Training time is also a problem that we are going to improve in the future. With techniques for extracting essential features and hardware development, we can improve credit scoring to be more accurate and efficient by applying machine learning.

References

1. Ahmed, M.S.I., Rajaleximi, P.R.: An empirical study on credit scoring and credit scorecard for financial institutions. International Journal of Advanced Research in Computer Engineering & Technology (IJARCET), vol. 8, no. 7 (2019)
2. Al Daoud, E.: Comparison between xgboost, lightgbm and catboost using a home credit dataset. Int. J. Comput. Inform. Eng. **13**(1), 6–10 (2019)
3. Altmann, A., Toloşi, L., Sander, O., Lengauer, T.: Permutation importance: a corrected feature importance measure. Bioinformatics **26**(10), 1340–1347 (2010)
4. Show All Code and Hide All Code. Deep learning for credit scoring in the era of big data (adapted from a research conducted by mis, banking academy of vietnam)
5. Dorogush, A.V., Ershov, V., Gulin, A.: Catboost: gradient boosting with categorical features support (2018)
6. Friedman, J.H.: Stochastic gradient boosting. Comput. Stat. Data Anal. **38**(4), 367–378 (2002)
7. Ghatasheh, N.: Business analytics using random forest trees for credit risk prediction: a comparison study. Int. J. Adv. Sci. Technol. **72**(2014), 19–30 (2014)
8. Huang, C.-L., Chen, M.-C., Wang, C.-J.: Credit scoring with a data mining approach based on support vector machines. Expert Syst. Appl. **33**(4), 847–856 (2007)
9. Jeni, L.A., Cohn, J.F., De La Torre, F.: Facing imbalanced data-recommendations for the use of performance metrics. In: 2013 Humaine Association Conference on Affective Computing and Intelligent Interaction, pp. 245–251. IEEE (2013)
10. Ke, G., et al.: Lightgbm: a highly efficient gradient boosting decision tree. In: Advances in Neural Information Processing Systems, pp. 3146–3154 (2017)
11. Liaw, A., Wiener, M., et al.: Classification and regression by randomforest. R. News **2**(3), 18–22 (2002)
12. Lobo, J.M., Jiménez-Valverde, A., Real, R.: AUC: a misleading measure of the performance of predictive distribution models. Glob. Ecol. Biogeogr. **17**(2), 145–151 (2008)
13. Zhou, L., Lai, K.K., Yu, L.: Least squares support vector machines ensemble models for credit scoring. Expert Syst. Appl. **37**(1), 127–133 (2010)

Bayesian Networks

Unsupervised Co-training of Bayesian Networks for Condition Prediction

Mathilde Monvoisin[1,2]($\boxtimes$), Philippe Leray[1]($\boxtimes$) (iD), and Mathieu Ritou[1]($\boxtimes$) (iD)

[1] Laboratory of Digital Sciences of Nantes (LS2N UMR CNRS 6004),
Université de Nantes, Nantes, France
{mathilde.monvoisin,philippe.leray,mathieu.ritou}@ls2n.fr
[2] IRT Jules Verne, Nantes, France

Abstract. The objective of Smart Manufacturing is to improve productivity and competitiveness in industry, based on in-process data. It requires reliable, explainable and understandable models such as Bayesian networks for performing tasks like condition prediction. In this context, a Bayesian network can be classically learned in a supervised, unsupervised way or a semi-supervised way. Here, we are interested in how to perform the learning when the ground truth isn't included in the learning data but is observable indirectly in another related dataset. This paper introduces a fully unsupervised variation of co-training that allows to include this second dataset, with two learning strategies (split and recursive). In our experiments, we propose one simple probabilistic graphical model used for predicting the state of a machine tool from results given by several sensors, and illustrate our unsupervised co-training strategies first with benchmarks available from the UCI repository, for which 4 out of 5 datasets have best results with the recursive strategy. Finally, the recursive strategy was validated by McNemar's test as being the best strategy on a real industrial dataset.

Keywords: Bayesian network · EM algorithm · Unsupervised learning · Co-training · Industry 4.0 · Condition-based maintenance

1 Introduction

Smart manufacturing is a promising research area to improve productivity and competitiveness in industry [1,2]. Indeed, it is crucial to detect any system failure as early as possible to reduce maintenance costs and downtimes. This is the reason why predictive maintenance is a key issue in industry 4.0 [3]. Approaches can be data-driven, model based or hybrid.

In our work, we are interested in discovering and understanding of the events leading to the damage of industrial production machine, and in predicting their failure, in a predictive maintenance perspective. In the application, we have been faced with a more general problem. Supervised learning is a classic approach for learning any predictive model when the ground truth is known. Unsupervised

© Springer Nature Switzerland AG 2021
H. Fujita et al. (Eds.): IEA/AIE 2021, LNAI 12799, pp. 577–588, 2021.
https://doi.org/10.1007/978-3-030-79463-7_49

learning aims at learning the same model when this ground truth is unknown. In our application, we consider the unsupervised scenario, but with an additional information provided about the system state during another phase.

Smart manufacturing can make use of supervised learning in order to build a predictive model, such as a Probabilistic Neural Network to classify broken tools and good tools [4] or Bayesian networks and Support Vector Machines for thermal modelling and prediction [5].

Improving the learning of a given model with the results of another one is one of the founding principle of the co-training. [6] and [7] proposed semi-supervised learning paradigm, which trains two naive Bayes classifiers respectively from two different views and lets the classifiers label some unlabeled data for each other. [8] used Bayesian undirected graphical model for co-training.

This paper introduces a fully unsupervised variation of co-training and several learning strategies are proposed, the first one to our knowledge. It includes a conditional linear Gaussian Bayesian Network structure and the learning strategies associated. The strategies were experimentally tested on 5 UCI datasets, and on a real industrial dataset dedicated to the diagnosis of machine tool. The result is the first generic framework for fully unsupervised diagnosis, which parameters are learned with co-training.

Section 2 proposes a formal description of the problem. Section 3 describes our unsupervised co-training framework, as well as three learning strategies. Section 4 is dedicated to the empirical evaluation of the proposal. In Sect. 4.1, we describe one simple hybrid Bayesian network dedicated to condition prediction. In Sect. 4.2, we will describe one first set of experiments with benchmarks available from the UCI repository, transformed for co-training task, in a controlled context where the ground truth is known. Section 4.3 presents an application on real industrial data, and Sect. 5 concludes on the contribution of this paper and our perspectives of research.

2   Problem Statement

$\{SensA_1, ..., SensA_n\}$ is a set of continuous variables, outputs of several sensors (potentially preprocessed) that are measured every day during the "production phase" (phase A) of the machine tool. The objective is to predict $State_A$, the (discrete) state of the system, by the mean of one model $Model_A$ learned from data.

A classic approach to this problem would be to learn the parameters of $Model_A$ in a supervised way, from a dataset containing observations of the sensors $\{SensA_1, ..., SensA_n\}$ and the ground truth about $State_A$; or in an unsupervised way, without measuring the ground truth. Let us denote D_A this dataset with the sensors information only.

In our problem, we consider the unsupervised scenario, but with an additional information D_B provided by another set of sensors about the system state during another phase (phase B). So, $\{SensB_1, ..., SensB_m\}$ is also a set of continuous variables, outputs of these other sensors (potentially preprocessed), that are also measured every day. This dataset can be used to predict $State_B$, the state of the system during phase B. States A and B of the system are assumed to be two estimations of the same underlying state of the machine. Our objective is to learn $Model_A$, with D_A, i.e. in an unsupervised way, without knowing the ground truth, but also by taking into account data D_B acquired during the second phase. As an example, in our application, D_A is the data from the process monitoring and D_B is the data collected during condition monitoring when the component signature are recorded.

As shown in a strong context by [6] or a weaker one by [9] for (supervised) co-training, we consider the following assumptions: (a) weak sufficiency, each of our views ($Model_A$ and $Model_B$) is at least approximately sufficient in itself to achieve good prediction, and (b) weak dependency, both views are not too highly correlated.

3   Unsupervised Co-training

3.1   Principle

In order to solve the problem described in the previous section, we propose to "enrich" $Model_A$ with another sub-model $Model_B$ dedicated to the prediction of $State_B$ from the other sensors $\{SensB_1, ..., SensB_m\}$ leading to an unsupervised co-training of both models that should agree about the state of the system.

We will consider that both models are probabilistic graphical models with continuous and discrete variables (and parameters θ_A and θ_B), and that unsupervised learning can be performed by the EM algorithm [10,11].

This unsupervised co-training can be performed with different learning strategies, in relation to the way the equality assumption between $State_A$ and $State_B$ is envisaged.

3.2   Split Learning

Instead of learning one unique model with all the sensors inputs, we propose to reduce the complexity of the parameter learning by splitting this task. i.e. learning one first sub-model in an unsupervised way with the help of the EM algorithm, and then the second one enriched with the results of the first one, obtained by probabilistic inference, as described in Algorithm 1. As described in Fig. 1, one model is then learned to "reproduce" the output of the second one.

In this case, $Model_A$ takes benefit of the $Model_B$ unsupervised learning. However, in a symmetrical way, a better learning of $Model_A$ would also help for learning $Model_B$.

3.3   Recursive Learning

The recursive method consists in using the previous method and iterating n_{step} times ($2n_{step}$ EM and probabilistic inference runs). Sub-model B is learned in

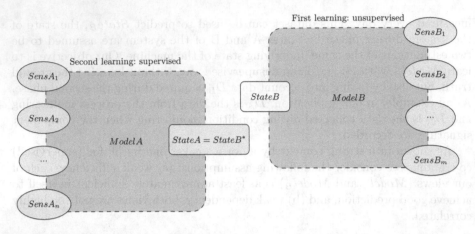

Fig. 1. Unsupervised co-training by split learning strategy. Firstly, $ModelB$ is learnt in an unsupervised way, then $ModelA$ is learnt in a supervised way, by considering that $StateA$ should be the optimal prediction of $StateB$ after $ModelB$ learning. The blue nodes denote variables observed during the learning task, where the white ones represent unobserved variables.

an unsupervised way, enabling the supervised learning of model A, and then of model B, etc. The procedure is detailed in Algorithm 2 where $P(D_A|\theta_A)$ is the likelihood of observing the data D_A for the model A, and symmetrically for model B.

For an optimal computation time, we break complexity by learning one model, and then learning the other model with the prediction of the first one, and repeating it n_{step} times. The model is learned in a sort of semi-supervised way, but without real labeled data such as in usual co-training framework.

Instead of controlling the number of steps, we can also monitor the likelihood and stop the iterations when it has stopped improving significantly.

Algorithm 1: Split strategy

Input: D_A, D_B
Output: θ_A^*, θ_B^*
1 $\theta_B^* = argmax\ P(D_B|\theta_B)$
2 $State_B^* = argmax\ P(State_B|D_B, \theta_B^*)$
3 $\theta_A^* = argmax\ P(D_A, State_A = State_B^*|\theta_A)$

Algorithm 2: Recursive strategy

Input: D_A, D_B
Output: θ_A^*, θ_B^*
1 $\theta_B^* = argmax\ P(D_B|\theta_B)$
2 **for** $i = 1$ to n_{step} **do**
3 $\quad$ $State_B^* = argmax\ P(State_B|D_B, \theta_B^*)$
4 $\quad$ $\theta_A^* = argmax\ P(D_A, State_A = State_B^*|\theta_A)$
5 $\quad$ $State_A^* = argmax\ P(State_A|D_A, \theta_A^*)$
6 $\quad$ $\theta_B^* = argmax\ P(D_B, State_B = State_A^*|\theta_B)$

---

4 Experiments

4.1 Model and Parameter Initialization

We propose to use probabilistic graphical models which are explainable models, and more especially Conditional Linear Gaussian Bayesian Networks (CLGBNs, [12]) that are able to deal with continuous and discrete variables.

Our unsupervised co-training framework proposes to use jointly or iteratively two models $Model_A$ and $Model_B$. We will consider here that the structure of both models is similar, and we will describe only the first one. As we are interested in applying this unsupervised co-training for condition prediction, the choice of the model used in the experiments and described in Fig. 2 is inspired from the following considerations.

In an industrial system, the physical measurements (power, temperature, etc.) corresponding to good operating conditions of the system are within a limited range of values. Therefore, values outside this small and frequently observed range probably indicate problems during the manufacturing. We are defining $State_A$ as a boolean variable with {OK, KO} values. Moreover, each sensor is usually able to discriminate some intermediate states. Let us define $DiscrA_i$ the local estimation of the state provided by $SensA_i$. This variable is a discrete variable with a larger domain, for instance {OK, degraded, KO}. As in usual CLGBNs, we consider that the distribution of each $SensA_i$ is a Gaussian distribution conditional on $DiscrA_i$.

In order to simplify the description of the model, we will also consider that low values of $SensA_i$ usually corresponds to $State_A = OK$, and the more the sensor values increase, the more the state of the system is *degraded* or *KO*.

Each conditional Gaussian distribution is initialized either by one application of EM for the joint distribution $P(SensA_i, DiscrA_i)$, or by using a classical grid initialization given in Eq. 1 for a mixture of k distinct Gaussians (with i from 0 to $k - 1$).

$$\mu_i = min(SensA_i) + \frac{0.5 + i}{k}(max(SensA_i) - min(SensA_i)) \qquad (1)$$

$$\sigma_i^2 = \frac{\sigma_{SensA_i}^2}{k}$$

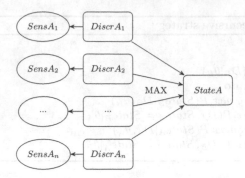

Fig. 2. Conditional Linear Gaussian Bayesian Network used in our experiments for process monitoring in smart manufacturing. Circles denote continuous variables and squares discrete ones.

We finally consider that the global state of the system is an aggregation of the local states estimated by each sensor. In a first approach that is very similar to a deterministic MAX function, we consider here that $State_A = KO$ when it has been diagnosed as *degraded* or *KO* by at least one sensor of the model.

4.2   Experiments on UCI Datasets

Dataset Adaptation for Co-training. Several benchmarks from the UCI repository [13] have been used. They were selected based on their similarity to our industrial context, with several numerical variables as inputs. The target variable was binarized such as the highest value corresponds to a failure if it wasn't already binary. These benchmarks are not dedicated to co-training. In order to adapt them for our task where we need two-viewed datasets, we followed a procedure described in [14] to split an "usual" one view dataset into two views by using an entropy based method. The two-views UCI datasets are shared on github[1] to create a public benchmark for co-training. [14] also introduces two measures to verify the two assumptions needed for co-training.

The sufficiency criterion δ_1 measures the fact that the two models should have sufficient information by itselves to predict the target variable. The independence criterion δ_2 measures the ability of predicting the attributes of the other dataset (given the value of the class variable). As shown in [14], the lower δ_1 and δ_2 are, the better the dataset is fit for co-training.

Table 1 summarizes all the benchmarks selected from UCI repository, with their properties (total number of input variables, data size, imbalance ratio) and the sufficiency and independence measurements (δ_1 and δ_2) estimated by using a decision tree as a baseline classifier and stratified 10-fold cross-validation.

---

[1] https://github.com/MathildeMonvoisin/Co-training-benchmark.

Table 1. UCI datasets characteristics in a co-training context. δ_1 and δ_2 are the respective measures for sufficiency and independence. n and m are the number of columns of views A and B, N is the number of samples in the dataset and IR is the imbalance ratio, i.e. the percentage of the positive class.

	δ_1	δ_2	n	m	N	IR
heart-statlog	0.33	0.12	7	6	270	45%
APS failure	0.11	0.39	5	5	758	36%
hydraulic stable	0.45	0.66	8	7	2206	34%
hydraulic valve	0.56	0.67	8	7	2206	67%
hydraulic leakage	0.19	0.67	8	7	2206	22%

Experimental Protocol. The implementation of the models described in Sect. 4.1 with our different learning strategies proposed in Sect. 3 has been performed with our library dedicated to Probabilistic Graphical Models (PILGRIM) with the help of ProBT[2] library.

We compare in these experiments our two learning strategies (Split and Recursive). As a baseline method, we also learned independently each model in an unsupervised way.

Parameters used during learning were: a threshold equal to 0.0001 on likelihood variation as stopping criterion for EM and $n_{step} = 30$ (chosen for guaranteeing convergence in all our experiments) for the recursive strategy.

The accuracy and sensitivity of each model (A and B) are estimated with 10-fold cross validation, and expressed as a value between 0 and 100%. Their average (between both models) is then considered as the global performance of each learning strategy (unsupervised, split learning and recursive learning).

Results. Table 2 shows us the variation both of our metrics (accuracy and sensitivity) for each dataset.

The recursive strategy is usually better than the simple split one, with an increase in terms of accuracy and sensitivity for all datasets excepted for one dataset (hydraulic stable). The recursive co-training strategy is also more interesting than the unsupervised learning (without co-training) for three datasets (heart-statlog, APS failure and hydraulic-valve) or equivalent (for hydraulic leakage, the increase of accuracy is counterbalanced by a decrease in sensitivity).

Both co-training strategies are not efficient for the hydraulic stable benchmark and not useful for another one (hydraulic leakage). Both datasets have one high value for δ_2, showing that one of the co-training usual assumption (independence here) is not verified with also one small imbalance ratio. In such imbalanced context, the first model seems to produce wrong results that are

---

[2] https://www.probayes.com/.

Table 2. Variation of accuracy and sensitivity between unsupervised learning and the split and recursive co-training strategies.

		Split vs. unsup	Rec. vs. split	Rec vs. unsup
Heart-statlog	Δ acc.	1.67	0.56	2.22
	Δ sens.	3.12	0.21	3.33
APS failure	Δ acc.	0.49	0.21	0.71
	Δ sens.	11.59	1.55	13.14
Hydraulic stable	Δ acc.	0.70	-1.82	-1.12
	Δ sens.	-0.92	-1.68	-2.60
Hydraulic valve	Δ acc.	1.74	1.43	3.17
	Δ sens.	4.79	2.66	7.45
Hydraulic leakage	Δ acc.	1.50	-0.06	1.44
	Δ sens.	-1.44	0.52	-0.92

given as a ground truth for the next model. This situation can lead to a negative feedback loop and progressively produces a decrease of the global performances.

4.3 Experiments on Real Data from Industrial Use Case

Data and Experimental Protocol. This use case concerns the machining industry and the component to be diagnosed is a machine tool spindle. The industrial dataset have been collected over more than one year, aggregated at a daily level and it is unlabelled. The results obtained by a previous study [15] which have been afterwards confirmed by an expert are considered as the ground truth.

The model A is dedicated to process monitoring during the machining phase: the four inputs are classical vibration criteria. The model B corresponds to the spindle condition monitoring: a vibration signature is performed once a day to evaluate it, with also four criteria.

Problems are uncommon in machining: from the process monitoring and the spindle monitoring datasets respectively only 7 (1.6%) and 5 (1.1%) events are considered as events that might have seriously damaged the spindle, from the previous study. Another issue in this real application is the fact that the two diagnosis don't coincide perfectly: only 3 of the 5 spindle damages are included in the 7 events detected during the process monitoring.

For this dataset, the sufficiency and independence criteria ($\delta_1 = 0.05$ and $\delta_2 = 0.49$) have been estimated by applying the ADASYN over-sampling algorithm from the package imbalanced-learn [16] because of the very low imbalance ratio ($\approx 1\%$). These values are in the range of values where co-training was efficient in our previous study on the UCI datasets.

We compare in these experiments our two co-training strategies (Split and Recursive). As a baseline method, we also learned independently each model in a unsupervised way without the help of the other model.

The evaluation of the learning strategies is done here by two confusion matrices comparing the predictions done by our $Model_A$ and $Model_B$ to the same ground truth. For each model, we also present the classic performance indicators (precision, recall, ...) and computation time for each model A and B. In our application, the sensitivity is a very important indicator because it measures how wrong the model was when predicting an OK, and there can be a big impact if we ignore a KO, depending on what was the damage suffered.

Results. Table 3 and Table 4 present the confusion matrices and the other performance indicators obtained for our two co-training strategies and the baseline unsupervised learning.

The recursive method converges to performances very similar to the split one on (B), and gives increased accuracy performances on (A) and they both have a very fast learning time (less than 10 s).

Table 5 presents the results of McNemar's statistical test [17] where the null hypothesis considers that the predictive performances of the two classifiers are equal (with a significance level of $\alpha = 0.05$). The tests were computed using the statsmodel python library [18]. This table shows that the split strategy improves the spindle diagnosis results, compared to the unsupervised one. Recursive learning is globally the best strategy, by significantly outperforming all the other strategies except the split one for the spindle condition diagnosis.

The fact that the recursive strategy is not always better than the split one means that repeating the learning iterations can decrease precision and sensitiv-

Table 3. Process diagnosis (A) and spindle condition diagnostic (B) confusion matrices for several unsupervised co-training strategies compared with a baseline independent learning of both models.

	A				B			
	FP	FN	TP	TN	FP	FN	TP	TN
Independent unsupervised learning	1	15	414	6	0	38	393	5
Unsupervised co-training (split)	1	15	414	6	0	9	422	5
Unsupervised co-training (recursive)	3	2	427	4	0	8	423	5

Table 4. Process diagnosis (A) and spindle condition (B) performance indicators (precision, sensitivity, recall, accuracy and computation time) for the split and recursive (rec.) unsupervised co-training strategies, compared with a baseline independent unsupervised learning of both models.

	A: Process diagnosis				B: Cond. monitoring				Time (s)
	Prec.	Sens.	Rec.	Acc.	Prec.	Sens.	Rec.	Acc.	
Unsupervised	99.7%	85.7 %	96.5%	96.3%	100%	100%	91.2%	91.3%	2.1
Split strategy	99.8%	85.7 %	96.5%	96.3%	100%	100%	97.9%	97.9%	2.8
Rec. strategy	99.3%	57.1%	99.5%	98.9%	100%	100%	98.1%	98.2%	9.8

Table 5. Results of McNemar's statistical test where the null hypothesis considers that the predictive performances of a pair of classifiers are equal (=) with a significance level of $\alpha = 0.05$. The classifiers were learned with our unsupervised co-training strategies or with a baseline independent unsupervised learning of both models.

	A : Process diagnostic			B : Spindle Condition Maintenance		
	unsupervised	split	recursive	unsupervised	split	recursive
unsupervised		=	≠		≠	≠
split			≠			=

ity in the process diagnosis classifier. This situation can be explained by several hypothesis: our unsupervised co-training is considering that both models should agree about their outputs, where the ground truth considered for the evaluation metrics is based on independent results for both models that disagree about some *KO* events. Some improvements addressing this situation are proposed in the following section.

A detailed study with a machining expert has validated a new incident in the data that was detected using the recursive strategy. This rare event has not been previously detected by other techniques that were used on this dataset.

5   Conclusion and Future Work

The paper focuses on learning a predictive model in a smart manufacturing context with an unsupervised framework where additional information is provided about the system state during another phase.

We have proposed one fully unsupervised variation of co-training framework with several learning strategies, which can be applied to various models and application fields.

These strategies have been illustrated with several benchmarks available from the UCI repository (and adapted for a co-training purpose), and have then been applied in a real application dedicated to the detection of machine tool failure when the ground truth is unknown. We have shown that our unsupervised co-training strategies can take profit from separate information in order to provide better results.

This present work can yet be extended or improved in several ways. In order to avoid the negative feedback loop observed during our experiments, the split and recursive strategies could be improved by not transferring from one sub-model learning to the second one the state predicted by the sub-model (cf. Eq. 1), but the probability distribution of the state as a soft evidence, as proposed in multi-agent context [19]. We can also inspire ourselves from the semi-supervised co-training strategies with only a partial transfer of information between the two learning tasks, as proposed in [7] where only the more confident prediction are transferred. As the sufficiency assumptions are not always met in real applications, we are also interested by extending our work with insufficient views, such as proposed for co-training in [20].

The model structure we proposed in a smart machining context is a very simple one, used to highlight the interest of the co-training strategies. This model can be improved by taking into account more complex deterministic aggregation functions (for instance the AtLeastK operator instead of the MAX one) or probabilistic ones like NoisyMax [21] or other causal independence models [22].

Acknowledgement. Thanks are addressed to the IRT Jules Verne, French Institute in Research and Technology in Advanced Manufacturing for the PhD PERFORM program. The authors would also like to thank people who laid the foundations of this project with Philippe Leray and Mathieu Ritou, in particular Victor Godreau, Abdal Moughit Idrissi and Guillaume Ferrand, and the industrial partners for supplying the experimental data.

References

1. Wang, J., Ma, Y., Zhang, L., Gao, R.X., Wu, D.: Deep learning for smart manufacturing: methods and applications. J. Manuf. Syst. **48**, 144–156 (2018). Special Issue on Smart Manufacturing
2. Tao, F., Qi, Q., Liu, A., Kusiak, A.: Data-driven smart manufacturing. J. Manuf. Syst. **48**, 157–169 (2018). Special Issue on Smart Manufacturing
3. Gao, R., et al.: Cloud-enabled prognosis for manufacturing. CIRP Ann. - Manuf. Technol. **64**(2), 749–772 (2015)
4. Huang, P.B., Ma, C.-C., Kuo, C.-H.: A PNN self-learning tool breakage detection system in end milling operations. Appl. Soft Comput. **37**, 114–124 (2015)
5. Ramesh, R., Mannan, M., Poo, A., Keerthi, S.: Thermal error measurement and modelling in machine tools. part ii. Hybrid Bayesian network–support vector machine model. Int. J. Mach. Tools Manuf. **43**(4), 405–419 (2003)
6. Blum, A., Mitchell, T.: Combining labeled and unlabeled data with co-training. In: Proceedings of the Eleventh Annual Conference on Computational Learning Theory, COLT 1998, pp. 92–100 (1998)
7. Nigam, K., Ghani, R.: Analyzing the effectiveness and applicability of co-training. In: Proceedings of the Ninth International Conference on Information and Knowledge Management, ser. CIKM 2000, pp. 86–93. Association for Computing Machinery, New York (2000)
8. Yu, S., Krishnapuram, B., Rosales, R., Rao, R.B.: Bayesian co-training. J. Mach. Learn. Res. **12**(80), 2649–2680 (2011)
9. Balcan, M.-F., Blum, A., Yang, K.: Co-training and expansion: towards bridging theory and practice. In: Advances in Neural Information Processing Systems, pp. 89–96 (2005)
10. Dempster, A.P., Laird, N.M., Rubin, D.B.: Maximum likelihood from incomplete data via the EM algorithm. J. R. Stat. Soc.: Ser. B **39**, 1–38 (1977)
11. McLachlan, G., Krishnan, T.: The EM Algorithm and Extensions. Wiley Series in Probability and Statistics, 2nd edn. Wiley, Hoboken (2008)
12. Lauritzen, S., Wermuth, N.: Graphical models for associations between variables, some of which are qualitative and some quantitative. Ann. Stat. **17**, 31–57 (1989)
13. Dua, D., Graff, C.: UCI machine learning repository (2017). http://archive.ics.uci.edu/ml

14. Ling, C.X., Du, J., Zhou, Z.-H.: When does co-training work in real data? In: Theeramunkong, T., Kijsirikul, B., Cercone, N., Ho, T.-B. (eds.) PAKDD 2009. LNCS (LNAI), vol. 5476, pp. 596–603. Springer, Heidelberg (2009). https://doi.org/10.1007/978-3-642-01307-2_58
15. Godreau, V., Ritou, M., Chové, E., Furet, B., Dumur, D.: Continuous improvement of HSM process by data mining. J. Intell. Manuf. **30**(7), 2781–2788 (2019)
16. Lemaître, G., Nogueira, F., Aridas, C.K.: Imbalanced-learn: a python toolbox to tackle the curse of imbalanced datasets in machine learning. J. Mach. Learn. Res. **18**(17), 1–5 (2017). http://jmlr.org/papers/v18/16-365
17. Dietterich, T.G.: Approximate statistical tests for comparing supervised classification learning algorithms. Neural Comput. **10**(7), 1895–1923 (1998)
18. Seabold, S., Perktold, J.: Statsmodels: econometric and statistical modeling with python. In: 9th Python in Science Conference, pp. 92–96 (2010)
19. Vomlel, J.: Probabilistic reasoning with uncertain evidence. Neural Netw. World **14**, 453–466 (2004)
20. Guo, X., Wang, W.: Towards making co-training suffer less from insufficient views. Front. Comput. Sci. **13**(1), 99–105 (2019)
21. Srinivas, S.: A generalization of the noisy-or model. In: UAI 1993 Proceedings of the Ninth International Conference on Uncertainty in Artificial Intelligence, pp. 208–215 (1993)
22. Díez, F.J., Druzdzel, M.J.: Canonical probabilistic models for knowledge engineering. UNED, Madrid, Spain, Technical report CISIAD-06-01 (2006)

BigData and Time Series Processing

Implementation of Neural Network Regression Model for Faster Redshift Analysis on Cloud-Based Spark Platform

Snigdha Sen[1,2]($\boxtimes$) (iD), Snehanshu Saha[3] (iD), Pavan Chakraborty[1] (iD), and Krishna Pratap Singh[1] (iD)

[1] Indian Institute of Information Technology, Prayagraj, India
[2] Global Academy of Technology, Bangalore, India
[3] CSIS and APPCAIR BITS Pilani K K Birla Goa Campus, Pilani, Goa, India

Abstract. Since observational astronomy has turned into data-driven astronomy recently, analyzing this huge data effectively to extract useful information is becoming an important and essential task day by day. In this paper, we developed a neural network model to analyze redshift data of million of extragalactic objects. In order to do that, two different approaches for faster training of neural networks have been proposed. The first approach deals with the training model using Lipschitz-based adaptive learning rate in a single node/machine whereas the second approach discusses processing astronomy data in a multinode clustered environment. This approach can scale up to accommodate multiple nodes when necessary to handle bulk data using Apache spark and Elephas. Additionally, this paper also addresses the scalability and storage issue by implementing the model on the cloud. We used the distributed processing capability of the spark that reads data directly from HDFS (Hadoop Distributed File System) of multiple machines and our experimental results show that using these approaches we can reduce training time and CPU time tremendously which is a crucial requirement while dealing with the extensive dataset. Although we have tested our experiment on a subset of huge data it can be scaled to process data of any size as well without much hurdle.

Keywords: Astronomical big data · Adaptive learning rate · Apache spark · Elephas · Distributed processing

1 Introduction

Astronomy is witnessing accelerated and terabyte range data [1] growth from multiple diverse sky surveys captured through sophisticated instruments and telescopic cameras. Upcoming LSST (Large Synoptic Survey Telescope) and SKA (Square Kilometre Array) are expected to generate data even in the higher range. To exclusively deal with astronomical big data and its challenges, a new interdisciplinary branch Astroinformatics has been proposed by Borne [2]. In

© Springer Nature Switzerland AG 2021
H. Fujita et al. (Eds.): IEA/AIE 2021, LNAI 12799, pp. 591–602, 2021.
https://doi.org/10.1007/978-3-030-79463-7_50

addition to rapid data surge, astronomical data is of very high dimension and complex in nature too. Hence a constant need arises to analyze these data efficiently which will further lead to the exotic discovery.

In this paper, we contemplate analyzing redshift data precisely. Broadly, Redshift is a very important cosmological parameter that helps us to measure the distance to galaxies from the earth and finally comprehend the structure of the universe better. Handling, accommodating, and manipulating this proliferated growth of data is beyond the capacity of the conventional data management system. Therefore astronomers are looking for an efficient and robust solution that has driven astronomy towards using machine learning and big data environment. Recently and over the years researchers are motivated to analyze astronomical data for solving various critical issues and subsequently making novel discoveries about the universe. Although a lot of work has been reported in this direction, most of the work was reported using a centralized system and limited data set. Traditional data processing system was enough until data size did not reach beyond the limit. It is observed and tested that traditional systems with limited capacity cannot handle this growth of data and maintaining an on-premise infrastructure system is becoming more expensive as well. Instead, cloud-based platform offers on-demand services and inexpensive solution.

Despite deep network is powerful in understanding features and data complexity well from large data, it suffers from prolonged training time because of its complicated large number of hyperparameters and heavy computation due to usage of high performing computers. This issue has been a hindrance in deep learning research. Working with a single node or machine won't be solving astronomical big data challenges anymore as a single machine's network complexity soars with oversized data.

Although high-performance GPU offers a solution but at the same time very expensive as well. On contrary, Apache Hadoop and spark provide a much cheaper solution with commodity hardware. Spark being an open-source distributed computing framework is much faster than Hadoop map-reduce because of its capability of in-memory processing. Big data technologies and ML (machine learning) algorithms collectively can be an excellent combination for providing optimal solutions to the problem. In order to mitigate the burden on a single machine, both ML and bigdata framework together will provide high-speed performance, lesser training time while developing the accurate model. The objective of our study is to build a neural network model to analyze and process vast astronomical data without elongated execution time. Hence utilization of spark-based cluster is a popular choice that will expedite distributed processing of bulky datasets across many nodes inside the cluster. Our approach will be fault-tolerant and reliable and can be scaled up to handle data of any size.

2   Related Work

Plenty of machine learning and big data approaches have been proposed by many researchers in this area. We discuss a few recent advancements here. Ball et al. [3]

first introduced the need for astronomical data mining and proposed various machine learning and data mining approaches for better data analysis. Kremer et al. [4] highlighted several challenges of data-rich astronomy and different machine learning and image analysis approaches tested on those data. The benefits and importance of Artificial intelligence and machine learning in astronomy have been illustrated by Fluke et al. [5] elaborately. The authors mentioned how ML algorithms can be used in analyzing petabyte-scale astronomy data. Baron et al. [6] primarily concentrated on unsupervised machine learning algorithm emphasizing principal component analysis (PCA) and K-means clustering etc. and application of those in astronomical data analysis.

In the context of galaxy morphological classification, Barchi et al. [7] evaluated a comparative study between machine and deep learning algorithms. Wadadekar [8] presented SVM based approach for redshift estimation whereas Collister et al. [9] discussed artificial neural network-based model. On the other hand, Garofalo et al. [10] depicted the issues of astronomical big data and tells the need for ML and big data in this context whereas a cloud-based astronomical data mining tool CANFAR+Skytree [11] which is considered first cloud project on astronomy, was suggested by Ball. CANFAR and Skytree offer high computing power along with petabyte range memory access.

Recently, Hong et al. [12] worked on a spark-based framework for the topological structure of gravitational clustering. VeljkoVujci et al. [13] experimented on real-time astrophysical data processing project GRIST that uses a grid computing approach internally and processes images. The benefits of using python 2.7 while working with cross-matching catalogs of an extensive dataset have been discussed by Juric. In a similar direction, Wiley et al. presented how Hadoop MapReduce helps to process large images captured from SDSS. Later, Brahem et al. [14] work is focused on developing an in-memory distributed software Astroide for astronomical data processing, query, and optimization.

Distributed data processing surely benefits astronomers in any respect. ADQL and data partitioning technique HEALPix pixilationcis are used to speed up query processing. Their work showed the benefit of spark over other solutions. Zhang et al. [15] suggested the image processing framework Kira which gives more efficient performance over supercomputer. Using an in-memory computation facility and streaming of spark, it assists in quicker data analysis. Investigating solutions in the same way, Zecevic et al. [16] used AstroPy packages and SQL statements and built spark-based open-source scalable astronomical data analysis framework AXS to query and analyze large astronomical catalogs. Data partitioning is done by AXS in a distributed manner. Williams et al. [17] has stored and analyzed huge data generated from PHAT survey data on AWS EC2 instance quite efficiently and effectively whereas Araya et al. [18] has developed a jupyter notebook-based interface which helps in astronomical data processing in the cloud and offers high-performance computing. Although spark has been applied in other applications of astronomy, analyzing redshift data is not been explored much.

The manuscript is organised as follows. Section 2 describes related work and Sect. 3 presents our contribution and approaches. In Sect. 4 and 5 we illustrate about dataset and experimental setup. Results and discussion have been discussed in Sect. 6. Finally we conclude with prospective future enhancements.

3   Our Contribution

In our paper primarily we contribute by adopting two distinct approaches.

1. We show the potential of Lipschitz constant based learning rate [19] for faster training of a neural network model
2. We show the usefulness of spark based distributed deep learning model for quicker training of a neural network model.

3.1   Learning Rate Setting Using Lipschitz Constant

As we are aware that during neural network training, learning rate plays a dominant role to reach global minima. With a very low learning rate, a neural network takes a long time to train whereas a larger learning rate often misses global minima. In our first approach, we try to use a novel adaptive learning rate scheme based on the Lipschitz constant which will help neural networks converge faster.

Basically Lipschitz constant sets a limit on how fast can a function change and it restricts a function from becoming discontinuous. We can call a function $g(y)$ Lipschitz continuous if a constant p exists in the function domain which will restrict the absolute slope value between two points from becoming greater than p. Therefore, Lipschitz constant will be the minimum value of p. In mathematics, the Lipschitz constant of function g, which depends on input y, can be written as $\|g(y_1) - g(y_2)\| \leq m \|y_1 - y_2\|$ where p is the Lipschitz constant. In this approach we have used Mean Absolute Error (MAE) as a loss function for our analysis and as MAE follows Lipschitz continuity in its domain, there should be a Lipschitz constant p. Because of mean value theorem , the supremum of the gradient, sup $\|\nabla g(y)\|$, will be there and the supremum of the gradient will be the Lipschitz constant.

As we know, we have a lesser value of gradient in the preceding layers than the last layer of a neural network and to obtain the maximum gradient value of a neural network we need to know the last layer gradient value. The following equation proves to be true

$$\max_{mn} \left\| \frac{\partial Error}{\partial w_{mn}^{[Last]}} \right\| \geq \left\| \frac{\partial Error}{\partial w_{mn}^{[l]}} \right\| \forall l, m, n$$

We can calculate the Lipschitz constant of the loss function, $max \|\nabla_w g\|$ and we restrain weight change using weight updating formula to $\triangle w \leq 1$ by using reciprocal of the Lipschitz constant as the learning rate of the model. with L set to Lipschitz constant, The gradient descent slowly decreases g if $\eta = 1/L$

$$\mathbf{w} = \mathbf{w} - \eta.\nabla_w g$$

where $\eta = \frac{1}{max\|\nabla_w g\|}$ and known as learning rate.

As discussed above we had chosen MAE as a error function for our neural network model on the basis of MAE is a Lipschitz continious function in L1-norm and it is very robust. In regression task MAE implies upper bound of the error. MAE is denoted as $MAE = 1/n \sum_{j=1}^{n} \|(y_1 - y_2)\|L^1$.

Proof. If we consider two values, y_1 and y_2 where $y_1, y_2 \in R^n$ and $D \in R^n$ then MAE can be written as $\|MAE(y_1 - D) - MAE(y_2 - D)\| = \|(y_1 - D - y_2 + D)\|$, from triangle inequality it will assume the following form: $\le \|(y_1 - D - y_2 + D)\|$ that is in turn $\le \|(y_1 - y_2)\|$.

Theorem 1. *Consider a composite function F where $F \in D^1$ of MAE loss function $M(E)$ and a linear regression function G, the difference can be bounded by $|F(y + h) - F(y)| \le P_{ED}\|(h)\|$ where $F(y) = MAE(G(y))$ and P_{ED} is some random constant.*

Proof. From triangle inequality theorem $|F(y + h) - F(y)| \le P_{ED} \|(y + h - y)\| = P_{ED}\|(h)\|_{L^1}$ where P_{ED} is known as Lipschitz constant.

3.2   Distributed Processing Using Spark

Being a part of the Hadoop ecosystem, Apache spark [20] is a distributed data processing and real-time streaming framework to deal with big data. Developed by UC Berkeley AMP Lab Spark's in-memory processing reduces large I/O overhead. Directed Acyclic Graph (DAG) of spark describes the parallel task and maintains data locality while task scheduling. It also helps to recover lost data through linage-based re-execution. In addition to reading data from HDFS, Spark can read data from AWS s3 also. We have deployed our model in spark clustered configuration as spark reduces execution delay. Multiple nodes together form a cluster and it works in the concepts of one master node and remaining data/workers nodes. Spark context is the main entry point of the spark program. We use Pyspark [21] for our implementation here which is a python API that facilitates developing a machine learning model in spark.

As there is no deep learning library in spark, in this approach we used Elephas to develop our distributed deep learning model. Elephas [22] is inherently an extension to Keras that can deal with massive data using spark. We use a data-parallel approach, where multiple worker nodes will be having distributed data, running parallelly across machines and all worker nodes will apply the same algorithm on different data set. Distribution has a hugely positive effect on the reduction of training time. In our approach data parallelization, asynchronous training, and data-parallel algorithms are implemented on Keras, using Spark's RDDs and data frames.

At the beginning of implementation, after installing Elephas, we create pyspark context and define the Keras neural network model. Only Elephas 0.4.5 version supports the regression task. Other versions of Elephas are mainly for solving a classification problem. Keras model is initialized on the driver, then serialization and distribution are done to worker nodes, while broadcasting data and model parameters. After getting a job, Worker nodes deserialize the model, train the data portion of their part and transfer their gradients back to the driver. The optimizer updates the master node by taking gradients from others either through synchronous or asynchronous communication.

As regular Keras library can't handle spark data frame while training model, Elephas is the solution that takes RDD (Resilient Distributed Dataset) as input data. In Spark, RDD offers an abstraction and logical partition of data distributed among multiple nodes. SparkModel is the elementary model in Elephas which takes compiled Keras model during training and the mode of parallelization either synchronous or asynchronous. Working of Spark and Elephas has been shown in Fig. 1 and 2 respectively. Then we discuss various components of proposed setup and their interconnection in Fig. 3.

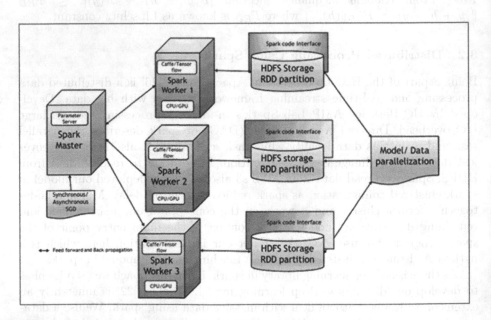

Fig. 1. How Spark works [20]

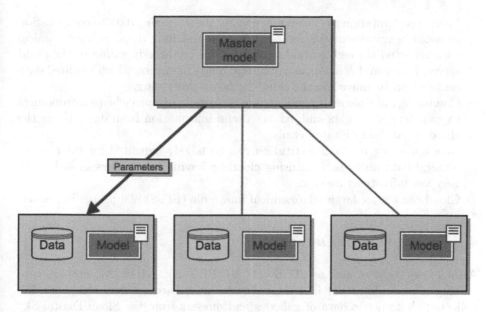

Fig. 2. How Elephas works [22]

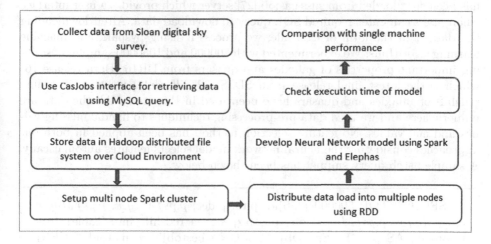

Fig. 3. Framework for fast astronomical data processing

3.3   Benefits of the Cloud for Astronomy

– It offers reliable and sustainable storage solution of astronomical big data problem which operates in any time anywhere concept on-demand basis
– Astronomers can make use of high-performance computers or supercomputers for data analysis without buying it that is much powerful than their personal machines. This way cost optimization can be done.

- Moving computation to data is much faster than bringing data to computation to avoid heavy downloads for large images and bulk data. So astronomical data collected through several telescopes can be directly stored in the cloud server. Heavy and complex astronomical query operation which required data centers, can be moved to the cloud for faster processing.
- Combining multiple astronomical data archives in one place helps astronomers to gain deeper insights and extract useful information from data. Using the cloud, it can be facilitated easily.
- New upcoming research institution can be hugely benefited for their astronomical data analysis work using cloud by having a web browser only with very low infrastructure cost.
- Cloud can enable large astronomical image file (FITS) [23] processing faster.

4 Description of Dataset

A lot of sky surveys such as SDSS [24], VIPERS [25], KIDS [26], etc. are generating massive data that is being collected by researchers over the years. We collected photometric data of galaxies and quasars from the Sloan Digital Sky Survey (SDSS), the most wide survey to date for our research. The real dataset has been downloaded from sdss casjob [27] server which provides a user interface where users can enter required SQL query to download data. After downloading the dataset in the form of CSV file, we process it using pyspark and machine learning algorithms. We experimented with 500000 and 1050000 samples describing important properties of galaxies and quasars from DR16 (Data release 16) which is the latest final release from SDSS. 32 different properties including redshift of galaxies and quasars have been used in this study. All the data are numeric here and we used data pre-processing techniques to handle missing values and null values. No feature selection method has been applied in both our approaches considering the neural network model selects features automatically. A sample batch query snippet has been shown below.

SELECT TOP 500000 p.objid, p.ra, p.dec, $p.psfMag\_u$, $p.psfMag\_g$, $p.psfMag\_r$, $p.psfMag\_i$, p.r, p.i, p.z, $s.z$ as redshift into Table1 from PhotoObj AS p JOIN SpecObj AS s ON s.bestobjid = p.objid WHERE s.class='GALAXY' OR s.class='QSO' AND clean=1

5 Experimental Setup

For Lipschitz based approach, we train our model in a single machine with 8 GB RAM. For the second approach, we design and implement and train our deep learning model in spark cluster. For our work, we used the services from leading cloud provider Amazon web services (AWS) [28] EC2 instances Ubuntu machine and set up multi-node spark cluster. The entire experiment has been carried out in a cluster environment with 1 Gateway node, 1 Master node, and 5 Data/slave nodes with 124 GB RAM. While setting up a cluster for master node and slave nodes, we generated valid AWS key pair for authentication and configured Yet Another Resource Negotiator (YARN) as a job scheduler.

When the cluster is ready, after reading data using the spark.read.csv function, we convert it into pandas for splitting the data. Then using Keras we developed the model. Elephas uses the spark model to train the dataset and this spark model takes rdd version of the dataset while training along with other parameters such as epochs and parallelization mode. Using tosimplerdd() we convert panadas dataframe to rdd. In Table 1 and 2 we had shown performance comparison between standalone system and cloud-based spark cluster. The result shows that a reduction in training time implies if the dataset grows also it will be able to handle these without much effort. Here we showed results improvement in two different aspects- reduction in training time and CPU time. To test our approach, we used samples of dataset although this model can be scaled properly to handle massive data. Sometimes people report hardware limitation issues but this can be easily avoided by executing the model on a cloud environment.

6 Results and Discussion

6.1 Lipschitz Based Approach

In this approach, we developed a neural network model on a single machine and trained using adaptive as well as constant learning rate of .1. Configuration of the network is done using 2 hidden layers with 18 and 15 neurons respectively. Relu is used as an activation function in hidden layers whereas soft sign is applied in the output layer. Here we have compared the performance of adaptive and constant learning rate using MAE as a loss function. Figure 4 depicts Lipschitz-based learning rate offers faster convergence of model, thus implying less training time. Time taken for execution is .82 min for 20 epochs and 1.70 min for 40 epochs.

6.2 Spark Based Approach

Here we trained the model using spark in a clustered setup as well as non clustered setup without spark. 2 hidden layers with 128 neurons have been used to build the model along with the Relu activation function. Tables 1 and 2 respectively present comparative performance evaluation. From these two tables, it is evident that processing data in a clustered setup provides a drastic reduction in training time as expected. After increasing the number of hidden layers to 3 and 4, we get training time .0635 min and .0775 min respectively. It indicates that a deep network also executes faster without much effort.

From Tables 1 and 2, we can see that CPU time is tremendously reduced from minutes to milliseconds in the case of clustered approach. Even for a very large number of samples also, it executes fast. Here CPU time implies the duration

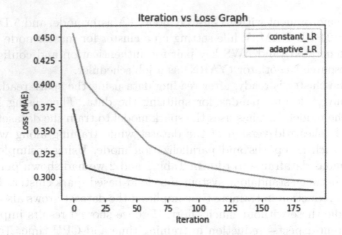

Fig. 4. Training of model

Table 1. Performance evaluation of non clustered environment

No. of samples	Epoch	Total time	CPU time
500000	20	1.17 min	1.53 min
500000	40	2.31 min	3.43 min

Table 2. Performance evaluation of clustered environment

No. of samples	Epoch	Total time	CPU time
500000	20	.076 min	381 ms
500000	40	.099 min	684 ms
1050000	20	.068 min	388 ms
1050000	40	.088 min	678 ms

CPU was busy. In the case of adaptive learning rate (LR) in Fig. 4, within a few iteration model is converging whereas constant LR needs a higher number of iteration. Reduction of training time subsequently helps in reducing carbon emission too which is a great concern in any AI and ML research.

7 Conclusion

Our suggested methods definitely gives faster results leveraging facility of adaptive learning rate and distributed computing among multiple nodes. With Apache spark integrated with Elephas library giving improvement in performance. Our result demonstrated the fact that efficient resource sharing leads to quicker convergence as well as less execution time. It will allow us to deal with colossal data in future. Various experiment using increasing or deceasing nodes and assessing performance will be our future study. Furthermore we are planning to implement the Lipschitz based neural network model in a multinode clustered environment and evaluate its performance improvement.

References

1. Tallada, P., et al.: CosmoHub: interactive exploration and distribution of astronomical data on Hadoop. Astron. Comput. **32**, 100391 (2020)
2. Borne, K.D.: Astroinformatics: a 21st century approach to astronomy. arXiv preprint arXiv:0909.3892 (2009)
3. Ball, N.M., Brunner, R.J.: Data mining and machine learning in astronomy. Int. J. Mod. Phys. D **19**(07), 1049–1106 (2010)
4. Kremer, J., et al.: Big universe, big data: machine learning and image analysis for astronomy. IEEE Intell. Syst. **32**(2), 16–22 (2017)
5. Fluke, C.J., et al.: Surveying the reach and maturity of machine learning and artificial intelligence in astronomy. Wiley Interdiscip. Rev.: Data Min. Knowl. Discov. **10**(2), e1349 (2020)
6. Baron, D.: Machine learning in astronomy: a practical overview. arXiv preprint arXiv:1904.07248 (2019)
7. Barchi, P.H., et al.: Machine and deep learning applied to galaxy morphology-a comparative study. Astron. Comput. **30**, 100334 (2020)
8. Wadadekar, Y.: Estimating photometric redshifts using support vector machines. Publ. Astron. Soc. Pac. **117**(827), 79 (2004)
9. Collister, A.A., Lahav, O.: ANNz: estimating photometric redshifts using artificial neural networks. Publ. Astron. Soc. Pac. **116**(818), 345 (2004)
10. Garofalo, M., Botta, A., Ventre, G.: Astrophysics and big data: challenges, methods, and tools. Proc. Int. Astron. Union **12**(S325), 345–348 (2016)
11. Ball, N.M.: CANFAR+ Skytree: a cloud computing and data mining system for astronomy. arXiv preprint arXiv:1312.3996 (2013)
12. Hong, S., et al.: Constraining cosmology with big data statistics of cosmological graphs. Mon. Not. R. Astron. Soc. **493**(4), 5972–5986 (2020)
13. Vujčić, V., Darko, J.: Real-time stream processing in astronomy. In: Knowledge Discovery in Big Data from Astronomy and Earth Observation, pp. 173–182. Elsevier (2020)
14. Brahem, M., Zeitouni, K., Yeh, L.: Astroide: a unified astronomical big data processing engine over spark. IEEE Trans. Big Data **6**(3), 477–491 (2018)
15. Zhang, Z., et al.: Kira: processing astronomy imagery using big data technology. IEEE Trans. Big Data **6**(2), 369–381 (2016)
16. Zečević, P., et al.: AXS: a framework for fast astronomical data processing based on Apache Spark. Astron. J. **158**(1), 37 (2019)
17. Williams, B.F., et al.: Reducing and analyzing the PHAT survey with the cloud. Astrophys. J. Suppl. Ser. **236**(1), 4 (2018)
18. Araya, M., et al.: JOVIAL: notebook-based astronomical data analysis in the cloud. Astron. Comput. **25**, 110–117 (2018)
19. Yedida, R., Saha, S., Prashanth, T.: LipschitzLR: using theoretically computed adaptive learning rates for fast convergence. Appl. Intell. **51**(3), 1460–1478 (2020). https://doi.org/10.1007/s10489-020-01892-0
20. Spark Homepage. https://spark.apache.org/. Accessed 29 Jan 2021

21. PySpark Homepage. https://spark.apache.org/docs/latest/api/python/index.html. Accessed 29 Jan 2021
22. elephas Homepage. https://github.com/maxpumperla/elephas
23. Pence, W.D., et al.: Definition of the flexible image transport system (fits), version 3.0. Astron. Astrophys. **524**, A42 (2010)
24. SDSS Homepage. https://sdss.org. Accessed 29 Jan 2021
25. VIPERS Homepage. http://vipers.inaf.it/. Accessed 29 Jan 2021
26. KIDS Homepage. http://kids.strw.leidenuniv.nl/. Accessed 29 Jan 2021
27. casjob Homepage. https://skyserver.sdss.org/casjobs/. Accessed 29 Jan 2021
28. AWS Homepage. https://aws.amazon.com/. Accessed 29 Jan 2021

Target Class Supervised Sample Length and Training Sample Reduction of Univariate Time Series

Sanjay Kumar Sonbhadra$^{(\boxtimes)}$, Sonali Agarwal , and P. Nagabhushan

IIIT Allahabad, Prayagraj 211015, India
{rsi2017502,sonali,pnagabhushan}@iiita.ac.in

Abstract. The anomaly/novelty detection in time series data analysis is one of the most admired area of research, which is specifically a one-class classification problem. Concerning univariate time series data, apart from a huge number of training samples the higher sample span (observation length) also adds computation overhead along with its intrinsic issue of curse of dimensionality (sample length is considered as dimension). In this context, the present research proposes a concurrent way of sample span (treated as dimension) and training sample reduction approach for univariate time series data under the supervision of target class samples. Data representation of time series decides the performance of any machine learning approach, therefore the present research utilizes dissimilarity-based representation (DBR) techniques for time series data representation and later to reduce the sample length, a knowledge grid is computed via eigen space analysis of variance-covariance of target class samples. This knowledge grid is further used to transform the original sample length to reduced one. Afterwards, the training samples are selected using prototype methods. For experiments 16 different DBR measures are used along with 11 prototype techniques. Finally, one-class support vector machine (OCSVM) and 1-nearest neighbour (1-NN) are utilized for classification to validate the performance of proposed approach over 85 UCR/UEA univariate datasets.

Keywords: Time series · Target class · One-class classification · Curse of dimensionality · Sample reduction · Dissimilarity-based representation · Prototype

1 Introduction

Time series are temporal arrival of data in an ordered manner. All real time applications such as sales, social behaviour, industrial applications, meteorology, geophysics, astrophysics etc., contain the time series observations [5]. In today's environment of big data and real time applications, the time series classification (TSC) is most interesting and challenging area of research in the field of pattern recognition and data mining [13,22,41]. Representation of raw time series data

© Springer Nature Switzerland AG 2021
H. Fujita et al. (Eds.): IEA/AIE 2021, LNAI 12799, pp. 603–614, 2021.
https://doi.org/10.1007/978-3-030-79463-7_51

is one of the major concern that decides computational resource requirement and performance of machine learning tasks [12,40]. In this paper, vector representation of time series is obtained through dissimilarity-based representation (DBR) [11] techniques to ensure information preservation [18] for further processing. Meanwhile, apart from massive sample space, huge dimensionality of the time series also leads computation overhead along with its own intrinsic problem of curse of dimensionality [38]. The objective of this research is to reduce the sample length along with the number of training samples to maximize the learning ability for minimum false-negative and false-positive concerning the target class. Therefore, this paper proposes a novel tweak of sample length reduction technique via knowledge grid obtained by eigen space analysis on only target class samples and demonstrates the effectiveness of prototype methods [27] for training sample selection. The present research utilizes OCSVM and 1-NN for classification in presence of most promising training samples with reduced sample span obtained by the proposed method. As per above discussion, following are the key contributions of this paper:

- Dissimilarity-based representation (DBR) techniques are used to represent the time series.
- Guided by the target class, a concurrent way of sample span and training sample reduction concerning to the target class is proposed, where:
  - Considering only the target class samples, a knowledge grid (K) is computed via eigen space analysis of variance-covariance matrix.
  - 11 different prototyping methods are used to reduce the number of training samples.
- For experiments, 85 UCR/UEA univariate time series datasets are utilized and selection of training sample size is done with 20%, 40% and 80% of the overall population.
- OCSVM and 1-NN are evaluated for classification performance (area under the receiver operating characteristics (AUROC) is used as performance metric) in presence of reduced training set with identified sample length via proposed approach.

The rest of the paper is organized as follows: Sect. 2 briefs the literature on data representation and one-class classification of time series. The proposed approach is discussed in Sect. 3, whereas experiments and results are discussed in Sect. 4. Concluding remarks and future scope are discussed in Sect. 5.

2   Related Work

Data representation of time series is an important area of research to enhance the performance of any machine learning algorithm [26]. In present research, dissimilarity based representation (DBR) techniques are utilized to represent the time series. The DBR techniques describe one unknown object through a direct pairwise comparison with a set of reference objects, and has been proven an effective alternative for the original feature space representation when addressing multi-class classification problems [8,32]. But for one-class classification very limited number of research works are reported till date concerning DBR representation. Specifically, for one-class classification problems, the effectiveness of DBR based representation is demonstrated by Mauceri et al. [23], where full sample span was considered for experiments, and 8 prototype selection methods were used to chose prototypes. The present research aims to use DBR techniques to obtain better feature vector representation for further processing. For experiments, 16 different DBR techniques have been used out of many as discussed by Giusti and Batista [17]. Later, to reduce the sample span; a novel feature transformation via knowledge grid method is proposed using eigen space analysis followed by sample reduction via prototype selection [27] methods.

In present research, the sample length (span) is considered as the dimension of samples. For time series data, many DR based research articles have been published towards binary and multi-class classification [3,14]. But, it is evident that concerning to target class guided dimensionality reduction for one-class classification tasks of time series, there is no research article published till date (to the best of our knowledge). It is also evident from deep insight into literature of univariate time series data analysis that there is no research accomplished towards sample length reduction (considered as dimensionality reduction). In this context, a novel way of sample length reduction method is proposed via eigen space analysis.

Aiming to the target class mining, one-class classifiers (OCCs) are the best practice to solve anomaly and novelty detection problems in several application domains like healthcare, industry, text mining, audio and video processing, intrusion detection, etc. [1,2,34,35]. Binary and multi-class classifiers may give biased outcomes, if the dataset suffers from severe class imbalance problem i.e. either the positive class (also known as target class or CoI) is well defined and the other classes are either absent or ill-defined. During past decades several one-class classification algorithms have been published like one-class random forest (OCRF), one-class nearest neighbour (1-NN), one-class support vector machine (OCSVM), support vector data description (SVDD), one-class neural network, etc. [6,20,24,29]. With deep insight into literature, it is evident that very limited research work has been done concerning time series one-class classification, and it is observed that 1-nearest neighbour is the most commonly used one-class classifier for time series analysis. Recently, deep learning models are becoming popular to perform anomaly detection task [42]. The performance of any classification model highly depends on the quality of the input features; therefore, this paper proposes a novel feature transformation model (sample length reduction approach) for target class mining along with sample reduction via prototype methods, whereas OCSVM and 1-NN are evaluated for classification performance.

3   Proposed Approach

The proposed approach is divided into four components:

- Data representation using DBR.

– Sample length reduction via knowledge grid (K).
– Training sample reduction using prototyping.
– One-class classification.

Data representation is the one of the important step for time series classification task. DBR is a feature based data representation approach that transforms the time series into feature-vectors to perform machine learning tasks. For data representation, 16 different dissimilarity based measures are used in this research. Apart from data representation, sample length and number of training samples play key roles in performance of machine learning algorithms. In the context of binary and multi-class classification of time series data, many dimensionality reduction techniques have also been proposed [33], but target class guided dimensionality reduction techniques have not been reported till date for time series analysis. Hence, the present research proposes a novel way of sample length reduction (can be considered as dimensionality reduction) of time series guided by the target class samples and later, the training samples are selected using 11 prototype selection methods to obtain best class representatives. Finally, with the help of reduced samples with most discriminating features, state-of-the-art one-class classification models are trained. Later, testing is done on all trainable, non-trainable in-class and out-class samples. Figure 1 shows the schematic of overall process.

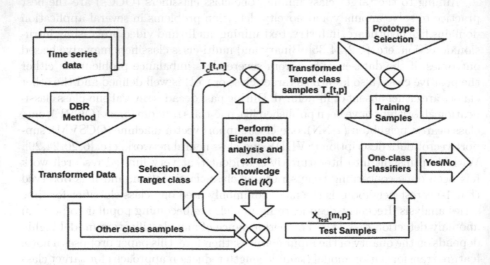

Fig. 1. Schematic of proposed approach

In this research, a time series is represented as a vector of dissimilarities using following 16 dissimilarity measure techniques: L_1 (Manhattan), L_2 (Euclidean), and L_∞ (Chebyshev), cosine dissimilarity, dynamic time warping (DTW), edit distance on real sequences (EDR), move split merge dissimilarity

(MSM), auto-correlation dissimilarity, Gaussian kernel, Sigmoid kernel, Kullback-Leibler, Wasserstein dissimilarity, maximum shifting correlation, Minkowski distance, Mahalanobis and Jaccard score [7, 10, 16, 19, 25, 30, 36, 39].

3.1 Sample Length (span) Reduction

The objective of this research is to reduce the length of samples of univariate time series that can be viewed as dimensionality reduction task. It is assumed that initially, only the target class samples (let T_c is the target class) are available, where the eigenspace analysis will be performed. This constitutes the problem of finding a function F to map the target class as $Y_{ESpace} \leftarrow F(T_c)$ which represents the transformed form of the target class. The objective is to find a suitable representation of the target class and also to help in accomplishing a reduction in the undesired features.

The eigen subspace obtained from the function F satisfies the following two basic objectives:

- Enhances the associativity among target class samples.
- Ensures target class discrimination over other class samples.

Statistically, both these objectives are contradictory to each other, because associativity measures the proximity of the target class samples from its mean denoted as A_{CoI} and the associativity within the intended class is reciprocal to the variance (a measure of the scattering of the data) i.e. $A_{CoI} \propto \frac{1}{var(CoI)}$. On the other hand, $significance(f_{discrim}) \propto var(CoI)$. The features satisfying the above conditions also follows the objectives indicated below:

- Maximize the target class density to avoid the false rejection of the target class.
- Minimize the false acceptance into the target class during the classification process. To accomplish this, the variance-covariance of target class samples is to be analysed.

Consider the dataset $X = [x_1, x_2, \ldots x_t]^T$ where $x_i = \{x_i^1, x_i^2, \ldots x_i^n\}$ and classes are $Y = \{C_1, C_2, \ldots C_m\}$. Initially, the target class (T_c) samples are available as training set and after normalization, covariance matrix is calculated using following:

$$Cov(T_c) = \frac{1}{t} T_C^T T_C \tag{1}$$

After diagonalization of matrix T_c following is obtained:

$$D[Cov(T_c)] = V \Sigma V^T \tag{2}$$

where the columns of the matrix V are the eigenvector (EV) of the covariance matrix and Σ is a diagonal matrix containing the respective eigenvalues in the increasing order as $\lambda_1, \lambda_2, \ldots, \lambda_n$. Let the range is λ is $[\underline{\lambda}, \overline{\lambda}]$

Eigen vectors (EV_s) are identified as follows:

$$EVs([T_c]) = [EV_1, EV_2, \ldots EV_n] \qquad (3)$$

The EV_s are further selected based on the variance, where the higher and lower valued EV_s are directly rejected (via Eqs. 5 and 6 respectively) because the lower valued EV_s do not contribute significant information and higher valued EV_s may split the target class itself. Cumulative variance of EV_s can be calculated as:

$$EV_{cum}^{var} = [EV_1^{var}, EV_2^{var}, \ldots, EV_n^{var}] \qquad (4)$$

$$EV_{reject}^{high} \xleftarrow{k} \sum_{i=1}^{k} EV_i^{var} \geq \sum_{i=k}^{n} EV_i^{var} \qquad (5)$$

$$EV_{reject}^{low} \xleftarrow{n-(p+k)} \sum_{j=p+1}^{n} EV_j^{var} \leq \sum_{i=k+1}^{p} EV_i^{var} \qquad (6)$$

After rejecting higher and lower valued eigenvectors, the remaining vectors are treated as knowledge matrix (K) identified as follows:

$$K([T_c]) = [EV_{k+1}, EV_{k+2}, EV_{k+3}, \ldots, EV_p] \qquad (7)$$

where $var(EV_{k+1}) > var(EV_{k+2})$. The knowledge matrix K is further used to transform the samples from original length (n) to reduced length (p) where $p << n$ (Eq. 8).

$$X'_{[t,p]} = X_{[t,n]}.K_{[n.p]} \qquad (8)$$

Transformed features obtained by Eq. 8 represents the CoI and are further used for one-class classification. Algorithm 1 describes the overall process.

3.2   Training Sample Reduction

It is evident that very limited literature is available concerning prototype methods in the context of DBR. This area is often analyzed in the context of nearest prototype classification [21] that suffers from storage overhead and low noise tolerance, therefore it is argued that by reducing the training set to a smaller set of prototypes, it is possible to mitigate all these weaknesses while improving generalization performance [37]. Pekalska et al. [27] demonstrated that the set of prototypes should be large and diverse enough to represent the class of interest. The prototype methods can be divided into two groups: methods that select samples from the training data [15], and methods that generate "synthetic" prototypes [37]. Following 11 prototype methods are used for experiments: borders, centers Gaussian-mixture (CGM), centers k-means (CKM), closest, furthest, percentiles, random, support vectors (SVs), Bayesian Gaussian-mixture (BGM), affinity propagation (AP) and mini Batch k-means (MKM) [23,28,31,43]. The number of prototypes (training samples) is considered as hyperparameter (N).

Algorithm 1. LTC-ES algorithm

Input: Target class (T_c) samples $T_c[t, n]$
Output: Knowledge grid (K) representing Target class
Step 1: Calculation of mean and variance-covariance matrix:
      1.1 Calculate the mean:
         $\overline{T_c} = \frac{\sum_{i=1}^{t} x_{i,j}}{t}$ where $j \in 1, 2, \ldots, t$;
      1.2 Calculate variance-covariance matrix:
         $Cov(T_c) = \frac{1}{t} \sum (T_c - \overline{T_c})^T (T_c - \overline{T_c})$
Step 2: Eigen Decomposition:
      Eigen values: $\{\lambda_i\}$ where $i \in \{1, 2, \ldots, n\}$
      Corresponding Eigen vectors: $w = \{V_i\}$ where $i \in \{1, 2, \ldots, n\}$
Step 3: Transformation of input feature space
      $X^T . w$
Step 4: Selection of eigenvectors (EVs)
      4.1 Cumulative variance of EVs:
         $EV_{cum}^{var} = [EV_1^{var}, EV_2^{var}, \ldots, EV_n^{var}]$
      4.2 Reject higher valued EVs:
         $EV_{reject}^{high} \overset{k}{\leftarrow} \sum_{i=1}^{k} EV_i^{var} \geq \sum_{i=k}^{n} EV_i^{var}$
      4.3 Reject lower valued EVs:
         $EV_{reject}^{low} \overset{n-(k+p)}{\leftarrow} \sum_{j=p+1}^{n} EV_j^{var} \leq \sum_{i=k+1}^{p} EV_i^{var}$
Step 6: Extraction of most promising eigenvectors:
      $K([T_c]) = [EV_{k+1}, EV_{k+2}, EV_{k+3}, \ldots, EV_p]$
Step 7: Return knowledge grid K for T_c

3.3 Data and Experiment Design

To validate the performance of the proposed approach, experiments have been performed on UCR/UEA archive [9] for 85 univariate time series data-sets. Presently, it has been upgraded to 128 data-sets, but for this research the original 85 univariate datasets are experimented. All these datasets contain labelled training/test samples of different length and have previously been examined in several binary and multi-class time series classification experiments [4]. All used univariate time series contain only real numbers. Every time series contains samples of fixed length within a given data-set, and are z-normalized. Each dataset is experimented individually and finally the average performance (AUROC) of all the 85 datasets is shown in the Tables 1 and 2.

4 Experimental Setup and Results

Initially, above discussed DBR techniques are applied on all datasets. Later, for a given dataset available in archive; proposed sample length reduction technique is applied on the "only target class" samples to extract knowledge grid (K). The extracted knowledge grid is further used for transformation of training and test samples. After that, the prototype methods have been applied for different variations of number of training samples to be selected (hyperparameter $N = 20\%$, 40% and 80% samples of total population). For classification OCSVM and

1-NN have been applied as shown in Table 1 and 2. Each cell shows the average AUROC score on all 85 datasets. Experiments have been performed in presence of complete length (CL) and reduced length (RL) obtained by the proposed method. The classification performance is also evaluated with raw data (original data) where training samples are randomly selected with different values of hyperparameter N: 20%, 40% and 80%. All target class and other class samples are considered for testing.

Table 1. Average AUROC of OCSVM

Dissimilarity Measure	Borders		CGM		CKM		Closest		Furthest		Percentile		Random		SVs		BGM		AP		MKM		Avg		Random Rawdata
DBR 20%	CL	RL	CL	RL	CL	RL	CL	RL	CL	RL	CL	RL	CL	RL	CL	RL	CL	RL	CL	RL	CL	RL	CL	RL	**20%**
Manhattan	70	71	74	72	78	79	73	74	74	75	73	75	75	76	76	76	78	73	75	74	73	74	74	74	76
Euclidean	72	70	73	70	73	74	69	69	74	74	70	68	71	73	71	72	81	78	73	71	71	70	73	72	73
Chebyshev	73	72	72	72	79	80	72	76	76	77	75	75	73	73	75	74	78	76	72	74	70	71	74	75	74
Cosine	69	69	73	77	78	76	76	76	78	73	75	74	74	76	77	73	74	74	75	75	75	74	75	75	75
DTW	69	73	76	78	75	76	76	77	76	75	73	72	70	70	77	76	79	76	76	78	76	77	75	75	76
EDR	72	70	73	70	73	74	69	69	74	78	71	74	73	74	76	77	81	78	73	74	77	75	74	74	72
MSM	70	71	74	72	78	80	80	82	79	79	73	72	72	73	71	72	81	78	73	71	71	70	75	75	75
Autocorrelation	71	71	74	72	77	78	73	77	77	77	75	77	75	76	77	76	77	76	76	74	73	75	75	75	73
Gaussian	69	73	76	78	75	76	77	74	74	76	75	71	71	73	73	76	73	74	77	75	76	74	75	74	74
Sigmoid	70	73	77	79	76	76	76	75	73	75	72	72	75	75	72	73	78	80	76	75	73	70	74	75	77
Kullback-Leibler	72	70	73	70	73	74	69	69	74	78	76	75	71	71	70	70	76	82	78	75	75	75	73	74	76
Wasserstein dissimilarity	71	69	75	76	77	77	74	79	73	72	75	76	75	76	76	76	79	80	76	75	73	74	75	75	76
Maximum shifting correlation	69	73	76	78	75	76	76	77	76	77	71	73	73	73	75	74	78	78	76	75	73	77	74	76	76
Minkowski Distance	71	71	74	72	78	79	73	74	77	77	73	75	74	73	76	74	78	79	74	75	74	73	75	75	76
Mahalanobis	72	74	73	74	73	74	74	75	78	80	75	73	74	79	77	76	82	84	76	78	75	76	75	77	76
Jaccard Score	72	70	73	70	73	74	69	77	74	75	73	74	71	69	74	73	75	75	75	73	74	74	73	73	73
Avg	71	71	74	74	76	76	73	75	75	76	73	74	73	74	75	74	78	78	75	75	74	74	74	75	75
DBR 40%																									**40%**
Manhattan	71	71	74	72	77	78	73	77	78	75	75	76	75	76	76	76	78	77	75	77	75	77	75	76	75
Euclidean	69	73	76	78	75	76	76	77	76	70	70	68	71	73	73	73	77	78	73	72	72	73	73	74	73
Chebyshev	70	73	77	79	76	76	76	75	75	75	73	75	75	73	75	74	78	76	72	74	70	73	74	75	74
Cosine	72	70	73	70	73	74	73	72	74	73	73	75	74	74	76	77	73	74	74	75	75	75	74	74	70
DTW	71	69	75	76	77	77	74	79	77	73	73	72	70	70	77	76	79	76	76	78	76	77	75	75	74
EDR	69	73	76	78	75	76	76	77	76	71	71	74	73	74	76	76	81	80	73	74	77	75	75	75	76
MSM	70	71	74	72	78	79	73	74	74	73	73	72	72	75	75	72	80	80	78	75	75	75	78	75	75
Autocorrelation	72	70	73	70	73	74	69	69	74	75	75	77	75	76	77	76	77	77	77	74	73	75	74	74	74
Gaussian	73	72	72	72	79	80	72	76	80	76	76	75	71	71	73	73	76	79	74	77	75	76	75	75	76
Sigmoid	69	69	73	77	78	76	75	76	76	72	72	72	75	75	72	78	78	80	76	75	73	70	74	75	76
Kullback-Leibler	69	73	76	78	75	76	77	76	76	76	75	71	71	71	70	70	76	82	78	75	75	75	74	75	76
Wasserstein dissimilarity	72	70	73	70	73	74	69	69	74	75	75	75	76	75	76	76	79	80	76	75	73	74	74	75	75
Maximum shifting correlation	66	66	73	73	74	74	72	73	71	73	72	73	73	73	75	74	78	78	76	75	74	77	73	74	74
Minkowski Distance	69	70	75	74	77	75	70	73	75	73	73	75	74	74	76	76	80	80	75	77	75	76	75	76	73
Mahalanobis	70	73	76	78	73	75	72	74	73	75	75	73	74	79	77	76	80	80	75	77	75	76	75	76	77
Jaccard Score	64	65	75	73	74	74	70	73	71	73	73	74	71	72	74	73	75	75	75	73	74	74	72	73	76
Avg	70	71	74	74	75	76	73	74	75	74	74	74	74	73	74	75	78	78	75	75	74	75	74	75	75
DBR 80%																									**80%**
Manhattan	70	71	74	72	77	78	73	77	78	75	75	76	75	76	76	76	78	77	75	77	75	75	75	75	75
Euclidean	71	73	76	78	75	76	76	77	76	70	70	68	71	73	71	72	77	78	73	74	73	72	74	74	74
Chebyshev	70	73	77	79	76	76	76	75	75	75	75	73	73	75	74	78	76	72	74	70	71	74	75	75	74
Cosine	72	72	73	73	73	74	73	73	74	73	73	75	74	74	76	77	73	76	76	75	75	75	74	74	71
DTW	71	69	75	76	77	77	74	79	77	73	73	72	70	70	77	76	79	76	76	78	76	77	75	75	74
EDR	69	73	76	78	75	76	76	77	76	71	71	74	73	74	76	76	81	80	73	74	77	75	75	75	73
MSM	70	71	74	72	78	79	73	74	74	73	73	72	72	75	75	72	80	80	78	75	75	75	78	75	75
Autocorrelation	72	70	73	70	73	74	69	69	74	75	75	77	75	76	77	76	77	77	77	74	73	75	74	74	70
Gaussian	73	72	72	72	79	80	72	76	80	76	76	75	71	71	73	73	76	79	74	77	75	76	75	75	72
Sigmoid	69	69	73	77	78	76	75	76	76	72	72	72	75	75	72	78	78	80	76	75	73	70	74	75	72
Kullback-Leibler	73	73	76	78	75	76	76	77	76	76	75	71	71	70	70	76	82	78	75	75	75	74	75	75	73
Wasserstein dissimilarity	72	70	73	70	73	74	69	69	74	75	75	76	75	76	76	79	80	76	75	73	74	74	74	74	73
Maximum shifting correlation	69	68	73	74	74	74	72	73	71	71	71	73	73	73	75	74	78	78	74	75	73	77	73	74	71
Minkowski Distance	69	69	75	74	77	75	70	73	75	73	73	75	74	74	76	77	78	79	74	75	74	75	74	73	73
Mahalanobis	72	73	76	78	73	75	75	76	73	75	75	73	74	79	77	78	81	83	78	77	75	76	75	77	77
Jaccard Score	63	64	75	73	74	70	70	73	71	73	73	74	71	69	74	73	75	75	75	73	74	74	72	72	76
Avg	70	71	74	75	75	76	73	75	75	74	74	74	74	73	74	75	78	79	75	75	74	75	74	75	73

From experiments it is observed that the proposed method identifies ~16% eigenvectors as most informative therefore, able to reduce the computation cost by ~84%. From results shown in Tables 1 and 2, it is evident that for all combinations of DBR and prototyping techniques, the reduced sample length performs nearly equal to full sample length and raw data. In presence of original and

Table 2. Average AUROC for 1-NN

Prototype Methods (Borders, CGM, CKM, Closest, Futhest, Percentile, Random, SVs, BGM, AP, MKM, Avg), each with CL and RL sub-columns; last column is Random Rawdata.

Dissimilarity Measure	Borders CL	Borders RL	CGM CL	CGM RL	CKM CL	CKM RL	Closest CL	Closest RL	Futhest CL	Futhest RL	Percentile CL	Percentile RL	Random CL	Random RL	SVs CL	SVs RL	BGM CL	BGM RL	AP CL	AP RL	MKM CL	MKM RL	Avg CL	Avg RL	Random Rawdata
DBR 20%																									**20%**
Manhattan	66	69	70	72	67	67	63	65	66	69	67	69	66	69	68	70	73	75	70	71	70	69	68	70	69
Euclidean	66	66	71	69	69	71	65	68	69	74	74	77	75	76	73	75	79	82	74	73	71	70	71	73	73
Chebyshev	68	70	70	73	70	70	71	70	73	71	70	73	74	77	73	78	78	78	72	74	70	72	72	73	73
Cosine	69	71	73	75	71	71	72	70	70	72	73	72	70	70	77	76	79	80	70	72	71	71	72	73	75
DTW	67	68	77	76	71	73	74	75	73	72	71	74	73	74	76	76	78	78	76	78	76	75	74	74	76
EDR	65	67	74	71	72	73	73	74	73	71	73	72	72	75	75	72	78	78	73	74	77	75	73	73	72
MSM	70	69	76	73	73	75	74	74	73	75	75	77	75	76	77	76	79	81	78	75	75	75	75	75	75
Autocorrelation	63	68	73	73	74	74	72	73	71	74	76	75	71	71	73	73	76	78	76	76	73	75	73	74	73
Gaussian	66	68	77	80	71	73	74	75	73	73	72	72	75	75	72	78	78	73	74	75	75	76	73	74	74
Sigmoid	65	64	73	73	74	74	72	73	71	74	76	75	71	71	70	70	76	78	76	75	73	70	72	72	70
Kullback-Leibler	65	68	73	73	73	71	74	74	73	72	75	76	75	76	76	79	79	79	78	75	75	77	74	74	76
Wasserstein dissimilarity	60	62	70	72	69	73	70	69	71	74	70	68	71	73	71	72	76	77	76	73	73	74	71	72	72
Maximum shifting correlation	65	67	74	71	72	73	73	74	73	71	75	75	73	73	75	74	74	73	76	75	73	77	73	73	74
Minkowski Distance	63	63	75	74	77	75	73	75	76	73	75	74	76	77	79	74	74	75	74	73	74	74	74	74	76
Mahalanobis	68	70	76	77	73	75	72	72	73	72	75	73	74	79	77	76	77	80	80	78	72	74	74	74	75
Jaccard Score	60	61	73	73	74	74	73	71	70	76	75	71	71	73	73	75	75	75	73	74	77	72	72	72	73
Avg	65	67	73	73	72	73	72	72	72	73	73	74	73	74	74	75	77	77	75	75	73	74	73	73	74
DBR 40%																									**40%**
Manhattan	67	68	73	73	73	71	74	74	73	72	75	76	76	76	76	78	73	75	77	75	77	74	74	75	75
Euclidean	65	67	70	72	69	73	70	69	71	74	70	68	71	73	71	72	81	78	73	71	71	70	71	72	73
Chebyshev	70	69	74	71	72	73	73	74	73	71	75	75	73	73	75	74	78	76	72	74	70	71	73	73	74
Cosine	63	68	75	74	77	75	75	76	73	75	75	74	76	77	73	74	74	75	75	75	73	74	73	74	70
DTW	66	68	73	75	71	71	72	70	70	72	73	72	70	70	77	76	79	76	76	78	76	77	76	73	74
EDR	65	64	77	76	71	73	74	75	73	72	71	74	73	74	76	76	81	78	73	74	77	75	74	74	73
MSM	65	70	74	75	72	76	73	74	73	77	73	72	72	75	75	72	78	76	78	75	75	78	73	75	75
Autocorrelation	63	68	74	73	73	74	74	74	73	75	75	77	75	76	77	76	77	76	74	76	74	73	75	74	70
Gaussian	66	68	73	73	74	74	73	71	74	76	75	71	71	73	75	72	78	73	74	77	75	76	73	73	72
Sigmoid	60	61	77	80	71	73	74	75	73	73	72	75	75	72	78	78	80	76	75	73	70	73	73	74	72
Kullback-Leibler	63	65	73	74	74	72	73	71	74	76	75	71	70	70	76	82	78	75	75	75	75	73	73	73	73
Wasserstein dissimilarity	61	61	73	73	73	71	74	74	73	72	76	75	76	76	79	80	76	75	73	74	73	73	73	73	70
Maximum shifting correlation	60	61	73	73	74	74	72	73	71	74	71	73	73	73	75	74	78	78	76	75	73	77	72	73	71
Minkowski Distance	63	63	75	74	77	75	73	75	76	73	75	74	76	77	78	79	79	74	73	74	73	74	73	73	73
Mahalanobis	68	70	76	78	73	75	72	74	73	72	75	73	74	79	77	76	80	80	75	77	75	76	74	75	77
Jaccard Score	60	61	73	73	70	70	73	73	71	74	74	73	71	69	74	73	75	75	75	75	74	73	74	72	76
Avg	64	66	74	74	73	73	72	73	72	74	74	73	73	74	75	75	78	77	75	75	74	75	73	73	73
DBR 80%																									**80%**
Manhattan	63	63	77	80	71	73	74	73	73	76	75	71	71	73	73	75	76	73	76	73	73	72	74	75	75
Euclidean	63	67	73	73	74	74	72	73	71	72	75	75	74	74	76	77	79	75	77	75	74	76	73	74	74
Chebyshev	60	61	77	77	71	73	74	75	73	74	76	72	71	70	70	76	75	70	75	70	73	70	72	72	72
Cosine	60	61	77	77	71	73	74	75	73	74	72	75	72	69	78	76	79	70	76	70	73	78	73	71	71
DTW	63	65	74	71	71	73	70	70	71	73	72	74	73	74	76	76	81	78	76	78	76	78	73	73	74
EDR	62	61	73	73	74	74	72	73	71	74	70	72	72	75	75	72	80	74	72	74	77	75	73	72	73
MSM	68	69	70	74	69	73	70	76	77	70	70	75	71	76	77	76	79	80	78	78	75	77	73	75	75
Autocorrelation	67	68	74	71	72	73	73	74	73	73	72	72	75	71	73	73	76	73	76	73	73	73	73	73	70
Gaussian	63	68	75	74	77	75	73	75	74	72	75	71	75	72	80	80	77	80	77	75	73	70	74	75	72
Sigmoid	66	68	73	75	71	71	72	70	70	73	72	75	71	70	70	76	75	70	75	70	73	70	72	72	72
Kullback-Leibler	65	64	77	76	71	73	74	73	73	72	76	75	74	76	76	73	80	75	73	75	76	74	74	73	73
Wasserstein dissimilarity	62	60	74	75	72	76	73	74	74	70	73	74	77	77	76	81	77	76	77	75	77	73	73	74	74
Maximum shifting correlation	63	65	76	78	73	75	72	74	73	74	71	73	73	75	74	80	75	74	75	73	75	73	74	71	71
Minkowski Distance	60	61	73	71	74	74	70	73	71	76	73	75	74	76	77	80	75	77	77	73	73	73	73	73	73
Mahalanobis	64	64	77	80	74	76	72	74	73	72	75	74	79	77	75	80	78	75	78	75	77	74	75	77	77
Jaccard Score	60	61	73	71	74	74	70	73	71	74	76	75	71	71	70	69	75	76	69	73	70	71	72	72	76
Avg	63	64	75	75	72	74	72	74	73	74	73	74	73	73	74	74	79	76	74	76	74	74	73	73	73

reduced data length, Mahalanobis measure and Bayesian Gaussian mixture pre-form significantly better than other combinations for all values of hyperparameter (N) for all the classifiers. The borders prototype methods performs worst among all and it is evident that for OCSVM it performs comparatively better than 1-NN.

It is also evident that in presence of reduced sample length, OCSVM performs slightly better than 1-NN. This research proves that data representation of time series via DBR becomes more robust in presence of reduced sample length obtained by the proposed method, whereas it is also observed that reduced length also empowered the prototyping method and therefore 20% of the training samples are sufficient enough to achieve better performance. Experiments have been also performed with 10% prototypes and the achieved average AUROC was below 50% for OCSVM; therefore not included for comparison. However, 1-NN is able to work in presence of 1 prototype too.

5   Conclusion

The present research uses DBR techniques for data representation and proposes a robust way of target class guided sample length reduction (can also be called dimensionality reduction) technique along with training sample reduction approach using prototyping methods. UCR/UEA archive is used for intense experiments, where 16 DBR representations along with 11 prototype selection strategies are utilized. The experiments have been performed considering both the original length and reduced sample length. On average ~16% eigenvectors are identified as knowledge grid representatives therefore the transformed data help to reduce the computation cost by ~84%. With exhaustive experiments, it is proven that DBR methods are more advantageous with proposed sample reduction approach because class membership depends on the time series shape. Correct choice of DBR/Prototype pair also plays a vital role in target class mining task. Results show that the 20% of the training samples are sufficient enough for better classification performance, therefore computation cost can be reduced by 80%. Two one-class classifiers: OCSVM and 1-NN are utilized to show the effectiveness of the proposed approach. For all scenarios, it is evident that Mahalanobis measure and Bayesian Gaussian mixture together exhibit better target class representation compared to other state-of-the-art approaches. After proper parameter tuning and intensive experiments, it is evident that OCSVM preforms slightly better than 1-NN. In future, the present work can be extended to multi-variate time series.

References

1. Alam, S., Sonbhadra, S.K., Agarwal, S., Nagabhushan, P.: One-class support vector classifiers: a survey. Knowl.-Based Syst. **196**, 105754 (2020)
2. Alam, S., Sonbhadra, S.K., Agarwal, S., Nagabhushan, P., Tanveer, M.: Sample reduction using farthest boundary point estimation (FBPE) for support vector data description (SVDD). Pattern Recognit. Lett. **131**, 268–276 (2020)
3. Badhiye, S.S., Chatur, P.: A review on time series dimensionality reduction. HELIX **8**(5), 3957–3960 (2018)
4. Bagnall, A., Lines, J., Bostrom, A., Large, J., Keogh, E.: The great time series classification bake off: a review and experimental evaluation of recent algorithmic advances. Data Min. Knowl. Discov. **31**(3), 606–660 (2016). https://doi.org/10.1007/s10618-016-0483-9
5. Cassisi, C., Montalto, P., Aliotta, M., Cannata, A., Pulvirenti, A.: Similarity measures and dimensionality reduction techniques for time series data mining. In: Advances in Data Mining Knowledge Discovery and Applications, pp. 71–96 (2012)
6. Chalapathy, R., Chawla, S.: Deep learning for anomaly detection: a survey. arXiv preprint arXiv:1901.03407 (2019)

7. Chen, L., Özsu, M.T., Oria, V.: Robust and fast similarity search for moving object trajectories. In: Proceedings of the 2005 ACM SIGMOD International Conference on Management of Data, pp. 491–502 (2005)
8. Costa, Y.M.G., Bertolini, D., Britto, A.S., Cavalcanti, G.D.C., Oliveira, L.E.S.: The dissimilarity approach: a review. Artif. Intell. Rev. **53**(4), 2783–2808 (2019). https://doi.org/10.1007/s10462-019-09746-z
9. Dau, H.A., et al.: The UCR time series archive. IEEE/CAA J. Automatica Sinica **6**(6), 1293–1305 (2019)
10. De Amorim, R.C., Mirkin, B.: Minkowski metric, feature weighting and anomalous cluster initializing in k-means clustering. Pattern Recognit. **45**(3), 1061–1075 (2012)
11. Duin, R.P., Pękalska, E.: The dissimilarity representation for pattern recognition: a tutorial. Tech. rep., Technical Report (2009)
12. Duin, R.P., Roli, F., de Ridder, D.: A note on core research issues for statistical pattern recognition. Pattern Recognit. Lett. **23**(4), 493–499 (2002)
13. Esling, P., Agon, C.: Time-series data mining. ACM Comput. Surv. (CSUR) **45**(1), 1–34 (2012)
14. Fu, T.C.: A review on time series data mining. Eng. Appl. Artif. Intell. **24**(1), 164–181 (2011)
15. Garcia, S., Derrac, J., Cano, J., Herrera, F.: Prototype selection for nearest neighbor classification: taxonomy and empirical study. IEEE Trans. Pattern Anal. Mach. Intell. **34**(3), 417–435 (2012)
16. Geun Kim, M.: Multivariate outliers and decompositions of Mahalanobis distance. Commun. Stat.-Theory Methods **29**(7), 1511–1526 (2000)
17. Giusti, R., Batista, G.: An empirical comparison of dissimilarity measures for time series classification, pp. 82–88 (October 2013). https://doi.org/10.1109/BRACIS. 2013.22
18. Hoi, S.C., Sahoo, D., Lu, J., Zhao, P.: Online learning: a comprehensive survey. arXiv preprint arXiv:1802.02871 (2018)
19. Jiang, G., Wang, W., Zhang, W.: A novel distance measure for time series: maximum shifting correlation distance. Pattern Recognit. Lett. **117**, 58–65 (2019)
20. Khan, S.S., Madden, M.G.: One-class classification: taxonomy of study and review of techniques. Knowl. Eng. Rev. **29**(3), 345–374 (2014)
21. Kuncheva, L.I., Bezdek, J.C.: Nearest prototype classification: clustering, genetic algorithms, or random search? IEEE Trans. Syst. Man Cybern. Part C (Appl. Rev.) **28**(1), 160–164 (1998)
22. Lin, J., Williamson, S., Borne, K., DeBarr, D.: Pattern recognition in time series. Adv. Mach. Learn. Data Min. Astron. **1**(617–645), 3 (2012)
23. Mauceri, S., Sweeney, J., McDermott, J.: Dissimilarity-based representations for one-class classification on time series. Pattern Recognit. **100**, 107122 (2020)
24. Mazhelis, O.: One-class classifiers: a review and analysis of suitability in the context of mobile-masquerader detection. S. Afr. Comput. J. **2006**(36), 29–48 (2006)
25. Mori, U., Mendiburu, A., Lozano, J.A.: Distance measures for time series in R: The TSdist package. R J. **8**(2), 451 (2016)
26. Nakano, K., Chakraborty, B.: Effect of data representation for time series classification—a comparative study and a new proposal. Mach. Learn. Knowl. Extr. **1**(4), 1100–1120 (2019)
27. Pękalska, E., Duin, R.P., Paclík, P.: Prototype selection for dissimilarity-based classifiers. Pattern Recognit. **39**(2), 189–208 (2006)

28. Peng, K., Leung, V.C., Huang, Q.: Clustering approach based on mini batch kmeans for intrusion detection system over big data. IEEE Access **6**, 11897–11906 (2018)
29. Pimentel, M.A., Clifton, D.A., Clifton, L., Tarassenko, L.: A review of novelty detection. Signal Process. **99**, 215–249 (2014)
30. Rakthanmanon, T., et al.: Searching and mining trillions of time series subsequences under dynamic time warping. In: Proceedings of the 18th ACM SIGKDD International Conference on Knowledge Discovery and Data Mining, pp. 262–270 (2012)
31. Rodríguez, C.E., Núñez-Antonio, G., Escarela, G.: A Bayesian mixture model for clustering circular data. Comput. Stat. Data Anal. **143**, 106842 (2020)
32. Serra, J., Arcos, J.L.: An empirical evaluation of similarity measures for time series classification. Knowl.-Based Syst. **67**, 305–314 (2014)
33. Sharma, A., Kumar, A., Pandey, A.K., Singh, R.: Time series data representation and dimensionality reduction techniques. In: Johri, P., Verma, J.K., Paul, S. (eds.) Applications of Machine Learning. AIS, pp. 267–284. Springer, Singapore (2020). https://doi.org/10.1007/978-981-15-3357-0_18
34. Sonbhadra, S.K., Agarwal, S., Nagabhushan, P.: Early-stage covid-19 diagnosis in presence of limited posteroanterior chest x-ray images via novel pinball-OCSVM. arXiv preprint arXiv:2010.08115 (2020)
35. Sonbhadra, S.K., Agarwal, S., Nagabhushan, P.: Target specific mining of covid-19 scholarly articles using one-class approach. Chaos Solitons Fractals **140**, 110155 (2020)
36. Stefan, A., Athitsos, V., Das, G.: The move-split-merge metric for time series. IEEE Trans. Knowl. Data Eng. **25**(6), 1425–1438 (2012)
37. Triguero, I., Derrac, J., Garcia, S., Herrera, F.: A taxonomy and experimental study on prototype generation for nearest neighbor classification. IEEE Trans. Syst. Man Cybern. Part C (Appl. Rev.) **42**(1), 86–100 (2011)
38. Verleysen, M., François, D.: The curse of dimensionality in data mining and time series prediction. In: Cabestany, J., Prieto, A., Sandoval, F. (eds.) IWANN 2005. LNCS, vol. 3512, pp. 758–770. Springer, Heidelberg (2005). https://doi.org/10.1007/11494669_93
39. Wang, X., Mueen, A., Ding, H., Trajcevski, G., Scheuermann, P., Keogh, E.: Experimental comparison of representation methods and distance measures for time series data. Data Min. Knowl. Discov. **26**(2), 275–309 (2013)
40. Wilson, S.J.: Data representation for time series data mining: time domain approaches. Wiley Interdiscip. Rev.: Comput. Stat. **9**(1), e1392 (2017)
41. Yang, Q., Wu, X.: 10 challenging problems in data mining research. Int. J. Inf. Technol. Decis. Mak. **5**(04), 597–604 (2006)
42. Yin, C., Zhang, S., Wang, J., Xiong, N.N.: Anomaly detection based on convolutional recurrent autoencoder for IoT time series. IEEE Trans. Syst. Man Cybern.: Syst. (2020)
43. Zhang, K., Gu, X.: An affinity propagation clustering algorithm for mixed numeric and categorical datasets. Math. Probl. Eng. **2014**, 1–8 (2014)

Information Retrieval and Relation Extraction

Improving Relation Extraction via Joint Coding Using BiLSTM and DCNN

Kaixu Wang[1], Qianqian Ren[1(✉)], Li Hui[1(✉)], Hui Xu[1], Shiyang Li[1], and Peng Xu[2]

[1] Department of Computer Science and Technology, Heilongjiang University, Harbin 150080, China
{renqianqian,huili}@hlju.edu.cn
[2] China Railway Harbin Group Co., Ltd., Harbin, China

Abstract. Neural network methods based on distant supervision has been widely used in studies concerning relation extraction, however, a traditional convolutional neural network can not effectively extract the dependency relationship and structured information between words in sentences. In order to solve this problem, we propose a novel approach to improve relation extraction results. Specifically, we propose to first apply a neural network-based model to encode sentences, feature vectors obtained are then fed into a one-dimensional dilated convolutional neural network to extract the relation. Finally, sentence-level attention mechanism is used to reduce the noise caused by the mislabeling problem of distant supervision. Our approach has been evaluated on real world datasets NYT10 and compared with a wide range of baselines. Experimental results show that: (1) our approach can improve the performance of neural network relation extraction based on distant supervision; (2) the proposed approach achieves outstanding results on the datasets.

Keywords: Relation extrction · LSTM · Dilated convolution

1 Introduction

In recent years, knowledge graphs has attracted continuous interest in various fields, resulting in a variety of large-scale knowledge bases (KBs), such as Freebase, DBpedia, YAGO, etc. [1–3]. These databases consist of a large number of facts in the form of triples such as (Barack Hussein Obama, place of birth, Honolulu). In real applications, the existing databases are far from enough, and a mass of knowledge margin still needs to be filled with triples extracted from the text. Therefore, relation extraction still plays an important role and need to be further studied.

Distant supervision is an efficient method to solve the problem that a supervised approach requires a large number of manual annotations [4]. It assumes that if two entities have a relationship in KBs, then all sentences containing these two entities are considered to express this relationship. Distant supervision implements automatic labeling of data, while its strong assumption will

H. Fujita et al. (Eds.): IEA/AIE 2021, LNAI 12799, pp. 617–628, 2021.
https://doi.org/10.1007/978-3-030-79463-7_52

bring noise that two entities in the sentence may be not express their relationship in KBs, which will cause many false tags and affect the performance of the algorithm. In order to reduce the noise existed in distant supervision-based method, Riedel et al. propose to use multiple instance learning [5], which contains the same entity to sentences in the same bag. In the process of learning, the uncertainty of the instance labels is taken into consideration. Lin et al. propose a sentence level selective attention mechanism [6], which reduces the impact of false label instances by assigning weights to each sentence.

In the process of relation extraction, the method of feature extraction has a great influence on the accuracy of extraction. In the early days, most methods used NLP tools such as POS Tagging, etc. However, error propagation and accumulation will inevitably occur in the training process when using NLP tools. In recent years, deep learning technique is incorporated to extract feature vectors in sentences and build a classifier to achieve relation extraction. Zeng et al. construct a piecewise max-pooling convolutional neural network (PCNN) [7]. It divides the feature vector obtained by convolution into three segments according to the positions of two entities for pooling, extracts the most important information of each segment, and reduces the noise effectively. However, these methods fail to take into account the dependencies between words in the sentence and lose the higher level structured information between words.

In this paper, we propose a novel framework for improving relation extraction using LSTM and dilated convolutional neural network. To do so, we first apply a deep neural network sequence model, which is a bidirectional long short-term memory (BiLSTM), to extract the long-term dependence relation between words in a sentence. Then, a dilated convolutional neural network (DCNN) is trained to extract the semantic unit information between words in a sentence, it can obtain the structure information of a higher level of the sentence. Finally, two feature vectors are joined for feature fusion and extraction to obtain the relation probability. We evaluate the effectiveness of our approach on NYT10 datasets, and compare our results with baselines including Mintz, MultiR, MIML, and PCNN. Experimental results show that the proposed approach achieves excellent results on the datasets. This shows that the proposed method can improve the performance of relation extraction.

The main contributions of our work are summarized below:

- We propose a novel sentence joint coding for relation extraction by using BiLSTM and DCNN to capture sentence semantic information and structural information.
- We incorporate the sentence joint coding with a selective attention mechanism to reduce the noise caused by distant supervision.
- In expetiments, we compare with several neural network baseline models, our model can effectively improve performance of relation extraction algorithm based on the distant supervision.

The rest of this paper is organized as follows: we introduce related work in Sect. 2; and then present the details of our approach in Sect. 3; next explain the results and analysis of the experiment in Sect. 4; finally we conclude this work in Sect. 5.

2   Related Work

In the early stage, the relation extraction method is divided into kernel-based method and feature-based method. The feature-based method converts the structured representation of sequence and analytic tree into feature vectors according to the appropriate feature set. The kernel-based method uses the features in the sentence (such as syntax parsing tree) to construct kernel functions, such as convolutional tree kernel function and dependent tree kernel function [8, 13]. However, both methods use traditional NLP tools and cannot obtain high quality feature vectors, which will inevitably generate false propagation and accumulation in the whole process. With the continuous development of deep learning and its wide application in various fields, scholars have also studied the use of neural networks to automatically learn sentence features and obtain more accurate semantic information. For example, Socher et al. uses a recursive neural network to transform each node in the sentence parsing tree into a vector representation [14]. Zeng et al. use piecewise convolutional neural network to extract sentence features and consider the structure information of entity position [7].

In recent years, relation extraction has been widely concerned. Many scholars have proposed a number of effective methods to optimize relation extraction model. First, supervised methods are widely used because of its more accurate results [8–10]. However, the supervision method requires a large number of labeled data for training, which requires a lot of time and manpower. Therefore, the distant supervision relation extraction algorithm was proposed [4]. This method aligns the corpus with the structured knowledge base, and assumes that sentences containing the same entity pair express the same relationship to achieve automatic labeling. However, the assumption of distant supervision is too strong, and the sentences in the corpus may not express the relation in KBs. Therefore, in order to reduce the impact of the mislabeling problem caused by distant supervision, many authors applied the idea of multi-instance learning to the relation extraction task [5, 11, 12]. Considered the reliability of each sentence lables, and successfully reduced the noise data. Based on this idea, Lin et al. proposed a sentence-level selective attention mechanism [6], which assigns higher weights to sentences with more information and lower weights to sentences with less information, further improve the accuracy of extraction results.

3   Methodology

We present our approach for improving relation extraction in this section. An overview of the approach is shown in Fig. 1. We first introduce the prepare vectors for model training (Sect. 3.1). Then, we describe BiLSTM model which extracts long term dependency information in sentence (Sect. 3.2), DCNN mode which

extracts structure information (Sect. 3.3) and fused with dependency information (Sect. 3.4). Finally, we assign different weights for each sentences in bags
(Sect. 3.5).

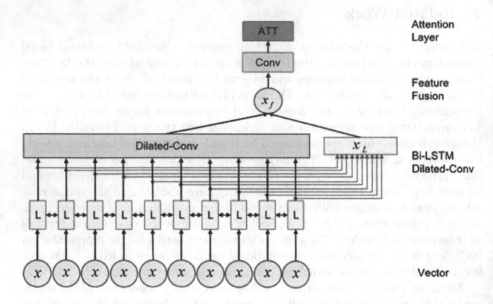

Fig. 1. The architecture of our model used for distant supervised relation extraction.

3.1 Preliminary

In this section, we prepare vectors for training in the next phases. To do this, we
convert the word representation into a low-dimensional vectors that can be recognized by the computer, the obtained vectors are input into the neural network.
We convert each word in the sentence into vectors by looking for the pre-trained
words embedding, and to show the position of the given entity pair in the sentence, we join the position embeddings of all words in the sentence in the vector
representations which can better express the word's semantics and structure in
the sentence.

Word Embeddings. The purpose of word embeddings is to map each word
in a sentence to a low-dimensional truth vector and transform the word into a
distributed representation. Some studies have shown that word embeddings can
well capture the syntactic and semantic information of words, and can converge
to a smaller local value when the neural network uses word embeddings initialization [15]. Therefore, the use of pre-trained word embeddings has become a
common practice in many NLP tasks. In recent years, researchers have proposed
several methods of training word embeddings [16–18]. This paper uses Skip-gram
model to train word embeddings [18].

Position Embeddings. Zeng et al. proved the importance of position feature PF in relation extraction task, and words closer to the target entity usually contain richer semantic information [7]. We use position embeddings to represent the position of each word. Specifically, it is the relative distance between the head and tail entities of each word. For example, in Fig. 2, the relative distances from born to (Obama) and (Honolulu) are 2 and −2, respectively. We randomly initialize the two position embedding matrix PF_1 and PF_2 (corresponding e_1 and e_2 respectively), and then convert the relative position to vector by looking them up.

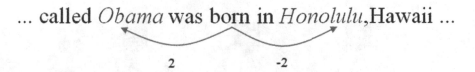

$$\dots \text{ called } \textit{Obama} \text{ was born in } \textit{Honolulu,}\text{Hawaii} \dots$$

2   -2

Fig. 2. The example of position embeddings.

We concatenate the word representation and position representation as the input of the neural network. Assuming that the size of word representation is d_w and the size of position representation is d_p, the final input vector we get is expressed $\omega = \{\omega_1, \omega_2, \cdots, \omega_m\}$, where $\omega_i \in \mathbb{R}^d\,(d = d_w + d_p \times 2)$, m is the number of words in a sentence.

3.2   BiLSTM Model for Dependency Information

In the task of relation extraction, semantic information is very important. The semantic information and syntactic information are hidden in the sequence of words in a sentence. In this paper, We use BiLSTM to extract the dependencies between words in sentences. LSTM was first proposed by Hochreiter and Schmidhuber (1997) in order to solve the problem of gradient disappearance in recurrent neural network, and is a kind of recurrent neural network. It can control each LSTM unit to retain part or all of the historical information, remember the current input information, and selectively retain characteristics according to the degree of importance through gate mechanism (input gate, output gate, forget gate) and cell state.

We input sentences into the LSTM as word sequences. Each word passing through the gate mechanism, constantly updating the cell state. As shown in Fig. 3, these word vectors represent x input into the LSTM, constantly update the cell state through the gate mechanism of LSTM, and finally output a new vector representation y. Through the input gate and forget gate, the cell state at the end of the previous word is combined with the current new input word and the previous hidden state to form a weight matrix to determine how much new information is added and how much old information is discarded. Through the output gate, the cell state after adding new information is taken as the current cell state, and the weight matrix is formed with the current input word and the previous hidden state to determine which information is output. And so on, until all the words are entered into the LSTM. Finally, we obtain feature vectors that take into account the implicit information in the sequence of words, which retain the important information in the sentence and forget the unimportant information. For sequential modeling tasks, future information at each moment is as important as historical information, and the standard LSTM model does not capture future information in its order. Therefore, this paper adopts the bidirectional LSTM (BiLSTM) model to add a reverse LSTM layer to the original forward LSTM network layer.

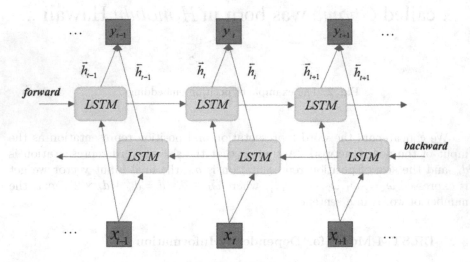

Fig. 3. The view of BiLSTM procession.

3.3   Dilated Convolution Model for Structure Information

Dilated convolution is a special form of convolution, which can increase the receptive field without pooling the loss of information, so that each convolution output contains a larger range of information. Receptive field is the region size of the pixel points on the feature map output by each layer of the convolutional neural network on the original image. The dilated convolution is mainly proposed to solve some problems in image segmentation. In FCN (fully convolutional networks), the image size is reduced by pooling to increase the receptive field, and then the image size is restored by up-sampling. However, precision loss is caused in this process, so the dilated convolution emerges at the right moment. In relation extraction, dilated convolution can solve the problem of information dependence in long sentences, and capture the structured information between contexts to extract the semantic unit information in sentences. We set dilation rate $= 2$, which can be understand as taking the number of every other line or column on the feature map to convolve with the convolution kernel which size is 3×3. As shown in Fig. 4, we extract the features of words in the sentence at intervals, so as to obtain the structural information between words and the semantic information between distant words.

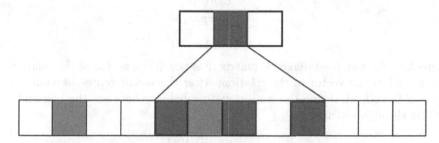

... called Obama was born in Honolulu, Hawaii on August 4 ...

Fig. 4. The view of dilated convolution procession.

3.4 Feature Fusion

In our model, the inputs of BiLSTM are vector representations of original data ω_i $(i = 1, 2, \cdots, m)$, the inputs of dilated convolution are the outputs of BiLSTM. We spliced the outputs of BiLSTM and dilated convolution together as the overall feature of a sentence, which combines the dependency relation between words in the sentence and the semantic unit information. After obtaining the fused feature vectors, we use Convolutional Neural Network to further extract the features of vectors. We set the window size to 3 and the padding to fill in the 0 vector outside the sentence boundary. For the pooling part, due to the position of entity pair contains additional information in the sentence, we pool the three segments divided by the head and tail entities separately and taking the maximum value of each segment. Finally, we use a nonlinear activation function tanh to enhance the power of the network.

3.5 Selective Attention Mechanism

In order to reduce the noise caused by the strong hypothesis of distant super-vision, we use the sentence-level selective attention mechanism proposed in [6]. We determine the weight of each sentence in the bag to a certain relation by calculating the matching degree between the sentence feature vector and the predicted relation. Suppose that a bag B contains n instances containing entity pairs($head, tail$), $B = \{b_1, b_2, \cdots, b_n\}$, where the sentence feature vector b_i after sentence encoding is $\mathbf{b_i}$, the feature vectors of all sentences is weighted sum to represent the bag vector $\mathbf{B}$:

$$\mathbf{B} = \sum_i \alpha_i \mathbf{b}_i \tag{1}$$

For the weight of each sentence vector α, we obtain by calculating the matching score between the input sentence b_i and the relation r to be predicted :

$$\alpha_i = \frac{exp\,(e_i)}{\sum_k exp\,(e_k)} \tag{2}$$

$$e_i = \mathbf{b_i}\mathbf{A}\mathbf{r} \tag{3}$$

where $\mathbf{A}$ is the weighted diagonal matrix, $\mathbf{r}$ is the query vector of the relation r, represented as the vector of the relation. After the vector representation of the bag is obtained, we define the conditional probability between the bag and the relation through softmax:

$$p\,(r|B,\theta) = \frac{exp\,(o_r)}{\sum_{k=1}^{n_r} exp\,(o_k)} \tag{4}$$

where n_r is the total number of relations, $\mathbf{o}$ is the neural network output which is corresponding score related to all relation types , it is defined as:

$$\mathbf{o} = \mathbf{M}\mathbf{B} + \mathbf{d} \tag{5}$$

where $\mathbf{d}$ is the bias vector, $\mathbf{M}$ is the representation matrix of the relation.

3.6   Training Objective

Suppose there are N bags in the training set $\{B_1, B_2, \cdots, B_N\}$, and their labels are $\{r_1, r_2, \cdots, r_N\}$ respectively, we define the objective function of the bag with cross entropy as follows:

$$J\,(\theta) = \sum_{i=1}^{N} \log p\,(r_i|B_i,\theta) \tag{6}$$

where N is the number of bags and θ is all the parameters in the model. In the training process, we select a small batch randomly from the training set for iteration, and adopt stochastic gradient descent (SGD) to minimize the objective function until convergence. At the same time, we use dropout in the output layer to enhance the generalization ability of the model and prevent overfitting.

4   Experiments

In this part, through the experiments on real dataset, we proved that our neural network joint encoding model can effectively reduce the error label problem of distant supervision, and make full use of the word's long-term dependence and higher level of structure information and semantic information in a sentence to extract relation. First we introduce the data sets used in the experiment, then we use cross-validation to determine the parameters in the model, and finally we compare the performance of our model with several baseline models.

4.1   Dataset

We evaluated our model on the widely used NYT10 dataset, which was generated by aligning Freebase with the New York Times corpus. In NYT10, the entity is obtained using the Stanford NER annotation and matching the entity name in Freebase. There are a total of 53 relations in Freebase, which are combined with the result of sentence alignment in the New York Times corpus in 2005–2006 as a training set, including 522,611 sentences, 281,270 entity pairs and 18,252 relationship facts. The results of sentence alignment after 2007 was used as the test set, containing 172,448 sentences, 96,678 entity pairs and 1,950 relationship facts. In addition, among the 53 relations, there is a special relation NA, which means that there is no relation between the head entity and tail entity. In terms of vector representation of sentences, we use word2vec to conduct pre-training on NYT corpus, and the embedding vector of original data is obtained and input into the neural network.

4.2   Experimental Setting

In our experiment, we used the three-fold validation on the training set to adjust the model. Select the dimension of word embedding d_w among $\{50, 100, 200, 300\}$, select the dimension of position embedding d_p among $\{5, 10, 20\}$, select the window size ω among $\{3, 5, 7\}$, select the number of feature maps of LSTM layer, dilated convolutional layer and convolutional layer n_l, n_d, n_c among $\{50, 60, ..., 230\}$, select the weight λ among $\{0.001, 0.01, 0.1, 0.5\}$, select the batch size among $\{100, 130, 160, 190\}$, and select the epoch among $\{30, 60, 120\}$. The best configurations is: $d_w = 50, d_p = 5, \omega = 3, n_l = 60, n_d = 120, n_c = 230, \lambda = 0.01$, batch size $= 160$, epoch $= 60$. For dropout setting, We following Hinton et al. in 2012, dropout $= 0.5$.

4.3   Result and Comparisons

We use held-out to evaluate our approach, compared the relation extraction results from the test set with the relation in Freebase, and report the accuracy/recall curve of the experiment. In order to evaluate the proposed method, we compare the model in this paper with the following traditional methods.

Mintz: Traditional model based on distant supervision proposed by Mintz et al. in 2009.

MultiR: Multi-instance learning method proposed by Hoffmann et al. in 2011.

MIML: Multi-instance multi-lable model proposed by Surdeanu et al. in 2012.

PCNN: The model of PCNN mechanism proposed by Zeng et al. in 2015.

The accuracy/recall curve for each method is shown in Fig. 5, we can see that our model performs better than the traditional method on the overall scale. In the entire recall rate range, our model achieve a higher accuracy. When the recall rate is less than 0.05, the accuracy of prediction reaches between 0.7 and 1. We also analyzed at the same time, when the recall rate is greater than 0.05, the accurate rate of our model can gradually smooth when recall rate rises. It proves that our approach can achieve a better performance sentence encoder to extract relation by effectively extract the long-term dependence relation between words in the sentence and the structured information. The experimental results on the real dataset show that our method is superior to the traditional methods.

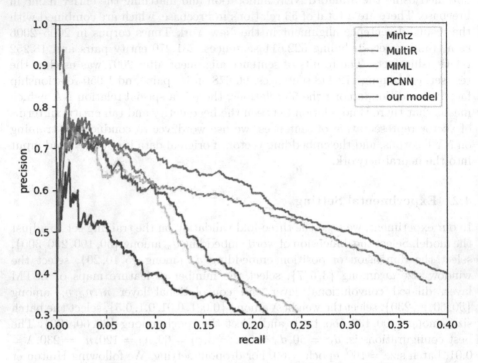

Fig. 5. Performance comparison of the proposed method with traditional approaches.

5   Conclusion

This paper has presented a novel sentence joint coding to improve relation extraction based on the distant supervision. The method employs BiLSTM to extract long term dependency information in sentence, and employs dilated convolution to extract sentence structure information. We fused two information as fused feature and extract relation from it using piecewise convolutional neural network. We also assign valid instances higher weights and invalid ones lower weights to reduce the noise. We have conducted experiments on NYT10 datasets in comparison with 4 other approaches. Empirical results show that our approach has further improvement compared with similar methods by combining various feature information.

Acknowledgement. This work was supported by the Natural Science Foundation of Heilongjiang Province (No. LH2020F043, JJ2019LH1096,F2018028), the Scientific Research Fund of Heilongjiang University (No. 2020-KYYWF-1010).

References

1. Suchanek, F.M., Kasneci, G., Weikum, G.: Yago: a core of semantic knowledge. In: Proceedings of the 16th International Conference on World Wide Web, pp. 697–706 (2007)
2. Auer, S., Bizer, C., Kobilarov, G., Lehmann, J., Cyganiak, R., Ives, Z.: DBpedia: a nucleus for a web of open data. In: Aberer, K., et al. (eds.) ASWC/ISWC -2007. LNCS, vol. 4825, pp. 722–735. Springer, Heidelberg (2007). https://doi.org/10.1007/978-3-540-76298-0_52
3. Bollacker, K., Evans, C., Paritosh, P., et al.: Freebase: a collaboratively created graph database for structuring human knowledge. In: Proceedings of the ACM SIGMOD International Conference on Management of Data, pp. 1247–1250 (2008)
4. Mintz, M., Bills, S., Snow, R., et al.: Distant supervision for relation extraction without labeled data. In: Proceedings of the Joint Conference of the 47th Annual Meeting of the ACL and the 4th International Joint Conference on Natural Language Processing of the AFNLP, pp. 1003–1011 (2009)
5. Riedel, S., Yao, L., McCallum, A.: Modeling relations and their mentions without labeled text. In: Balcázar, J.L., Bonchi, F., Gionis, A., Sebag, M. (eds.) ECML PKDD 2010. LNCS (LNAI), vol. 6323, pp. 148–163. Springer, Heidelberg (2010). https://doi.org/10.1007/978-3-642-15939-8_10
6. Lin, Y., Shen, S., Liu, Z., Luan, H., Sun, M.: Neural relation extraction with selective attention over instances (2016)
7. Zeng, D., Liu, K., Chen, Y., et al.: Distant supervision for relation extraction via piecewise convolutional neural networks. In: Proceedings of the 2015 Conference on Empirical Methods in Natural Language Processing, pp. 1753–1762 (2015)
8. Bunescu, R., Mooney, R.: A shortest path dependency kernel for relation extraction. In: Proceedings of Human Language Technology Conference and Conference on Empirical Methods in Natural Language Processing, pp. 724–731 (2005)
9. Zelenko, D., Aone, C., Richardella, A.: Kernel methods for relation extraction. J. Mach. Learn. Res. 3(2), 1083–1106 (2003)
10. Zhou, G.D., Su, J., Zhang, J., et al.: Exploring various knowledge in relation extraction. In: Proceedings of the 43rd Annual Meeting of the Association for Computational Linguistics (acl 2005), pp. 427–434 (2005)
11. Hoffmann, R., Zhang, C., Ling, X., et al.: Knowledge-based weak supervision for information extraction of overlapping relations. In: Proceedings of the 49th Annual Meeting of the Association for Computational Linguistics: Human Language Technologies, pp. 541–550 (2011)
12. Surdeanu, M., Tibshirani, J., Nallapati, R., et al.: Multi-instance multi-label learning for relation extraction. In: Proceedings of the 2012 Joint Conference on Empirical Methods in Natural Language Processing and Computational Natural Language Learning, pp. 455–465 (2012)
13. Qian, L., Zhou, G., Kong, F., et al.: Exploiting constituent dependencies for tree kernel-based semantic relation extraction. In: Proceedings of the 22nd International Conference on Computational Linguistics (Coling 2008), pp. 697–704 (2008)
14. Socher, R., Huval, B., Manning, C.D., et al.: Semantic compositionality through recursive matrix-vector spaces. In: Proceedings of the 2012 Joint Conference on Empirical Methods in Natural Language Processing and Computational Natural Language Learning, pp. 1201–1211 (2012)

15. Erhan, D., Courville, A., Bengio, Y., et al.: Why does unsupervised pre-training help deep learning? In: Proceedings of the Thirteenth International Conference on Artificial Intelligence and Statistics. JMLR Workshop and Conference Proceedings, pp. 201–208 (2010)

16. Bengio, Y., Ducharme, R., Vincent, P., et al.: A neural probabilistic language model. J. Mach. Learn. Res. **3**, 1137–1155 (2003)

17. Collobert, R., Weston, J., Bottou, L., et al.: Natural language processing (almost) from scratch. J. Mach. Learn. Res. **12**(ARTICLE), 2493–2537 (2011)

18. Mikolov, T., Chen, K., Corrado, G., et al.: Efficient estimation of word representations in vector space. arXiv preprint arXiv:1301.3781 (2013)

19. Hinton, G.E., Srivastava, N., Krizhevsky, A., et al.: Improving neural networks by preventing co-adaptation of feature detectors. arXiv preprint arXiv:1207.0580 (2012)

A Possible Worlds Interpretation
of Many-Sorted Theory for IR

Mohammed Sadou[1]([✉]) [iD], Yassine Djouadi[1], and Allel Hadj-Ali[2]

[1] RIIMA Laboratory, Department of Computer Science, USTHB University,
Algiers, Algeria
{m.sadou,y.djouadi}@univ-alger.dz
[2] LIAS/ENSMA, Poitiers, France
allel.hadjali@ensma.fr

Abstract. Many-sorted theory for Information retrieval were proposed
to provide a generic model of the different items of an information
Retrieval system, the IR process is then seen as a proof of theorems based
on a set of five axioms. The authors have proved that three of the classical IR models satisfy the theory: boolean, vector space and fuzzy-set
models. However, it is not proved that the theory satisfies the modal-
logic based IR models. In this paper we propose a new interpretation
of the theory, this interpretation is based on possible worlds semantics
where a document is a possible world and the accessibility relation is the
transformation of the document. It will be proved that the interpretation
proposed satisfies the many-sorted theory for IR, thus consolidating its
consistency and genericity.

Keywords: Information retrieval · Modal logic · Possible worlds
semantics · Axiomatic theory · Many-sorted logic

1 Introduction

The main purpose of Information Retrieval (IR) is how to find a relevant set of
documents from a collection, such as responding to a user query expressing a
need of information. The most important part of the IR research area is document modeling and IR process. Several IR models have been proposed in the
literature: the boolean, the vector space, the fuzzy and the probabilistic models
are the most known. It has been proved that these models offer simplistic and
specific representation of information [4,5,8]. The limitations of these models
have pushed the researchers to propose new models. The logical models quickly
emerged. The logical models for IR have been proposed to provide a generic
representation of the IR process. Zerarga and Djouadi [10] have proposed an
axiomatic theory independently of any model, it has been proven that three
classical models of IR, Boolean, fuzzy and the vector space models satisfy the
theory. The modal interpretation has not been studied for the theory.

In this paper we propose at the first stage, a new interpretation for the
Many-Sorted theory for IR [10]. This interpretation is based on possible worlds

© Springer Nature Switzerland AG 2021
H. Fujita et al. (Eds.): IEA/AIE 2021, LNAI 12799, pp. 629–635, 2021.
https://doi.org/10.1007/978-3-030-79463-7_53

semantics, where a document is a possible world. As a second stage, we prove that this interpretation is a model of the theory.

The remainder of this paper is structured as follows. Throughout Sect. 2, we give a brief introduction of logical models in the field of IR and a theoretical interpretation based on possible worlds semantics. Whilst Sect. 3 presents the many-sorted theory for IR, vocabulary, formulas and the axioms of the theory have been given. The possible worlds interpretation of the theory is given in Sect. 4, the satisfaction of the theory is proven. Finally, we conclude and offer some issues for the future.

2   Logical Models for IR

2.1   Classical and Non-Classical Logic for IR

The basic idea of using logic in IR is to consider the correspondence between a query and a document as an inference process. In a classical logic, inference is associated with a logical implication, let a document d and a query q, d is relevant to q if $d \rightarrow q$ (d implies q). This implication is too rigid, either it returns several documents that are not all relevant to the query or it returns too few documents, disregarding some relevant documents. The need to use other logic is quickly made it felt. In 1986, Van Rijsbergen [8] proposes to capture the uncertainty in the evaluation of the implication $d \rightarrow q$ using the following famous logical uncertainty principle: "*Given any two sentences x and y; a measure of the uncertainty of* $y \rightarrow x$ *related to a given data set is determined by the minimal extent to which we have to add information to the data set, to establish the truth of* $y \rightarrow x$". Two years later, Van Rijsbergen proposed to estimate the uncertainty by Imaging process [9], a detailed version of the imaging process is proposed in [2]. Imaging process enables to evaluate the uncertainty degree of $d \rightarrow q$ according to a possible worlds semantics where a term is a possible world.

Another version of this principle has been proposed by Nie [7] under the documents transformation principle. The principle is based on possible worlds semantics where a document is a possible world.

2.2   Possible Worlds Semantics for IR

The possible worlds semantics is the structure $\mathcal{M} = (W, R, V)$ proposed by Kripke [3] as a semantic of the modal logic [1], where W set of worlds, R is an accessibility relation spanning over a world and V a valuation function that assigns truth values to propositional variables at world. Based on this structure, Various models of IR have been proposed. The variation concerns how formulas, worlds and the accessibility relation are represented in the components of Information Retrieval System.

For our purpose, we will interest in the proposition of Nie (details can be found in [6]). The set of possible worlds corresponds to the finite set $\mathcal{D} = \{d_1, d_2, ..., d_n\}$ of documents. The set $\mathcal{T} = \{t_1, t_2, ...t_n\}$ of terms corresponds to propositional variables in the modal logic considered, and the function

V allows to assign for each term $t \in \mathcal{T}$ a sub-set $V(t) \subseteq \mathcal{D}$. Thus, if $t_i \in \mathcal{T}$ is true in the world $d_j \in \mathcal{D}$, then $d_j \in \mathcal{V}(t_i)$.

A document d is relevant to a query q, if q is true in the world d, i.e. $d \vDash q$, or the query q is true in an another document d' which is accessible to the former document. This relation is represented in modal logic by the following notation: $d \vDash \Diamond q$ ($d_0 \vDash \Diamond q$, iff $\exists d_1 \in \mathcal{D}, d_0 \mathcal{R} d_1$ and $d_1 \vDash q$). Dually, The notation $d \vDash \Box q$ means that q is necessary in the document d ($\mathcal{M}, d_0 \vDash \Box q$, iff $\forall d_1 \in \mathcal{D}, d_0 \mathcal{R} d_1 \Rightarrow d_j \vDash q$). The expression $d_0 \mathcal{R} d_1$ means that the document d_1 is accessible from the document d_0. What is suggested in this semantics is that a given document should be revised in a minimal way and look for the truth of the query in the new revised document. If q is not satisfied in the world d_1 accessible from the document d_0, we change the document d_1 to another document d_2 and so on, until d_n with $d_n \vDash q$. For each document is associated a set of documents which all have the same distance.

3   Many-Sorted Theory for Information Retrieval

The Many-sorted theory [10] (denoted $\mathfrak{T}$) is concerned by the universe of discourse $\mathfrak{D} = \{\mathcal{X}, \mathcal{Y}, \mathcal{Z}\}$ composed of three types of objects, namely documents, terms and queries. The language of the theory consists of well-formed formulas, constructed over the vocabulary presented in the following:

Constants : $y_\perp \in Y$ and $z_\perp \in Z$. Three types of Variables: x_i range over X,
  $y_j \in Y$ and $z_l \in Z$. Connectives: $\wedge$ and $\Rightarrow$.
Functions: $\oplus, \otimes : Y * Y \rightarrow Y$
  $\sqcap, \sqcup : Z * Z \rightarrow Z$
  $\ominus : Y \rightarrow Y$
  $\sim : Z \rightarrow Z$
  $f : X \rightarrow Y$
Predicate : $S(.,.)$

The formulas are inductively constructed using the rules defined below. The notation $x : \mathcal{X}$ means that the variable x is of the sort $\mathcal{X}$.

- each variable is a term,
- if t is a term, then $f(t)$ is a term,
- if t_1, t_2 are terms, then $\ominus t_1, t_1 \oplus t_2, t_1 \otimes t_2, t_1 \sqcap t_2, t_1 \sqcup t_2, \sim t_1$ are terms,
- if t_1, t_2 are terms, then $S(t_1, t_2)$ is an atomic formula,
- each atomic formula is well formed formula(wff).
- if A, B are wff then $A \wedge B$ and $A \Rightarrow B$,
- if v is variable, $\mathcal{D}$ a sorted domain, then $\forall v : \mathcal{D}$ is wff.

The theory $\mathfrak{T}$ is based on the following five axioms :

(A1) $S(y_\perp, z_\perp)$

(A2) $\forall x : \mathcal{X} \, S(f(x), x)$

(A3) $\forall y_1, y_2 : \mathcal{Y}, \forall z_1, z_2 : \mathcal{Z} \, (S(y_1, z_1) \wedge S(y_2, z_2) \Rightarrow S((y_1 \otimes y_2), (z_1 \sqcap z_2)))$

(A4) $\forall y_1, y_2 : \mathcal{Y}, \forall z_2, z_2 : \mathcal{Z} \, (S(y_1, z_1) \wedge S(y_2, z_2) \Rightarrow S((y_1 \oplus y_2), (z_1 \sqcup z_2)))$

(A5) $\forall y : \mathcal{Y}, \forall z : \mathcal{Z} \, S(y, z) \Rightarrow S(\ominus y, \sim z)$

and on two inference rules: Modus Ponens (MP)$(A, A \rightarrow B \vdash B)$ and conjunction introduction (CI)$(A, B \vdash A \wedge B)$.

4   IR-modal Semantic Proposal to the Theory $\mathfrak{T}$

The underlying semantics of the modal model consists of the structure $\mathcal{M}_M = \langle [\mathfrak{D}]^{I_M}, I_M \rangle$, such that $[\mathfrak{D}]^{I_M} = [\{\mathcal{X}, \mathcal{Y}, \mathcal{Z}\}]^{I_M} = \{\mathcal{T}, 2^{\mathcal{D}}, \mathcal{Q}\}$, where $\mathcal{Q}$ is a set of queries, $\mathcal{D}$ a set of documents, and $\mathcal{T}$ a set of terms, whereas the interpretation $\mathcal{I}_{\mathcal{M}}$ is given in Table 1:

Table 1. The interpretation I_M

Syntax	Interpretation
$y_\perp$	$\emptyset_D$ (the empty set of documents)
$z_\perp$	$\emptyset_Q$ (the empty query)
$f(x)$	$\{d_i, i = 1...n | \exists d_j \in \mathcal{D}, (d_i \mathcal{R} d_j) \text{ and } d_j \vDash x^{I_M}\}$
$y_1 \otimes y_2$	$y_1{}^{I_M} \cap y_2{}^{I_M}$
$y_1 \oplus y_2$	$y_1{}^{I_M} \cup y_2{}^{I_M}$
$\ominus y$	$D \setminus y^{I_M}$
$z_1 \sqcap z_2$	$z_1{}^{I_M} \wedge z_2{}^{I_M}$
$z_1 \sqcup z_2$	$z_1{}^{I_M} \vee z_2{}^{I_M}$
$\sim z$	$\neg z^{I_M}$
$S(y, z)$	$(\forall d \in [y]^{I_M}, \exists d' \in \mathcal{D} | ((d \mathcal{R} d') \text{ and } (d \vDash z^{I_M}))$
	(i.e. $d \vDash \Diamond z^{I_M}$) $\wedge (\forall d \in \mathcal{D}, d \vDash \Diamond z^{I_M} \Rightarrow d \in y^{I_M})$

The following theorem establishes that $\mathcal{M}_M$ is a model of the theory $\mathfrak{T}$.

Theorem 1. $\mathcal{M}_M \vDash \mathfrak{T}$

Proof. We have to prove that all axioms of $\mathfrak{T}$ are satisfied in the model $\mathcal{M}_{\mathcal{M}}$.

(A1) It is well known that in an IR system, the result of an empty query is an empty set of documents then we have $\mathcal{M}_M \vDash S(y_\perp, z_\perp)$.

(A2) we have : $[f(x)]^{I_M} = \{d_i, i = 1...n | \exists d_j \in \mathcal{D}, (d_i \mathcal{R} d_j)$ and $d_j \vDash x^{I_M}\}$

$\implies \forall x^{I_M} : [f(x)]^{I_M} = \{d_i, i = 1...n | \exists d' \in \mathcal{D}, (d_i \mathcal{R} d')$ and $d' \vDash x^{I_M}\}$

$\implies \forall d \in [f(x)]^{I_M} : \exists d' \in \mathcal{D}, (d \mathcal{R} d')$ and $d' \vDash x^{I_M}$

$\implies [S(f(x), x)]^{I_M}$ is true

$\implies \mathcal{M}_M \vDash \forall x : \mathcal{X} \ S(f(x), x)$

(A3) Let us suppose that $\mathcal{M}_{\mathcal{M}} \vDash S(y_1, z_1) \wedge S(y_2, z_2)$, then we have :

(i) $\mathcal{M}_{\mathcal{M}} \vDash S(y_1, z_1) \wedge S(y_2, z_2)$

$\implies (\forall d \in [y_1]^{I_M}, \exists d' \in \mathcal{D}|((d \mathcal{R} d'))$ and $(d' \vDash z_1^{I_M}))$ and

$(\forall d \in [y_2]^{I_M}, \exists d'' \in \mathcal{D}|((d \mathcal{R} d''))$ and $(d' \vDash z_2^{I_M}))$

$\implies (\forall d \in ([y_1]^{I_M} \cap [y_2]^{I_M}), \exists d', d'' \in \mathcal{D}|(d \mathcal{R} d'), (d \mathcal{R} d''), (d' \vDash z_1^{I_M})$ and $d'' \vDash z_2^{I_M}))$

$\implies (\forall d \in ([y_1]^{I_M} \cap [y_2]^{I_M}, \exists d''' \in \mathcal{D}|(d \mathcal{R} d'''), (d''' \vDash z_1^{I_M} \wedge z_2^{I_M}))$

(ii) $\mathcal{M}_{\mathcal{M}} \vDash S(y_1, z_1) \wedge S(y_2, z_2)$

$\implies \forall d \in \mathcal{D}, d \vDash \Diamond z_1^{I_M} \Rightarrow d \in y_1^{I_M} \wedge \forall d \in \mathcal{D}, d \vDash \Diamond z_2^{I_M} \Rightarrow d \in y_2^{I_M}$

$\implies \forall d \in \mathcal{D}, d \vDash \Diamond (z_1^{I_M} \wedge z_2^{I_M}) \Rightarrow d \in (y_1^{I_M} \cap y_2^{I_M})$

(i) and (ii) $\implies S([y_1]^{I_M} \cap [y_2]^{I_M}, z_1^{I_M} \wedge z_2^{I_M})$

$\implies [S(y_1 \otimes y_2, z_1 \sqcap z_2)]^{I_M}$ is true using the modal interpretation

$\implies \mathcal{M}_{\mathcal{M}} \vDash S(y_1 \otimes y_2, z_1 \sqcap z_2)$

i.e. if there exists a transformation of the document d for the satisfaction of $z_1^{I_M}$ and a transformation for the satisfaction of $z_2^{I_M}$, then there exists a transformation of the document d in favor of the satisfaction of the query z_1 and z_2.

(A4) Let us suppose that $\mathcal{M}_{\mathcal{M}} \vDash S(y_1, z_1) \wedge S(y_2, z_2)$, then we get :

(i) $\mathcal{M}_{\mathcal{M}} \vDash S(y_1, z_1) \wedge S(y_2, z_2)$

$\implies (\forall d \in [y_1]^{I_M}, \exists d' \in \mathcal{D}|((d \mathcal{R} d'))$ and $(d' \vDash z_1^{I_M}))$ and

$(\forall d \in [y_2]^{I_M}, \exists d'' \in \mathcal{D}|((d \mathcal{R} d'')$ and $(d' \vDash z_2^{I_M}))$

$\implies (\forall d \in [y_2]^{I_M} \cup [y_1]^{I_M}, \exists d' \in \mathcal{D}|((d \mathcal{R} d')$ and $(d' \vDash z_1^{I_M} \vee d' \vDash z_2^{I_M}))$

$\implies (\forall d \in [y_2]^{I_M} \cup [y_1]^{I_M}, \exists d' \in \mathcal{D}|((d \mathcal{R} d')$ and $(d' \vDash z_1^{I_M} \vee z_2^{I_M}))$

$\implies (\forall d \in [y_2]^{I_M} \cup [y_1]^{I_M}, (d \vDash \Diamond z_1^{I_M} \vee \Diamond z_2^{I_M}))$

$\implies (\forall d \in [y_2]^{I_M} \cup [y_1]^{I_M}, d \vDash \Diamond (z_1^{I_M} \vee z_2^{I_M}))$

(ii) $\mathcal{M}_{\mathcal{M}} \vDash S(y_1, z_1) \wedge S(y_2, z_2)$

$\implies \forall d \in \mathcal{D}, d \vDash \Diamond z_1^{I_M} \Rightarrow d \in y_1^{I_M} \wedge \forall d \in \mathcal{D}, d \vDash \Diamond z_2^{I_M} \Rightarrow d \in y_2^{I_M}$

$\implies \forall d \in \mathcal{D}, d \vDash \Diamond (z_1^{I_M} \vee z_2^{I_M}) \Rightarrow d \in (y_1^{I_M} \cup y_2^{I_M})$

(i) and (ii) $\implies S([y_2]^{I_M} \cup [y_1]^{I_M}, z_1^{I_M} \vee z_2^{I_M})$

$\implies S([y_2] \cup [y_1], z_1 \vee z_2)$ is true in the interpretation $\mathcal{I}_{\mathcal{M}}$

$\implies \mathcal{M}_{\mathcal{M}} \vDash S(y_1 \oplus y_2, z_1 \cup z_2)$

(A5) Let us suppose that $\mathcal{M_M} \vDash S(y, z)$, then we have :

$\mathcal{M_M} \vDash S(y, z)$

$\implies (\forall d \in [y]^{IM}, \exists d' \in \mathcal{D}|((d\mathcal{R}d'))$ and $(d' \vDash z^{IM})) \wedge (\forall d \in \mathcal{D}, d \vDash \Diamond z^{IM} \implies d \in y^{IM})$

$\implies (\forall d \notin [y]^{IM}, \forall d' \in \mathcal{D}$ and $d\mathcal{R}d' \implies (d' \vDash \neg z^{IM})$

$\implies (\forall d \in \mathcal{D} \setminus [y]^{IM}, \forall d' \in \mathcal{D}$ and $d\mathcal{R}d' \implies (d' \vDash \neg z^{IM})$

$\implies (\forall d \in \mathcal{D} \setminus [y]^{IM}, d \vDash \Box \neg z^{IM}$

$\implies (\forall d \in \mathcal{D} \setminus [y]^{IM}, d \vDash \neg \Diamond z^{IM}$

$\implies S(\mathcal{D} \setminus [y]^{IM}, \neg z^{IM})$

$\implies \mathcal{M_M} \vDash S(\ominus y, \sim z)$

We have proved that the model of IR based on documents as possible worlds satisfies the five axioms of the theory $\mathfrak{T}$, and we know that the two inference rules (MP and CI) preserve validity, so we conclude that the theorem given above establishes that the model of IR based on documents as possible worlds satisfies the theory $\mathfrak{T}$.

5   Conclusion and Perspectives

In this paper, we have proposed a new interpretation of the many-sorted theory for IR. The interpretation is based on possible worlds semantics where a document is a possible world. The satisfaction of the theory has been established, which strengthens the basic principle of the theory which is to suggest a generic framework and then establishes its consistency.

An immediate perspective is concerned with the implementation of the theory in the modal interpretation and experimental comparisons of the others IR models. We intend also to study the theory's fulfillment in another interpretation of the accessibility relation and the world.

References

1. Chellas, B.F.: Modal Logic: An Introduction. Cambridge University Press, Cambridge (1980)
2. Crestani, F., van Rijsbergen, C.J.: Information retrieval by logical imaging. J. Documentation **51**(1), 3–17 (1995)
3. Kripke, S.A.: Semantical analysis of modal logic i normal modal propositional calculi. Math. Logic Q. **9**(5–6), 67–96 (1963)
4. Lalmas, M.: Logical models in information retrieval: introduction and overview. Inform. Process. Manag. **34**(1), 19–33 (1998)
5. Nie, J.: An outline of a general model for information retrieval systems. In: Proceedings of the 11th Annual International ACM SIGIR Conference on Research and Development in Information Retrieval, pp. 495–506 (1988)
6. Nie, J.: An information retrieval model based on modal logic. Inform. Process. Manag. **25**(5), 477–491 (1989)

7. Nie, J.: Un modèle logique général pour les systèmes de recherche d'informations: application au prototype RIME. Ph.D. thesis, Joseph Fourier - Grenoble I (1990)
8. Van Rijsbergen, C.J.: A non-classical logic for information retrieval. Comput. J. **29**(6), 481–485 (1986)
9. Van Rijsbergen, C.J.: Towards an information logic. In: Proceedings of the 12th Annual International ACM SIGIR Conference on Research and Development in Information Retrieval, pp. 77–86 (1989)
10. Zerarga, L., Djouadi, Y.: A many-sorted theory proposal for information retrieval: axiomatization and semantics. Knowl. Inform. Syst. **55**(1), 113–139 (2017). https://doi.org/10.1007/s10115-017-1074-9

Author Index

rinted in the United States
by Baker & Taylor Publisher Services